Reading John
with St. Thomas Aquinas

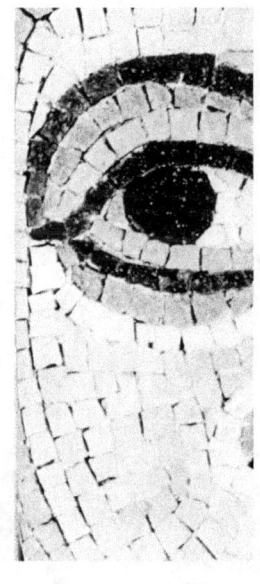

Reading John with St. Thomas Aquinas

Theological Exegesis and Speculative Theology

edited by
Michael Dauphinais and
Matthew Levering

The Catholic University of America Press • Washington, D.C.

Copyright © 2005
Reprinted in paperback 2010
The Catholic University of America Press
All rights reserved

The paper used in this publication meets the minimum requirements of American National Standards for Information Science—Permanence of Paper for Printed Library Materials, ANSI Z39.48-1984.
∞

LIBRARY OF CONGRESS CATALOGING-IN-PUBLICATION DATA
Reading John with St. Thomas Aquinas : theological exegesis and speculative theology / edited by Michael Dauphinais and Matthew Levering.
p. cm.
Rev. and expanded versions of papers delivered at a conference sponsored by Ave Maria College and the Aquinas Center for Theological Research.
Includes bibliographical references and index.
ISBN-13: 978-0-8132-1405-4 (cloth : alk. paper)
ISBN-13: 978-0-8132-1870-0 (pbk)
1. Bible. N.T. John—Criticism, interpretation, etc.   2. Thomas, Aquinas, Saint, 1225?–1274. Super Evangelium S. Joannis lectura.   I. Dauphinais, Michael, 1973–
II. Levering, Matthew Webb, 1971–   III. Title.
BS2615.52.R43 2005
226.5′07—dc22

2004007255

To Stephen F. Brown and David B. Burrell, C.S.C.

Contents

Acknowledgments xi
Introduction xiii

PART 1. REVELATION

JOHN F. BOYLE
1. Authorial Intention and the *Divisio textus* 3

STEPHEN F. BROWN
2. The Theological Role of the Fathers in Aquinas's *Super Evangelium S. Ioannis Lectura* 9

PART 2. THE TRIUNE GOD

GILLES EMERY, O.P.
3. Biblical Exegesis and the Speculative Doctrine of the Trinity in St. Thomas Aquinas's *Commentary on St. John* 23

BRUCE D. MARSHALL
4. What Does the Spirit Have to Do? 62

MATTHEW LEVERING
5. Does the Paschal Mystery Reveal the Trinity? 78

MICHAEL WALDSTEIN
6. The Analogy of Mission and Obedience
A Central Point in the Relation between *Theologia* and *Oikonomia* in St. Thomas Aquinas's *Commentary on John* 92

PART 3. GOD AND THE WORLD

DAVID B. BURRELL, C.S.C.
7. Creation in St. Thomas Aquinas's *Super Evangelium S. Joannis Lectura* 115

MATTHEW L. LAMB
8. Eternity and Time in St. Thomas Aquinas's Lectures on St. John's Gospel   127

STEVEN A. LONG
9. Divine Providence and John 15:5   140

PART 4. THE MORAL LIFE

CARLO LEGET
10. The Concept of "Life" in the *Commentary on St. John*   153

MICHAEL SHERWIN, O.P.
11. Christ the Teacher in St. Thomas's *Commentary on the Gospel of John*   173

JANET E. SMITH
12. "Come and See"   194

RICHARD SCHENK, O.P
13. *And Jesus Wept*
    Notes towards a Theology of Mourning   212

PART 5. THE PERSON AND WORK OF JESUS CHRIST

BENEDICT M. ASHLEY, O.P.
14. The Extent of Jesus' Human Knowledge according to the Fourth Gospel   241

PAUL GONDREAU
15. Anti-Docetism in Aquinas's *Super Ioannem*
    St. Thomas as Defender of the Full Humanity of Christ   254

PIM VALKENBERG
16. Aquinas and Christ's Resurrection
    The Influence of the *Lectura super Ioannem* 20–21 on the *Summa theologiae*   277

PART 6. CHURCH AND SACRAMENTS

FREDERICK CHRISTIAN BAUERSCHMIDT
17. "That the Faithful Become the Temple of God"
    The Church Militant in Aquinas's *Commentary on John*   293

MICHAEL DAUPHINAIS
18. "And They Shall All Be Taught by God"
    Wisdom and the Eucharist in John 6   312

SERGE-THOMAS BONINO, O.P.
19. The Role of the Apostles in the Communication of Revelation according to the *Lectura super Ioannem* of St. Thomas Aquinas   318

About the Contributors   347
Selected Bibliography   351
Index   363

Acknowledgments

 First and foremost, we should thank the contributors to this volume, whose dedicated scholarship made possible this book. The essays included in the volume are revised and expanded versions of papers delivered at a conference sponsored by Ave Maria College and the Aquinas Center for Theological Renewal. To all who assisted in the success of the conference, and to the numerous participants who made it a memorable event, we extend our warm appreciation. Without the support of Nicholas Healy Jr., now president of Ave Maria University, and Dominic Aquila, then provost of Ave Maria College, the event would never have come to pass. Betsy Dalton, Carole Carpenter, and Diane Eriksen, among others, played an important role in orchestrating the conference, and merit recognition. Nancy Dauphinais and Joy Levering were more than wonderful, as always; we owe a unique debt to them. At The Catholic University of America Press, we owe profound thanks to David McGonagle and Gregory LaNave, who quickly recognized the importance of the volume, and to Susan Needham, who assisted us in preparing it. We also offer our gratitude to the broader community of scholars who care about the intersection of biblical exegesis and systematic theology, and who value the insights of our forebears in the faith. In this vein we wish to draw particular attention to the distinguished careers of our teachers and mentors, Stephen F. Brown and David B. Burrell, C.S.C. Would that all students were privileged to have such caring and learned instructors in the task of entering into the Church's theological conversation. May God continue to bless their lives and labors.

Introduction

 Like all medieval biblical commentaries, Aquinas's *Commentary on John* consists to a significant degree in speculative theological questioning inspired by the biblical text. Proceeding on the assumption that it would not have been possible for St. John to have written what he wrote without the ecclesial light of faith and without engaging speculative questions, Aquinas's commentary recommends a similar movement in the thought of the biblical interpreter: speculative thinking about divine realities emerges from within biblical exegesis itself. The circular movement from biblical exegesis to speculative theology and back again must be a continual one for the health of both exegesis and theology. The present volume, as a speculative theological commentary upon Aquinas's biblical commentary, further displays the fruits of this circular movement. By way of contributing to the reintegration of biblical studies and speculative theology, *Reading John with St. Thomas Aquinas* seeks to illumine and recover the convergences between the scriptural words, exegetical commentary, and theological analysis.

Insofar as biblical exegesis and speculative theology are distinct, the essays in *Reading John with St. Thomas Aquinas* are the latter, as speculative theological reflection upon St. Thomas's biblical exegesis. Yet the two tasks indwell one another. St. Thomas's biblical exegesis is constituted by his procedure of continually moving, within the exegetical task, from exegesis proper to speculative theological questioning and back again. In this dynamic process of exegesis, he brings to bear not only parallel interpretive texts from throughout the Bible, but also the accumulated insights of the Fathers. Biblical exegesis depends upon the exegete's gifts as a speculative theologian, which in turn depend upon the exegete's acquaintance with not merely the particular text at hand but indeed the whole Scriptures as illumined in faith by the Fathers and interpreted doctrinally by the Church. This expansive view of exegesis and of the exegete is justified by Aquinas's understanding of *sacra scriptura* as *sacra doctrina*, sacred teaching, in which the Church's teachers participate.

The present volume, therefore, should contribute to developing the rationale for contemporary exegetical approaches that interpret Scripture primarily through the historical lens of tradition and with a speculative intention. As a theological commentary, furthermore, *Reading John with St. Thomas Aquinas* emphasizes the congruence of biblical exegesis and systematic theology in Aquinas's thought by adopting the basic structure of Aquinas's *Summa theologiae*. A brief sketch of the contents of the volume will draw out this pattern.

In the volume's first section—on Revelation, taking up issues found in I, q.1, of the *Summa theologiae*—John F. Boyle proposes, *pace* Beryl Smalley's view that Aquinas's interest in the literal sense anticipates modern historical-critical exegetical approaches, that Aquinas is actually not concerned to determine precisely what the author meant. Drawing upon the *De potentia*, Boyle finds that Aquinas, influenced by Augustine, instead poses two negative principles for interpreting the literal sense: one cannot hold something contradictory to the truth, especially the truth of faith, to be the meaning of Scripture, and one cannot insist upon one's own interpretation if other interpretations may be valid. These principles enable Thomas to admit that the literal sense of a particular passage may admit of many meanings. Unlike modern biblical exegetes, then, rather than pursue arduously the exact meaning of the literal sense of a passage, St. Thomas uses the method of *"divisio textus"* to focus upon the intention or goal with which the author wrote, namely the salvation of human beings.

Stephen F. Brown seeks to uncover the role of Aquinas's citations of the Fathers in the *Commentary on John*. Drawing upon the work of the fourteenth-century theologians Durandus and the Franciscan Peter Aureoli, who establish a distinction between deductive theology and declarative theology, Brown surveys how Aquinas in the *Commentary on John* uses the work of the Fathers to expose central articles of the faith. In contrast to Durandus and other late thirteenth- and early fourteenth-century theologians, who considered Aquinas's theology to be primarily an effort to deduce further truths from the articles of faith, Brown argues (in agreement with Aureoli) that Aquinas practices declarative theology, that is, theology whose purpose is to defend, clarify, and explain the articles of faith. Examining both the Commentary and Aquinas's numerous discussions elsewhere about the nature of theology, Brown shows that Aquinas's practice of declarative theology relies heavily upon his use of the Fathers.

The second section of the volume concerns the triune God. Gilles Emery, O.P. analyzes the relationship of biblical exegesis and speculative theology within the *Commentary on John*. Emery compares the trinitarian content of the *Commentary on John* with that of the *Summa theologiae*. Treating Aquinas's trinitarian theology as a whole, Emery shows that with the exception of questions 32 and 38, Aquinas discusses in rich detail the themes of every question from *Summa theologiae* I, qq.27–43, in his *Commentary on John*. Aquinas's exegesis addresses speculative considerations about the Son and his generation, the Spirit and his procession, the Father, the equality of the divine persons, and the mission of the persons. Indeed, Emery finds that the speculative teaching of the Commentary is at certain points, especially the doctrine of the Word and the soteriological dimension of trinitarian theology, significantly more developed than in the *Summa theologiae;* yet the Commentary confirms and deepens, rather than alters, what we learn from the speculative synthesis in the *Summa*. Above all, Emery's thorough comparison makes clear that biblical theology and speculative theology are not separated by St. Thomas. For Aquinas, to comment adequately upon the meaning of Scripture requires engaging speculative questions, that is to say, requires the *habitus* of the theologian.

Bruce D. Marshall investigates Aquinas's account of the action of the Holy Spirit in light of the unity of the triune God's acts *ad extra*. In response to the common argument that Latin trinitarian theology is marred by a "pneumatological deficit," Marshall first demonstrates that Aquinas's *Commentary on John* reserves an important role for the Spirit's action. Marshall identifies the numerous places in the Commentary where the Spirit's action, irreducible to Christ's, is emphasized by Aquinas. Aquinas, Marshall shows, focuses on two actions of the Spirit in particular: making us adopted children of the Father and manifesting to us the truth. Having established the uniqueness and spontaneity of the Spirit's action according to the Commentary, Marshall then inquires into the effect of the axiom that the works of the Trinity *ad extra* are undivided and common to the three Persons. Drawing in particular upon Peter Geach's notion of relative identity, he inquires into how one might conceive of Aquinas's doctrine of appropriations in the most convincing way. If each of the divine Persons takes part distinctly in the one divine action *ad extra,* is the divine action still one? Marshall concludes that here we have reached a limitation of the human *modus significandi* in our efforts to articulate the action of the triune God. While we can correctly assert that the divine Persons are identical with the divine essence yet not with each other, we cannot clearly understand how this can be the case.

Matthew Levering and Michael Waldstein both seek to place Aquinas's theological insights in his *Commentary on John* within the context of concerns brought to the fore by the thought of Hans Urs von Balthasar. In light of the concern of contemporary biblical exegetes and theologians that discourse about the Trinity be grounded in the concrete revelation of God through the passion, death, and resurrection of Jesus Christ, Levering argues that Aquinas's *Commentary on John* makes clear that for Aquinas the Paschal mystery reveals the Son as perfect self-gift and therefore as the perfect image of the Father in the Holy Spirit. Levering begins by analyzing the view of the biblical exegete N. T. Wright, who argues that Greek metaphysics prevented classical Christian thinkers from recognizing the radical redescription of "god" made necessary by revelation. In Wright's view, Western theology has suffered from a "kyriarchal" understanding of God that conceived of God as aloof and uninvolved, despite the Cross. Levering suggests that Aquinas's *Commentary on John,* far from instantiating such an aloof god, presents the Paschal mystery as the highest revelation of the self-giving constitutive of the Trinity. Levering argues that Aquinas's understanding of the Paschal mystery fits the biblical data better than does the idea, increasingly popular today, that the Cross signals an intra-divine rupture bridged by the Holy Spirit.

Michael Waldstein examines the concepts of mission and obedience in the *Commentary on John,* and argues that "obedience" may be analogically applied to the Son in his eternal relation (of love) to the Father. Waldstein explores how the divine economy (Oikonomia) reveals the immanent Trinity (Theologia) by focusing our attention upon passages in the Gospel of John that unite the two. The mission and obedience of the Son in the Oikonomia, Waldstein finds, provides an analogy for the immanent personhood of the Son in the Theologia, because mission cannot be separated from the note of obedience. Although Waldstein recognizes that Aquinas regularly distinguishes Christ's obedience as belonging to his human will, rather than to his divine will (since will is one in God), nonetheless Waldstein identifies passages that appear to indicate that obedience may also be applied analogously to Christ in his divinity. In the *Commentary on John*, Waldstein notes, Aquinas describes the Father's generation of the Word as a communication that, in a sense, commands what the Word speaks. The Word himself is thus "obedient," both within the Trinity and in his temporal mission, to this generative command. As adopted sons in the Son, human beings come to share, by the Holy Spirit, in this obedient Sonship.

The third section of the volume, following the order of the *Summa theologiae,* addresses God and creation. David B. Burrell, C.S.C. treats the theology of creation from the perspective of Aquinas's *Commentary on John*. Burrell argues that Aquinas in the *Summa theologiae* uses philosophical and theological arguments in an inextricably intertwined manner, rather than doing philosophy at one point and theology at another. Surveying the (highly philosophical) discussions in the *Commentary on John* of "Verbum" and the act of creation, Burrell identifies a similarly rich interplay of philosophical and theological argumentation. He focuses his attention upon Aquinas's investigation of the meaning of the Johannine "Logos" or "Verbum." If the act of knowing always involves the generation of a "word," Burrell asks, does John's use of this name for the Son make God's triunity accessible to reason? Aquinas shows that the answer is no: The divine knowing, as a supreme knowing-by-identity, does not necessarily require the expression of a word. Thus the philosophical analogy serves divine revelation by illumining its cogency and the fittingness of John's inspired language. As Burrell shows, Aquinas then undertakes a similar analysis of John's testimony that all things are created "through" the Word, in which Aquinas uses philosophical argumentation to preserve the radical distinction between God's creative activity and the efficient causality of creatures, thereby underscoring the non-duality of God and creatures. Without being able to grasp it fully in a concept, we can affirm with Aquinas the supreme causality of God that enables him to cause free creatures who depend entirely upon his causality.

Matthew L. Lamb engages the theme of eternity and time as understood by Aquinas in the Commentary. The metaphysical and the historical, Lamb notes, are often contrasted as if the former were merely "conceptual" while the latter was "concrete." In contrast, Aquinas recognizes that metaphysics describes realities that are the basis for the reality possessed by finite history. Concerned especially to illumine the mystery of the eternal Word incarnate in time, Lamb reviews the history of philosophical speculation on eternity and time, focusing upon the breakthroughs achieved by Augustine, Boethius, and Aquinas, who move beyond the Platonic and Plotinian antithesis of the eternal and the temporal. Lamb argues that realist metaphysics, as exemplified by Aquinas in his analysis of the mind and its knowing, alone enables us to grasp the meaning of the passages in the Gospel of John about the divine Word and about the relation of the spatio-temporal universe to the Word incarnate. Only such a metaphysics can move beyond our tendency to envision reality solely in terms of extension and duration. Thus Lamb notes how, for Aquinas, Arius's and Sabellius's errors stemmed from their failure to grasp the processions in God in immaterial terms. Similarly, since eternity, properly understood, is not "before" time, Aquinas is able to expose the intimate presence of the incarnate Word, according to St. John, in all time.

Steven A. Long examines God's Providence and human freedom in light of John 15:5, "Without me you can do nothing." Long points out that these words of Jesus refer not only to Jesus in his humanity, but also to Jesus in his divinity. We can do nothing without the divine Word. It follows, as Aquinas teaches in many places, that God's causality is absolute. In arguing that there is only Pure Act and created act, with literally nothing in between, Long addresses some of the thorny questions that arise from a strong doctrine of divine Providence. If God causes everything, are human beings free? Long notes that divine causality must not be conceived as coercive or violent. Rather, God, unlike any created efficient cause, moves contingent things contingently. Distinguishing between self-determination and absolute independence, Long shows that creatures are never free of God's causality in the sense of absolute independence, and yet our free acts are truly self-determination. For Long, therefore, evil is the relinquishing by God of the creature to its own defectibility for the sake of a higher good—contrary to contemporary efforts to treat "nothingness," negation, and deprivation in the creature as though they were themselves beings. Long concludes by connecting this understanding of divine causality and human freedom to the relationship of divine Providence and natural law. Building upon the work of Russell Hittinger, Long points out that a metaphysics of moral action that supposes that human agency is in some way outside divine causality breaks the link between divine Providence and natural law. The metaphysical error has as its consequence the notion of an alien God who threatens, rather than authors and perfects, human freedom and virtue.

Section four concerns the moral life. Seeking a theologically rich avenue for investigating the multiple facets of Aquinas's understanding of "life," Carlo Leget shows that Aquinas's Prologue to the Commentary provides, as might be expected given its place as a hermeneutical framework for the Commentary, an evocative lens through which to explore the concept. By employing Aquinas's Prologue as a lens, Leget exposes how Aquinas sets forth the relationship of temporal life to the eternal life that the divine Word, as St. John repeatedly emphasizes, shares with us. Leget finds that Aquinas, in marked contrast to the modern world, orders corporeal (temporal) life to spiritual (eternal) life. This way of understanding "life" in the Gospel has hermeneutical consequences for the entire reading of Scripture. For Aquinas, the Gospel should be read as a continual call to conversion, to renewing one's inner, spiritual life by means of the biblical and Eucharistic Word. Drawing upon Ricoeur and Stephen Fowl, Leget shows that this understanding of the spiritual ordering of "life" also informs Aquinas's understanding of the spiritual sense as necessary for entering into the tradition of Catholic reading of Scripture.

Leget thereby demonstrates the significance of Aquinas's scriptural exegesis for renewing contemporary biblical exegesis.

Michael Sherwin, O.P. and Janet E. Smith both take up the theme of how moral education occurs. Sherwin does this by exploring the Commentary's presentation of the theme of Christ the teacher. Aquinas presents Christ, the Holy Spirit, and the Father as teachers (masters) who instruct us through interior and exterior teaching. Discipleship, then, is a "divine apprenticeship" by means of faith and the other virtues, which we learn from Christ and to which the Father draws us. This understanding of the role of the "Magister," which centers upon wisdom, differs greatly from modern emphases on power. Sherwin discusses how Aquinas's Commentary depicts the disciples' growth in faith under the instruction of Christ's pedagogy (his words, deeds, and example). By means of the teaching of Christ, the Holy Spirit, and the Father, we are drawn and attracted to wisdom, rather than impelled by extrinsic power. As Sherwin notes, for Aquinas therefore the Last Supper and the Cross constitute the summit of this teaching, which is received by those who are formed in charity by the Holy Spirit. Christ teaches ultimately by his suffering and sacrifice, because his teaching is wisdom, not extrinsic or arbitrary power. Those whom Christ instructs become his friends, in the deepest sense of friendship, and are thus enabled to teach others about wisdom and charity. The teacher (Christ) becomes, as the perfect embodiment of divine wisdom and charity, what is taught.

Janet E. Smith attends to a related question raised by the Commentary: Why is it that some hear this teaching, and others do not? Her answer has to do with moral connaturality. She reminds us that we should not expect Aquinas's use of Aristotle to be absent from his commentary on Scripture. Identifying Aristotle's understanding of habituation as a key to Aquinas's depiction of the moral life, she argues that Aquinas in the *Commentary on John* emphasizes that whether individuals follow Jesus depends significantly upon whether they are formed by the moral virtues. As both Aristotle and Scripture point out, "like knows like." To put it in terms of the medieval axiom, "what is received, is received according to the mode of the receiver." It follows, Smith holds, that moral goodness assists one in making right judgments about all aspects of reality. On the basis of a close reading of passages in the commentary, she concludes that without moral goodness, it may well be that one cannot even *recognize* the truth that is Christ. The disciple John, as understood by Aquinas, is a prime example: because of his charity, he is able to see further into the mysteries of Christ. Similarly, Aquinas repeatedly comments that wicked people, caught up in the love of the world, are unable to recognize Christ. Since the distortion of the will in vice clouds the intellect, the encounter with Christ that leads to conversion proceeds differently in people depending upon whether they have acquired the moral virtues. In elaborating this point about the moral condition of Christ's interlocutors, Smith guides us through Aquinas's interpretation of the central stories of conversion in the Gospel of John.

The section on the moral life begins with "life" and ends, appropriately, with death and the theology of mourning. Contrasting the Christian ambivalence about death with Stoic and neo-Platonic certainties, Richard Schenk, O.P. discusses Aquinas's anthropology in light of his treatment, in the *Commentary on John,* of the sadness of Christ, especially Christ's mourning for Lazarus in John 11. Schenk first discusses Augustine's ambivalent attitude toward mourning in his *Confessions,* and then turns to Aquinas's theological anthropology, whose holistic scope provides Aquinas with the resources to take seriously mourning for the loss of a fully human life. Building upon the systematic and historical contributions of Norbert Luyten, Anton Charles Pegis, and Mary F. Rousseau, Schenk develops by means of an analysis of the *Commentary on John* a theology of mourning not only for death but also for sin and injustice as losses of properly human goods. Schenk focuses upon Aquinas's treatment of passages in the Gospel that include the verb *tarásso,* to shake or disturb, especially regarding Jesus' distress at the death of his friends, disciples, and himself, beginning with John 11. Schenk compares Aquinas's interpretation to those of modern exegetes such as Bultmann and Schnackenburg. Whereas Bultmann denies that St. John intends to imply that Christ experienced sadness, Schnackenburg and Aquinas affirm it. Attending to the five reasons that Aquinas gives at different times for the fittingness of Jesus' sadness, Schenk explores the resources that Aquinas's account provides for contemporary understandings of the Church's relationship to the goods of this life.

The fifth section treats the Person of Christ. Benedict M. Ashley, O.P. discusses the Christological contribution of Aquinas's *Commentary on John* as an alternative to the view of Gerald O'Collins, S.J. and Daniel Kendall, S.J. (among many others) that Jesus possessed faith, not the vision of God. After reviewing the difficulties with Aquinas's position, as well as relevant magisterial texts, Ashley notes that Aquinas, despite being well aware of the difficulties, consistently held that Christ possessed the vision. The *Commentary on John,* in Ashley's view, assists us in understanding why Aquinas continued to affirm this position. Ashley pays particular attention to Aquinas's comments on John's affirmation that Christ was, in his earthly life, full of grace and truth. Aquinas approaches the Incarnation as a mystery that must be described in light of Christ's salvific mission, including the role that he possesses in his humanity as Head (that is, fount of grace) of his mystical Body. Given the mystery of the Incarnation, Christology must avoid the temptation to conform Christ to our expectations of what constitutes human nature in such a way as to deprive him of the fullness of his status as Head. Examining texts from both the Commentary and the *Summa theologiae,* Ashley argues that Christ's headship requires a fullness of grace and truth compatible only with vision: Christ's humanity is the source, during his earthly life as well as after the resurrection, of beatitude in us. Ashley responds to a wide range of views that argue that possession of vision would be incompatible with Christ's earthly humanity. Suggesting that Christ's vision is analogous to the highest level of mystical experience, Ashley concludes that the vision would have enhanced, not destroyed, Christ's freedom, and would have enabled Christ to possess the self-awareness of his divinity that he exhibits in the Gospels.

Also treating Christ's human nature, Paul Gondreau identifies the centrality, in the Commentary, of Aquinas's anti-docetic Christology, his critique of those tendencies in Christian thought that seek to deny the full humanity of Christ. As Gondreau points out, Aquinas's realist account of the Incarnation enables him to defend Christ's full human consubstantiality, to offer a credible depiction of Jesus in his humanity, and to defend the real presence of Christ in the Eucharist (John 6). Proposing that Aquinas's exegesis provides a model for contemporary efforts to unite biblical exegesis and speculative theology, Gondreau demonstrates that Aquinas's attention to Christ's humanity flows from his theological exegesis of Scripture and is aided by his Aristotelian metaphysics of human nature. As is well known, the docetist heresies turn upon the question of whether the divinity could enter truly into substantial union with a material reality. Elucidating John 1:14, "And the Word was made flesh," Aquinas affirms that such an event indeed has happened. In the *Commentary on John,* as in the *Summa theologiae,* Aquinas emphasizes the soteriological significance of Christ's flesh, in particular his bodily suffering (passion) and resurrection: Christ's humanity is the "instrument" of his divinity, and so it is through his real humanity that we receive the grace of eternal life. In order for there to be a Mystical Body, Christ must first truly possess a fleshly body, as well as a full rational soul. He must therefore possess real passions, without manifesting the moral effects of sin. After surveying the manifold texts in the Commentary that reveal Aquinas's concern to refute docetic heresies in order to display the salvific truth that Jesus' human actions are real rather than illusory, Gondreau concludes by extending this insight to

Aquinas's exegesis of John 6: the real presence of Christ's body and blood in the Eucharist depends upon the incarnate reality of Christ's historical body.

Pim Valkenberg addresses the Commentary's treatment of Christ's resurrected body. Valkenberg, indebted to Michel Corbin, identifies links between Aquinas's Commentary and his *Summa theologiae* as regards the theology of Christ's resurrection. While praising Aquinas for recognizing that John is a theologian whose aim is to speak about Christ not simply in his humanity but also in his divinity, Valkenberg cautions that Aquinas's *Commentary on John* should be read in light of his other biblical commentaries in order to avoid theological misconceptions that might arise from reading John's Gospel alone. Valkenberg focuses his study upon Aquinas's interpretation of John 20 and 21 in comparison with *Summa theologiae* III, qq. 53–56, where Aquinas systematically explores Christ's resurrection. He shows that Aquinas's exegesis combines two medieval genres, *expositio* and *quaestio:* In Aquinas's exposition of the biblical text, he frequently pauses to explore certain questions in a speculative manner. Likewise, although the *Summa theologiae* is composed of a series of *quaestiones,* Valkenberg finds a marked influence of the genre of *expositio* upon the *Summa,* due to Aquinas's increasing familiarity with Scripture over the course of his career. Examining ways in which Aquinas's *Commentary on John* may have influenced his theology of the resurrection in the *Summa theologiae,* Valkenberg identifies the *Summa* as a prime exemplar of biblical theology.

The sixth and final section of the volume treats the Church. Although Aquinas did not write a treatise on the Church, Frederick Christian Bauerschmidt reminds us that we should expect to learn something about the Church from the *Commentary on John,* since Aquinas in the Prologue to the Commentary writes that the "end" or goal of the Gospel of John is "that the faithful become the temple of God and be filled with the majesty of God" by coming to understand the humanity and divinity of Christ. Bauerschmidt explores the significance of contemplation in the Commentary, showing that Aquinas ties contemplative life, modeled by John, intimately to sanctification through the sacramental and ascetical practices of the Church, by participating in which we become the Church as the community of friends of God. In the same vein, Bauerschmidt explores Christ's "theandric" teaching, in which his divine Person is communicated to his disciples. Christ and the Holy Spirit make the Church to be an "army" whose emblem is love and humility, made visible by concrete practices. These practices include works of mercy as well as the apostolic ordering of the community. Bauerschmidt further shows how St. Thomas's exegetical method (his pattern of integrating speculative

Introduction   xxiii

theology into exegesis by means of careful *divisio textus*) conforms with John's own speculative structuring of the gospel narrative. Bauerschmidt concludes by reflecting upon the Church's holiness and unworthiness, in light of the goal of the Church, salvation—a goal that no human community can bring about, but that requires the return of the Lord. For Bauerschmidt, Aquinas models the way in which theologians recognize the Church to be holy without Platonically instantiating a Church other than the concrete Church of saints and sinners.

Michael Dauphinais explores the insights of St. Thomas's interpretation of John 6 as an alternative to the interpretation of Raymond Brown. In Brown's view, the Bread of Life discourse in John 6 is composed of two strands: John 6:35–50 forms the original discourse, to which John 6:51–58 is a later addition. The former is primarily sapiential, whereas the latter is Eucharistic. Dauphinais argues that Aquinas unites the sapiential and Eucharistic dimensions of the Bread of Life discourse, thereby displaying the literary and theological unity of John 6. Aquinas achieves this unity because of his theological understanding of Christ's Incarnation: as the incarnate Word, Christ is spiritual or sapiential food. If the Eucharist is not received as divine Wisdom, then its grace unto eternal life is not received. Yet, this spiritual food comes to us, because of our epistemological reliance upon sensibles, as the incarnate One, in the Eucharistic body and blood. By integrating a speculative theological approach with a literary exegetical approach, Aquinas thus brings together what Brown sees as disparate.

Serge-Thomas Bonino, O.P. in the concluding essay of the volume, meditates upon perhaps the most striking aspect of the Church: God has chosen human beings, with all their faults and imperfections, to communicate the Revelation that comes from God in Jesus Christ. Revelation comes from Christ the Teacher, but is mediated by human teachers. God's teaching reaches its perfection when those to whom it is communicated can also teach it. God communicates to creatures a share in his own perfection. In exploring this mystery of faith as articulated in Aquinas's *Commentary on John*, Bonino begins with Christ's human knowledge. For Christ, in his human nature, to be the *source* of divine teaching, his human mind must be replete with the knowledge of the truth about God. The apostles have a direct and preeminent participation in Jesus' knowledge. For this reason, the Church is founded upon the faith of the apostles. Having established these basic points, Bonino proceeds to elaborate the Commentary's profound theology of the apostolic ministry, with special attention to how Aquinas's interpretation is shaped by his practice of interpreting Scripture through other texts of Scripture as well as through the Fathers, by the role played in his conceptual analysis by the metaphysics of causality and participation, and by his view of the apostles as archetypes of the Christian spiritual life to be imitated by the young Dominicans to whom Aquinas was lecturing.

A final note: The text of the *Commentary on John* is a *reportatio*. During Aquinas's second period of teaching in Paris, between 1270 and 1272, his faithful scribe and Dominican brother, Reginald of Piperno, copied it down from Aquinas's lectures. At the time Aquinas was in his mid forties, and as a "Master of the Sacred Page," he had the primary duty of teaching Scripture. We have Aquinas's Dominican brothers also to thank for the preservation of the *Commentary on John,* as Reginald tells us by way of introducing his *reportatio.* Aquinas delivered these lectures just as he was beginning the *tertia pars* of the *Summa theologiae,* that is, the section on Christ and the sacraments.[1]

The English text of the Commentary, translated by Fabian Larcher, O.P. and James Weisheipl, O.P., that is used in *Reading John with St. Thomas Aquinas* (along with the Marietti version of the Latin text), is not a critical edition. The translators used the Parma, Vivès, and Marietti editions; the French critical edition by M.-D. Philippe, in contrast, benefits from the corrections made to the first eight chapters by the Leonine commission (the Leonine edition remains incomplete).[2] Weisheipl points out that the Commentary was a popular one in the medieval period, with the result that "[s]cattered throughout the world there still exist thirty three complete and thirteen incomplete manuscript copies of this work."[3]

Although Bartholomew of Capua, Tolomeo of Lucca, and Bernard Gui, all early biographers of Aquinas, state that Aquinas himself revised this *reportatio* for publication, the most recent intellectual biography of Aquinas, that of Torrell, argues against this possibility. Nonetheless, Torrell notes that this *reportatio* is particularly carefully done.[4] As to its theological value, Torrell classifies the *Commentary on John,* along with those on Job and Romans, as Aquinas's most significant. Quoting M.-D. Philippe, who translated and edited the Commentary (through Book VIII) in French, Torrell remarks that some "do not hesitate to say that it holds among them [the biblical commen-

---

1. Jean-Pierre Torrell, O.P., *Saint Thomas Aquinas,* vol. 1: *The Person and His Work,* trans. Robert Royal (Washington, D.C.: The Catholic University of America Press, 1996), 198.
2. See Torrell, 200 n. 9.
3. James A. Weisheipl, Introduction, in Thomas Aquinas, *Commentary on the Gospel of St. John,* Part 1, trans. James A. Weisheipl and Fabian R. Larcher (Albany: Magi Books, 1980), 3.
4. Ibid., 199. Weisheipl accepts the testimony of the early biographers that Aquinas corrected this Commentary and even wrote out himself the first five chapters. See ibid., 3, 8.

taries] a 'unique place,' and that we could even say that it is 'the theological work par excellence by Saint Thomas.' This statement can be explained if we recall that 'John's gospel contains the ultimate in revelation.' . . . Thomas reveals himself here as one of the contemplatives of whom St. John is the model."⁵

5. Ibid., 200–201.

PART I
Revelation

ONE

Authorial Intention and the *Divisio textus*

JOHN F. BOYLE

 Beryl Smalley in her landmark book, *The Study of the Bible in the Middle Ages,* sought to show, among other things, that not all of those who commented on the Bible in the Middle Ages were, in her words, theologians. Some were also scholars.[1] The mark of the scholar was an interest in the literal sense apart from and in contrast to the Middle Ages' seeming fixation on the spiritual or mystical senses of Scripture. In particular, Smalley was interested in those scholars whose work was a kind of anticipation of modern biblical scholarship, especially of an historical critical flavor. She found, as we know, two such forward-looking John the Baptists: a modest son of the abbey of St. Victor by the name of Andrew and, far more significantly, the intellectual luminary of the Order of Preachers, St. Thomas Aquinas. Smalley would come to have her doubts about St. Thomas. Although his instincts in interpreting the literal sense were sound, according to Smalley, St. Thomas was still too drawn to the dark side, or at least the silly side, of the medieval interpretive project.[2] Smalley was correct.

The medieval quirks and oddities in St. Thomas's interpretation of Scripture, however, extend beyond his fascination with the mystical senses. They extend as well into his understanding and interpretation of the literal sense. Not even here is Thomas particularly modern. Thus a disappointment to Smalley, St. Thomas may nonetheless be of some value to the modern interpreter of Scripture, precisely because he is not one of us.

Thomas's conception of the literal sense of Scripture is not particu-

---

1. Beryl Smalley, *The Study of the Bible in the Middle Ages,* 2nd ed. (Notre Dame: University of Notre Dame Press, 1964), xv–xvi.

2. Beryl Smalley, *The Gospels in the Schools, c. 1100–c. 1280* (London: Hambledon Press, 1985), 265–66.

larly novel; it is, however, articulated in a particularly clear way. Thomas says that the literal sense of Scripture pertains to those things that the words of Scripture signify.[3] It is concerned with the *sensus*—let us translate *sensus* here as "meaning"—of the words. The task of the interpreter of the literal sense of Scripture is to articulate that meaning—the *sensus*—of the words.

Getting at the meaning of the words is not always an easy task. As is clear throughout the tradition, and here in Thomas's commentary on the Gospel according to St. John, the interpreter is confronted with different interpretations of the meaning of the words, of the literal sense of Scripture. What is one to do? Fortunately, Thomas does, once, address this question. It is tucked away in an article of his disputed questions *De potentia,* in which he asks whether the creation of unformed matter precedes in duration the creation of things. We need not worry here about unformed matter. As for how one is to read the literal sense of Scripture, Thomas poses two negative principles: first, one ought not assert something false to be found in Scripture, especially what would contradict the faith; and second, one ought not to insist upon one's own interpretation to the exclusion of other interpretations which in their content are true and in which what Thomas calls "the circumstance of the letter" is preserved.[4] I take this latter to mean, minimally, that the interpretation more or less fits the words and their context. Thus for an interpretation to be true it cannot be contrary to the truth, and it must fit the circumstance of the letter.

What is missing from Thomas's criteria, and notably so to moderns, is any consideration of what the author meant. This is not a momentary lapse. Such consideration is not absent only in theoretical discussions, but also in practice. If we look for an expression such as the "meaning of the author" *(sensus auctoris),* we do not find it, with one notable exception to be discussed below. This begs the obvious question: why is it that when Thomas considers an ambiguous passage of Scripture, he shows no interest in determining what the author meant when he wrote it. Might not the question of what the author meant be of some help? I think that Thomas would simply answer no. One need only recall Book XII of Augustine's *Confessions,* known to and cited by St. Thomas.[5] In Book XII, Augustine struggles with the opening chapter of

---

3. *Summa theologiae* [hereafter *ST*] I, q. 1, a. 10.
4. St. Thomas Aquinas, *Quaestiones disputatae de potentia* [hereafter *De pot.*] 4.1 in *Quaestiones disputatae,* ed. P. Bazzi et al., vol. 2 (Turin: Marietti, 1949), 102–10; English translation in *On the Power of God,* trans. English Dominican Fathers, vol. 2 (London: Burns, Oates and Washbourne, 1932), 1–23.
5. See *De pot.* 4.1. resp.; *ST* I, q. 1, a. 10.

Genesis, a biblical dark continent defying the most ambitious and determined cartographers. Some had criticized Augustine's interpretation of Genesis 1 on the grounds that it was not what Moses meant. Augustine's reply was the counter question: How do his critics know what Moses meant? Do not Augustine and his critics share the same letter? Does not Augustine's interpretation fit the letter? Augustine says nothing contrary to the faith (a sure indicator of a false interpretation). So on what basis do his critics claim his interpretation is not the one meant by Moses? Apart from some secret knowledge, some Gnostic or Straussian decoder ring, they have no basis. The appeal to what the author meant in such contentious cases is simply a dead end. In this concern with the meaning of the author, Thomas seems to be in full accord with Augustine.

If Thomas's disinterest in the meaning of the author is, from our vantage point, a notable quirk in his reading of the literal sense, it is not the only one. It is just the beginning.

If a given passage of Scripture admits of two different interpretations, two different meanings such that they satisfy Thomas's modest criteria of legitimate interpretation—not contrary to truth and fitting the circumstance of the letter—what is one then to do? Which interpretation is the right one? The opportunities for this question abound in Thomas's commentary on the Gospel according to St. John. Time and time again, Thomas provides two or more patristic interpretations for a single scriptural passage. He does not judge one to be correct, the other not; by his own criteria no such judgment can be made.

So in answer to the question, "Which is the true meaning of the letter?" the answer is simply, all of the above. What Thomas does in practice by presenting multiple interpretations of the letter, he affirms in principle: the literal sense admits of many meanings. Recall the principle from *De potentia:* one ought not insist upon one's own interpretation to the exclusion of other interpretations which in their content are true and in which the circumstance of the letter is preserved. If Thomas is, at least to us, surprisingly uninterested in pursuing what is the meaning of the author as such, he is also uninterested in determining a single meaning of the letter. If the former is a dead end, the latter is simply the wrong question: There is not necessarily one single meaning for each passage of Scripture. Some admit of more.

Thomas does recognize that such is odd. So he asks, might not the human author mean all of these meanings in a given passage? Augustine raised the same question about Moses. And with Augustine, Thomas says yes. In the *De potentia,* Thomas says, "It is not unbelievable that it could be divinely granted to Moses and the other authors of Sacred Scripture to know the diverse truths which men would be able to understand, and that they might signify those truths under one letter such that whichever of these meanings is the meaning of the author."[6] This apparently unique instance of the phrase "meaning of the author" *(sensus auctoris)* in the works of Thomas is notably found here in a context in which Thomas affirms the very possibility of the multiplicity of such meanings under one letter.

But if the author did not so mean all of those meanings, it does not matter. And it does not matter for one simple reason: the primary author of Scripture is God. Thomas has a fine sense of human authorship in the writing of Scripture; but he never loses sight of his theological first principles, one of which is that God is the author of Scripture. God could mean all of the literal meanings, and thus one would have multiple literal meanings, but without any such meanings on the part of the human author.[7]

Having avoided for understandable reasons the quagmire of human authorial meaning, Thomas has nonetheless returned to authorial meaning with his final appeal to divine authorship. Why? If we were to consider Thomas as a commentator on Aristotle, we would find something rather different. Certainly passages of Aristotle are difficult, and multiple interpretations might fit the text both narrowly and more broadly; this would, I think, be taken as a defect in the case of Aristotle. It is clearly not a defect in the case of Sacred Scripture. In the *De potentia,* Thomas says: "This pertains to the dignity of divine Scripture that it contains many meanings *(sensus)* under one letter, so that it thus would be fitting to the diverse intellects of men, such that each might marvel that he can find in divine Scripture the truth which he conceives in his mind."[8]

For Thomas, the purpose of Scripture is to make known those truths necessary for salvation.[9] Scripture is ordered to an end. The divine intention is to bring the rational creature into union with Himself, but as always in ways that are accommodated to the reality of that creature. Are not the manifold meanings of the letter in fact fitting given the divine intention of Scripture as communicating the truth requisite for eternal beatitude with God? Do not the manifold possibilities of scriptural reading—and this just on the literal level—suggest in a dim but analogical way the manifold actualities of beati-

---

6. *De pot.,* 4.1. resp.
7. *ST* I, q. 1, a. 10.
8. *De pot.,* 4.1. resp.
9. *Quaestiones de quolibet* 7.6.1. resp., in *Opera omnia iussu Leonis XIII P. M. edita* fs24, vol. 25.1 (Rome: Commissio Leonina, 1996), 28.

tude which Scripture signifies and to which it is ordered? Such multiplicity is no defect, but the unique dignity of Sacred Scripture.

If the *sensus auctoris* is missing from St. Thomas's commentaries, *intentio auctoris*—the intention of the author—is not. It is precisely here that the modern reader of St. Thomas must be particularly careful. Insofar as the modern reader is inclined to think that authorial intention is simply "what the author meant," he is not of one mind with St. Thomas. So how are we to understand "intention of the author" according to Thomas?

In the *Summa theologiae*, St. Thomas tells us that intention, to intend, is an act of the will insofar as the will moves to some end or goal, embracing not only the willing of that end, but also the willing of those things that are ordered to that end.[10] When Thomas speaks of the "intention of the author," it is precisely in this way.

Consider the opening sentence of the first lecture on the first chapter of the Gospel according to St. John: "John the Evangelist principally intends to show the divinity of the incarnate Word." Thomas here states a reason why St. John wrote his Gospel, the end St. John was pursuing. Such a consideration is not unimportant; in providing the end intended by St. John, Thomas gives the frame for his interpretation of the Gospel as a whole. Because to intend is not only to will an end, but also to will those things that are ordered to that end; a knowledge of the intention of St. John provides the context for understanding a given passage of his Gospel, since the whole Gospel will be read as ordered to the end intended.

The articulation of the author's intention is particularly powerful when yoked as it is in Thomas's commentary on St. John to that splendid scholastic device, the division of the text. In a division of the text, a commentator states some theme that serves as an interpretive key for his commentary. St. Albert the Great uses the lion and its attributes as the starting point for his commentary on the Gospel according to St. Mark. The Franciscan John of La Rochelle uses a passage from Isaiah as the starting point for his commentary on the Gospel according to St. Matthew. With the theme stated, the commentator begins to divide the text, dividing each division in turn into smaller and smaller parts down to the verse or even smaller. Thus, St. Albert divides the Gospel according to St. Mark into seven initial parts according to seven properties of the lion.

The division of the text provides a sustained structural analysis by which the parts of the Gospel stand in relation both to the whole and to each other.

---

10. *ST* I-II, q. 12, a. 1, ad 4.

No verse stands in isolation, but rather each stands in a rich and organic set of relations to the rest of the Gospel. The division maintains the integrity of the Gospel in the midst of careful, detailed, and often word for word interpretation. In the *De potentia,* Thomas stated that one of the criteria for considering the legitimacy of a given interpretation of Scripture is that "the circumstance of the letter" is preserved. By providing a context that reaches not only to the surrounding verses or even chapters, but to the Gospel as a whole, the division of the text articulates in a highly formal way the circumstance of the letter.[11]

In his *Commentary on John,* Thomas yokes the division of the text to the intention of the author. I quoted above the opening sentence of the commentary: "John the Evangelist principally intends to show the divinity of the Word incarnate"; but this is only the first part of the sentence, which significantly concludes, "and thus this Gospel is divided into two parts: for first, he presents the divinity of Christ; second, he makes it known through those things which Christ accomplished in the flesh." In the Commentary on the Gospel according to St. John, the intention becomes the defining note of the division. Thus the whole and its parts are ultimately seen in relation to John's end of making known the divinity of the Word Incarnate. Since, intention embraces not only the end but also the means to the end, the manifold subdivisions of the text ultimately relate to the first division and its signal theme. Each part of the Gospel is now structurally related as a means to the end of making known the divinity of the incarnate Word, that is, to the intention of the author.

Authorial intention thus has a place in Thomas's interpretation of the Gospel according to St. John. While it does not directly answer the question, what did St. John mean when he wrote a particular passage, it does answer this question: to what ultimate end did St. John write this particular passage. In this, authorial intention is invaluable to the interpreter of the Gospel.

---

11. I have developed this point at more length in "The Theological Character of the Scholastic 'Division of the Text' with Particular Reference to the Commentaries of Saint Thomas Aquinas," in *With Reverence for the Word: Medieval Christian Exegesis in Judaism, Christianity and Islam,* ed. Jane Dammen McAuliffe, Barry D. Walfish and Joseph W. Goering (Oxford: Oxford University Press, 2002), 276–83.

TWO

The Theological Role of the Fathers in Aquinas's *Super Evangelium S. Ioannis Lectura*

STEPHEN F. BROWN

 Many modern studies on the nature of theology according to St. Thomas Aquinas have been centered on his claim for a scientific study of divine revelation. This stress perhaps to a great extent is due to our modern concentration on the opening question of the *Summa theologiae,* where the second article asks: "Whether sacred doctrine is a science?" The immediate context is the preceding article: "Whether besides the philosophical disciplines any further doctrine is required?" By placing sacred doctrine in contrast to the teachings of the philosophical disciplines, Aquinas invites us to compare the kind of science that each provides: in short, which science, philosophy or theology, is more scientific. Theology is more certain, based as it is on divine revelation. Yet, philosophy has, in a sense, a certain advantage: it starts with sources that are evident, not on authority.

Still, the focus on theology as a scientific discipline is due not only to our present-day perspective. Even in Aquinas's own time, one can find that his answer to the question "Whether sacred doctrine is a science?"—namely, that sacred doctrine is a subaltern science whose principles or premises are based most essentially on the authority of divine revelation—was challenged. The discussion, carried on in especially strong terms in the works of Henry of Ghent and Godfrey of Fontaines,[1] shortly after Aquinas's time, led to a certain division con-

---

1. Henricus de Gandavo, *Summa quaestionum ordinariarum,* a. 7, qq. 4–5 (Paris: 1520), f. 52rB–54rH. Cf. S. F. Brown, "Henry of Ghent's Critique of Aquinas's Subalternation Theory and the Early Thomistic Response," in *Knowledge and the Sciences in Medieval Philosophy,* Proceedings of the Eighth International Congress of Medieval Philosophy: Annals of the Finnish Society for Missiology and Ecumenics 55, vol. 3

cerning the meaning of the word "theology." Durandus, in the early fourteenth century, tells us that the word "theology" has three meanings.[2] The first meaning contrasts the "theology" of Aristotle, that is, his first philosophy or metaphysics, with Christian theology, that is, God's revelation in sacred Scripture. This first meaning of "theology," God's divine revelation in the Scriptures, is the fundamental meaning of theology for Durandus and all medieval Christian theologians: they accept what God has revealed because He has revealed it. God is the First Truth. He Himself is the ground of Christian faith. God's authority is the ultimate guarantee of truth, not any experience we ourselves might have undergone.

Given this most fundamental meaning, however, Durandus tells us that the more common meaning given to the word "theology" in his time presents theology as "a lasting quality of the soul by means of which it deduces further things from the articles of the faith and the sayings of sacred Scripture in a way that conclusions are deduced from principles." In short, this form of theology is deductive. For many of the late-thirteenth- and early-fourteenth-century theologians, Thomas Aquinas was the principal exponent for this second form of "theology."

The third meaning of "theology" for Durandus is what he calls at one time "*defensive* or *persuasive* theology," and at another "a habit that *clarifies* and *defends* the articles of the faith." Parallel to his description of deductive theology, he portrays declarative theology as "a lasting quality of the soul by means of which the faith and those things handed down in sacred Scripture are *defended* and *clarified* by using principles that we know better." In the early fourteenth century the author most associated with this declarative theology is the Franciscan Peter Aureoli.

AQUINAS AND DECLARATIVE THEOLOGY

Peter Aureoli is the author who spoke most explicitly of declarative theology as that which ought to be the principal type of theology. It is the habit a theologian develops "from the kind of theological study by which those things we believe are supported by probable arguments taken from other sciences, doubts concerning them are removed, terms expressing them are clarified, and sacred Scripture is explained."[3] Aureoli saw the need for such a de-

---

(Helsinki: 1990), 337–45. Godefridus de Fontibus, *Quodlibet IV*, q. 10 (Louvain: 1904), 262. Cf. P. Tihon, *Foi et théologie selon Godefroid de Fontaines* (Paris: 1966), 120–31.

2. Durandus, *Commentaria in Petri Lombardi Sententias Theologicas* (Venetiis 1571), prol. q. 1, f. 2.

3. Petrus Aureoli, *Scriptum in I Sententiarum*, prooem., sect. 1, n. 92, ed. E. M. Buytaert (St.

clarative theology because of the types of problems encountered by believers. These difficulties, according to Aureoli, are fourfold:

> First, because terms are not properly understood. Secondly, because there are reasons supporting the opposite of Christian belief that confuse the intellect and prevent it from reconciling these reasons with beliefs. Thirdly, because believers lack examples, helps, and analogies to support the truths of the faith. Fourthly, because probable reasons are not available to support Christian beliefs; in other words: even though one can believe something to be true by the power of the will, still if probable reasons are not available, then faith is not viewed as having intellectual support.[4]

These difficulties prompted the development of declarative theology throughout Christian history, according to Aureoli. Even though he criticizes Aquinas's position on deductive theology, he claims that in fact Aquinas's theology is not only deductive, it is also declarative, as is that of all the great doctors:

> But, for sure, this Doctor in his *Summa,* and generally all doctors of theology, formulate questions concerning the articles of faith, and then they go on to give solutions to these questions, and they provide clarification concerning them, and they add arguments supporting them, as when they ask: whether God is only one, or whether in God there is a trinity of persons, or whether the incarnation is possible.[5]

In brief, Aureoli claims that Aquinas practiced both deductive theology and declarative theology. Declarative theology does not focus on principles or premises as supplying the materials for deducing new truths. It focuses on the principles or articles of the faith and clarifies these principles themselves. We might add: Aquinas not only does so, as Aureoli indicates; he also indicates throughout his works why it is necessary to do so.

We might begin with his *Commentary on Boethius's De Trinitate,* where he examines how a theologian deals with the principles or starting points of theology, the articles of the faith. His answer is:

Bonaventure, N.Y.: 1952), I, 159: "ex huiusmodi studio theologico, quo videlicet ea quae credimus rationibus probabilibus sumptis ex aliis scientiis deducuntur, et dissolvuntur omnia dubia, declarantur termini, et explicatur Scriptura."

4. Ibid., n. 113 (I, 165): "Primo quidem quia termini non capiuntur. Secundo vero quia in oppositum sunt rationes intellectum involventes et impedientes ne possit componere quod credit. Tertio quoque quia non sunt exempla, manuductiones, et similitudines ad illud quod creditur.... Quarto vero, cum non sunt probabiles rationes ad illud; licet enim illud credatur esse verum ex imperio voluntatis, non tamen bene capitur aut concipitur ductu intellectus."

5. Petrus Aureoli, *Scriptum,* n. 24, 139: "Sed certum est quod iste Doctor, in *Summa* sua, et universaliter omnes doctores theologi, formant quaestiones de articulis fide, et ad eas dissolvendum, declarandum et concludendum procedunt, ut cum quaeritur: Utrum Deus sit tantum unus, vel: Utrum in Deo sit trinitas personarum; vel: Utrum Incarnatio sit possibilis."

Now, in divine science the articles of faith are like principles and not like conclusions. They are *defended* against those who attack them, as the Philosopher (*Metaph.* IV, 4–6, 1005b 35–1011b 22) argues against those who deny principles. Moreover, they are *clarified* by certain analogies, just as principles that are naturally known are made evident by induction but not proved by demonstrative reasoning.[6]

Aquinas, then, also has an approach to theology where he defends its principles or the articles of the faith by opposing errors or heresies and where through analogies he makes an effort to clarify or make manifest the truths of the faith. Aureoli had announced, as we have said, the list of difficulties throughout Christian history that have demanded diverse responses:

1. Terms are not properly understood.
2. Arguments opposing Christian belief need to be refuted.
3. Believers themselves need examples and analogies to help them better grasp the realities they believe in.
4. In order for faith to be not only an act of the will but also an act of the intellect, arguments are necessary on its behalf.

In the statement of his *Commentary on Boethius's De Trinitate*, Aquinas already spoke of the need for items 2 and 3. Item 1 can be exemplified in q. 13 of the *Prima pars* of his *Summa,* where Thomas gives an instance where he stresses the importance of understanding terms properly: "When we say 'God is good' the meaning is not 'God is the cause of goodness,' or 'God is not evil.' The meaning is 'Whatever good we attribute to creatures, pre-exists in God, and in a more excellent and higher way.'"[7] This is just one of the innumerable instances throughout his works where Thomas clarifies the meaning of terms. Item 4 can be illustrated by the first question of Aquinas's treatise on faith in the *Secunda-secundae* of the *Summa theologiae.* There he tells us:

The arguments employed by holy men to prove things that are of faith are not demonstrations; they are either persuasive arguments showing that what is proposed to our faith is not impossible or else they are proofs drawn from the principles of faith, i.e., from the authority of Holy Scripture, as Dionysius declares. Whatever is based on these principles is as well proved in the eyes of the faithful as a conclusion

---

6. Thomas Aquinas, *In Boetii De Trinitate,* ed. R. M. Spiazzi, *Opuscula theologica* II (1954), prooem., q. 2, a. 2, ad 4um, p. 331: "Articuli autem fidei in hac scientia non sunt quasi conclusiones, sed quasi principia, quae etiam defenduntur ab impugnantibus, sicut et Philosophus IV *Metaph.* disputat contra negantes principia, et manifestantur per aliquas similitudines contra principia naturaliter nota per inductionem, non autem ratione demonstrativa probantur."

7. Thomas Aquinas, *ST* I, q. 13, a. 2: "Cum igitur dicitur 'Deus est bonus,' non est sensus: Deus est causa bonitatis vel Deus non est malus. Sed est sensus: id quod bonitatem dicimus in creaturis praeexistit in Deo, et hoc secundum modum altiorem."

drawn from self-evident principles is in the eyes of all. Hence, again, theology is a science, as we stated at the outset of this work.[8]

In *Quodlibet IV,* Thomas even goes further: he goes to the heart of what Durandus and Aureoli call declarative theology, especially in regard to item 4. In article 18 of this *Quodlibet* Aquinas asks whether a master in determining theological questions should more use reason or authority? He answers:

A disputation can be ordered to a twofold end. Some disputations are set up in order to remove doubts about whether something is true *(an ita sit),* and in such disputations authorities are more often used. . . . Other disputations are more characteristic of the way a master teaches in the schools. The end or purpose is not to remove errors but to instruct the listeners so that they may be led to an understanding of the truth on which the master is centering his attention. To achieve this end, it is then necessary to support one's self on reasons that get to the root of the truth and which make one know *how* that which is true is true. Otherwise, if a master determines a question by using pure authorities, then the listener will be guaranteed that something is true *(ita est),* but he will acquire nothing of science or understanding and he will go away with an empty head.[9]

Aquinas's portrait of this second type of disputation is very reminiscent of the portrait William of Auxerre gave of "understanding" in the prologue of his *Summa aurea:*

Now, when someone has true faith and also has reasons by which faith can be illustrated, he himself does not rely on the First Truth because of these reasons. Rather, he assents to these reasons because they agree with the First Truth and confirm it. . . . The more faith a person has, the more quickly and clearly he sees such reasons, since faith is an illumination of the mind that helps us to see God and divine things. And the more a soul is illuminated by faith, the more it sees not just *that* something is as it be-

---

8. Thomas Aquinas, *ST* II-II, q. 1, a. 5, ad 2: "Dicendum quod rationes quae inducuntur a Sanctis ad probandum ea quae sunt fidei non sunt demonstrativae, sed persuasiones quaedam manifestantes non esse impossibile quod in fide proponitur, vel procedunt ex principiis fidei, scilicet ex auctoritatibus sacrae Scripturae, sicut dicit Dionysius, II cap. *De divinis nominibus.* Ex his autem principiis ita probatur aliquid apud fideles sicut etiam ex principiis naturaliter notis probatur aliquid apud omnes. Unde etiam theologia scientia est, ut in principio Operis dictum est."

9. Thomas Aquinas, *Quodlibet IV,* a. 18: "Utrum magister determinando quaestiones theologicas magis debeat uti ratione vel auctoritate? . . . Disputatio autem ad duplicem finem potest ordinari. Quaedam enim disputatio ordinatur ad removendum dubitationem 'an ita sit"; et in tali disputatione theologica maxime utendum est auctoritatibus. . . . Quaedam vero disputatio est magistralis in scholis non ad removendum errorem, sed ad instruendum auditores ut inducantur ad intellectum veritatis quam intendit. Et tunc oportet rationibus inniti investigantibus veritatis radicem, et facientibus scire quomodo sit verum quod dicitur: alioquin si nudis auctoritatibus magister quaestionem determinet, certificabitur quidem auditor quod ita est, sed nihil scientiae vel intellectus acquiret, et vacuus abscedet."

lieves it to be, but *how* it is as it believes it to be, and *why* it is as it believes it to be. This is the definition of understanding.[10]

DECLARATIVE THEOLOGY IN AQUINAS'S *SUPER EVANGELIUM S. IOANNIS LECTURA*

The *Commentary on the Gospel of St. John* was probably given in Paris in 1270–1272, and Thomas was well-prepared for his work by his *Glossae super evangelia* or *Catena aurea*, which he began at Orvieto toward the end of 1262 or the beginning of 1263.[11] The *Commentary on John* depends heavily on the Fathers of the Church, so our brief examination will focus on how the Fathers contribute to the declarative theology we find in these lectures. In Aquinas's own prologue, he reports the judgment of Augustine concerning the four evangelists: "The other evangelists instruct us in their Gospels on the active life; but John in his Gospel instructs us also on the contemplative life" (*Ioan.* prol., n. 1). John does not start with the earthly life of Christ, but with His heavenly or divine life: "In the beginning was the Word. . . ." For Aquinas, the subject matter of this Gospel is presented in these terms:

For while the other Evangelists treat principally of the mysteries of the humanity of Christ, John, especially and above all, makes known the divinity of Christ in his Gospel. . . . Still, he does not ignore the mysteries of his humanity. He did this because, after the other Evangelists had written their Gospels, heresies had arisen concerning the divinity of Christ, to the effect that Christ was purely and simply a man. (*Ioan.* prol., n. 10)

Peter Aureoli did not invent declarative theology. He claimed the opposite: that Aquinas and all other *doctores theologi* practiced it. We will examine Thomas's *Commentary on John* to see to what degree this claim is true in regard to this particular work of St. Thomas. The subject matter is the divinity

---

10. Guillelmus Altissiodorensis, *Summa aurea*, ed. J. Ribaillier (Paris-Grottaferrata: 1980), I, prol., I, 16: "Cum autem habet quis veram fidem et rationes quibus ostendi possit fides, ipse non innititur primae veritati propter illas rationes, sed potius acquiescit illis rationibus quia consentiunt primae veritati et ei attestantur. . . . Quanto autem maior est in aliquo fides, tanto citius et clarius videt huiusmodi rationes, quoniam fides mentis est illuminatio ad Deum videndum et res divinas. Et quanto magis illuminatur, tanto clarius videt anima non tantum quod ita est ut credit, sed quomodo ita est et quare ita est ut credit; quod est intelligere."

11. Cf. J.-P. Torrell, *Saint Thomas Aquinas*, vol. 1: *The Person and His Work*, trans. R. Royal (Washington, D.C.: The Catholic University of America Press, 1996), 198–201 and 136–40. On studies on this commentary, see ibid., 201, n. 10. On the relation between the *Catena aurea* and the *Super evangelium S. Ioannis Lectura*, see the detailed study of C. G. Conticello, "San Tommaso ed i Padri: La *Catena aurea super Ioannem*," *Archives d'histoire doctrinale et littéraire du moyen âge* 65 (1990): 31–92.

and humanity of Christ. We will search for its form or method of procedure by following the list of items that make up declarative theology according to the description given by Aureoli. Essentially, it is an examination of Thomas's use of the Fathers, who are for him the custodians of John's Gospel, to see in what way they help him in his declarative efforts.

1. The proper use of terms

Right from the beginning of his work, Aquinas makes us aware of the importance of terms, and uses the text of John and the comments of the Fathers to bring about this precision. In approaching this issue of the proper use of language, we may find it helpful to look at an earlier attempt to deal with John the Evangelist's opening words, "In the beginning was the *Word*." "Word" is our English translation of the Greek "Logos." For Latin Christians an appropriate expression for Greek words required some effort. The Roman Stoic philosophers had already translated *logos* by *ratio*, the universal and divine reason, of which human reason *(ratio)* is a spark. But in *Adversus Praxean* 5,[12] Tertullian seemed deliberately to hesitate regarding the already existing Roman philosophical term *ratio* when searching for a corresponding Latin expression for *logos*. He chose instead the first of two alternatives used by the Church in Africa for *logos*, namely *sermo* and *verbum*. And although Tertullian himself at a technical level might have wished to distinguish between the divine *logos* as *verbum* (immanent in God before creation) and *logos* as *sermo* (the *logos* as expressed in creation), he selected *sermo*, because the Old Latin African Bible (with its "In primordio Sermo erat apud Deum") was so familiar to African Christian communities, whereas only a few learned individuals could grasp the subtle theological distinction that Tertullian himself made between *verbum*, expressing the immanent *logos* of God, and *sermo*, expressing the *logos* of God as manifested in creation.[13]

---

12. Tertullian, *Adversus Praxean*, 5 (CCSL II, 1163–64): "Rationalis enim Deus et ratio in ipsum prius et ita ab ipso omnia. Quae ratio sensus ipsius est. Hanc Graeci logon dicunt, quo vocabulo etiam sermonem appellamus ideoque iam in usi est nostrorum per simplicitatem interpretationis sermonem dicere in primordio apud Deum fuisse, cum magis rationem competat antiquiorem haberi, quia non sermonalis a principio sed rationalis Deus etiam ante principium, et quia ipse quoque sermo ratione consistens priorem eam ut substantiam suam ostendat. Tamen et sic nihil interest. Nam etsi Deus nondum sermonem suum miserat, proinde eum cum ipsa et in ipsa ratione intra semetipsum habebat, tacite cogitando et disponendo secum quae per sermonem mox erat dicturus. Cum ratione enim sua cogitans atque disponens sermonem, eam efficiebat quam sermone tractabat."

13. Cf. Stephen F. Brown, "Medieval Philosophy and Theology," in *Medieval Latin: An Introduction and Bibliographical Guide*, ed. F. A. C. Mantello and A. G. Rigg (Washington, D.C.: 1996), 267–87.

Aquinas is more precise than Tertullian, and it is not just because St. Jerome has given him John's opening words as "In principio erat Verbum." He has further reasons. He notes that the Word spoken of by John differs from our own word in three ways. The first difference derives from Augustine's *De Trinitate*:[14] our word is formable before it is formed. We go through a process of cogitation or discourse before we arrive at a complete and perfect grasp of a thing and have a word. Our word is first in potency before it is in act. The Word of God, in contrast, is always in act. The second difference likewise comes from Augustine. Our word is imperfect: it takes many words to express our thoughts—whereas the divine Word is most perfect: "If there were less in the Word than the One speaking it, the Word would be imperfect; but it is most perfect; therefore, it is only one" (*Ioan.* 1, lect. 1, n. 27). The third difference has as its source John of Damascus's *De fide orthodoxa*:[15] our word is not of the same nature as we; but the divine Word is of the same nature as God. Since our soul is not its own operation, to understand is not the same as the nature of the soul. In God, to understand and to be are the same, so the Word is not an accident, but belongs to its nature. The Word is consubstantial with the Father—whereas our interior words are only concepts of the mind. From these considerations it is clear that the Word is co-eternal with that from which it issues; and that it is equal to the Father, since it is perfect and expressive of the whole being of the Father; and that it is co-essential and consubstantial with the Father, since it is His substance (*Ioan.* 1, lect. 1, nn. 26–28).

Certain aporiae concerning the Word that the Fathers present help us clarify matters even further. The first question comes from John Chrysostom, who Aquinas tells us is of such great authority among the Greeks as an expos-

---

14. Augustine, *De Trinitate* XV, c. 11 (CCSL LA, 488): "Perveniendum est ergo ad illud verbum hominis, ad verbum rationalis animantis, ad verbum non de deo natae sed a deo factae imaginis dei, quod neque prolativum est in sono neque cogitativum in similitudine soni quod alicuius linguae esse necesse sit, sed quod omnia quibus significatur signa praecedit et gignitur de scientia quae manet in animo quando eadem scientia intus dicitur sicuti est."

15. John of Damascus, *De fide orthodoxa* I, 6 (PG 94, 803): "At Deus, cum sempiternus perfectusque sit, perfectum quoque et subsistens, vereque exsistens Verbum suum habet; et quod semper sit, et vivat, et omnia habeat, quae Pater habet. Sicut enim sermo noster ex mente progrediens, nec prorsus cum mente idem est, nec rursum omnino ab ea diversus (quatenus enim ex mente, hactenus alius est a mente; quatenus vero mentem ipsam palam profert, non jam prorsus a mente diversus est, verum natura quidem est unum cum ea, subjecto autem ab illa diversum): ad eumdem modum Dei quoque Verbum, quatenus per se subsistit, ab eo distinguitur, a quo habet ut per se subsistat: quatenus autem eadem in ipso ostendit, quae in Deo conspiciuntur, idem natura cum ipso est. Quemadmodum enim omnimoda undique perfectio in Patre perspicitur, eadem etiam in Verbo ex ipso genito spectatur."

itor of Scripture that they do not admit other expositions if Chrysostom has given one (*Ioan.* 1, lect. 2, n. 94). The question is: Why did the Evangelist begin his Gospel by omitting the Father and begin with the Son, saying: "In the beginning was the Word"? This question has two answers: the Father was known to everyone in the Old Testament, not under the aspect of Father, but as God. So, in the New Testament, which is concerned with our knowledge of the Word, he begins with the Word or Son. Another answer to Chrysostom's query is that we are brought to know the Father through the Son. So, the Evangelist fittingly began with the Son, to lead the faithful to a knowledge of the Father (*Ioan.* 1, lect. 1, n. 30).[16]

The second question also derives from Chrysostom: Why did he not say "In the beginning was the Son" instead of "In the beginning was the Word"? Again there are two answers: "Son" means something begotten, and when we hear of the generation of the Son, someone might suppose that this generation is the kind he can comprehend, that is, a material and changeable generation. Thus, he did not say "Son," but "Word," which signifies an intelligible proceeding, so that it would not be understood as a material and changeable generation. By showing that the Son is born of the Father in an unchangeable way, he eliminates a faulty conjecture (*Ioan.* 1, lect. 1, n. 31).[17]

A third query comes again from St. Augustine—and it brings us back to Tertullian's difficulty about translating *logos*. The difference is that Augustine provides fewer options *(ratio* and *verbum* instead of *sermo, ratio,* and *verbum),* and his economy effectively brings clarity. Augustine asks: Why did the translators pick *Verbum* instead of *ratio,* since both are interior? Aquinas, following Augustine, answers that *ratio* does not signify a relation to anything exterior, whereas *Verbum* does. Because the Evangelist intended to signify not only a reference to the Son's existence in the deity but also the operative power of the Son, by which, through Him, all things were made, Augustine says: "Our predecessors preferred to translate it as 'Word' which implies a reference to something exterior" (*Ioan.* 1, lect. 1, n. 32).[18]

With the help of his Patristic predecessors, Aquinas has brought some precision to the use of terms and has applauded the Gospel's writer and translators for helping us avoid faulty conjectures. In a way that might go unnoticed, he also was doing other declarative activities—warding off heresies, showing the analogies used by sacred Scripture and the Fathers, and provid-

---

16. Cf. John Chrysostom, *Homiliae LXXXVIII Ioannem,* II, 12 (PG 59, 34).

17. Cf. John Chrysostom, *Homiliae.*

18. Cf. St. Augustine, *De diversis quaestionibus octaginta tribus capitula,* q. 63 (CCSL XLIVA, 136).

ing reasons that bring intellectual support for the Christian beliefs about the Son of God, the eternal, perfect Word who is consubstantial with the Father. But let us move on to more explicit and noticeable efforts at dealing with items 2–4 concerning declarative theology.

2. The defenses against heresies and errors

In Thomas's Prologue he tells us that John wrote his Gospel after the others and that, without setting aside the humanity of Christ, he in a special and primary way spoke of Christ's divinity, since many heresies arose after the time of the synoptic Gospels (*Ioan.* prol., n. 10).

> And so John the Evangelist, who drunk of the truth of the divinity of Christ from the very Fountain of the divine breast, at the requests of the faithful, wrote that Gospel in which he handed down the teaching of Christ's divinity and refuted all the heresies concerning Christ. (*Ioan.* prol., n. 10)

Again, at the end of Lecture 1, Aquinas notes succinctly that the opening words of John's Gospel ("In the beginning was the Word; and the Word was with God; and the Word was God; He was in the beginning with God") "clearly destroy all the errors of the heretics and of the philosophers" (*Ioan.* 1, lect. 1, n. 64). "In the beginning was the Word" refutes the errors of the Ebionites, Cerinthus, Photinus, and Paul of Samosata, who claimed that Christ had no existence before he was born of the Virgin and thus was purely a man. The words "And the Word was with God" overcome the claim of Sabellius, who argued that the Father and the Son were identical persons. Eunomius's contention that the Son was not like the Father is refuted by the third statement, "And the Word was God." And finally, Arius's effort to subordinate the Son, making him less than the Father, is discounted with the words "He was in the beginning with God" (*Ioan.* 1, lect. 1, n. 64).

Thomas also points out that the same verses refute the teachings of the classical philosophers. The Pre-Socratics, who asserted that the world was unconnected to an intellect or to reason and thus was due to chance, are refuted by the opening line, "In the beginning was the Word." Plato's claim that the reasons of things are found in the Ideas separated from God is voided by the words "And the Word was with God." Following a lead from John Chrysostom, Aquinas notes that the Platonists, who subordinated Mind to God, are challenged by John's declaration "And the Word was with God." Even Aristotle's contention that the world is eternal is refuted by the words "He [alone] was in the beginning with God" (*Ioan.* 1, lect. 1, n. 65).

The Fathers play a leading role throughout Thomas's *Commentary on John* in his effort to show how the whole Gospel is a refutation of early Church heresies. Chrysostom, Hilary, Augustine, and Gregory the Great are invoked against Arius and the Arians (*Ioan.* nn. 69, 477, 978, 1794, 1999). Augustine and Gregory likewise expose the errors of the Manicheans (*Ioan.* nn. 1279, 1580). Gregory, furthermore, attacks the heresy of Eutyches (*Ioan.* n. 2559). Yet, these attacks and defenses against heresies and errors are not purely negative. As they dispute with their opponents, the Fathers often explain and clarify issues, as is especially clear in the case of Augustine (*Ioan.* nn. 1794, 1999). Quite likely, this positive accent in dealing with heretics led Peter Aureoli to truncate Durandus's "theologia declarativa et defensiva" to the simpler "theologia declarativa."

3. The uses of analogies and examples

The pattern for patristic and medieval theologians is to envision the Book of the Scriptures as the revelation of God's wisdom and providence, which they at times called the Book of Life. Since the Scriptures are a revelation to men, they are written and preached in human words and provide natural examples. The Book of Nature supplies the materials we need to dig deeper into the Scriptures that reveal the wisdom and providence of God. John's Gospel speaks of Christ washing the feet of his disciples (13:4–10), and also of "light," "life," and "Word." To understand the Gospel message, it is necessary to examine the scriptural examples. They help us to see better the wisdom of God revealed in the Scriptures.

Aquinas might go to different sources to mine the riches of this Gospel. To understand "Word" he goes to Aristotle's *Perihermeneias,* where the Philosopher tells us the "words" are "signs of passions of the soul" and of things (*Ioan.* 1, lect. 1, n. 25). But, as we have seen, he also goes to Augustine and John of Damascus to discover the ways in which the divine Word differs from our human words. To understand "light," he turns to "Augustine and many others" (*Ioan.* 1, lect. 3, n. 96; 8, 2, n. 1142), especially Ambrose, in order to grasp something about spiritual light and about Christ as the "light that shines in darkness," and "the life that is the light of men" (1, 4–5). And, in contrast, he will follow Augustine in his attempt to explain to the Manicheans the many meanings of "darkness" (*Ioan.* 1, lect. 3, nn. 102–3; 8, 2, n. 1142). He will even undercut the analogies and examples of heretics, such as Eutyches, and show that they not only limp, but totally distort the revealed realities of true Christian faith (*Ioan.* 1, lect. 7, n. 166). The use of analogies is inescapable when one wants to understand the Scriptures.

4. Arguments supporting the faith

Aquinas often supplies reasons or arguments to support his interpretation of John's Gospel. Against Arius and Apollinaris he argues:

> The falsity of this opinion is obvious, both because it is in conflict with Sacred Scripture, which often mentions the soul of Christ. . . . Also, God cannot be the form of a body. Nor can an angel be unified to a body as its form, since an angel, according to its very nature is separated from body, whereas a soul is united to a body as its form. Consequently, the Word of God cannot be the form of a body. . . . The same conclusion [that Christ has an intellectual soul] can be reached by reason. For as there is no flesh without a soul, so there is no human flesh without a human soul, which is an intellectual soul. So, if the Word assumed flesh which was animated with a merely sensitive soul to the exclusion of a rational soul, he did not assume human flesh; consequently, one could not say: "God became man." Besides, the Word assumed human nature in order to repair it. Therefore, he repaired what he assumed. But if he did not assume a rational soul, he would not have repaired it. Consequently, no fruit would have accrued to us from the incarnation of the Word; and this is false. (*Ioan.* 1, lect. 7, nn. 167–68)

Not only does Aquinas supply reasons for his own positions, but he also provides the reasons or arguments that the Fathers give for their interpretations. They are authorities, but they are often authorities that back up their interpretations with reasons. We noted this, as we have seen a number of times, when he gave Augustine's and Damascene's reasons for distinguishing human words from the Divine Word. We also see it when he treats the knowledge men have of God, where he invokes Pseudo-Dionysius (*Ioan.* 1, lect. 11, nn. 211–12). It is likewise to the arguments of Augustine that Aquinas turns when he speaks of the different types of grace (*Ioan.* 1, lect. 10, nn. 205–6).

CONCLUSION

Aquinas does indeed practice a declarative theology. He realized that the conclusions of any deductive theology received whatever light or understanding they had from the light beyond faith found in the principles or premises. The premises of faith are not accepted because of the declarative efforts of a theologian, but these efforts on the part of the believer do provide some understanding of the truths of the faith. These declarative efforts are made by Aquinas himself, but to a very great extent he was assisted and inspired in his efforts, especially in his *Commentary on John,* by the earlier efforts of the Fathers of the Church, especially Augustine, Chrysostom, Hilary, Gregory the Great, and John of Damascus—as the indexes and texts well indicate.

PART 2

The Triune God

THREE

Biblical Exegesis and the Speculative Doctrine of the Trinity in St. Thomas Aquinas's *Commentary on St. John*

GILLES EMERY, O.P.

 The theological exposition of the Gospel of St. John is certainly to be considered the most fully complete and most profound commentary that St. Thomas Aquinas has left us.[1] According to M.-D. Philippe, the *Commentary on St. John* is "the theological work par excellence of St. Thomas": this commentary enables us to enter into the theological intelligence of St. Thomas, even better than does the *Summa theologiae* or the *Summa contra gentiles*.[2] This special value of the *Commentary on the Gospel of St. John* is to be found notably in the importance of the speculative developments of the biblical exposition, which count among the characteristic features of this work. This general observation raises a question: Is the biblical exegesis of St. Thomas in his *Commentary on St. John* different than his speculative teaching in the *Summa theologiae*, and if so, what is the difference?

To try and give a partial response to this question, the present contribution proposes to consider the commentary's Trinitarian doctrine. Our approach does not examine the details of St. Thomas's teaching on particular points of Trinitarian doctrine, but it considers rather the body of the commentary's Trinitarian doctrine under the aspect of the whole and of its organic unity. The choice of Trinitarian theology is not without reasons: it concerns a cornerstone of the speculative theol-

---

1. This essay appears as chapter 7 of Gilles Emery, O.P., *Trinity in Aquinas* (Ypsilanti, Mich.: Sapientia Press, 2003).
2. Marie-Dominique Philippe, "Préface" to *Thomas d'Aquin, Commentaire sur l'Évangile de saint Jean*, vol. 1 (Paris: Cerf, 1998), 10–11. Cf. J.-P. Torrell, *Saint Thomas Aquinas*, vol. 1: *The Person and His Work*, 200.

ogy of St. Thomas and, as such, gives a number of clues for measuring the connection between exegesis and speculative theology. Our comparative study will try to find the answers to three specific questions: (1) What is the Trinitarian doctrinal content of the *Commentary on St. John* in relation to that of the *Summa theologiae*? (2) What is St. Thomas's exegetical and theological method in the Trinitarian teaching of the *Commentary on St. John*? (3) What does the *Commentary on St. John* bring to our understanding of the Trinitarian doctrine of St. Thomas?

THE TRINITARIAN DOCTRINE OF THE *COMMENTARY OF ST. JOHN* AND THE *SUMMA THEOLOGIAE*

To verify the extent of the Trinitarian themes treated in the *Commentary on St. John*, the comparison with the treatise of the Trinity in the *Summa theologiae* (*Prima pars,* qq. 27–43) is very instructive. As a matter of fact, most of the themes expounded in the *Summa* are present in the *Commentary on St. John*: they are not only mentioned indirectly, but they are expressly expounded or discussed by St. Thomas. The results of our comparison have been gathered together in the synoptic table that follows. This table, however, is not exhaustive; numerous allusions and evocations have not been included here. The passages indicated are sometimes composed of a short insight on a theme, sometimes a more extensive account: the references are, for this reason, often of unequal value (the numbers in boldface type indicate the most important passages; the numbers in parentheses point to some themes that are mentioned by St. Thomas but that are not a subject of discussion; a hyphen indicates no direct mention of the same theme). This table therefore gives only an approximate material idea; it allows us, however, to measure the amplitude of the Trinitarian doctrine of the *Commentary on John* (passages of the commentary are indicated following the numeration used in the Marietti Edition and in the English translation by J. A. Weisheipl and F. R. Larcher)[3] compared with that of the *Summa theologiae* (qq. 27–43):

---

3. St. Thomas Aquinas, *Super Evangelium S. Ioannis lectura,* ed. Raffaele Cai (Turin/Rome: Marietti, 1952). *Commentary on the Gospel of John,* Part 1, trans. Weisheipl and Larcher; *Commentary on the Gospel of John,* Part 2, trans. Fabian R. Larcher (Petersham, Mass.: St. Bede's Publications, 1999).

TABLE I

Q. 27, a. 1: nn. **24–33, 41,** 56, 769, 2107, 2064, 2114, **2161,** 2172; a. 2: nn. **29, 31** (24–33), 41–42, 46, 218, 547, **750,** 768, 782, 977, 978, 1462, 1869, 2161, 2262; a. 3: n. 2064; a. 4: nn. 545, 753, 2064; a. 5: -.

Q. 28, a. 1: n. 2113; a. 2: n. **2113; a. 3:** n. **2063, 2112–13;** a. 4: -.

Q. 29, a. 1: -; a. 2: -; a. 3: - (nn. 28, 49); a. 4: -.

Q. 30, a. 1: - (nn. 64, 2248); a. 2: -; a. 3: - (nn. 1450–51, 1462, 2050, 2172); a. 4: -.

Q. 31, a. 1: - (nn. 64, 1946); a. 2: nn. 1451, 1911–12; a. 3: n. 2187; a. 4: nn. 1154, 2172, 2187–88.

Q. 32, a. 1: -; a. 2: -; a. 3: -; a. 4: -.

Q. 33, a. 1: nn. 36, 1183, 1971, 2213; a. 2: nn. 1278, 1922, 2195; a. 3: nn. 36, 390, 741, 1060, 1278, 1922, 2195, 2520–21; a. 4: n. 747.

Q. 34, a. 1: nn. 24–33 [28–29], 41, 46, 49, 50–51, 54, **55,** 56–59, 534, 540, 754, 780, 1874, 1878, 1893; a. 2: nn. **25,** 28–29, 33, 42, 754, 1720, 1726, 1869, 1951; a. 3: nn. 7–8, **27, 32, 35,** 38, **68–78** [76–77], **79–88, 89–94, 118,** 133–34, 135, 136, 740, 761, 1183, 1450, 1553, 1695, **1723,** 1781, 1869, 1879, 2201.

Q. 35, a. 1: n. 1879 (nn. 1712, 1878, 1951); a. 2: -.

Q. 36, a. 1: n. 452, 1916, 1955, 2062, **2064;** a. 2: nn. 543, 753, 1092, **1916,** 1956–57, **2062–65, 2107–15,** 2538; a. 3: n. 2064 (nn. 74–76); a. 4: nn. 1183, 2065 (2115).

Q. 37, a. 1: nn. 357, 545, 753, 1004, 2060, 2064, 2262; a. 2: n. 2214.

Q. 38, a. 1: -; a. 2: -.

Q. 39, a. 1: nn. 2113, 2209; a. 2: - (nn. 1450–51, 1794, 1929); a. 3: - (nn. 187, 2188); a. 4: nn. 44, 58, 59, 187, 1851; a. 5: n. **44;** a. 6: -; a. 7: -; a. 8: nn. 1912, 1961, 2365 (nn. 76, 77, 90, 207, 533, 1192, 1290, 1869).

Q. 40, a. 1: n. 2113; a. 2: nn. **2063, 2064, 2111–13;** a. 3: - (n. 2063); a. 4: -.

Q. 41, a. 1: -; a. 2: nn. 545, 753, 2114, 2262; a. 3: nn. 162, 202, 2108, 2115; a. 4: - (n. 543); a. 5: -; a. 6: -.

Q. 42, a. 1: - (cf. a. 4); a. 2: nn. 37–39, 41, 62, 66–67, 70, 750, 783, 1059–1060, 2161; a. 3: nn. **34,** 2064, **2107, 2112–13;** a. 4: nn. 11, 59, 64, **741–47,** 769, 783, 1278, 1451, 1875, 1970–71, 2192, 2208; a. 5: nn. 36, 49, 50, 54, **1466,** 1880–81, 1887, **1891,** 1926–29, 2161, 2172, 2214, 2239; a. 6: nn. 62, 69, 71, 76, 452, 748, 749, **751–53,** 761, 786–87, 797, 817, 1304, 1450–51, 1743, 1775, 1999.

Q. 43, a. 1: nn. 144, 769, 1794, 1944, 2061, 2088–2090, 2161–62; a. 2: nn. 1236, 2061, 2161–62, 2204; a. 3: nn. 176, 292, 541–544, 1853, 1915, 1920, 1930, 1943–47, 1958, 1961, 2061, 2246–47, 2248, 2269–70; a. 4: nn. 176, 1192, 2248; a. 5: nn. 292, 946, 1930, 1961, 2090; a. 6: - (cf. a. 3); a. 7: nn. 1662, 2538–40; a. 8: nn. 1794, 1911, 1956–57, 1958, 2059, 2061, 2248.

The Trinitarian themes of the *Commentary on St. John*

The most important Trinitarian accounts in St. Thomas's *Commentary on John* concern the five following fields: (1) the person of the Son and his generation (in particular the doctrine of the Word); (2) the person of the Spirit and his procession; (3) the person of the Father; (4) the equality of the persons; (5) the mission of the persons (this corresponds to the teaching in the questions 33, 34, 36, 42, and 43 of the *Prima pars* of the *Summa theologiae*).

The most remarkable case is without a doubt the doctrine of the Word. Except for a few details, the whole doctrine of question 34 of the *Summa* is to be found in the *Commentary on St. John*: the meaning of the word *verbum* explained on the basis of Aristotle's *Perihermeneias*, the relationship between the inner word and the exterior word, the mode of procession of the Word in God, the differences between the human and divine Word, the exclusively personal signification of the name *Verbum* in God, the relationship of the Word to the Father who says it (coeternity, consubstantiality, etc.), the distinction of the Word and of the Father, the relational character of the Word that constitutes the property of the Son, and so forth. The speculative account of the *Commentary on St. John* is more developed than that of the *Summa* on several points: this shows in the numerous explications that concern the creative action of the Word,[4] but also in the affirmation of the *necessity* of a word in all intellectual nature, and in the conception of the word as the relative object of intellection ("that in which the intellect knows *[in quo intellectus intelligit]*") (*Ioan.* 1, lect. 1, n. 25).[5] The doctrine of the Word, in the *Commentary on St. John*, gives a characteristic example of a highly speculative point of view that is treated in such amplitude as to be comparable, even superior to, the *Summa theologiae*. It is also very near to the *Summa contra gentiles*, in which the exposition dedicated to the Word is structured by the *Prologue* of St. John (IV, ch. 11).[6]

The study of the person of the Father and of the Holy Spirit manifests equally the extent of the Trinitarian doctrine in the *Commentary on St. John*: St. Thomas, in a way close to that of the *Summa theologiae*, expounds in what

---

4. See the above table under the rubric: q. 34, a. 3.

5. On these two points, see Yves Floucat, "L'intellection et son Verbe selon saint Thomas d'Aquin," *Revue Thomiste* 97 (1997): 650–54 and 684–91.

6. See Emery, "The Treatise of St. Thomas on the Trinity in the *Summa contra gentiles*," in *Trinity in Aquinas*, 93–106 (the section entitled "Approaches to a Theological Understanding of the Mystery"). St. Thomas's commentary on St. John does not cover the exclusion of the name "Verbum" to designate the Holy Spirit (*ST* I, q. 34, a. 2, ad 5); but this doctrinal point stays attached to biblical exegesis, as the commentary on the Epistle to the Hebrews explicitly witnesses (*Super ad Hebraeos* 1:3; Ed. Marietti, n. 34).

way the word "principium" applies to the Father, giving the precision that paternity constitutes the personal property of the Father. It gives details in several places of the analogic extension of the name "Father" that applies to the Trinitarian relation of the Father to the Son and then to the relationship that the Father has with the creatures, in the order of creation and in the order of grace. For that which concerns the Father, only the study of the innascibility seems to be less developed in the *Commentary on St. John* in comparison to the *Summa theologiae* (q. 33, a. 4). As to the Holy Spirit, the Johannine commentary presents also a teaching very similar to that of question 36 in the *Summa theologiae:* apart from the explanation of the proper name *"Spiritus Sanctus,"* St. Thomas develops in a very broad way the doctrine of the procession of the Holy Spirit *a Filio,* as well as that of the unity of the Father and the Son as principle of the Spirit, treating the procession *per Filium* more briefly. The *Commentary on St. John* (especially in the exegesis of John 14:15, John 15:26, and John 16:14–15) presents a highly speculative technical doctrine, which brings to light all the major themes of the doctrine of the *Summa:* the mode of procession of the Son and the Spirit, the personal distinction by relative opposition depending on the origin, the unity of the Father and of the Son who are the one principle of the Spirit, the theme of Love, Trinitarian order, the identity of the principle of communication and of the reality communicated. The biblical exegesis brings St. Thomas to demonstrate that, *Trinitate posita,* it is necessary to recognize that the Spirit proceeds from the Father and the Son (*Ioan.* 15, lect. 5, n. 2063).[7] More developed in the *Commentary on St. John* than in the *Summa theologiae,* the doctrine of the *Filioque* also provides the place where par excellence St. Thomas sets forth his doctrine on the various types of distinction, in particular about the real relation depending on the origin that alone distinguishes the persons in God. The exegesis of St. John gives the occasion for an exposition of the *Filioque* that involves all essential elements of the doctrine of relation, as found in question 28 of the *Prima pars.* It is again in the exegesis of these pneumatological passages that St. Thomas expounds several elements concerning the relationship of the persons to the essence, or the relationship of the persons to properties and relations: the real identity of the person with the essence, the real identity of the relation with the essence, as well as the necessity to pose the relation of origin (relative opposition) to be able to conceive the distinct persons (cf. *Prima pars,* qq. 40 and 41). We can observe here again the proximity of the *Commentary on St. John* to the *Summa contra gentiles:* in the

---

7. *Ioan.* 15, lect. 5, n. 2063, cf. 2064–5; 16, lect. 4, nn. 2110–15). On these arguments, see Emery, "The Procession of the Holy Spirit *a Filio* according to St. Thomas Aquinas," in *Trinity in Aquinas,* 209–69.

Summa contra gentiles, indeed, it is equally in the study of the procession of the Holy Spirit (Book IV, chs. 24–25) that St. Thomas placed his most complete exposition about the relations of origin in God.[8]

The equality of the divine persons and the mission of the persons constitute the two last particularly large Trinitarian themes developed by the *Commentary on St. John*. Except for the general reflection on the notion of equality in God (I, q. 42, a. 1), the largest part of the doctrinal contents of question 42 of the *Prima pars* of the *Summa theologiae* is found in the *Commentary on St. John*: the co-eternity of the Father and the Son, the Trinitarian order, the equal greatness of the Father and the Son, the mutual immanence of the Father and the Son, as well as the equality of power in the Father and the Son. The attention given to the equality of the persons corresponds to the general subject of the fourth Gospel, following St. Thomas: whereas the other gospel writers are particularly attentive to what Christ accomplishes in his flesh, St. John "gazes on the very deity of our Lord Jesus Christ, by which he is equal to the Father" (*Ioan.* prol., n. 11). Apart from the mutual immanence of the Father and of the Son, which reveals the divine unity of the persons, we must observe the numerous developments concerning the equality of power and of operation of the Father and the Son. St. Thomas gives us the reason: "For the clearest indication of the nature of a thing is taken from its works. Therefore, from the fact that he does the works of God it can be very clearly known and believed that Christ is God" (*Ioan.* 10, lect. 6, n. 1466). The attention given to the equality of the Father and the Son expressly aims at manifesting the divinity of Christ, which constitutes the trait proper to the fourth Gospel.

Lastly, the long developments concerning the mission of the persons give place to complete expositions on the concepts of *"processio"* and of *"missio,"* on the visible and invisible missions, and on the indwelling of the persons by grace. It is in the context of missions, for example, that St. Thomas explains in a broad way the notion of eternal procession *(exitus)*, which carries the double aspect of the identity of nature (immanent action) and the personal distinction (*Ioan.* 16, lect. 7, n. 2161; cf. 15, 5, n. 2062). With the exception of article 6 of question 43 of the *Prima pars,* where St. Thomas establishes that the mission of the divine persons has place in all those who live from grace, the biggest part of the doctrinal contents of question 43 is found in the *Commentary on St. John*. It is hardly surprising that this teaching is placed, in its essentials, in the exegesis of the passages of St. John that concern the announcement of the sending out of the Holy Spirit and the coming of Christ

---

8. See Emery, "The Treatise of St. Thomas on the Trinity in the *Summa contra gentiles,*" in *Trinity in Aquinas.*

to the faithful (chs. 15–17 of the fourth Gospel). It must be added that, in the expositions of the Word and the Spirit, as well as in the discussion of the missions, the *Commentary on St. John* includes most of the explanations concerning the procession in God treated by the three first articles of question 27 of the *Prima pars*.

St. Thomas's *Commentary on St. John* treats several other technical themes. We have already mentioned diverse doctrinal points that touch on the rapport of persons, of relations, and of the essence. It must be added that, in the context of anti-Arian criticism, St. Thomas shows the necessity of the notional act of generation (divine will is not the formal principle of the generation of the Word) and the substantial principle of a notional act (the Son does not proceed *de nihilo*, but he is engendered from the substance of the Father). Treated in question 41 (aa. 2 and 3) of the *Prima pars*, in the section on notional acts, these problems are exposed by the *Commentary on St. John* in the context of the generation of the Son and the procession of the Holy Spirit. Here St. Thomas underlines, with remarkable rigor, the identity of the principle of communication and the reality communicated that is divine substance (*Ioan.* 16, lect. 4, n. 2115). Lastly, several problems of Trinitarian language hold St. Thomas's attention while he comments on St. John. Whereas the *Summa theologiae* gathers these language problems in two defined sections (*Prima pars*, qq. 31 and 39), the *Commentary on St. John* explains them according to the texts of the fourth Gospel: the personal otherness meant by the word *"alius,"* the use of exclusive words qualifying essential or personal names (*"solus"*), the technical logic of *"suppositio"* in Trinitarian language, and the practice of Trinitarian appropriations. We are in the presence, in the middle of a biblical commentary, of a body of Trinitarian doctrine especially well developed.

Absent or Less Developed Trinitarian Themes

Before trying to evaluate the relationship of St. John's commentary and the *Summa theologiae*, we must note that the Commentary does not pay the same attention to all Trinitarian themes. The comparison with the *Summa theologiae* shows that certain themes, to which St. Thomas gives over a question or an article in his systematic work, are not given the same place in the *Commentary on St. John*. Among these less developed themes, we must first of all bring out the definition of the person, that is to say the signification of the word "persona" and the justification of the use of this term in Trinitarian theology. The *Commentary on St. John* frequently employs the word "persona" or "hypostasis" to speak about the Father, Son, and Holy Spirit. St. Thomas indicates that these two words both mean the same reality in God, and he specifies that the divine persons are distinct in virtue of their relations (or personal properties). But he does not explain the signification of the word "persona" and does not develop the speculative study of the concept of person in the context of Trinitarian faith. The statements about hypostatic union employ as frequently the words "person" or "hypostasis," but without precisely defining the concept of person.[9] The famous definition of person given by Boethius is absent from the *Commentary on St. John,* as it is absent from St. Thomas's commentaries on St. Matthew and St. Paul. In reality, despite the fact that St. Thomas does not use the definition of the person made by Boethius, he employs a very precise concept when speaking of the divine Word as "something that subsists in the divine nature *(aliquid subsistens in natura divina)*" (*Ioan.* 1, lect. 1, n. 28).[10] St. Thomas's explanations focus on a distinct reality, in virtue of a relation or a property, which subsists in the manner of a hypostasis in the identity of the divine nature. If we take into account the affirmation of the distinction of hypostasis, which St. Thomas recalls in the same place, we can ascertain that the expression *"aliquid subsistens in natura divina"* corresponds to the formal signification of the word "person" in God, despite the fact that St. Thomas does not specify it in his commentary.[11]

Thus, when he comments on the Gospel of St. John (as well as on St. Matthew and the Epistles of St. Paul), St. Thomas uses a very clear notion to expose the hypostatic subsistence in God, but without discussing the word "person" and its signification. This silence is not exceptional: St. Thomas has a similar discretion concerning the word "person" in the Trinitarian treatise of the *Summa contra gentiles*.[12] It is not easy to evaluate the motives for this discretion. Aquinas knows that the Bible does not apply the word "persona" to the Three Divine: the Trinitarian concept of person comes from the defense of faith by the Fathers in face of heresies.[13] But the non-biblical origin of the

---

9. The *Index thomisticus* allows one to discover 238 uses of the lemma "persona" in the commentary on St. John. For example: "persona Verbi seu suppositum" (n. 170); "hypostasis seu persona, quae est eadem utriusque naturae in Christo" (n. 175); "Trinitas personarum ... tres personae" (n. 357); "si igitur Filius et Spiritus Sanctus sunt personae distinctae procedentes a Patre, oportet quod aliquibus proprietatibus oppositis distinguantur" (n. 2063); "cum personae divinae relationibus distinguantur" (n. 2113); and so on.

10. Cf. n. 49: "Verbum erat in principio, non ut accidens: sed erat apud Deum, ut subsistens, et hypostasis divina."

11. See for example *De pot.,* q. 9, a. 4: "persona vero divina, formali significatione, significat distinctum subsistens in natura divina."

12. See Emery, "The Treatise of St. Thomas on the Trinity in the *Summa contra gentiles*," in *Trinity in Aquinas,* 114–18 (the section entitled "Problems of Trinitarian Theology").

13. *ST* I q. 29, a. 3, ad 1.

concept of person does not suffice to explain St. Thomas's reserve, for the *Commentary on St. John* abundantly develops other doctrines issued from Patristic controversies (the doctrine of Trinitarian relations for example). At the risk of surprising, we must rather conclude that the specific study of the word "person" (the study of the word, and not of the reality) does not constitute an indispensable element of a doctrine on the Trinity by St. Thomas (biblical commentaries and *Summa contra gentiles*).

A further point is the absence of other important elements of St. Thomas's speculative doctrine. Thus, whereas the exposition of the Word is extremely well developed and complete, the parallel explications concerning the Holy Spirit as Love are quite thin. In his *Commentary on St. John,* St. Thomas several times designates the Holy Spirit as Love.[14] Aquinas specifies that the Holy Spirit proceeds as Love by the mode of will,[15] and distinguishes essential Love from personal (or notional) Love in God.[16] St. Thomas expressly excludes that the Son proceeds by mode of Love: Love is the reason of the procession of the Holy Spirit but not that of the Son, who proceeds by mode of nature or of intellect.[17] He also specifies that the Holy Spirit is the mutual *"dilectio"* of the Father and the Son, their "mutual bond."[18] The Father and the Son love each other though the Holy Spirit.[19] But St. Thomas does not expound his doctrine of the presence of "God loved in God who loves," that is to say the loving *"impressio"* or *"affectio"* that springs up in the will when it loves (which allows one to give account, by analogy, of the personal name *Love* that we give to the Holy Spirit): this doctrine, in the *Summa contra gentiles* and in the *Summa theologiae* (as well as in the *Disputed Questions De potentia* and in the *Compendium theologiae*), has in the study of the Holy Spirit a role comparable to the doctrine of the Word in the study on the Son.[20] However, despite the fact that the doctrine of the Word is very well developed in the *Commentary on St. John,* the elaboration of the parallel doctrine of Love is very summary, or even absent: the *Commentary on St. John* by St. Thomas designates several times the Holy Spirit as Love, without ever giving

14. See for example *Ioan.* 15, lect. 5, n. 2060.
15. *Ioan.* 15, lect. 5, n. 2064 "persona procedens per modum voluntatis ut amor." The Son is designated as "persona procedens per modum naturae ut Filius" (ibid.).
16. *Ioan.* 5, lect. 3, n. 753; 17, 6, n. 2262.
17. *Ioan.* 3, lect. 6, n. 545; 5, 3, n. 753; 15, 5, n. 2064.
18. *Ioan.* 3, lect. 6, n. 545: "dilectio Patris ad Filium est Spiritus Sanctus"; cf. *Ioan.* 6, lect. 8, n. 1004: "Spiritus Sancti, qui est amor Patris et Filii, et nexus utriusque."
19. *Ioan.* 17, lect. 4, n. 2214: "Pater et Filius diligunt se Spiritu Sancto."
20. Cf. *ST* I, q. 37, a. 1; see Emery, "The Treatise of St. Thomas on the Trinity in the *Summa contra gentiles*" and "The Treatise on the Trinity in the *Summa theologiae,*" chs. 3 and 4 of *Trinity in Aquinas*.

its speculative reason. This difference may be explained by the fact that the Prologue of the fourth Gospel expressly mentions the *Word* and thus gives the textual opening for an exposition on the Word, whereas it is not the same for Love. One can make the same observation about the commentary on St. Matthew and the commentary on St. Paul's Epistles. Despite the close links that attach the doctrine of the Word to that of Love in systematic works by St. Thomas, the *Commentary on St. John* suggests that these two doctrines are not exactly on the same level. We can observe also that the personal name *"Donum,"* a proper name of the Holy Spirit to which the *Summa theologiae* gives up a whole question (I, q. 38), is not treated in the *Commentary on St. John*: the theme of "Gift" is present, but St. Thomas does not explain the personal feature of this name.[21]

The absence of speculative developments on other Trinitarian themes is less surprising. Thus the *Commentary on St. John* presents a very concise doctrine concerning the name *"Image"* to which the *Summa theologiae* gives a whole question (I, q. 35). St. Thomas does not give the elements that contribute to define the Image, and does not expose the reason for the personal signification of the word "Image." He explains, however, that the Son is the perfect Image of the Father, in a conformity of nature, because he is his Word: it is why the Son makes known the Father.[22] If the *Commentary on St. John* is rather reticent concerning this theme of the Image, it is without doubt because the fourth Gospel does not offer a textual occasion for such an exposition. Indeed, other biblical commentaries by St. Thomas offer complete expositions on the personal property of *"Imago,"* broader and more developed than question 35 of the *Prima pars*: this is the case, of course, of the commentary on the Epistle to the Colossians.[23] The same observation can be applied to the position of natural reason facing the Trinitarian mystery. Whereas the *Summa theologiae* gives an article to this question (I, q. 32, a. 1), the *Commentary on St. John* does not discuss the limits of the knowledge of the Trinity by natural reason, although St. Thomas does remind us of the prerogatives of faith. This theme, however, is not absent from the biblical commentaries of St. Thomas: one can find a brief statement in the commentary of the Epistle to the Romans.[24]

---

21. The commentaries on St. Matthew and on St. Paul mention the theme of the Spirit as *Gift*, but do not offer any more speculative explanation about this proper name of the third person.

22. *Ioan.* 14, lect. 2, nn. 1878–79; cf. 12, 8, n. 1712.

23. See the commentary of St. Thomas on Col 1:15 (Marietti ed., nn. 31–37), but also his commentary on 1 Cor 11:7 (Marietti ed., n. 604) and on 2 Cor 4:4 (Marietti ed., n. 126).

24. See the commentary of St. Thomas on Rom 1:20 (Marietti ed., n. 122).

Lastly, one realizes without much surprise that several technical problems are absent from the commentary, or only evoked without being discussed. The *Commentary on St. John* does not cover the questions that touch on the reasons for the number of processions, the number of persons and of real relations in God (I, q. 27, a. 5; q. 28, a. 4; q. 30, aa. 1–4), neither on the Trinitarian notions (I, q. 32), nor on the conceptual priority of notional acts (I, q. 40, a. 4) nor on certain problems touching notional acts and the notional power in God (I, q. 41, aa. 1, 4, 5 and 6). As well, the *Commentary on St. John* does not discuss certain questions of language such as the signification of the word "Trinitas" (I, q. 31, a. 1), the attribution of essential terms to the persons or the attribution of personal names to essential terms (I, q. 39, aa. 3 and 6). Although St. Thomas does use Trinitarian appropriations when he comments on St. John, he does not give any speculative justification of the practice of appropriations (I, q. 39, aa. 7 and 8); some elements are given in other biblical commentaries.[25] These academic problems are not the core of Trinitarian theology. They concern precisions about the conceptual technical tools that the theologian put to the service of the Trinitarian doctrine. The removal of these technical problems in the *Commentary on St. John* is then not surprising and does not prejudice the richness of the Trinitarian teaching of the *Commentary on John*.

Evaluation

As intermediary assessment, one can conclude that the Johannine commentary by St. Thomas contains the essential of the Trinitarian doctrine as taught in the *Summa theologiae:* the notion of procession, the modes of immanent procession of the Son and the Holy Spirit (mode of intellect or of nature, and mode of Love or of will), personal subsistence, the doctrine of the Word, the origin of the Spirit, the relative opposition and the distinction of persons by the relations, the doctrine of real relation depending on the origin, the personal properties, the relationship of the persons with the essence and with the relations, the equality of the persons, the order of nature *(ordo naturae)* in God, the relationship of the divine persons to the creatures, the mission of the persons as well as several problems of Trinitarian language, are expounded in detail. The absence of a study of the signification of the word "person" occurs elsewhere in St. Thomas and reveals that St. Thomas is able to show the subsistence proper to the Father, to the Son, and to the Spirit in divine nature, without specifying the meaning of the word that theological

---

25. See notably the commentary of St. Thomas on 2 Cor 13:13 (Marietti ed., n. 544).

tradition has forged to say this subsistence. The disparity of the treatment of the personal names "Word" and "Love" shows on its side that the doctrine of immanent procession is built principally on the study of the emanation by intellectual mode, that is to say on the Christological doctrine of the Word. The doctrine of the procession of the Spirit as Love, by mode of will, is much less clear to our mind (cf. *Ioan.* 15, lect. 5, n. 2064).

As regards the essential elements of Trinitarian theology, the *Commentary on St. John* shows in a brilliant way that St. Thomas does not separate biblical Trinitarian theology and speculative Trinitarian theology: It is the same theology, that is to say the same teaching of Holy Scripture reflected on and expounded, which one can find in the biblical commentary and in the theological synthesis of the *Summa*.[26] The doctrinal resources are similar. The principal difference is the order of exposition: whereas the *Summa theologiae* follows the *ordo disciplinae,* which allows one to grasp the speculative bases of Trinitarian theology in their coherence and internal organization,[27] the biblical commentary develops the doctrinal themes as they come up in the text, without losing sight of the internal speculative arrangement of particular expositions, as we shall see later.

The comparison of the doctrinal content of the Johannine commentary with that of the *Summa theologiae* helps us to understand the very aim of Trinitarian theology. The main themes of the commentary are, as we noted above, the study of each divine person, the mutual relations of the persons, and their action in the world. All the other themes are subordinated to the study of the persons and their agency. Such a priority of the divine persons is reinforced by the fact that, in the commentary, the discussion of processions and relations is directly integrated into the study of the persons. This observation confirms the "personalism" of Aquinas in the structure of the treatise on God in the *Summa theologiae:* Trinitarian theology aims to manifest the

---

26. In his doctoral dissertation, Wilhelmus G. B. M. Valkenberg notes that "Aquinas's commentaries on the Gospels bear a greater resemblance to his sermons than to his other systematic theological works." (*Did Not Our Heart Burn? Place and Function of Holy Scripture in the Theology of St. Thomas Aquinas* [Utrecht, 1990], 247). This does not seem to us to be verified in the *Commentary on St. John*, which, concerning Trinitarian theology, is very close to the *Summa theologiae* and even closer to the *Summa contra gentiles.*

27. The *Summa theologiae* presents firstly the notion of procession, then the relation, and then the concept of person (I, q. 27–29), because the theological intelligence of a divine person presupposes that of the relation (the person signifies the relation that subsists), which in turn presupposes the notion of procession (the procession is that which our spirit perceives as the foundation of the relation): that order of speculative exposition is not the one of the discovery of the mystery, but that of the expounding of concepts that allows one to grasp the Trinitarian faith. Cf. *ST* I, q. 27, prol.

divine persons in their proper subsistence and in their mutual relations,[28] in order to clarify the economy of creation and salvation by the divine persons.[29] The Johannine commentary thereby invites us to rediscover the unity of the *Summa*'s Trinitarian treatise centered on the persons.

The more developed themes in the *Commentary on John*

When comparing the *Commentary on John* and the *Summa theologiae*, one can see that the commentary develops several themes that the *Summa* examines in the Trinitarian treatise without giving them a comparable amplitude. Without pretending to be complete, we can gather these themes of the commentary into three groups: (1) the unity of knowledge and will of the Father and the Son; (2) the action of the divine persons in the world; and (3) the soteriological dimension of Trinitarian thought.

1. *The first theme is the unity of knowledge and love of the Father and the Son.* The *Summa theologiae* is very clear on the essential unity of the three divine persons whose common attributes are studied in the section concerning the divine essence (I, qq. 2–26). As to the Trinitarian treatise, it indicates well the unity of knowledge and of love of the persons, but only briefly. The unity of science and will is included in the affirmation of the identity of the person and the essence (I, q. 39, a. 1), as in the affirmation of the mutual immanence of the persons (I, q. 42, a. 5), but without being explicitly developed. The unity of the knowledge of the Father and of the Son is more expressly mentioned in the answer to an objection concerning the Word (I, q. 34, a. 1, ad 3) and in the answer to an objection concerning the equality of the Father and the Son (I, q. 42, a. 6, ad 2); their unity of will and of love appears in the study of the property of the Holy Spirit (I, q. 37, aa. 1–2). But the explanations of St. Thomas on the knowledge and will of the Son are sober and are not the object of an ample exposition. It is different in the *Commentary on St. John*. St. Thomas, following the biblical text, explains in many places that the Son knows the Father perfectly.[30] By his eternal generation, the Son receives from the Father divine knowledge, identical to his nature. The Son understands the Father in a way that is proper to him, in mutual comprehension.[31]

---

28. See Gilles Emery, "Essentialism or Personalism in the Treatise on God in Saint Thomas Aquinas?," *Thomist* 64 (2000): 531–53.

29. *ST* I, q. 32, a. 1, ad 3.

30. See *Ioan.* nn. 216–19, 534, 754, 1037, 1062–65, 1228, 1286, 1414, 2017–18.

31. *Ioan.* 10, lect. 4, n. 1414: "Cognoscere Patrem sicut cognitus est ab eo, est proprium solius Filii, quia solus Filius cognoscit Patrem comprehendendo, sicut Pater comprehendendo cognoscit Filium." The Son knows and sees the Father insofar as he proceeds as the personal Word of the Father's intellect (n. 534).

That is why the Son is the "doctrine of the Father."[32] In the same way, St. Thomas notes several times the unity of the will of the Father and of the Son,[33] by specifying that the Son accomplishes the will that he receives eternally from the Father (*Ioan.* 5, lect. 5, n. 798). This unity is twofold: it consists in the unity of nature, and in the unity of love.[34] In the wake of the knowledge and of the will, St. Thomas expounds the unity of action of the Father and the Son.[35]

In the *Summa theologiae,* several aspects of the unity of knowledge and of will of the Father and the Son have been placed under Christology *(Tertia pars),* in the study of the knowledge of Christ and his double will (divine and human). The *Commentary on St. John* does not present such a distinction of Trinitarian doctrine and Christology, and thus it illumines the Trinitarian roots of Christological affirmations. At the same time, the *Commentary on St. John* helps to better perceive the soteriological dimension of the Trinitarian unity. St. Thomas explains that the mutual knowledge of the Father and the Son is the basis for the illuminating and revealing work of the Word, and the source of the salvific activity of the Word: the Son knows the salvific will of the Father that he accomplishes, procuring for the faithful the security of faith.[36] In a similar way, St. Thomas notes the soteriological dimension of the unity of the Father and of the Son. The double aspect of unity (unity of nature and unity of love) flows from the Father and the Son to mankind by similitude, that is to say by participation: The human unity in the Church is a participation in the divine unity of the Trinity.[37]

2. *The* Commentary on St. John *also develops, much more so than the* Summa theologiae, *diverse themes that concern the actions of the divine persons in the world.* These themes are not absent from the *Summa,* where St. Thomas gathers them together in the study of certain questions: the personal and the essential sense of the name "Father" (I, q. 33, a. 3), the relationship to creatures carried by the name "Verbum" (I, q. 34, a. 3), the Holy Spirit as the Love by which the Father and the Son love each other and love us (I, q. 37, a. 2, ad 3),

---

32. *Ioan.* 7, lect. 2, n. 1037: "Cum doctrina uniuscuiusque nihil aliud sit quam verbum eius, doctrina Patris est ipse Filius."

33. See, for example, n. 60 ("concordia voluntatis"), n. 798 ("eadem voluntas"), n. 1553.

34. *Ioan.* 17, lect. 5, n. 2240: "In Patre et Filio est duplex unitas, scilicet essentiae et amoris." Cf. *Ioan.* 17, lect. 3, n. 2214.

35. See *Ioan.* nn. 752, 761–63, 2246.

36. *Ioan.* 10, lect. 4, n. 1414; cf. 1, 11, n. 221; 15, 3, nn. 2017–18.

37. *Ioan.* 17, lect. 3, n. 2214: "There is a twofold unity in God. There is a unity of nature . . . and a unity of love in the Father and Son. . . . Both of these unities are found in us, not in equal way, but with a certain likeness." Cf. 17, 5, nn. 2239–41.

Biblical Exegesis and the Speculative Doctrine of Trinity

and the divine missions (I, q. 43). In all these areas that touch the action of the three divine persons, one must note the vast teaching of the commentary.

The action *ad extra* of the Word is the object of the most numerous explanations of St. Thomas. Without coming back here to the creative role of the Word in John 1:3, one must first observe that the commentary gives great attention to the illuminating role of the Word and to the participation of human knowledge in the Word. St. Thomas often explains that all natural human knowledge is a participation in the Word[38] and that the knowledge of the mystery of God derives from the Word by grace, in virtue of an illuminating action of the Word who communicates to man, by interior inspiration or revelation, a similitude to himself.[39] "Because every imperfect thing derives from the perfect, all our knowledge is derived from the Word" (*Ioan.* 8, lect. 8, n. 1284). These explanations are founded on the doctrine of participation (exemplarity) and on the personal property of the Word: As the Word is in person the concept of the intellect of the Father, it comes to him to manifest the truth by communicating a part of his personal property in the Trinity. As the Son, in virtue of his property (he is the Word of the Father), expresses perfectly all the being of the Father and all the Father contains,[40] he is also in person the Truth that communicates and manifests the Father.[41] By the participation in the personal property of the Word who is the Son, St. Thomas explains, the faithful are deified and are being made "connoisseurs of truth" and "sons of God" by participation.[42] This teaching is particularly useful to perceive the soteriological repercussions of the *Summa theologiae* on the Word.

---

38. *Ioan.* 1, lect. 13, n. 246: "He shines in everyone's understanding; because whatever light and whatever wisdom exists in men has come to them from participating in the Word." See nn. 95–103, 125, 129, 1869, 2267.

39. See *Ioan.* nn. 95, 104–6, 125, 130, 136, 820, 1162, 1384, 1775, 1874, 1879, 2267. This kind of knowledge is the proper effect of the Word's mission: "Effectus missionis huiusmodi est ut faciat homines participes divinae sapientiae, et cognitores veritatis" (*Ioan.* 14, lect. 6, n. 1958).

40. *Ioan.* 1, lect. 1, n. 27: "Unicum Verbum divinum est expressivum totius quod in Deo est, non solum personarum, sed etiam creaturarum." "Verbum . . . totius *esse* Patris expressivum" (n. 29). Cf. *Ioan.* 1, lect. 4, n. 118: "Cum . . . omnes formae sint per Verbum, quod est ars plena rationum viventium, est ergo lumen, non solum in se, sed omnia manifestans. . . . Dei Verbum, quo Pater dicit se et omnem creaturam."

41. *Ioan.* 14, lect. 6, n. 1869; cf. *Ioan.* 16, lect. 25, n. 2150. Inasmuch as the Word is the concept of the Father and the perfect expression of the whole being of the Father (who contains the creatures), the Word is personally the Truth, that is to say the Truth as it is expressed by the Father. But in the aspect where the truth is an attribute common to the three persons, St. Thomas explains that the truth derives of all the Trinity (n. 1156). It is precisely to join these two aspects (personal and essential aspect) that St. Thomas explains that the truth is appropriated to the Word.

42. *Ioan.* 1, lect. 8, n. 187; 14, 6, n. 1958.

As to the Holy Spirit, it is almost impossible to pick out exhaustively all the actions that St. Thomas mentions in the *Commentary on St. John*. The Holy Spirit fills the earth, inspires and illuminates hearts, saves from slavery and from sin, gives freedom, procures the charity or the dilection whereby we love God and our neighbor, drives to that which is just and right, gives life, procures grace and forgiveness of sins, gives the unction, instructs and teaches interiorly, lifts up to higher good and gives one the taste for divine things, makes one act according to the truth, sanctifies the Church and constitutes its unity, intercedes and makes one pray, sheds multiple gifts (joy, consolation, love, etc.) and charismata (tongues, prophecies, miracles, etc.), inspires the Scriptures and enables the faithful to live in conformity with the revelation, glorifies Christ, makes known the Father and the Son, says the truth and makes the truth known, renders the faithful capable to receive the doctrine of Christ, makes one invoke the name of Christ, configures the faithful to Christ and renders them sons of God, lives in the saints in whom he dwells intimately by grace, gives confidence and the power to witness and to announce Christ, makes one merit resurrection, gives the glory of eternal life, and so forth.[43] The exposition of the works of the Spirit is much more complete in the *Commentary on St. John* than in the Trinitarian treatise of the *Summa theologiae*.[44]

In this vast fresco of the works of the Spirit, St. Thomas puts into play two major doctrinal principles. The first principle is the property of the Holy Spirit as Love: it is because he is personally Love that the Holy Spirit accomplishes the works of which love is the source.[45] The second systematic principle lies in the procession of the Holy Spirit *a Filio:* the Holy Spirit leads to the Son and makes manifest the Son; he deepens the teaching of the Son, because he proceeds from the Son (*Ioan.* 14, lect. 4, n. 1916). We can grasp here the soteriological stakes of the *Filioque:* "For since the Holy Spirit is from the Truth, it is appropriate that the Spirit teach the truth, and make those he teaches like the one who sent him" (*Ioan.* 16, lect. 3, n. 2102). "For everything which is from another manifests that from which it is" (*Ioan.* 16, lect. 4, n.

---

43. See *Ioan.* nn. 452–56, 972, 973, 992, 1092–95, 1520, 1909–20, 1957–59, 2060–62, 2066–67, 2099–107, 2321, 2541, 2605. Cf. Giuseppe Ferraro, *Lo Spirito e l'"ora" di Cristo: L'esegesi di San Tommaso d'Aquino sul quarto Vangelo* (Vatican City: Libreria Editrice Vaticana, 1996).

44. So as to balance the comparison, one should, however, consider all the pneumatological teaching spread through diverse parts of the *Summa theologiae*. See specifically, for the *Prima secundae*, Albert Patfoort, "Morale et pneumatologie," in *Saint Thomas d'Aquin, Les clefs d'une théologie* (Paris: FAC Editions, 1983), 71–102. The works of the Spirit are organized in a more complete systematic way in the *Summa contra gentiles* (Book IV, chs. 20–22).

45. See for example *Ioan.* 14, lect. 4, n. 1916; 15, 5, n. 2060.

2107). The *Commentary on St. John* reveals with great amplitude the soteriological repercussions of the doctrine of Love and of the *Filioque*, and, by applying these doctrinal principles to the works of the Spirit, it shows the breadth of the action of the Spirit, about whom a more formal account is given in the three questions of the *Summa* (qq. 36–38). One can make a similar observation concerning the person of the Father, despite the fact that the teaching of St. Thomas on the action of the first person is more reticent. The Father acts in the world in conformity with his property as principle of the Son and the Holy Spirit: the Father acts in a *personal* way, a way that is *proper* to him (not only by appropriation) as such that he is Father: the Father acts *through his Son*.[46] The Father creates, accomplishes everything through his Word and his Spirit, gives his Son and glorifies him, attracts mankind to the Son, adopts them by sending his Son and the Holy Spirit, lives in the saints with the Son and the Holy Spirit, and so forth.[47]

St. Thomas formulates on this basis an organizing doctrinal principle, which takes into account the Trinitarian economy in a synthetic way: "Just as the effect of the mission of the Son was to lead us to the Father, so the effect of the mission of the Holy Spirit is to lead the faithful to the Son" (*Ioan.* 14, lect. 6, n. 1958). This rule is inspired by the teaching of some Fathers of the Church (we could cite here St. Irenaeus of Lyons or St. Basil of Caesarea), but St. Thomas takes it more directly from St. Albert the Great, who formulates it in similar terms: "The Spirit who is sent brings back *(convertit)* to himself and to the Son, the Son brings back to himself and to the Father. . . . The person who proceeds from another person brings back to that other person, according to the order of nature, what it has from that other person."[48] This fundamental structure of Trinitarian economy rests on the doctrine of the Trinitarian order in God. The same structure of order of origin was already at work in the explanations on the glorification of the Father and the Son: "Now we see the reason why the Holy Spirit will glorify Christ: it is because the Son is the principle of the Holy Spirit. For every thing which is from another manifests that from which it is. Thus the Son manifests the Father because he is from the Father. And so because the Holy Spirit is from the Son, to glorify the Son is proper *(proprium)* to the Spirit" (*Ioan.* 16, lect. 4, n.

---

46. *Ioan.* 1, lect. 2, n. 76. The commentary here gives all its vigor to the briefer explanation of the *Summa* (*ST* I, q. 39, a. 8).

47. See notably, *Ioan.* nn. 76, 176, 935–37, 997, 1192, 1648, 2189–92, 2248.

48. Albert the Great, I *Sent.* d. 31, a. 14, ad quaest. 2: "Spiritus missus convertit in se et in Filium, et Filius in se et in Patrem. . . . Persona enim quae est ab alia, refert in eam per naturae ordinem quod habet ab ea." Albert is fully conscious of the rapport of this fundamental structure with the *Filioque* (ibid.: "et ideo constat errare Graecos").

2107).⁴⁹ "The Holy Spirit leads to the knowledge of truth, because he proceeds from the Truth" (*Ioan.* 14, lect. 4, n. 1916).

One can perceive very well that the doctrine of Trinitarian economy ("economic Trinity"), in St. Thomas, is not limited to a mere description of the works of the Trinity as told by the Scriptures. The doctrine of Trinitarian economy appears when the biblical data are explained in the light of a speculative principle that allows St. Thomas to organize the biblical texts and to show their profound reason. St. Thomas formulates himself this philosophical and theological rule: "What acts in virtue of another tends in its effect to reveal that other: for the action of a principle which proceeds from another principle manifests this principle" (*Ioan.* 17, lect. 1, n. 2185). This rule brings together the metaphysics of participation and the metaphysics of order. It is included in the doctrine of *"reductio,"* which was dear to St. Bonaventure, who found in it the heart of his doctrine of the return to God, and which St. Thomas applies often in Trinitarian theology.⁵⁰ According to that metaphysical rule, the reality that proceeds from a principle returns or leads to this principle, in virtue of the *order* that it has with this principle. We could mention many examples. Thus, when he explains that Christ is the source of all things *(principium)*, St. Thomas puts into action the similar rule of *"maxime tale."* The creative causality of the Son is manifested by the rule of the causality of the *primum:* that which sovereignly possesses a perfection is the cause of that which has this perfection in a secondary way (by participation). "Our Lord says that he is the source or beginning with regards to all creatures; for whatever is such by essence is the source and the cause of all those things which are by participation."⁵¹ The doctrine of Trinitarian economy rests on metaphysical principles that St. Thomas applies to the teaching of the Bible so as to make manifest its signification and profound truth.

Theological literature today more often distinguishes the doctrine of the "immanent Trinity," resulting from the speculative effort inaugurated by the Fathers of the Church, and the doctrine of the "economic Trinity." Very often, the doctrine of the economic Trinity is identified with biblical teaching, whereas the study of the immanent Trinity is viewed as constructed by later

---

49. Cf. *Ioan.* 1, lect. 14, n. 268: "As the Son, existing by the Father, manifests the Father, so the Holy Spirit, existing by the Son, manifests the Son."

50. See Gilles Emery, *La Trinité créatrice* (Paris: Vrin, 1995), 221–27.

51. *Ioan.* 8, lect. 3, n. 1183. This principle is often applied to the Son or to the Trinity in the commentary of St. Thomas on the *Sentences:* "Sicut trames a fluvio derivatur, ita processus temporalis creaturarum ab aeterno processu personarum ... semper enim id quod est primum est causa eorum quae sunt post" (I *Sent.*, prol.). Cf. Emery, *La Trinité créatrice*, 273–85. The same principle is found in the *quarta via* of our natural knowledge of God's existence (*ST* I, q. 2, a. 3).

dogmatic or systematic reflections on the eternal being of the Trinity. The reading of St. Thomas does not lead us to reject the distinction between the immanent and economic Trinity (Thomas speaks of the Trinity "in itself" and of the Trinity in its rapport to creatures or in its work), but it invites us rather to question the identification of biblical teaching as a doctrine of the "economic Trinity."[52] Indeed the *Commentary on St. John* demonstrates that there is only a veritable teaching on the economic Trinity when we can clarify and organize, through speculative thought, the agency of the divine persons taught by Scripture. For Aquinas, the simple identification of biblical teaching with the economic Trinity is an error. The Trinitarian doctrine of economy (doctrine of the action of the Father by the Son and by the Spirit), according to the Commentary on St. John, rests on the doctrine of the Trinity in itself, as taught by the Scriptures, which is necessary to understand the biblical text in depth. The doctrine of the economic Trinity is no less speculative than that of the immanent Trinity. The revelation of the Trinity by its works is admittedly first in the order of our discovery of the mystery. But the *doctrine* of the economic Trinity is not only the starting point of a theological reflection: It is rather the last fruit of a reflection founded in the speculative reading of the documents of revelation, when doctrinal speculative principles are applied to the agency of the persons as taught by Scriptures.

According to our reading of the *Commentary of St. John* by Aquinas, Trinitarian theology consists of three steps: (1) the discovery of the mystery of the Trinity, by faith, through the action of the Trinity as taught by Scriptures; (2) a speculative reflection on the being and properties of the divine persons (doctrine of the "immanent Trinity"); and (3) a speculative reflection on the creative and salvific action of the persons in the world (doctrine of the "economic Trinity") in the light of the properties and relations of the persons. In other words: The doctrine of the economic Trinity (third step) is achieved when a speculative reflection on the divine persons (second step) is applied to the agency of the persons discovered in the reading of Scripture (first step). In this way, Trinitarian theology moves from Scripture to Scripture.

3. *The Commentary on St. John also shows how we come to the knowledge of the eternal Trinity by considering its works in the world.* On the basis of the preceding explanations, so as to make manifest the divinity of the Son and the Spirit, St. Thomas brings into play the "soteriological argument," dear to St. Athanasius of Alexandria and other Greek Fathers. The best example con-

---

52. See on this matter the interesting remarks made by David Coffey, *Deus Trinitas: The Doctrine of the Triune God* (Oxford: Oxford University Press, 1999), 9–45.

cerns the Holy Spirit: "He from whom men are spiritually reborn is God; but men are reborn through the Holy Spirit, as it is stated here; therefore, the Holy Spirit is God" (*Ioan.* 3, lect. 1, n. 44). St. Thomas presents this reflection as an argument *(ratio)* that theological reasoning forms from John 3:5: "Unless one is born again of water and the Holy Spirit, he cannot enter the kingdom of God." The same argument is applied to the divinity of the Son:

> It is clear that a person by participating in the Word of God becomes god by participation. But a thing does not become this or that by participation unless it participates in what is this or that by its essence.... Therefore, one does not become god by participation unless he participates in what is God by essence. Therefore, the Word of God, that is the Son, by participation in whom we become gods, is God by essence.[53]

In the *Summa theologiae*, St. Thomas explains the secondary reality (our salvation) from the primary reality (the divinity of the Father and the Son): the Son deifies, the Spirit vivifies, because the Son and the Spirit are God; this is the order of the doctrinal statement that the *Summa theologiae* follows. But here, in the *Commentary on St. John*, St. Thomas follows the inverse order: He establishes the primary reality (the divinity of the persons) from the secondary reality (our salvation). Using St. Hilary's argument, but also that of St. John Chrysostom and St. Augustine (as the *Catena aurea* shows on these passages), Aquinas starts from the experience of salvation through faith, that is to say the true and real re-creation and divinization of the believer, so as to establish the divinity of the persons: Only the true God can divinize and re-create. We find here the way of Trinitarian theology, which starts from the action of the persons so as to show, by reasoning, a truth concerning the eternal Trinity in itself (the "immanent Trinity"). These explanations are of great value for rediscovering, behind the *ordo disciplinae* of the *Summa*, the Patristic roots of Aquinas's Trinitarian theology and its foundations in the economy of salvation.

The reflection on power and operation gathers together, on a more general level, the principles of this soteriological way of thought. In virtue of the mode of human knowledge, St. Thomas explains, "It is natural for man to learn of the power and natures of things from their actions, and therefore our Lord fittingly says that the sort of person he is can be learned through the works he does" (*Ioan.* 5, lect. 6, n. 817). For that reason, the works of Christ bear witness to him. In chapter 5, this witness concerns the judgment and, in

---

53. *Ioan.* 10, lect. 6, n. 1460; 17, lect. 1, n. 2187: "Because the Son exercises the true activities of divinity, it is clear that the Son is true God."

particular, the life-giving power of the Son. St. Thomas explains: "Here we should point out that in the Old Testament the power is particularly emphasized by the fact that God is the author of life" (*Ioan.* 5, lect. 4, n. 761). As the Son has the power to give life, the power of God himself, he is therefore himself true God. In neighboring passages, St. Thomas notes that "the clearest indication of the nature of a thing is taken from its works," "different actions indicate different natures" (*Ioan.* 10, lect. 6, n. 1466; 14, 4, n. 1912). Applied to Christ, this principle leads to the following conclusion: "Therefore, from the fact that he does the works of God, it can be clearly known and believed that Christ is God" (*Ioan.* 10, lect. 6, n. 1466).[54] St. Thomas's argument associates most often operation and nature, but it also applies to the relationship of *power* and of nature. Thus, as "All things were made through him," we know that the Word possesses the divine omnipotence. St. Thomas conceives power as the principle of action, and he specifies that "to be the principle of all things that are made is proper to the great omnipotent God. . . . Thus the Word, through whom all things were made, is God, great and co-equal to the Father" (*Ioan.* 1, lect. 2, n. 69). Here again, Aquinas's arguments come from his anti-Arian and anti-Eunomian Patristic sources: notably St. Hilary and St. John Chrysostom.[55]

Furthermore, St. Thomas integrates this teaching on power and operation in his doctrine of relative personal properties. The Son receives from his Father the power and the operation: "The Son, just as he does not have his being *(esse)* except from the Father, so he cannot do anything *(posse facere aliquid)* except from the Father. For in natural things, a thing receives its power to act from the very thing from which it receives its being." When John 5:19 says that the Son cannot do anything of himself, "no inequality is implied, because this refers to a relation" (*Ioan.* 5, lect. 3, n. 749). Therefore it is the doctrine of relation that allows one to grasp the power of the Son under its two aspects, namely its equality with the power of the Father, and its reception *a Patre* by eternal generation. The exposition concerning the "other Paraclete" in John 14:16 gives place to more ample precisions. The Son and the Holy Spirit are both called "Paraclete," but they do not exercise their action of Paraclete in the same way. As diversity of action is the sign of a diversity of nature, does it not signify that the nature of the Spirit is different from that of the Son? St. Thomas answers this question by introducing the property of the

---

54. Cf. *Ioan.* 17, lect. 1, n. 2187.

55. On the Patristic argument about divine power, see Michel René Barnes, *The Power of God: Dunamis in Gregory of Nyssa's Trinitarian Theology* (Washington, D.C.: The Catholic University of America Press, 2001).

persons: the Son and the Holy Spirit exercise the same action, but each one acts in his own distinct mode.

> The Holy Spirit is called a consoler because *(inquantum)* he is formally Love. But the Son is called a consoler because *(inquantum)* he is the Word. . . . Thus the word "another" does not indicate a different nature in the Son and in the Holy Spirit. Rather, it indicates the different way *(modus)* each is an advocate and a consoler. *(Ioan.* 14, lect. 4, n. 1912)

The divine persons therefore exercise the same action of consolation, but in a distinct mode, namely in the mode of their personal properties (Word and Love). We find again here, precisely, the heart of the teaching of St. Thomas on Trinitarian action: The three persons act inseparably in the same action, in virtue of their common nature and of their mutual relations, but each person acts in a distinct mode following the personal property. When commenting on St. John, St. Thomas integrates Patristic exegesis on nature and power, and clarifies this teaching by his own reflection on relations and properties in the Trinity.

This way of Trinitarian thought is confirmed by several explanations of the commentary concerning the divine missions. Indeed, St. Thomas explains, "The mission indicates the origin" *(Ioan.* 5, lect. 4, n. 769). Aquinas goes back on this subject to the teaching of St. Augustine by explaining: "[The Holy Spirit] is said to be sent *(mitti)* to indicate his procession from another, for the fact that he sanctifies the rational creature by indwelling he has from that other, from whom he has it that he is (*a quo habet ut sit*)" (*Ioan.* 15, lect. 5, n. 2061).[56] The mission (temporal procession) of the Son and of the Spirit is thus the way to the knowledge of eternal procession.[57] The *Commentary on St. John,* by giving details of the action of the divine persons in the world, allows us to grasp better the economic foundation of Trinitarian theology.

EXEGETICAL METHOD AND SPECULATIVE THEOLOGY

To evaluate the contribution that the commentary brings to the Trinitarian doctrine of St. Thomas, it is necessary to specify St. Thomas's method. For our subject, three principal aspects merit to be retained: the forms of speculative exposition, the place given to the Fathers of the Church, as well as the role of errors and heresies to make manifest the truth.

---

56. Cf. St. Augustine, *De Trinitate* IV, XX, 28.
57. See also *Ioan.* 3, lect. 2, n. 464: "If you do not believe in a spiritual generation occurring in time, how will you believe in the eternal generation of the Son?"

The Forms of Speculative Exegesis

The speculative Trinitarian expositions of the *Commentary on St. John*, putting on one side a few rare exceptions, do not concern the spiritual or mystical sense of Scripture,[58] but they concern the literal exegesis of the text, as it is exclusively on this literal sense that theological arguments are properly founded, following the hermeneutics of St. Thomas.[59] The lecture of St. Thomas spreads over the three levels or stages of literal exposition formulated by Hugh of Saint-Victor: the *littera* in the strict sense (textual analysis, grammatical and linguistic, a brief explanation of the words according to their content and their immediate sequence), the *sensus* (analysis of the signification of each element), and then the *sententia* (the true understanding of the text that extricates the profound theological and philosophical content of a text).[60] This *sententia*, that is to say the development of theological and philosophical themes that make up the doctrine provided by the finished exposition, takes on two principal forms in the Trinitarian exegesis of the *Commentary on St. John*.

1. Following a first form, the speculative doctrine intervenes in the continuous explanation of the commented pericope, where a strict exegesis of the words allows St. Thomas to extract the immediate sense so as to come to the doctrine contained in the text. This method often includes several intermediate approaches, among which we can count the following ones: (a) preliminary precisions concerning the biblical vocabulary, which can include a definition of words;[61] (b) a research for the reasons why the Gospel writer (or the person speaking, Christ for example) brings such a precision by using such words;[62] (c) preliminary or complementary doctrinal preci-

---

58. When St. Thomas introduces a mystical or spiritual sense, it usually is on Christological themes (mysteries lived out by Christ in his flesh), but also eschatological or moral. The Trinitarian themes are not absent but are much more rare in the context of spiritual exegesis; see for example the mystical Trinitarian sense of the "three measures" in John 2:6 (n. 357), or the "causa mystica et allegorica" in the exegesis of John 9:6–7 (n. 1311).

59. Cf. *ST* I, q. 1, a. 10.

60. See Gilbert Dahan, *L'exégèse chrétienne de la Bible en Occident médiéval, XIIe–XIVe siècle* (Paris: Cerf, 1999), 239–97; Marie-Dominique Chenu, *Introduction à l'étude de saint Thomas d'Aquin*, 70–71 and 214. Cf. Hugh of Saint-Victor, *Didascalicon* VI, 8: "Expositio tria continet: litteram, sensum, sententiam," ed. C. H. Buttimer (Washington, D.C.: The Catholic University of America Press, 1939), 125.

61. See, for example, *Ioan.* 1, lect. 1, n. 25 (definition of the name "Word"), n. 34 (precisions on the word "principium"), n. 44 (signification of the word *"Deus"*), n. 45 (signification of the preposition *"apud"*); on John 1:3, n. 46 (signification of the preposition *"per"*), and so on.

62. See, for example, *Ioan.* 1, lect. 1, n. 59 (the reason why the word *"Deus"* in John 1:1c does

sions;[63] (d) indication and refutation of the errors and heresies that a good exegesis must avoid.[64] Going against a too widely spread prejudice, one must insist on this point: the speculative reflection of an exegete does not necessarily take the form of a scholastic question. We can easily see it in, for example, the exegesis of the word "Verbum" in John 1:1 (nn. 25–29): the complete speculative exposition of St. Thomas details the sense of the words and brings doctrinal precisions in the form of a continuous explanation where the academic sort of *quaestio* does not appear.

2. Following a second form, the speculative doctrine is the object of *quaestiones, obiectiones,* or *dubitationes* raised in the text. The vocabulary is, then, that of the scholastic question, comprising the terms of the question and the master's own answer.[65] One must note however that these *quaestiones* do not always concern speculative doctrinal points developed in the manner of the *Summa theologiae*. Very often these questions are rather of a strictly exegetical order, or discuss diverse Patristic interpretations of a verse of St. John.[66]

3. In other more developed passages, the speculative exegesis of St. Thomas associates these two forms and takes on a complex figure that combines the continuous exposition (form 1) and the questions (form 2), so as to

---

not carry an article), or John 5:19, n. 750 (the reason why the Gospel talks of the communication of wisdom to the Son by generation). The motive of such a word is often given in reference to errors that the evangelical text removes, as one can see for example in the exegesis of John 1:1–2 (nn. 60–66), then in John 1:3 (n. 69), and so on.

63. See, for example, *Ioan.* 5, lect. 3, n. 753 (preliminary precision on the role of fatherly dilection in the generation of the Son, then on the distinction between the essential sense and notional sense of "love" in God), on John 16:14, n. 2107 (analogical sense of the word *"recipere"* applied to the creatures and to God), on John 16:15, n. 2114 (on the relationship between the agent and the formal principle of action), and so on.

64. See, for example, *Ioan.* 1, lect. 1, nn. 58–59; 1, 1, nn. 60–66, 1, 2, nn. 69–70, 73–75). We shall come back later to the place of errors and heresies.

65. See, for example, *Ioan* 1, lect. 1, concerning the Word (n. 41: "potest aliquis quaerere," "ad quod dicendum est"; nn. 46–50: "sunt quatuor obiectiones"); on John 3:34 concerning the gift of the Holy Spirit (n. 542: *"responsio"*); on John 16:15 concerning the relation in God (n. 2113): "sed quaeritur utrum," "dicendum"), and so on. The question can be presented as a *dubitatio* (see for example *Ioan.* 16, lect. 3, nn. 2103–4, concerning the Holy Spirit) or as a notice ("sed nota," "notandum"): see for example *Ioan.* 16, lect. 4, nn. 2108, 2112.

66. There is a good example in the four *quaestiones* that St. Thomas asks about John 1:1 (nn. 30–33), concerning the reason for the words chosen by St. John according to John Chrysostom, Augustine, and Origen. See also *Ioan.* 1, lect. 1, n. 54 (the order of the words in the statement "Et Deus erat Verbum," according to Origen) and nn. 55–56 (Patristic discussion on two objections); on John 5:19 (nn. 745–751: the action of the Son and his relationship to the Father, following Augustine, Hilary and Chrysostom); and so on. In other passages, St. Thomas speaks of *"quaestio litteralis"* to designate a question searching for the reason of a word in the Gospel (see, for example, *Ioan.* 1, lect. 15, n. 306, or *Ioan.* 3, lect. 4, n. 498, etc.).

Biblical Exegesis and the Speculative Doctrine of Trinity 47

come to a synthetic conclusion that summarizes the doctrine taught, as one can observe, in particular, in the first verses of the Prologue and in the interpretation of the passages about the origin of the Holy Spirit.

Thus, the exegesis of the first words of the Prologue *("In principio erat Verbum")* details the analysis of each term. For the first word *(Verbum)*, the exposition of St. Thomas has the following structure: (a) philosophical and theological explanation of the word *Verbum;* (b) application of the results of this analysis and determination of the sense of the word *Verbum* in the Prologue; (c) precisions on the differences of the human word and of the divine Word; (d) theological conclusion on the exclusively personal sense of the name *Verbum* in God and on the properties of the divine Word (the divine Word is the perfect expression of the Father, coeternal and consubstantial with the Father). At this stage St. Thomas has shown the profound meaning of *Verbum* in the first verse of the Gospel, but he continues his exegesis: (e) discussion of four *quaestiones* that are raised by the name "Word." These four questions come from the Patristic documentation of St. Thomas (St. John Chrysostom, St. Augustine, and Origen).

The exegesis of the following word *("principium")* proceeds in a similar way: (a) philosophical and theological exposition of the sense of the word *principium;* (b) application of this sense in the Prologue of St. John, with indication of three possible interpretations (all originally Patristic); (c) doctrinal conclusion on the properties of the divine Word manifested in the exegesis of *"principium"* (causality, consubstantiality, and co-eternity of the Word and the Father). As to the interpretation of the third word *("erat"),* it comprises: (a) the exposition of the signification of the past imperfect; (b) a precision taken from the *Glossa;* (c) a theological question *("sed potest aliquis quaerere")* on the eternity of the generation in God; (d) a conclusion on the names that express the property of the Son.

The exegesis of John 16:14–15, which gives place to a remarkable speculative exposition on the procession of the Holy Spirit *a Filio,* reveals a similar complex structure (nn. 2105–14): (a) a first explanation of the biblical text concerning the glorification of the Son by the Holy Spirit; (b) a theological explanation of the reasons for the Son's glorification by the Spirit; (c) a theological precision on the way that the Holy Spirit "receives" from the Son; (d) a theological precision on the consubstantiality signified by the preposition *"de";* (e) a theological precision on the way that a divine person possesses *(habet)* something; (f) objection and answer concerning the personal property of paternity; (g) a complementary precision on the order *("ordo")* of the persons in God; (h) a speculative question on the relation in God; (i) a conclusion on the procession of the Holy Spirit *a Filio*, with an argument founded on the concept of procession and on the essence in God.

These examples manifest that by associating all the resources of theological reading, St. Thomas integrates exegesis and speculative reflection in a complex unity. It is not sufficient to say that St. Thomas goes from biblical exegesis to theology, because speculative reflection intervenes to offer the profound sense of the text that the exegesis is looking for. Questions and theological precisions are neither juxtaposed nor superimposed on biblical exegesis, but they are integrated into biblical exegesis, in such a way so as to be fully part of the exegesis practiced by St. Thomas. The arguments brought out by the reading of the biblical text aim at making clear the profound doctrine taught by the Gospel in its literal content.[67] The theologian exercises his speculative reflection in the very act of the literal interpreting of the Gospel. This exegetical practice is founded on the understanding of the nature of *sacra doctrina:* we shall come to that later.

Patristic exegesis

The Trinitarian doctrine of St. Thomas's *Commentary on St. John* carries no explicit reference to scholastic authors from the twelfth and thirteenth centuries. This is a remarkable difference of method between the commentary on the fourth Gospel and the Trinitarian doctrine of the *Summa theologiae*. The Trinitarian treatise of the *Summa theologiae* (I, qq. 27–43) names Peter Lombard, Gilbertus of Poitiers, Richard of Saint-Victor, Joachim of Fiore, Praepositinus of Cremona, as well as older medieval authors (Boethius). The *Commentary on St. John* does not mention any of these theologians. It is not easy to evaluate the reasons for their absence from the Commentary. St. Thomas's reserve may stem from the dignity of Holy Scripture and from the sort of scriptural exposition: the biblical exposition mainly brings to light the Fathers of the Church *(doctores)* who constitute a "proper" authority of sacred doctrine (sacred Scripture), which is not the case for the other authors.[68] St. Thomas's silence on these mediaeval theologians makes Aristotle's presence all the more remarkable: Aristotle is mentioned nearly fifteen times in the *Commentary on St. John,* and intervenes from the exegesis of the first verse in the exposition of the name *"Verbum."*[69] The same reference to Aristotle's *Per-*

---

67. In his general survey on exegesis in medieval universities, G. Dahan distinguishes on one side the *expositio*, and on the other the *quaestiones* (Dahan, *L'exégèse chrétienne de la Bible*, 112). The commentary by St. Thomas on St. John does not separate these two elements.

68. Cf. *ST* I, q. 1, a. 8.

69. *Ioan.* 1, lect. 1, n. 25 (two occurrences.) The philosophers are present from the *Prologue*

Biblical Exegesis and the Speculative Doctrine of Trinity 49

ihermeneias appears, in an identical context, in the *Summa theologiae* (I, q. 34, a. 1): this parallel underlines the close relationship of the *Commentary on St. John* and the *Summa theologiae*. The references to Aristotle are not, however, without criticism, for the *Commentary on St. John* makes up part of the works in which St. Thomas qualifies as error the teachings of Aristotle on the eternity of the world (*Ioan.* 1, lect. 1, n. 65).

The only Christian authors to whom Aquinas refers in the exegesis of Trinitarian passages are the Fathers of the Church. St. Augustine, St. John Chrysostom, Origen, and St. Hilary occupy the first place.[70] But St. Thomas also refers to St. Basil of Caesarea, Didymus the Blind, St. Ambrose, Pseudo-Dionysius, St. John Damascene, St. Gregory the Great, as well as Bede and Alcuin.[71] The Fathers occupy a very considerable place in the Trinitarian exegesis of St. Thomas, from the very first verses. Thus, for example, the interpretation of *"In principio"* consists mainly of the exegeses of Origen, Chrysostom, Basil, and Hilary (*Ioan.* 1, lect. 1, nn. 35–37). The four *quaestiones* raised by "Verbum erat apud Deum" are asked and answered with Basil, Hilary, Chrysostom, Alcuin, Bede, and Origen (*Ioan.* 1, lect. 1, nn. 47–52). The utility of the precision *"per eum omnia facta sunt"* goes back to the explanations of Chrysostom and of Hilary, and the theological sense of this expression is developed with reference to Augustine, Origen, Chrysostom, and Hilary (*Ioan.* 1, lect. 2, nn. 84–88). One could easily add numerous other examples. Often St. Thomas multiplies the Patristic exegeses, which offer diverse and complementary interpretations of the text.[72] Sometimes, the exposition of a verse by St. Thomas is limited to an introduction and presentation of Patristic exegesis: this is the case, among many examples, on John 13:20 on the faithful receiving the Father, or on John 17:22 on the gift of glory to the Son by the Father.[73] In some other places, the reference to the Fathers is used to introduce

---

by St. Thomas, who mentions the *"antiqui philosophi"* when explaining our ways to the knowledge of God (n. 3).

70. The Fathers the most quoted in the commentary on St. John are St. Augustine (426 times) and St. John Chrysostom (259 times), many more than Origen (91 times), St. Gregory the Great (54 times), and St. Hilary of Poitiers (46 times). For a more complete comparative table, see Leo J. Elders, "Santo Tomás de Aquino y los Padres de la Iglesia," *Doctor Communis* 48 (1993): 55–80 (table on page 66).

71. Bede and Alcuin are considered as *"doctores"* like the Fathers: they are often quoted by St. Thomas in his *Catena* on the Gospels. The *Catena* does not mention St. Anselm, whose opinion concerning the "cogitatio" is corrected by St. Thomas in *Ioan.* 1, lect. 1, n. 26; his criticism of St. Anselm, in the context of the Word, is identical in the *Summa theologiae* (*ST* I, q. 34, a. 1, ad 2).

72. See, for example, *Ioan.* 1, lect. 1, nn. 35–37; 1, 2, nn. 84–88; and so on.

73. *Ioan.* 13, lect. 3, n. 1793; 17, lect. 5, nn. 2245–49: Augustine and Chrysostom.

St. Thomas's own exposition.[74] The Fathers are again often invoked on the occasion of a *quaestio* or of a complementary precision, as one can see several times in the exegesis of John 1:1–3.[75] The commentary of St. Thomas benefits greatly from his *Catena aurea* on St. John, from which he integrates a considerable number of Patristic sources.

This massive material presence of the Fathers constitutes a characteristic of the Trinitarian doctrine of the *Commentary on St. John* when compared to Aquinas's systematic works *(Summa theologiae, Commentary on the Sentences, De potentia).* Let us take an example among many other Trinitarian themes: the equality of power of the Father and of the Son. In the *Summa theologiae,* the article given over to this problem (I, q. 42, a. 6) mentions several texts from St. John in the objections (John 5:19, John 5:20, John 5:30, John 14:31) and in the argument *sed contra* (John 5:19). The main response of St. Thomas does not indicate any Patristic authority, despite there being a reference to Augustine's *Contra Maximinum* in the third objection as well as a reference to Hilary's *De Trinitate* (Book IX) in the response to the first objection. The *Commentary on St. John* is much more instructive about St. Thomas's Patristic sources. The commentary on John 5:19 ("The Son cannot do anything of himself, but only what he sees his Father doing") presents in a very complete way an anti-Arian exegesis from the *De Trinitate* (Book VII) by St. Hilary, who, by associating power and nature, shows that the Son receives power from the Father as he receives from him his nature, his being and operation, without any inequality.[76] The commentary also recalls the exegesis of St. Augustine, who takes in the interpretations of St. Hilary and St. John Chrysostom.[77] The commentary allows one then to discover that, in the *Summa theologiae,* St. Thomas's response to the objections taken from John 5:20 and John 5:30 comes principally from St. Augustine (in his *Homilies on John* notably): When it is said that the Son has received a commandment from the Father, or that the Son receives knowledge from the Father to whom he listens, it concerns Christ in his human nature, or it concerns the eternal generation by which the Father communicates science and divine will to the Son.[78] As to the relations or the personal properties that cannot be communicated

---

74. See, for example, *Ioan.* 16, lect. 4, n. 2114 on the relation of the Holy Spirit to the Son: Hilary and Didymus.

75. See also, for example, *Ioan.* 14, lect. 3, nn. 1886–90.

76. *Ioan.* 5, lect. 3, n. 749; cf. *Catena Ioan.* 5:19 (pp. 401–3). This enlightens the response of *ST* I, q. 42, a. 6, ad 1.

77. *Ioan.* 5, lect. 3, nn. 747, 751.

78. *Ioan.* 5, lect. 3, n. 754, and *Ioan.* 5, lect. 5, n. 795; cf. *Catena Ioan.* 5:20 and 5:30 (pp. 402–3 and 407–8). This enlightens the response of *ST* I, q. 42, a. 6, ad 2.

(the Son receives the essence from the Father but not the personal property of paternity), the commentary shows that the answer given by the *Summa* is taken from the *Treatise on the Holy Spirit* by Didymus.[79]

In this way, one can see that the *Summa* organizes and summarizes the Patristic teaching of the *Catena aurea*, which the *Commentary on St. John* (posterior in time) presents in greater detail. The commentary allows one to measure the deep Patristic roots of the *Summa*'s doctrine on the subject of the equality of power of the Father and the Son. One could multiply similar examples: the exegesis of the commentary is guided by the inheritance of the Fathers, and aids us to rediscover the Patristic foundation, both Latin and Greek, of the Trinitarian theology of the *Summa*.

Trinitarian Heresies

Trinitarian errors deserve a special place in this Patristic file. The attention paid to heresies is far from being secondary or marginal: the *Commentary on St. John* mentions and discusses nearly fifty times the errors of Arius and the Arians, and sixteen times the error of Sabellius and the Sabellians. In Trinitarian matters, it indicates too the error of Eunomius of Cyzicus, of Macedonius and the Macedonians, as well as the error of Photinus of Sirmium and of Paul of Samosata.[80]

The list of errors with which Arius is reproached is complex and detailed: the negation of the eternity of the Son (very often repeated), that is to say the rejection of the co-eternity of the Father and the Son, the affirmation of the superiority of the Father *(maior)* and the inferiority of the Son *(minor)*, the negation of the equality of the Father and the Son, the negation of their consubstantiality, the negation of their identity of nature and unity of essence, the affirmation of the diversity of the Father and the Son, the negation of the all powerfulness of the Son, the negation of the equality of power of the Father and the Son, the negation of the true divinity of the Son, the negation of the incomprehensibility of the Son, and the conception of the Son as "God by participation" or as creature.[81] Against the Arians *(ariani)* St. Thomas crit-

---

79. *Ioan.* 16, lect. 4, n. 2111, cf. n. 2114; cf. *Catena Ioan.* 16:15 (541). This enlightens the response of *ST* I, q. 42, a. 6, ad 3.

80. One can count in the commentary respectively 32 explicit mentions of Arius, 17 of the *Ariani*, 14 of Sabellius and 2 of the *Sabelliani*, 1 mention of Macedonius and 1 mention of the *Macedoniani*, 1 mention of Eunomius, as well as 4 mentions of Photinus and 3 mentions of Paul of Samosata.

81. For the details of Arius's errors in the commentary on St. John, see nn. 61, 62, 64, 69, 126, 262, 477, 769, 935, 978, 1355, 1451, 1696, 1794, 1879, 1888, 1895, 1970, 2181, 2183, 2240, 2248, 2520. St. Thomas also refutes the Christological error of Arius on the human soul of Christ

icizes the affirmation of the superiority of the Father and the inferiority of the Son, the negation of the eternity of the Son and of the equality of the Father and the Son, the affirmation of the essential diversity of the Father and the Son, the conception of the Son as creature, as well as the generation of the Son by will rather than by nature.[82]

St. Thomas distinguishes very well the error of Arius and the error of Eunomius of Cyzicus, the latter having radicalized Arianism by teaching the total dissimilarity of the Father and the Son (*Ioan.* 1, lect. 1, n. 64). The precision of these historical details of the Trinitarian doctrine makes the *Commentary on St. John* "our most fruitful source for St. Thomas's account for Arianism."[83] The important discussion of Arianism in the *Commentary of St. John* is materially linked to the place of the Fathers of the Church: the Commentary conveys the anti-Arian (and anti-subordinationist) purpose of Patristic exegesis from the fourth century. For this reason, the Commentary aids us to discover the sources of Aquinas on Arianism. These sources are taken mostly from St. Hilary, but also from St. John Chrysostom and St. Augustine.[84]

Concerning semi-Arianism, St. Thomas mentions the error of Macedonius and the Macedonians. He notes correctly that the Macedonians undermined the divinity of the Holy Spirit under the aspect of the *power* of the Spirit, as they conceived the Spirit as an instrument or "minister" of the Father and the Son.[85] There again, the commentary and the *Catena* allow us to identify St. Thomas's sources, namely St. John Chrysostom and Theophylactus, who are among the principal authors of Aquinas's oriental documentation.

The precisions concerning Sabellius and Sabellianism are a little less detailed. According to St. Thomas, Sabellius denied the personal distinction and the personal plurality in the Trinity, by affirming that the Father and the Son are the same person and are distinguished only by their names: Sabellius confused the persons by attributing the incarnation to the Father.[86] In the wake of Sabellius, the Sabellians taught the personal identity of the Father

---

(negation of a human soul in Christ, because the divine Word takes the place of a soul in Christ): nn. 167, 168, 1654.

82. See, in the commentary on St. John, nn. 41, 61, 198, 545, 742, 745, 783, 1278, 1290, 1451, 1456, 1704, 1929, 1999, 2187.

83. Peter Worrall, "St. Thomas and Arianism," *Revue théologie ancienne et médiévale* 23 (1956): 211.

84. Ibid.

85. See *Ioan.* nn. 452, 2089.

86. See *Ioan.* nn. 64, 769, 783, 1154, 1237, 1451, 1696, 1887, 1895, 1911, 2181, and 2248.

Biblical Exegesis and the Speculative Doctrine of Trinity 53

and the Son, holding that the Son is inengendered.[87] The *Commentary on St. John* and the *Catena* on the fourth Gospel allow us to identify fairly easily St. Thomas's sources concerning Sabellianism: St. Augustine, St. Hilary, and St. John Chrysostom principally.

St. Thomas also reproaches Photinus of Sirmium for having taught that Christ is a mere man whose existence started in the womb of the Virgin Mary and who merited divinity (this does away with faith in the Trinity).[88] Among his sources on Photinus, one discovers Augustine and Chrysostom. But a more detailed study has allowed us to show that St. Thomas's principal source on Photinus is a work of Vigilius of Thapsus transmitted under the name of St. Athanasius.[89] It is from these sources that St. Thomas must have associated a little too closely Photinus with Paul of Samosata, neglecting Photinus's Sabellianism and his links to Marcellus of Ancyra. St. Thomas reproaches Origen for having taught that the Son is inferior to the Father, in the way of an instrument of the Father who is not God by essence but only by participation. Origen's exegesis concerning the absence of an article for the word "God" in John 1:1c ("Et Deus erat Verbum") is ruled out by going back to St. John Chrysostom.[90] Still concerning the Word, St. Thomas dismisses the Gnostic error of Valentinus, for whom the Word is the cause of the creating act of the Father (it is because of the Word that the Father created the world): St. Thomas owes the knowledge of this thesis and its refutation to having read Origen.[91]

The exclusion of heresies is present, in a significant way, in all the principal Trinitarian sections of the Commentary of St. Thomas: in the exegesis of the Prologue on the Word, in the teachings on the gift of the Spirit in chapter 3, in the exposition on the action of Christ in chapter 5 and in chapter 10, in the exposition of the speech after the Last Supper in chapters 14 through 17 (the immanence of the Son and the Father, the promise of the Paraclete, the work of the Spirit, the glorification of the Father and of the Son). St. Thomas indicates sometimes, depending on his Patristic sources, that a heretical doctrine comes from the wrong interpretation of such and such a verse,[92] or that

---

87. On the *"sabelliani,"* see *Ioan*. nn. 749, 1037.

88. See *Ioan*. nn. 64, 126, 783, 786, 935.

89. Gilles Emery, "Le photinisme et ses précurseurs chez saint Thomas," *Revue Thomiste* 95 (1995): 371–398.

90. See *Ioan*. 1, lect. 1, n. 58; 1, 2, n. 75; 1, 5, n. 126, as well as the *Catena aurea* on John 1:1–3 (p. 329). On this subordinationism in Origen, see *Super Boetium De Trinitate*, q. 3, a. 4.

91. *Ioan*. 1, lect. 2, n. 73; cf. *Catena Ioan*. 1:3 (p. 331).

92. See, for example, *Ioan*. 1, lect. 1, nn. 58, 60; *Ioan*. 1, lect. 2, n. 80: "Three heresies came from this," cf. n. 83; *Ioan*. 1, lect. 9, n. 198: "It is from this text [1:15] that the Arians took occa-

the heretics tried to found or confirm their heresy on this or that particular verse of St. John.[93] He refutes Arianism and Sabellianism by using the exegesis of one of the Fathers of the Church, or indicates several Patristic authorities that dismiss the heretical interpretation,[94] indicating sometimes that the letter of the Gospel excludes such an interpretation.[95]

Sometimes, the heretical opinion is the object of a particular question (*quaestio, obiectio*) raised by the biblical text,[96] but most often the indication of the heretical exegesis appears in the course of a continuous exposition. St. Thomas rules out the heretical interpretation by showing the motives of the error and by giving a correct exposition of the Gospel with the Fathers: it is by showing the truth of the Gospel that one excludes errors. In any case, the exclusion of errors is closely linked to the exposition of the truth of the Gospel, to such a degree that the manifestation of the truth and the rejection of errors are indissociable. One finds a good example at the end of the commentary on John 1:1–2, where St. Thomas presents a long list of errors excluded by the two first verses of the Gospel and concludes: "If one considers these four propositions well, he will find that they clearly destroy all the errors of the heretics and of the philosophers."[97] As well, St. Thomas explains many times that it is *to exclude an error* that the Gospel text uses such a word or gives such an explanation: "To exclude this, the Evangelist says . . . ," "To exclude this the Evangelist added . . . ," "To avoid such an understanding, the Evangelist John added . . ," "So you do not understand this teaching in that way, the Evangelist says. . . ."[98] The exclusion of heresies does not concern only the subject of the theologian, but it concerns already the subject of Scripture itself.

---

sion for their error"); *Ioan.* 8, lect. 2, n. 1161; *Ioan.* 12, lect. 7, n. 1696: "From this word Sabellius took occasion for his error."

93. See, for example, *Ioan.* 5, lect. 3, n. 745: "The Arians use what Christ said here, 'the Son cannot do anything of himself,' to support their error that the Son is less than the Father"; *Ioan.* 14, lect. 3, n. 1887: "Sabellius made this statement the basis of his error"; *Ioan.* 14, lect. 3, n. 1895: "Two heresies were based on the above texts"; *Ioan.* 17, lect. 5, n. 2240: "Arius uses this passage to argue that . . ."; *Ioan.* 20, lect. 3, n. 2520: "Arius based his error on these words."

94. See, for example, *Ioan.* 5, lect. 4, nn. 747–51, where St. Thomas refutes the Arian interpretation of this verse using the exegeses of St. Hilary, St. Augustine, and St. John Chrysostom.

95. *Ioan.* 5, lect. 2, n. 742: "Sed per ea quae dicta sunt in ipso textu, aliter etiam manifestum est"; cf. *Ioan.* 14, lect. 3, n. 1888, and 14, lect. 8, n. 1970.

96. See, for example, *Ioan.* 1, lect. 1, nn. 46–48: "duplex obiectio fit ab haereticis"; cf. n. 55.

97. *Ioan.* 1, lect. 1, n. 64, cf. nn. 65–66; see also, for example, *Ioan.* 5, lect. 5, n. 783: "Destruuntur autem per haec verba tres errores, secundum Hilarium."

98. See, for example, *Ioan.* 1, lect. 1, nn. 60, 61, 62; 1, 2, n. 84; 1, 7, n. 174; 5, 3, n. 749; 5, 4, n. 769; and so on.

The place given to heresies in the commentary of St. Thomas has two principal motives. In the first place, the refutation of heresies is linked to Patristic exegesis: by resuming the exegesis of the Fathers, St. Thomas takes on their concern to eliminate heretical interpretations of the Scriptures. Furthermore, St. Thomas knows that heresies were the historical motive for the development of the Trinitarian dogma.[99] But in second place, one must observe a deeper motive: to make manifest the truth and to exclude errors are the two faces of one and the same subject. This is the goal of Christian wisdom, the task of the wise person that St. Thomas expresses and systematically puts to work in the *Summa contra gentiles:* to announce and make manifest the contemplated truth, and to discard errors that contradict this truth.[100] We find here, again, one of the aspects of the astonishing likenesses between the *Commentary on John* and the *Summa contra gentiles*. It is by showing the truth that one excludes errors, and the truth is not fully made clear unless one is able to show the falseness of the errors that oppose it. One must remark on this subject that, except for the "error" of the Greeks on the procession of the Holy Spirit,[101] St. Thomas does not mention contemporary medieval errors on Trinitarian faith (neither errors of theologians nor errors of medieval religious groups). He argues only against the errors of antiquity. The reason for this choice is probably of a speculative order: if one considers the intelligence of faith, the error allows one to better grasp the truth to which it is opposed, in the measure that, by contrast, it lights up the truth. From then on, as R.-A. Gauthier has so well explained, "an error is not all the more interesting because it is more widespread, but it is all the more interesting when it opposes a deeper truth."[102] The interest for the heresies is not therefore only historical, nor is it motivated only by Patristic documentation, but it is properly systematic with a speculative aim.

In the Prologue of his *Commentary on St. John,* St. Thomas presents this Gospel as the fruit of the Apostle's contemplation: the portrait of St. John is that of a contemplative par excellence, whose contemplation was "high, full and perfect." It is about the contemplation of God, more precisely the "contemplation of the nature of the divine Word and of his essence" and of "the

---

99. See notably *De pot.,* q. 9, a. 5.

100. *Summa contra Gentiles* [hereafter *SCG*], ch. 1 (n. 7) and Book IV, ch. 1 (n. 3348). See especially R.-A. Gauthier, *Saint Thomas d'Aquin, Somme contre les Gentils, Introduction* (Paris: Editions universitaires, 1993), 143–63. One can see the same attention given to errors in other works of St. Thomas, in his *De articulis fidei* for example: see Gilles Emery, *Saint Thomas d'Aquin, Les raisons de la foi et les sacrements de l'Eglise* (Paris: Cerf, 1999), 200–8.

101. *Ioan.* 15, lect. 5, n. 2063–65.

102. Gauthier, *Sainte Thomas d'Aquin, Somme contre les Gentils,* 142.

power of the Word as it extends to all things," that is to say of the "very deity of our Lord Jesus Christ, by which he is equal to the Father."[103] According to St. Thomas, "John represents those who are devoted to the contemplation of truth."[104] We must remember here that, for St. Thomas, the words "contemplative" and "speculative" are practically equivalent and designate the same reality (*speculativus* is employed in the treatises inspired by Aristotle, whereas St. Thomas uses the word *contemplativus* in the treatises that have Christian sources).[105] Theological science is speculative because its end is the contemplation of the truth.[106] The fourth Gospel appears thus to be a privileged source of speculation. The attention given to Trinitarian heresies, in the context of this speculative exegesis, is therefore not surprising. It shows that the aim of the exposition of the fourth Gospel is identical to the subject of theological wisdom formulated in the *Summa contra gentiles:* to make manifest the contemplated truth and get rid of the errors that oppose this truth.[107]

We find here again, exactly, the aim or the goal of Scripture (or *sacra doctrina*), such as St. Thomas explains it from the start of his *Scriptum super Sententiis:* "We make our way to three things in Sacred Scripture *(in sacra Scriptura),* namely: to the destruction of errors . . . ; it also proceeds to the instruction of moral actions . . . ; third, it proceeds to the contemplation of truth in questions of Sacred Scripture."[108] In the *Summa theologiae,* St. Thomas shows that *sacra doctrina* is principally speculative, and states also the equivalence of *sacra doctrina* and *sacra Scriptura* when he explains that "Sacred Scripture disputes with one who denies its principles."[109] For St. Thomas, the expressions "sacra doctrina," "theologia," and "sacra Scriptura" are employed as synonyms and designate the whole of divine teaching founded on the revelation.[110] The aims of theological reflection are those of holy Scripture, as St. Albert the Great already explained on the subject of the modes of exposition of holy Scripture *(de modis exponendi sacram Scripturam):* holy Scripture carries a double aim *(duplex finis),* that is to say the ex-

---

103. *Ioan.*, prol., nn. 1–11.
104. *Ioan.* 20, lect. 1, n. 2487.
105. Servais Pinckaers, "Recherche de la signification véritable du terme 'spéculatif,'" *Nouvelle Revue Théologique* 81 (1959): 673–95.
106. I *Sent.*, prol., q. 1, a. 3, qla 1; cf. *ST* I, q. 1, a. 4.
107. This subject is not foreign to the *Summa theologiae,* whose Trinitarian treatise begins precisely by indicating the reasons for the Arian and Sabellian errors, and the ways to avoid such errors (I, q. 27, a. 1).
108. I *Sent.*, prol., q. 1, a. 5.
109. *ST* I, q. 1, a. 8.
110. Henri Donneaud, "Insaisissable sacra doctrina?" *Revue Thomiste* 98 (1998): 179–224.

hortation in the holy doctrine and the refutation of those who wish to contradict it.[111] In this way, exegesis and theological reflection dismiss errors as the Scripture discards errors. Biblical exegesis is speculative as holy Scripture is speculative; it leads one to the contemplation of truth, because such is the aim of Scripture itself.

CONCLUSION: THE CONTRIBUTION OF THE *COMMENTARY ON JOHN*

Our study of the *Commentary on John* by St. Thomas has not examined in detail the particular Trinitarian themes: it has been limited to considering the body of the Trinitarian doctrine, taken as a whole and with its inner coherence, by comparing it to the *Summa theologiae*. This general approach offers the following results, which can help to renew our reading of St. Thomas's Trinitarian theology.

1. The comparison with the Trinitarian treatise of the *Summa theologiae* shows the amplitude of the Trinitarian doctrine in the biblical commentary. The speculative doctrine of the Trinity, even in its technical elements, is very broad in the exposition of the Gospel. All the principal doctrinal themes are present in the commentary on the fourth Gospel. Let us remember them: the notion of procession, the immanent procession of the Son by mode of intellect or of nature, the eternal procession of the Holy Spirit, the personal subsistence in God, the doctrine of the Word, the origin of the Spirit, the property of the Father, the unity of the Father and the Son as principle of the Holy Spirit, relative opposition and the distinction of the persons by the relations, the doctrine of the real relation according to the origin, the personal properties, the order of nature in God, the necessity of notional acts, the relationship between the divine persons and creatures, the mission of the persons, as well as several problems about Trinitarian language. The most developed themes concern the three divine persons and their properties (with an accent on the doctrine of the Word, and on the procession of the Holy Spirit *a Patre et a Filio*), as well as the equality of the persons, their mutual relationships, the mission of the persons, and their action in the world. The commentary invites us to reread the Trinitarian treatise of the *Summa* in the light of these principal themes, which occupy the first place in the theologian's subject.

2. The *Commentary on St. John* allows us to identify the biblical context of several doctrinal themes. These biblical places are obvious for the doctrine of

---

111. Albert the Great, I *Sent.*, d. 1, a. 5.

the Word, the procession of the Spirit, or the unity and immanence of the persons, as Aquinas's teaching on these themes, even in the *Summa theologiae*, is directly attached to the Gospel text. But the commentary also reveals other biblical places: thus, for example, it is in the study of the procession of the Holy Spirit that the Commentary on St. John gives the most complete exposition on relative opposition. The statement on the personal subsistence in God is found principally in the study on the Word. Likewise, the study of the notion of procession is particularly developed in the exposition on the divine missions. The *Summa theologiae* treats the procession, the relation, and the properties in special questions, at the risk of suggesting a certain isolation of these themes if one omits to consider their place in the structure of the Trinitarian treatise. The *Commentary on St. John,* very close to the *Summa contra gentiles* in this aspect, indicates on its side that these doctrinal themes are attached to the study of the persons and their agency, and invites a rereading of the Trinitarian treatise of the *Summa* centered on the persons.

3. The *Commentary on St. John* reveals a more special attention given to certain themes, which the *Summa theologiae* also treats but without giving them such amplitude: the knowledge and mutual love of the divine persons, the action of the divine persons in the world, and the knowledge of the eternal Trinity through the actions of these persons. The *Commentary on St. John* develops the soteriological repercussions of the Trinitarian doctrine: the property of the Word and the mutual knowledge of the Father and the Son are the source of the illuminating and revealing role of the Son, the Trinitarian unity is the source of human and ecclesial unity, and so forth. By explaining the agency of the Son and of the Holy Spirit in the light of their personal property, St. Thomas shows that the speculative doctrine of the Word and Love does not constitute a formal "psychological" reflection detached from the history of salvation. The speculative study of the Word and Love not only has for its aim the manifestation of the distinction of the persons in the unity of divine essence, but also allows one to account for the work of the divine persons in the world and to organize the biblical teachings on the acts of the persons.

4. By exposing the actions of the divine persons in the world, St. Thomas does not content himself with the enumeration of the works of the Father, the Son, and the Spirit, but he organizes and explains these works in a doctrine on Trinitarian activity *ad extra* ("economic Trinity") by means of speculative principles, namely: the relative properties of the persons, but also the Trinitarian order, and the metaphysics of action and participation. The *Commentary on St. John* invites one to criticize the thesis, widespread today, that identifies purely and simply biblical teaching as a doctrine of the "economic

Trinity," whereas the doctrine of the "immanent Trinity" would be the result of a second and posterior reflection. In St. Thomas, the teaching on the economic Trinity is as speculative as the teaching on the immanent Trinity. The doctrine of the "economic Trinity" appears to be rather the fruit of a reflection that, benefiting from the study of the Trinity in itself, explains the Trinitarian economy in the light of the eternal being of the Trinity. The doctrine of Trinitarian economy is not first: it constitutes rather the last stage of Trinitarian theology.[112] The *Commentary on St. John* suggests that one should perceive the development of Trinitarian theology in the following way: (a) revelation of the Trinity through its actions in the world (economy of salvation) according to the witness of Holy Scriptures; (b) speculative reflection on the persons in their distinction and their unity; (c) speculative reflection on the agency of the persons in the world. Trinitarian theology starts from the agency of the divine persons in the world and comes back to this agency, in the same way that it starts from Scripture to return to Scripture.

5. The *Commentary on St. John* manifests the deeply Patristic roots of the Trinitarian doctrine of St. Thomas. Without having been able to give in detail here the extraordinary amplitude of this Patristic inheritance, we have given some examples. The comparison shows that certain articles from the *Summa theologiae*, when reread in the light of the *Commentary on St. John*, are taken directly from Patristic exegesis (even when, in the *Summa*, St. Thomas omits explicit references to the Fathers of the Church). The exegesis of the Trinitarian passages of the Gospel benefits massively from the work of the *Catena aurea:* it is led principally by the reading of the Fathers of the Church. The Trinitarian exegesis of St. Thomas is clearly presented as a resumption of the Patristic exegesis, prolonged in a personal way.

6. The Trinitarian exposition on St. John gives great attention to errors and heresies. The commentary furnishes one of our principal sources for appreciating, in a detailed way, the place of Trinitarian heresies in St. Thomas's thought. These heresies, present in all the important sections on the Trinity, all come from antiquity and manifest the Patristic roots of St. Thomas's exegesis. The interest in Trinitarian heresies is not only of a documentary order. It belongs first of all to the subject of Scripture itself, which teaches the truth and excludes errors. It is inscribed, in St. Thomas, in the speculative enterprise of the manifestation of truth. St. Thomas is interested in heresies because the exposition of Scripture aims at manifesting the catholic faith, and

---

112. For this reason, the *Summa theologiae* treats the mission of the persons at the end of the Trinitarian treatise, in the last question (*ST* I, q. 43): The study of the works of the person benefits from all the preliminary reflection.

because the manifestation of truth is intrinsically linked to the exclusion of errors. Commenting on St. John, St. Thomas seeks to accomplish the task of Christian wisdom, which consists in exposing the truth that one has meditated upon and in excluding errors. This subject is not foreign to the *Summa theologiae,* but it is more like the Trinitarian treatise of the *Summa contra gentiles.*

7. The *Commentary on St. John* can help one to perceive the unity of the *sacra doctrina* in St. Thomas better. The subject he pursues in exposing the Scriptures is identical to the aim of the Scriptures themselves and to that of Christian theology: to teach the revealed truth and to banish errors, to perceive that which we hope to contemplate one day in full light. The speculative reflection comes in then, in the *Commentary on St. John* as well as in the *Summa theologiae,* to manifest (that is to say *make more manifest for our spirit*) the truth taught by the revelation. The most speculative reflections on personal properties and Trinitarian relations is not superimposed on biblical teaching, but is included in biblical exegesis, because it has for its aim to extract the profound sense of the text by the means of intellectual resources, in faith.

8. One must conclude that the principal difference of the Trinitarian doctrine of the commentary and that of the *Summa theologiae* does not reside in the themes treated nor in the aim that consists in exposing the truth, neither in the conceptual tools, but simply in the organization of the matter. Whereas the *Summa theologiae* presents the Trinitarian doctrine according to the *ordo disciplinae* that manifests the internal arrangement and coherence (the order of exposition where the different aspects and concepts of the Trinitarian doctrine are connected according to their mutual implications), the *Commentary on St. John* presents the same teaching following to the letter the biblical text. One can see it easily in the examination of the soteriological foundations of the knowledge of the eternal Trinity (soteriological argument, reflection on power and operation, manifestation of a person by the person who proceeds from him). The *Commentary on St. John* reveals the way to elaborate a Trinitarian doctrine, which the *Summa* on its side organizes in a systematic way.

It is perhaps in this last point that we find the principal contribution of the commentary of St. Thomas on St. John. In the nineteenth and twentieth centuries, neo-scholastic Trinitarian theology gave itself the task of explaining dogmatic formulas, recalling that the dogma constitutes the norm of the reading of Scripture. The development of exegesis and historical sciences, as well as the influence of contemporary philosophical currents, have led many to argue against the pertinence and value of classical Trinitarian dogmatics. If we want to follow St. Thomas today, our first task is to show the deep biblical and Patristic foundations of his Trinitarian doctrine. The movement has been, in a way, inversed. The commentary of St. Thomas on St. John allows us to return along the path by showing how the speculative doctrine of St. Thomas is inscribed in the reading of Scripture. This speculative doctrine of the Trinity is one with the reading of the biblical text and, put to the service of the intelligence of Scripture, it does not look for anything else than the manifestation of the deep sense of the Gospel.

FOUR

What Does the Spirit Have to Do?

BRUCE D. MARSHALL

 ## A PNEUMATOLOGICAL DEFICIT?

From the West as well as the East, among Roman Catholics as well as Protestants, Christian theologians now regularly suggest that western theology suffers from a "pneumatological deficit." The Western theological tradition accounts for the temporal actions of the triune God, so these critics worry, without giving the Holy Spirit anything to do. In contrast to the Father and especially the Son, the Spirit has no action of his own, and no property, effect, or relationship to us that is unique to him. As a result, the Spirit himself tends to vanish.[1] Where we should expect traditional theology to speak of the Spirit, we find instead talk of various created substitutes for the Spirit: grace, the Church, the Virgin Mary, and so forth. This purported deficit not only affects Western theology's understanding of the Spirit's action, but insinuates itself into traditional views of the Spirit's being, as evinced by teachings such as the *Filioque* and the *vinculum amoris* (which, so the argument goes, threaten to efface the fully hypostatic or personal character of the Spirit). Augustine is usually assigned the chief blame for this unhappy state of affairs, with Thomas Aquinas a close second.

It is striking to observe, therefore, how freely Thomas assigns particular temporal actions and outcomes to the Holy Spirit in his *Commentary on John,* and in other biblical commentaries as well. To begin

---

1. Thus, *inter alia,* Robert W. Jenson: "The common factor in Western problems with the Spirit, one may suggest, is a tendency of the Spirit simply to disappear from theology's description of God's triune action, often just when he might be expected to have the leading role." *Systematic Theology,* vol. 1: *The Triune God* (New York: Oxford University Press, 1997), 153. Jenson also thinks the Christian East has noteworthy pneumatological problems.

at the end. Donated by Christ in the upper room (Jn 20:22) and on the day of Pentecost (Acts 2:33), the Holy Spirit himself gives the grace of Christ to the apostles.[2] The Spirit was "sent upon" Christ in two ways—the baptismal dove and the cloud of transfiguration—in order to signal both the sacramental and the doctrinal way in which Christ's grace would reach us. In just the same fashion, the Spirit is sent upon the apostles in two ways—the breath in the upper room and the flaming tongues of Pentecost—in order to signal that the apostles would themselves spread this grace abroad by both sacrament and teaching. But their work too is the Spirit's doing; it happens only once the apostles are "filled with the Holy Spirit" (*Ioan.* 20, lect. 4, n. 2539).

As the one who gives the grace of Christ, the Spirit naturally forgives sins. This is the "fitting effect" of the Holy Spirit's coming *(conveniens effectus Spiritus sancti),* since "the Spirit himself is love and by him *(per eum)* love is given to us" (*Ioan.* 20, lect. 4, n. 2541). Interestingly the text of Thomas's commentary here uses "caritas" for the love that the Spirit is (as well as that which the Spirit gives us), rather than "amor," which is Thomas's more typical way of talking about the Spirit's love. The reason for this lexical oddity immediately becomes clear. Thomas ties the gift of the Spirit to the apostles in the upper room, upon which he here comments, directly to Romans 5:5—the divine love (*caritas,* in Thomas's Vulgate), poured into our hearts by the Holy Spirit. The forgiveness of sins links John 20:22 to Romans 5:5, since the remission of sins entrusted to the apostles "happens," Thomas argues, "only by love" (*Ioan.* 20, lect. 4, n. 2541). In his own commentary on this Romans passage, Thomas specifies the bond between the *amor* that the Spirit is and the love that he gives us.

The Holy Spirit, who is the love of the Father and the Son, is given to us in order to lead us to share in that love which is the Holy Spirit himself. By this very participation we are made lovers of God.[3]

Here both the crucial saving action that leads us to love God (forgiveness of sins) and the effect of that action (our very love for God) belong to the Spirit. Both the act and the effect belong to the Spirit, it appears, precisely in virtue of a characteristic that is proper *(proprium)* to the Spirit, that is, unique to him—his being as *amor ipse,* the "amor Patris et Filii."[4] For just this reason

---

2. "Gratia Christi . . . datur per Spiritum sanctum." *Ioan.* 20, lect. 4, n. 2539.

3. *In Roman.* 5, lect. 1, n. 392.

4. On love in God, taken "personally" or "notionally," as unique or "proper" to the Holy Spirit, see *ST* I, q. 37, a. 1. On the Spirit as thus *amor ipse,* see, e.g., *Ioan.* 14, lect. 4, n. 1916: "The Holy Spirit is nothing but *amor*"; also the text cited below, note 29.

the divine act of forgiving sins belongs to the Spirit in particular, as his own *conveniens effectus*.

That Christ gives—or, more precisely, sends—the Holy Spirit does not mean, Thomas also observes, that the Spirit's coming is anything less than his own free action. So when Christ speaks of the Paraclete "coming" (Jn 15:26), Thomas argues, we learn something important about the basis of every temporal action the Spirit undertakes: "one is rightly said 'to come' who goes spontaneously and by his own authority. This is true of the Holy Spirit, 'who blows where he wills'" (*Ioan.* 15, lect. 5, n. 2059). The Son and the Father of course send the Spirit, but not in such a way that the Spirit is a mere instrument or servant of the Father and the Son. Rather the Spirit's mission inevitably upholds his own power and spontaneity. Thomas is quite explicit about this, in his interpretation of John 3:8.

It is in virtue of his own power of free choice that [the Spirit] blows where he wills, and when he wills, illuminating hearts. . . . Thus is refuted the error of the Macedonians, who claimed that the Holy Spirit is a servant *(ministrum)* of the Father and the Son. For if that were the case he would not blow where he wills, but where he was commanded to go. (*Ioan.* 3, lect. 2, n. 452)[5]

Therefore, Thomas argues, "That Christ says 'I will send the Spirit,' indicates not coercion, but origin" (*Ioan.* 15, lect. 5, n. 2059). The principle that a di-

---

5. From this it follows that the Holy Spirit can in no way be an *instrument* of the Father and the Son, a point the *Commentary on John* develops at the outset in connection with the Son's relation to the Father. Prompted by Jn 1:3 ("All things have been made through him"), Aquinas reflects in detail on the logical grammar of the Latin causal preposition *per* ("through," "by," or "with"). He points out that "per" sometimes denotes the cause or means by which an agent brings about an effect, in contrast to the cause that moves the agent to act. Thus we say, for example, "The carpenter makes the bench with *(per)* an axe." When it comes to created action, causes like the axe are indeed instruments, with the implication of inferiority to the agent who uses them. But the Word or Son through whom all things are made is not the Father's instrument, because he acts by numerically the same power *(virtus)* as the Father, received from the Father through eternal generation, rather than by a numerically distinct (and so created) power. For this reason, being the one through whom all things were made is not appropriated to the Son, but proper to him (on all this see *Ioan.* 1, lect. 2, n. 76).

All this applies equally to the Spirit, as Thomas's interpretation of Jn 3:8 shows. He seems to say as much in the passage I have just been analyzing, where the Marietti text has "Thus it is obvious that neither the Holy Spirit nor the Son is . . . the servant or instrument *(minister seu instrumentum)* of the Father, as Origen dreamed" (*Ioan.* 1, lect. 2, n. 76). But this appears to be a mistake in the "vulgate" text of Aquinas, which the Marietti ed. largely reproduces. The recent French translation of the first half of the *Commentary on John* incorporates many corrections of the Marietti ed. on the basis of the still forthcoming Leonine text. It renders the passage just quoted like this: "Thus it is obvious that the Holy Spirit was not made . . . and that [the Son] is neither the servant nor the instrument of the Father, as Origen said." This makes perfect sense in context of the passage, since Thomas's analysis of instrumental causality here focuses entirely

vine person can be sent only by one from whom he originates in no way limits, in other words, the spontaneous freedom of the one who is sent.[6] Mission implies origin, but origin preserves spontaneity.

ACTION UNIQUE TO THE SPIRIT

This pattern recurs throughout Thomas's *Commentary on John*. He attributes a wide range of actions and effects to the Spirit in particular, and roots these attributions in the Spirit's *propria*, especially *amor* as a personal characteristic of the Spirit. He seems untroubled by his own suggestion that these actions and effects belong to the Spirit alone, and not to the Father and the Son.

Thus "in the spiritual person," Thomas argues, "are the properties *(proprietates)* of the Holy Spirit," namely freedom, audible presence, hidden origin, and hidden goal. We do not simply possess copies of the Spirit's characteristics, created in the remote likeness of an absent source, but a participated likeness of the Spirit's very own uncreated attributes: they are in us "just as the properties of fire are in a piece of burning wood" (*Ioan.* 3, lect. 2, n. 456). Indeed "everyone who is born of the Spirit is just like *(sicut)* the Holy Spirit" (*Ioan.* 3, lect. 2, 456). The Spirit's own unity makes the Church one.[7] The Spirit "raises up our hearts from love of the present age to a spiritual resurrection, in order that they might find their way totally into God" (*Ioan.* 7, lect. 5, n. 1095). The Spirit cleanses the hearts of the apostles so that they may convict the world of sin (*Ioan.* 16, lect. 3, n. 2093). He consoles us in the face of the uproar of this world and the memory of our past sins, by making us love God (since he himself is love) and giving us the hope of pardon. He moves our hearts to obey God, and consecrates us to God (*Ioan.* 14, lect. 6, n. 1955). Just because he is the *amor Dei* in person, the Spirit tastes sweet; "he gives us contempt for earthly things and makes us cling to God, so driving out from us despair and sadness and granting us joy in God" (*Ioan.* 15, lect. 5, n. 2060). Indeed the Spirit—"*amor* taken notionally"—is "the source *(principium)* of all the gifts which are given to us by God" (*Ioan.* 5, lect. 3, n. 753).

It seems, then, that for Thomas the Holy Spirit actually has quite a lot to

---

on the Son, but he had earlier (n. 74) discussed the view, which he attributes to Origen, that the Spirit was created or made *(factum)*. See Thomas d'Aquin, *Commentaire sur l'évangile de saint Jean*, vol. 1, ed. M.-D. Philippe (Paris: Éditions du Cerf, 1998), 85a. On the textual basis of this translation, see 29.

6. On this Trinitarian principle, by which Thomas links temporal mission to timeless procession, cf. *ST* I, q. 43, a. 1 and ad 1; a. 2, ad 3; a. 4.

7. "Unitas Spiritus sancti facit in Ecclesia unitatem." *Ioan.* 1, lect. 10, n. 202.

do. But in his commentary on John, Aquinas tends to focus above all on two particular actions of the Spirit: he makes us the Father's adopted children, and he teaches us the truth. In both cases the action of the Spirit is to bring about a specific relationship of human beings to the Son.

The Spirit's mission is of course unique to him; only he is sent by both the Father and the Son. "The name 'Spirit,'" Thomas argues, "implies a certain power of movement *(impulsionem)*, and every motion has an effect appropriate to its source . . . consequently the Holy Spirit makes those into whom he is sent similar to him whose Spirit he is" (*Ioan.* 15, lect. 5, n. 2062). As the one originating from, and therefore sent by, both Father and Son, the Holy Spirit gives us a share in Jesus' own eternal sonship. In Thomas's words, he "has conformed *(configuravit)* us to the Son, in that *(inquantum)* he adopts us as children of God" (*Ioan.* 14, lect. 6, n. 1957).

Thomas gives a detailed treatment of the Spirit's adoptive action elsewhere, in connection with his account of our adoptive sonship in Christ.[8] The John commentary is especially striking for its account of the Spirit's teaching action.[9] The Spirit's act, Thomas repeatedly argues, is to manifest the Son, to make him known. The Johannine Spirit of truth (Jn 15:26) makes known the Johannine truth, which is simply the person of the Son (Jn 14:6). The action of the Spirit, like his mission, is to be distinguished clearly from that of the Son. "As the effect of the Son's mission," Thomas argues, "was to lead us to the Father, so the effect of the Spirit's mission is to lead the faithful to the Son." The Spirit does this by making us capable of receiving what the Son has to teach: "The Son hands on his teaching to us, since he is the Word, but the Holy Spirit creates room in us for his teaching *(doctrinae eius nos capaces facit)*" (*Ioan.* 14, lect. 6, n. 1958; cf. 16, 4, n. 2106). The Spirit begins to manifest the Son at the Son's baptism; he teaches the apostles about Jesus' divinity and humanity; in due course he teaches them about the Son's resurrection and our own (*Ioan.* 1, lect. 14, nn. 268, 270; 16, 3, n. 2096; 7, 5, n. 1095).

Here too the Spirit's temporal act of manifesting the Son depends on unique features of the Spirit's own being: not only his proper characteristic of love, but also, as Thomas here stresses, his procession from the Son. The two are, of course, related. "Anything which is from another," Thomas claims, "manifests that from which it is" (*Ioan.* 16, lect. 4, n. 2106). "The Spirit leads

---

8. Cf. *ST* III, q. 23, especially a. 2, ad 3. On this see Bruce D. Marshall, "Action and Person: Do Palamas and Aquinas Agree about the Spirit?" *St. Vladimir's Theological Quarterly* 39 (1995): 379–408, especially 390–92, 397–99.

9. Of course the Father and the Son have a teaching action as well; on this see Michael Sherwin's essay in this volume.

us to the knowledge of the truth," therefore, "because he proceeds from the truth," namely Christ the Son, who rightly says, "I am the truth" (*Ioan.* 14, lect. 4, n. 1916). The Spirit, moreover, comes forth from the Father and the Son quite particularly as love. As love for the truth springs from knowledge of the truth, so in God the Holy Spirit proceeds as the Father's love for the Son, the truth whom the Father brings forth. "Just as, in us, from a truth conceived and grasped there follows love of this very truth, so in God when the truth, which is the Son, gets conceived, love comes forth."[10] At the same time the Spirit proceeds as the Son's love for the Father, whose truth the Son has been brought forth to be. As Thomas observes in his commentary on the transfiguration story in Matthew: "Love itself"—the Holy Spirit—"proceeds from the Father delighting in the Son, and from the Son delighting in the Father."[11]

Now "it belongs to love," Thomas says, "to reveal what is hidden"—above all, of course, the deep things of God (cf. 1 Cor 2:10). Therefore, Thomas

---

10. "In Deo concepta veritate, quae est Filius, procedit Amor" (*Ioan.* 14, lect. 4, n. 1916). On the Father's love for the Son eliciting the procession of the Spirit, see also *ST* I, q. 27, a. 4, ad 2. In God the eternal *processio amoris*—the Spirit's way of coming forth—differs in kind from the Son's generation. The Son comes forth precisely as the perfect likeness *(similitudo)* of the one who generates him. "But love," Thomas observes, "is not itself a likeness. Rather likeness is the basis of loving *(principium amandi),*" that is, it elicits or calls forth love. Thus, Thomas concludes, "it does not follow that love is begotten, but that the begotten one is the basis of love *(non sequitur quod amor sit genitus, sed quod genitus sit principium amoris)."* In other words: it is precisely the begotten who elicits love from the begetter, the Son who elicits the *processio amoris* from the Father, and so the person of the Spirit himself. (In this context "genitus sit principium amoris" clearly does not mean that the begotten one is the *source* of the Spirit—viz., that the Spirit proceeds from the Son—since the present point is to locate the elemental distinction between the two modes of procession in God: that the second is called forth from the source of both by the term of the first.) Since the Father's love for the Son brings forth the Spirit, it follows that the Spirit proceeds *to* the Son, and not only *from* him. The Spirit is "the love of the Father reaching out to the Son *(tendens in Filium)"* and in just this sense is "the love by which the Father loves the Son" *(Scriptum super libros Sententiarum* [hereafter *Sent.* with book number] I, d. 14, q. 1, a. 1, c. Cf. I, d. 15, q. 4, a. 3, ad 2: "In a certain way it may be granted that the Holy Spirit eternally proceeds from the Father to the Son" *[procedat a Patre in Filium ab aeterno]).* The Spirit therefore proceeds from the Father so as to rest in the Son; that the Spirit abides in the Son is not a feature of the Spirit's temporal mission alone. "The Holy Spirit is said to rest in the Son . . . just as the love of the lover [viz., the Father] rests in the beloved" *(ST* I, q. 36, a. 2, ad 4). The *Commentary on John,* by contrast, thinks of the Son's possession of the Spirit from the Father primarily in terms of the Son's "capacity and power of breathing the Holy Spirit" *(Ioan.* 3, lect. 6, n. 543). But Thomas sees no conflict here. The Son abides in the Father, from whom he comes forth; surely the Spirit can come forth from the Son, in whom he abides (cf. *ST* I, q. 36, a. 2, ad 4).

11. *Super Matthaeum* 17, lect. 1, n. 1436: "Ipse Amor procedit a Patre diligente Filium, et a Filio diligente Patrem."

concludes, "to manifest the truth belongs uniquely to the Holy Spirit" *(convenit proprietati Spiritus sancti) (Ioan.* 14, lect. 4, n. 1916). The Spirit's temporal action of teaching the truth apparently belongs to him alone, just as much as his proper characteristic of love and his procession from the Son. Labeling this action a *proprium* of the Spirit, as here in the interpretation of John 14:17, is not an entirely isolated feature of Thomas's commentary. When he returns to the issue in his remarks on John 16:14, he says the same thing. "Since the Holy Spirit is from the Son, it is proper for him to glorify the Son" *(proprium est ut clarificet eum) (Ioan.* 16, lect. 4, n. 2107).

Striking as it is for Thomas to label a temporal *action* of one person of the Trinity as unique or proper to him, the thought is clearly present in the *Commentary on John* even where the word is not used.[12] As we have seen, throughout his commentary Thomas attributes to the Holy Spirit actions that have characteristics or features different from the actions of the Father or the Son: the characteristic from which the acts spring in the agent is different, the quality of the acts is different, the term or result of the acts is different. This naturally leads one to think that the actions themselves are different. If actions x and y (say, the Son's act of leading us to the Father, and the Spirit's act of leading us to the Son)[13] have at least one feature or attribute not shared by both, then presumably they are different actions—actions not numerically the same. Discernible, x and y are not identical. So there seems good reason to say that (for example) the Son's act of leading and the Spirit's act of leading are not the same act.

Of course Thomas's official position is precisely that all of the temporal actions of the divine persons are numerically identical, and thus common to

---

12. On this score actions may pose a more difficult problem than relations. One divine person can clearly be the subject of a relation with a temporal term of which the other two are not the subjects. The standard example is the Son's relation of union to a human nature, which is of course unique to him (cf. *ST* III, q. 3, a. 4). But the same applies to the Spirit's relation ("being manifested by") to the dove that manifests him. This relation is unique to the Spirit (the dove does not manifest the Father or the Son), though of course it is a different *kind* of relation than hypostatic union (Thomas discusses this point *Ioan.* 1, lect. 14, n. 270; cf. *ST* III, q. 39, a. 6, ad 2). In both cases Thomas holds that the relation brought about by the relevant divine action is unique to one of the persons, while the action that brings it about is common to the three (although, as we will discuss momentarily, in a way different for each). For Thomas this is especially clear in Jesus' baptism. "Just as the dove, and the human nature assumed by Christ, are the work of the whole Trinity *(columbam . . . tota Trinitas operata est)*, so also is the sound of the voice. Nevertheless in the voice the Father alone is revealed, as the speaker, just as the Son alone has assumed human nature, and the Holy Spirit alone is made manifest in the dove *(in columba solus Spiritus Sanctus demonstratus est)." ST* III, q. 39, a. 8, ad 2; cf. *Ioan.* 1, lect. 14, nn. 268, 270; 16, 3, n. 2096.

13. Cf. *Ioan.* 14, lect. 6, n. 1958, cited above.

the three persons. "The exterior works of the Trinity are undivided" *(opera trinitatis ad extra indivisa sunt)*, runs the ancient trinitarian axiom, which Thomas clearly endorses.[14] For Thomas, like the Cappadocians and Augustine before him, the unity of God hangs on this axiom. In the John commentary this emerges with particular clarity when Thomas discusses Christ's saying that the Holy Spirit will be "another Comforter" (14:16). A comforter's action is to console, so when Christ speaks of *another* comforter, he apparently introduces a second act of consolation, alongside the one he himself already performs. But this cannot be, since "difference of action indicates difference of nature" *(alietas operationis designat alietatem naturae)* (*Ioan.* 14, lect. 4, n. 1912). The problem, it seems, is that positing a numerical difference of action between Christ and the Holy Spirit would multiply the divine essence and so destroy the unity of God. If Christ and the Spirit (together, of course, with the Father) are to be one God, they have to have, and undertake, one action—an action that is numerically, and not just qualitatively, the same for each. What we want, as Thomas puts it elsewhere in the *Commentary on John,* is "not to distinguish the action, but the persons" (*Ioan.* 17, lect. 5, n. 2246).[15]

APPROPRIATION AND UNITY OF ACTION

As Thomas clearly realizes, however, a problem arises here. As his own exegesis of John repeatedly shows, the actions of the divine persons in time are qualitatively different. On this hangs at least our ability to recognize them as distinct persons. Had they no differences of action or attribute that they made available to us, they would be indiscernible for us—we would have no way of distinguishing them from one another. So the exegetical and dogmat-

---

14. "Exterior," that is, in the sense that they terminate in some created, rather than divine, reality; for the sake of brevity I have here been calling these the "temporal" acts of the divine persons. On the axiom just cited see, e.g., *ST* III, q. 3, a. 4, obj. 1; q. 32, a. 1, obj. 1.

15. One might reasonably wonder why God's action has to be numerically one, like his nature, rather than being allowed to float free of the unity of nature. After all, "actions belong to individual subjects" or "supposits" *(actus sunt suppositorum),* as Aquinas insists (*ST* I, q. 39, a. 5, ad 1; cf. I, q. 29, a. 1; III, q. 19, a. 1, obj. 3; q. 20, a. 1, ad 2). So since there are three persons or supposits in God, why not eliminate the problem by letting there be three actions? For Aquinas perhaps the clearest response to this question is that while numerical unity of action indeed goes with unity of person or supposit *(ab unitate hypostasis est unitas [operationum] secundum numerum)*—we normally count actions by counting agents—the *kinds* of action of which an agent is capable depend on its nature *(a diversitate . . . naturarum est diversa species operationum)* (all from *ST* III, q. 19, a. 1, ad 3). Since there is (numerically) only one nature in God, there can be only one capacity to act divinely (one *operatio* of the divine kind), which has to be shared by three different persons. Thus the problem.

ic requirements of Christian faith in the Trinity commit us, as Thomas recognizes, to believing both that the actions of the divine persons are qualitatively different and that they are numerically identical. How can this be?

Of course the converse poses no problem. We have no difficulty supposing that objects can be qualitatively identical but numerically distinct—a bagful of white marbles, which we can easily count, even though they all look the same. But if objects or actions are numerically identical, how can they nonetheless be qualitatively different?

Thomas's chief answer to this question is his teaching on appropriations. It is a sophisticated answer, which has been widely misunderstood and unvalued in recent theology (not least under the influence of Karl Rahner).[16] For the moment we can simply look at one place in the John commentary where he develops this teaching. It comes precisely in answer to a question about how there can be no *alietas operationis* between Christ and the Spirit, even though their actions are manifestly different.

According to Thomas each of the two, Son and Spirit, is consoler and advocate. Each undertakes the single divine action of consoling, and the single action of advocating, but each consoles and advocates "in a different sense *(alia et alia ratione)* . . . if we take it by appropriating [the action] to the persons." Thus "Christ is called 'advocate' in that, as a human being, he intercedes for us with the Father, the Holy Spirit, however, in that he causes us to pray." Likewise the Spirit "is called 'consoler' in that he formally has the characteristic of *amor*, the Son in that he is the Word" (here again the distinctive character of each person's action depends on his *propria*, the features that only he possesses, from all eternity). As *Verbum*, Christ consoles both by his teaching and by himself giving the Holy Spirit, "thereby inflaming our hearts with love." Since the Son's consolation is to give the fire of love that is the Spirit himself, and since the Spirit does not give or send himself, it is clear that each person has to undertake the one divine act of consoling (or, yet more precisely, of inflaming the heart) in a different way. The Son consoles by sending the Spirit, the Spirit by inflaming the hearts of those to whom he is sent. Thus the difference between the Son's action and the Spirit's does not

---

16. On Rahner's disregard for what he habitually calls "mere" appropriations, and some curiosities about Rahner's own view of this matter, see Bruce D. Marshall, *Trinity and Truth* (Cambridge: Cambridge University Press, 2000), 255 n. 23. Modern Catholic theology has included a complex debate about appropriation, much of it in the context of the long-running argument (which reaches as far back as Lessius and Petavius in the early seventeenth century) over whether the Holy Spirit has any "proper" relationship to the justified. Here we cannot sort out that debate, but will simply try to clarify Thomas's position.

"indicate a [numerical] difference of nature between the Son and the Holy Spirit, but indicates a different *way (alium modum)* in which each is consoler and advocate."[17] No danger here that the Spirit will have nothing of his own to do, yet the action of Father, Son, and Spirit remains single, not multiple.

Whether Thomas's solution is, as it stands, an entirely convincing one is another matter. If an action x is undertaken in one way by this person, and in a different way by that person, it still looks rather like x designates two different actions (or, more precisely, a class of action multiply instantianted by multiple agents). One person's x apparently remains discernible from the other person's x, so the numerical unity of the action x remains a bit of a puzzle.

THE ACTS OF THE TRIUNE GOD AND PROBLEMS ABOUT IDENTITY

While evidently indispensable to the coherence of his Trinitarian theology, Thomas's teaching on appropriations apparently poses some serious problems about identity. It seems to fall afoul of a quite basic truth about identity, sometimes called "Leibniz's law": x and y are identical—are one and the same—just in case they have all the same properties (or, as it is sometimes put, just in case whatever is true of x is true of y). Thomas has deep Trinitarian reasons for saying not only that for any action of the Father *ad extra* there is also an action of the Son and of the Holy Spirit, but that these are one and the same action. Given Leibniz's law, this should entail that the actions of the Son and of the Spirit share all and only the properties of the Father's action. Yet this Thomas denies, for equally deep Trinitarian reasons. He holds that

---

17. All from *Ioan.* 14, lect. 4, n. 1912; my emphasis in the last phrase. In some passages Thomas apparently tries to reconcile numerical unity of divine action with qualitative difference in the way each agent acts by suppressing qualitative difference. When, e.g., he treats Jesus' statement that he has given to his followers the glory that the Father gave to him (Jn 17:22), Thomas declines to take the former gift as an action of Jesus, and the latter as an action of the Father. Rather he regards both as actions common to the Father and the Son, and so as actions of the Trinity (cf. *Ioan.* 17, lect. 5, n. 2246). Perhaps passages like these prompt the worry of Rahner and others that "appropriation" obscures each divine person's distinct manner of action, and so the distinction of persons itself. But the difficulty is more apparent than real. Thomas takes the creation of Christ's glorified humanity and the imparting of this glorified humanity to others as two different divine actions (whether this position is exegetically wise in the context of Jn 17 is beside the present point). Precisely because these *actions* are numerically distinct, they must be common to the three divine persons, who always share numerically single divine actions *ad extra*. But each of the persons still undertakes each of these divine actions in a way qualitatively different from the other two persons. So the Son, e.g., gives glory to believers "through his own humanity," which of course the Father does not (*Ioan.* 17, lect. 5, n. 2246). The logic of the issue remains that spelled out in the passage we have just been interpreting (n. 1912).

the Son acts in a different way *(alium modum)* than the Father, and the Spirit than the Father and the Son; their actions thus fail to share all the same properties.

However we deal with this problem (which is not Thomas's alone), we should, I think, avoid the sort of merely verbal solution to which we theologians are unfortunately prone. It is sometimes suggested, for example, that on Thomas's view the actions of the divine persons (or perhaps their modes of action) are *distinct,* but not *different.* This helps not at all. In order for x and y to be distinct, they have to differ in at least one respect; they must, in other words, fail to share at least one property. They cannot be distinct except by being different. But if they are different, then they are *numerically* distinct, which is just what we do not want in the case of divine action.

Theologians who worry about a "pneumatological deficit" in Western theology tend not to offer a merely verbal solution to this problem, but no solution at all. Their characteristic pattern is rather to take the actions of Father, Son, and Spirit as three distinct deeds, which are the same only in kind, or generically, and not in number. Its advocates sometimes seem to count this as needed Trinitarian or pneumatological boldness; why it should not also be counted as tritheism is usually less clear.

There is no room here for an adequate treatment of the problems about identity suggested by Thomas's account of what the Spirit has to do. I will conclude simply by pointing out two different directions a possible solution might take.[18]

1. It is now regularly observed that what seems like quite legitimate talk about identity and sameness in ordinary language does not always satisfy the requirements of Leibniz's law, even when it is clearly numerical identity we are talking about. The most obvious cases are entities that are identical for a time, but then cease to be identical (or, equally, began to be identical, but previously were not). It seems straightforward to say that the ring on my finger is identical with a certain lump or small quantity of gold. The gold and the ring currently share all the same properties. At some time in the future, however, the ring might be melted down and made into a coin. In that case, the lump of gold would have properties, like bearing the imprint of a former U.S. president, which the ring does not have. By the stringent requirements of Leibniz's law, therefore, the ring and the lump of gold are not identical af-

---

18. My observations in *Trinity and Truth* (256) about contexts in which terms referring to the divine persons can and cannot be substituted *salva veritate* are, I now realize, no solution to this problem. They simply specify the results that have to follow from any theologically acceptable solution.

ter all. But this does not, of course, lead us to say that the ring on my finger and the lump of gold it is made of are actually two entities, rather than one and the same entity. We thereby grant that some common and unproblematic cases of numerical identity do not meet the requirements of Leibniz's law, and take up the slack between the two by noting the capacity of some sorts of things to acquire different properties over time.

This gives us some purchase on the thought that claims about numerical identity may sometimes fall afoul of Leibniz's law and still be not only intelligible, but true. But this will not by itself help us with the case of temporal acts of the triune God that are differently appropriated to each of the three persons. When it comes to the works of the Trinity *ad extra* we clearly do not have a case where one and the same action is first identical with a deed of the Father, then later with a somewhat different deed of the Son, and finally with a deed of the Spirit, also different in at least one respect from the actions of the first two. Rather we want to say, if we are of Thomas's party on this matter, that one and the same divine action is at the same time identical with the action of the Father, the action of the Son, and the action of the Spirit, yet the actions of the three are not identical with each other, since each undertakes the same divine action in a different way from the other two. This is clearly a more difficult case than the gold and the ring.

P. T. Geach has, however, proposed a theory of identity that would also make the acts of the Trinity unproblematic, if the theory works. Geach argues that numerical identity is always relative to some sort or kind. That is: to ask whether x and y are one and the same is not to pose an adequately formed question, one that admits of an answer as it stands. In order to answer the question, we first have to ask, "One and the same *what?*" Armed with clarity on this point, we can then decide whether x and y are one and the same cat, coffee bean, divine act, or whatever. Geach maintains that identity is always relative to kind in this way. There simply is no "absolute" or "strict" identity of the sort usually thought to be required by Leibniz's law.[19] Thus on Geach's account it is quite possible for "x is the same A as y" to be true, while "x is the same B as y" is false—for x and y to be numerically identical relative to one sort or kind, and numerically distinct relative to another sort or kind. The

---

19. In Geach's own formulation: "I am arguing for the thesis that identity is relative. When one says 'x is identical with y,' this, I hold, is an incomplete expression; it is short for 'x is the same A as y,' where 'A' represents some count noun understood from the context of utterance." *Logic Matters* (Oxford: Basil Blackwell, 1972), 238. For Geach's vigorous defense of relative identity, cf. ibid., 238–49. He introduced the notion in *Reference and Generality*, first published in 1962; cf. the 3rd ed. (Ithaca: Cornell University Press, 1980), 63–64, 179–82.

ring is the same lump of gold as the coin, but not the same piece of goldsmith's work as the coin; if Geach is right, we can make sense of such cases even where time is not involved.

The application of this view to the problem at hand is not difficult to see. We seek a way of saying that the temporal actions of the three divine persons are numerically identical, yet have different features. On a standard notion of strict or absolute identity this is perplexing at best, but given the notion of relative identity it falls nicely into place: for each kind of action *ad extra* undertaken by the Father, the Son, and the Spirit, the act itself is the same, but the mode or manner of action is not. Recall Thomas's example, the consolation of the faithful by the triune God (though in reflecting on Jn 14:15, Thomas concerns himself explicitly only with the Son and the Spirit). The Son's consoling is the same act as the Father's consoling, but the Son's way of consoling is not the same as the Father's. Likewise, the Holy Spirit's consoling is the same act as the Son's (and the Father's), but the Spirit's way of consoling is not the same as the Son's (or the Father's). This accounts for the seemingly curious Christian practice of counting or distinguishing the divine persons as agents in time not by their actions (which are always one and the same), but by the distinct manner of acting that each presents.

The problem about identity posed by the temporal acts of the Trinity naturally puts us in mind of the most familiar and basic conceptual problem about the Trinity, namely how the three persons can be one God—or, more precisely, how the three persons can be numerically distinct from each other, but numerically identical with the one God.[20] Relative identity makes this seem less puzzling than it would be otherwise. Father, Son, and Spirit are the same *A*, but not the same *B*, the same nature, but not the same person.[21] Thomas himself sometimes makes much the same logical move in order to block the unhappy consequences of Leibniz's law (though not under that name) in this Trinitarian context.[22] Applying the relative identity thesis to the

---

20. On Thomas's account, indeed, the one follows quite closely from the other. The three divine persons are in reality identical with their one divine nature, but each possesses, indeed *is*, that nature in a manner unique to him: "the same essence which is paternity in the Father is filiation in the Son" (*ST* I, q. 42, a. 6, ad 3; cf. a. 4, ad 2, also *Ioan*. 16, lect. 4, n. 2112). Since actions get their species or kind for Aquinas from the nature (rather than the subject or suppositum) of the agent (cf. above, note 15), and the nature is, as it were, "stamped" differently by each divine person, it follows that any action the three persons undertake in virtue of their common nature will be performed by each in a manner unique to him.

21. Peter van Inwagen argues the case for this application of relative identity in detail; see "And Yet They Are Not Three Gods but One God," *God, Knowledge, and Mystery* (Ithaca: Cornell University Press, 1995), 222–59.

22. Cf. *ST* I, q. 28, a. 3, ad 1; also q. 39, a. 1, ad 1–2.

actions of the Trinity *ad extra* is an extension of its application to the more basic issue of personal distinction in unity of nature.

All this looks promising, as we observed, if the theory works. On this score, however, there is considerable controversy.[23] Although vigorously defended by some, the notion of relative identity has not found wide acceptance. Critics argue that to relativize the application of Leibniz's law to countable kinds is simply to dispense with it altogether. From this follow insupportable paradoxes. Not so, Geach replies; indeed, greater paradoxes follow from accepting absolute identity.[24] The logical waters here run deep, and I will make no attempt to enter them at this point. We may simply note the undesirability, if it can be avoided, of hanging the coherence of our account of the triune God's actions in the world on a controverted piece of logical theory. Of course we could say that the theory must be right because it makes our Trinitarian theology cohere, but that would be cheating.

2. As we have just noticed, Thomas himself occasionally appeals to relative identity, or at least notions quite like it, in order to solve Trinitarian problems. Yet even if the concept of relative identity can be made logically compelling, one may reasonably wonder whether it represents the sort of solution on which Thomas would prefer to rely, at least primarily. As a device for blocking unwanted conclusions about numerical identity, relative identity works as well for divine persons and their modes of action as it does for lumps of gold and rings. Far from being an attraction, this degree of lucidity makes relative identity seem like a questionable instrument for dealing with theological problems. From Thomas's point of view, it looks like all too univocal a solution to the difficulty at hand.

The problem, tersely put, is that no concept can apply as well to God as it does to gold. The infinite difference between God and creatures, and thereby the basic inadequacy of everything that we can know and say about God in this life, blocks the way. We can know and name God only from creatures, Thomas everywhere insists, and this applies as much to what we know and say about God at the heart of Christian faith as it does to what we might know about God by natural reason. That our knowledge and language are thus impeded in their effort to speak of divine things does not mean that we are unable to make true statements about God. It does mean, however, that precisely those names or terms that rightly apply to God "fail to represent

---

23. For some of the literature on this topic, see van Inwagen, "Not Three Gods," 231–32.
24. W. V. Quine in particular has made much of the philosophical role of identity, strictly conceived; Geach tries to disarm some of Quine's arguments in the pages from *Logic Matters* cited above.

him" *(deficiunt a repraesentatione ipsius)*.[25] Even the names that are true of God "have a mode of signifying which is suited to creatures," and not to the God whom we signify by them; they "introduce corporeal conditions, not in the signification of the name, but in the mode of signifying."[26] In particular, on Aquinas's account, our thought and talk about God imports various kinds of composition that are real in creatures, but that are not real in God. This applies not only to our account of God's being and attributes, but in the most basic Trinitarian case. In God relation, and so person, "is not different from the essence in reality, but only in our way of thinking."[27]

Although we can rightly assert that the three divine persons are identical with the divine essence, we cannot help *thinking* of the persons and the essence as distinct. We lack, in Thomas's terminology, a *modus significandi* for the identity of persons and essence (or nature) in God. As a result we are bound to run into problems about identity when we seek to understand faith's conviction that Father, Son, and Holy Spirit are but one God. If we take our cues from our composite mode of signifying, in which the persons are not identical with the essence, we will naturally infer that they must be three gods. Troubled by this, we will assert—correctly—that the persons and the essence are in reality one and the same. But given our creaturely *modus significandi* for identity, we will naturally, yet incorrectly, infer from this assertion that the persons are identical with each other.

The same problem crops up when we think about the temporal actions of the Trinity. Just because we have no *modus significandi* for the identity of persons and essence in God, we run into problems when we try to understand how one and the same act can be carried out in three irreducibly different ways. The modes of action are different because the persons are three, but the act is the same because the essence is one. Faced with this, we will naturally want to conclude that the actions must be three because the persons are, or that the mode of action must be single because the essence is. If we had a way of signifying identity that was suited to God, and not only to creatures, we could avoid these dialectical standoffs; they would never get off the ground. But that we cannot have, at least in this life. The best we can do is block these unwanted inferences by observing that they originate not in the way things are *in divinis*, but in the limitations imposed by our creaturely way of think-

---

25. *ST* I, q. 13, a. 2. Thomas regularly makes this point in Trinitarian contexts. See, e.g., I, q. 28, a. 2, ad 2–3.

26. *ST* I, q. 13, a. 3, ad 3.

27. *ST* I, q. 39, a. 1: "Relatio autem ad essentiam comparata non differt re, sed ratione tantum."

ing about God.²⁸ Or so, at least, we may conclude if we read John with Thomas Aquinas, and find that the Spirit has a work of his own to do, yet not another work from that of the Father and the Son.

---

28. All of this raises very large problems about epistemology, the philosophy of language, and the application of both in theology. For a stimulating approach to some of these questions in Aquinas, see David B. Burrell, *Aquinas: God and Action* (Notre Dame: University of Notre Dame Press, 1979). For more on the Trinitarian application of the *modi significandi* in Aquinas, cf. Bruce D. Marshall, "In Search of an Analytic Aquinas: Grammar and the Trinity," in *Grammar and Grace*, ed. Robert MacSwain and Jeffrey Stout (London: SCM Press, forthcoming).

FIVE

Does the Paschal Mystery Reveal the Trinity?

MATTHEW LEVERING

When a biblical scholar such as N. T. Wright, a confessing Christian with a deserved reputation for theological depth, faults Patristic and medieval theology for a distortion of the biblical portrait of God, his argument deserves attention from theologians.[1] This is even more the case when his view corresponds to a movement in Protestant (Barth, Moltmann) and Catholic (Mühlen, Balthasar) Trinitarian theology to employ the Paschal mystery of Jesus Christ as the fundamental datum for speculation into the life of the Trinity.[2] Anne Hunt, in her study of this theological movement, speaks for many of these theologians in arguing that before the twentieth century, theologians focused on the "divine being *ad intra*" with the result that the historical events of salvation did not shape their speculative conclusions about the Trinity.[3] Hunt indicates surprise that this situation lasted as long as it did: "Why then is the Trinity not considered in terms of Jesus' death and resurrection? In retrospect it seems an astonishing omission in

---

1. Portions of this essay are found in Matthew Levering, *Scripture and Metaphysics: Aquinas and the Renewal of Trinitarian Theology* (Oxford: Blackwell, 2004). See Thomas G. Weinandy, O.F.M. Cap., *Does God Suffer?* (Notre Dame: University of Notre Dame Press, 2000), 1–74, for a survey of contemporary theological/exegetical critiques of the doctrine of divine impassibility and an account of the Old and New Testaments that suggests that metaphysical investigation is in fact required by Scripture itself as a necessary medium through which to understand the events of salvation history.

2. In order to grasp the links between Protestant and Catholic theologians on this point, as well as to understand their philosophical underpinnings, see David Coffey, *Deus Trinitas: The Doctrine of the Triune God* (Oxford: Oxford University Press, 1999), 105–50; and Samuel M. Powell, *The Trinity in German Thought* (Cambridge: Cambridge University Press, 2001). For a brief critical introduction to Balthasar's approach, see my "Balthasar on Christ's Consciousness on the Cross," *Thomist* 65 (2001): 567–81.

3. Anne Hunt, *The Trinity and the Paschal Mystery: A Development in Recent Catholic Theology* (Collegeville, Minn.: Liturgical Press, 1997), 2.

classical Trinitarian theology. Apparently the interconnection of the Trinity with Jesus' death and resurrection is simply not a question at this stage in the tradition."[4] In the work of Hans Urs von Balthasar and numerous of his contemporaries, Hunt recognizes something new, namely an interpretation of the Trinity that finds in Christ's passion and resurrection, rather than in the metaphysical structure of spiritual act, the foundation for speculation about the inner-Trinitarian mystery. As Balthasar argues in his multi-volume trilogy, Christ's Paschal mystery reveals, in the immanent Trinity, "such an incomprehensible and unique 'separation' of God from himself that it *includes* and grounds every other separation—be it never so dark and bitter."[5] The Cross reveals the inner life of the Trinity.

Although the profound connections between Aquinas's theology of the triune God and his soteriology have been exposed by, among others, A. N. Williams,[6] nonetheless Aquinas, in his formal discussions of the triune God in himself, makes little direct or explicit reference to Christ's passion and resurrection. The concerns raised by contemporary exegetes and theologians, and their call for a different approach, are thus understandable. If Christ cru-

---

4. Ibid., 5; cf. vii–viii.

5. Hans Urs von Balthasar, *Theo-Drama*, vol. 4, *The Action*, trans. Graham Harrison (San Francisco: Ignatius Press, 1994), 325; cf. 362 and elsewhere. The relationship of Hans Urs von Balthasar's thought to Aquinas's is a complex one, but in the areas of Trinitarian theology, Christology, and soteriology there is a marked divergence. Commenting on Balthasar's interpretation of Aquinas's historical role in *The Theology of Karl Barth* (263–66), Fergus Kerr, O.P., has noted, "Much as with de Lubac, Thomas is admitted to be a 'transitional figure': before him the one and only concrete spiritual order governed all theology, ahead of him lay the *duplex ordo*, culminating at Vatican I. 'Whoever does not realise how Thomas was open both to the past and to the future will misunderstand his position in the history of human thought.' Yet, if de Lubac encouraged us to read Thomas as the inheritor of the patristic conception of natural desire for God, Balthasar (here at least) preferred us to read Thomas more in terms of what was to come. The notion that philosophy and theology should divide and go their separate ways is the 'authentic spirit of Thomism'. In the event, the three treatises that did *not* interest Aquinas—*de Deo Trino* (excellent formal training but no shaping influence on the project of the *Summa theologiae*), *de Christo* (carefully done but with no influence on all that precedes in the *Summa*), and *de Ecclesia* (simply absent)—are, Balthasar contends, precisely what Christian theology is about. In other words, Thomas' focus was already opening him to the standard account in terms of theistic proofs, natural law, etc. His predominantly philosophical methodology prevents him from doing Christian theology properly. Above all, as he says, theology does not deal with *singularia:* the very particular historical events are treated as mere examples. Thus, in the end, Balthasar chooses Barth over Aquinas, because Barth's methodology means theology practised as *scientia de singularibus*." (Fergus Kerr, O.P., "Thomas Aquinas: Conflicting Interpretations in Recent Anglophone Literature," in *Aquinas as Authority,* ed. Paul van Geest, Harm Goris, and Carlo Leget [Leuven: Peeters, 2002], 169.)

6. A. N. Williams, *The Ground of Union: Deification in Aquinas and Palamas* (Oxford: Oxford University Press, 1999).

cified and risen is the heart of revelation, should not reflection upon his Paschal mystery guide reflection upon all other theological topics? Should not the Paschal mystery strikingly illumine the reality of God-in-himself? If the answer is yes, as I think it is, then contemporary exegetes and theologians have exposed a central neglected area in the theology of the triune God.

This essay addresses the concerns of the "Paschal mystery"[7] exegetes and theologians. First I will examine the biblical exegesis of N. T. Wright, whose investigation of the biblical "identity of God" leads him to criticize traditional theological approaches to the divine identity. I will then attempt to clarify the issue at stake by exploring the theological significance of Christ's Paschal mystery according to Aquinas. Aquinas's treatise on Christ's passion can help us to understand what it means to say that the Paschal mystery is the prime locus of revelation about God. Third, using both Aquinas's *Summa theologiae* and his *Commentary on the Gospel of John,* I will argue that for Aquinas, Christ's Paschal mystery, as a manifestation of self-giving love, reveals the Trinity.

N. T. WRIGHT ON JESUS AND THE IDENTITY OF GOD

N. T. Wright[8] has remarked, "Long before anyone talked about 'nature' and 'substance,' 'person,' and 'Trinity,' the early Christians had quietly but definitely discovered that they could say what they felt obliged to say about Jesus (and the Spirit) by telling the Jewish story of God, Israel and the world, in the Jewish language of Spirit, Word, Torah, Presence/Glory, Wisdom, and now Messiah/Son."[9] For Wright, narrative theology—theology that seeks insight into Israel's God by retelling the story of Israel and placing Jesus within that story, as does the biblical narrative—offers the most accurate portrait of God. Wright conceives of his exegesis as dependent upon this form of narrative theology. In Wright's words, "if you start with the God of the Exodus, of Isaiah, of creation and covenant, of the Psalms, and ask what that God might be like, were he to become human, you will find that he might look very much like Jesus of Nazareth, and perhaps never more so than when he dies

---

7. This name has been applied to them by David Coffey.

8. Wright is hardly alone in his views among biblical scholars. For very similar arguments, see for example Richard Bauckham, *God Crucified: Monotheism and Christology in the New Testament* (Grand Rapids, Mich.: Eerdmans, 1998). Bauckham, a New Testament scholar, also qualifies as a systematic theologian, as the author of two books on the theology of Jürgen Moltmann.

9. N. T. Wright, "Jesus and the Identity of God," *Ex Auditu* 14 (1998): 48–49.

on a Roman cross."[10] Speculative theology is suspect—at the very least to be normed and corrected by narrative theology.

Given this starting point, Wright warns against the tendency of Christians to speak about a "God" abstracted from this Jewish story. Although he thinks that a "high christology" belonged to the Christian message from the outset,[11] Wright is wary of translating the language of the New Testament authors into the terms of the later creedal formulations. The phrase "Son of God" exemplifies this mistake for Wright: "Later Christian theologians, forgetting their Jewish roots, would of course read this as straightforwardly Nicene christology: Jesus was the second person of the Trinity."[12] In fact, Wright suggests, the early Christians were simply making use of a phrase found frequently in the "Jewish story" of their milieu, in order to convey Jesus' messianic identity.

As Wright argues in a number of places, the key to the worldview or story of Jesus' Jewish milieu was that "YHWH would comfort and restore his people after their exile, would pour out his wrath upon the pagans who had held them captive, and would return in person to Zion to reign as king."[13] Wright interprets Jesus' actions in light of this Jewish narrative. On the basis of an analysis of Jesus' actions, as recorded in the synoptic gospels, Wright concludes that Jesus "believed that it was his own task not only to announce, but also to enact and embody, the three major kingdom-themes, namely, the return from exile, the defeat of evil, and the return of YHWH to Zion."[14] By enacting and embodying these three tasks, Jesus was doing (or claiming to do) what only YHWH could do.

For Wright, Jesus' resurrection explains the shift in "worldview" that occurred among Jesus' disciples after his death. In light of his resurrection, his disciples recognized that in Jesus YHWH had actually returned to Zion and renewed the covenant, now ordered around Jesus himself, as the true interpreter of Torah and true embodiment of the Temple, in whom the exile of Israel was over and through whom sins were forgiven.[15] Given the validation of

---

10. Wright, "Jesus and the Identity of God," 54.
11. See, e.g., N. T. Wright, *The Climax of the Covenant: Christ and the Law in Pauline Theology* (Minneapolis: Fortress Press, 1992), 18–136.
12. Wright, "Jesus and the Identity of God," 48.
13. N. T. Wright, *Jesus and the Victory of God* (Minneapolis: Fortress Press, 1996), 588. See also Wright, *The New Testament and the People of God* (Minneapolis: Fortress Press, 1992), 145–338.
14. Wright, *Jesus and the Victory of God*, 481; cf. "Jesus and the Identity of God," 52–53 (and elsewhere throughout Wright's corpus).
15. Wright, *Jesus and the Victory of God*, 538–39.

Jesus' messianic actions, it became necessary to "speak of him within the language of Jewish monotheism."[16] The resurrection confirms that Jesus' enactment and embodiment of YHWH's work was truly the presence of YHWH, the God revealed in the Jewish Scriptures, restoring and renewing (as promised by the prophets) Israel and the world. Wright summarizes this perspective: "In Jesus himself, I suggest, we see the biblical portrait of YHWH come to life."[17]

For Wright, the early Christians were not only challenging the worldview or story of their Jewish milieu; they were affirming it, announcing its fulfillment, and redescribing God by insisting that "[Jesus] and his Father belonged together within the Jewish picture of the one God."[18] On this basis, he critiques views of God that seem to him to be unbiblical: "Western orthodoxy has for too long had an overly lofty, detached, high-and-dry, uncaring, uninvolved, and (as the feminists would say) kyriarchal view of god. It has always tended to approach the christological question by assuming this view of god and then fitting Jesus into it."[19] The "kyriarchal" god, he implies, would never have become truly incarnate—in other words, never would have entered into the messiness of enacting and embodying the restoration and renewal of Israel. The "kyriarchal" god of "Western orthodoxy" remains fundamentally ahistorical, even when the Incarnation is affirmed as dogma. He suggests that "[w]e could only ask the 'kenotic' question in the way we normally do—did Jesus 'empty himself' of some of his 'divine attributes' in becoming human?—if we were tacitly committed to a quite unbiblical view of God, a high and majestic God for whom incarnation would be a category mistake and crucifixion a scandalous nonsense."[20] Instead, rather than beginning with theological or philosophical *a priori* claims, theologians, aided by historical methodology, should contemplate Jesus' (Jewish) humanity, as presented in the synoptic gospels, in order to "see, as Paul says, the glory of God in the face of Jesus Christ."[21] In Jesus, Israel's God is fully revealed.[22]

---

16. Wright, "Jesus and the Identity of God," 52; cf. *Climax of the Covenant*, 99–136.
17. Wright, "Jesus and the Identity of God," 53.
18. Ibid. 19. Ibid.
20. Ibid., 54–55. 21. Ibid., 55.
22. Wright remarks, "I do not think Jesus 'knew he was God' in the same sense that one knows one is tired or happy, male or female. He did not sit back and say to himself 'Well I never! I'm the second person of the Trinity!'" (Wright, "Jesus and the Identity of God," 53.) Wright adds that the "category of 'vocation' [is] the appropriate way forward for talking about what Jesus knew and believed about himself." (Ibid.) Although Wright's critique is aimed at the patristic and medieval tradition, for Aquinas, Jesus' human knowledge of his divinity certainly belongs to his vocation of preaching about divine mysteries. This knowledge could not trivialize

DOES THE PASCHAL MYSTERY REVEAL THE TRINITY?

Does Aquinas fall into the mistake that Wright, along with many contemporary theologians, finds in "Western orthodoxy," the mistake of bypassing the historical Jesus in describing the Trinity? In light of Wright's thesis that traditional Trinitarian theology, because of its non-narrative character, "has always tended to approach the christological question by assuming this [ontological] view of god and then fitting Jesus into it,"[23] I will explore how, according to Aquinas, Jesus' Paschal mystery determines our understanding of the Trinity.

What is meant when scholars speak about the revelatory power of Jesus' Paschal mystery? What is the salient aspect (or aspects) of Jesus' cross and resurrection that might illumine the inner life of the Trinity? Wright suggests that the salient aspect is the way in which Jesus' historical experience is precisely the opposite of what one would expect to find from a "kyriarchal" God, that is, from "an overly lofty, detached, high-and-dry, uncaring, uninvolved" God that, in Wright's view, emerges out of the tradition of Western metaphysics. Jesus' historical experience, and in particular his Paschal mystery, reveals a God who is lowly, attached, present, caring, and involved. The Paschal mystery reveals the inner Trinitarian life as one of humility, self-giving, presence, and love.

Aquinas's treatise on God's essence (what is common to the Persons) is representative of the tradition of Western metaphysical reflection upon God. What, then, does Aquinas think that the Paschal mystery reveals? This is the topic of question 46, article 3 of the *tertia pars* of the *Summa theologiae*. The question posed is "Whether there was any more suitable way of delivering the human race than by Christ's passion?" It would seem, Aquinas notes, that there were more suitable ways than Christ's bloody death. First, "God could have liberated mankind solely by His Divine will."[24] Not only would this have been easier—and would have spared the life of his incarnate Son—but also it seems more fitting on another ground, that of the divine power. Injustice is typically righted by a superior power: thus courts of law have the power to deprive the criminal of his freedom in order to restore the order of jus-

---

Jesus' human thinking (as in "Well I never! . . ."). On the contrary, Jesus' exalted human knowledge—as a spiritual communion—rules out such trivializing self-reflection.

23. The words are Wright's ("Jesus and the Identity of God," 54) but could equally be spoken by Hunt and the numerous theologians to whom she refers.

24. *ST* III, q. 46, a. 3, obj.1.

tice by means of this retributive punishment. If the court of law does not or cannot exercise this superior power, the criminal continues to act with impunity. Thus, "it seems more suitable that Christ should have despoiled the devil solely by His power and without the Passion."[25]

As these arguments or objections show, Aquinas too possesses the notion of a "kyriarchal" God (although it seems unlikely that Aquinas would have used "lordly" in a pejorative sense) that Wright both opposes and links with metaphysically sophisticated treatises. In his answers to the objections, however, Aquinas rejects this portrait of God quite as strongly as Wright does. Christ's Paschal mystery reveals a different God, not a God "on high" who rules by divine decrees or a God who comes down to earth to demonstrate his absolute power. Aquinas states that indeed Christ's passion was the most suitable, or fitting, manner of redeeming the human race on the grounds that Christ's passion teaches us about the God who saves us. He states, "In the first place, man knows thereby how much God loves him, and is thereby stirred to love him in return, and therein lies the perfection of human salvation."[26] Christ's Paschal mystery reveals to humankind the extraordinary depth of God's love. Without Christ's passion, humankind would not have known the superabundance of God's love. Therefore, the Paschal mystery reveals the Trinity (God-in-himself) first of all in terms of wondrous love, to the point of the Son of God giving his own life for the salvation of sinners, that is, for the salvation of those who by pride had cut themselves off from God.

Christ's Paschal mystery reveals the divine life by means of other attributes as well. Aquinas gives a second reason for the fittingness of Christ's passion as the way that God chose to redeem humankind: by his passion, Christ "set us an example of obedience, humility, constancy, justice, and the other virtues displayed in the Passion, which are requisite for man's salvation. Hence it is written (1 Pet 2:21): *Christ also suffered for us, leaving you an example that you should follow in His steps.*"[27] Obedience is ultimately the conforming of one's human will to the will of God, who is love; humility is the opposite of pride, and means that one loves each thing in accord with its goodness, rather than proudly rejecting the goodness of other things. In this way, Christ's passion reveals the Trinity not only as constant and just, but also as perfect love and perfect humility, since God in Christ actively loves (rather than dominates) the creatures he has made. Lastly, Aquinas comments on the fittingness found in the symmetry of God's plan: "as man was overcome and deceived by the devil, so also it should be a man that should overthrow the devil; and as

---

25. *ST* III, q. 46, a. 3, obj. 3. 26. *ST* III, q. 46, a. 3.
27. Ibid.

man deserved death, so a man by dying should vanquish death."²⁸ This symmetry of God's plan (his divine Providence) manifests the wisdom of God, who orders all things rightly.

Like Wright, then, Aquinas has recourse to Jesus' cross in order to dispel the myth of what Wright calls the "kyriarchal," or aloof and uncaring, God. The Paschal mystery of Jesus Christ reveals a God of superabundant and active love, humility, and wisdom. Moreover, the Paschal mystery manifests at the same time the Trinitarian nature of this God. Aquinas observes, "Christ suffered voluntarily out of obedience to the Father."²⁹ The incarnate Son, in his humanity, obeys the Father's will. The Son is thus revealed in his passion to be the perfect image of the Father. Yet, does the fact that Christ suffered out of obedience to the Father mean that God the Father abandoned the Son to a state of God-forsakenness, or poured out his wrath upon the Son? Aquinas states that the Father "abandoned" the incarnate Son in the sense of not shielding him from those who would crucify him. The incarnate Son did not, however, undergo the deeper sense of abandonment by God, the experience of God's wrath. As Aquinas points out in answer to an objection, "It is indeed a wicked and cruel act to hand over an innocent man to torment and death against his will. Yet God the Father did not so deliver up Christ, but inspired him with the will to suffer for us."³⁰ The Father inspired Christ's human will with this perfect charity by infusing Christ's humanity with the fullness of the grace of the Holy Spirit. In Christ's passion, therefore, we see manifested the incarnate Son's obedience to the Father through the Holy Spirit. The Paschal mystery of Jesus Christ reveals God's wisdom and love in Trinitarian form.

If we now return to Anne Hunt's comment—"Why then is the Trinity not considered in terms of Jesus' death and resurrection? In retrospect it seems an astonishing omission in classical trinitarian theology"—it should be apparent that her critique misses the way in which Aquinas interprets Christ's Paschal mystery as the revelation of God's Trinitarian wisdom and love. As Aquinas writes in his *Commentary on John*, "And just like one of us who wants to be known by others by revealing to them the words in his heart, clothes these words with letters or sounds, so God, wanting to be known by us, takes his Word, conceived from eternity, and clothes it with flesh in time. And so no one can arrive at a knowledge of the Father except through the Son."³¹ Only

---

28. Ibid.
29. *ST* III, q. 47, a. 3.
30. Ibid., ad 1.
31. *Commentary on the Gospel of Saint John*, Part 2, trans. Weisheipl and Larcher, ch. 14, lect. 2, n. 1874.

the revelation of Jesus Christ provides humankind with knowledge of the Trinity. By natural reason we can know God analogously, insofar as he is cause or principle of things. This mode of knowing rules out natural knowledge of the Trinity, for Father, Son, and Holy Spirit are distinguished only by intra-divine processions, and thus the three Persons are *one principle* of creatures.

It should also be apparent, however, that faith in the God manifested by the Paschal mystery may lead believers to seek deeper understanding of how the divine Persons are at once distinct and a perfect unity. The Paschal mystery does not reveal all that faith, seeking understanding, wishes to know about the mystery of the triune God. Nonetheless, it can be said that Jesus' Paschal mystery gives the central clue by directing the believer to meditate upon God's wisdom and love. From this perspective, Aquinas's use of the psychological analogy, which flows from his attempt to understand Jesus' words "From God I proceeded" without making "procession" an outward act, possesses evident legitimacy. The goal of the treatise on the Trinity is to gain insight into the God manifested by the Paschal mystery: the God who is named Father, Son (Word, Image), Holy Spirit (Love, Gift).

To this point I have focused upon Aquinas's *Summa theologiae*. In Aquinas's *Commentary on John,* we find three steps by which the revelatory function of Christ's Paschal mystery is addressed. These "steps" are not, in the commentary, an organized argument, but rather are issues that Aquinas takes up when prompted by the exegetical task. In one set of passages, Aquinas discusses the Father's generation of the Son in terms of self-giving. In a second, he explores how Christ is sent to manifest the Father. In a third, he identifies the Paschal mystery as the central way in which Christ manifests his Father and the Trinity. I will briefly treat each of these "steps" in turn.

Aquinas speaks of an "astonishment of devotion" that should characterize the believer who, "considering the great things of God, sees that they are incomprehensible to him; and so he is full of astonishment: 'The Lord on high is wonderful' (Ps 93:4), 'Your testimonies are wonderful' (Ps 118:129)."[32] Nowhere is this astonishment more fitting than in reflection upon the Father's eternal generation of the Son.

In generating the Son, the Father gives or communicates everything to the Son. Since scholars at times imagine that the modern period invented the theology of self-gift and self-communication, it is necessary to emphasize that

---

32. *Commentary on the Gospel of Saint John,* Part 1, trans. Weisheipl and Larcher, ch. 3, lect. 2, n. 449.

this language, which is ultimately biblical, appears in Aquinas.[33] Commenting on John 5:20, Aquinas notes that "because the Father perfectly loves the Son, this is a sign that the Father has shown him everything and has communicated *(communicaverit)* to him his very own power and nature" (*Ioan.* 5, lect. 3, n. 753). Similarly, commenting on John 3:34, Aquinas conceives of the Father's generation of the Son in terms of gift: "For God the Father is said to give *(dare)* the Holy Spirit without measure to Christ as God, because he gives to Christ the power and might to spirate the Holy Spirit, who, since he is infinite, was infinitely given him by the Father: for the Father gives it just as he himself has it, so that the Holy Spirit proceeds from him as much as from the Son. And he gave him this by an everlasting generation" (*Ioan.* 3, lect. 6, n. 543). The generation of the Son is the Father's self-gift or self-communication. Further, Aquinas interprets John 5:20, "For the Father loves the Son, and shows him everything that he does" by connecting the Father's love with the Father's generative communication or gift.

How can this be, given that the Father generates by the divine nature?[34] Aquinas notes, "If love is taking essentially [pertaining to God's oneness], it indicates the divine will; if it is taken notionally [pertaining to the distinction of Persons], it indicates the Holy Spirit" (*Ioan.* 17, lect. 6, n. 2262). The generation of the Son does not pertain to either of these kinds of love, because the Father generates neither by the divine will nor by the Holy Spirit, but by the divine nature. Aquinas explains that when we link the Father's generation of the Son (his self-gift) with the Father's love, this refers not to the power of generation, but to the fruit of generation. Because the Father generates the Son by giving him everything he has—by speaking the entire Trinity in his Word—the Son is the perfect image of the Father. As image (Heb 1:3, Col 1:15), the Son must be perfectly loved by the Father. Aquinas states, "For since likeness is a cause of love (for every animal loves its like), wherever a perfect likeness of God is found, there also is found a perfect love of God" (*Ioan.* 5, lect. 3, n. 753). The Father's love is a sign of what he has done for the Son in giving him everything that he, the Father, possesses. It is love that manifests a giver who has generated his perfect likeness.

This understanding of the character of the Father's generative self-gift undergirds Aquinas's affirmation that the Son, with the Father, is the principle of the Holy Spirit in the order of divine processions. Aquinas explains this doctrine (the *filioque*) in various ways, but it is the aspect of self-giving that I

---

33. The gift of "self" is the gift of all that the Person is, excepting the personal property.
34. On the *potentia generandi*, see John Boyle's masterful treatment in *Thomist* 64 (2000): 581–92.

wish to highlight here. In generating the Son, the Father gives himself absolutely. Only the order of generation differentiates Father and Son: the Father is begettor, the Son begotten. Does the Father, then, communicate to the Son his spirative power? If his self-giving is absolute, the answer must be yes. The "astonishment of devotion" comes from awareness of the love signified by the Father's absolute gift.

If the Father's begetting of the Son is characterized by this absolute self-giving, then if Christ is to make the Father known, he will have to do so by giving himself. Aquinas repeatedly affirms that manifesting the Father, making him known, is the task of the incarnate Son. Following Chrysostom, he interprets John 17:6, "I have manifested your name to the men" as suggesting "the characteristic work of the Son of God, who is the Word, and the characteristic of a word is to manifest the one speaking it: 'No one knows the Father except the Son and any one to whom the Son chooses to reveal him' (Mt 11:27); 'No one has ever seen God; the only Son, who is in the bosom of the Father, he has made him known' (John 1:18)" (*Ioan.* 17, lect. 2, n. 2194). Before Christ's coming, the people of Israel knew God the Father, but they knew him only as Father in the sense of Creator, and as the one and only God. Christ's disciples, on the other hand, are able to know the Father by faith (by the grace of the Holy Spirit) as the Father of the only-begotten Son (*Ioan.* 17, lect. 2, n. 2195).[35]

In exploring how Christ manifests his Father, Aquinas emphasizes the disciples' friendship with Christ. The figure of the apostle John is paradigmatic for Aquinas, since he was uniquely beloved by Christ. Interpreting mystically John's closeness to Jesus at table, Aquinas writes that "we can see from this that the more a person wants to grasp the secrets of divine wisdom, the more he should try to get closer to Christ, according to 'Come to him and be enlightened' (Ps 34:5)" (*Ioan.* 13, lect. 4, n. 1807). The sign of friendship is that friends reveal their secrets to each other, and thus when we have become friends of God in Jesus Christ he reveals to us what belongs to his infinite wisdom. Christ's wisdom is nothing less than the Trinity: in speaking his Word (the Wisdom of God), the Father speaks the whole Trinity. Thus Aquinas notes that if someone were to ask, "The Father will manifest himself, will he not?" the answer is "Yes, both the Father and the Son. For the Son manifests himself and the Father at the same time, because the Son is the Word of the Father: 'No one knows the Father except the Son' (Mt 11:27)"

---

35. Cf. *Ioan.* 1, lect. 8, nn. 179–86, which discusses the glory of Christ as the glory manifested to those who recognize, in faith, his divinity.

(*Ioan.* 14, lect. 5, n. 1937). Since Christ is the Wisdom of God, his wisdom is the Trinity, and learning his wisdom, as his friend, means to share in his Trinitarian life (*Ioan.* 15, lect. 3, n. 2016).

Christ, then, reveals the Trinity to his friends. As incarnate Wisdom, he does so by teaching through his words and actions. Aquinas frequently describes Christ's "eagerness to teach" (*Ioan.* 9, lect. 4, n. 1355). Yet, Jesus' words cannot be understood simply by hearing or reading them, as can the words of other teachers. Rather, in order for true teaching to occur, we must hear or read his words in the Holy Spirit. As Aquinas writes, "The root and fountain of our knowledge of God is the Word of God, that is, Christ. . . . From this knowledge of the Word, which is the root and fountain, flows, like rivulets and streams, all the knowledge of the faithful" (*Ioan.* 17, lect. 6, nn. 2267–68). This knowledge requires not merely hearing, but rather a participation in the Word by faith through the power of the Holy Spirit.[36]

In addition to words, Jesus teaches effectively by what he does. Commenting on John 5:36—"The very works which my Father has given me to perform—those works that I myself perform—they bear witness to me that the Father sent me"—Aquinas remarks that "the sort of person he [Christ] is can be learned through the works he does" (*Ioan.* 5, lect. 6, n. 817).[37] His definitive work is his passion. As the "way," Christ opens up for us friendship with the Father; as the "truth" and "life," Christ is the end or destination of the way, and thus is the consubstantial Son (*Ioan.* 14, lect. 2, nn. 1867–70). In revealing himself by his works, Christ thus reveals the Father: "the Father was seen in the incarnate Christ: 'We have beheld his glory, glory as of the only Son from the Father' (Jn 1:14)" (*Ioan.* 14, lect. 2, n. 1881).

Thus far, our discussion of Aquinas's *Commentary on John* has suggested two things. First, Aquinas holds that the Trinity is constituted by absolute self-giving. Second, Aquinas holds that Christ's mission, as the incarnate Word, was to reveal the Father by teaching through words and deeds. Now we arrive at the third step: through his Paschal Mystery, Jesus Christ manifests the Father in a supreme way.

Aquinas states that Christ "carried his cross as a teacher his candelabrum,

---

36. Cf. *Ioan.* 3, lect. 1, nn. 431–43, where Aquinas interprets Jesus' words to Nicodemus about being "born again." Aquinas writes that in order to know Christ truly, "It is necessary that one be [spiritually] generated in the likeness of the one generating; but we are regenerated as sons of God, in the likeness of his true Son. Therefore, it is necessary that our spiritual regeneration come about through that by which we are made like the true Son; and this comes about by our having his Spirit" (n. 442, p. 187).

37. Aquinas makes the same point later in discussing how Christ teaches through his action of prayer: "For every action of Christ is a lesson for us" (*Ioan.* 11, lect. 6, n. 1555).

as a support for the light of his teaching, because for believers the message of the cross is the power of God" (*Ioan.* 19, lect. 3, n. 2414). His cross and resurrection reveal the true meaning of his oral communication, and so the Paschal events are the culmination of his teaching. Following Augustine, Aquinas remarks, "Christ hanging on the cross is like a teacher in his teaching chair" (*Ioan.* 19, lect. 4, n. 2441). Christ, in his humanity, teaches the obedience that springs from love (*Ioan.* 14, lect. 8, n. 1976). This obedient love (or human self-giving) gives access to the Father: "For just as the love which the Father has for him is the model or standard of Christ's love for us, so Christ wants his obedience to be the model of our obedience.... Christ shows that he abided in the Father's love because in all things he kept the Father's commandments" (*Ioan.* 15, lect. 2, n. 2003). When we come to understand Christ's love, manifested on the cross, he reveals for us the Father's love—the love expressed (as we have seen) as the absolute self-giving that begets the Son, the Father's Word or Image.

In short, it is by attending to Christ's passion and resurrection that we truly learn who God is. By suffering on the cross, Christ obediently does the Father's will; he abides in the Father's love. This love is manifested by Christ, through his human act of supreme suffering, as absolute self-giving. By his resurrection, Christ, as man, reveals the fruit (the glory) of this absolute self-giving: the fruit is the glory of friendship with the Father, since like loves its like (*Ioan.* 17, lect. 1, nn. 2190–92). When we are conformed to his (self-giving) image, we manifest his glory and are glorified with him. As Aquinas explains, commenting on John 3:16, Christ "indicates the immensity of God's love in saying, 'have eternal life': for by giving eternal life, he gives himself. For eternal life is nothing else than enjoying God. But to give oneself is a sign of great love: 'But God, who is rich in mercy, has brought us to life in Christ' (Eph 2:5)" (*Ioan.* 3, lect. 3, n. 480). Christ, whose Paschal Mystery is God's gift of himself to us, thus reveals that "eternal life" (God himself) is absolute self-giving—a self-giving that is, unlike human self-giving, without risk, suffering, or loss, in other words a self-giving that is glory.

CONCLUSION

The Paschal mystery is Christ's ultimate teaching about his Father, and at the heart of this teaching is self-giving. In a way that differs from that of the "Paschal mystery" theologians such as Balthasar, who see the cross as a sign of intra-divine abandonment, and yet agree with their emphasis on self-giving, the Paschal mystery does indeed reveal the Trinity according to Aquinas. This does not mean that one can simply "read off" the Trinity from the structure of Christ's suffering, death, and resurrection. For Aquinas, as for Wright, the Paschal mystery must be approached through the pedagogy with which God had instructed Israel (for Aquinas this means largely the testimony to God's unity and other attributes), and through Christ's oral teaching before his passion, death, and resurrection. To understand this divine pedagogy, Wright employs historical and literary methods. Aquinas's philosophically sophisticated approach in his *Summa theologiae,* as in his *Commentary on John,* has the same intent: it is not a means of constructing an aloof "kyriarchal" idol, but is undertaken precisely in order to maintain faithfulness to YHWH's command that Israel avoid idolatry and worship the God revealed as "I am." What is revealed by the Paschal mystery must be articulated with the aid of philosophical precisions. Christ's Paschal mystery reveals that his claim to be the Son of the Father—his claim to be the perfect image of the Father whose love is signified by his absolute gift of himself—is indeed the very truth manifested by the incarnate Word's suffering, death, and resurrection. This truth, revealed by Jesus Christ, is articulated theologically by metaphysically sophisticated analogies for the Trinity that preserve the mystery of the Son as the consubstantial, yet distinct, Word and Image of the Father. As ways of instilling within believers greater understanding of the mystery of the Trinity, reflection upon the Paschal mystery and the psychological analogy, as metaphysically advanced by Aquinas, thus complement one another.

SIX

The Analogy of Mission and Obedience
A Central Point in the Relation between *Theologia* and *Oikonomia* in St. Thomas Aquinas's *Commentary on John*

MICHAEL WALDSTEIN

INTRODUCTION: THE ANALOGY OF MISSION AND
OBEDIENCE IN JOHN

Obedientia est maxima virtutum, "Obedience is the greatest of all virtues," St. Thomas Aquinas says, citing Gregory the Great with approval.[1] At least, as he is careful to point out in another place, it is the greatest of all the moral virtues. Only the theological virtues are greater.[2] Again citing Gregory he says, *Obedientia non tam est virtus quam mater omnium virtutum,* "Obedience is not so much a virtue, but the mother of all the virtues."[3] Or in a more sweeping judgment, *Omne bonum, quantumcumque bonum est per se, per obedientiam redditur melius,* "Every good, however good it is in itself, is made better by obedience."[4] In short, *Per obedientiam homo perfectus redditur in vita activa et contemplativa,* "Through obedience man is made perfect in the active and the contemplative life" (*Ioan.* 11, lect. 1, n. 1473).

Such a judgment on obedience is second nature, one would think, for anyone who has engraved in his heart the words of Paul in Romans and Philippians, "For just as by the one man's disobedience the many were made sinners, so by the one man's obedience the many will be made just" (Rom 5:19). "He became obedient to the point of death—even death on a cross. For this reason God highly exalted him and gave him the name that is above every name" (Phil 2:8–9), namely, the divine name, κύριος (cf. Phil 2:11). Obedience is the hinge around

1. II *Sent.,* d. 44, q. 2, a. 1, sc. 2. 2. Cf. *ST* II-II, q. 104, a. 3.
3. II *Sent.,* d. 44, q. 2, a. 1, ag 6. 4. *Super Phil.* 2, lect. 3, n. 74.

The Analogy of Mission and Obedience 93

which the glorification of Jesus and therefore the salvation of the world turns.

The Gospel of John is distinctive among the Gospels in deepening and unfolding the link between the economy of salvation and the theology of the Trinity. As St. Thomas puts it at the very beginning of his lectures on John, "The evangelist John intends principally to show first of all the divinity of the incarnate Word." John considers the obedience of Jesus not only in its saving power, but as something rooted in the eternal relation between the Father and the Son. Of particular importance in the general link between *oikonomia* and *theologia* is the little adverb καθώς = as, which one could call the adverb of analogy. Here are twelve examples:

1. As (καθώς) I hear, I judge; and my judgment is just, because I seek not my own will but the will of him who sent me (5:30).

2. As (καθώς) the living Father sent me, and I live through the Father, so he who eats me will live through me (6:57).

3. When you have lifted up the Son of Man, then you will know that I AM, and that I do nothing of myself, but as (καθώς) the Father taught me, these things I speak (8:28).

4. I know my own and my own know me, as (καθώς) the Father knows me and I know the Father (10:14–15).

5. I know that his commandment is eternal life. Therefore, what I speak, as (καθώς) the Father has told me, thus I speak (12:50).

6. A new commandment I give to you, that you love one another, as (καθώς) I have loved you, that you too love one another (13:34).

7. So that the world may know that I love the Father, I do as (καθώς) the Father has commanded me (14:31).

8. As (καθώς) the Father has loved me, so I have loved you. Remain in my love. If you keep my commandments, you will remain in my love, as (καθώς) I have kept my Father's commandments and remain in his love (15:9–10).

9. Protect them in your name . . . so that they may be one, as (καθώς) we are one (17:11).

10. . . . that they may all be one, as (καθώς) you, Father, are in me and I am in you (17:21).

11. The glory you have given to me I have given to them, that they may be one as (καθώς) we are one. I in them and you in me, that they may be completed into one, so that the world may know that you have sent me and have loved them as (καθώς) you have loved me (17:22–23).

12. As (καθώς) Father has sent me, so I send you (20:21).

Among these twelve passages, the most central seem to be those that deal with love and with something closely related to love, namely, unity. We are to love one another as Jesus loves us. He loves us as the Father loves him. Our unity with each other and with him therefore follows the exemplar of the eternal unity between the Father and the Son. This analogy of love and of unity is closely related to the analogy of mission and obedience. "As (καθώς) the Father has sent me, so I send you" (20:21). These are the words of the risen Jesus immediately before he breathes the Holy Spirit into his disciples, enabling them to obey and carry out their mission. The depth of this mystery of mission is indicated by the Eucharistic sending passage, "As (καθώς) the living Father sent me, and I live through the Father, so he who eats me will live through me" (6:57). Obedience is a necessary aspect of this mystery. "If you keep my commandments, you will remain in my love, as (καθώς) I have kept my Father's commandments and remain in his love" (15:10). Living through the Father, being sent by the Father, obeying his command (ἐντολή), and remaining in his love lie closely together for the Son of God. For us who "have life in his name" (20:31), living through him, eating his flesh, receiving his Spirit, being sent and therefore obeying his commandments so as to remain in his love, lie likewise closely together.

Given the systematic speculative power of St. Thomas and his careful attention to the details of the text of Scripture, it is antecedently likely that he would have much to say about the analogy of mission and obedience in John. In fact, in his treatment of the divine missions, he explains the exact point of intersection that is at stake in the analogy of mission and obedience. In one who is sent, sending always involves two aspects, a relation to the one who sends and a relation to the place to which he sends. In the mission of the Son of God, the first of these is identical with the eternal procession of the Son from the Father, and the second is a new respect in which the Son becomes present in his creation, namely, as a man who fulfills a certain task.[5] In the mission of the Son, theology and economy are thus closely intertwined. Inasmuch as Jesus visibly lives out his mission in obedience, he in some way manifests his eternal relation to the Father as the one who proceeds from the Father. And since the divine persons are subsistent relations distinct from each other by relative opposition in relations of origin, obedience is closely related to the very person of the Son. This is the main principle that establishes an analogy of obedience between Christ and us. St. Thomas, as we will see, unfolds this analogy in the course of his reading of John.

---

5. I *Sent.*, d. 15, q. 1, a. 1; *ST* I, q. 43, a. 1.

OBEDIENCE ONLY *"SECUNDUM HUMANITATEM"*

Can one truly speak, according to St. Thomas Aquinas, of an analogy of obedience? If such an analogy involves attributing obedience to the Eternal Son in relation to the Father, it appears that St. Thomas rejects it. St. Thomas quotes St. John Damascene as saying, *Christus non est obediens patri nisi secundum quod homo,* "Christ is not obedient to the Father except as man."[6] In his expositio fidei, John Damascene writes, "It is not as God, but as man that the Lord became obedient to the Father. As the divinely inspired Gregory (Nazianzen) says, As God he was neither obedient nor disobedient. These are proper to people under (someone's) hand."[7]

To turn from the Eastern to the Western lung of the Church, St. Thomas also quotes St. Augustine: "In what Christ says, 'Not what I will, but what You will,' he shows that he willed something else than his Father; and this he would have been able to do only by his human heart, since He did not transfigure our weakness into his divine will but into his human will."[8]

St. Thomas speaks in a similar manner in commenting on Paul's statement in the hymn of Philippians 2, "He became obedient unto death." "But how did he become obedient? Not in the divine will, which is itself the rule, but in the human will which is ruled in all things according to the Father's will. As he says in Matthew 26:39, 'Yet not what I want but what you want.'"[9] St. Thomas follows the theological tradition in seeing in the agony of Jesus and, in particular, in the contrast, "Not my will, but your will," *the* classical expression of Jesus' human will submitting itself in obedience to the Father's divine will. The divine will of the Father and the Son is one. It seems impossible for Jesus to say about his divine will, "Not my will, but yours."

In this manner St. Thomas reads many obedience passages in John. Does this manner of reading do full justice to the text of John? I believe it does not. In fact, St. Thomas himself interprets a number of Johannine obedience texts as applying to Jesus both in his humanity and in his divinity.

First, some points about obedience in general. St. Thomas offers detailed

---

6. I *Sent.*, d. 15, q. 1, a. 1, ag 3.

7. John Damascene, *Expositio fidei*, 3,13; TLG 58,110–115. ὑπήκοος δὲ γενόμενος τῷ πατρί ὁ κύριος ου καθο θεὸς γέγονεν, ἀλλὰ καθο ἄνθρωπος, "Καθὸ γὰρ θεὸς οὔτε ὑπήκοος οὔτε παρήκοος. τῶν ὑπὸ χεῖρα γὰρ ταῦτα," καθὼς ὁ θεηγόρος ἔφη Γρηγόριος.

8. Augustine, *Contra Maximinum*, 2, cap. 20. ML 42, 789: in hoc quod christus ait, non quod ego volo, sed quod tu, aliud se ostendit voluisse quam pater. Quod nisi humano corde non posset, cum infirmitatem nostram in suum, non divinum, sed humanum transfiguraret affectum.

9. *Super Phil.* 2, lect. 2, n. 65.

discussions of obedience in two main contexts, in the context of the virtue of justice and in the context of the counsels for perfection in love.

OBEDIENCE AS A SPECIFIC VIRTUE

There are several virtues, St. Thomas argues, that should be seen as connected with justice, even though they do not possess all the defining marks of justice.[10] Justice is the virtue that governs generally how we relate to persons other than ourselves. It consists in giving other persons their right *(ius)*, which involves a certain equality.[11] For example, someone who works three hours for me has a right to corresponding or equal pay. In some relationships with other persons, however, it is in principle not possible for us to achieve equality in paying our debt. St. Thomas, following Cicero, mentions three virtues that govern such disproportionate debts. The first is the virtue of religion, which is concerned with the debt we owe to God as the highest good and the source of all our good. The proper activity of this virtue, namely, the divine cult, is what we offer to God as due to him, but without ever being able to render something fully equal to God.[12] The second is the virtue of *pietas,* whose proper activity is the cult of our parents and our fatherland. (In contemporary English, the word "piety" has come to coincide with "religion," though often in a narrow or even derogatory sense.) St. Thomas, following Cicero, calls the third virtue *observantia.* It governs the cult that we render to persons of dignity or authority, for example, to a political leader or a bishop.

What makes all three of these virtues so interesting for interpreting the Gospel of John is that all three of them have to do with fatherhood and therefore with sonship.

According to the various excellences of persons to whom something is due, there must be a corresponding distinction of virtues in a descending order. Now just as a father in the flesh shares in a particular way in the notion of beginning, while God is beginning in a universal way, so too a person who in some way exercises providence over us, shares in the notion of father in a particular way, *since a father is the beginning of generation, of education, of learning and of whatever pertains to the perfection of human life.* A person who is in a position of dignity is something like a beginning of government with regard to certain things: for instance, the governor of a state in civil matters, the commander of an army in matters of warfare, a teacher in matters of learning, and so on. Hence it is that all such persons are called "fathers," because of a likeness in caring, as the servants of Naaman said to him (2 Kings 5:13), "Father, if the

---

10. See *ST* II-II, q. 80.
11. See *ST* II-II, q. 57, a. 1.
12. See the lengthy discussion of religion in *ST* II-II, qq. 81–100.

prophet had asked you to do some great thing," etc. Therefore, just as beneath religion, by which cult is given to God, we find *pietas,* by which we offer cult to our parents, so beneath piety we find *observantia,* by which we pay cult and honor to persons in positions of dignity.[13]

Observantia, St. Thomas goes on to argue, contains two virtues in itself, *dulia* and obedience. *Dulia* is a cult of honor offered to persons of dignity; obedience is the cult of consent with their will as they exercise their office of government over us. It is important to focus exactly on the formal object that is required for defining obedience as a specific virtue. This formal object is a precept issued to us by someone who has a particular office of providential care over us, a precept that therefore imposes on us a duty or debt of consent: *Obedientia est specialis virtus, quia attendit specialem rationem, scilicet praeceptum cum debito consentiendi,* "Obedience is a specific virtue, because it is concerned with a particular notion, namely, precept with the debt of consent."[14]

OBEDIENCE AS A COUNSEL OF PERFECTION

In his opusculum *De perfectione vitae spiritualis,* St. Thomas begins the discussion of the vow of obedience with a consideration of the dynamism of love.

For the perfection of love, it is not only necessary that a person casts off what is exterior: he must also in some way leave himself behind. Denys, in Chapter IV of *On the Divine Names,* says, "Divine Amor (Eros) is ἐκστατικός, it brings ecstasy," that is, it places a person outside of himself, "not allowing him to belong to himself, but to that which he loves." Paul, writing to the Galatians (2:20), shows an example of this thing in himself when he says, "I live, no longer I, but Christ lives in me," as if he considered his life not his own, but Christ's, because he spurned all that he possessed, in order to cling to Christ. He shows that this is complete in some; for he says to the Colossians (3:3), "You are dead, and your life is hidden with Christ in God." He also exhorts others to reach this point when he says to the Corinthians (2 Cor 5:15), "Christ died for all that those who live might no longer live for themselves, but for him who died for them." And therefore, in Luke 14:26, after he had said, "If anyone comes to me and does not hate his father and mother and wife and children and brothers and sisters" he continues as if adding something even greater, "and even his own life (ψυχή), he cannot be my disciple."[15]

---

13. *ST* II-II, q. 102, a. 1.
14. II *Sent.,* d. 44, q. 2, a. 1.
15. *De Perfectione Vitae Spiritualis,* c. 11 (Leonine numbering), ll. 1–28: Non solum autem necessarium est ad perfectionem caritatis consequendam, quod homo exteriora abiciat, sed etiam quodammodo se ipsum derelinquat. Dicit enim dionysius, 4 cap. De divinis nominibus, quod divinus amor est extasim faciens, id est hominem extra se ipsum ponens, non sinens

"The observance of this saving denial and loving hatred" *(Huius autem salubris abnegationis et caritativi odii observatio)*,[16] he goes on to argue, is most complete in the martyrs, who give their life for love of Christ. Thomas quotes from a sermon on martyrdom by Augustine: *Nulli enim tantum impenderunt quam illi qui seipsos impenderunt,* "No one gives as much as those who give themselves."[17] Close to the completeness of this gift of self in martyrdom, he continues, is the totality of gift involved in obedience. Apart from life, *nihil . . . est homini amabilius libertate propriae voluntatis,* "nothing is more loveable to a person than the freedom of his own will."[18]

Religious life, St. Thomas says in the *Secunda secundae,* has three main aspects: it is a kind of learning or training *(disciplina vel exercitium)*[19] for growth toward the fullness of love; it is a quieting of life, an elimination of what distracts from the love of Christ; third, and most important, *est quoddam holocaustum, per quod aliquis totaliter se et sua offert Deo,* "It is a kind of holocaust by which someone completely offers himself and what belongs to him to God."[20] Obedience is necessary for all three of these aspects: it is necessary for training in love, because it helps in overcoming the disorder of a sinful will; it is necessary for quieting life, because it eliminates worry about decisions; third, and most important, it is necessary for the holocaust of love, because by our will we use all our powers.[21] By giving our will, we therefore give ourselves as a whole.

How is the religious vow of obedience related to the virtue of obedience? Since the vow of obedience is part of the dynamism of love, in particular of the total self-donation or holocaust of love, it is compared to the virtue of obedience as universal is to particular. "This obedience compared to the other is as universal to particular. . . . Those who live in the religious state give themselves totally to God. . . . For this reason their obedience is universal."[22]

---

hominem sui ipsius esse, sed eius quod amatur: cuius rei exemplum in se ipso demonstravit apostolus dicens ad Gal. II, 20: vivo ego, iam non ego, vivit vero in me christus, quasi suam vitam non suam aestimans, sed christi: quia quod proprium sibi erat contemnens, totus christo inhaerebat. Hoc etiam in quibusdam esse completum ostendit, cum dicit ad Col. III, 3: mortui estis, et vita vestra abscondita est cum christo in deo. Exhortatur etiam alios ut ad hoc perveniant, cum dicit II ad Cor. V, 15. Pro omnibus mortuus est christus: ut et qui vivunt, iam non sibi vivant, sed ei qui pro ipsis mortuus est. Et ideo, ut habetur Luc. 14,26, postquam dixerat: si quis venit ad me et non odit patrem suum et matrem et uxorem et filios et fratres et sorores: tanquam aliquid maius addens subdit: adhuc autem et animam suam; non potest meus esse discipulus.

16. Ibid., lin. 32.
17. Ibid., lin. 82–85; cf. Augustine, *Sermo 31*.
18. Ibid., lin. 116–17.
19. *ST* II-II, q. 186, a. 5.
20. *ST* II-II, q. 186, a. 7.
21. Cf. ibid.
22. *ST* II-II, q. 186, a. 5.

The Analogy of Mission and Obedience 99

OBEDIENCE ALSO *"SECUNDUM DIVINITATEM"*?

There are no occurrences in John of the words usually translated as obey, obedience, and obedient: the verb ὑπακούω, the noun ὑπακοή, or the adjective ὑπήκοος. Although these words are not present in John, the reality of obedience clearly is. St. Thomas uses the words *obedire, obedientia,* and *obediens* 140 times in his commentary, which is perfectly reasonable since he is engaged in exegesis of the text, not in simple repetition of it.

John expresses the obedience of Jesus in a variety of ways. The clearest formulation is closely akin to the Synoptic formulation in the agony of Jesus, though in a characteristic Johannine conjunction with the sending motif: I came not to do my own will, but the will of him who sent me (twice). Similarly clear are texts that speak of the commandment (ἐντολή or ἐντέλλομαι) of the Father that Jesus carries out (five times). Precept or commandment, if you remember, is the formal object of obedience according to St. Thomas. A frequent and characteristically Johannine formulation is that Jesus does not act of himself (ἀφ᾽ ἑαυτοῦ; more frequently in the first person ἀπ᾽ ἐμαυτοῦ), but according to the Father's teaching or commandment (seven times). The most frequent concept, of course, is that of mission. More than sixty (60) texts in John speak about the Son being sent and about the Father as "the one who sent me." Mission is close to the notion of commandment and commandment requires obedience in the one sent. Leaving aside these numerous mission texts, here are the main texts that make use of the other concepts or phrases.

1. It is my food to do the will of him who sent me (4:34).
2. The Son can do nothing of himself (ἀφ᾽ ἑαυτοῦ), but only what he sees the Father doing (5:19).
3. I can do nothing of myself (ἀπ᾽ ἐμαυτοῦ). As I hear, I judge; and my judgment is just, because I seek not my own will but the will of him who sent me (5:30).
4. He who speaks of himself (ἀφ᾽ ἑαυτοῦ) seeks his own glory; but he who seeks the glory of him who sent him is true, and in him there is no falsehood (7:18).
5. I have come down from heaven, not to do my own will, but the will of him who sent me (6:38).
6. I have not come of myself (ἀπ᾽ ἐμαυτοῦ), but the one who sent me is true (7:28).
7. When you have lifted up the Son of man, then you will know that I

AM, and that I do nothing of myself (ἀπ' ἐμαυτοῦ), but speak as the Father taught me. And the one who sent me is with me; he has not left me alone, for I always do what is pleasing to him (8:28–29).

8. I proceeded and came forth from God; I came not of myself (ἀπ' ἐμαυτοῦ), but he sent me (8:42).

9. I have power to lay down my life, and I have power to take it again; this commandment (ἐντολή) I have received from my Father (10:18).

10. Now my soul is troubled. And what should I say—Father, save me from this hour? No, it is for this reason that I have come to this hour. Father, glorify your name (12:27–28).

11. I have not spoken of myself (ἀπ' ἐμαυτοῦ); the Father who sent me has himself given me commandment (ἐντολή) what to say and what to speak. And I know that his commandment (ἐντολη) is eternal life. What I speak, therefore, I speak just as the Father has told me (12:49–50).

12. The words that I say to you I do not speak of myself (ἀπ' ἐμαυτοῦ); but the Father who remains in me does his works (14:10).

13. So that the world may know that I love the Father, I do as the Father has commanded (ἐντέλλομαι) me (14:31).

14. If you keep my commandments (ἐντολή), you will remain in my love, as I have kept my Father's commandments (ἐντολή) and remain in his love (15:10).

It is a characteristic of St. Thomas's exegesis that he casts his net very far and deep for possible meanings. One might say his main exegetical principle is what Jesus says to the unsuccessful fishermen, *duc in altum* (Luke 5:4). In contrast to classical historical critical scholars, who attempt to pinpoint the meaning of texts as narrowly as possible in accord with some historical context, St. Thomas allows many alternate interpretations to stand next to each other. This open approach is most evident in the manner in which he handles the different readings proposed by the Fathers, both Greek and Latin. He is content for the most part to present the various readings and to leave them standing next to each other in some suitable order as equally valid, even when they disagree with each other. It is only occasionally that he tips his hand to say, Chrysostom (etc.) says *melius,* better. The underlying principle seems to be that there is a multiple sense of the letter in Scripture. "Something else is found only in Scripture, namely, that there are many meanings of the letter in it, and that every one of them is true. In other writings only one meaning is true, namely, the meaning which the author intends. Since Sacred Scripture is handed [to us] by the Holy Spirit, and nothing can be thought out in it which the Holy Spirit has not thought out, whatever one says about Sacred

The Analogy of Mission and Obedience

Scripture, as long as it does not contradict the faith, truly belongs to it, as Augustine says."[23]

When one surveys St. Thomas's reading of the obedience texts in John one finds in many instances an apparently opposite approach. By default, as it were, St. Thomas interprets many obedience texts as applying to Jesus only as man. Yet there are also many passages in which he casts his net further into the deep. Here are seven of these latter texts.

(1) I can do nothing of myself (ἀπ' ἐμαυτοῦ). As I hear, I judge; and my judgment is just, because I seek not my own will but the will of him who sent me (5:30).

The first point, when he says, I cannot do anything of myself, can be understood in two ways, even according to Augustine.

First, as referring to the Son of Man . . .

Secondly, it is explained as referring to the Son of God; and then the aforesaid division still remains the same. Thus Christ, as the Divine Word showing the origin of his power, says: I cannot do anything of myself, in the way he said above, "the Son cannot do anything of himself" (5:19). *For his very doing and his power are his being (esse); but being (esse) in him is from another, that is, from his Father. And so, just as he is not of himself (a se), so of himself he cannot do anything:* "I do nothing of myself" *(below 8:28).*

His statement, I judge only as I hear it, is explained as his previous statement, "only what he sees the Father doing" (above 5:19). For we acquire science or any knowledge through sight and hearing (for these two senses are those most used in learning). But because sight and hearing are different is us, we acquire knowledge in one way through sight, that is, by discovering things, and in a different way through hearing, that is, by being taught. But in the Son of God, sight and hearing are the same; thus, when he says either "sees" or "hears," the meaning is the same so far as the acquisition of knowledge is concerned. And because judgment in any intellectual nature comes from knowledge, he says significantly, I judge only as I hear it, i.e., as I have acquired knowledge together with being from the Father, so I judge: "Everything I have heard from my Father I have made known to you" (below 15:15).

Showing the justness of his judgment he says: and my judgment is just: the reason being, because I am not seeking my own will. *But do not the Father and the Son have the same will?*

I answer that the Father and the Son do have the same will, but the Father does not have his will from another, whereas the Son does have his will from another, i.e., from the Father. *Thus the Son accomplishes his own will as that of another, i.e.,*

---

23. St. Thomas Aquinas, I *Sent.*, a. 4, qc. 1., ad 3; Oxford Bodleian, Lincoln College lat. 95; transcription by M. Jordan. "Item aliud proprium est quia in ista sunt plures sensus litterales et quilibet est uerus. In aliis autem unus solus sensus est uerus, ille scilicet quem auctor intendit. Cum enim sacra scriptura tradita sit per spiritum sanctum et nichil in ipsa possit excogitari quod non excogitauerit Spiritus Sancuts quicquid dicitur de sacra scriptura, dummodo non contradicat fidei, est proprium sibi, sicut dicit Augustinus (Conf. 12)."

as having it from another; but the Father accomplishes his will as his own, i.e., not having it from another. Thus he says: I am not seeking my own will, that is, such as would be mine if it originated from myself, but my will, as being from another, that is from the Father. (*Ioan.* 5, lect. 5, nn. 794–98)

(2) *This commandment (ἐντολή) I have received from my Father (10:18).*

The Word did not receive the command by a word, but in the only-begotten Word of the Father there is every word. When the Son is said to receive what he has substantially, the power is not lessened, but his generation is shown. For to the Son, whom he generates as a perfect Son, the Father *gave everything by begetting.*[24]

(3) *The Father who sent me has himself given me commandment (ἐντολή) what to say and what to speak (12:49).*

All the divine commandments are in the mind of the Father, since these commandments are nothing other than the patterns of things to be done. And so just as the patterns of all creatures produced by God are in the mind of the Father and are called ideas, so the patterns of all things to be done by us are in his mind. And just as the patterns of all things pass from the Father to the Son, who is the Wisdom of the Father, so also the patterns of all things to be done. Therefore the Son says, *The Father who sent me has himself given me, as God, the commandment, that is, by an eternal generation he has communicated to me* what to say within and what to speak without. . . . (*Ioan.* 12, lect. 8, n. 1723)

(4) *I know that his commandment (ἐντολή) is eternal life (12:49).*

The Father gave the commandment, not that the Son did not have it, but in the Wisdom of the Father, which is the Word of the Father, there are all the commandments of the Father. *The commandment is said to be given, because the one to whom it is given is not of himself,* and this is to give to the Son that without which he never was Son, which is to beget the Son, who never was not.[25]

In these four texts, St. Thomas takes all the key Johannine concepts and phrases that express the obedience of Jesus and interprets them as applicable to Jesus in his divinity. Again, if we leave aside the concept of mission, these are the concept of the "commandment" (ἐντολή and ἐντέλλομαι) that the Father gives and the Son receives and follows, the phrase "not my own will, but the will of him who sent me," and the phrase "not of myself" (ἀπ' ἐμαυτοῦ) or "not of himself" (ἀφ' ἑαυτοῦ). As far as I can see, St. Thomas never applies the terms *obedientia, obedire,* or *obediens* to Jesus in his divinity.

The reason why St. Thomas does not use this term, the reason why he understands many obedience texts as applying to Jesus only in his humanity,

---

24. *Catena aurea Ioan.* 10, lect. 4.
25. *Catena aurea Ioan.* 12, lect. 7.

can perhaps be understood, at least partly, from the following argument and resolution in the *Summa*.

(5) The Father teaches and commands

It seems that the Son is not equal to the Father in power. . . . The power of one who commands and teaches is greater than the power of the one who obeys and learns. But the Father commands the Son, "I act as the Father commanded me" (14:31). The Father also teaches the Son, "The Father loves the Son and shows him all that he himself is doing" (15:20). In a similar way, the Son hears, "As I hear I judge" (5:30). Therefore the Father has greater power than the Son.

Ad 2: In the Father showing and the Son hearing one understands only that the Father communicates knowledge to the Son, as also the essence. And to the same point one can refer the commandment of the Father, through this that from eternity by generating him he gave him the knowledge and the will of what is to be done. Or, *preferably, it should be referred to Christ according to human nature.*[26]

Caution against the danger of Arianism seems to be one of St. Thomas's motives in the theory and practice of the principle, "preferably, it should be referred to Christ according to human nature." This caution is reasonable, because Arianism is not a limited historical phenomenon, but a general tendency of the human mind, unless the greatest care is taken when it thinks of distinct persons in the Trinity. This caution is particularly important in an age in which personalist approaches to the Trinity have been widely adopted and many speak in unguarded ways of the Trinity as a community of persons, and so on.

Caution, however, is one thing; an excessive narrowing of exegetical options to the point of violence to the text is another. St. Thomas's anti-Arian stance most certainly does not make him a reductionist in reading John. His exegesis remains remarkably supple and multi-layered. Take, for example, the most notorious Arian proof text, "The Father is greater than I" (14:28). After saying with great decision in his commentary that this text ought to be understood of Jesus in his humanity, St. Thomas then proceeds calmly to apply it to him in his divinity as well, gathering up absolutely essential dimensions of the text of John in the process.

(6) "The Father is greater than I" (14:28)

One could also say, as Hilary does, that even according to the divine nature the Father is greater than the Son, yet the Son is not inferior to the Father, but equal. For the Father is not greater than the Son in power, eternity and greatness, but by the authority of a giver or beginning. For the Father receives nothing from another, but the Son, if I may put it in this way, receives his nature from the Father by

---

26. *ST* I, q. 42, a. 6, ag 2 and ad 2.

an eternal generation. So, the Father is greater, because he gives, yet the Son is not inferior, but equal, because he receives all that the Father has: "God has given him the name that is above every name" (Phil 2:9). No less than the giver is he to whom one and the same being is given. (*Ioan.* 14, lect. 8, n. 1971)

This text beautifully articulates the fundamental principle that returns in all of St. Thomas's accounts of obedience texts applied to Jesus in his divinity. One and the same mystery shines through all these texts, namely, the mystery of the eternal begetting, the eternal gift of the complete divine nature to the Son, the reception of this nature by the Son.

Although St. Thomas avoids the term *obedience,* he is willing to employ the closely related terms *subiectio* and *pietas,* which he defines in their applicability to the eternal Son, following Hilary, as "recognition of paternal authority." Commenting on the same text in the *Summa,* he writes,

(7) *"The Father is greater than I" (14:28),*

> These words are understood as said of Christ according to human nature, in which he is less than the Father, and subject to him; but according to the divine nature he is equal to the Father. This is what Athanasius says, Equal to the Father according to divinity; less than the Father according to humanity.
>
> Or, following Hilary: By the authority of the giver, the Father is greater; but no less is he to whom one and the same being is given; and (De Synod.): *The subjection of the Son of nature is pietas, that is, recognition of paternal authority;* whereas the subjection of all others is the weakness of creation.[27]

St. Thomas defines *pietas* as a human virtue, you will remember, in a manner parallel to obedience and religion. *Pietas* in relation to one's parents corresponds to *religio* in relation to God, and to *dulia* as well as obedience in relation to one's superiors. What unites these virtues as their object is "fatherhood" in its analogical application to God, to human fathers and to those who have particular offices of providential guidance. The *pietas* of the eternal Son in the Trinity, St. Thomas says with Hilary in the text just quoted, is a subjection that consists in the Son's recognition of the paternal authority. The term *obedience* is not far away at this point, it seems to me. It remains a fact that St. Thomas never applies this term to Jesus in his divinity. This fact must be respected. Still, what St. Thomas does say comes quite close. Here is again the most penetrating and telling formulation, which is found in St. Thomas's comments on 5:30: "I can do nothing of myself (ἀπ' ἐμαυτοῦ). As I hear, I judge; and my judgment is just, because I seek not my own will but the will of him who sent me." St. Thomas comments, *Filius implet voluntatem suam*

---

27. *ST* I, q. 42, a. 4, ad 1.

ut alterius, idest ab alio habens; pater vero ut suam, idest non habens ab alio, "The Son accomplishes his own will as that of another, that is, as having it from another; but the Father accomplishes his will as his own, that is, as not having it from another" (*Ioan.* 5, lect. 5, n. 798).

OBEDIENCE AND LOVE

"So that the world may know that I love the Father, I do as (καθώς) the Father has commanded me" (14:31). According to this statement, the obedience of Jesus must be understood in terms of the dynamism of love between the Father and the Son. This dynamism is frequently described by John in terms of gift. "The Father loves the Son and has given everything in his hand" (3:35). "The Father loves the Son and shows him everything that he is doing" (5:20). "Father, I want those you have given me to be with me where I am so that they may see my glory which you have given me before the foundation of the world because you loved me" (17:24). In these texts, the Father's love appears as the final source from which the gift of everything, of the entirety of divine life, proceeds to the Son. "As the Father has life in himself, so has he given to the Son to have life in himself" (5:26).

That the Father's love is the ultimate source from which the gift of the divine nature proceeds to the Son cannot mean, of course, that the Son is begotten by will rather than nature, because this would make him a creature, as St. Thomas points out in his commentary on 3:35 and 17:24 as well as in the article in the *Summa* that asks whether the notional acts are voluntary.[28] That the Father's love is the ultimate source can only mean that the act of giving that constitutes the person of the Father is necessary, because in his eternity "God is love" (1 Jn 4:8, 16) or communion, κοινωνία (1 John 1:3). This communion reaches its completion in the person of the Holy Spirit. In the words of Pope John Paul II,

> In his intimate life, God "is love," the essential love shared by the three divine Persons: personal love is the Holy Spirit as the Spirit of the Father and the Son. Therefore he "searches even the depths of God," as uncreated Love-Gift. It can be said that in the Holy Spirit the intimate life of the Triune God becomes totally gift, an exchange of mutual love between the divine Persons and that through the Holy Spirit God exists in the mode of gift. It is the Holy Spirit who is the personal expression of this self-giving, of this being—love. He is Person-Love. He is Person-Gift.[29]

The important point in the present context is that the gift that lies in this love is complete: "All that is mine is yours and what is yours is mine," Jesus

---

28. Cf. *Ioan.* 3, lect. 6, n. 545; *Ioan.* 17, lect. 6, n. 2262; *ST* I, q. 41, a. 2.
29. John Paul II, *Dominum et Vivificantem*, 10.

prays to his Father in John 17:10. The filial *pietas* or obedience of the Son who receives himself in this gift is equally complete. "I always do what is pleasing to him" (8:29). It is almost a definition of his own eternal person when Jesus says, "He who speaks of himself (ἀφ' ἑαυτοῦ) seeks his own glory; but he who seeks the glory of him who sent him is true, and in him there is no falsehood" (7:18). What is the truth of the Word that was with God at the beginning? At least one aspect of its truth, according to the text just quoted, lies in an answering love that seeks only the glory of the Father. This point is the hinge around which the close relation between theology and economy turns in John. The obedience that Jesus lives as a man is rooted in his very identity as the Son of God and eternal Word. The holocaust of love that he offers as man is the expression of the infinitely total answering love that he offers as God to the Father.

Before we return to St. Thomas's *Commentary on John* to see how he unfolds this central point of Johannine theology, an objection against this account of love between the Father and the Son should be considered. According to St. Thomas, the Father generates the Word, properly speaking, by speaking the word of his own intelligible likeness of himself. When one says, the Father loves the Son and the Son returns this love in obedience, one is speaking metaphorically, as the Psalms do when they address God as my rock and my fortress or when they mention God's right arm. Since God has only one act of knowing and willing, one cannot be speaking according to the proper meaning of terms when one speaks about the divine persons as standing vis-à-vis each other, performing various acts between I and you as we human beings do, who are not consubstantial with each other. One should not psychologize the divine persons. In particular, the act of consent to the will of another that lies in obedience presupposes two wills. Since the three divine persons have only one will, one cannot speak of obedience, properly speaking. "Obedience" is a metaphor, at best. After all, St. Thomas did not follow the path of Richard of St. Victor, whose interpersonal account of the Trinity is largely metaphorical in this manner. The Catechism of the Council of Trent says, "Among the different comparisons employed to throw light upon the mode and manner of this eternal generation, that which is borrowed from thought seems to come nearest to its illustration. Hence St. John calls the Son the Word. For the human mind, in some sort looking into and understanding itself, forms an image of itself which theologians express by the term word."[30] If, therefore, one really wants to understand the Johannine

---

30. *Roman Catechism* (Boston: St. Paul Editions, 1984) Article 2, section 9; p. 41.

obedience texts in their application to Jesus in his divinity, if one wants to use truly analogous terms, rather than mere metaphors, one must delve into how the inner word proceeds in our mind, not into how distinct human beings relate to each other. It is misleading to talk about the procession of the Son in terms of love. Procession by way of love is proper to the Holy Spirit. And even there it cannot mean interpersonal love as we know it.

There is much to be said in answer to this objection, particularly with regard to St. Thomas's relation to Richard of St. Victor. A first response can match authority with authority. Speaking of the communion of persons in marriage and the family, Pope John Paul II writes, "In the whole world there is no image more perfect or more complete of what God is: unity, communion. There is no other human reality that corresponds better to this divine mystery."[31] I do not think this statement should be seen as contradicting the statement in the Roman Catechism that the psychological analogy is the best. In fact, there is a certain inverse symmetry between the difficulties and strengths that attach to the two ways of speaking, to the so-called psychological analogy and the analogy of love between distinct human persons.

> An abyss separates the soul and its God: in us the faculties or acts belong only to one person, while in God the generation of the Word and the procession of the Holy Spirit constitute three persons. On the other hand . . . the analogy of friendship between human beings is insufficient, because in our experience there is never an absolute unity among the lovers, while in God the three persons are one substance. Thus inter-subjective love fails, because it leaves us many; and intra-subjective love fails, because it leaves us single. Plurality of "we"; solitude of "I."[32]

The analogy of the inner word, therefore, does not have a decisive advantage over the analogy of love between distinct human beings. The two analogies are necessary complements of each other. To adopt only one and reject the other leads to distortions.

I think one has to go one step further without denying what was just said. If there is a fault in Nedoncelle's judicious remarks, it is that they place the two ways of speaking too much on the same level. The account of the generation of the Word in terms of the inner word in us human beings is *a theological account,* while the other way of speaking, namely in terms of love between distinct human persons, is the normal way of speaking in the Gospel of John. In his commentary, St. Thomas follows that normal way of speaking. He makes necessary qualifications as possible difficulties arise. In particu-

---

31. John Paul II, Sermon on December 30, 1988, Feast of the Holy Family.
32. Maurice Nedoncelle, "L'intersubjectivité humaine est-elle pour saint Augustin une image de la Trinité?" in *Augustinus Magister,* vol. 1 (Paris: Études Augustiniennes, 1954), 600.

lar he always guards against the danger of dividing the divine nature in the manner in which human nature is divided between distinct human persons. There is, however, not a shred of evidence that St. Thomas believes the Gospel of John is mired in metaphor and that exegesis can free itself from this swamp to reach the level of the proper meaning of truly analogous terms only when it explains Johannine obedience texts in terms of the inner word in human knowing. Such a reading of John would invert the proper relation between the text of Scripture and a theological account. Even while he unfolds the speculative account of the psychological analogy in the *Summa*, St. Thomas does not eliminate language taken from relations between distinct human beings. According to St. Thomas's own understanding of *sacra doctrina*, the *Summa* must be read in the light of his Scripture commentaries. In this respect, St. Thomas is the opposite of a system builder such as Spinoza or Hegel who latches on to one idea and logically builds it up into a system, that is, to the ultimately absurd solitude of that one idea that has managed to squeeze out whatever does not fit into it.

To return to the objection about obedience in particular. It is not true that what is needed for obedience is two wills. In Christ there are two wills, but it would not be correct to say that Christ as man obeys Christ as God (see *ST* III, q. 30, a. 2). What is needed for obedience is a distinction of persons and, on the one hand, a command, on the other consent. Both of these can be properly and analogously said of the Son of God. *Qui misit me pater, ipse mihi dedit, inquantum deus, mandatum, idest per aeternam generationem communicavit, quid dicam, interius, et quid loquar, exterius*, "The Father who sent me has himself given me, as God, the commandment, that is, by an eternal generation he has communicated to me what to say within and what to speak without" (*Ioan.* 12, lect. 8, n. 1723). *Filius implet voluntatem suam ut alterius, idest ab alio habens; pater vero ut suam, idest non habens ab alio*, "The Son accomplishes his own will as that of another, that is, as having it from another; but the Father as his own, that is, as not having it from another" (*Ioan.* 5, lect. 5, n. 798).

CONCLUSION: THE ANALOGY OF MISSION AND OBEDIENCE

In a masterful article entitled "Essentialism or Personalism in the Treatise on God in Saint Thomas Aquinas?" Gilles Emery considers the charge that St. Thomas's teaching on the Trinity falls into essentialism and is not sufficiently personalist. St. Thomas, so the charge, derives the divine persons from the one divine essence, in particular from the one act of knowing and the one act of loving in the divine nature, so that the divine persons are mere aspects or functions of the nature, as in fact our own inner word and the procession of love are. He convincingly refutes this charge, showing that St. Thomas is always concerned to speak about God both according to the unity of essence and according to the distinction of persons. There must always be an irreducible doubling back of our thought over itself *(redoublement)* to gather up both of these aspects. He also shows that this doubling back of thought holds true for St. Thomas's account of the relation between the Trinity and the order of creation and redemption. In particular, he shows that contrary to a widespread reading of St. Thomas that places all the emphasis on the unity of the divine essence in God's activities *ad extra,* in the economy of creation and redemption,

> This rule of the unity of operation of the persons *ad extra* (a principle shared by East and West) does not constitute the sole aspect of Thomas's doctrine on this point. If he holds firmly the unity of divine action, in virtue of the unity of the principle of operation (the divine nature) required by the consubstantiality of the Trinity, he maintains equally clearly another principle: "the procession of the divine persons is the cause and the reason of the procession of creatures." This thesis is found in all of Thomas's works. The connection of the double rule (unity of operation *ad extra* and causality of the Trinitarian processions) comes not from a modern interpretation, but is explicitly posed by Thomas. Thus, the causality of the Trinitarian going-forth *(processus)* in the order of efficiency and of exemplarity unites the divine activity *ad extra* to the eternal generation of the Son and to the procession of the Holy Spirit: it furnishes from this fact the "motive" of the divine economy. The elaboration of the doctrine of the Word and of Love at the core of the Trinity finds itself verified by its capacity to take account of the activity of the Son and of the Holy Spirit in the world and on behalf of mankind: the Father accomplishes all things by his Word and by his Love. We touch here the necessity of a *redoublement* of Trinitarian language in Thomas: it is imperative to consider the double perspective of the common nature and the Trinitarian relations if one is to take account fully of Trinitarian faith.[33]

Let me now use Emery's insight as a guiding light to understanding St. Thomas's interpretation of the obedience of Jesus in the Gospel of John and to the close relationship between *theologia* and *oikonomia* that it implies.

1. *The Identity of Person, Procession, and Mission*

The argument can suitably begin with the key principle mentioned in the introduction, namely, St. Thomas's thesis of the identity of person and mission in Jesus. In one who is sent, he argues, sending always involves two aspects, a relation to the one who sends and a relation to the place to which he

---

33. Gilles Emery, "Essentialism or Personalism in the Treatise on God in Saint Thomas Aquinas." *Thomist* 64 (2000): 521–63, at 527–28.

sends. In the mission of the Son of God, the first of these is identical with the eternal procession of the Son from the Father; the second is a new respect in which the Son becomes present in his creation, namely, as a man who fulfills a certain task.[34] The first of these aspects, the relation to the Father as origin, is identical with the person of the Son, correlative with the person of the Father. It is therefore not surprising that Jesus can summarize the faith of the disciples as follows: "Now they have come to know that all you have given me comes from you; for the words you gave me I have given to them and they have accepted and have truly come to know that I came from you, and have come to believe that you sent me" (17:7–8). To see this utter and complete relational character of the Son is to see his glory, which is not of himself, but of the Father. The fullness of vision in the future wedding of the lamb will continue what the eyes of faith perceive now. "Father, I want those you have given me to be with me where I am so that they may see my glory which you have given me before the foundation of the world because you loved me" (17:24). In this way the disciples understand the truth of the Word of God. "He who speaks of himself (ἀφ' ἑαυτοῦ) seeks his own glory; but he who seeks the glory of him who sent him is true, and in him there is no falsehood" (7:18). This is the comprehensive mode of the Son's being. St. Thomas says following Hilary, *Filius nihil habet nisi natum,* "The Son has nothing except as born."[35] He comments on "Now they have come to know that all you have given me comes from you, . . . , and have truly come to know that I came from you, and have come to believe that you sent me" (17:7–8): "Now, this also, namely, that they kept your word, redounds to your glory, Father, for this is my word, that everything, whatever I have, is from you, and they themselves have now come to know that everything which you gave me, as to a man who is your Son, is from you. 'We have seen his glory, the glory as of the only-begotten of the Father' (1:14), that is, we saw him as having everything from the Father. And thus by what they have come to know the Father is glorified in their minds" (*Ioan.* 17, lect. 2, n. 2199).

2. Exemplar and Participation

In this respect, namely proceeding from another, creatures are made after the exemplar of the eternal Son in his eternal procession. This exemplarity, which is fundamental in the natural order of creation, continues in the supernatural order of grace and divinization: created persons gain life by union with the Son, by participation in his sonship. By the power of the Holy Spir-

---

34. I *Sent.,* d. 15, q. 1, a. 1; *ST* I, q. 43, a. 1.
35. *ST* I, q. 40, a. 3, sed contra. *Ioan.* 5, lect. 5, n. 782.

The Analogy of Mission and Obedience

it they are adopted as sons in the Son to cry Abba, Father. St. Maximus Confessor is extremely helpful at this point. He distinguishes the λόγος τῆς φύσεως, the account of the nature of Christ, his human nature and his divine nature that he shares without division with the other persons, from the τρόπος τῆς ὑπάρξεως, the mode of being, by which the person of the Son is distinct from the other divine persons, namely sonship. He then shows that the human will of Christ is utterly divinized, that it is shaped entirely by the Son's mode of existence, τρόπος τῆς ὑπάρξεως. Thirdly and finally, he shows that by grace we come to participate in this mode of being. Commenting on Jesus' statement "As (καθώς) living Father sent me, and I live through the Father, so he who eats me will live through me" (6:57), St. Thomas writes something quite similar to St. Maximus:

Here he posits the minor premise, namely, that the one who is joined to Christ has life. He brings in this premise by showing a certain likeness, which is as follows. Because of the unity he has with the Father, the Son receives life from the Father. Therefore, the one who is united with Christ receives life from Christ. . . .

If this text is applied to Christ as Son of God, then the word "as" (καθώς, *sicut*) implies a similarity of Christ with the creature in a certain respect, not in all respects, but in respect of being from another. In another respect it is dissimilar. For the Son has something proper to him, namely that he is from the Father in such a way that still he receives the entire plenitude of divine nature, so much so that whatever is natural to the Father is also natural to the Son. The creature, on the other hand, receives a certain particular perfection and nature. "As the Father has life in himself, so has he given to the Son to have life in himself" (5:26) (*Ioan*. 6, lect. 7, n. 977).

3. *Redoublement* in the Derivation of Life

When St. Thomas explains in another place how we come to participate in the life of the Son, one can observe the *redoublement* observed by Emery throughout St. Thomas's works. Commenting on, "Preserve them in your name . . . so that they may be one, as (καθώς) we are one" (17:11), St. Thomas writes:

They are preserved for this goal, namely, to be one. For, our entire perfection consists in the unity of the Spirit, "Take every care to preserve the unity of the Spirit by the peace that binds you together" (Eph 4:3). "How good and joyful it is when brothers dwell in unity!" (Psalm 133:1).

But he adds, "as we are one." There is a difficulty in this statement. They are one in essence; therefore we will also be one in essence. But this is not true.

Response: The perfection of each being is nothing other than a participation in the divine likeness. For we are good to the degree in which we are made like God. Our unity, therefore, is perfective precisely in the degree to which it participates in the divine unity.

Now, there is a twofold unity in God, namely, the unity of nature (cf. "The Father and I are one." John 10:30) and *the unity of love in the Father and the Son which is the unity of the Spirit.* Both of these are in us, not in equality of rank, but by a certain likeness. For the Father and the Son are numerically of one nature, but we are one in nature according to our kind. Again, they are one by a love that is not derived from the gift of someone else, but [by a love] that proceeds from them. For the Father and the Son love each other by the Holy Spirit, but we by a love in which we participate as something derived from a higher source [i.e., the Holy Spirit]. (*Ioan.* 17, lect. 3, n. 2214)

CONCLUSION: THE ANALOGY OF OBEDIENCE

In conclusion, the three steps just taken can be arranged in inverse order to show the full logic of St. Thomas's reading of the Gospel of John.

3. We participate in the divine unity both with respect to the unity of God's nature and with respect to the distinction of persons. Our participation in the latter unity is a participation in the Holy Spirit, who is the unity of love between the Father and the Son. This participation in the Holy Spirit allows us to fulfill the twofold command of love, love of God and love of neighbor. It thereby brings us into God's own life, into the communion between the Father and the Son.

2. Since, as creatures, we are similar to the Son of God in being from another, our share in the life of the Spirit is in particular a share in the life of the Son. It has a filial character. The Son of God, as Son, is in this respect the divine idea according to which we are fashioned and refashioned. Our love for the Father must therefore have the form of *pietas* or of obedience. Even our love of neighbor must have the character of a service undertaken in obedience to the Father.

1. By sharing in this mode of life, we are not slaves overpowered by external force, but we participate in the hypostatic mode of the person of the Son of God in whom procession from the Father and mission are, with respect to his relation to the Father, identical. It is on this basis that Christians ultimately understand the often maligned virtue of obedience and the holocaust intended in the religious vow of obedience. The ultimate source and norm of these human realities, according to St. Thomas, is the filial *pietas* of the Son of God, that is, as he puts it following Hilary, the Son's recognition of the Father's authority, which is an authority of love.

"As (καθώς) the Father has loved me, so I have loved you. Remain in my love. If you keep my commandments, you will remain in my love, as (καθώς) I have kept my Father's commandments and remain in his love" (15:9–10).

PART 3

God and the World

SEVEN

Creation in St. Thomas Aquinas's
Super Evangelium S. Joannis Lectura

DAVID B. BURRELL, C.S.C.

It will hardly seem strange to remind ourselves that appropriating Aquinas for our times may well require deconstructing appropriations effected in other intellectual climes, especially those of the last century. Indeed, an outstanding note of these earlier readings had been their unilateral focus on Aquinas the philosopher, generating a fast distinction between "philosophy" and "theology"—a distinction that hardened into an institutional separation between such faculties in Catholic colleges and universities. There emerged a bridging discipline, to be sure, called "natural theology," which purported to treat theological issues from "reason alone." Yet the issues so treated—typically the existence of God and the immortality of the soul—were not considered part of theology as such, which operated from premises of faith, but rather deemed to be "preambles to faith." Proving such matters by reason was said to facilitate one's acceptance of truths of faith, though philosophical demonstrations of the required sort could never be regarded as a prerequisite for a responsible assent to faith. They were rather thought to be useful ploys for fending off skeptical objections, and so handy to have available on demand but hardly a necessary part of every believer's intellectual equipment. Under the general rubric of apologetics, such inquiries could take place under the aegis of a theology faculty as "fundamental theology" or in a philosophy faculty as "natural theology"—where "natural" contrasted with "supernatural" as reason to faith. The firm distinction between "theology" and "philosophy" remained intact, however, leaving a yawning gap in the purported "bridge" between them; as philosophical demonstrations intended to supply "motives of credibility" could lead up to but never quite suffice to bring one into faith, which always required the action of grace. But a seminal article by Guy de Broglie, S.J., in 1958 challenged this picture as an accurate reading of Aquinas's use of the expression *preambula fidei* ("preambles to faith"), thus implicitly undermining the entire conceptual and institutional edifice firmly separating philosophical inquiries from theological investigations.[1] An influential English collection of articles published soon after under the title *New Essays in Philosophical Theology* served to coin a phrase for an authentic bridging discipline, "philosophical theology," whose implications continue to be explored, but which challenges the neat separation implied by the predecessor title of "natural theology," with the collateral effect of vastly expanding the range of topics treated in this domain.[2] Instead of confronting us directly with the "natural/supernatural" distinction, this descriptive phrase makes it clear that the subjects to be considered will be theological in character, while the mode of treatment will be philosophical. So it tends to be inclusive rather than exclusive, allowing premises from revelation to work in tandem with rational arguments.[3]

That description, of course, could accurately depict Aquinas's procedure in his *Summa theologiae*, and so threaten the handy distinction-become-separation between the two disciplines named. Yet it is precisely that later distinction-become-separation which must be recognized to be the construction that it is, and so effectively dismantled, yet without losing the penetrating edge that philosophical rigor brings to theological inquiry. Once we have dispensed with the demand to know whether Aquinas is doing "philosophy" or "theology" in a particular text, we have a better chance to recognize what he is actually doing. A decisive incentive to deconstruct the earlier appropriation of Aquinas will come from recognizing its roots in modernity, which put great store in "reason alone," whereas following the ways in which Aquinas actually proceeds will allow us to acknowledge how his use of reason is imbedded in presuppositions of faith. And once we have accomplished that, it will become clear that his mode more nearly matches ours, as we follow both Gadamer and Wittgenstein into paths of inquiry that utilize convictions of varying provenance in an inescapably intertwining manner. We will be able, we shall see, to distinguish diverse strands of inquiry, yet not be constrained to separate them. Indeed, the distinction we need can be found in an article of the *Summa theologiae* that will provide a key to our inquiry into

1. Guy de Broglie, S.J., "La vraie thomiste des *praeambula fidei*," *Gregorianum* 34 (1953): 341–89.
2. Anthony Flew, ed., *New Essays in Philosophical Theology* (London: SCM Press, 1955).
3. "Theology and Philosophy," in *Blackwell Companion to Modern Theology*, ed. Gareth Jones (Oxford: Blackwell, 2003).

Aquinas's *Commentary on the Gospel of St. John:* "Can the trinity of divine persons be known by natural reason?"[4] The answer, we already suspect, is *no,* since reason has no other way to proceed to God except as "origin and goal of all things";[5] and since "the creative power of God is common to the entire trinity," no distinction of "persons" could ever be detected by this route. Yet the responses to the objections will prove germane to our inquiry. The second objection induces typical theological investigations, citing examples of those who use reason to "prove *(ad probandum)* the trinity of persons from the infinity of divine goodness" (Richard of St. Victor), or to "manifest *(ad manifestandum)* the trinity of persons from the procession of word and of love in our mind" (Augustine). Aquinas distinguishes this use of reason from the "sufficient reason employed in natural science to prove that the motion of the heavens will always be of uniform velocity," identifying the theological use with what Charles Sanders Peirce called abduction: "once the root has been posited, one can show how the effects will be congruent, as astronomers employ epicycles to 'save the appearances' once [erratic] heavenly motions have been ascertained."[6] If we can judge teachers by the quality and appropriateness of the examples they offer, Aquinas scores high here. By identifying two ways in which reason is employed within scientific investigation, and indicating how the second is more appropriate to theological inquiry, he avoids contrasting faith with reason, or supernatural with natural, since each use of reason plays a role in rational inquiry; yet he also makes clear that inquiries predicated on the assent of faith will not have the perspicuity attending a purported "reduction to first principles," presumably *per se nota.* So where "philosophy"—whether natural or metaphysical—can conform to that stringent Aristotelian model for "scientific inquiry," it will clearly distinguish itself from "theology," yet the inclusion of another form of reasoning ("abduction") within scientific inquiry itself serves to relativize the *Posterior Analytics* paradigm, as indeed Aristotle's own practice does as well. (Indeed, Aquinas notes in his commentary on that work that only the "constructed science" of geometry satisfies the paradigm.)[7] We shall see how the lectures on John satisfy this second use of reason, usually called "fittingness" and often relegated to second place by Thomists dedicated to distinguishing philosopher from theologian in Aquinas, yet which Aquinas's own example here suggests we re-evaluate, notably in the light of work in the history and philosophy of science that

---

4. *ST* I, q. 32, a. 1.   5. *ST* I, q. 2, prol.
6. *ST* I, q. 32, a. 1, ad 2. There are many sources for *abduction* in Peirce, but see "Hume on Miracles," in *Collected Papers,* ed. Charles Hartshorne and Paul Weiss (Cambridge, Mass.: Belknap Press of Harvard University Press, 1960), VI.522–47 (356–69).
7. *In Posteriorum Analyticorum* 1.1 [10] (Turin: Marietti, 1955), 151.

confirms Peirce's identification of *abduction* as normal form for modern scientific inquiry.

If the response to the second objection lays bare the method employed in Aquinas's lectures when dealing with the "Word through whom all things are made," the response to the third objection lays bare their content. The objection itself is so oddly generic (that is, "dialectical") as to be beside the point, so we may treat it as a set-up for Aquinas's startling response. The anonymous questioner notes that "it seems superfluous even to consider what cannot be known by human reason, yet since divine tradition regarding knowledge of the trinity can hardly be said to be superfluous, the 'trinity of persons' must be able to be known by human reason." (Just try to be faithful to the pedagogic form of the *Summa,* and ask yourself what you would do with an objection like that one!) Aquinas "takes the objection seriously" by neatly overlooking its purported argument form, yet proceeds directly to counter the charge of "superfluity" by adopting Anselm's use of "necessary reason": "it must be said that knowledge of divine persons was necessary for us in two ways: first, for a proper way of regarding *(ad recte sentiendum)* the creation of things. For by the fact of our saying that God made all things by his Word, the error of positing that God produced things by the necessity of [the divine] nature is excluded. And by the fact that we posit in God a procession of love, it is shown that God did not produce creatures according to any need nor according to any other extrinsic cause, but according to the love of God's own goodness." He then associates this duplex procession with the text of Genesis 1, linking "God says 'Let there be light'" to manifestations of the divine Word, and "God saw that the light was good" to showing the approbation of divine love—where this is clearly an accommodation of a text that Aquinas would never take to have revealed the "trinity of persons." "The other way [in which it must be said that knowledge of divine persons was necessary for us] is yet more significant: for a proper way of regarding *(ad recte sentiendum)* the salvation of humankind, which is executed through the Son incarnate and through the gift of the Holy Spirit."[8] That Aquinas insists that a proper way of regarding salvation is more important than getting creation straight is one more confirmation of Leonard Boyle's locating the heart of the *Summa* in its second part, but since our topic is creation, we shall focus on the first way in which knowledge of divine persons was necessary for us to have a proper regard *(ad recte sentiendum)* for the creation of things. This is the textual source for what Josef Pieper's astute reading of Aquinas had

---

8. *ST* I, q.32, a. 1, ad 3.

brought him to notice: that "creation is the hidden element in the philosophy of Saint Thomas"—an assertion that quite by itself (abetted by Pieper's towering authority) deconstructs the distinction-become-separation of "philosophy" from "theology" in Aquinas.[9]

I shall employ this strategic text from the *Summa* to elucidate two dimensions of the *Commentary on John:* the first concerning method it employs, and the second directed to its teaching. For in the *Commentary on John,* Aquinas apparently proceeds as though we could know the consubstantiality of the Word with God by reason. But we shall see how those appearances are misleading, since the lectures do not proceed from reason to truths of faith, but rather use reason to show the plausibility of the revelation of John, as well as to clear a path for the proper understanding of that revelation. This represents, of course, the Augustinian understanding of theological inquiry as "faith seeking understanding" *(fides quaerens intellectum),* and also illustrates the second way in which our key text identified reason functioning in inquiry. I shall then show how Aquinas employs revelation to lead us as close as we can come to ascertaining the way in which creation takes place. Indeed, as his response to the third objection (in our key text) intimates, revelation of the trinity of persons not only keeps us from getting creation wrong, but also suggests what it might be to get it right. This is delicate, however, since our language has no way of expressing the way in which creation takes place, since as the "emanation of all of being from the universal being,"[10] creation involves no change[11] and hence no discernible process. For there is no *becoming* involved in "the production of existing itself *(producere esse absolute).*"[12] Yet while these stark reminders of the *Summa* forbid us offering any image to bolster our insistence that God creates the universe, the lectures nevertheless succeed in offering complementary analogies that can help us to penetrate the mystery as best we can.

VERBUM IN DIVINIS

Commenting on the opening line of the gospel, "In the beginning was the Word *(in principio erat Verbum),*" Thomas cites two of his favorite authorities, Augustine and John of Damascus (the Damascene), inferring from their remarks that "Word, properly speaking, must always be taken *personally* in

---

9. Leonard Boyle, *The Setting of the Summa Theologiae of St. Thomas* [Etienne Gilson Series 5] (Toronto: Pontifical Institue of Mediaeval Studies, 1982); Josef Pieper, *Silence of St. Thomas* (New York: Pantheon, 1957): "The Negative Element in the Philosophy of St. Thomas," 47–67.

10. *ST* I, q. 45, a. 4, ad 1; cf. q. 45, a. 1.   11. *ST* I, q. 45, a. 2, ad 2.

12. *ST* I, q. 45, a. 5.

God, since it simply means something expressed by one who understands" (*Ioan.* 1, lect. 1, n. 29). Reasoning to this conclusion by contrast with our "imperfect word," he notes that "we need to form many imperfect words, through which we express all that we know in an articulated fashion *(divisim),* since we are unable to express all of our conceptions in a single word, whereas this is not the case with God. For when God understands, in a single act, both God's own self and whatever God understands through [understanding] His essence, a single divine Word is expressive of all that is in God—not only of the 'persons' but of creatures as well; otherwise God would be imperfect" (*Ioan.* 1, lect. 1, n. 27). And that capacity for expressing all in a single word stems from the fact that God need not reason things out, proceeding as our words do from potency to act, but "the Word of God is always in act" (*Ioan.* 1, lect, n. 26). Thomas's reasoning here is so seamless that one might presume that a proper understanding of God as "origin and goal of all things, and especially of rational creatures"[13] would lead ineluctably to God's creative knowing coming forth in a single Word, but if that were the case, then at least the second "person" of the triune God could be rationally inferred from the leading formula that identifies how the creator can be a subject of human discourse. Yet that cannot be the case, since (as we have seen) "the trinity of divine persons [cannot] be known by natural reason."[14] Rather, God's knowing perfectly fulfills the Aristotelian paradigm of knowing-by-identity, so there is no need for God, in knowing God's own self, to express any word at all—even a single one—to express that all-embracing act of knowing. As Aquinas makes clear in the *Summa theologiae* I, q. 17, a. 1, John's opening verse, identifying the divine person of Jesus as "the Word," provides the best analogy we can employ for understanding divine triunity as a distinction of "persons" or of "subsistent relations." Yet the austere reasoning found in questions 3–11 of the *Prima pars* of the *Summa theologiae,* which establishes *simpleness* as the identifying metaphysical mark of the One who is "origin and goal of all things," could never conclude to a divine Word eternally expressed; there would simply be no need for such a Word, given what we must say about divine knowing.[15] So Aquinas is proceeding from revelation to show its cogency by way of this prescient analogy already introduced by John, and later elaborated by Augustine.

By way of underscoring its appropriateness, he will also show why "Word" is a better name than "Son," which was Jesus' own self-description, leading

---

13. *ST* I, q. 2, prol. 14. *ST* I, q. 32, a. 1.
15. Bernard Lonergan, S.J., *Verbum: Word and Idea in Aquinas,* ed. David Burell, C.S.C., (Notre Dame, Ind.: University of Notre Dame Press, 1967), ch. 5, "*Imago Dei,*" 194f.

spontaneously to addressing God as "Father." The Gospel of John departs from the other three Gospels in this regard, and Thomas shows how using the "name 'Word'" removes any "faulty conjecture" of a "material or changeable generation in God by supplying an intelligible procession" (*Ioan.* 1, lect. 1, n. 31). And by rendering the Greek *logos* into Latin as *verbum* rather than *ratio* (for Augustine had noted that it can properly be translated as either term), Thomas notes that "*ratio* properly refers to a concept of the mind, in so far as it is in the mind, even though nothing might come of it outside the mind, whereas *verbum* bespeaks a relation to things external [to the mind]. And since the evangelist, in using *logos,* intended not only to make reference to the existence of the Son in the Father, but also to the operative power of the Son, 'by which all things are made through Him,' our predecessors preferred to translate it as *verbum,* which implies a reference to external things" (*Ioan.* 1, lect. 1, n. 32). By highlighting the phrase subsequently incorporated into the Nicene creed—"by Whom all things are made," Thomas securely grounds the argument in the tradition of revelation, while his astute remarks regarding a preferable translation of *logos* remind us of the way he carefully anchors the word spoken to create in the Word proceeding within divinity, as its eternal pattern.[16] His summary comments on this pregnant initial verse—"In the beginning was the Word *(in principio erat Verbum)*"—utilize a battery of authorities—Chrysostom, Origen, Basil, Hilary, and Augustine—to delineate the three ways in which this verse may be parsed: to assert the causality of the Word, and the consubstantiality as well as the co-eternity of Word with Father (*Ioan.* 1, lect. 1, n. 38, reprising nn. 35–37). He will wait until parsing verse 4, however, where John asserts "this [Word] to be in the beginning with the Father *(hoc erat in principio apud Deum),*" to head off any misperceptions of divine self-knowing and creative knowing that could think of God's word in impersonal terms, as though divine knowing required expression in a word, or as though the universe so expressed would have to be co-eternal with God. So the way in which the Word is *with (apud)* God is utterly unique to this revealed divinity, as Aquinas shows by using John's expression to correct the misunderstandings of both Christian heretics and pagan "Platonists" (*Ioan.* 1, lect. 1, nn. 64–65).

---

16. Cf. *ST* I q. 34, a. 3; q. 45, a. 6, ad 2; Gilles Emery, O.P., *La Trinité créatrice: Trinité et création dans les commentaires aux 'Sentences' de Thomas d'Aquin et de ses précurseurs Albert le Grand et Bonaventure* (Paris: Vrin, 1995).

ANALOGIES FOR THE CREATING ACT

Having secured a proper understanding of *Verbum* in God, Thomas can proceed to the act of knowing all that is not God, creation, as it is modeled on that unique procession within God. He carries this out by parsing verses 3–4a: *Omnia per ipsum facta sunt. Et sine ipso factum est nihil. Quod factum est in ipso vita erat,* "All things are made through Him, while without Him nothing is made; and what is made is life in Him." Aquinas will proceed to show how these verses can be taken to offer analogies to help us appreciate the way in which creation happens—something that will otherwise totally escape us. He will use the initial phrase to display what Robert Sokolowski has shown to be the crux of Christian theology, "the distinction" of creator from creatures, followed by a penetrating analysis of the strategic use of *"per"* (through). The second phrase can either be considered to reinforce the first, or taken (with Augustine) to underscore that evil can be taken to be only a metaphysical "black hole," and never *something* that would then have to find its source in the creator. The last phrase, as we shall see, will open us, in Aquinas's hands, to the only way we can properly construe this crucial "distinction": namely, as a "non-duality."

The "distinction" is secured by various commentaries on this key verse— "all things are made through Him," including those of Chrysostom and Augustine, both of whom conclude (against Arius) that "if all things are made through the Word, the Word itself cannot be said to be made; for if it were made, it would have to be made through another Word, since 'all things are made through the Word'" (*Ioan.* 1, lect. 2, n. 71). Indeed, understood in this way, the phrase confirms "the equality of the Word to the Father, with Chrysostom; co-eternity with Hilary, and consubstantiality with Augustine" (*Ioan.* 1, lect. 2, n. 72), as well as

alerting us to three errors [regarding creation itself] to be avoided: that of Valentinus, who took the phrase to mean that the Word proffered to the creator the cause of His creating the world, so that all things were made through the Word as if the father's creating the world came from the Word. This seems to lead to the position of those who have said that God produced the world by way of some external cause, which contradicts Proverbs 16:4: "the Lord made all things for Himself." Origen exposed the falsity of their position when he noted that were the Word to have served the creator as a cause by supplying material for making things, [the gospel verse] would not have said "all things are made through Him," but rather that all things are made through the creator by the Word. (*Ioan.* 1, lect. 2, n. 73)

This clarification leads Aquinas to explore the crucial preposition *"per"* as a way of gesturing toward the manner in which God's creation is carried out—

"through the Word." If "through" denotes a formal cause, then creation will simply be "appropriated to" the Son as the wisdom through which God creates—*wisdom* being the divine attribute appropriated to the second person of the triune God; "whereas if 'through' denotes causality from the standpoint of the thing produced, then when we say that the Father does all things through the Son, this is not a [mere] appropriation but proper to the Word, because the fact that He is a cause of creatures is had from someone else, namely the Father, from whom He has His being" (*Ioan.* 1, lect. 2, n. 76). The reasoning is subtle here, since the analogy that Aquinas is using for the use of "through" "from the standpoint of the things produced" is that of an instrument, as we can say the pictures were hung on the wall through using a hammer to secure the nails on which to hang them. So he must go on to clarify that "it does not follow that the Word is an instrument of the Father," since "the Father gives the Son the same power which He [the Father] has, by which the Son operates." So while the analogy offered to help us understand the manner through which the Son is said to create all things is that of an instrument, in this unique activity the Son cannot be reduced to an instrumental role. What his role underscores, Aquinas will note later, is that creation "does not amount to producing things by way of natural necessity, but by intellect and will, by which manner things are also governed" (*Ioan.* 1, lect. 2, n. 94).

The moves Aquinas makes here deserve close attention. To say that the Word is the one "through Whom all things are made" does not simply allude to the fact that the creator acts intelligently, or through divine wisdom, for that would have to be part of a monotheistic account of creation, or even a pagan one such as Plotinus's; the One from whom all things come cannot be mindless, certainly. So the "intellect and will" referred to here hearken us back to our key text, where

> knowledge of divine persons was [deemed] necessary . . . for a proper way of regarding *(ad recte sentiendum)* the creation of things. For by the fact of our saying that God made all things by his Word, the error of positing that God produced things by the necessity of [the divine] nature is excluded. And by the fact that we posit in God a procession of love, it is shown that God did not produce creatures according to any need nor according to any other extrinsic cause, but according to the love of God's own goodness.[17]

The reduplication in the final phrase—"the love of God's own goodness"—is of special significance here, for it blocks the simple argument from the Neoplatonic axiom "*bonum est diffusivum sui*" ("good is self-disseminating") for

---

17. *ST* I, q. 32, a. 1, ad 3.

creation as coming forth from God's goodness *tout court*.[18] Yet there is a reduplication here as well regarding the Word, for emanation "by necessity of nature" would also have to be intelligent, modeled as it is on axiomatic deduction. Once the intentional analogy of intellect and will has been used to offer a kind of explication of the revelation of "persons" in divinity, however, intelligence will be yoked to will in a way unsuspected by those (like Plotinus) who would also have to insist that the One could not overflow mindlessly. So we have a gesture toward characterizing what free creation amounts to by allusion to its eternal model: the procession of the Word within God. At the same time, however, we cannot really see *how* this free creation happens, for the instrumentality of the Word in creation is unlike any instrumentality we know within creation, for this instrument is "of one substance with the Father."

"Without Him nothing has been made *(sine ipso factum est nihil)*" has been understood in Manichean fashion, to gesture toward a dimension of the universe that is intrinsically evil and so knows a source other than creation through the Word of God, and where Augustine identified evil with nonbeing (or *nihil*) precisely to avoid this dualistic picture of origins, some might read John to support it. So Aquinas follows Chrysostom again to insist that this phrase but intensifies the initial part of the same verse, and so "is introduced to manifest how total is the causality" of the Word (*Ioan.* 1, lect. 3, n. 84). So he turns to the initial part of the following verse: *Quod factum est in ipso vita erat* ("what is made is life in Him"), to display just how unique is the causality operative in creation. After noting some unacceptable readings of this enigmatic verse, Aquinas has recourse to a known homily source entitled *Vox spiritualis* as a way of expounding it:

"What is made in him," i.e., through him, "is life" not in each thing itself but in its cause. For in the case of all things that are caused, it is always true that effects, whether produced by nature or by will, exist in their causes not according to their own existence, but according to the power of their proper cause. Thus, lower effects are in the sun as in their cause, not according to the existence proper to them but according to the power of the sun. Therefore, since the cause of all effects produced by God is a certain life and an art full of living archetypes *(rationum viventium)*, for this reason "what is made in Him," i.e., through him, "is life" in its cause, i.e., in God (*Ioan.* 1, lect. 2, n. 90).

The background here is the *Liber de causis*, the Proclean text that insists that God's first creation is *esse* (existing), which then permeates to all levels of in-

---

18. See Norman Kretzmann, "A General Problem of Creation: Why Would God Create Anything at All?" in *Being and Goodness*, ed. Scott MacDonald (Ithaca, N.Y.: Cornell University Press, 1991), 208–28; a position that he reasserts in his *Metaphysics of Theism* (Oxford: Clarendon Press, 1997), 233–26.

dividual beings, for as the most general of terms semantically (in this Neoplatonic scheme) it must also be the most influential existentially.[19] Without adopting the entire picture, Aquinas will insist that the "effect most proper to the first cause of all is *esse* (existing) itself."[20] The import of this gloss, which Aquinas appropriates to explicate this difficult verse, is to remind us that creatures can never be separated from their creator, as (for example) offspring become quite separate from their parents. And since generation is the best example of Aristotelian efficient causality, creation must be something other; quite ungraspable in Aristotelian categories and more akin (as Sara Grant has shown) to what Sankara identified as *non-duality*.[21] The uniqueness of the creator/creature relation is a corollary of "the distinction," of course, and corroborated in these same lectures when Aquinas comments on John 15:5: *sine me nihil potestis facere* ("without me you can do nothing"):

Our actions are either from the power of nature or from divine grace. If from the power of nature, all natural movements are from the very Word of God, for no nature can be moved to do anything without Him. And if from grace, since He is the author of grace, for "grace and truth are realized through Jesus Christ (John 1:17), it should be clear that no meritorious action can take place without Him." (*Ioan.* 15, lect. 1, n. 1993)

The earlier exposition continues to address our topic with reference to the apparently innocuous verse 10: *in mundo erat* ("He was in the world"), where Aquinas is intent on expounding the manner in which the Word through whom all things are made is *in* the world. Passing over the obvious senses of being contained in or being a part of something, Aquinas asserts:

The true light was in the world in a third way, i.e. as an efficient and preserving cause: "I fill heaven and earth" as said in Jeremiah 23:24. However, there is a difference between the way God acts and causes all things and the way in which other agents act. For other agents act as things existing externally [to what is acted upon]: since they do not act except by moving and altering in some fashion what is extrinsic to a thing, they work from without. But God acts in all things as one acting from within, because He acts by creating. Now to create is to give *esse* (existing) to the thing created. So, since *esse* is innermost in each thing [*ST* I, q. 8, a. 1], God, who by acting gives *esse*, acts in things as one acting from within. Hence God "was in the world" as giving *esse* to the world (*Ioan.* 1, lect. 5, n. 133).

---

19. Annotated English translation by Vincent Gualiardo, O.P., Charles Hess, O.P., and Richard Taylor, of St. Thomas Aquinas, *Commentary on the Book of Causes* (Washington, D.C.: The Catholic University of America Press, 1996).

20. *ST* I, q. 45, a. 5.

21. See the revised edition, edited by Bradley Malkovsky, of Sara Grant, R.S.C.J., *Toward an Alternative Theology: Confessions of a Non-Dualist Christian* (Notre Dame, Ind.: University of Notre Dame Press, 2001).

It should be clear that Aquinas is using "efficient cause" in his comments in a generic way, without direct reference to Aristotle. His comment on the remainder of verse 10, *et mundus per ipsum factus est* ("and the world was made through Him"), makes even more explicit the intimate connection of creatures with creator, such that creatures can never *be* without the creator. Linking this verse with the preceding *erat lux vera* ("He was true light"), Aquinas identifies the aim of the universe made through Him to be "that light itself might be manifested in it":

> For as a work of art manifests the art of the artisan, so the whole world is nothing else than a certain representation of the divine wisdom conceived within the mind of the Father: "He poured her [wisdom] out upon all his works," as is said in Sirach 1:10. (*Ioan.* 1, lect. 5, n. 136)

This appears to be the most he can say about how creation might be construed by us creatures, yet what is particularly significant is the way it veers away from the kind of causality found among creatures to one that belongs to God alone and that enters so intimately into the existential constitutions of creatures as to make them literally unintelligible without recourse to this relation. Yet that same relation/"distinction" resists formulation, so its mode remains strictly speaking unknowable. One can only gesture by analogies, the most appropriate of which are supplied by Scripture, as he noted already in *Summa theologiae* I, q. 12, a. 13:

> By grace we have a more perfect knowledge of God than we have by natural reason. The latter depends on two things: images derived from the sensible world and the natural intellectual light by which we make abstract intelligible concepts from these images. In both these respects human knowledge is helped by the revelation of grace. The light of grace strengthens the intellectual light and at the same time prophetic visions provide us with God-given images which are better suited to express divine things than those we receive naturally from the sensible world. Moreover God has given us sensible signs and spoken words to show us something of the divine, as at the baptism of Christ when the Holy Spirit appeared in the form of a dove and the voice of the Father was heard saying, *this is my beloved Son* (Mt 3:17).

It is hardly accidental that the image that Aquinas notes to illustrate the way in which Aristotelian epistemology can be employed to elucidate knowing-by-faith is one that gestures toward what reason cannot itself know: the triune God.

EIGHT

Eternity and Time in St. Thomas Aquinas's Lectures on St. John's Gospel

MATTHEW L. LAMB

 In commenting on John 3:24 "For he gives the Spirit without measure," Aquinas makes the startling affirmation that the grace of Christ is not only more than sufficient to save the entire world, but that it is more than sufficient to save "even many worlds, if they were to exist" (*Ioan.* 3, lect. 6, n. 544). To understand the concrete universality of Jesus Christ, the reader must overcome an all too contemporary tendency, rooted in nominalism, to oppose the universal and the particular, the metaphysical and the historical, as if one was only "conceptual" and the other "concrete." In Trinitarian theology this tendency leads to a disjunction between the mission of the Word Incarnate and the mission of the Spirit. Such disjunctions and oppositions are nowhere to be found in Aquinas's work. I shall explore how Aquinas understands eternity and time in his lectures on John. This is the context for understanding of the concrete universality of salvation in the Word Incarnate.

Among the Gospels John is the most cited in the writings of St. Thomas Aquinas—over thrice as often as each of the Synoptic Gospels. Indeed, it seems that among cited *"auctoritates,"* references to the writings of St. John and St. Paul may only be surpassed by those to St. Augustine.[1] The Gospel of John corresponded to the contemplative and theoretical concerns of St. Thomas Aquinas. It contemplatively patterns the *"exitus—reditus"* framework of his *Summa theologiae*. In his own prologue Aquinas sets out the perfection of John's

---

1. Cf. Roberto Busa, S.J., *Thomae Aquinatis Opera Omnia cum hypertextibus in CD-ROM,* 2nd ed. (Milan: Licosa-Editel, 1996).

contemplative knowledge of God, containing in a "most perfect way" the ancient philosophical knowledge of God gained from the authority of God governing all things to His end, as well as gained from reflections on His eternity, on His supreme dignity, and on the incomprehensibility of His truth (*Ioan.* prol, nn. 1–11). The inner Trinitarian life is revealed in the prayers of Jesus to the Father and the promise of the Paraclete (*Ioan.* 1, lect. 1, nn. 23–67; 14, 1–17, nn. 1848–2270).[2] The creation of all through the Word is followed with the rejection of God by intelligent creatures, and the redemptive return to God in the life, death, and resurrection of Jesus Christ. John's Gospel unites the visible and invisible missions of the Word Incarnate and the Holy Spirit, showing how these missions are continued down the ages in the apostolic mission of the Church carrying forward the Word of God in her sacraments and Scriptures until the whole of history is consummated in the eternal life of the Father with the Word in the Spirit.[3]

To read the Gospel of John with Aquinas can occur genuinely only when we realize that faith and intelligence, wisdom and scholarship, are united in his theological exegesis.[4] The teachings of the Scriptures and the Church are truly and fully known only in the light of a charity-informed faith by which we participate in the redemptive visible and invisible missions of the Son and Holy Spirit:

Just as the effect of the mission of the Son is to lead us to the Father, so the effect of the mission of the Holy Spirit is to lead the faithful to the Son. Now the Son, since He is begotten Wisdom, is Truth itself: "I am the way, and the truth, and the life" (14:6). And so the effect of this kind of mission is to make men sharers in the divine

---

2. On the Trinitarian spirituality of Aquinas, cf. Jean-Pierre Torrell, O.P., *Saint Thomas d'Aquin, maître spirituel* (Paris: Éditions du Cerf, 1996), 31–298.

3. *Ioan.* 1, lect. 10, nn. 205–7; *Ioan.* 4, lect. 4, nn. 638–55; *Ioan.* 6, lect. 7, nn. 971–81; *Ioan.* 14, lect. 6, nn. 1952–1960; *Ioan.* 17, lect. 1, nn. 2177–92; *Ioan.* 17, lect. 5 and 6, nn. 2232–70; *Ioan.* 21, lect. 6, nn. 2652–60.

4. On Aquinas's approach to Scripture, cf. Thomas Aquinas, *Commentary on Ephesians*, trans. M. Lamb (Albany, N.Y.: Magi Books, 1966), 3–36, and John F. Boyle, "St. Thomas Aquinas and Sacred Scripture," *Pro Ecclesia* 4 (1995): 92–104; for a contemporary perspective on Aquinas, cf. J. A. DiNoia, O.P., and Bernard Mulcahy, O.P., "The Authority of Scripture in Sacramental Theology: Some Methodological Observations," *Pro Ecclesia* 10 (2001): 329–45. A theological exegesis requires faith in the truth of the Word of God so that one does not stop at texts alone, but knows by faith the realities the texts affirm. This also applies to the study of theology. No theology can be done by bracketing out one's faith, for then there is no knowledge of the sacred realities, but only a comparative textology, a comparative study of religious texts, but not theology. For an excellent example of a truly theological study of St. Thomas that develops a genuinely Thomistic soteriology, see Matthew Levering, *Christ's Fulfillment of Torah and Temple: Salvation according to Thomas Aquinas* (Notre Dame: University of Notre Dame Press, 2002).

wisdom and knowers of the truth. The Son, since He is the Word, gives us teaching (*doctrinam*); but the Holy Spirit makes us capable of receiving His teaching. (*Ioan.* 14, lect. 6, n. 1958; my translation)

Why does Aquinas state in the prologue to his lectures that the contemplation of John offers us the most perfect knowledge of God relative to the ancient philosophical knowledge of divine eternity? In the first lectures on John Aquinas outlines his profound appropriation of both philosophical and theological sources. He communicates the metaphysical, cognitional, and theological requirements of an adequate theological interpretation of the truth of the Gospel doctrine or teaching on the eternal Word incarnate in time.

In his prologue Aquinas does not name the "ancient philosophers" who arrived at knowledge of God from His eternity. From other writings, especially his exposition on the *Liber de causis,* he acknowledges the common elements in both platonic and peripatetic philosophers, and singles out Proclus, whose *Elementatio theologica* had been translated by William of Moerbeke in 1268.[5] For Aquinas, as for the Patristic traditions, it was clear that revelation had provided a far more perfect knowledge of God than any philosophy alone could attain. Eternity is not simply an abstraction, eternity is the Triune God. Moreover, eternity is not opposed to time, eternity creates and redeems time.

As God is simple, infinite understanding and loving, so God is eternal. There is no extension or duration in God. This divine eternity, as divine infinity and simplicity, cannot be imagined; nor can it be understood and conceived, except by God. We can, however, affirm that God is eternal and understand analogically that affirmation. There are major breakthroughs in the philosophical and theological grasp of this analogical understanding of the affirmation that God is eternal. Those breakthroughs are in the works of Augustine, Boethius, and Thomas Aquinas. A contrast with ancient philosophers on this theme might bring out their achievement.

Divine eternity was not adequately understood outside the context of revealed religion. For the Eternal God revealing Himself in time meant that it was not enough to appeal to the spiritual character of acts of intelligence and conceptualization as an analogue for knowing God. Augustine emphasized the importance of *Veritas* and judgments of truth, along with a meditative appropriation of human intelligence as an immaterial *imago Dei* as the highest analogue for understanding the Trinitarian mystery. Aquinas clearly differen-

---

5. Cf. Torrell, *Saint Thomas Aquinas,* vol. 1: *The Person and His Work,* 222. Thus the work was available to Aquinas when he lectured on the Gospel of John, which occurred according to Torrell in 1270–72; ibid., 198–99.

tiated the first and second acts of the mind, articulating how it is only in true judgments that being, *esse*, is known. Without a clear attainment of judgment as affirming and denying being, as a positing of the synthesis of subject and predicate, the efforts of philosophers to understand the divine either make the divine into some type of Absolute Idea, infinitely remote from all finite beings, or make the divine into an Absolute Intelligence that pantheistically informs the whole universe. Only in the light of revelation was the proper theological understanding of divine transcendence and immanence elaborated.

Parmenides and Zeno, in acknowledging the "all at once" character of the one, argued against the reality of change. In Plato the divine eternal is a unity beyond, and in opposition to, all multiplicity. In Aristotle the divine eternal is the νόησις νοήσεως as the immanent unmoved mover of all that is. Where Plato can contrast the eternal and the temporal to the point of opposing them, Aristotelian scholarship has been unable to determine if he ever decisively differentiated the eternal and temporal. This has been a philosophical dialectic ever since: transcendence without immanence or immanence with a very questionable transcendence. This dialectic could be resolved only by adverting to what is implied in the activity of judging, of knowing the truth, as distinct from understanding and thinking. Neither Plato nor Aristotle, it seems, understood the act of judgment as more than the synthesis of concepts, of subject and predicate. Hence the notion of being was in some way a conceptual content, an essence, without distinguishing that from existence or *esse*. This distinction would result from adverting to judging as a positing of the synthesis. The positing of the synthesis would have led, as it did in Arab and Christian philosophers, to grasping a real distinction between essence and existence.[6]

Unaided philosophical speculation on a divine eternity reached a high point in the seventh chapter of Plotinus's *Third Ennead*. The divine eternal selfsame is the whole as present without extension or duration. This is contrasted with the mutability of time. Similar to Plato and Aristotle, Plotinus could treat of judgment only as a synthesis of subjects and predicates, so that the notion of being was a conceptual content to be known by a direct act of

---

6. Cf. E. Gilson, *Being and Some Philosophers,* second corrected edition (Toronto: PIMS, 1952); John F. Wippel, *The Metaphysical Thought of Thomas Aquinas: From Finite Being to Uncreated Being* (Washington, D.C.: The Catholic University of America Press, 2001), 23–62, 585–94; C. Fabro, *Participation et causalité selon S. Thomas d'Aquin* (Louvain: Publications Universitaires de Louvain, 1961); Rudi A. te Velde, *Participation and Substantiality in Thomas Aquinas* (Leiden: E. J. Brill, 1995); Bernard Lonergan, *Verbum: Word and Idea in Aquinas* (Toronto: University of Toronto Press, 1997), 60–105.

understanding (ἐννοεῖν) rather than by the indirect way of analogically understanding that we know in judgment. The divine eternal being is that which "always exists" beyond all extension and duration. The eternal and the temporal are opposites, and the task of the true philosopher or mystic is to leave behind all the temporal for the super-intuition of the eternal. Eternity is "intelligible nature" (Φύσις νοητική), which is contrasted with and transcends time, which is identified as the whole order of the heavens and earth. The antithesis of understanding and what is understood is heightened into the antithesis of the eternal and the temporal. Plotinus did not overcome but only intensified the contrast between the eternal and the temporal in Plato.[7] Proclus then sought to explain how the eternal One, as the unknown and imparticipable cause of all, is super-eminent and produces all the eternal beings-unities or gods, who know all things immediately: wholes and parts, beings and nonbeings, things eternal and things temporal. So Proclus would introduce the mediation of the Roman gods.[8]

In a proposition of Proclus Aquinas captures the conceptuality and limitations of his stance insofar as it does not move beyond grammar and logic to realist metaphysics:

For Proclus introduces this proposition according to Platonist suppositions that posit the abstraction of universals: the more abstract and universal something is they placed that much more prior to *esse*. For it is clear that the noun eternity is more abstract than eternal; for the noun eternity designates the essence of eternity, whereas the word eternal is that which participates in eternity.[9]

To understand eternity required both an appropriation of intelligence as not intrinsically conditioned by space or time and a grasp of the concreteness of being known by judgment. Only if these came together would there be the proper analogue for understanding God as the eternal creating the temporal. Attempting any metaphysics of divine eternity based only upon a logic of concepts leads to an emanationism that requires gods and/or world soul to account for finite intelligibilities, and matter to account for temporality and evil.

---

7. Cf. Pierre Hadot, *Plotinus and the Simplicity of Vision*, trans. Michael Chase (Chicago: University of Chicago Press, 1993). Plotinus distinguished the Divine One from Divine Mind in order to allow an intellectual mysticism that would not, however, bring multiplicity into the Divine One. Augustine saw the inadequacy of this Plotinian position; on the consequences for political philosophy, cf. Fortin, *The Birth of Philosophic Christianity*, ed. Brian Benestad (Lanham, Md.: Rowman and Littlefield, 1996), 181–87.

8. Proclus, *Elements of Theology*, Greek text with English trans. by E. R. Dodds (Oxford: Oxford University Press, 1933).

9. *Expositio super Librum de causis* 2.

So in his first lecture on John, the opening sentence of the Gospel, "In the beginning was the Word, and the Word was with God, and the Word was God," leads Aquinas to set forth briefly how a faith-informed assent to the truth of this revelation requires a proper understanding of intelligence if one is to understand the doctrine on the Word. Because words are both external and internal, and inner words precede outer, he distinguishes the human mind as a power or faculty from the species of the thing understood as its form, and both these from the operation *(intelligere)* of the mind. "That therefore is properly termed an inner word that the one understanding forms [by the act of] understanding" *(Ioan.* 1, lect. 1, n. 25).[10] Because there are two operations of the mind (understanding and judging), Aquinas draws on Augustine to indicate how the inner word relevant to John's Word is not just the concept formed by the first operation of the mind, but the full inner word in which *(in quo)* the mind knows the reality understood. Moreover, the proper analogue is not the human mind knowing things outside itself, but, again following Augustine, the image of the Trinity is the mind truly understanding itself, because "when the intellect understands itself, then this kind of word is the likeness and intelligibility *(ratio)* of the intellect" *(Ioan.* 1, lect. 1, n. 25).[11]

With the proper analogue established, Aquinas can then show how Augustine indicates three major differences between created intelligence and the divine intelligence. First, inner words in us are first only in potency, and only by reflecting further about a thing in discursive inquiry do we come to know the thing truly in a judgment that forms a "word that is already formed in accord with a perfect contemplation of the truth." But the divine Word is always in act *(Ioan.* 1, lect. 1, n. 26). Second, our inner words are always imperfect,

> For since we cannot express all our conceptions in one word, we must form many imperfect words through which we separately express all that is in our knowledge. But it is not that way with God. For since He understands both Himself and everything else through His essence, by one act, the single Divine Word is expressive of all that is in God, not only of the Persons but also of creatures; otherwise it would be imperfect *(Ioan.* 1, lect. 1, n. 27).

Third, when our mind knows itself, the inner word is not our nature. But the Divine Word is of the same nature with God, subsisting in the divine nature *(Ioan.* 1, lect. 1, n. 28).

Aquinas then proceeds to show that *in principio* can be taken to teach three things about the Word: he is the origin of all creatures; he is consub-

---

10. *Illud ergo proprie dicitur verbum interius, quod intelligens intelligendo format.*
11. *Quando intellectus intelligit se, tunc huiusmodi verbum est similitudo et ratio intellectus;* my translation.

stantial with the Father, and the Word is co-eternal with the other Divine Persons. The co-eternity of the Word indicates how the relations of time to eternity cannot be defined by physical or imaginative space-time. Just as the Father generating the Son is not like a human generation, where fathers pre-exist their sons, so Aquinas warns his readers not to fall into a picture thinking, imagining that the eternity is a duration, or that the Word being "with" *(apud)* God designated spatial extension. Aquinas shows how neither grammar (verb tenses) nor logical concepts drawn from quantitative space-time suffice of themselves. Only a mind tutored in realist metaphysics is able to do justice to the truth expressed grammatically and logically in the texts of John.

[T]he sense of "In the beginning was the Word" is that the Word was before all things, as Augustine explains it. According to Basil and Hilary, this phrase shows the eternity of the Word. The phrase "in the beginning was the Word" shows that no matter which beginning of duration is taken, whether of temporal things which is time, or of aeviternal things which is the aeon, or of the whole world, or any imagined span of time reaching back for many ages, at that beginning the Word already was. (*Ioan.* 1, lect. 1, n. 37)

Eternity transcends the four-dimensional world of past, present, future, and place. And it is the eternal Word who creates the four-dimensional universe of space and time. So Aquinas indicates both how John uses the past imperfect *(erat)* to refer to eternal realities that already were in whatever past and still exist and how the present tense, alluding to Augustine's exploration of intelligent presence of a mind being knowingly present to itself, is most appropriate for signifying eternity:

But in so far as concerns the notion of the present, the best way to designate eternity is the present tense, which indicates that something is in act, and this is always the characteristic of eternal things. And so it says in Exodus (3:14): "I am who am." And Augustine says: "He alone truly is whose being does not know a past and a future." (*Ioan.* 1, lect. 1, n. 39)

Aquinas shows how the text of John tutors the mind of a faithful reader to transcend imaginative distortions because implicit in the text is a realist metaphysics of *esse* that has overcome a false confusion of reality with extension and duration. A key for Aquinas is realizing how John reveals an intellectualist generation of the Son by the Father. It is neither by thinking *(cogitatio)* nor by willing that the Son is generated, but by true understanding that transcends any succession or duration:

Again, it is impossible that the generation of the Word involve succession: for then the divine Word would be unformed before it was formed (as happens in us who form words by "cogitating"), which is false, as was said. Again, we cannot say that the

Father pre-established a beginning of duration for His Son by His own will, because God the Father does not generate the Son by His will, as the Arians held, but naturally: for God the Father, understanding Himself, conceives the Word; and so God the Father did not exist prior to the Son. (*Ioan.* 1, lect. 1, n. 41)

Aquinas then proceeds to emphasize how the knowledge of God implicates a realism that transcends the limitations of extension and duration:

You say that the Word was in the beginning, i.e., before all things. But before all things there was nothing. So if before all things there was nothing, where then was the Word? This objection arises due to the imaginings of those who think that whatever exists is somewhere and in some place. But this is rejected by John when he says, "with God" . . . not in some place, since He is not circumscribable, but He is with the Father, who is not enclosed by any place. . . . From whom is the Word if He exists before all things? The Evangelist answers: "the Word was with God," i.e., although the Word has no beginning of duration, still He does not lack a *principium* or author, for He was with God as His Author. (*Ioan.* 1, lect. 1, nn. 47–48)[12]

The first lecture ends appropriately by indicating how the opening sentences of the Gospel refute pagan polytheism, as well as the errors of heretics. Aquinas shows, for example, how Arius misreads the opening sentences of John because, unlike the orthodox Fathers, he does not acknowledge that the Son is consubstantial and co-eternal with the Father. These errors, along with others such as those of Sabellius, stem from an infidelity whereby the light of the true Catholic faith is darkened and imaginative durations and subordinations distort the Gospel (*Ioan.* 1, lect. 1, nn. 60–64). How the light of faith heals the light of reason can be glimpsed in how the Gospel excludes errors of some ancient philosophers. Pre-Socratic materialists such as Democritus held that the universe results by mere material chance, so that the original cause is not reason and intelligent purpose, but matter in flux. Among idealist errors were those of Plato, that separate intelligible Ideas, separated from God, were the cause of all things, and those of some of his school, which held that only the Father was supreme God and that the Ideas were subordinated to Him. And, while Aristotle recognized the identity of intellect, the act of understanding, and the object understood, and so thought of the Ideas as in God, he seems to have made the world co-eternal with God (*Ioan.* 1, lect. 1, n. 65).[13]

---

12. *Incircumscriptibile* is translated as "not circumscribable" rather than with "unsurroundable."

13. Note that this error Aquinas attributes to Aristotle is not the same as the sempiternity of the world that could be philosophically maintained. The sempiternity of the world does not make the world co-eternal with God. In the *De aeternitate mundi* Aquinas makes this point: "And so it is said that in no way can anything be coeternal with God, because nothing is

But, as Aquinas concludes, the Word of God exceeds all times: present, past, and future (*Ioan.* 1, lect, n. 67).[14]

In the *Summa contra gentiles* much use is made of Aristotle in the proofs for existence of God: how we know God *via remotionis,* then a series of chapters dealing with how God transcends all finite beings, beginning with God as eternal and ending with divine simplicity and perfection.[15] In the *Summa theologiae* the order is reversed, indicating how the simplicity, perfection, and goodness of God leads to the divine presence immanent in all being, and ending with God as immutable and eternal.[16] Aquinas clearly states that "not only is God eternal, but God is his eternity."[17] Only God is eternity as the fullness of being *(esse)* or life totally present.[18] God's ubiquitous presence is really the presence of all finite existence in the act of God creating, which act is identical with God's own being. Because God is pure being *(esse),* understanding *(intelligere),* and loving *(amare),* the act of creating all things is a supremely free act, since God in no way depends on creatures, while all of creation depends utterly on God. As eternity is identified most properly with God, so too is time identified most properly with material creation.[19]

In the second lecture on chapter 1 of John, Aquinas explicates the various meanings of "all things were made through Him, and without Him was made nothing that was made." What has to be kept in mind is that by "all things" is meant precisely that. God creates the totality of the spatio-temporal universe; everything that is not God is totally dependent upon Him. The whole span of time, all singular things and events of all the past, all the present, and all the future exist and are known in the eternal Triune God:

Since therefore God is eternal, His knowledge must have the mode of eternity, which is to be totally at once without succession. Hence even though all time is successive, nonetheless His eternity is present to all times by one and the same and indivisible eternal now; so also His knowledge intuits all temporal things. . . . Hence Boethius remarks that [God's knowledge] is better called providence than pre-knowledge: because it is not as it were of the future, but He sees all things by one glance as present,

---

immutable but God alone, as is evident in what Augustine says in Book XII of the *City of God,* chapter 15: 'time, because it runs through constant changes cannot be coeternal with immutable eternity.'"

14. John says "the Word was" "in order to show that the Word of God exceeds all times, namely present, past, and future. It was as if he said: He was beyond present, past, and future time."

15. *SCG* I, chs. 14–28.

16. *ST* I, qq. 3–11.

17. *ST* I, q. 10, a. 2.

18. Augustine in *Confessions* XI, 11 refers to God alone as *totum esse praesens.*

19. Cf. Brian J. Shanley, "Eternity and Duration in Aquinas," *Thomist* 61 (1997): 525–48.

as it were from the mirror of eternity. It can, however, be called pre-knowledge inasmuch as He knows what is future for us but it is not future for Him.[20]

Aquinas often called attention to the hypothetical necessity of true judgments about all contingent free events:

For pre-knowledge does not impose necessity on things neither insofar as it is a cause, since it is the first cause, whose conditioning does not have an effect, but the proximate causes; nor [is necessity imposed] by reason of the conformity of the thing known which is required by reason of the truth and certitude of the knowledge; because that conformity is present to God's knowledge of a thing, not according to how the thing is in its causes, in which it is only a possible future thing, but [the conformity in God's knowledge] to the thing is insofar as it itself is, having a determinate *esse*, as it is present, and not as a future.[21]

The eternal Triune God creates the totality of all things, and so the divine act of creating embraces all created things and events. Yet this does not impose any necessity on the things or events because the eternal God is not "before" time in any temporal sense of "before." God knows what is going to happen, and which choices every human being is going to make, next year, next century, and so on. While these events are future to us, they are all present to God in His eternal *esse-intelligere-amare*.[22]

The lectures on John reference this theological understanding of eternity and time. In a beautiful reflection on the revelation of creation by the Word, Aquinas indicates that the divine Word is intimate to all that is.

However, there is a difference between the way the Word acts and causes all things and the way in which other agents act. For other agents act as existing externally: since they do not act except by moving and altering a thing qualitatively in some way

---

20. I *Sent.*, d. 38, q. 1, a. 5 (my translation). On the divine knowledge of singulars, cf. *ST* I, q. 14, a. 11; also Frederick Crowe, "Rethinking Eternal Life," *Science et Esprit* 45 (1993): 25–39 and 145–59, on the four-dimensional universe.

21. Thomas Aquinas, I *Sent.*, d. 40, q. 3, a. 1; my translation. This line of argument runs throughout Aquinas's writings, e.g., *ST* I, q. 14, a. 13; *Expositio super Librum de causis* 11, 30. Cf. Brian Shanley, "Eternal Knowledge of the Temporal in Aquinas," *American Catholic Philosophical Quarterly* 71 (1997): 1–28.

22. Cf. Lonergan, *Grace and Freedom: Operative Grace in the Thought of St. Thomas Aquinas* (Toronto: University of Toronto Press, 2000), 107: "If the future is known with certainty, then necessarily it must come to be; and what necessarily must come to be, is not contingent but necessary. But St. Thomas denies that God knows events as future. He is not in time but an eternal 'now' to which everything is present. Hence, when you say, 'If God knows this, this must be,' the 'this' of the apodosis must be taken in the same sense as the 'this' of the protasis. But the 'this' of the protasis is present; therefore, the 'this' of the apodosis is present; it follows that 'this must be' is not absolute but hypothetical necessity: 'necesse . . . est Socratem currere dum currit.'"

with respect to its exterior, they work from without. But God acts in all things from within, because He acts by creating. Now to create is to give existence *(esse)* to the thing created. So, since *esse* is innermost in each thing, God, who by acting gives *esse*, acts in things from within. Hence God was in the world as One giving *esse* to the world. . . . He is present everywhere by His essence, because His essence is innermost in all things. For every agent, as acting, has to be immediately joined to its effect, because mover and moved must be together. Now God is the maker and preserver of all things, with respect to the *esse* of each. Hence, since the *esse* of a thing is innermost in that thing, it is plain that God, by His essence, through which He creates all things, is in all things. (*Ioan.* 1, lect. 5, nn. 133–4)

The whole universe and each and every being in it finitely participate in *esse*, and so God is in all that is since his essence alone is *esse*. This is not any form of pantheism, for only God's essence is his existence. The absolute and unique transcendence of God grounds his intimate immanence. God is not world-soul or form, God is *esse*, and so all creatures can exist only by, in, with, and for God.

Following Origen, Aquinas illustrates this by an analogy. As the human vocal sound is to the inner word in the mind, so are creatures to the divine Word: as vocal sounds are the effects of inner words conceived in our mind, so creatures are the effect of the Word conceived in the Divine Mind, "For He spoke, and they were created" (Ps 148:5).

Hence, just as we notice that as soon as our inner word vanishes, the sensible vocal sounds also cease, so, if the power of the divine Word were withdrawn from things, all of them would immediately cease to be at that very instant. (*Ioan.* 1, lect. 5, n. 135; my translation)

The presence of all of creation in the Word was spurned by intelligent creatures that turned away from the light of the divine presence. The darkness of sin and disordered desires are not the result, as it was for ancient philosophers, of matter (e.g. Plotinus) or cosmic rivalry among gods (e.g. Proclus). Evil results from intelligent creatures willfully turning away from the light, loving themselves and the world apart from the Word (*Ioan.* 1, lect. 5, nn. 137–41). Having spurned the divine presence in the world, the Father sent his Son to redeem fallen creatures. In the Incarnation the Person of the Divine Word is made flesh.

So we come to the startling statement of Aquinas with which the essay began. The Word is now present not only as cause of all that is but in his own Person united to a human nature in Jesus Christ, born of the Virgin Mary, now visibly present in time and space. The eternal Word embraces all human beings throughout all time, and the grace of Christ as Head of the Church is literally "infinite in its influence," for Christ can save not only all human beings in this world, but also "those of many worlds if they were to exist."

Thus, the soul of Christ has infinite grace and grace without measure from the fact that it [the soul of Christ] has united to itself the Word, which is infinite and unfailing source of the entire emanation of all created things. For what has been said, it is clear that the grace of Christ which is called capital grace, insofar as He is head of the Church, is infinite in its influence. For from the fact that He possessed that from which the gifts of the Spirit could flow out without measure, He received the power to pour them out without measure, so that the grace of Christ is sufficient not merely for the salvation of some men, but for all the people of the entire world . . . (1 Jn. 2:2), and even for many worlds, if they were to exist. (*Ioan.* 3, lect. 6, n. 544; my translation)

For any and all worlds are created and so whatever and however many worlds exist they are by, in, and for the Triune God. The influence of Christ, the Word Incarnate, extends to all that exists.

This infinite influence of Christ as Head of the Church with its strong emphasis on his universal mediation of salvation is firmly rooted in Aquinas's theology of the hypostatic union. His notion of how the eternal Word incarnate through his human nature has an infinite influence comes out in his lectures on chapter 6 when discussing the sacraments and the Eucharist. The Church with her Scriptures and sacraments continues the visible and invisible missions of the Son and Holy Spirit. Aquinas points out how the other sacraments have singular effects, whereas the Eucharist, because it contains the whole Christ (body, soul, divinity) in his immolation on the cross and his resurrection has a universal effect. For the effect of the Eucharist is the effect of the passion, death, and resurrection of Christ: the destruction of death and the restoration of life. The sacraments, and primordially the Eucharist, participate in the universal efficacy of the paschal mystery of the risen Christ by being present and effective visibly in particular places at specific times (*Ioan.* 6, lect. 6, nn. 961–64). The universality of salvation in Christ Jesus is not an "abstract" or "classicist" or "idealist" universality; it is the concrete universality of the Word Incarnate to whom all times and places are present in all their concrete singularity.

All times are present to this concrete universality of the eternal Word incarnate in Jesus Christ. It extends as well to the past. Thus in lecturing on chapter 8 on "Abraham rejoiced to see my day. . . . Amen, Amen I say to you, before Abraham came to be, I AM," Aquinas sees a twofold "day of Christ": the eternal day of his proceeding from the Father, and the temporal day of his Incarnation. The "I AM" of Exodus 3:14 is Jesus Christ, the Word Incarnate, "for eternal existence knows neither past nor future time, but embraces all time in one indivisible presence" (*Ioan.* 8, lect. 8, nn. 1287–90; my translation).

There are many other ways in which Aquinas's understanding of eternity and time influences his theological interpretation of the truth of John's Gospel. It informs his treatment of the passion and death of Christ for the sins of all, with a suffering and pain *(dolor)* that is greater than any other suffering because of who Jesus Christ is. It comes out in the ways the risen body of the Lord transcends the earthly limitations of space and time while embracing them all. His mission and that of the Holy Spirit are continued in the concrete catholicity (universality) of the apostolic succession as the Church renders visible the Word of God Incarnate in the Eucharist and his sacraments and teachings. Clearly, the contemplative wisdom revealed in the Gospel of John is the most perfect knowledge of the eternal Word. But "even an infinite number of human words cannot equal *(attingere)* one Word of God" (*Ioan.* 21, lect. 6, n. 2660).

NINE

Divine Providence and John 15:5

STEVEN A. LONG

"Without me you can do nothing" (Jn 15:5). One of the chief meanings of these words according to St. Thomas Aquinas is—as he writes in chapter 67 of the first part of the third volume of the *Summa contra gentiles*—"That in all things that operate God is the cause of their operating." St. Thomas further writes in chapter 67:

> Hence it is clear that in all things that operate God is the cause of their operating. For everyone that operates is in some way a cause of being, either of essential or of accidental being. But nothing is a cause of being except in so far as it acts by God's power. Therefore everyone that operates acts by God's power.

This teaching remains the source of great difficulties for those who wish to preserve theism while denying divine omnipotence. And this category of brow-furrowed theists contains more occupants than may at first be apparent. Speech about human freedom often supposes that the reality of a free act cannot be caused by God. It is widely thought that if God is a cause of the free human act, then this cause must be only a remote precondition—a sort of deistic stage-setting—and not a causality that extends as far as moving the human person freely to act, actualizing the person's free self-determination. Yet the denial that God activates and moves human creatures freely depicts divine causality as coercive or violent, and defines human freedom in metaphysical terms more proportioned to God than to a creature that can neither be nor act apart from God.

This strongly contrasts with the teaching of St. Thomas, who describes the divine causality of freedom as follows:

> Free-will is the cause of its own movement, because by his free-will man moves himself to act. But it does not of necessity belong to liberty that what is

free should be the first cause of itself, as neither for one thing to be cause of another need it be the first cause. God, therefore, is the first cause, Who moves causes both natural and voluntary. And just as by moving natural causes He does not prevent their acts being natural, so by moving voluntary causes He does not deprive their actions of being voluntary: but rather is He the cause of this very thing in them; for He operates in each thing according to its own nature. (*ST* I, q. 83, a. 1, ad 3)

Far from moving the human will violently, God is the cause of the natural motion of the will, constituting it as what it is. He articulates the same point more starkly in the following lines from *De malo,* q. 3, a. 2, ad 4:

When anything moves itself, this does not exclude its being moved by another, from which it has even this that it moves itself. Thus it is not repugnant to liberty that God is the cause of the free act of the will.

Indeed, apart from God the natural motion of the will could neither be—it is not self-existent—nor be applied to action, since the act of the will represents a surplus of actuality that itself must be reducible to the first cause. Everything that moves from potency to act is moved by another in act—indeed, *quod movetur ab alio movetur* is for St. Thomas an evident principle.

Thomas considers that God is the first author both of the will's being and of its natural motion and free choice. God moves necessary things necessarily, and contingent things contingently.[1] He puts the point pronouncedly when he writes:

Man is master of his acts, both of his willing and not willing, because of the deliberation of reason, which can be bent to one side or another. And although he is master of his deliberating or not deliberating, yet this can only be by a previous deliberation; and since this cannot go on to infinity, we must come at length to this, that man's free choice is moved by an extrinsic principle, which is above the human mind, namely by God, as the Philosopher proves in the chapter on *Good Fortune.*[2]

God is the first mover, the first object of appetite, and the first willer. Thus as he puts it, "every application of power to action is chiefly and primarily from God."[3] On this account the positive substance of our own willing is, like our very existence, simultaneously most our own while being simultaneously most a gift.

Freedom of the will, for St. Thomas, is rooted in the intellect. He teaches that the will has the natural character of being undeterminable by finite goods,[4] as this pertains to the motion of the will as an *inclinatio sequens for-*

---

1. Cf. *ST* I-II, q. 10, a. 4, ad 1.
2. *ST* I-II, q. 109, a. 2, ad 1.
3. *SCG* III, ch. 67.
4. *ST* I q. 82, a. 2, ad 2.

mam intellectam, an inclination following the form of reason.[5] Because the object of the will is universal or rational good, no finite good is so compelling that reason is bound to command the will to embrace it. Every limited or finite good is, in some respect, perceivable as *not good.* For instance it is good to get up in the morning—but it is bad to do so because one is weary. It is good to read a great work of literature—but it is bad, because it strains the eyes. It is good for you at the conference to listen to the papers, but it is bad, because I am verbose, or you need coffee, or—God forbid—you prefer the philosophy of Jean-Paul Sartre. Every finite good is by its nature limited and from some point of view not-good: no created good *is* the subsisting universal good.[6]

As St. Thomas everywhere makes clear, freedom is defined not in relation to God and to a spurious liberty of indeterminacy with respect to divine causality—which is a metaphysical impossibility—but rather it is defined in relation to the will's finite terrestrial objects.[7] Since we affirm or negate God primarily in our response to created things, and naturally lack a direct knowledge of God, the human person's response to God is free. But if one achieves the beatific knowledge of God, then God is known as he is: the perfect Good who is in no way undesirable, and who answers and fulfills the order divinely instilled in the human heart. This divine ordering of the person is not subject to human dominion or caveat. Thus if one were to merit the beatific vision there could be no possibility of refusing God because the will would be utterly perfected in cleaving to perfect Good.

It must be noted that there are many implications of Thomas's teaching

---

5. *Quaestiones Quadlibetales,* Quodlibet 6, q. 2, a. 2.

6. Every finite good is by its nature limited and from some point of view not-good: no created good *is* the subsisting universal good. Were willing held *not* to be an inclination following the form of reason, this would curiously imply either that the will were itself an intellect, or else that we could will without any object of will.

7. St. Thomas makes clear that human freedom is defined vis-à-vis its natural objects, and not in relation to God. Cf. Leonine *De malo,* 16, 7, ad 15: "Et hoc quidem quantum ad scientiam patet ex his que supra dicta sunt: sic enim se habet diuina scientia ad futura contingentia sicut se habet oculus noster ad contingentia aue in presenti sunt, ut dictum est; unde sicut certissime uidemus Sortem sedere dumsedet, nec tamen proper hoc sit simpliciter necessarium, ita etiam ex hoc quod Deus uidet omnia que eueniunt in se ipsis, non tollitur contingentia rerum. Ex parte autem uoluntatis considerandum est quod uoluntas diuina est uniuersaliter causa entis et uniuersaliter omnium que consequntur <<ipsum>>, unde et necessitatis et contingentie; ipsa autem est supra ordinem necessarii et contingentis sicut est supra totum esse creatum. Et ideo necessitas et contingentia in rebus distinguitur non per habitudinem ad uoluntatem diuinam que est causa communis, set per comparationem ad causas creatas, quas proportionaliter diuina uoluntas ad effectus ordinauit, ut scilicet necessariorum effectuum sint cause intransmutabiles, contingentium autem trnasmutabiles."

that account for the tendency to reject it. Some authors believe it too deeply implicates God in the scandal of moral evil; others think it insufficiently safeguards human liberty, or that salvation would be more accessible were it more wholly a function of a human act not indebted for its being to divine causality; and of course, continental a priorists live off the artificial dichotomy of nature and reason. All these objections cannot be fielded here. I will limit myself to a compressed consideration of two prime objections: first, a brief consideration of an objection founded on the confusion of self-determination with absolute independence; and second, a more lengthy but still quite limited consideration of a confusion that has clouded the understanding of the relation of God and the will by misconstruing Thomas's teaching regarding God and the permission of evil.

As to the first objection, the denial of God's causality of free human acts seems predicated on the confusion of self-determination with absolute independence. But as St. Thomas points out, an agent may be self-determining and still not be the *first cause* of that self-determination, just as an agent may be a *cause* of being without being *the first cause.*

The actuality of a thing is not a static possession, but is at each instant received from and preserved by God. As this is true of first act, it is alike true of second act or operation. Were we not caused to be, and caused to be rational and free; did our wills not receive their natural motion from God; and were this natural motion not then further activated and applied by the superior agency of God, *then* we would neither cause ourselves to exist, nor bestow upon our wills their nature and natural motion, nor apply the natural motion of our wills without being moved from potency to act with respect to that very act whereby we determine ourselves. That self-determination has *conditions* does not detract from the fact that it is self-determination—although it does detract from the rationalist claim of absolute independence.[8] Further, a thing can only act as it *is,* and the creature is a creature—which is to say, dependent on God for its being. So, its action will ineluctably manifest such dependence. God causes necessary things necessarily, and contingent things contingently. That the motion supplied by God—who is the Author of the natural motion of the will, and so befittingly applies it to act—is not violent, but the creature's own motion, saves this teaching from any hint of occasionalism. For the will to determine itself, it must move from potency to act with respect to that determination: and it is this same motion which it receives

---

8. Thus speaking of voluntary causes (*ST* I, q. 83, a. 1, ad 3), Thomas argues that God "does not deprive their actions of being voluntary: but rather is He the cause of this very thing in them."

from God. The very motion by which the creature determines itself is that motion which it receives from God.

Secondly, as for the objection regarding God and the permission of evil, this profound questions calls for fuller treatment elsewhere.[9] But the principles that regard this great mystery are clearly and eloquently articulated by St. Thomas in his *Commentary on the Gospel of John:*

> Our choice is caused by some already existing good; while God's choice is the cause of an influx of good, greater in one than in another. Since choice is an act of the will, then according as the will of god and the human will are differently related to the good, so the character of their choice will be different. Now God's will is related to a created good as its cause: "How would anything have endured if thou hadst not willed it?" (Wis 11:25). And so goodness is dispensed to created things from the will of God. Accordingly, God prefers one person to another insofar as he confers more good on that one than on another. But the human will is moved to something by a preexisting good which has become known. Therefore in our choices it is necessary that one good exist before another. The reason why God confers more good on one than on another is so that there might be a splendor of order in things. This is clear in material things where prime matter of itself is uniformly disposed to all forms. Also, before things themselves exist, they are not disposed to this or that existence; rather, they receive different forms and existences from God so that an order can be established among them. It is like this among rational creatures where some are chosen for glory and some are rejected for punishment: "The Lord knows who are his. . . . In a great house there are not only vessels of gold and silver but also of wood and earthenware, and some for noble use, some for ignoble" (2 Tim 2:19). And so we see a diversified order: the mercy of God shines forth in those whom, without any previous merits, he prepares for grace; in others we see the justice of God when, because of their own guilt, he allots them punishment, yet less than is deserved. So, I have chosen you by predestining you from all eternity, and by calling you to the faith during your lifetime. (*Ioan.* 15, lect. 3, n. 2024)

It is worthy of note that while punishment presupposes guilt, Thomas states that *being chosen* for glory or *rejected* for punishment is "like" the "reception of different forms and existences from God so that an order can be established among them"—a phrase immediately followed by "It is like this among rational creatures where some are chosen for glory and others for punishment": *Ipsae etiam res antequam sint, non sunt dispositae ad hoc vel illud esse; sed ut servetur ordo in eis, diversas formas et diversum esse sortiuntur a Deo. Et* similiter *in creatura rationali quidam eliguntur ad gloriam, quidam reprobantur ad poenam.*[10] One observes that *there is no reference to this presup-*

---

9. For a detailed analysis see my "Providence, liberté et loi naturelle," *Revue Thomiste* 102 (2002): 355–406.

10. Emphasis added.

posing sin, but on the contrary it is expressly said to be like "the reception of different forms and existences from God so that an order can be established among them."

Thus sin presupposes the divine permission of evil, a permission understood as God's, for the sake of a higher good, not sustaining the creature in good. Nor may it be cogently objected that this passage refers only to the diffusion of diverse degrees of being and good, and not to evil—for evil is precisely the deprivation of a good, such that the degree of good that one possesses who suffers either physical or moral evil *is limited.* And the passage in question pertains to how it is that the good enjoyed by one creature is a lesser or more limited good than that of another, and is directly applied within this same passage to those in whom God's mercy shines forth, as opposed to the guilty in whom God's justice is manifest. In other words, absolutely speaking, God ordains being and good from eternity, and likewise permits evil not as creatures "permit," but in the sense of not sustaining the creature in good and thereby relinquishing the creature to its own defectibility for the sake of some higher good. Many more passages exist throughout St. Thomas's writings indicating that this is indeed his teaching. For example:

> To sin is nothing else than to fall from the good which belongs to any being according to its nature. Now as every created thing has no being unless from another, and considered in itself is nothing, so does it need to be conserved by another in the good which pertains to its nature. For it can of itself fall from good, just as of itself it can fall into nonbeing, unless it is conserved by God (*ST* I-II, q. 109, a. 2, ad 2).

Observe the sense of the "can" in the above passage: that is, it is not that a thing may or may not fall out of being if God does not sustain it in being; and "just as" with being, it is not as though a thing may or may not fall from good if it is not conserved in good by God. If not conserved in being and good, the thing will fail of its being and good. One notes again that far from Thomas affirming that this presupposes the datum of sin in this passage—a frequent rhetorical objection—rather, this passage is phrased, just as is his observation from the Commentary, *in absolute terms.* This is, in a nutshell, the core of the teaching of negative reprobation: reprobation is not positive—not something God actively *does* or *causes*—but rather something God permits in relinquishing the creature to its own defectibility when he does not sustain it in good. This is always for the sake of some higher good, because it is impossible that God—who is the infinite subsistent Good—should will evil as such. And, to cite one other text of St. Thomas, from *Summa theologiae* I, q. 20, a. 4:

> It should be stated that it is necessary to say, according to what has been said before, that God loves more the better things. For it has been shown that God's loving one

thing more than another is nothing else than His willing for that thing a greater good: because God's will is the cause of goodness in things. And thus the reason why some things are better than others, is that God wills for them a greater good. Hence it follows that He loves more the better things.

"As every created thing has no being unless from another, and considered in itself is nothing, so does it need to be conserved by another in the good which pertains to its nature. For it can of itself fall from good, just as of itself it can fall into nonbeing, unless it is conserved by God." "And thus the reason why some things are better than others, is that God wills for them a greater good." Some of the greatest Thomists of the twentieth century have blanched before St. Thomas's words, unable to accept their plain meaning and affirmation of negative reprobation (as opposed to the positive reprobation of the Calvinists, with which certain authors perpetually confuse it).

Thus, Jacques Maritain suggested that God moves man by impedible motions that can be "shattered" by a negation of the creature that he refers to as the creature "noughting" or "nihilating." This view, were it true, would enable one to hold that evil does not infallibly flow from the divine permission. Rather than divine permission consisting in non-sustenance in good, divine permission would then approximate the "permission" given by one creature to another, which latter creaturely permission is consistent with acting or not acting. Several authors seem to hold such views, and there is dispute about the origin of Maritain's account. But in any case the root incompatibility with Thomas's text here and elsewhere is clear. This type of explanation involves the view—expressly held by Maritain—that "non-negation" is *formally prior* to the reception of divine motion. As Maritain puts it:

It is proper to remark here that if "not to nihilate" and "to consider the rule" come practically to the same thing, nevertheless there is, formally, a clear distinction between the two, and the first formality is the condition of the second.[11]

Yet it is clearly true—and equally clearly held by St. Thomas Aquinas—that *in a real subject* the negation of negation (i.e., "non-negation") is not really different from something positive. If one does not *not* have a nose, this is no different than saying that one does have a nose. To put it in St. Thomas's words, "the destruction of non-white is not really different than the coming to be of white" (cf. *De veritate* III.28).[12] Hence to say that "non-negation" of

---

11. Jacques Maritain, *Existence and the Existent,* trans. Lewis Galantiere and Gerald B. Phelan (New York: Pantheon Books, 1948), p. 100, note #10.

12. Leonine *De veritate* [hereafter *De. ver.*] III, 28, resp.: "Quaedam vero opposita sunt quorum alterum tantum est natura quaedam, reliquum vero non est nisi remotio vel negatio ipsius,

divine motion is formally *prior* to receiving the divine motion is to forget that "non-negation" of the divinely bestowed motion *is not really different than this motion of the creature itself.* In other words, the view that non-negation of divine motion is prior to the divine motion in the creature is a clear fallacy, for non-negation is not really distinct from the motion bestowed upon the creature.

It is not, as some have thought, a question of fallible or infallible motions from God. For any fallible motion is fallible either because of something positive (and God is the cause of all being) or something negative (and hence something that God does not deign to cause). Hence, as God ordains from all eternity the whole sum of creation, and knows what he causes, he knows evil indirectly in two ways: first in the permissive decree in which he does not sustain a defectible creature in good for the sake of some higher good. For he knows exactly what he causes, and the decree determining this good is indeed such as to exclude that good which creaturely evil excludes, an evil divinely permitted only for the sake of some higher good related to the manifestation of the divine mercy and justice. And secondly God knows evil indirectly in his eternal knowledge of all created things as present, whereby he knows them with the limits of that being and good which he efficaciously ordains for them. That God permits evil is not for God to cause evil, any more than for a wise man not to counsel the ignorant is for him to be the cause of ignorance. And this is the great lesson of humility: that of ourselves we cannot sustain ourselves in good, anymore than of ourselves we can sustain ourselves in being.

The retreat from negative reprobation, under the assumption that it makes God responsible for sin, or shares in the Calvinist error of the natural corruption of man, forgets that insofar as we can say sin has a cause it is precisely the creature's own defectible nature. Nor does this mean that the creature is of itself evil, but only that the creature is of itself defectible—it is able to be moved to the end, and also able not to be so moved. This might be thought to imply that God treats persons merely as means to an end. But persons are treated with utterly condign mercy and justice insofar as they receive

---

sicut patet in oppositis secundum affirmationem et negationem, vel secundum privationem et habitum; et in talibus negatio oppositi quod ponit naturam aliquam, est realis quia est alicuius rei, negatio vero alterius oppositi non est realis, quia non est alicuius rei, est enim negatio negationis; et ideo haec negatio negationis quae est negatio alterius oppositi, nihil differt secundum rem a positione alterius; unde secundum rem idem est generatio albi et corruptio non albi. Sed quia negatio, quamvis non sit res naturae, est tamen res rationis, ideo negatio negationis secundum rationem sive secundum modum intelligendi est aliud a positione affirmationis; et sic corruptio non albi secundum modum intelligendi est aliud quam generatio albi."

far more than their due in good, and far less than their due in punishment (as noted by St. Thomas in his Commentary as cited above). Further, all intellectual creatures should see that the end of creation is the manifestation of the *summum bonum*. Although no finite universe is such that it could not be made better, still the infinitely Good God permits evil only for the sake of a more befitting manifestation and communication of the ultimate good.

To deny negative reprobation will be, in the end, to deny the convertibility of being and good, and to treat the creature's negation as though it were a positive being. It also will be to suppose that the divine permission is like a mere creature's permission, which allows of different outcomes. But, *sed contra:* if God for the sake of a higher good permits a rational creature to fall in the sense of not upholding that being in good, then that being will not be upheld in good, and will act freely and viciously; whereas, if God does ordain that a rational creature be upheld in good, then that creature will act freely and virtuously. One discerns once more the importance of Thomas's teaching that freedom is defined vis-à-vis the contingent objects of the will, and not in relation to God or to a spurious liberty of indeterminacy with respect to divine causality.

This finally brings us to a decisive implication of rejecting the Thomistic interpretation of the words, "Without me you can do nothing." If one denies that the human will receives not only its being, but also its natural motion and application to action from God, one makes of the will a *demiurgically unmoved first mover.* Divine providence extends only so far as the divine causality. It follows that if the human will is not subject to divine power then naturally it is not subject to the divine government. But natural law is nothing other than a mode of the divine government through secondary causality.

Thus if our free human acts escape dependence upon God for their coming-to-be, it will be an axiomatic inference to separate the governance of these acts from the divine government. Human action then comes to represent a zone of being and good *beyond the divine power and outside the scope of divine government.* This is contrary to the divine omnipotence and for this reason alone a foolish conclusion. But it also implies the impossibility of natural law.

Since the natural law is nothing other than a rational participation in the eternal law; and since man cannot be subject to divine ordering inasmuch as he is outside the divine power; it will then also follow that man's moral actions cannot be subject to natural law. The absolute and unconditional autonomy of the human will is incompossible with natural law. This is precisely the anti-theistic conclusion drawn by much of modernity and postmodernity.

Recall that on St. Thomas's account of the natural law, man first passively participates in the divine ordering of nature. All creatures receive their being, natures, and natural ordering passively from God. But because man is created rational, he receives being, nature, and natural ordering not only passively, but also—and by the very nature of this passive participation—receives these *actively, preceptively, and rationally:* as providing reasons to act or not to act. It is this finely delineated metaphysic of moral order that is jeopardized by suggesting that human agency is causally outside the sphere of divine governance. For how can a rule govern something that is outside the power of the ruler? The legislature of Michigan does not pass laws governing the molecular structure of carbon, nor does the Senate of the United States deliberate whether to command angels to pay more taxes. And although it may censure or disbar him, even the Supreme Court does not command Bill Clinton to be continent.

Once the Thomistic metaphysic of morals is denied, the implications for the moral life cascade. The normativity of the natural law will no longer reside in the identity of absolute being, truth, and good in God, but instead in the determinations of autonomous human reason. Nature and reason go from being manifestations and expressions of divine order to being either antipodes of divine order or perhaps to opposing one another in an endless and fruitless dialectic. God moves from being the author and perfector of human liberty and virtue, to being a threat to authentic human freedom and an alien distortive influence upon morality. The symmetry of these implications with Kantian autonomism is arresting. Yet unlike the express rationalism of Kant, these implications flow from an intra-Catholic source: metaphysical failure to reconcile divine providence and human freedom.

Somehow, the ensuing absolutely autonomous kingdoms of the will are brought under a different regime of divine law in revelation. Russell Hittinger has amusingly and profoundly described this problem as that of "Cartesian minds somehow under Church discipline."[13] If there could be a being utterly independent of divine causality and hence not ordered by or toward God, why would it then require divine direction?

Once human freedom is held to be causally independent of God, the conditions for the separation of natural and eternal law are achieved: the "prenuptial agreement" of their temporary cohabitation guarantees future calamitous conflict. Eternal law then is brought in—if it is brought in at all—only as a theological gloss on an already sufficiently constituted moral

---

13. Russell Hittinger, "Natural Law and Catholic Moral Theology," in *A Preserving Grace*, ed. Michael Cromartie (Grand Rapids, Mich.: Eerdmans, 1997), 1–30.

order, rather as the limits of jurisdiction of one sovereign power help to demarcate the limits of an adjacent kingdom.

This denial of God's causality over human freedom—not as we find it in the minds and with the motives of Catholic theologians such as Molina,[14] but simply in its objective character—thus appears to be a critical intra-Catholic contribution to the evolution of secularist anti-theism in the moral realm. For what do we mean by secularism save the claim that the public order is outside the jurisdiction of divine rule? And what could more directly imply this posture than the claim that our free actions are outside the divine government? It is the moral implications of this autonomism that Pope John Paul II addresses and corrects in *Veritatis splendor*.

"Without me you can do nothing." As Thomas writes of this passage in his *Commentary*, "Look at what our Lord says here! He says that without him we cannot do anything great, nor anything small, indeed, we cannot do anything at all" (*Ioan*. 15, lect. 1, n. 1993). Thus also St. Thomas concludes chapter 67 of the first part of the third book of the *Summa contra gentiles*:

Hence it is said (Isa. xxvi. 12): Lord, Thou hast wrought all our works in us: and (Jo. xv. 5): Without Me you can do nothing: and (Philip. ii. 13): It is God who worketh in us both to will and to accomplish, according to His good will. For this reason Holy Writ often ascribes natural effects to the divine operation: because He it is who works in every agent, natural or voluntary.

---

14. For an anticipation—and rejection—by St. Thomas of Molina's type of explanation (i.e., of the *scientia media*), see *Ioan*. 15, lect. 3, n. 2023: "Others say that it is true that our actually existing merits are not the cause of our predestination, but those merits preexisting in the foreknowledge of God are. Thus they say that because God knew that certain persons would be good and make good use of grace, he decided to give them grace. But if this were so, it would follow that the reason he chose us was because he foreknew we would choose him. And so our choice would be prior to the divine choice; which is contrary to our Lord's statement."

PART 4

The Moral Life

TEN

The Concept of "Life" in the *Commentary on St. John*

CARLO LEGET

The concept of "life" is without any doubt a key word in both Aquinas's theology and the Gospel of St. John. This can easily be shown as regards both statistics and content.[1] In this essay I will address two questions. The first question is how Thomas deals with this concept in his *Commentary on St. John*. In answering this question I will refer to other works of Aquinas where he deals with the concept of "life" and show how these interrelate. The second question concerns the way Aquinas's exegesis relates to doing theology at the threshold of the third millennium. This question is about hermeneutics, about the relationship between exegesis and systematic theology, and about the role of tradition in contemporary theology.

THE CONCEPT OF "LIFE" IN AQUINAS'S *COMMENTARY ON ST. JOHN*

Introduction

Since the fourth Gospel focuses on the divinity of the incarnate Word and the concept of "life" is a keyword in this Gospel, it seems

---

1. As regards the Gospel of John, George R. Beasley-Murray says: "In the teaching of Jesus, as in the writings contemporary with the New Testament, the supreme blessing of the Kingdom of God is 'life.' . . . It is of no small significance that the term 'life,' or 'eternal life,' occurs many more times in the Fourth Gospel than in any of the first three Gospels. Indeed, it is not too much to say that the key term of Jesus for salvation appropriated is the key term of the Gospel of John." (G. R. Beasley-Murray, *The Gospel of Life: Theology in the Fourth Gospel* [Peabody, Mass.: Hendrickson Publishers, 1991], 2). For the theology of Thomas Aquinas cf. my *Living with God: Thomas Aquinas on the Relation between Life on Earth and "Life" after Death* (Louvain: Peeters, 1997).

likely that the word "life" offers a special opportunity for communicating the mysteries of God. As a matter of fact, it does indeed, and grasping this special appropriateness, one should begin by noticing that "life" is a name of God. But "life" is also a word that indicates our mode of being. The task of the theologian consists in exploring the various uses and meanings of the word and its ramifications.

There are a few places in the *Commentary on St. John* where Thomas offers short sketches of different aspects of the concept of "life." In two places, he refers to the various grades of life. Explaining John 1:4, "And that life was the light of men," Thomas connects the grades of life with grades of knowledge:

For some things live, but do so without light, because they have no knowledge; for example plants. Hence their life is not light. Other things both live and know, but their knowledge, since it is on the sense level, is concerned only with individual and material things, as is the case with the brutes. So they have both life and a certain light. But they do not have the light of men, who live, and know, not only truths, but also the very nature of truth itself. Such are the rational creatures, to whom not only this or that are made manifest, but truth itself, which can be manifested and is manifestive to all. (*Ioan.* 1, lect. 3, n. 97)[2]

Commenting on chapter 5, Thomas distinguishes four grades of life: plants, animals that only sense, perfect animals that move, and those who understand (*Ioan.* 5, lect. 4, n. 771).

Thomas's discourse on the grades of life in the *Commentary on St. John* is in line with several of his other works.[3] It is connected with three meanings of the word "life," all of which can be traced back to Aristotle, that can be found in his works.

In a first meaning of the word, "life" refers to the existence of a being that possesses the ability to move itself in a certain manner. In this first meaning "life" is a substantial predicate, referring to the being of the subject, as is reflected in Aristotle's definition *vivere viventibus esse est*.[4] Thomas sees this basic dimension reflected in the order of prologue to the Gospel:

We find a fitting order in the above. For in the natural order of things, existence *(esse)* is first; and the Evangelist implies this in his first statement, "In the beginning was the Word." Secondly, comes life *(vivere);* and this is mentioned next, "In him was life." Thirdly comes understanding *(intelligere);* and that is mentioned next; "And that life was the light of men." (*Ioan.* 1, lect. 3, n. 100)

---

2. All English translations of fragments of Aquinas's *Commentary on John* are taken from or based upon the *Commentary on the Gospel of St. John*, trans. Weisheipl and Larcher.

3. Cf. *ST* I, q. 18, and *SCG* I, chs. 97–99.

4. II *De anima* 7 (415b13): "vivere autem viventibus est esse, causa autem et principium horum anima" (quoted in *ST* I, q. 18, a. 2, s.c.).

In a second meaning, which is less familiar to us than the first and the third, "life" refers to a specific act of a living substance that is characteristic for its mode of being. Thus the volitional and cognitive acts of human beings can be called their "life": these acts are characteristic for the human mode of being regarded as self-movement.[5] Again, we find this meaning of the concept "life" in Thomas's commentary on the fourth Gospel (cf. *Ioan.* 1, lect. 3, n. 97; 5, 4, n. 771; 14, 2, n. 1869). Commenting on the famous verse "I am the way, I am truth and life" (Jn 14:6), for example, he says:

Everything that has some activity from itself is said to be living, while non-living things do not have motion from themselves. Among the activities of life the chief are called the intellectual activities. Thus, the intellect *(intellectus)* itself is said to be living, and its activities are a certain kind of life *(et actio ejus est vitae quaedam)*. (*Ioan.* 14, lect. 2, n. 1869)

In a third meaning, the word "life" signifies the chief occupation or direction of a human being. Thus one can lead a honorable life, a contemplative life, and the like.[6] This third meaning of the word "life" can be found in a passage such as his commentary on the discussion between Christ and Nicodemus where Thomas explains:

For there is a sentient life that some living things share in common, and this life has a sentient vision or knowledge. And there is also a spiritual life by which man is made like God and other holy spirits; and this life enjoys a spiritual vision. (*Ioan.* 3, lect. 1, n. 432)

These three meanings in which the word "life" is used are closely connected by the notion of 'self-movement.' Since the human mode of being is an in-

---

5. IX *Eth.* 11 (1170a16): "Vivere autem determinant animalibus potentia sensus, hominibus autem sensus vel intellectus. Potentia autem ad operationem reducitur; principale autem in operatione. Videtur autem vivere esse principaliter sentire vel intelligere." Aquinas comments (*In* IX *Eth.* 11): "in omnibus animalibus communiter determinatur vivere secundum potentiam sensus, in hominibus autem determinatur secundum potentiam sensus, quantum ad id quod habet commune cum aliis animalibus, vel secundum potentiam intellectus, quantum ad id quod est proprium sibi. Omnis autem in potentia reducitur ad operationem sicut ad propriam perfectionem: unde id quod est principale consistit in operatione et non in potentia nuda, actus enim est potior quam potentia, ut probatur in IX Metaphysicae. Et ex hoc patet quod principaliter vivere animalis vel hominis est sentire vel intelligere."

6. I *Eth.* 5 (1095b14–19): "Bonum enim et felicitatem non irrationabiliter videntur ex his quae huius vitae sunt existimare. Multi quidem et gravissimi voluptatem. Ideo et vitam diligunt voluptuosam. Tres enim sunt maxime excellentes, et quae nunc dicta est et quae civilis est et tertia quae contemplativa est." Aquinas comments (*In* I *Eth* 5): "unusquisque id ad quod maxime afficitur reputat vitam suam, sicut philosophus philosophari, venator venari et sic de aliis. Et quia homo maxime afficitur ad ultimum finem, necesse est quod vitae diversificentur secundum diversitatem ultimi finis."

telligent mode of being, one could even say that, in the case of human beings, these meanings of the word "life" imply each other. The species *homo* is differentiated from the genus *animal* by the predicate *rationale* that refers to the intellectual operations; the nature of these operations determines the specific nature of human existence. In other words: the life (in the third meaning) we lead follows from our free deliberate choices ("life" in the second meaning) that follow from our mode of being ("life" in the first meaning).[7] This intertwinement of the three meanings of the concept of "life" will be met again and again in Thomas's explanation of the Gospel.

However much helpful this first orientation might be, Aquinas's commentary on the fourth Gospel remains a great puzzle as regards the many contexts and ways in which the concept is used. So where do we go from here? I propose to follow the directions Thomas himself gives in the prologue to his commentary (*Ioan.* prol., nn. 1–11). My choice for this approach is motivated by several reasons. In the first place it provides us with a framework in which the many ramifications of the concept of "life" can be organized. In the second place, it helps us to approach the concept of "life" through the lens of Aquinas's own hermeneutics. This has two advantages: first, it puts our interpretation in line with Aquinas's own method of working. And, second, it informs us about Aquinas's own hermeneutic presuppositions and points of departure. This will contribute to addressing the second part of this paper, where the question of contemporary relevance is discussed.

Aquinas's Prologue to the *Commentary on John*

Thomas begins his prologue with a verse of Isaiah 6:1:

> I saw the Lord seated on a high and lofty throne,
> and the whole universe was full of his majesty,
> and the things that were under him filled the temple.

He proposes to contemplate this verse, because it will help us understand the special nature of St. John's Gospel. According to Augustine, namely, the fourth Gospel adds something to the first three Gospels: whereas they are concerned with the active life *(vita activa)*, John also informs us about the

---

7. In *In* IX *Eth* 7 the connection of the different meanings can be detected: "Esse autem nostrum consistit in quodam actu, esse enim nostrum est vivere et per consequens operari (non enim est vita absque vitae operatione quacumque), unde unicuique est amabile operari opera vitae; faciens autem in actu est quodam modo ipsum opus facientis, actus enim moventis et agentis est in moto et patiente; ideo itaque diligunt opus suum et artifices et poetae et benefactores, quia diligunt suum esse."

The Concept of "Life" in the *Commentary on St. John*

contemplative life *(vita contemplativa)*. Thus, if the verse of Isaiah is taken as if it were said by John *(si capiantur quasi ex ore Joannis)*, a threefold characteristic of John's contemplation can be discovered: it is high *(alta)*, full *(ampla)*, and perfect *(perfecta)* (*Ioan.* prol., n. 1).

The height *(altitudo)* and sublimity *(sublimitas)* consists in the contemplation and knowledge of God. Characteristic of John is that he transcends the created world and reaches the Creator. In his approach, John includes the four ways in which the philosophers of the ancient world arrived at knowledge of God: by God's *auctoritas, aeternitas, dignitas,* and *incomprehensibilitas*. John's Gospel displays a full contemplation by showing not only the cause, but also the effects of this cause. The contemplation of God in this Gospel is perfect because it rises and really attains the object of contemplation, in the sense that it is adhered and assented by affection and understanding *(inhaerendo et assentiendo per affectum et intellectum veritati contemplatae)* (*Ioan.* prol., nn. 2–8).

From all this, Aquinas continues, the formal object *(materia)* of the fourth Gospel can be concluded: it deals especially with the divinity of Christ, in order to correct the various heresies that appeared after the first three Gospels had been written. As concerns the order of the matter, Thomas sees a parallel between the three parts of Jesaja's verse and the development of the prologue in the Gospel. As regards the aim of the Gospel: it was written so that the faithful might form the temple of God and be filled with God's majesty. In the words of John 20:31: "These things are written so that you may believe that Jesus is the Christ, the Son of God" (*Ioan.* prol., n. 10).

Thomas concludes his prologue with four remarks about the condition of the author (*Ioan.* prol., n. 11). They should be mentioned, because they are not without hermeneutical relevance. The name of the writer of the fourth Gospel is "John," which means "in whom is grace" because, as Aquinas says "only those who are full of God's grace can see the secrets of the divinity" (1 Cor 2:11). John's virtuousness is linked to this meaning of his name, because John was a virgin and only those who have a pure heart will see the Lord (Mt 5:8). As for the symbol that is associated with John: John flies like an eagle above the cloud of human weakness and looks upon the light of unchanging truth with the most lofty and firm eyes of the heart. The fourth remark concerns the privilege of John, who was the most loved of the disciples. The hermeneutic importance of this remark is contained in the idea that friends are the ones to whom secrets are revealed. The closer one's friend, the better an address for secrets such a person is.

Considering the lines drawn in Aquinas's prologue to the Gospel, the contours of a framework appear that determine the way in which Thomas interprets the text of St. John. This framework can be rephrased as follows:

- The Gospel of John deals primarily with the divinity of the Word incarnate.
- It does so in the most high, full and perfect way, even reaching the divine object with affect and intellect.
- Its intention is promoting faith in Christ.
- Its author displays some specific conditions for grasping the kind of knowledge that is communicated in the Gospel: God's grace, purity of heart, and an intimate relationship of friendship with Christ.

Focusing on the concept of "life" in the *Commentary on St. John,* we are now in a position to explore the way in which it is developed, looking through the hermeneutic lens of Thomas's prologue.

Reading through the Lens of the Prologue

Altitudo (height)

Analyzing the height and sublimity of John's contemplation, Thomas distinguishes four ways that led the early philosophers to God and that are incorporated and surpassed by John.

1. The first way concerns God as the author *(auctor)* of creation. The early philosophers came to the conclusion that there should be something higher by which the things of nature are directed to an end and governed, because even the creatures that lack intelligence somehow know how to act in accordance with their nature. In the Gospel of John this indirect way of proceeding to knowledge of God is replaced by the testimony of verses 3 and 4a of the first chapter, which proclaim about the Word:

> (3) All things were made through him, and without him nothing was made. What was made
> (4a) in him was life.

Striking here is the fact that Thomas uses a different punctuation than we are familiar with. Reading his explanation of the verse, one learns that also in Thomas's day there was a discussion about the question as to which punctuation and interpretation should be followed: the one given by Manichaeus, Augustine, Origen, Hilary, or Chrysostom? (*Ioan.* 1, lect. 2, nn. 89–95).

Striking here is also the fact that the life of the Word, God's life, is connected with God as author of creation. The link between the two is constituted by appreciating "life" as knowledge (the second meaning). When read against the background of God's simplicity, the verse "What was made in him was life" *(Quod factum est in ipso vita erat)* becomes intelligible. Since the intellect, the object known and the act of knowing are the same in God *secundum rem*, the content of what is known by God is identical with His essence. In fact, all creatures are known by God even before they come into existence, as we have seen. Thus, all created being, as God knows it, cannot be distinguished from God's essence *secundum rem*. Since God's essence is life, all creatures are life in God.[8]

2. The second way of the philosophers that is incorporated by John concerns God's eternity *(aeternitas)*. Thomas relates this to the thought that the lower realms of being are marked by mutability, whereas the first principle is immutable. Thinking about a connection between the concept of "life" and God's eternity, of course one immediately thinks of the concept of eternal life *(vita aeterna)*. And indeed, the concept of eternal life plays an important role in the Gospel. In John 3:16 it is said:

For God so loved the world that he gave his Only Begotten Son, so that whoever believes in him should not perish, but have eternal life.

In John 17:2–3 Jesus asks the Father to glorify his Son, that his Son may glorify him:

For you granted him authority over all people that he might give eternal life to all those you have given him. Now this is eternal life: that they may know you, the only true God, and Jesus Christ, whom you have sent.

In his commentary on both passages, Thomas explains that eternal life is nothing but God himself. And the way in which human beings can "have" God is by knowing him. Thus the gift of eternal life appears as an expression of the immensity of God's love. "For by giving eternal life, he gives himself. For eternal life is nothing else than enjoying God" (*Ioan.* 3, lect. 3, n. 480).[9]

In his exegesis of John 17:3 Aquinas's explanation is more technical (*Ioan.* 17, lect. 1, n. 2186). First he explains that all activities to which one moves oneself can be called operations of life. The more actual and perfect these op-

---

8. Cf. *ST* I, q. 18, a. 4: "Respondeo dicendum quod, sicut dictum est, vivere Dei est eius intelligere. In Deo autem est idem intellectus et quod intelligitur, et ipsum intelligere eius. Unde quidquid est in Deo ut intellectum, est ipsum vivere vel vita eius. Unde, cum omnia quae facta sunt a Deo, sint in ipso ut intellecta, sequitur quod omnia in ipso sunt ipsa vita divina."

9. "In hoc autem quod dicit 'habeat vitam aeternam' [Jn 3:16], indicatur divini amoris immensitas: nam dando vitam aeternam, dat seipsum. Nam vita aeterna nihil aliud est quam frui Deo. Dare autem seipsum, magni amoris est indicium; Eph 2:4–5: 'Deus autem qui dives est in misericordia, convivificavit nos in Christo,' idest fecit nos habere vitam aeternam."

erations are, the more one speaks of "life." Because knowing *(intelligere)* is the highest of these operations, the act of knowing can be called "life" in the best sense *(operatio intellectus maxime est vita)*. Thus, when knowing is living, knowing an eternal object is eternal life. God is eternal, so knowing God is eternal life.

3. The third way of the philosophers concerns the dignity of God—or God's life. Thomas relates this way to the idea of Platonism that all things that are by participation can be reduced to being by essence. This idea plays an important role in Aquinas's interpretation of the fourth Gospel. The Word incarnate is life, life by essence, and principle of life.

Commenting on the fifth chapter, Thomas argues that it is impossible that the first and foremost life *(prima vita)* could be the life of plants or animals *(Ioan.* 5, lect. 4, n. 771). The reason for this is that all corporal life is participated life: a living body is not life itself, but participates in life. This means that the first and foremost life cannot be but intellectual or spiritual life. Since Christ is the Word, the Wisdom of God, he himself is life per se. He is the source of life.

This line of thought is prolonged in Aquinas's interpretation of John 5:26: "just as the Father possesses life in himself, so he has given to the Son to have life in himself." Thomas explains that

In every genus of things, that which is something through its essence is the cause of those things that are it by participation, as fire is the cause of all things afire. And so, that which is life through its essence is the cause and principle of all life in living things. Accordingly, if something is to be a principle of life, it must be life through its essence. And so our Lord fittingly shows that he is the principle of all life by saying that he has life in himself, i.e. through his essence. *(Ioan.* 5, lect. 5, n. 782)

4. The fourth way of the ancient philosophers concerns the *incomprehensibilitas Dei,* or—in this case—the incomprehensibility of divine life. Thomas connects this with the verse "No one has ever seen God." Commenting on the first chapter he explains why:

Each thing is knowable to the extent that it has being and truth: while one is a knower according to his amount of cognitive power. Now a created intellectual substance is finite; hence it knows in a finite way. And since God is infinite in power and being, and as a consequence is infinitely knowable, he cannot be known by any created intellect to the degree that he is knowable. And thus he remains incomprehensible to every created intellect. *(Ioan.* 1, lect. 11, n. 213)

As a consequence one might either turn to agnosticism or stress the need for God's grace in order to overcome the barrier of the limited capacity of the created intellect. And thus, as we shall see below, Thomas holds that only the life of grace can help one to learn to know God. This life of grace is perfected in eternal life, in which God is seen as he is (cf. *Ioan.* 1, lect. 10, n. 206).

Summarizing these four themes—God's *auctoritas, aeternitas, essentia,* and *incomprehensibilitas*—with respect to which the height of John's contemplation can be demonstrated, and connecting these themes with Aquinas's approach of God's life in his commentary on the fourth Gospel, one can discern the same lines of reasoning that are developed systematically in *Summa theologiae* I, q. 18.[10] God's life is life in essence, and the ultimate criterion of what life essentially is. As long as we dwell in our mortal bodies, we do not have access to God's life to a degree that makes us understand what life in the fullest sense is. Thus we can only point in a certain direction without fully understanding what we say when we confess God as the source of life. To put it differently: as concerns our knowledge, reality is turned upside down. The only way in which our knowledge of God can increase is by participating in his divine knowledge. This brings us to the second characteristic of John's contemplation: its fullness.

Amplitudo (fullness)

The second characteristic of Johannine contemplation is its fullness: the fact that it concerns the power of the essence of life according to its effects. According to Thomas's analysis of the fourth Gospel's structure, chapters 2–21 deal with the *effectus et opera* of Christ. At first sight the concept of "life" plays a role here in the sense that according to Aquinas, chapters 2–11 deal with the life of Christ, and chapters 12–21 with his passion and death.

In chapters 2–11 the concept of "life" appears to be a keyword as regards both structure and context. After chapter 2—on the wedding of Cana and the cleansing of the temple and dealing with Christ's power over nature *(dominium supra naturam)* (*Ioan.* 2, lect. 1, n. 335)—chapters 3–11 focus on the effects of Christ's grace. Thomas develops his explanation of the structure of these chapters on the framework of human internal and external life, a parallel that is well known from his treatise on the sacraments.[11] He divides chapters 3–11 in two parts: the spiritual regeneration (as concerns the Jews [chapter 3] and the Gentiles [chapter 4]) and, in the same line of thought, the three *beneficia* that—according to Aristotle—children receive from their parents: life, nourishment, and instruction (*Ioan.* 5, lect. 1, n. 699).[12] The Greek

---

10. For an elaborate reading of this *quaestio,* cf. Leget, *Living with God,* 25–46.
11. Cf., e.g., *SCG* IV, c. 58; *ST* III, q. 65, a. 1; *De art.* 2. For the relation with Christ's incarnation and a discussion of John 3 and 6, cf. Leget, *Living wth God,* 132–40.
12. Aristotle says this in VIII *Eth.* 7.5 (1162a6): cf. III *Sent.,* d. 29, q. 1, a. 7, sc 2; IV *Sent.,* d. 26, q. 1, a. 1; IV *Sent.,* d. 42, q. 2, a. 2, ad 3; *ST* I-II, 67, q. 8, a. 2; *De duobus praec caritatis,* a. 6.

philosopher proves to be a surprising help in explaining the structure of the fourth Gospel.

A few remarks in line with the preceding are helpful in understanding the "logic" of life that Aquinas adopts in his commentary on the fourth Gospel. We have seen that Thomas considers corporeal life as a form of participated life: it can never be the source of life. This primacy of the invisible, intellectual, spiritual over the visible, sensate, and corporeal is a characteristic feature of the discourse in John. Throughout the *Commentary on St. John* one can find some very strong formulations of this structural hierarchy. Commenting on the sixth chapter, for example, Aquinas states the following:

In this respect we should point out that material things are likenesses of spiritual things, since they are caused and produced by them; and consequently they resemble spiritual things in some way. Now just as the body is sustained by food . . . (. . .) This food is God himself, insofar as he is the truth that is to be contemplated and the Goodness which is to be loved, which nourish the spirit. (*Ioan.* 6, lect. 3, n. 895)

A little further on, we read:

Now there are two parts in man: the chief part is the soul, and the second is the body. It is the soul which makes man to be man, and not the body; and so that truly is the food of man which is the food of the soul. (*Ioan.* 6, lect. 7, n. 895)

And the same "reversal" goes for light, as we learn from his explanation of John 1:5, "And light shines in the darkness":

According to Augustine and many others, light is more properly said *(magis proprie dicitur)* of spiritual things than of sensible things. (*Ioan.* 1, lect. 3, n. 96)

The parallelism of internal and external life turns out to be part of an important set of oppositions that mark the Gospel: corporal versus spiritual, visible versus invisible, external versus internal, and temporal versus eternal. All of these oppositions relate to the concept of life, and all of them have to do with the incarnation of the Word and the effects of the life of Christ. Following the metaphor of the life, nourishment and instruction, the reversal of our criterion of knowledge that was encountered in the preceding paragraph, is combined with a reversal as concerns the basic characteristics of human existence. Reality is turned not only upside down, but also inside out. How does Aquinas proceed?

First of all, Thomas deals with spiritual regeneration. John 3—where the conversation with Nicodemus is reported—deals with the reformation through grace. Reformation through grace comes about through spiritual generation. The conversation between Nicodemus and Christ is about this regeneration, but it also shows the importance of this regeneration as an indispensable prerequisite for those who are willing to understand what Christ means. Thomas paraphrases Christ's answer to Nicodemus's misunderstanding as follows:

> It is not strange that you regard me as a mere man, because one cannot know these secrets of the divinity unless he has achieved a spiritual regeneration. (*Ioan.* 3, lect. 1, n. 431)

Thomas continues explaining that since vision is an act of life, according to the diverse kinds of life there will be diversity of vision. The sentient life has a sentient knowledge or vision. But there is also a spiritual life, by which human beings are made like God, and by which they enjoy a spiritual vision. This is the work of the Holy Spirit (*Ioan.* 3, lect. 1, n. 432).

Thomas explains that although Christ brings about a spiritual regeneration that enables us to see the work of God that cannot be seen by our natural vision, this regeneration is not perfect. We are only regenerated inwardly by grace. We remain mortal human beings that will have to hope and wait for outward regeneration in heaven (*Ioan.* 3, lect. 1, n. 433). This is expressed by the use of water in the sacrament of baptism. Human beings are a unity of soul and body. In order to express that the spiritual regeneration—brought about by the Holy Spirit—is extended to the body as well, something bodily is involved: water (*Ioan.* 3, lect. 1, n. 443).

In these reflections about spiritual regeneration Thomas uses the direct relation between knowing (the second meaning of "life") and being (the first meaning of "life") in order to explain the reversal that is brought about between the inward and the outward dimension of human existence. In natural life our knowing follows our being; in our spiritual regeneration our being follows upon our knowing. In other places in his oeuvre Thomas works this out in the appreciation of faith as the beginning of eternal life *(inchoatio vitae aeternae)*.[13]

The analogy between natural generation and spiritual generation comprises more than entering a new realm of being and knowing. It also entails a likeness of the one generating (*Ioan.* 3, lect. 1, n. 442). We are regenerated as sons of God, in the likeness of his true Son. And this comes about by having his Spirit. Thus spiritual regeneration must come from the Holy Spirit.[14] As Thomas explains later in his discussion of the sixth chapter:

---

13. Cf. *ST* II-II, q. 4, a. 1: "fides est habitus mentis, qua inchoatur vita aeterna in nobis, faciens intellectum assentire non apparentibus."

14. At the end of *Ioan.* 3, lect. 1, n. 448, Thomas discerns a threefold generation: one that is materially and effectivly from the flesh; one that is according to the spirit; and a third that is

For as the body lives its bodily life through a bodily spirit, so the soul lives a spiritual life through the Holy Spirit: "Send forth your Spirit, and they will be created" (Ps 103:30). *(Ioan.* 6, lect. 8, n. 993)

After having dealt with the spiritual regeneration of the Jews (chapter 3) and the Gentiles (chapter 4), the *Commentary on John* focuses on the three benefits of those who are spiritually reborn.

1. The first benefit is spiritual life. Chapter 5, which is—according to Aquinas's interpretation—dedicated to this benefit, begins with the healing of a man who had been sick for thirty-eight years and who was lying near a pool. As Thomas explains in the first lecture on this chapter:

This is the usual practice in this Gospel: to always join to the teaching of Christ some appropriate visible action, so that what is invisible can be made known through the visible. *(Ioan.* 5, lect. 1, n. 699)

The discourse on the life-giving power of the Son is in line with the spiritual regeneration that was dealt with in chapter 3. An important feature of this chapter is the emphasis on the equality of the Son and the Father as regards their divine power. Because in the Old Testament the divine power is particularly emphasized by the fact that God is the author of life (cf. 1 Sam 2:6 and Deut 32:39), in John 5:21 the power to raise the dead and grant life is equally assigned to the Son *(Ioan.* 5, lect. 4, n. 761).

A second line of reasoning concerns the twofold resurrection of body and soul *(Ioan.* 5, lect. 4, n. 779). The resurrection of the soul from the death of unbelief to the life of faith can happen here and now. The resurrection of the body will happen in the future. Reasoning from the logic according to which the external and the internal, the corporeal and the spiritual are reversed, it is clear that the resurrection of the body—however much spectacular to carnal eyes—is only a secondary effect of the spiritual life-giving power of the Son here and now.[15]

2. Christ not only gives spiritual life to those who are born again, he also sustains their life by spiritual food. This brings us to the second benefit: nourishment. Again we find a visible sign—the miracle of the loaves and fishes—followed by a discourse where Christ calls himself living bread *(panis vivus)* and bread of life *(panis vitae).*

---

midway: the unique case of Christ who was born materially from the flesh but effectively from the Holy Spirit.

15. The question whether the Gospel of John has a future or a present eschatology, or a juxtaposition of both (Beasley-Murray, 5–7) does not make much sense from the perspective of Aquinas's exegesis. Cf. for the ongoing discussion H.-C. Kammler, *Christologie und Eschatologie. Joh 5, 17–30 als Schlüsseltext johanneischer Theologie* (Tübingen: Mohr Siebeck, 2000).

Taking the spiritual food provided by Christ is of vital importance, for as Thomas explains:

> Just as material food is so necessary for bodily life that without it you cannot exist ... so spiritual food is necessary for the spiritual life to such an extent that without it the spiritual life cannot be sustained. (*Ioan.* 6, lect. 7, n. 968)

There is no doubt for Aquinas that the spiritual food Christ is referring to is primarily the sacrament of the Eucharist. As it is the application of Christ's suffering to us, the importance of this sacrament is enormous. It is the way in which Christ is corporeally present among us, and it is the cause for the restoration of our life: both the spiritual and the corporeal life (*Ioan.* 6, lect. 6, nn. 963–4).

Taking the bread of life, one takes Christ within oneself. In a concise and clear passage Thomas explains this in the following manner:

> Now Christ is within us in two ways: in our intellect through faith, so far as it is faith; and in our affections through love, which informs or gives life through our faith: "He who abides in love, abides in God, and God in him" (1 Jn 4:16). So he who believes in Christ so that he tends to him, possesses Christ in his affections and in his intellect And if we add that Christ is eternal life, as is stated in "that we may be in his true Son, Jesus Christ. This is the true God and eternal life" (1 Jn 5:20), and "In him was life" (above 1:4), we can infer that whoever believes in Christ has eternal life. He has it, I say, in its cause and in hope, and he will have it at some time in reality. (*Ioan.* 6, lect. 6, n. 950)

The result of this is the reverse of what happens when corporeal nourishment is taken. When one takes corporeal food, the food is transformed in the one who eats. When one takes spiritual food, however, the one who takes it is transformed in the food (*Ioan.* 6, lect. 7, n. 972; further developed in nn. 974–78). In fact it is the very idea of being reborn in the likeness of the Lord, which is extended to the metaphor of spiritual food.

3. The third benefit that children receive from their parents is instruction. After chapter 7 has dealt with the origin of Christ's instruction, chapters 8 to 11 focus upon the usefulness and power of Christ's instruction. This power is twofold: enlightening and life-giving. Again we find the concept of "life" functioning in both contexts.

The enlightening power of Christ's doctrine—expressed in the verse "I am the light of the world. Whoever follows me will not walk in darkness, but he will have the light of life" (Jn 8:12) and chasing away the threefold darkness of ignorance, guilt, and eternal damnation—shows the relation between knowledge and life. Thomas explains that the light of Christ is life giving, because we live insofar as we have knowledge, and this knowledge participates in the divine light of Christ. And the perfection of our life is nothing else than the perfection of our capacity to know God by grace (*Ioan.* 8, lect. 2, n. 1145).[16] And of course there is no clearer confirmation of Christ's teaching than by the healing of the man born blind in John 9.

Chapters 10 and 11 deal with the life-giving power of Christ. Again Thomas recognizes the structure of a discourse (about the good Shepherd) confirmed by a miracle (the resurrection of Lazarus). The words "I am the resurrection and the life" (John 11:25) refer to Christ's power: the very power by which all will resurrect, the power that gives life to the souls and the bodies, the power that has its origin in the fact that Christ is "life," as we learned from John 1:4 (cf. *Ioan.* 11, lect. 4, nn. 1516–17).

Summarizing what we have learned so far, one could say that the Gospel of John turns reality inside out. Showing how the corporal life is at the service of the spiritual, the visible leading to the invisible, the external pointing to the internal, and the temporal founded upon the eternal, the Gospel can be read as a continuous invitation to conversion; a permanent training in penetrating into the spiritual, invisible, internal, intimate, and eternal core of reality. This marks the theological character of the fourth Gospel, drawing the reader to join the movement toward inner life. It brings us to the next characteristic of John's contemplation.

Perfectio (perfection)

John's contemplation is said to be perfect because it actually reaches the object of contemplation, adhering and assenting God by affection and understanding. If we think of the content of the Gospel—teaching about spiritual regeneration, nourishment, and instruction—and if we think of Aquinas's characterization of the disciple whom Jesus loved, we must conclude that the writer of the Gospel was in an intimate way familiar with what he wrote. This reflection of the content on the author, however, goes one step further and cannot but reflect on the reader of the Gospel as well. Thus Aquinas's assessment of John's Gospel as containing the most perfect contemplation—reaching God himself—reveals a great deal about his own theological hermeneutics.

We have seen that the objective of the Gospel is that its readers might

---

16. "Lumen vero istud vitam dat, quia vivimus inquantum intellectum habemus, qui est quaedam participatio illius lucis. Quando autem lux illa perfecte irradiabit, tunc habebimus vitam perfectam: Ps 35:10: 'Apud te est fons vitae, et in lumine tuo videbimus lumen'; quasi dicat: Tunc ipsam vitam perfecte habebimus quando ipsum lumen per speciem videbimus."

The Concept of "Life" in the *Commentary on St. John* 167

come to faith in Jesus Christ (John 20:31). Any reader who wants to penetrate to the spiritual sense of the Gospel, who wants to hear the Word of God that is communicated to us through the text, should be spiritually reborn, nourished, and instructed by Christ. Such a person should lead a life that is consonant with the message that is communicated. Thus we find a theological version of the hermeneutical circle, which is typical for theological or spiritual reading: the aim of reading the Scripture is conversion, but one can understand what is communicated in its deepest (spiritual) sense only after such a conversion. As Henri de Lubac formulates it:

> It is certain that the Christian mystery is not something to be curiously contemplated like a pure object of science, but is something which must be interiorized and lived. It finds its own fullness in being fulfilled in souls. . . . But the converse is just as true: the spiritual meaning of a mystery, is the meaning we discover—or rather, into which we penetrate—by living that mystery. Still more fundamentally, the entire process of spiritual understanding is, in its principle, identical to the process of conversion. It is its luminous aspect. . . . The Word of God, a living and effective word, acquires true fulfillment and total significance only by the transformation which it effects in the one who receives it. This is why the expression "passing on to spiritual understanding" is equivalent to "turning to Christ"—a conversion which can never be said to have been fully achieved.[17]

This paradoxical logic is met time after time in John's Gospel, as the conversations with Nicodemus, the scribes, and the Samaritan woman witness.[18] Considering that the word "life" offers a special opportunity for communicating the mysteries of God, how does the keyword "life" play a role in dealing with this circle?

I think it does by the word *vivificare:* the Gospel "gives life" when we understand what is being communicated.[19] Thus *vivificare* can be considered as a hermeneutic category: it expresses what is taking place in the one "understanding" the theological depth of the text.[20] Understanding this theological

---

17. Henri de Lubac, "Spiritual Understanding," in *The Theological Interpretation of Scripture: Classic and Contemporary Readings*, ed. Stephen E. Fowl (Oxford: Blackwell, 1997), 13.

18. Cf. e.g. *Ioan.* 3, lect. 1, n. 437: "Et ideo, quia Nicodemus carnalis adhuc, et animalis erat, non potuit quae dicebantur, nisi carnaliter intelligere. Et ideo ea quae Dominus dixerat de regeneratione spirituali, ipse de regeneratione carnali intelligebat."

19. The words *vivificare* and *vivificativus* are typical words of the *Commentary on John*: whereas the *Scriptum super libros sententiarum* and the *Summa theologiae* are approximately 4? times as large as the *Commentary on John*, the word *vivificare* occurs only 71 times in the *Scriptum*, 76 times in the *Summa*, against 68 times in the *Lectura*; the word *vivificativus* is used only 48 times in Thomas's entire oeuvre, 26 times of which in the *Commentary on John*, 5 times in the *Summa*; it is not used in the *Scriptum* (the *Catena aurea* holds second place with 14 times).

20. Cf. e.g. *Ioan.* 6, lect. 8, nn. 992–93: "et sic intellecta, vita sunt, scilicet animae: nam sicut

depth is more than an activity of the intellect: it is "adhering and assenting it by affection and understanding." Understanding is a transforming experience by which the message that is communicated actually works in the one who receives the message. Of course the "life" communicated thus is the life of grace, and the one who animates our spiritual life is the Holy Spirit.[21]

Reframing these insights in terms of "life," one could say that by understanding the spiritual sense of the Scripture, one participates in the object understood. Understanding can be called "life" in the second sense: it is the characteristic activity of human beings. Such activity perfects a human being's knowledge, which has consequences for leading a certain "life" (in the third sense) in the world.

AQUINAS'S EXEGESIS AND CONTEMPORARY THEOLOGY: BREAKING THE BARRIERS

Having sketched the meaning and role of the concept of "life" in Aquinas's *Commentary on John*, we now ask, what does it mean for doing exegesis and systematic theology today? How are we to "break the barriers that separate modern from pre-critical exegesis and speculative theology"? A first step, I think, is to become aware of the complexity of the problem, which is—eventually—a hermeneutical one. Comparing Aquinas's exegesis with contemporary commentaries on John, for example, simply will not do without having clarified the differences in hermeneutical approach of the authors involved and having determined one's own position in this respect. For this reason, the second part of this essay has a rather formal character. I hope to contribute to paving the way for a good interpretation rather than going all the way myself.

Aquinas's Hermeneutics versus a Contemporary Theological Reading

As regards Aquinas's hermeneutics, the work of Eugene Rogers Jr., for example, has made clear that ultimately Aquinas's hermeneutics leaves the meaning of the text underdetermined.[22] Thomas is interested in the spiritual

---

corpus vivit vita corporali per spiritum corporalem, ita et anima vivit vita spirituali, per Spiritum sanctum; Psal. 103, 30: 'Emitte spiritum tuum, et creabuntur.'"

21. The connection between the concept of "life" and the Holy Spirit in Thomas's *Commentary on St. John* deserves more attention than I can give within the limits of this contribution. I limit myself to calling into remembrance that within the Trinity "life" is attributed to the Spirit, and the Spirit is connected with *amor* and the theological virtue of *caritas*, the mother and root of all virtues.

22. Eugene F. Rogers, Jr., "How the Virtues of an Interpreter Presuppose and Perfect Hermeneutics: The Case of Thomas Aquinas," *Journal of Religion* 76 (1996): 64–81. Cf. also his

sense of Scripture, the one that informs us about the Mystery of God, the way we reach God (moral sense) or our final reunion with God (anagogical sense). As we have seen—and in this respect my reading of Thomas's commentary on John confirms Rogers's findings—this sense is not open to just anyone who is able to determine the literal sense of the words.[23]

If we look at the development of biblical exegesis in the second half of the twentieth century, one can see the focus shifting from issues behind the text (historical-critical method), to issues in the text (structuralism), and finally to issues in front of the text (all post-structuralist readings that focus on the reader as the one who constructs meaning).[24] I follow Paul Ricoeur, and others, in the view that any interpretation that tries to limit the meaning of a text to one of these three dimensions exclusively is not very fruitful. Looking at Aquinas's exegesis from this perspective, one must conclude that one cannot follow him on the level of "behind the text" issues: our knowledge of the context within which the Gospels have been written has increased since the thirteenth century, and Thomas would agree with us that this is of importance on the level of the *sensus litteralis*. This goes also for the analyses of textual structures, the "in the text" issues. Where Thomas explained the instructions of Christ on the framework of the *Magister* teaching his disciples, and where he draws heavily on Aristotle (as we have learned from his view on "life"), we have various more defensible methods that can bring the text into relief, taking notice of the standards of literary composition in biblical times.

But what about the third level? What about the reader? It is here that the really hard questions arise. For whatever knowledge one has of "behind the text" and "in the text" issues, this knowledge is never a guarantee that the text has any theological meaning to the reader. In my reading as a Christian, ancient Egyptian texts on Osiris do not have the same impact on me as the story of Abraham has, nor would they even if I knew everything there is to know about ancient Egypt. The story of Abraham has a different impact on me, because it is part of a larger story that is constitutive for the community within

---

Thomas Aquinas and Karl Barth. Sacred Doctrine and the Natural Knowledge of God (Notre Dame, Ind.: University of Notre Dame Press, 1995), chs. 3–6.

23. Cf. also Aquinas's own remarks about the inaccessible character of Holy Scripture in *ST* I, q. 9, on the use of metaphorical language in Scripture: "occultatio figurarum utilis est ad exercitium studiosorum, et contra irrisiones infidelium; de quibus dicitur 'Nolite sanctum dare canibus'" (ad 2) and "per hujusmodi, divina magis occultantur indignis" (ad 3).

24. Cf. Max Turner and Joel Green, "New Testament Commentary and Systematic Theology: Strangers or Friends?" in *Between Two Horizons: Spanning New Testament Studies and Systematic Theology,* ed. Joel B. Green and Max Turner (Grand Rapids, Mich.: Eerdmans, 2000), 1–22, at 4–6.

which the biblical stories are read. Here we enter a triple hermeneutical circle, as Paul Ricoeur reminds us, that touches the foundation of the Christian tradition on the Word of God.[25]

The first circle concerns the relation between the Word of God and Holy Scripture: the Word of God is considered to be the founding instance of Holy Scripture; simultaneously, however, Scripture is considered to be the place where the Word is revealed. Thus the Word of God cannot be the foundation of Scripture without Scripture being its first place of manifestation.

The second circle concerns the relation between the first one (comprising the circular relation between Word of God and Holy Scripture) and the community of the Church. The Church understands itself as being founded upon the Word of God as received through a particular reading of Scripture; at the same time, however, it is the community that sets the standards and rules for interpreting Scripture.

Both circles are repeated and enclosed within the soul of the individual who reads Scripture and tries to understand the meaning of a certain text for his or her own life. One can only grasp the meaning of a scriptural passage for one's own life by understanding oneself departing from the passage as it is read within a certain tradition.

The three hermeneutical circles sketched by Ricoeur make clear that there is no smooth or natural transition between whatever exegetical method focuses on "behind the text" or "in the text" issues on the one hand, and a theological reading on the other. In order to enter the triple circle, one has to make a choice. Ricoeur calls this the existential circle: "hazard transformed into destiny through a continuous choice."[26]

Of course this does not imply that any theological reading should not engage in insights that flow from historical-critical, structuralist, and other methods of interpretation. The point is, however, that these latter methods can never be exhaustive for interpretation: they leave enough room for a theological reading. Stephen Fowl, in his book *Engaging Scripture,* speaks of an "underdetermined" interpretation that leaves room for a theological reading that has its criteria elsewhere.[27] On this point, I think, Thomas Aquinas enters the scene. Why do I think that his view is still important, and which in-

---

25. Paul Ricoeur, "Expérience et langage dans le discours religieux," in *Phénoménologie et Théologie,* ed. J.-L. Chrétien et al. (Paris: Criterion, 1992), 21–25.

26. Ricoeur, "Expérience et langage," 25: "Tel est le cercle existentiel: un hasard transformé en destin à travers un choix continu."

27. Stephen Fowl, *Engaging Scripture: A Model for Theological Interpretation* (Oxford: Blackwell, 1998), 56–61.

sights concerning the concept of "life" in his commentary on John do I consider to be still of great value?

The Role of Aquinas and the Importance of the Concept of "Life"

The more formal reason why I think Thomas's view is important is because he plays a constitutive role in the tradition I am part of. As one of the Teachers of the Church he is considered to be a faithful witness with respect to the interpretation of the mysteries of faith. Thus his theological reading of, for example, the bread of life passage in John 6 can help me develop a theological understanding of the mystery of the Eucharist, the celebration of which is part of the living tradition I am partaking in and because of which I am interested in understanding the Scripture. It can even do so reasonably when—as some exegetes say—Aquinas "misreads" John 6:51–58 by interpreting the bread of life as referring to the sacrament of the Eucharist instead of to the person of Christ:[28] when I read Thomas's more systematic theological reflections in, for example, the *Summa theologiae,* the inseparable connection between the person of Christ and the Eucharist is so evident that this "misreading" has more the character of a "detour" than a "mistake."[29]

The continuity between Thomas's view on theological reading and ours lies in the fact that we have seen that he joins an ancient tradition that is—framing it in terms of "grace"—aware of the hermeneutical circles that play a role, and that puts the ultimate criterion of the meaning of a text in the degree to which it helps us in becoming more intimate with God. As regards his treatment of the concept of "life," I see the following insights of importance for contemporary theology, all three of them marked by the eschatological dimension inherent in the concept of life.

Cognition: Reality Upside-down

In the first place, Thomas's view on the concept of "life" turns reality upside down. Although our knowledge of the concept of "life" is real, based on what we know from creatures that move themselves, the ultimate criterion of "life"—God who is the source of life—remains beyond our grasp. Nevertheless, we are created in his threefold image: *imago naturalis, imago gratiae,* and *imago gloriae.* By placing the criterion above the top of what we can know, the knowledge of our world is turned upside down. Being created for a destination that lies beyond our grasp, we must confess that we hardly understand

---

28. Cf. e.g. M. J. J. Menken, "John 6,51c–58: Eucharist or Christology?," *Biblica* 74 (1993): 1–26: reprinted in *Critical Readings of John 6,* ed. R. A. Culpepper (Leiden: Brill, 1997), 183–204.

29. I am alluding here to St. Augustine, I *De doctrina christiana.*xxxvi 40 [86]–41[88].

what we are living unto. In this sense our entire life—in the first meaning (as mode of being)—is something the depth of which can be understood only by reaching its fulfillment in eternal life. This should promote our humility in knowing, but also in acting. The consequences of this reach unto the very fragile beginnings of human life.

Moral Action: Reality Inside-out

But Thomas's commentary on the Gospel of John has a second important lesson for us. The continuous conversion from the outside world to the inside makes our natural life appear as pointing to an invisible, spiritual, inner life that is the real core of our existence. Thus the Gospel of John can be read as a pedagogical version of the truths expressed in Aquinas's eschatology: this world will be recreated, but then departing from its hidden core: the relationship with God.[30] Living as a Christian is leading a way of life in which this eschatological dimension becomes reality right here and now. Making this inner dimension visible is a great task for us who live in a culture that is so obsessed with the material and visible world.

Theological Hermeneutics: The Access to the Mysteries of Faith

As a consequence of all this, Thomas's commentary on the fourth Gospel has an important hermeneutical lesson as regards our access to the mysteries of faith. Above all we learn that only God's grace can open our eyes and make us see how our life is embedded in and heading for divine life. Once this is appreciated, one cannot fail to notice that the Gospel of John ("in whom is grace") has itself this poetic and fascinating power. Reading the Gospel, no reader is left unattached. It is hard to keep distance, because as a reader one becomes involved and one is—as it were—drawn into the text. The concept of life plays an important role in this dynamism. Thanks to Thomas we learn why this is so.

---

30. This is worked out in greater detail in Leget, *Living with God,* ch. 4.

ELEVEN

Christ the Teacher in St. Thomas's *Commentary on the Gospel of John*

MICHAEL SHERWIN, O.P.

> "Do not let yourselves be called teacher *(magister)*, because one alone is your teacher, the Christ." (Mt 23:10)

The first chapter of the Gospel of John describes an encounter between Jesus and two disciples of John the Baptist. These two disciples are following Jesus when suddenly Jesus turns to them and asks, "What do you seek?" The disciples respond, "Rabbi [which is translated as 'teacher' in English, or *magister* in Latin], where do you dwell?" (Jn 1:38). In his *Commentary on the Gospel of St. John,* Thomas Aquinas portrays this encounter as a model of all encounters with Christ that lead to discipleship. Aquinas regards it as initiating a unique relationship, the relationship between Christ, the master, and his followers, the disciples (see *Ioan.* 1, lect. 15, nn. 290–94). In the pages that follow we shall investigate Aquinas's description of this relationship and the theory of moral education it implies.[1]

THE MEANING OF THE TERM *MAGISTER*

The first difficulty we must surmount is how to translate the term *magister.* In common English parlance, "master" is regularly paired with servant or slave. A master is one whom we must obey. Although in the Latin of Aquinas a *magister* is also one whom we obey, this is

---

1. For an extended treatment of this theme that complements the present essay, see the doctoral dissertation of Michael Dauphinais, *The Pedagogy of the Incarnation: Christ the Teacher according to St. Thomas Aquinas* (Notre Dame: University of Notre Dame, 2000).

not its primary connotation. *Magister* connotes not so much dominion over another as expertise in a domain of knowledge. A *magister* is one who has mastered a discipline.² Aquinas himself, for example, was deemed a *magister in sacra pagina,* a title signifying that he was proficient in the study of sacred Scripture and had acquired an expert understanding of the unique *disciplina* it contains, the *disciplina spiritualis* known as *sacra doctrina*.³ It is in this context that we can also grasp the meaning of the term *"discipulus." Disciplina* and *discipulus* both derive from *"discere,"* a Latin verb meaning "to learn." A person's identity as a disciple comes from his status as a learner of a specific discipline. It is this desire to learn that is the hallmark of the true disciple. Indeed, in Aquinas's view, the honest desire to learn from the Lord distinguishes a true disciple of Christ from those who follow him out of curiosity or only in order to test him (see *Ioan.* 8, lect. 2, n. 1160). Perhaps a helpful way to convey in English the nuance of these terms and the relationship they express is by appealing to apprenticeship.⁴ Aquinas's description of discipleship with Christ is akin to apprenticeship with a master: Christ is the master craftsman of the moral life, and his followers are apprentices in the trade of right living. With these terms better in focus, we can turn our attention to St. Thomas's conception of how Christ, the master, guides his people in this divine apprenticeship.

---

2. The contrast between the English word "master" and the Latin term *magister* emerges vividly when we compare the Latin of the Vulgate Bible with the English of the Revised Standard Version. Although in English we sometimes translate the Greek word *kyrios* as Lord and sometimes as Master, the Latin of the Vulgate never translates *kyrios* as *magister*. The Vulgate exclusively employs *dominus* to translate *kyrios,* reserving *magister* to translate *didascalos.* For example, although the RSV makes "master" the correlative of "slave," for the Vulgate, as for Aquinas, the correlative of *servus* is not *magister* but *dominus,* such as in the biblical phrases, *non est servus maior domino suo* (Jn 13.16) and *servus nescit quid facit dominus euis* (Jn 15.15).

3. T. C. O'Brien, "*Sacra Doctrina* Revisited: The Context of Medieval Education," *Thomist* 41 (1977): 475–509; James Weisheipl, "The Meaning of *Sacra Doctrina* in *Summa theologiae* I q. 1," *Thomist* 38 (1974): 49–80; Marie-Dominique Chenu, *Toward Understanding Saint Thomas,* trans. A. M. Landry and D. Hughes (Chicago: Henry Regnery, 1964), 233, 235–38; J. de Ghellinck, "'Pagina' et 'Sacra pagina.' Histoire d'un mot et transformation de l'objet primitivement désigné," in *Mélanges Auguste Pelze études d'histoire littéraire et doctrinale de la scholatique médievale* (Louvain: Bibliothèque de l'Université, 1947), 23–59.

4. The analogy of apprenticeship is suggested by the early modern philosopher of education, Johann Comenius in his *Great Didactic,* ch. 21, n. 7, and ch. 27, n. 1. See John Amos Comenius, *The Great Didactic,* trans. M. W. Keatinge (London: Black, 1896). Cited in John Edward Sadler, *J. A. Comenius and the Concept of Universal Education* (New York: Barnes and Noble, 1966), 224 and 251.

THE FATHER AS A TEACHER WHO CALLS AND ATTRACTS US TO DISCIPLESHIP

The first reference to the term *"magister"* in St. Thomas's *Commentary on John* appears in his analysis of the opening phrase of the Gospel: "In the beginning was the word." Thomas considers the ways in which Christ is a "beginning," a *principium*. He explains that in any discipline there is a twofold order: an order proper to the nature of the subject and an order that belongs to it in relation to us. Consequently, in the discipline of the Christian life *(disciplina christiana)* Christ is the beginning and principle of our wisdom in two ways. According to his proper nature in his divinity as the Word of God, he is wisdom itself. In relation to us, however, as the Word made flesh in the incarnation, he becomes a wisdom attainable by us *(Ioan.* 1, lect. 1, n. 34). Both as the Word and as the Word-made-flesh, therefore, Christ is the principle and wellspring of all our wisdom.

This description of Christ places God the Father in the role of the teacher and Christ in the role of what is taught. Indeed, elsewhere in his *Commentary*, Aquinas describes Christ as the *"ars patris,"* the embodiment of the Father's redeeming art. Just as the Word was the pattern *(exemplar)* according to which the Father created the world, so too the Word is the pattern *(exemplar)* according to which we are justified *(Ioan.* 13, lect. 3, n. 1781). Aquinas holds that Christ himself addresses the Father's role as the teacher of salvation in the Bread of Life discourse. There, Christ quotes Isaiah (54:13), "They shall all be taught by God," adding that "Everyone who listens to my Father and learns from him comes to me" (Jn 6:45). For St. Thomas the crucial feature of the Father's pedagogy is the way in which it leads us to a relationship of loving trust with his Son. The Father does not merely teach us about the Son, he leads us to him; as Christ himself states, "no one can come to me unless the Father who sent me draw him" (Jn 6:44).

Aquinas asserts that the Father does this in the gift of faith. Although the act of faith is something we do, it is primarily a gift of God, who "draws" us to believe in his Son. By responding to this gift through an act of loving trust in Christ, one begins to be a disciple of Christ and enter into the apprenticeship of the Christian life.

This drawing by the Father is most effective, because, "every one who has heard the Father and has learned, comes to me." Here he mentions two things: first, what relates to a gift of God, when he says, "has heard," that is, through God who reveals; the other relates to a free decision *(liberum arbitrium)*, when he says, "and has learned," that is, by an assent. These two are necessary for every teaching of faith.

"Every one who has heard the Father," teaching and making known, "and has learned," by giving assent, "comes to me." (*Ioan.* 6, lect, n. 946)

The disciples hear what the Father reveals about his son through the Father's revealing grace, but they only learn what this means through a loving assent of the will. In other words, although faith is a gift that enlightens the intellect, we only truly learn what faith reveals when we respond in God's gift of love. Aquinas is careful here to strike a balance between knowledge and love in the act of faith: although the intellect's hearing requires the learning of love, love's learning also requires the intellect's hearing.

In each way [that one comes to Christ] it is necessary that one hear and learn. The one who comes through a knowledge of the truth must hear when God inspires: "I will hear what the Lord God will speak within me" (Ps 84:9); and he must learn through affection, as was said. The one who comes through love and desire—as the Lord describes below (Jn 7:37), "if any one thirsts, let him come to me and drink"— must hear the word of the Father and grasp it, in order to be moved in his affections. For that person learns the word who grasps it according to the meaning of the speaker. But the Word of God the Father breathes forth love. Therefore, the one who grasps it with eager love, learns. "Wisdom goes into holy souls, and makes them prophets and friends of God" (Ws 7:27). (*Ioan.* 6, lect. 5, n. 946)

In order to love, the intellect must first hear. Nonetheless, to learn what the intellect hears, we must love what we hear.[5]

Lastly, Aquinas affirms that the Father's pedagogy leads to action. This hearing and learning lead the disciple to right action in imitation of Christ. Just as in speculative reasoning one who learns is led to affirm the right conclusion, so too in practical reasoning, one who learns is led to engage in right action (*Ioan.* 6, lect. 5, n. 946). Consequently, in Aquinas's view, the Father's pedagogy leads us to Christ in a threefold way: "by the knowledge of truth, the affection of love, and the imitation of action" (*Ioan.* 6, lect. 5, n. 946).

We began our analysis of the Father's role in the call to discipleship by noting that St. Thomas portrays the Father as a teacher and Christ as what is taught. Elsewhere in his *Commentary*, however, we learn that as the wisdom of God, Christ is also our teacher. "As the wisdom of God he teaches everyone" (*Ioan.* 13, lect. 3, n. 1775). Not only does he teach us in his humanity by his words and deeds, but as God he teaches us interiorly, illuminating our minds. Indeed, although for Aquinas, the Father, Son, and Spirit are all equally our teachers (*Ioan.* 16, lect. 3, n. 2103), through the incarnation the

---

5. See Jean-Pierre Torrell, *Saint Thomas d'Aquin, maître spirituel, Initiation 2* (Paris: Éditions du Cerf, 1996), 8.

Son becomes our teacher in a unique way. He it is who calls us to enter into a unique apprenticeship of trust.

FAITH IN THE MASTER AS THE CORNERSTONE OF DISCIPLESHIP

The Role of Faith in Learning

In the *Summa theologiae,* St. Thomas explains the necessity of faith by analogy with the process of learning in the sciences. "In order for someone to arrive at the perfect vision of happiness, he must first believe God, as a disciple believes the master who is teaching him."[6] In order to learn from another, we must first believe that the other is trustworthy and knowledgeable in the subject at hand. Aquinas elsewhere explains that this is true at all levels of human learning.[7] In his *Conferences on the Creed,* he states:

> If a person were willing to believe only those things that he could know with assurance, he would not be able to live in this world. How would anyone be able to live unless he believed someone? How would he even know who his own father was? One must, therefore, believe someone about those things that he cannot know perfectly by himself.[8]

Aquinas offers a similar argument in his *Commentary on John:*

> This intellectual life is made perfect by the true knowledge of divine wisdom, which is eternal life: "this is eternal life: that they know you, the only true God, and Jesus Christ, whom you have sent" (Jn 17:3). But no one can arrive at any wisdom except by faith. Hence it is that in the sciences, no one acquires wisdom unless he first believes what is said by his teacher. Therefore, if we wish to acquire this life of wisdom, we must believe through faith the things proposed to us by it. "He who comes to God must believe that he exists and rewards those who seek him" (Heb 11:6); or as we read in another verse of Isaiah, "if you do not believe, you will not understand" (Is 28:16). (*Ioan.* 5, lect. 4, n. 771)

Like students everywhere, an apprentice in the Christian life must first trust his teacher, trust that his master knows the way of holiness and union with God, and desires to share that knowledge with us.

---

6. *ST* II-II, q. 2, a. 3.

7. For a contemporary investigation of the role of faith in learning, see Jerry Gill, *Learning to Learn: Toward a Philosophy of Education* (Atlantic Highlands, N.J.: Humanities Press, 1993), especially page 58.

8. *Collationes Credo in Deum* 1.

The Disciples' Growth in Faith

St. Thomas notes that in John's Gospel the followers of Jesus grow in their faith. For example, Thomas explains that when Nicodemus calls Christ "Rabbi," he recognizes Christ's office as a teacher; when Nicodemus further states that "no one could perform the signs you perform, unless he had God with him" (Jn 3:2) he affirms Christ's power. Yet, Nicodemus goes no further. Consequently, although Nicodemus believes that Christ is a true teacher who comes from God and is empowered by God to perform signs, he is silent about whether Christ is God. In St. Thomas's view, Nicodemus has the gift of faith but still remains in the ignorance of an imperfect faith. For this reason, it was appropriate for Nicodemus to come to Jesus at night. "Night was appropriate to his ignorance and the imperfect knowledge he had of Christ" (*Ioan.* 3, lect. 1, n. 427). Aquinas adds, however, that the literal reason Nicodemus visits him at night was his imperfect love. Nicodemus, he explains,

> was one of those of whom it is said that they "believed in him; but they did not admit it because of the Pharisees, so that they would not be expelled from the synagogue" (Jn 12:42). Their love was not perfect, so it continues, "For they loved the glory of men more than the glory of God." (*Ioan.* 3, lect. 1, n. 427)

Here again Aquinas establishes a close connection between knowledge and love. Nicodemus approaches the Lord in darkness, a darkness caused by an imperfect faith and a faulty love.

St. Thomas portrays Mary Magdalene as another example of a disciple whose faith is imperfect. She recognizes the resurrected Christ as her teacher, and hence calls him Rabbi, but she is still ignorant of his divinity. Hence, in Aquinas's view, when the Lord tells her not to cling to him, he is telling her not to cling to her partial understanding of who he is (see *Ioan.* 20, lect. 3, n. 2517). We should note that Aquinas apparently does not see her partial faith as blameworthy. In the *Summa theologiae,* Aquinas allows that as with all students, the disciples' understanding is partial in the beginning, but grows over time.

> Progress in knowledge can occur in two ways. In one way, on the part of the teacher, be he one or many, who advances in knowledge, through a temporal succession. This is how knowledge advances in the sciences by means of human discovery. In another way, progress in knowledge occurs on the part of the learner, as when a teacher who knows the whole art does not give it all to the student from the beginning, because the student would not be able to grasp it all, but, adjusting himself to the student's capacities, gives it to him gradually. This is the reason why the human person ad-

vances in the knowledge of faith through a temporal succession. Hence, the Apostle compares the period of the Old Testament to childhood (Gal 3–4).[9]

Aquinas identifies concrete examples of the disciples' growth in faith in his analysis of the Johannine account of the Last Supper. When Jesus tells the disciples that they know both where he is going and how to get there, Thomas the Apostle balks at this and exclaims, "Lord, we do not know where you are going, how can we know the way?" (Jn 14:5). Aquinas explains that although the disciples deny it, they do already on one level know where Jesus is going and the way to get there, because they already know Jesus who is both our goal and the way to it. "Christ is at once both the way and the destination. He is the way by reason of his human nature and the destination because of his divinity" (*Ioan.* 14, lect. 2, n. 1868). Yet, their knowledge of Jesus is still imperfect. "They knew, but they did not know that they knew" (*Ioan.* 14, lect. 2, n. 1866). Aquinas explains this apparent paradox by appealing to the distinction between principles and conclusions.

One and the same thing can be known perfectly and imperfectly, as is clear in the sciences, where one who knows all the principles of a science is said to know that science, although imperfectly, ... because everything that belongs to that science is virtually contained in its principles. But one knows that same science more perfectly when he knows the individual conclusions that were virtually in the principles. In this way also we can have a twofold knowledge of divine matters. One is imperfect and is gained by faith, which is a foretaste of that other future knowledge and happiness which we will have in our heavenly homeland. (*Ioan.* 15, lect. 3, n. 2018)

Consequently, at this point in their journey with Christ, the disciples know Jesus and have learned from him the fundamental principles of the faith—"for they knew many things about the Father and the Son which they had learned from Christ"—but they do not yet grasp the implications of this teaching (*Ioan.* 14, lect. 2, n. 1866). They still do not grasp that Jesus and the Father are one; hence, even at this late date Philip asks, "show us the Father" (Jn 14:8). He still does not understand that he who sees Jesus sees the Father (see *Ioan.* 14, lect. 3, n. 1886). Nonetheless, Aquinas holds that the Lord does not fault them for this ignorance, because knowledge of the Father and of Christ's relationship to him is difficult to grasp. "For it is difficult to go to the Father, nor is it surprising that they did not know the way, because although they perfectly knew Christ as man they did not perfectly understand his divinity" (*Ioan.* 14, lect. 2, n. 1866).

St. Thomas also draws on St. Paul's distinction between the "spiritual

9. *ST* II-II, q. 1, a. 7, ad 2.

man" and the "natural man" to explain the manner of the disciples' growth in understanding. At first, the disciples fail to grasp Christ's teaching because of their purely natural mindset. Later, however, after they receive the grace of the Spirit they begin to acquire a spiritual perspective. This spiritual perspective enables them grasp the content of Christ's message.

> The natural person receives spiritual teachings as mere figures of speech, not because they were spoken to him that way, but, since his mind does not have the power to rise above material things, spiritual things remain hidden to him: "the natural person does not perceive the things that belong to the spirit of God" (1 Cor. 2:14). Yet, the spiritual person receives spiritual teachings as spiritual. In the beginning, the disciples themselves had a purely natural mindset, and what was said to them remained obscure to them. They received it as mere figures. But, after they were made spiritual by Christ and were taught by the Holy Spirit, they began to grasp spiritual things clearly as spiritual. (*Ioan.* 16, lect. 7, n. 2152)

This passage reveals that the transition from purely natural to spiritual understanding becomes possible only through the action of the Holy Spirit in the gift of grace. We shall look at the Spirit's role in this divine pedagogy more fully in a later section. Here, however, the key feature to recognize is the role of faith. In Aquinas's view, we grow in our understanding of Christ only by trustingly clinging to him.

> If, therefore, you ask by what way you should go, accept Christ, for he is *the way*: "this is the way, walk in it" (Is 30:21). As Augustine says: "walk by means of the man and you will come to God. For it is better to limp along on the way than to walk rapidly off the way." Because he who limps on the way, even if he makes little progress, is approaching his goal; but if one ambles off the way, the faster he runs the further he gets from his goal. Yet, if you ask where you should go, adhere to Christ, because he is *the truth* at which we desire to arrive. "My mouth will meditate upon the truth" (Prov. 8:7). If you ask where you should remain, adhere to Christ because he is *the life*. "He who finds me finds life and shall have salvation from the Lord" (Prov. 8:35). (*Ioan.* 14, lect. 2, n. 1870)

Since Christ is "the way, the truth and the life" (Jn 14:6), it is by slowly walking in his way, clinging to his truth, and remaining in his life that we advance on the way, grow in knowledge of the truth, and begin to be fully alive.

According to Aquinas, this growth in faith occurs in and through an ongoing dialogue with Christ. Some people pose questions out of a lack of faith, as when Zechariah questions the angel. Others, however, question out of a zeal to learn (*studium addiscendi*). The Virgin Mary is the classic example of this studious desire. Indeed, even Nicodemus is motivated by a sincere desire to learn, and for this reason he merits an answer from the Lord (*Ioan.* 3, lect. 2, n. 458). The dialogue between master and disciple also entails the Master asking questions of his disciples. For example, in the Bread of Life discourse Jesus asks Philip, "where shall we buy bread that these may eat?" (Jn 6:44). Commenting on the Evangelist's explanation that Jesus posed this question in order to test Philip, Thomas affirms that this questioning was part of the teacher's method of teaching others by means of questions (see *Ioan.* 6, lect. 1, n. 850). The role of such questions is to prompt the disciples to reflect (*Ioan.* 13, lect. 3, n. 1773). Aquinas asserts that "we should meditate on the works of God because they are profound" (*Ioan.* 13, lect. 3, n. 1773). To this end, Christ questions the disciples in order to "rouse their understanding" (*Ioan.* 13, lect. 3, n. 1773). For example, the questions Jesus poses both to Martha at the tomb of her brother Lazarus and to Peter at the lakeshore after the resurrection lead the disciples to come to deeper understanding. Specifically, the questions reveal the effect of God's grace in the lives of his followers: they bring to light Martha's faith and Peter's love (*Ioan.* 11, lect. 4, n. 1518; 21, 3, n. 2617). Indeed, St. Thomas goes so far as to describe Peter's encounter with the Lord as an examination *(examinatio de dilectione)* (*Ioan.* 21, lect. 3, n. 2617).

Aquinas recognizes that the questioning dialogue between the master and his disciples can at times become heated. The classic example of this occurs in Christ's relationship with Peter. Aquinas describes Peter's exchange with the Lord over the washing of his feet as a confrontation between master and disciple *(Concertationem discipuli et magistri)* (*Ioan.* 13, lect. 2, n. 1751).[10] Nevertheless, because Peter confronts his teacher from a sincere and loving desire to learn, Christ explains to Peter the meaning of his actions (see *Ioan.* 13, lect. 2, nn. 1752–54).

10. The term *concertatio* is rarely employed by Aquinas. The translators of the English edition of the *Commentary* translate it as "encounter," but this is too weak. In the thirteen instances Aquinas uses the term it always caries the connotation of a conflict out of which someone emerges victorious. In other words, *concertatio* always implies a *victor* and a *victum*. In its strongest form it is synonymous with *pugna*, as when Thomas employs it to describe the conflict between the good and bad angels (II *Sent.*, d. 11, q. 2, a. 5, sc. 2), or when he speaks of the *"concertatio bellorum"* proper to warfare (*Expositio super Iob ad litteram*, ch. 29). In this same vain, Thomas explicitly regards it as a synonym for *"pugna pugilum"* and *"monomachia"* which we would normally translate as boxing or wrestling (*ST* II-II, q. 95, a 8, obj. 3, and *ST* I-II, q. 32, a. 6, ad 3). In its weakest form, it signifies a verbal argument *(concertatio verborum)*, such as the ones that occur between lawyers (*ST* II-II, q. 188, a. 3, obj. 2). This seems to be the sense of *concertatio* in the *Commentary*. Peter is arguing with Jesus in a confrontative manner. Note that St. Thomas does not fault Peter for his confrontative manner. On the contrary, he describes Peter's actions as flowing from his intense love and friendship for Christ (*Ioan.* 13, lect. 2, n. 1753); moreover, Thomas portrays Peter's question to Jesus as "words that have great depth," *verba magnum pondus habent* (*Ioan.* 13, lect. 2, n. 1755). What St. Thomas does find blameworthy in Peter's behavior is his stubborn refusal to conform himself to the wisdom and will of Christ (*Ioan.* 13, lect. 2, n. 1758). For Aquinas, therefore, the questioning and probing heart is no danger as long as it is a humble heart willing to commend itself to the wise care of Christ.

In Aquinas's view, the process by which the disciple grows in knowledge ultimately leads from the knowledge of faith to the knowledge of glory.

> The ultimate happiness of the human person consists in the supernatural vision of God. The human person cannot come to this vision except through being taught by God, as is stated in John's Gospel: "everyone who has heard and learns from my Father comes to me." But this instruction *(disciplina)* makes the human person participate in this knowledge, not all at once, but successively, according to the manner proper to his nature. For everyone who would learn such things must believe in order to come to perfect knowledge, as the Philosopher also affirms, stating that "the learner must believe." Consequently, in order for someone to arrive at the perfect vision of happiness, he must first believe God, as a disciple believes the master who is teaching him.[11]

According to Aquinas, therefore, when the Lord leads the disciples to grow in their understanding, he does so gradually, in the way a teacher guides his students from faith to clear sight.

THE MASTER'S METHODS

St. Thomas's General Theory of Teaching

Scattered throughout his *Commentary on John,* St. Thomas offers brief observations concerning the nature of learning. For example, when commenting on the assertion from *John* chapter 7 that "whoever speaks on his own seeks his own glory" (Jn 7:18), Thomas states that all our knowledge is from another, explaining that we acquire knowledge in three ways: by way of discovery, by way of revelation, or by way of instruction *(disciplina).* In discovery, we learn from the things we are investigating; hence Paul states that "the invisible things of God are clearly known by the things that have been made" (Rm 1:20). In revelation, we learn directly from God. When we learn from a *disciplina,* however, we learn from a teacher (*Ioan.* 7, lect. 2, n. 1040). St. Thomas presents elsewhere what he means by a *disciplina.* A *disciplina* is any demonstrative science in which we acquire knowledge from demonstrations offered by a teacher *(magister).*[12] In the *Summa theologiae,* we learn that a *disciplina* need not refer merely to speculative knowledge. There are also practical disciplines. For example, Thomas describes religious life as a *disciplina vel exercitium,* contending that "whoever wishes to learn or to train for a goal,

---

11. *ST* II-II, q. 2, a. 3.

12. *In Boethii De Hebdomadibus* 1: "ex huiusmodi autem principiis intendit concludere et facere nota omnia quae consequenter tractanda sunt, sicut fit in geometria, et in aliis demonstrativis scientiis, quae ideo dicuntur disciplinae, quia per eas discipulis aggregatur scientia ex demonstratione quam magister proponit."

must follow the direction of someone under whose guidance they learn and are trained, as disciples learn from a master."[13] Knowledge acquired from a *disciplina*, therefore, is knowledge acquired in a relationship with a teacher, with one who is a master in that domain of knowledge.

We also find in the *Summa theologiae* Thomas's description of how a master teaches a discipline. "Whoever teaches leads a student from things he knows to the knowledge of things he does not know, as is stated in the *Posterior Analytics:* 'every doctrine and every discipline causes knowledge from pre-existing principles.'"[14] Thomas states that a teacher does this in two ways. The teacher either offers aids to learning, such as sensible examples or less universal propositions, that help the student reason from what he knows to what he does not know, or the teacher guides the student step by step through the stages of reasoning from principles to conclusion, much the way one might trace on a map the stages of an itinerary. In the first way, the teacher is helping the student reason by himself from principles to conclusions; in the second way, the teacher guides the student through a process of reasoning that he could not achieve on his own.[15]

Thomas notes, however, that both these ways of teaching presuppose the presence of principles within the student that the teacher does not cause. For this reason, the role of the teacher is akin to the role of the physician. Just as a physician leads the patient to health by helping the principles of health within the patient do their work in healing, so too the teacher leads the student to knowledge by helping the principles of learning do their work in reasoning to conclusions.[16] In other words, as is the case with the physician, a teacher is merely the external cause of the student's learning. The essential work of learning is done by the student himself in and through his natural gifts.

Aquinas holds, however, that Jesus is an exception to this rule. Following the conclusions St. Augustine reaches in the *De Magistro* (Augustine's famous dialogue with his son, Adeodatus), Aquinas contends that Jesus teaches both exteriorly, in the ways described above, and interiorly in his divinity, as the cause of the inner principles of learning. He teaches externally through instruction and internally through illumination, enlightening the mind with the principles of wisdom and knowledge.[17]

The twofold character of Christ's teaching provides Aquinas a way to interpret the words of Jesus in Matthew's Gospel, "Do not let yourselves be called teacher *(magister)*, because one alone is your teacher, the Christ" (Mt

---

13. *ST* II-II, q. 186, a. 5.   14. *ST* I, q. 117, a. 1.
15. *ST* I, q. 117, a. 1.   16. *ST* I, q. 117, a. 1, ad 1.
17. See *De ver.*, q. 11, a. 1 *corpus* and ad 8; Augustine, *De Magistro* (*PL* 32: 1193–1220).

23:10). Christ alone is the true teacher because in his divinity he is the first cause of all our learning, teaching us interiorly as the cause of our inner principles of learning. Christ's disciples, on the other hand, can be called teachers only by extension. They merit this title only to the extent that they participate in Christ's teaching mission. They are the external instruments of Christ's interior teaching action.[18] St. Thomas gives us a poignant account of this truth in his inaugural lecture, delivered in the Spring of 1256 when he was assuming the responsibilities of a *magister* for the first time. After describing the exalted nature of the teaching office, he adds,

> But "who is capable of this?" (2 Cor. 2:16). . . . Yet, although no one is adequate for this ministry by himself and from his own resources, he can hope that God will make him adequate. "Not that we are capable of a single thought on our own resources, as if it came from us, but our adequacy is from God" (2 Cor. 3:5). So the teacher should ask God for it. "If people lack wisdom, they should beg for it from God and it will be given them" (James 1:5).[19]

He concludes by beseeching his audience, "let us pray that Christ may grant this to us."[20] Christ, therefore, is the one true teacher. In his divinity he is the first cause of all learning. Yet, in the greatness of his power and providence he is able to employ his creatures as instruments and secondary causes of his teaching. They thus become teachers by participation and truly merit the title *magistri*.[21] Consequently, since it is by God's good design that they can become teachers, their attitude toward Christ must always be one of prayer. They must ask Christ the teacher for the insights they need as the instruments of his instruction.

Christ the Teacher

In his *Commentary on John*, St. Thomas is true to his Christ-centered theology of education. Thomas portrays Jesus as a teacher instructing his disciples about the way to eternal life. Aquinas affirms that Jesus teaches both by word and by example (*Ioan.* 2, lect. 2, n. 375). By the example of his submission to the Law, Jesus teaches humility to his disciples, (*Ioan.* 2, lect. 2, n. 375) while with his challenging words to Nicodemus he teaches Nicodemus this same virtue (*Ioan.* 3, lect. 2, n. 460). By the example of his obedient love of

---

18. *De ver.*, q. 11, a. 1 ad 1.
19. *Principium 'Rigans montes de superioribus.'*
20. *Principium 'Rigans montes de superioribus.'* For the addition of the *"quod"* see Simon Tugwell, *Albert and Thomas: Selected Writings*, trans. and ed., with an introduction by Simon Tugwell, Classics of Western Spirituality (New York: Paulist Press, 1988), 360 n. 16.
21. *De ver.*, q. 11, a. 1 ad. 9.

the Father, Jesus teaches his disciples the character of the obedient love they should extend to him (*Ioan.* 15, lect. 2, n. 2003). Like other teachers, Jesus both instructs the faithful and refutes his adversaries (*Ioan.* 8, lect. 1, n. 1118). Unlike other teachers, however, his teaching during his earthly ministry had the power to illumine and to vivify the faithful—"because his words are spirit and life"—and to overcome and hold at bay those who wished to destroy him (*Ioan.* 8, lect. 2, n. 1118; 8, 2, n. 1163).

The Summit of Christ's Teaching Mission

Although Thomas portrays several events in the Gospel—such as Christ's actions at the feast of booths—as emblematic examples of Christ's teaching, Thomas seems to regard the events of the Last Supper and of the passion as the summit of Christ's teaching ministry. Indeed, Aquinas follows Augustine in proclaiming that "Christ hung from the cross the way a teacher sits in his chair *(sicut magister in cathedra)*" (*Ioan.* 19, lect. 4, n. 2441).[22] John's description of the passion as Christ's glorification seems to suggest to Aquinas this educational role. Aquinas regards glorification as a type of revelatory teaching. One who is glorified is "known with clarity" (*Ioan.* 13, lect. 6, n. 1826). In Aquinas's view, the glorification of Christ is what reveals both the merit of his humanity and the fullness of his divinity. Specifically, it reveals the perfectly obedient love of God and neighbor present in Christ's human nature and the full divinity present in his divine nature (*Ioan.* 13, lect. 6, n. 1829).[23] "He began to have this glory [in other words, he began to be known with clarity] at his passion and resurrection, when people began to recognize his power and divinity" (*Ioan.* 13, lect. 6, n. 1830). Aquinas has in mind here the acts of faith expressed by such people as the centurion at Christ's death, Mary Magdalene at the tomb, and Thomas the Apostle in the upper room. The glorification of Christ makes his perfect humanity and full divinity known in the gift of faith. In Aquinas's view, the revelatory properties of these events are so profound and universal they are how all people in the gift of faith come to knowledge of God. "All who know God owe this to Christ" (*Ioan.* 13, lect. 6, n. 1830).

Aquinas also tells us here that the events of the passion begin the moment Judas leaves the upper room (*Ioan.* 13, lect. 6, n. 1827). Consequently, the Last Supper is also the moment when Christ's true identity begins to be recog-

---

22. For example, his care for his mother during his suffering on the cross teaches us the importance of coming to the aid of our parents (*Ioan.* 19, lect. 4, n. 2441).
23. For his treatment of the merit of his humanity glorifying God, see *Ioan.* 13, lect. 6, n. 1828. For his treatment of the glorification of his divinity, see *Ioan.* 13, lect. 6, n. 1829.

nized clearly, as Christ himself states from his place at the table: "Now is the Son of man glorified" (Jn 13:31; *Ioan.* 13, lect. 6, n. 1827). This fact seems to lead Aquinas to portray the events of the Last Supper as something akin to a graduate seminar on the Christian life. He views every word and deed of Christ on that night as belonging to a rich pedagogy of perfection.

The Role of Christ's Example

Aquinas discerns an order of presentation in Christ's pedagogy. "The sequence found in this exhortation is that Christ later taught in words what he had first done by his actions" (*Ioan.* 13, lect. 3, n. 1769). Christ first acts and then explains his actions. Aquinas holds that this procedure is fitting because the example of one's life teaches more powerfully than the eloquence of one's words.

> For when we are dealing with the conduct of people, example has more influence than words. A person chooses and does what seems good to him, and so what one chooses is a better indication of what is good than what one teaches should be chosen. This is why when someone says one thing and does another, what he does has more influence on others than what he has taught. Thus it is especially necessary to give example by one's action. (*Ioan.* 13, lect. 3, n. 1781)

Aquinas reminds us that the purpose of Christ's teaching is to lead us to the Father. This fact shapes Christ's behavior during the Last Supper. "Since Christ is going to God, it is special to him to lead others to God. This is done especially by humility and love; and so he offers them an example of humility and love" (*Ioan.* 13, lect. 1, n. 1743). Since humility and love are what especially lead us to God, Christ offers them the humble and loving example of washing their feet.

St. Thomas affirms that Christ's example of humble love is meant first of all to prepare them for the events of his crucifixion and death (*Ioan.* 13, lect. 1, n. 1738). Thomas adds, however, that the act of washing their feet is also meant to teach them the nature of the service they should render to each other. Indeed, Thomas regards Christ's actions as offering a perfect symbol of true service. A good servant always strives to notice whatever might be lacking at the table; hence, the servant stands in order to survey the needs of all the guests. Moreover, to be unencumbered in this service, a good servant wears a minimum of clothing. Lastly, a good servant always has on hand what he needs to serve his master well. According to Aquinas, John's Gospel tells us that Jesus exhibited each of these traits. Jesus stood, removed his garments, and placed a towel around his waist to dry his disciples' feet. Christ, therefore, is the good servant, giving his disciples an example to follow.

The Implications of Christ's Clothing and Posture

St. Thomas later contrasts Christ's behavior when washing his disciples' feet with his behavior when explaining to them the meaning of these actions. When washing their feet he embodies the symbols of a servant; when explaining his actions, however, he takes on the symbols of a teacher. Thomas draws our attention to both Christ's clothing and posture. Indeed, he points out that the Evangelist himself is careful to note both of these. In Thomas's view, clothing and posture are both important. Clothing is important because "different clothing is suitable to different people depending on the different activities appropriate to each. Thus, Sirach states, 'a man's attire . . . shows what he is' (Sir 19:30)" (*Ioan.* 13, lect. 3, n. 1770). Aquinas continues:

> One sort of attire is suitable for a servant, and another for a teacher. Now because a servant must be ready to serve, he does not have any superfluous clothing; and so Christ, when he wished to serve, "rose from supper, and laid aside his garments." Yet, it is proper for a teacher, who should have gravity and should emanate authority, to be suitably attired. Thus, when our Lord begins to teach, he "puts on his garments." (*Ioan.* 13, lect. 3, n. 1770)

Aquinas addresses what he seems to regard as an evident truth. What a teacher or preacher wears affects how his message is received. Aquinas, however, is silent concerning the character of this clothing. He tells us that teachers should be "suitably attired"—literally that they should be "suitably ornate of clothing," *vestium decens ornatus*—but offers no description of the type of clothing that would serve this purpose.

St. Thomas next addresses the pedagogical significance of Christ's posture, of his decision to recline while teaching them the meaning of his actions.

> When Christ began to serve he rose; thus [the Evangelist] says that Christ "rose from supper." Yet now, about to teach, he reclines; hence [the Evangelist] says "when he had reclined again, he said to them." The reason for this is that *doctrina* should take place in tranquility. (*Ioan.* 13, lect. 3, n. 1770)

Aquinas defends the connection between tranquility and learning by adding a line from Aristotle's *Physics:* "it is by sitting down and by being quietly at rest that the soul becomes wise and prudent" (*Ioan.* 13, lect. 3, n. 1770).[24] In his *Commentary on the De Anima,* Aquinas makes this reference to Aristotle explicit:

---

24. *Physics* 7.3 (247b10).

Understanding is best compared to quiet rest. Aristotle himself teaches this in book seven of the *Physics* (7.3) where he states that one cannot become wise until he rests and becomes quiet. This is why it is not easy to find wisdom among the young and the restless. Instead, one finds wisdom when he is quietly at rest. Hence, Aristotle says that it is by sitting down and by being quietly at rest that the soul becomes wise and prudent.[25]

The environment proper to the *disciplina* that is *sacra doctrina*, therefore, is to recline and be at rest with the Lord, like the disciples in the upper room. Consequently, for St. Thomas, the upper room at the Last Supper becomes the ideal model for theological instruction.

St. Thomas adds that Christ's act of washing the disciples' feet is not merely an example; it is also a mystery (*Ioan.* 13, lect. 2, n. 1756). This washing is a mystery that "signifies a interior cleansing" (*Ioan.* 13, lect. 2, n. 1756). Indeed, Thomas follows the Fathers of the Church in discerning layers of meaning in Christ's every action while washing the disciples' feet (see *Ioan.* 13, lect. 2, nn. 1746–48). The reference to mystery points to the Holy Spirit's role as the interior master who will teach the disciples the deeper meaning of Christ's actions after the resurrection.

The Holy Spirit as an Internal Teacher

We noted earlier that St. Thomas describes Christ as a teacher who teaches both exteriorly by his words and actions and interiorly as the cause of the intellectual principles by which the disciples understand these words and actions. Later in his *Commentary*, however, Thomas explains that Christ's interior teaching occurs through the Holy Spirit. "No one learns without the Holy Spirit teaching" (*Ioan.* 14, lect. 6, n. 1959). Christ in his humanity teaches exteriorly, but this exterior teaching is rendered intelligible through the Holy Spirit. "The Son, since he is the Word, gives teaching to us; but the Holy Spirit enables us to grasp it" (*Ioan.* 14, lect. 6, n. 1958). The Spirit, "in a hidden way aids our ability to know" (*Ioan.* 14, lect. 6, n. 1960). Aquinas seems to regard the Spirit's action as necessary in any act of understanding.

---

25. *In De Anima* 1, lect. 8, n. 125: "[intelligentia] magis assimiletur quieti quam motui, patet, quia, sicut ipse dicit in septimo physicorum, non potest fieri aliquis sapiens, quando motus eius non resident nec quiescunt. unde in pueris, et in omnibus in quibus motus non quiescunt, non de facili invenitur sapientia. sed tunc aliquis sapientiam acquirit, quando quiescit: unde dicit, quod in quiescendo et sedendo, anima fit sapiens et prudens." See also *ST* I-II, q. 33, a. 3 obj. 1. Aquinas appears to be quoting the Physics from memory, because in his commentary on the Physics he renders the line slightly differently: "sed scientia, quae est cognitio speculativa, et prudentia, quae est ratio practica, adveniunt animae per quietationem et residentiam corporalium motionum et sensibilium passionum" (*In Physic.* 7, lect. 6, n. 925).

No matter what a person may teach by his exterior actions, he will have no effect unless the Holy Spirit gives an understanding from within. For unless the Spirit is present to the heart of the listener, the words of the teacher will be useless: "the inspiration of the Almighty makes him understand" (Job 32:8). (*Ioan.* 14, lect. 6, n. 1958)

Aquinas is here offering a window into the role of love in learning. He seems to be saying that unless there is love in our hearts we cannot truly understand what our teachers are telling us. At this point, Thomas says no more about this interesting educational principle. Instead, he chooses to underline that Christ in his humanity is no exception to this rule. "This is true even to the extent that the Son himself, speaking by means of his human nature, is not successful unless he works from within by the Holy Spirit" (*Ioan.* 14, lect. 6, n. 1958). Christ teaches exteriorly by his words and actions, but interiorly through the action of the Holy Spirit.

In commenting on Jesus' statements that he will send them the Spirit "who will teach them all truth" (Jn 14:26), Thomas discerns two stages in the Spirit's presence among the disciples. There is the initial presence of the Spirit that sanctifies them and gives them a partial understanding of Christ's words and actions. St. Thomas holds that the disciples already had received the Holy Spirit in this way before the events of the Last Supper. This is the meaning of Christ's statement that only their feet need to be washed (Jn 13:10; *Ioan.* 13, lect. 2, nn. 1762–65). Moreover, this preliminary presence of the Spirit is what prepares them to receive the fullness of the Spirit after the resurrection. Thomas explains that to be prepared to receive the fullness of the Holy Spirit the disciples must be loving and obedient. "The disciples needed a twofold preparation: love in their hearts and obedience in their work" (*Ioan.* 14, lect. 4, n. 1908). Both of these are from the Holy Spirit.

No one can love God unless he has the Holy Spirit: because we do not act before we receive God's grace, rather, the grace comes first: 'he first loved us' (1 Jn 4:10). We should say, therefore, that the apostles first received the Holy Spirit so that they could love God and obey his commands. But it was necessary that they make good use, by their love and obedience, of this first gift of the Holy Spirit in order to receive the Spirit more fully. (*Ioan.* 14, lect. 4, n. 1909)

One characteristic of God's gifts is that "if one makes a good use of a gift given to him, he deserves to receive a greater gift and grace" (*Ioan.* 14, lect. 4, n. 1909). Consequently, the Holy Spirit, by empowering the disciples to love God and to obey him in their actions, prepares them to receive the fullness of the Spirit after the resurrection.

Thomas holds that the Spirit's role in the Son's teaching mission is fitting because of the way the Spirit proceeds from the Father and the Son.

The Holy Spirit leads to the knowledge of the truth, because he proceeds from the Truth, who says, 'I am the way, the truth and the life' (Jn 14:6). In us, love of the truth arises when we have conceived and considered truth. So also in God, Love proceeds from conceived Truth, which is the Son. And just as Love proceeds from the Truth, so Love leads to knowledge of the truth. (*Ioan.* 14, lect. 4, n. 1916)

The love that proceeds from truth leads to knowledge of the truth because "it is love that impels one to reveal one's secrets" (*Ioan.* 14, lect. 4, n. 1916). The Son is Wisdom and Truth itself. The Spirit, as proceeding from the Truth, comes to us to make us sharers in the divine wisdom and knowers of the truth. This is what makes the Holy Spirit a teacher. "The Spirit teaches because he makes us share in the wisdom of the Son" (*Ioan.* 14, lect. 6, n. 1960). Earlier we noted that the Father draws us to himself through the teachings of the Son. Now we find that the Father's action through the Son occurs in and through the action of the Spirit. The Father speaks a Word that breaths forth Love. In the incarnation this Word speaks in human words, words that are vivified and made effective by the love of the Spirit.

FRIENDSHIP WITH GOD AS AN INTIMATE APPRENTICESHIP

St. Thomas later describes the disciples' participation in divine wisdom by analogy with human friendship. He portrays the relationship between Christ and his disciples on the eve of his passion as a life of "companionship with Christ" *(societas Christi)* that entailed "freedom from the burdens of material things," and established them in a "mode of life that holds everything in common" (*Ioan.* 16, lect. 8, n. 2171). Thomas offers here a concise description of the Early Dominican conception of the "Apostolic life."[26] The only missing feature is the apostolic vocation to proclaim the Gospel. Thomas has not forgotten this aspect of the apostolic life. Instead, true to the witness of the Gospels, he portrays the general commission to preach the Gospel as arising only after the resurrection, when the disciples receive the fullness of the Spirit.

Aquinas holds that when the apostles abandoned Christ during his passion, they suffered a threefold loss. They lost their companionship with Christ, their freedom from material care, and their common life together. Yet, after the resurrection of Christ and their reception of the Holy Spirit,

---

26. For the early Dominican conception of the apostolic life, see Simon Tugwell, *Early Dominicans: Selected Writings*, ed. with an introduction by Simon Tugwell (New York: Paulist Press, 1982), 16–27; Simon Tugwell, *The Way of the Preacher* (Springfield, Ill.: Templegate Publishers, 1979), 22–32, 42–53, 82–96.

they not only regain their friendship with God and with each other, they are emboldened by the Spirit to go out and teach the nations. Not surprisingly, therefore, when St. Thomas describes the friendship with Christ that the Spirit establishes among the disciples, he focuses on two educational aspects of this friendship: Divine friendship is the context within which (1) God teaches the disciples, and (2) the disciples put this teaching into practice by teaching others.

Christ Reveals his Secrets to his Friends

St. Thomas follows Aristotle in asserting that "the true sign of friendship is that a friend reveals the secrets of his heart to his friend" (*Ioan.* 15, lect. 3, n. 2016). This is so because the intimacy existing between friends creates confidence. Since friends are "of one mind and of one heart," what one friend says to the other seems to remain hidden in one's heart. Aquinas explains that something similar occurs when we become the friends of God. As God unites our hearts and minds to himself, "God reveals his secrets to us by letting us share in his wisdom: 'In every generation [Wisdom] passes into holy souls and makes them friends of God and prophets'" (Wis 7:27; *Ioan.* 15, lect. 3, n. 2016). Although it is God's love that establishes us in divine friendship, it is only by responding to this love that our friendship grows. Specifically, it is only by loving God in return (in and through the grace of the Holy Spirit) that we grow in our knowledge of God. "The secrets of divine wisdom are principally revealed to those who are united to God by love" (*Ioan.* 13, lect. 4, n. 1807). According to Aquinas, the love poured into our hearts by the Spirit is so powerful that it renders the words of Christ as effective today as they were when Christ first spoke them. Because we love Christ's words, they remain alive within us and are able to teach us (*Ioan.* 15, lect. 1, n. 1995). They also empower us to teach others.

The Friends of Christ Become Teachers of the Gospel

Although St. Thomas is clear that the ultimate goal of Christ's teaching is to lead the disciples to the joy of heaven (*Ioan.* 16, lect. 8, nn. 2173–74), he nonetheless also affirms that one of the reasons Christ educates his disciples is to incorporate them into his mission of leading people to himself. Thomas affirms that in his actions, Christ "most of all wanted to instruct [his disciples] who were going to be the teachers of the whole world *(magistri orbis terrarum)*" (*Ioan.* 6, lect. 1, n. 864). As the "Spirit of Truth," the Holy Spirit "teaches the truth and makes those he teaches like the one who sent him" (*Ioan.* 16, lect. 3, n. 2102). The disciples become like the Truth by becoming teachers. "The Spirit will give them the confidence to preach clearly and openly" (*Ioan.* 16, lect. 4, n. 2106). The process whereby "they become fit for bearing the fruit of teaching" entails keeping Christ's words dwelling in their hearts (*Ioan.* 15, lect. 1, n. 1996). Thomas describes this as a fourfold process: *"amando, credendo, meditando et implendo"* (*Ioan.* 15, lect. 1, n. 1995). His words remain in the disciples when they love them and believe them, meditate upon them and accomplish them. These four actually reduce to the twin stages of contemplating and giving the fruits of our contemplation to others.[27] We are to contemplate what we believe and love, and then embody it in our actions *(implendo)*. We embody the words of Christ "by living well" and "by teaching well" (*Ioan.* 15, lect. 1, n. 1996). Thomas describes each of these as glorifying God. Thomas takes special care to note that teaching well "also glorifies God," citing Isaiah: "Glorify the Lord by teaching" (Is 23.15; *Ioan.* 15, lect. 1, n. 1996). As we noted earlier, Aquinas describes glorification as a revelatory action. What is glorified is known clearly. Thus, Thomas is saying that the good news of Christ remains in the disciples when they make God known by the tenor of their lives and the quality of their teaching.

CONCLUSIONS

In this study we have seen that St. Thomas presents Christ as a *magister*. As sent by the Father and working through the Spirit, Christ is the master of the spiritual life. He teaches the disciples the way to eternal happiness and how to grow to full stature as teachers themselves. In the process of presenting Christ as a teacher, Thomas also advances a fairly developed philosophy of education. To learn a practical *disciplina* one must have a mentor who embodies the skills of this discipline and who knows how to teach it to others. Students need to begin by trusting their master, by having faith in his knowledge and abilities. They must also love the subject they are learning in order truly to grasp what it means. The process of acquiring this skill occurs gradually. In learning a task, students naturally pass through stages of understanding and competence. Consequently, when teaching a practical discipline, the master recognizes and respects each student's ability and level of understanding, teaching each one according to his or her capacities. This apprenticeship occurs in an atmosphere of dialogue, where, because of the trust established between master and disciple, the student is able to question and challenge as well as be questioned and challenged. This method of teaching also establishes a camaraderie between the master's students. Together, they grow to know

---

27. See *ST* II-II, q., 188, a. 6.

and love their subject more deeply and acquire a zeal to share this knowledge and love with others.

St. Thomas apparently regards these characteristics as the component features of any authentic method of teaching, of any method that respects human nature. When Thomas presents Christ as a teacher, he portrays him as respecting these natural facets of teaching and learning. Christ both embodies the human role of a *magister* and elevates this role, drawing it into the life of grace. In the incarnation, the eternal Word begins to speak in human words and fills these words with his eternal Love. He speaks these human words in a human way: in a community of companionship, where his disciples learn gradually, in dialogue with their master, with the goal of one day participating in their master's mission to proclaim the good news. By proceeding in this way, Christ respects how humans learn. He respects the developmental, affective, and social facets of human learning. In short, St. Thomas regards the Christ of John's Gospel as the model Christian educator, a model for all those involved in education to follow.

TWELVE

"Come and See"

JANET E. SMITH

Why is it that some people accept Christ as the Son of God and their Savior and others do not? Why is it that some respond to evangelization and others do not? Certainly, sometimes inadequate knowledge or unpersuasive arguments make an evangelizer ineffective. Perhaps the evangelizer's own life is not a model of what he is preaching and thus his teaching is unattractive. But when Christ is the evangelizer, none of these negatives could possibly apply. Is there any explanation why some recognize Christ for who he is when they are invited to "Come and see" and others do not?

ARISTOTELIAN PRINCIPLES

Throughout his *Commentary on the Gospel of St. John,* Aquinas employs the philosophical principles of Aristotle. It would be a mistake to think that Aquinas's allegiance to Aristotle is largely confined to his philosophical commentaries on Aristotle's works and is absent from his more theological works, including his commentaries on Scripture. Indeed, one cannot read far into the *Commentary on John* without seeing the influence of Aristotle everywhere and, indeed, without sensing that here is a refresher course in Aristotelian principles.[1] In the Prologue and the first *lectio* alone, Aquinas draws upon principles from the *Physics,* the *Metaphysics,* the *De Anima,* the *De Interpretatione,* and the *Posterior Analytics,* and there may be other undetected influences.

For instance, as is his common practice, Aquinas employs Aristo-

---

1. For an illuminating discussion on the form and intention of medieval and particularly Thomistic commentary on Scripture, see chapter 7 of Chenu, *Toward Understanding St. Thomas,* especially 249–53. He remarks that Aquinas in his practice of division of the text, for instance, occasionally treats Scripture as a text of Aristotle.

"Come and See"   195

tle's four causes as an interpretive principle in explaining the Gospel of John.[2] Aquinas tells us that the "matter" of the Gospel is the divinity of Christ; he sketches out the order or "form" as moving from the Word as the beginning, to the Word as the creator, and thirdly to the Word Incarnate; the end or "final" cause is "that the faithful become the temple of God, and become filled with the majesty of God" (*Ioan.* prol., n. 10). John, as author, is the "efficient" cause. Aquinas begins the commentary with the observation that John wrote as a contemplative and that his contemplation was "full, high, and perfect." Aquinas's observation that "these three characteristics of contemplation belong to the different sciences in different ways" reflects his acceptance of the Aristotelian division of the sciences; Aquinas tells us that moral science, natural science, and metaphysics are all contained in contemplation and thus in the Gospel of John.[3]

Now, for all my claims of the influence of Aristotle on Aquinas, the influence of Aristotle's *Ethics* on Aquinas's *Commentary* is more implicit than explicit. This should not be surprising since the focus of Aristotle's *Ethics* is on habituation, on the effect of repeated deliberate action in forming one's character, whereas the *Gospel* is much more a report of the workings of grace than of the effects of human choice and action. Nevertheless, the importance of human choice and action lurks near the surface; for instance, Aquinas notes that John presents those who respond favorably to Christ's message as those who are "well-disposed," as those who have the "proper intention" (*Ioan.* 1, lect. 15, nn. 285, 289).[4]

Here I wish to concentrate on the role of moral goodness in an individual's ability to see Christ for who He is. Aquinas's initial focus on the holiness of John plays right into this theme, for Aquinas clearly believes that John has special insight into the person of Christ because he is holy. It is striking that in his commentary on various scenes of conversion in the Gospel of John Aquinas regularly remarks on the role of the moral state of the interlocutor in his or her response to Christ—an element that one might say does not exactly leap out of the text for the casual and perhaps even the discerning reader. Aquinas seems intent on driving home the point that is made repeatedly

---

2. Chenu notes that Aquinas does the same "at the beginning of the Paulinian corpus, of the Epistle to the Ephesians, of the book of Jeremiah" (ibid., 252).

3. Note also, for instance, his review of basic Aristotelian teleology, adapted to a Christian worldview (sec. 3); his discussion of mutable and immutable being (sec. 4); his claim that those who understand a cause understand its effects (sec. 7).

4. All citations from Aquinas's commentary are from *Commentary on the Gospel of St. John*, trans. Weisheipl and Larcher.

throughout the Gospel, that those in a more perfect moral state, either a state of virtue or heightened awareness of their unworthiness, are more easily able to recognize Christ's divinity.

Aquinas's interest in explaining why some individuals respond to Christ's divinity and others do not belongs to the part of scriptural commentary concerned with giving the reasons for things. Aquinas, following Augustine, identified as one of the senses of Scripture the "etiological sense," which he defines as "assigning a cause"; he gives as an example: "as when Our Lord gave the reason why Moses allowed the putting away of wives—namely, on account to the hardness of men's hearts."[5] We shall see that Aquinas delves into various elements, such as names, backgrounds, questions asked, and so on in his commentary on encounters to help draw out the cause of conversion or lack of conversion.

The importance of moral goodness is touched upon early in the *Commentary*. We are somewhat prepared for finding connections between moral philosophy and the commentary when Aquinas, in commenting on the importance of understanding that John was a contemplative, remarks that "the perfection of contemplation is found in Moral Science, which is concerned with the ultimate end" (*Ioan.* prol., n. 9). What Aquinas means here is that it is the job of moral science to discover the end of man, which has been found to be contemplation. Here surely is an echo of Aristotle's *Nicomachean Ethics*, in which we learn both that man's ultimate end is contemplation and that one needs the moral virtues; one needs to have one's passions under control, in order to engage in contemplation, which, Christianity tells us, is perfected in seeing God. Again, Aquinas notes that John's moral state enables him to be the perfect contemplative: "As concerns his virtue, John saw the Lord seated, because he was a virgin; for it is fitting that such persons see the Lord: 'Blessed are the pure in heart' (Mt 5:8)" (*Ioan.* prol., n. 11; 13, 4, n. 1804; 21, 5, n. 2639); John, the contemplative, achieved man's ultimate end, to the extent possible, even in this lifetime; thus in the *Gospel of John*, we are being taught morality by one who successfully achieved the end of morality.

EPISTEMOLOGICAL PRINCIPLE: LIKE KNOWS LIKE

The connection between one's moral character and one's cognitive responses is, of course, part of a larger epistemology. One extremely important view shared by Aristotle and Aquinas is their understanding that there is an

---

5. *ST* I, q. 1, a. 10, ad 2. All translations of the *Summa* are from *Summa Theologica*, trans. by the Fathers of the English Dominican Province (Benzinger Brothers, 1947).

objective reality that is knowable by man and that by nature the human person is designed to receive the truths of reality. In Aquinas's view, God gave man the "equipment" (senses, passions, passive and agent intellects, for instance) to grasp the truths he needs to know—both particular and universal truths. The mistakes we make in reading reality—that is, the reality accessible to us—are because of defects, such as defects in our senses or in our intelligence, and—what will be the focus of this essay—also in our character.

Indeed the epistemological principle explained above and justifying the point just made—that good people are better able to recognize the good—is an instance of the principle that "like knows like."[6] By this Aristotle means that there must be some commonality (not identity) between an object known and the knower; Aristotle discusses the principle primarily in references to the senses and the agent intellect, but, as we shall see, he also uses it in reference to discernment of moral goodness; that is, there must be some goodness in the soul to be able to respond to goodness; some goodness to be able to desire goodness. This principle is also expressed by Aquinas as "everything is received in the manner of the receiver." We find an excellent statement of it in his *Commentary on the De Anima:*[7]

[W]e should note that while the sense-faculty is always the function of a bodily organ, intellect is an immaterial power—it is not the actuality of any bodily organ. Now everything received is received in the mode of the recipient. If then all knowledge implies that the thing known is somehow present in the knower (present by its similitude), the knower's actuality as such being the actuality of the thing known, it follows that the sense-faculty receives a similitude of the thing sensed in a bodily and material way, whilst the intellect receives a similitude of the thing understood in an incorporeal and immaterial way. Now in material and corporeal beings the common nature derives its individuation from matter existing within specified dimensions, whereas the universal comes into being by abstraction from such matter and all the individuating material conditions. Clearly, then, a thing's similitude as received in sensation represents the thing as an individual; as received, however, by the intellect it represents the thing in terms of a universal nature. That is why individuals are known by the senses, and universals (of which are the sciences) by the intellect. (*Ioan.* 2, lect. 2, n. 377)

In respect to physical reality, the principle that everything is received in the manner of the receiver seems quite uncontroversial. It certainly means

---

6. This principle pervades the *De Anima;* Aristotle labors to demonstrate that his predecessors misunderstood the principle in thinking that it meant that the receptor had to be identical to the received (wood could perceive only wood) rather than meaning that the medium of perception or cognition had to be in some way suitable to grasp an object. (See, for instance, 405b15; 407b19; 409b27; 410a27; 411a25; 424a1; 426b9; 429a14.)

7. See also *ST* I, qq. 84–85.

that we must have a certain "equipment" to grasp reality; it also means that that "equipment" must be in good shape. For instance, it clearly means that we can hear only if we have ears and only the sounds that are in the range of our auditory abilities; we can see only if we have eyes and only the colors in the range of our optical abilities. The range of all human beings is limited; there are more sounds, colors, and smells than we can perceive by our senses. Even what is within our range as human beings is perceived differently to some extent by particular human beings because of the quality of their senses.

The scope of our intellects is infinitely greater than the powers of our senses, since the intellect is unencumbered by matter. There are various abilities in this realm as well; those with higher IQs and sharper intellects can comprehend a greater range of information about the world. And as with our senses, we who are in possession of agent intellects that are like the divine in their immateriality and immortality are constituted to grasp something of the divine as well when our "equipment" is in proper shape.

The principle of "like knowing like" and "everything being received in the manner of the receiver" is therefore not limited only to our physical means and instruments for grasping physical reality and to the quality of our intellects. Aristotle and Aquinas maintained that living a good moral life (and in Aquinas's thought this means acknowledging one's sinfulness) assists one in grasping reality, especially in grasping what is morally good; similarly disorderly passions can distort one's reading of and response to reality. Thus being moral, that is, having one's passions ordered, assists one in perceiving reality, moral goodness in particular, correctly. Having our passions ordered not only calms us enough to allow us the peace and serenity to be truly responsive to realities before us, it also enhances our intellectual abilities or cognitive capacities, much as a pair of glasses restores order to our visual powers and enables us to see better. When our receptors of reality are in good shape we perceive reality better and thus have better data with which to think. Disordered desires warp our perception of reality and thus provide erroneous information to our intellects and lead us often to mistake apparent goods for real goods.[8]

My claim here is that a theme of the Commentary is the epistemological importance of a good character, and in this case, the salvific importance of being able to discern the truth. It is those who are good or aware of their lack of goodness who are able to respond favorably to Goodness Itself, even in disguise.

---

8. See for instance, Aristotle's *Nicomachean Ethics* III.5, and book VII passim.

CONNATURALITY

That the principle of "like knowing like" extends to moral character can be seen in the explanation of the principle of connaturality, the principle that things are naturally inclined to the good that is natural to them and that they take pleasure in what is good for them.[9] That is, things have natural appetites, natural desires, and, one might even say, a natural love for what is good for them. The word "love" used here perhaps seems peculiar, but when one understands that by "love" Aquinas understands a desire for union or possession, it make sense to speak of things loving what is good for them.[10] Aquinas would not hesitate to speak of tomato plants, for instance, loving sunshine.

The principle of connaturality bears resemblance to the principle that "like is known by like"; it explains both why we are drawn to something and why we take delight in it. Certainly Aquinas makes it clear that we have a connaturality to what is good; what is good attracts us and evil repels us:

> Now, in the movements of the appetitive faculty, good has, as it were, a force of attraction, while evil has a force of repulsion. In the first place, therefore, good causes, in the appetitive power, a certain inclination, aptitude or connaturalness in respect of good: and this belongs to the passion of "love": the corresponding contrary of which is "hatred" in respect of evil. Secondly, if the good be not yet possessed, it causes in the appetite a movement towards the attainment of the good beloved: and this belongs to the passion of "desire" or "concupiscence": and contrary to it, in respect of evil, is the passion of "aversion" or "dislike." Thirdly, when the good is obtained, it causes the appetite to rest, as it were, in the good obtained: and this belongs to the passion of "delight" or "joy"; the contrary of which, in respect of evil, is "sorrow" or "sadness."[11]

An important conjunction of the principles of "like knowing like" and of "like loving like" is found in Aquinas's response to the question "Whether likeness is a cause of love?,"[12] a passage that includes reference to a supporting biblical passage from Ecclesiasticus:

---

9. See, for instance, *ST* I, q. 26, a. 1. Response: "Now in each of these appetites, the name 'love' is given to the principal movement towards the end loved. In the natural appetite the principle of this movement is the appetitive subject's connaturalness with the thing to which it tends, and may be called 'natural love': thus the connaturalness of a heavy body for the centre, is by reason of its weight and may be called 'natural love.' In like manner the aptitude of the sensitive appetite or of the will to some good, that is to say, its very complacency in good is called 'sensitive love,' or 'intellectual' or 'rational love.' So that sensitive love is in the sensitive appetite, just as intellectual love is in the intellectual appetite. And it belongs to the concupiscible power, because it regards good absolutely, and not under the aspect of difficulty, which is the object of the irascible faculty."

10. See for instance, *ST* I-II, q. 23.   11. *ST* I-II, q. 23, a. 4.
12. *ST* I-II, q. 27, a. 3.

I answer that, likeness, properly speaking, is a cause of love. But it must be observed that likeness between things is twofold. One kind of likeness arises from each thing having the same quality actually: for example, two things possessing the quality of whiteness are said to be alike. . . .

Accordingly the first kind of likeness causes love of friendship or well-being. For the very fact that two men are alike, having, as it were, one form, makes them to be, in a manner, one in that form: thus two men are one thing in the species of humanity, and two white men are one thing in whiteness. Hence the affections of one tend to the other, as being one with him; and he wishes good to him as to himself.

This passage is explaining why one good man desires the good for another, but it can also be understood to indicate that it is the good man who can discern goodness in another and is drawn to that other. As is common in the *Summa theologiae,* Aquinas uses Scripture to supplement philosophical analysis. The *sed contra* to this article makes reference to a biblical passage, "Every beast loveth its like" (*Ecclus.* 13:19), a passage that is evoked at key points in the *Commentary on John.* (We shall look at a few of these passages momentarily.) Indeed, the biblical passage becomes a "tag" for the philosophical principle. It tells us that those who share the same quality are as one—"in a manner" they share a "form"—and thus, in a sense are "one self"; one loves and knows the other as one loves and knows one's self.[13]

The efficacy of virtue for a positive response to what is good and true is stated explicitly in response to the question "Whether wisdom is in the intellect as its subject?":

[W]isdom denotes a certain rectitude of judgment according to the Eternal Law. Now rectitude of judgment is twofold: first, on account of perfect use of reason, secondly, on account of a certain connaturality with the matter about which one has to judge. Thus, about matters of chastity, a man after inquiring with his reason forms a right judgment, if he has learnt the science of morals, while he who has the habit of chastity judges of such matters by a kind of connaturality.[14]

Aquinas speaks of two kinds of knowledge here, the knowledge of the science, which knows the causes, and the knowledge of connaturality, which is based on affinity of the knower and the object. This passage focuses on the ability of the chaste individual to make proper judgments about chastity, but it is just a particular example of a more universal principle: namely that the one who is good makes better judgments about what is good because of his connaturality to the good.

---

13. This claim is clearly reminiscent of Aristotle's discussion of friendship, *Nicomachean Ethics* IX.8.

14. *ST* II-II, q. 45, a. 2.

"Come and See" 201

The philosophical works of Aristotle lurk in the background of these passages and provide justification for attributing epistemological value to moral goodness. We find in the *Metaphysics* this key passage:

[I]t is also foolish to occupy oneself equally with both opinions and with the fanciful statements of those who argue against themselves, because it is evident that one or the other of them must be wrong. This is clear from the facts of sensory perception; for the same thing never appears sweet to some and the opposite to others unless in some the organ of the sense which distinguishes the above mentioned savors has been impaired or injured. And such being the case, some must be taken as the measure and others not. And I say that the same thing applies *in the case of good and evil*, of beautiful and ugly, and of the other attributes of this kind. For to maintain this view is not different from maintaining that what appears to those who push their finger under their eye and make one object appear to be two must therefore be two because it appears to be so many, and yet that it must be one because to those who do not move their eye the one object appears to be one. (1062b33–a10; my emphasis)[15]

Aquinas comments on this passage:

And what is evident in the case of sensory perception must also be said to apply in the case of good and evil, of beautiful and ugly, and of all the attributes of this kind which are apprehended by the intellect. For if some conceive a thing to be good and others evil, the judgment of those whose intellect has not been impaired by some bad habit or by some bad influence or by some other cause of this kind must be the norm.[16]

In these texts we see a principle derived from assessing the reliability of sense data applied to the reliability of aesthetic and moral judgments; if one's senses are faulty, one will judge physical reality wrongly; if one's habits (or morals) are bad one will judge moral matters wrongly.

This principle is certainly a guiding principle of the *Nicomachean Ethics*. Throughout the *Nicomachean Ethics,* especially in Book VII in the discussion of *akrasia* or moral weakness, Aristotle teaches that the virtuous man is better able to discern what is good and true, precisely because he takes pleasure in what is good; because his appetites are working correctly he can perceive reality correctly. Correspondingly, those who are vicious have a difficult time discerning what is good and true because their intellects are clouded by the fact that their disordered appetites take pleasure in what is not good.

Throughout the *Ethics* an analogy is made between the sick man and his false reading of physical reality and the vicious man and his taking pleasure in

---

15. This translation is from the *Commentary on Aristotle's Metaphysics,* trans. John P. Rowan (Notre Dame, Ind.: Dumb Ox Books, 1995).

16. Ibid., n. 2231.

base actions, and also between the healthy man whose taste buds are operating correctly and the virtuous man who loves good deeds. A concise and clear statement of this principle is found in Book III:

For the good man that thing is an object of willing which is truly good; for the vicious man that thing is an object of willing which seems pleasing to him. Thus when men are in good bodily health those things are healthful which are such in reality, but for men who are ill, it is otherwise. The same applies to bitter, sweet, warm, and heavy things and to others of this kind. The virtuous person correctly passes judgment on each individual thing and in each case what appears to him is truly good. Those things which are proper to each habit seem pleasurable to it. *The good man perhaps is much different in his capacity to see what is truly good in individual matters, being as it were a norm and measure of these things.* Many men are apparently deceived because of pleasure. What is not good seems good, so they desire as good the pleasurable and seek to avoid the painful as evil.[17]

Both Aristotle and Aquinas maintain that there are natural human pleasures, both physical and moral, and that those in a good condition physically and morally respond rightly to those pleasures.[18]

---

17. This translation is from the *Commentary on Aristotle's Nicomachean Ethics*, trans. C. I. Litzinger, O.P. (Notre Dame, Ind.: Dumb Ox Books, 1964), 159; 1113a25–b2; my emphasis.

18. Aquinas's commentary basically restates Aristotle's text: " [Aristotle] says that for the good man that thing is an object of willing which is truly worthy of being willed, i.e., good in itself. But for the wicked or vicious man that thing is the object of willing which attracts him, i.e., whatever seems pleasing to himself. He exemplifies this in things of the body. We see that for men whose bodies are in good health those things are healthful that are really so. But for the sick, certain other things are healthful, namely, those that moderate their diseased condition. Likewise things really bitter and sweet seem bitter and sweet to those who have a healthy taste, things really warm seem warm to those who have a normal sense of touch. Those who have normal bodily strength properly estimate the weight of objects; those who are weak think light objects are heavy" (n. 493). "[Aristotle] says that the virtuous person correctly passes judgment on individual things that pertain to human activity. In each case that which is really good seems to him to be good. This happens because things seem naturally pleasurable to each habit that are proper to it. That is, agree with it. Those things are agreeable to the habit of virtue that are in fact good because the habit of moral virtue is defined by what is in accord with right reason. Thus the things in accord with right reason, things of themselves good, seem good to it. Here the good man differs very much indeed from others, for he sees what is truly good in individual practicable matters, being as it were the norm and measure of that is to be done because in these cases a thing must be judged good or bad according as it seems to him. [494]

. . . [Aristotle] says that for many, the vicious, deception in the distinction between good and evil occurs, especially because of pleasure. As a consequence of this it happens that they desire as good the pleasurable, which is not good, and seek to avoid as evil what is for them painful but in itself good. The explanation is that they do not follow reason but the senses" (n. 495).

Passages making this point could be multiplied. See, for instance, 1114a–b25; virtually all of Book 7; and 1175a–76a29.

PRINCIPLES APPLIED TO THE GOSPEL OF JOHN

The philosophical principles explained above are operative in key ways in the *Commentary on John*. For instance, the principle that "like knows like" is evoked when Aquinas is explaining the mutual love of the Father and the Son (John 5:20a):

> For since likeness is a cause of love (for every animal loves its like), wherever a perfect likeness of God is found, there also is found a perfect love of God. But the perfect likeness of the Father is in the son, as is said: "He is the image of the invisible God" (1:15); and "He is the brightness of the Father's glory, and the image of his substance" (Heb 1:3). (*Ioan.* 5, lect. 3, n. 753)

When Aquinas explains why Christ so perfectly knows the will of the father and why not even a vision of the divine will do the same for a human being, he states:

> The reason for this, of course, is that all vision or knowledge comes about through a likeness: creatures have a knowledge of God according to the way they have a likeness to him. Thus the philosophers say that the intelligences know the First Cause according to this likeness which they have to it. Now every creature possesses some likeness to God, but it is infinitely distant from a likeness to his nature, and so no creature can know him perfectly and totally, as he is in his own nature. That Son, however, because he has received the entire nature of the Father perfectly, through an eternal generation, sees and comprehends totally. (*Ioan.* 6, lect. 5, n. 947)[19]

Aquinas seems to have this principle much in mind, and as is befitting a biblical commentary, he uses what he finds to be a scriptural formulation of it. In *Ioan.* 8, lect. 7, n. 1258 Aquinas notes that Christ has a "reasonable and true starting point" when he says "he who is of God hears the words of God." Again, here he cites the supporting passage: "Every creature loves its like." (Ecclus. 13:15). Aquinas uses the reference to this scriptural passage as an occasion to discourse on the difference between the love of friendship and the love of concupiscence. When commenting on John 15:18–19—"If the world hates you, know that it has hated me before it has hated you. If you were of the world, the world would love its own; but because you are not of the world, but I chose you out of the world, therefore the world hates you"— Aquinas explains, "The reason why some are loved by the world is that they are like the world; If you were of the world, the world would love its own.

---

19. See also, 7, 3, n. 1065: "Now all knowledge comes about through some likeness, since nothing is known except insofar as there is a likeness of the known in the knower."

Like loves like: 'Every creature loves its like' (Sir 13:15)" (*Ioan.* 15, lect. 4, n. 2034). In a subsequent section he explains that

> with the love of concupiscence we draw external things or persons to ourselves, and we love these others insofar as they are useful to us or give us pleasure. But in the love of friendship we have the opposite, for we draw ourselves to what is external to us, because those we love in this way we treat the same as ourselves, sharing ourselves with them in some way. Thus, likeness is a cause of love, when we are speaking of the love of friendship, for we do not love a person in this way unless we are one with the person: and likeness is a certain way of being one. (*Ioan.* 15, lect. 4, n. 2036)

While this discussion is designed to explain why the world hates those who love Christ, it also explains why the good are able to love Christ and why the evil are not.[20]

Let me stress here that I am not focusing on the truth that sinners reject Christ because he requires that they change their ways. This is certainly true, and it is stressed throughout the commentary, most explicitly perhaps at 3:20–21: "Everyone who practices evil hates the light, and does not approach the light for fear that his deeds might be exposed. But everyone who practices the truth comes to the light, to make clear that his deeds are done in God." About this passage Aquinas states:

> So he says: The reason why they did not love the light is that their works were evil. And this is plain because everyone who practices evil hates the light. He does not say, "practiced," but rather practices: because if someone has acted in an evil way, but has repented and is sorry, seeing that he has done wrong, such a person does not hate the light but comes to the light. But everyone who practices evil, i.e., persists in evil, is not sorry, nor does he come to the light, but he hates it; not because it reveals truth, but because it reveals a person's sins. For an evil person still wants to know the light and the truth; but he hates to be unmasked by it. "If the dawn suddenly appears, they regard it as the shadow of death" (Jb 24:17). And so he does not approach the light; and this for fear that his deeds might be exposed. For no one who is unwilling to desert evil wants to be rebuked; this is fled from and hated. "They hate the one who rebukes at the city gate" (Am 5:10); "A corrupt man does not love the one who rebukes him" (Prv 15:12). (*Ioan.* 3, lect. 3, n. 494)

Certainly there are evil people who can recognize truth if it is obvious and blatant enough—even *moral* truth— but who refuse, nonetheless, to accept it if it requires that they change their ways. Yet, these are not the individuals that interest me here; rather, my point is that sometimes, immoral individuals are not even able to recognize the truth, precisely because of their immoral

---

20. The same point is made in *Ioan.* 17, lect. 3, n. 2223.

ways. (We shall see this point brought out in Aquinas's commentary on various "conversion" scenes.)

Aquinas compares those who are evil to those who do not use the full range of their abilities to grasp reality. In reference to a passage from John 1:9–10, "He [the Word] was the true light, which enlightens every man coming into this world. He was in the world, and through him the world was made, and the world did not know him," he comments on two kinds of sensuality that prohibit individuals from knowing Christ. One group are those who limit their data base to the evidence of their senses and are not open enough to spiritual truths; the others are those who are morally corrupt. Certainly the inability is not necessarily a product of immorality but can be the result of an intellectual deficiency in the face of some kinds of evidence. Aquinas often notes that some of those who interact with Christ or who hear about him cannot grasp his message because they are too sensual, and by this he seems to be pointing not to a moral but to an intellectual deficiency; they cannot rise above the evidence of their imagination (material evidence) to the level of the evidence of their intellects (immaterial evidence). Nonetheless he also attributes the inability to rise above sensuality to a deficient character:

> But if this lack is attributed to man's guilt, then the phrase, the world did not know him, is a kind of reason why God was not known by man; in this sense world is taken for inordinate lovers of the world. It is as though it said, The world did not know him, because they were lovers of the world. For the love of the world, as Augustine says, is what chiefly withdraws us from the knowledge of God, because "Love of the world makes one an enemy to God" (Jas 4:4); "The sensual man does not perceive the things that pertain to the Spirit of God" (1 Cor 2:14).
>
> From this we can answer the question of the Gentiles who futilely ask this: If it is only recently that the Son of God is set before the world as the Savior of men, does it not seem that before that time he scorned human nature? We should say to them that he did not scorn the world but was always in the world, and on his part is knowable by men; but it was due to their own fault that some have not known him, because they were lovers of the world. (*Ioan.* 1, lect. 5, nn. 138–39)

Aquinas, here, finds the sensuality of inordinate lovers of the world an obstacle to their perceiving things of the spirit. They cannot love or know things of the spirit because they love things of the flesh too much.

CONVERSION STORIES

Aquinas's *Commentary* makes clear that those who do not live a moral life cannot participate in the light of Christ; indeed it is very difficult for them even should they be able to acknowledge the truth of His claims, to find Him and His message appealing, let alone to embrace it (*Ioan.* 1, lect. 3, n. 101). Again, what I want to emphasize is that some reject Christ not because his message is too strange, that is, too much beyond the senses, or even because of the demand that they must leave aside sinful ways. Rather I want to stress that the vicious are often unable to get a sure read on who Christ is: vice clouds the intellect and prevents the vicious from seeing what is to be seen, from hearing what is to be heard; goodness, on the other hand, enhances receptivity to truth.

Aquinas finds evidence of this truth and uses it as a hermeneutical principle to explain why some individuals in the Gospel are quick to recognize Christ as divine and others are not. He makes much of the moral condition of those whom Christ encounters and shows that Christ interacts differently with individuals of different moral conditions; in several early encounters, we see him moving from interacting with those who seem exceptionally good to those who are still living in a state of serious sin. We see that either goodness and/or willingness to recognize and abandon one's sinfulness make individuals responsive to the grace of conversion and faith.

It is not insignificant that the first three encounters Christ has with individuals involve the words "Come and see." These words emphasize that faith involves a personal encounter of some kind; it requires immediacy and some ability to see.[21]

The first conversion story is told very briefly and indirectly; John tells us that two men became disciples of Christ upon hearing John's testimony about Christ at his baptism. Aquinas notes that not everyone who was witness to the baptism converted, but only those who were "well-disposed" (*Ioan.* 1, lect. 15, n. 285). In response to the question "Where do you live?" Christ first utters the words "Come and see." Aquinas comments upon the literal, the allegorical, and the moral sense of this question; he says the disciples want to know the physical location of his dwelling; they want to know where he is leading us (i.e., heaven) and they want to know what qualities they need to possess to be worthy to have Christ dwell within them (*Ioan.* 1, lect. 15, n. 290). In explicating the mystical way, Aquinas notes that Christ asks the disciples to "Come and see," "because the dwelling of God, whether of glory or grace, cannot be known except by experience; for it cannot be explained in words." "Come" means "believe and work," "see" means "experience and understand." Aquinas explains that we can come to know God in

---

21. Aquinas speaks of seeing as connoting a more immediate way of knowing than hearing: see *Ioan.* 12, lect. 7, nn. 1693f.

four ways: (1) by doing good works; (2) by rest or stillness of the mind; (3) by tasting the divine sweetness; and (4) by acts of devotion (*Ioan.* 1, lect. 15, n. 293). Clearly moral goodness contributes to all four ways of coming to know God.

Andrew, who heard these words, immediately goes to get his brother Simon, to bring him to see Christ. Aquinas, always interested in names as revealing reality, tells us that the name "Simon" means "obedient" (*Ioan.* 1, lect. 15, n. 303). Aquinas tells us that Christ wins over Simon by revealing hidden knowledge to him—he knew Simon's name, he knew his past, he knew his future; such was enough to convert Simon, for Simon was obedient. It seems we are to draw the inference that Simon's obedience, a kind of "good work," made him able to "taste divine sweetness" and thus come to know God.

Aquinas tells us that the name "Nathanael" means "gift of God"—and it is "God's gift if anyone is converted to Christ." He tells us that Nathanael was someone learned in the law of Moses and the prophets. As we recall, Nathanael was skeptical about Philip's claim that Jesus was the one Moses spoke of in the law, since he doubted that anything good could come out of Nazareth. Yet shortly thereafter, to Christ's apparent surprise and our own, Nathanael proclaims his belief in Christ simply because Christ tells him he saw him sitting under the fig tree.

Nathanael's approach to Christ followed upon Philip's invitation to "Come and see." Aquinas tells us that Philip knew that Nathanael "would no longer argue with him if he tasted the words and teaching of Christ" (*Ioan.* 1, lect. 16, n. 319). At this point Aquinas tells us that there are two ways by which men are converted to Christ. First some are converted "by miracles they have seen and things experienced in themselves or others" (*Ioan.* 1, lect. 16, n. 320). Aquinas tells us that the way of miracles can be dangerous, because devils and those who receive their help can simulate miracles. It is the second mode of conversion that he identifies as "more efficacious," that of being "converted through internal insights, through prophecy and the foreknowledge of what is hidden in the future." Aquinas maintains that this is the mode of Nathanael's conversion—that he is converted because Christ makes things known that are hidden; things of three kinds—"things of the heart; past facts; and future heavenly matters" and that knowing these things is "not a human but a divine achievement."

What Christ knew of the heart of Nathanael is that he was a "true Israelite, in whom there is no guile." Aquinas seems to accept two explanations of this insight, both indicating that Nathanael was a righteous man or at least a man who knew he was a sinful man. Aquinas understands Christ's comment that

Nathanael was under the fig tree in a symbolic way; he maintains that the fig tree represents sin, and as proof for this understanding he refers to "the fig tree that would produce no fruit" and the fact that Adam and Eve used the leaves from a fig tree to hide their shame. He understands Christ to be calling Nathanael away from sin and to be looking upon him with divine mercy, as one predestined from eternity. Again, to our and Christ's surprise, Nathanael immediately pronounces Christ the Son of God. In an earlier passage when Aquinas commented on the baptism of Christ where the Holy Spirit rested upon him, he states that the Holy Spirit will not rest on those in a state of sin, so it seems right to think that Nathanael, because of his lack of guile, his awareness of his own sinfulness, was a worthy recipient of the grace of conversion that Christ bestowed upon him (*Ioan.* 1, lect. 14, n. 273). Although Nathanael became a believer, he did not become an apostle. Aquinas explains that Christ did not choose Nathanael to be an apostle because "Christ did not want the conversion of the world to the faith to be attributed to human wisdom, but solely to the power of God." Nathanael was "very learned in the law; [Christ] rather chose simple and uneducated men" (*Ioan.* 1, lect. 16, n. 334). The point seems to be that education and sophistication are not key to recognizing Christ—goodness is.

The next "attempted conversion" scene is that with Nicodemus, and it is the first "failed" conversion of an individual. Christ tells Nicodemus he must be "born again" or he cannot see the kingdom of God. Aquinas explains that the sensual man cannot perceive those things that pertain to the spirit but that one needs spiritual regeneration and spiritual vision to see the kingdom of God (*Ioan.* 3, lect. 1, n. 432). Aquinas understands Christ to chide Nicodemus, the sensual man, for his slowness in grasping that he is speaking about spiritual regeneration. He cites 1 Corinthians 2:14: "The sensual man does not perceive those things that pertain to the Spirit of God." And he comments further, "so because Nicodemus was yet carnal and sensual, he was unable to grasp, except in a carnal manner, the things that were said to him" (*Ioan.* 3, lect. 1, n. 437). Aquinas gives the fact of Nicodemus's sensual character as one of the three reasons for Nicodemus's slowness (*Ioan.* 3, lect. 2, n. 462). Since Nicodemus is learned in Jewish law and should, therefore, be prepared to readily accept the statements of the wise and those who possess great authority, Aquinas finds his hesitancy especially reprehensible.

Because Nicodemus is more corrupt, he needs more teaching, and indeed we do not learn in this passage what is Nicodemus's ultimate response. As of yet, he is too attached to the flesh to understand Christ's spiritual message.

The next one-on-one encounter that Christ has is with the Samaritan woman at the well. Aquinas sees a progression here, a move from giving the message to the Jews to delivering it to the Gentiles. Again, the point is made that carnal and sensual creatures mistake Christ's message; the woman did not understand that Christ was speaking of spiritual water when He spoke of the living water He was able to give her. What Aquinas represents as her saving grace was her willingness to admit what Christ accused her of—having many husbands and living with one who was not her husband. Upon hearing that Christ knows secrets about her, she recognizes that he is a prophet (*Ioan.* 4, lect. 2, n. 596). Aquinas admires the woman for continuing her questioning about where one should worship: "Here we should admire the woman's diligence and attention: for women are considered curious and unproductive, and not only unproductive, but also lovers of ease, whereas she did not ask Christ about world affairs, or about the future, but about the things of God" (*Ioan.* 4, lect. 2, n. 596). Aquinas tells us that Christ revealed himself to this woman because she truly wanted to know and because of her simplicity. She then exhibits what Aquinas takes to be a sign of a genuine conversion: she goes to find others and tells them to "come and see"; she needs to share the truth with others.

The next conversion, that of the official seeking a cure for his son, shows us another conversion employing a miracle but also shows us a process of self-recognition that leads to a recognition of Christ's divinity. Aquinas's interpretation of the moral sense of this passage views the official as representing reason and his son as representing sinful affections:

In a moral sense, in the kingdom of the soul, the king is reason itself: "The king, who sits on his throne of judgment" (Prv 20:8). But why is reason called the king? Because man's entire body is ruled by it: his affections are directed and informed by it and the other powers of the soul follow it. But sometimes it is called an official [not the king], that is, when its knowledge is obscured, with the result that it follows inordinate passions and does not resist them: "They live with their foolish ideas, their understanding obscured by darkness" (Eph 4:17). Consequently, the son of this official, i.e., the affections, are sick, that is, they deviate from good and decline to what is evil. If reason were the king, that is, strong, its son would not be sick; but being only an official, its son is sick. This happens at Capernaum because a great many temporal goods are the cause of spiritual sickness: "This was the crime of your sister Sodom: richness, satiety in food, and idleness" (Ez 16:49; *Ioan.* 4, lect. 7, n. 678).

Aquinas tells us that Christ did not heal the son immediately because the father's faith was imperfect. The father gradually comes to believe in Christ as God who can heal at a distance. This belief follows upon Christ's healing of the father of sin. Aquinas reads Christ's admonition: "Go, your son lives" as directed as much to the father's sins as the son's illness. He tells us:

> He [Christ] orders the official to go: hence he says, Go, i.e., prepare to receive grace by a movement of your free will toward God: "Turn to me, and you will be saved." (Is 45:22); and by a movement of your free will against sin. For four things are required for the justification of an adult sinner: the infusion of grace, the remission of guilt, a movement of the free will toward God, which is faith, and a movement of the free will against sin, which is contrition. (*Ioan.* 4, lect. 7, n. 688)

The official's willingness to return home is understood as growth in faith because he does what Christ tells him to do; the father learns that this faith is rewarded when his servants come to announce to him that his son was going to live. Aquinas comments:

> In the mystical sense, the servants of the official, i.e., of reason, are a man's works, because man is master of his own acts and of the affections of his sense powers, for they obey the command and direction of reason. Now these servants announce that the son of the official, that is, of reason, lives, when a man's good works shine out, and his lower powers obey reason, according to: "A man's dress, and laughter, and his walk, show what he is" (Sir 19:27). (*Ioan.* 4, lect. 7, n. 693)

Aquinas reads the son's healing as symbolic of the healing of the father of his sinfulness, of a reassertion of reason over sinful affections. That the healing happened at the seventh hour signifies the gifts of the Holy Spirit, the forgiveness of sins, and the peace and life that comes with goodness (*Ioan.* 4, lect. 7, n. 695).

I suspect few would immediately see that Christ's healing of the blind man with spittle involved the moral condition of the blind man. Yet Aquinas (following Augustine) sees a gradual spiritual growth in the blind man as he is healed (*Ioan.* 9, lect. 2, n. 1319) and as he testifies to what happened to him. He seems to be healed gratuitously, but his culminating belief in Christ is attributed to his devotion to the truth. Aquinas notes that under cross-examination by the Pharisees, the blind man "does not deviate from the truth" (*Ioan.* 9, lect. 2, n. 1324) and that although "he did not yet profess that Christ was the Son of God, he firmly expressed what he thought, and did not lie" (*Ioan.* 9, lect. 2, n. 1329). The blind man does not capitulate when they attempt to get him to deny the truth (*Ioan.* 9, lect. 3, n. 1336; cf. 9, 4, n. 1355). The Pharisees condemn the blind man, Aquinas says, because of "untruth, pride and injustice" (*Ioan.* 9, lect. 3, n. 1353). Because they refuse to acknowledge the divinity of Christ, they are the truly blind ones; Aquinas cites Augustine, who cites Scripture: "those who think they see do not see, and those who do not think they see, see. Now we are said to be blind, spiritually, insofar as we sin: 'Their wickedness blinded them' (Wis 2:21)" (*Ioan.* 9, lect. 4, n. 1360).

Not only in his presentation of Christ interacting with individuals does Aquinas find the moral condition of the "interlocutor" significant; he also has ample opportunity to make his point about the epistemological value of moral goodness when he comments on some of the longer discourses of Christ. About Jesus' claim that "My sheep hear my voice" (10:27), Aquinas notes:

> [Unbelief] is imputed to [unbelievers] because they are the cause why [belief] is not given to them. Thus, I can not see the light unless I am enlightened by the sun. Yet if I were to close my eyes, I would not see the light; but this is not due to the sun but to me, because by closing my eyes I am the cause of my not being enlightened. Now sin, for example, original sin, and in some persons, actual sin, is the cause why we are not enlightened by God through faith. This cause is in everyone. Thus, all who are left by God are left by reasons of the just judgment of God, and those who are chosen are lifted up by God's mercy. (*Ioan.* 10, lect. 5, n. 1447)

Aquinas is denying that some sort of 'eternal election' explains why some hear the shepherd's voice and some do not; rather it is the receptivity of the agent, the degree of the enslavement to sin, and the devotion to truth or goodness that enables one to recognize and follow the shepherd's voice.

John explains the failure of many to respond to the signs of Christ by referencing Isaiah, "Lord, who has believed our report, and to whom has the arm of the Lord been revealed?" (12:38). John concludes, "Therefore, they could not believe" (12:39). Aquinas comments that they could not believe because "they had a will clouded over by their wickedness" (*Ioan.* 12, lect. 7, n. 1698). Aquinas uses an analogy to demonstrate that failure to believe is not because God failed to provide the necessary graces: "It is like a person who closes the shutters of his house, and someone says to him: 'You cannot see because you lack the light of the sun.' This would not be due to a failure of the sun, but because he shut out the light of the sun. In the same way we read here that they could not believe, because God blinded them, that is, they were the cause why they were deprived of sight as in 'Their wickedness blinded them'" (*Ioan.* 12, lect. 7, n. 1698).

The influence of some key Aristotelian principles on the *Commentary on John* is subtle but pervasive. While in no way distorting Scripture or inappropriately forcing revelation into a philosophic mold, they enable Aquinas to elucidate incidences that might otherwise remain obscure, in this case, the reason why some who encounter Christ recognize him as divine and why others do not.

THIRTEEN

And Jesus Wept

Notes towards a Theology of Mourning

RICHARD SCHENK, O.P.

 IMAGINING THE GOAL OF THE INVESTIGATION

To investigate historical texts with systematic intent demands at the start that we develop a rough idea of the goal that might be served by the texts that we plan to examine more closely. In the best case, the sense of where we are headed will make us aware of those texts most relevant to our question. This anticipation of a plausible end is also the condition of the possibility of ever being taught by the texts that an initial aim is untenable; the preconception of a systematic goal is what makes possible its verification or falsification along with the focus on certain texts within the vast forests of traditional writings. It is what will allow those texts to attain, to correct, to complete, or possibly to deny that interpretive *desideratum* which at first must remain somewhat vague.

In imagining at the beginning of our investigation the need for and the character of a theology of mourning, we face the same problem in looking back at Thomas's writings that he himself faced in looking at the tradition that he had received: the lack of a clear idea in advance as to what a genuinely Christian theology of mourning could and should be. If the thesis of this paper can be sustained, this deficit of today means that the theology of mourning that Thomas had once been working towards has still not yet been adequately identified or received, something that can be remedied in part by greater attention to his *Commentary on the Gospel of St. John*. What the following investigation seeks can be sketched already by the first of three systematic contexts related to a theology of mourning. The context most immediate and explicit, for Thomas as well as for us, regards the Christian reaction to the loss of personal loved ones.

A certain long-standing and widespread, though unexamined, habit of speaking, especially common at funeral services, implies that Christians should not mourn at all; at best, mourning is to be tolerated as a brief concession to our weak-sighted humanity, a concession directly in tension with our faith, rather than a demand of Christian faith, hope, and love. The sadness about death is said to come from a lack of vision into the reality of what has happened in death to the departed person. This attitude is reflected in part at the end of *The Tragedy of King Lear:*

> The weight of this sad time we must obey,
> Speak what we feel, not what we ought to say.[1]

The final speaker in *Lear*, Edgar, expresses here a dialectic between "ought" and "ought," not uncommon in everyday reflections on mourning: the tension between what we assume that we are expected to profess ("what we ought to say") and a more basic and pressing ought, the feelings whose need for expression we also "must obey," although they are thought to conflict with more social or ecclesial expectations.

This dialectic is at least as old as Augustine's *Confessions* (dated to ca. 396–398). Augustine's description of his own and his son's mourning at the death of Monica[2] displays one of the most insightful and detailed ancient phenomenologies of mourning. Augustine notes the waves of mourning, unimpressed by most of the therapies that would later be listed by Thomas Aquinas in the *Summa theologiae* as "remedies" for sadness,[3] and punctuated all too shortly by sleep.[4] Augustine mentions the solace provided the mourner by his continued concern for the well-being of the soul of the deceased;[5] the contribution of mourning towards slowing the final disappearance of the dead from our lives and towards that intertwining of concern for the deceased with a sense of one's own loss, revealing the irreplaceable uniqueness of and our need for the deceased in the very moment of their loss to our own

---

1. William Shakespeare, *The Tragedy of King Lear*, 5.3, in W. Shakespeare, *The Complete Works*, ed. Stanley Wells et al. (Oxford: Oxford University Press, 1988), 974.

2. St. Augustine, *Confessionum Libri XIII*, lib. IX, cap. 12 (32) *CChrL* XXVII (Turnholt: Brepols, 1990), lib. IX, cap. 11–13.

3. Compare Thomas Aquinas, *ST* I-II, q. 38, a. 5, on baths and sleep, with St. Augustine, *Confessionum*, 151f., ll. 50–70; on tears, compare a. 2 with ll. 69ff.; on the company and compassion of friends, compare a. 3 with ll. 25ff.; on the meditation of truth, compare a. 4 with l. 32.

4. St. Augustine, *Confessionum*, ll. 55ff.

5. St. Augustine, *Confessionum*, IX, 13 (34–37).

lives: "And I found solace in my weeping in Your sight both about her and for her, about myself and for myself."[6]

Augustine is not interested in a neutral phenomenology of mourning; and yet, his evaluation here is ambivalent. Immediately following the Plotinian scene of their meditation at Ostia with all the blessed detachment from corporeality which that implied,[7] Augustine had just praised Monica's "contempt of this life and the attraction of death":[8] at most, an indifference to death and burial that was all the more striking, given the customary excesses of North African funeral practices and burial plans at that time.[9] "What am I still doing here?" is repeatedly cited by Augustine as Monica's rhetorical question.[10] Augustine's ontology of death here approximates a simple denial of death: "For we felt that it was not fitting that her funeral should be solemnized with moaning and weeping and lamentation, for so it is normal to weep when death is seen as sheer misery or as complete extinction. But she had not died miserably, nor did she wholly die" (*At illa nec misere moriebatur nec omnino moriebatur*).[11] Death is the release of the soul from the body.[12]

Given this view of death, Augustine apologizes for his mourning. "I felt new grief at my grief and so was afflicted with a two-fold sorrow."[13] He checks his weeping not just in front of Monica or Adeodatus[14] but before his readers as well;[15] he relishes Monica's favoring remarks for his understanding of her indifference, in contrast to the objections of his brother.[16] Augustine tries to play down his sorrow as merely reflecting his own need to adjust to the loss of Monica's habitual companionship;[17] he seeks to channel his mourning largely into prayers for her soul.[18] Augustine admits, though perhaps not without irony, that his readers might nevertheless see his grief as sinful,[19] a sign of "too much earthly affection."[20]

And yet, readers of Augustine's *Confessions* would be misled, were they to

---

6. *The Confessions of St. Augustine*, trans. Frank J. Sheed (New York: Sheed and Ward, 1943), 205.

7. *Confessionum*, IX, 10 (23–26).

8. Ibid., IX, 11 (28) l. 32, Sheed, 202f., literally with the title words of Ambrose's work, "de . . . bono mortis."

9. Cf. Peter Brown, *Augustine of Hippo* (Berkeley: University of California Press, 1967), 128–31.

10. "Quid hic facio?" Augustine, *Confessions*, IX, 10, l. 61; and 11, l. 29.

11. Ibid., IX, 12 (29) l. 11f., Sheed, 203. 12. Ibid., IX, 11 (28) l. 38f., Sheed, 203.
13. Ibid., IX, 12 (31) l. 38–41, Sheed, 204. 14. Ibid., IX, 11.
15. Ibid., IX, 12 (33) ll. 74ff. 16. Ibid., IX, 11 (27), ll. 8ff.
17. Ibid., IX, 12 (30) ll. 14f. 18. Ibid., IX, 13.
19. Ibid., IX, 12 (33) ll. 75f.
20. Ibid., IX, 13 (34) l. 2, literally, "carnalis affectus," Sheed, 206.

pay attention only to these self-critical remarks within Augustine's reflections on his time of mourning. In the text just cited, only that reader could dismiss Augustine's mourning as wrong who "sees it as a sin that for so small a portion of an hour I wept for my mother, now dead and departed from my sight, who had wept so many years for me that I should live ever in Your sight."[21] Augustine asks the skeptic for prayers but suggests more than merely mitigating circumstances. Augustine expands his self-critique to the hypocrisy of cutting short for Monica's grandson the same kind of mourning that would benefit her son.[22] This phase of mourning is portrayed by Augustine as more than just another detour from his path to God, even though here, just before the turn of the century, Augustine cannot yet find adequate words to describe what he confesses as "weeping in Your sight" as a demand of Christian existence.

Two of Augustine's pastoral experiences lead him to revise still further the earlier Platonic assumptions that had prevented his development of a comprehensive theology of mourning. Along with the influx of Roman refugees into North Africa came also a revival of interest in the thought of Porphyry, who had been one of the chief channels for Augustine's Platonism as well. The revival, however, actualizing Porphyry's anti-Christian polemic, makes Christianity responsible for the fall of Rome in 410. *De civitate Dei* (written over the years 413–425) is Augustine's response to these charges and includes a critical re-evaluation of Platonism. Augustine begins to identify Porphyry's chief mistake as an axiom that he himself had followed too easily: *corpus est fugiendum*.[23] Augustine draws out the consequences of his rejection of this principle for a more genuinely Christian understanding of death and resurrection, though only slowly and never completely. Augustine approaches his Platonic sources dialectically, combining the necessity of corporeality that had been stressed in classically Platonic theories of reincarnation with Porphyry's innovation of the possibility of human perfection beyond any necessity for continued change or further reincarnation. Augustine harmonizes these viewpoints of opposing Platonic schools to argue for the profound humanity

---

21. Ibid., IX, 12 (33) ll. 74–77, Sheed, 205.
22. Ibid., IX, 13.
23. Augustine, *De civitate Dei*, xii 27f.; cf. R. Schenk: *Die Gnade vollendeter Endlichkeit. Zur transzendentalen Auslegung der thomanischen Anthropologie* (Freiburg: Herder, 1989), 251–53. Contrast the consequences suggested by Augustine's late criticism of Porphyry, implying a more positive view of the sexual and social dimensions of earthly existence, with the implications of Augustine's earlier views, summarized by H. Dörrie, "Das Verhältnis des Neuplatonismus und Christlichen in Augustins 'De vera religione,'" *Zeitschrift fuer neutestamentliche Wissenschaft und die Kunde der aelteren Kirche* 23 (1924): 64–102.

implied by the hope for resurrection and its ideal of perfected corporeality.

The second pastoral experience comes when hostilities have drawn closer to Augustine than the events at Rome: the experience of a bishop whose own province was now being raided and seized, whose own flock was being violated in the extreme, leading Augustine to shift still further away from the Platonic rhetoric displayed by his mentor, Ambrose, *de bono mortis*. "The sudden descent of war-bands on a fertile province had made people realize, not that the world was ugly and unsure, but had caused them to experience the sheer, desperate tenacity of their love of life."[24] Augustine shows understanding for these sentiments: "I know you want to keep living. You do not want to die. And you want to pass from this life to another in such a way that you will rise again not as a dead man, but fully alive and transformed. This is what you desire. This is the deepest human feeling: mysteriously, the soul itself wishes and instinctively desires it."[25] Neither Augustine nor the Platonic tradition of Christianity following his lead (including the more embodied model of Platonism espoused after Proclus by Dionysius the Pseudo-Areopagite)[26] ever managed to explicate the potential theological depth of this "instinct," but both articulated enough of a Christian ambivalence toward death to justify later attempts to conceive of a more adequate theology of mourning. Both Thomas and we today have inherited this ambivalent tradition.

THOMAS AND THE PHILOSOPHICAL CONTEXT OF HIS INTERPRETATION OF DEATH

Before turning to Thomas's *Commentary on John,* it is important to recall first how Thomas's philosophy made the need for a theology of mourning all the more acutely felt. Thomas would be forced into a confrontation with the theological meaning of death by the weight of his key philosophical insight. From his first works on, Thomas displays a programmatic interest in showing the compatibility and unexpected correspondence between the gospel and an anthropology that would not only situate human being at the ontological border *(horizon et confinium)* between angels and animals, but would correct the frequently all too spiritualistic reading of humanity by a new stress on the animal basis of human life. This programmatic goal led Thomas to give new answers to those three questions that, taken together, have always constituted

---

24. Cf. Brown, *Augustine,* 431.
25. Cited here with Brown, *Augustine,* from Augustine, *Serm. 344,* 4.
26. Schenk, *Die Gnade,* 130–206, 253–83.

the broader question, What is human being? Long before Immanuel Kant's formulation, this overarching question, at once speculative and practical, was articulated by three regional questions: What can I know? What should I do? What may I hope for? Thomas's starting point for an epistemology not reliant upon the *a priori* reception of divine ideas, together with the initial orientation of human knowledge towards beings other than God (who is no longer seen as the *primum cognitum*), was seen by many of Thomas's contemporaries as a *novum,* perhaps even a shocking *novum,* certainly as an intended one. Thomas's new starting point for anthropology led him as well to a view of freedom more reliant than for his contemporaries upon the dynamics of passion and upon the necessarily discursive labors of conscience. Thomas admits that acknowledging a greater degree of animality behind the claims to knowledge and freedom had misled some (like the most avid disciples of Averroes) to deny—understandably but mistakenly—the immortality of the human soul: *non irrationabiliter de immortalitate ipsius dubitatur.*[27] Unlike his teacher, Albert, Thomas did not see the immortality of the soul as a truth accessible to faith alone.[28] As all truths constituted by human spontaneity transcend the senses, so does the soul transcend the body. But as human truth also remains in dialectical unity with internalized sense, so, too, does the soul separated from the body remain a mere part of the lost whole it has survived; it retains a desire for that unique body of which it is the form. The separated soul is not the person nor a substantial whole of any kind; it remains a mere part of its lost whole. And although the soul's survival as a part or partial principle of the whole person can be demonstrated, proof of the resurrection is impossible; the desire of the soul for resurrection, but not the gift of resurrection, not even the gift of infused knowledge consoling us prior to resurrection, can be demonstrated from experience or self-reflection. Philosophy knows the immortality of the soul, but not its beatitude; it knows of hope, not of fulfillment.

Writing around 1278, William de la Mare, a Franciscan disciple of

---

27. Leonard A. Kennedy, "A New Disputed Question of St. Thomas Aquinas on the Immortality of the Soul," *Archives d'histoire doctrinale et littéraire du moyen-âge* 45 (1978): 205–23, here from the *corpus articuli,* 213. The text continues: "Convenit enim cum substantiis incorruptibilibus in hoc quod est intelligens; et hoc videtur incorruptibilis esse. Convenit cum substantiis corruptibilibus ex hoc quod est corruptibilis corporis forma; ex quo videtur et ipsa corruptibilis esse." While the verdict about Thomas's authorship of the question is not yet final, there can be little doubt that the *determinatio* expresses the early Thomistic answer to the problem.

28. Cf. I. Craemer-Ruegenberg, "Albert le Grand et ses démonstrations de l'immortalité de l'âme intellective," *Archives de Philosophie* 43 (1980): 667–73.

Bonaventure and the "first systematician" of the neo-Augustinian reaction,[29] inaugurated with his *Correctorium fratris Thomae* the so-called correctories dispute. The controversy focused attention to a large extent on these three anthropological implications of Thomas's programmatic thesis about the unicity of the substantial form in the human: the soul, constitutively the unique *forma substantialis corporis*, shares in many of the body's animal limitations, lending a specific character to human knowing, willing, and hope.[30] Already apparent in 1277 with Robert Kilwardby's prohibition of Thomistic theses at Oxford[31] and with the case at Paris against Aegidius Romanus,[32] these anthropological controversies gave shape to the reception of Thomas's thought in the first fifty years after his death. They continue to influence the common conception of what "Thomism" is about. And while the theological significance of Christ's body in the tomb provided a test case for Thomas's anthropological theses, this issue did not of itself unlock the theological view of death envisioned by Thomas. Even recent scholarship has understood more about the challenge to Thomas's theology rather than about the reply by it in connection with his anthropological reflections on the unicity of the substantial form,[33] including the "Krueppelwesen" seemingly implied by

---

29. Fernand Van Steenberghen, *La philosophie au XIIIe siècle*, 2nd ed. (Leuven: Peeters, 1991).

30. Cf. Theodor Schneider, *Die Einheit des Menschen. Die anthropologische Formel anima forma corporis im sogenannten Korrektorienstreit und bei Petrus Johannis Olivi. Ein Beitrag zur Vorgeschichte des Konzils von Vienne* (Muenster: Aschendorff, 1973).

31. Besides Schneider, ibid., cf. Daniel Callus, *The Condemnation of St. Thomas at Oxford* (Westminster, Md.: Newman Bookshop, 1946); as well as Frederick J. Roensch, *The Early Thomistic School* (Dubuque: Priory Press, 1964).

32. Cf. Aegidius Romanus, *Apologia*, in *Opera omnia* III, 1, ed. R. Wielockx (Florence: Leo S. Olschki, 1985), together with the introduction and commentary by the editor. Unlike the question of the unicity of forms, Thomas's anthropology of death does seem to have been an issue in the Parisian condemnation of March 7, 1277; cf. Roland Hissette, *Enquête sur les 219 Articles Condamnés à Paris le 7 Mars 1277* (Paris—Louvain: Publications universitaires, 1977), especially 304–7. But even during these months at Paris in the spring and summer of 1277, the Thomistic thesis on unicity continued to be a concern as well; besides Wielockx, cf. also for the references to the interventions by the papal legate, Simon de Brie, the later Pope Martin IV: Ludwig Hoedl, "Neue Nachrichten ueber die Pariser Verurteilungen der thomanischen Formlehre," *Scholastik* 39 (1964): 178–96.

33. Cf. *ST* I, q. 29, a. 1, ad 5: "Ad quintum dicendum quod anima est pars humanae speciei: et ideo, licet sit separata, quia tamen retinet naturam unibilitatis, non potest dici substantia individua quae est hypostasis vel substantia prima; sicut nec manus, nec quaecumque alia partium hominis. Et sic non competit ei neque definitio personae neque nomen"; cf. *ST* I, q. 75, a. 4, ad 2, and also *SCG* IV, 79: "Anima autem a corpore separata est aliquo modo imperfecta, sicut omnis pars extra suum totum existens; anima enim naturaliter est pars humanae naturae. Non igitur homo potest ultimam felicitatem consequi, nisi anima iterato corpori coniungatur"; as well as *Compendium theologiae* [hereafter cited as *Comp. theol.*] I, 151, and *ST* II-II, q. 83, a. 11, obj. 5

Thomas's philosophical ideas on the privations suffered by the soul's activities with the loss of the soul's bodily expression and personal wholeness:

> Soul and body are intelligible realities only within the context of the unity of the human composite. This composite controls not only the relations of soul and body but also the relations of immortality and death. Given the unity of man, we cannot simply identify immortality with the separation of the soul from the body, nor can we think of death as an event that takes place in physical nature. The result is certainly a mystery, not to say several mysteries. But it is, in St. Thomas's teaching at least, no more and no less a mystery than man himself.[34]

Following Pegis, but going well beyond him, Mary F. Rousseau writes insightfully of Thomas's view of the "natural" impoverishment of the immortal soul inflicted by death. But she then contrasts this "philosophical" doctrine to Thomas's supposedly "optimistic" theology of death,[35] never reconciling the two. Admittedly, Thomas is not as programmatic in bringing out the theological significance of the negativity of death; in some themes, such as the stress on the beatific vision of the separated soul, his arguments seem to run counter to his philosophical assertions.[36] This tension within the *corpus* of

---

et ad 5: "Anima Petri non est Petrus. Si ergo animae sanctorum pro nobis orarent quandiu sunt a corpore separatae, non deberemus interpellare sanctum Petrum ad orandum pro nobis, sed animam eius. Cuius contrarium Ecclesia facit. Non ergo sancti, ad minus ante resurrectionem, pro nobis orant.... Ad quintum dicendum quod quia sancti viventes meruerunt ut pro nobis orarent, ideo eos invocamus nominibus quibus hic vocabantur, quibus etiam nobis magis innotescunt. Et iterum propter fidem resurrectionis insinuandam: sicut legitur *Ex.* 3: *Ego sum Deus Abraham,* etc."

34. Cf. Anton C. Pegis, "Between Immortality and Death: Some Further Reflections on the *Summa contra gentiles,*" *Monist* 58 (1974): 1–15, here 15; cf. also A. C. Pegis, *St. Thomas and the Problem of the Soul in the Thirteenth Century* (Toronto: Pontifical Institute of Mediaeval Studies, 1976); idem, "The Separated Soul and its Nature in St. Thomas," in A. A. Maurer et al., eds., *St. Thomas Aquinas 1274–1974. Commemorative Studies,* vol. I (Toronto: Pontifical Institute of Mediaeval Studies, 1974), 131–58; idem, "St. Thomas and the Meaning of Human Existence," in A. Parel, ed., *Calgary Aquinas Studies* (Toronto: Pontifical Institute of Mediaeval Studies, 1978), 49–64. Cf. also the conclusion of Norbert A. Luyten, "Das Phaenomen des Sterbens konfrontiert uns sozusagen in ueberdimensionierter Weise mit dem Paradox, welches der Mensch eigentlich schon immer ist: Er ist zugleich wesentlich leiblich und uebersteigt das Leibliche. Bei der Frage nach der Identitaet des Menschen muß diese Paradoxie immer mitbedacht werden. Was die Sache natuerlich nicht vereinfacht!" in Luyten, ed., *Tod—Ende oder Vollendung?* (Freiburg: Alber, 1980), 193.

35. Mary F. Rousseau, "The Natural Meaning of Death in the *Summa theologiae,*" in G. F. McLean, ed., *Immateriality* (Washington, D.C.: American Catholic Philosophical Association, 1978), 87–95; idem, "Elements of a Thomistic Philosophy of Death," *Thomist* 43 (1979): 581–602.

36. Cf. the ontological statements such as *Comp. theol.* I, 151: "Natura enim animae est ut sit pars hominis ut forma. Nulla autem pars perfecta est in sua natura nisi sit in suo toto. Requiritur igitur ad ultimam hominis beatitudinem ut anima rursum corpori uniatur"; but also episte-

Thomas's writings was felt, for example, at the beginning of the *visio Dei* controversy in the fourteenth century about the sense in which fulfillment could be claimed for souls before the final resurrection.[37] But even within today's hermeneutical situation, the starting point for our interpretation of Thomas's work as a contribution towards a genuinely theological understanding of death remains characterized by this unresolved ambivalence.[38] Thomas's *Commentary on John*, while often overlooked as a locus of Thomas's theology of death, provides key insights into how Thomas himself addressed this ambivalence.

THOMAS AND THE SADNESS OF CHRIST IN HIS *COMMENTARY ON JOHN*

One feature of the Gospel of John that has never ceased to be a focus of interest and controversy is the Evangelist's use of the verb *tarásso*, to shake, trouble, or stir up, with reference to the apparently emotional response of Jesus and his disciples to the intrusion of death or persecution into their lives. It occurs in this sense five times in four consecutive chapters, beginning with the scene of mourning for Lazarus in John 11. As Thomas knows, the paradigm of such upheaval is the storm at sea, which churns up the ocean's waters.[39] As Thomas points out, this *mare turbatum* is still slightly reflected in the Gospel by the waters of the pool of Bethesda, which were thought to be

---

mological statements about the knowledge of the *anima separata* as "in quadam universalitate et confusione": *QD De anima* XX co; cf. *ST* I, q. 89, a. 4. The frequent use of the pejorative term *universaliter* to describe the vagueness of the knowledge of which the separated soul would be capable by its own powers especially in regards to the concrete beings, events, and persons experienced in the past, as well as the continued validity of the principle "omne enim receptum determinatur in recipiente secundum modum recipientis" (*QD De anima*, ibid.), underline the theological problem posed by Thomas's anthropology. Early disciples of Thomas, such as Bernhard de Trilia, were still quite aware of this implication: "Sed efficacia virtutis intellectivae animae separatae non est proportionata universalitati formarum influxarum, sed magis est proportionata formis a rebus acceptis, propter quod naturale est ei corpori uniri. Et ideo anima separata per huiusmodi species influxas non cognoscit omnes species rerum naturalium perfecte et complete sicut angeli, sed in universali et incomplete": *Quaestiones de cognitione animae separatae a corpore* II, ed. Stuart Martin (Toronto: Pontifical Institute of Mediaeval Studies, 1965), 68.

37. Cf. Friedrich Wetter, *Die Lehre Benedikts XII. vom intensiven Wachstum der Gottesschau* (Rome: Universitas Gregoriana, 1958); and Christian Trottmann, *La vision béatifique: des disputes scolastiques à sa définition par Benoît XII* (Rome: Ecole française de Rome, 1995).

38. It is this ambivalence that was behind the controversy between Theodor Schneider and Klaus Benrath as to whether Thomas, despite himself, winds up portraying human perfection in angelic terms; cf. Schneider, *Die Einheit des Menschen*, 30–42.

39. Thomas Aquinas, *Ioan.* 13, lect. 4, n. 1796; cf. already *Ioan.* 12, lect. 5, n. 1651: "proprie dicitur turbari aliquid quando commovetur: unde et mare commotum dicimus esse turbatum."

"disturbed" (RSV) or stirred up at times by an angel of healing (John 5:7; in some texts, including Thomas's, also 5:4).⁴⁰ Troubled waters were ever an easy metaphor for a troubled mind, which could be confused, agitated, or disturbed. Whole governments and states, too, just as individuals, could be caught by such upheaval and thrown into grave disorder or even anarchy.⁴¹ In that synoptic gospel most closely related to the Gospel of John, Luke uses the verb to describe how Zachariah was "startled" (RSV) at the sight of the angel (1:12) and how the apostles were "startled" (RSV) at the sight of the risen Lord (24:37); "shaken" might have been the closer translation. John uses the term to describe Christ immediately prior to his raising of Lazarus ("When Jesus saw her weeping and the Jews who were with her weeping, he was moved with indignation and *deeply distressed*": 11:33) as well as Christ predicting his imminent passion ("Now my soul *is in turmoil*": 12:27) and his betrayal through Judas ("Jesus exclaimed *in great distress,* 'In very truth I tell you, one of you is going to betray me'": 13:21). Twice Christ refers to the turmoil felt by the apostles ("Set your *troubled* hearts at rest": 14:1, 27). The Vulgate uses some form of the verb *turbare* to translate each of these Johannine passages.⁴²

Revealing Thomas's programmatic interest in reading these passages for their potential contribution to a theology of mourning, two dimensions of his exegesis stand out in contrast both to his biblical and Patristic sources and to our own contemporary exegesis today: Thomas interprets *turbatio* resolutely as *tristitia;* and he identifies behind the thus established *fact* of Christ's sadness five features of its *significance* for us. As Thomas himself articulates this twofold analysis: "And thus we need to see first what this upheaval in Christ is; and then why he willed to undergo it."⁴³ But, here, too, one of Thomas's favorite lines from Aristotle is valid: "finis, etsi sit postremus in executione, est tamen primus in intentione agentis." Indeed, it is because of

---

40. Ibid., "turbatio designat commotionem quamdam: et hoc apparet in hoc quod habetur supra, V, 4: *Angelus Domini descendebat secundum tempus in piscinam, et movebatur aqua,* et postea sequitur: *Domine, hominem non habeo, ut, cum turbata fuerit aqua, mittat me in piscinam:* quod pro eodem accipit aquam turbari et moveri. Secundum hunc etiam modum dicimus mare turbatum, quando est commotum. Turbatio ergo animi eius commotionem designat."

41. Cf. Henry George Liddell, Robert Scott, and Henry Stuart Jones, et al., eds., *A Greek-English Lexicon (LSJ)* (Oxford: Clarendon Press, 1985), 1757f.; and William F. Arndt and F. Wilbur Gingrich, *A Greek-English Lexicon of the New Testament and Other Early Christian Literature* (Chicago: University of Chicago Press, 1965), 812f.

42. *turbavit:* John 11:33; *turbata est:* John 12:27; *turbatus est spiritu:* John 13:21; *non turbetur:* John 14:1; 14:27.

43. *Ioan.* 12, lect. 5, n. 1650: "et ideo videndum est primum quid sit haec turbatio in Christo; secundo quare voluit eam subire."

Thomas's ultimate sense of why Christ should be shown to be sad in the face of death that Thomas first insists on *tristitia* as the main (but not the only) constituent of Christ's *turbatio*. Thomas' *hermeneutics* of facticity implicitly precedes here his resolute insistence on the *fact* of Christ's sadness; he argues decisively for the *fact* of Christ's sadness only because he can imagine and anticipate its *significance*. Even the statistical evidence on Thomas's vocabulary suggests the programmatic nature of his remarks: in these same *lectiones* where Thomas mentions some thirty-four times some form of the word *tristis*, the corresponding texts of the *Vulgata* and the *Catena aurea* do not employ the term even once (with the exception of an isolated reference by John Chrysostom to some future hearer of the Gospel as possibly "contristatum").[44] While the sadness of Christ is thematized by both Thomas and his texts with the use of some other expressions as well, the relative proportions of their uses of this key term, *tristitia,* is telling.

Turbatio as *Tristitia:* Arguing for the Fact of Christ's Sadness

That Christ is shaken here precisely by his sadness seems to be a possible, in places even quite a plausible, reading, but that reading is in no way the necessary or even the self-understood meaning of John. Many of today's most respected exegetes deny flatly, if without much argumentation, that this kind of upheaval was meant to consist of sadness at all.[45] Sometimes it is even said that a "pyschologizing explanation is inappropriate"[46] altogether, which does not prevent such authors from noting the evangelist's portrayal of "Jesus' apparently contradictory emotions"[47] or from emphasizing his "angry inward emotion."[48] This insistence of recent exegesis that, without a theological or at least a dramatic purpose, the Evangelist would not have mentioned that Christ was shaken, is an altogether plausible view that corresponds well to that Patristic and medieval insistence on Christ's sovereignty which was shared by Thomas and the sources he had gathered into the *Catena:* because Jesus could have avoided difficult emotions of this kind, he must have had some reason or purpose for choosing to suffer them. Whether this singular revelatory purpose is attributed also to Jesus or merely to the Evangelist, it becomes in either case all the more urgent, in order to grasp the Gospel's point,

---

44. *Catena aurea Ioan.,* XII, lect. 4 (497b).
45. Cf. Rudolf Bultmann, *The Gospel of John: A Commentary* (Philadelphia: Westminster Press, 1964), 406ff.
46. Rudolf Schnackenburg, *The Gospel according to John,* vol. 2 (New York: Crossroad, 1982), 334.
47. Ibid.; cf. the similar tension at 387.
48. Ibid., 336.

that we identify the emotions mentioned here. What does the Gospel want to tell us about Jesus' confrontation with death?

In their reading of John 11, recent exegetes have given primary emphasis to the double occurrence of *enebrimésato/embrimómenos* (11: 33 and 38), the first of which precedes and is qualified by the five words following it: *to pneúmati kai etáraksen heautón* ("He was moved with indignation and deeply distressed," so the RSV; or, perhaps more literally: "he growled/groaned inwardly and was shaken"). The verb, which refers generally to nonverbal utterances, such as the barking of dogs and the roaring of lions,[49] is often, though not always, associated with anger. The Vulgate translates the phrase with *fremuit spiritu et turbavit se ipsum.* Schnackenburg roughly follows Luther's suggestion here for underlining this sense of anger: "ergrimmet er im Geist und betrübt sich selbs":[50] ". . . ergrimmte er im Innern und erregte sich."[51] Those exegetes who were still confident of our ability to distinguish here the written "*semeia*-Quelle" from the Evangelist's own work assigned *enebrimésato* to the earlier work on Christ's miracles and the following words, *to pneúmati kai etáraksen heautón*, to the Evangelist. Unfortunately, they rarely dwell on what that addition was meant to convey by way of changed emphasis. The parallels to the use of this verb for articulate expressions of rebuke in Synoptic miracle stories (Mk 1:43; Mt 9:30) have led some to see in the pre-Gospel account "Traces of Thaumaturgic Techniques in the Miracles."[52] All this serves to confirm the reference to anger in the first term, but does little to explain the intent of the Gospel revision; few recent commentaries attempt to name the redactional point. Some of them, however, assuming the incompatibility of anger and sadness, and seeing Christ's anger documented here, bluntly reject that Christ is portrayed in chapter 11 as saddened. That leaves them with few options for interpreting the short sentence of John 11:35: *edákrusen ho jesous. Et lacrimatus est Jesus.* "And Jesus wept." R. Bultmann's interpretation is typical for that "irritation" which Schnackenburg describes as representative of the modern exegesis of v. 35, coming so close after the anger expressed in v. 33. Bultmann first notes the difference between the generic term for weeping, *edákrusen*, said here of Jesus (the only time this verb is used in the NT), and the more specific term for wailing, *klaíousan, klaíontas*, applied to Mary and

49. *LSJ*, 540; Bauer, 254; cf. LXX, Lam 2,6; Dan 11:30.
50. Wittenberg 1545.
51. Rudolf Schnackenburg, *Das Johannesevangelium*, 2. Teil (Freiburg: Herder, 1985), 419ff.
52. So the title by C. Bonner, *Harvard Theological Review* 20 (1927): 171–81; cf. R. Bultmann, *Gospel of John*, 406, n. 4, who sees even in the second expression the pneumatic excitement of an ecstatic miracle-worker; and, seemingly against this view ("Fehldeutung," even for the Gospel source?), Schnackenburg, *Johannesevangelium*, 421.

the Jews who accompany her in v. 33. From this difference, Bultmann constructs a diametrical contradiction.

The wailing of Mary and the Jews provokes the height of agitation in Jesus (v. 33). In this context, it cannot be otherwise interpreted than his wrath over the lack of faith, expressed in the wailing that is raised in his presence about the death of Lazarus. . . . The statement that Jesus wept (v. 35)—where the weeping must be understood as a sign of agitation in the sense of v. 33—has hardly any other purpose than to provoke the utterance of the Jews (vv. 36f.) and so to set in a yet brighter light the motif of the faithlessness in the presence of the Revealer. Jesus—again in that anger over the faithless—comes to the grave, which is blocked up by a stone.[53]

For Bultmann, the weeping of Jesus might be intended merely as a dramatic occasion for some of the Jews to question how serious Jesus' love for Lazarus might be: "Could not this man, who opened the blind man's eyes, have done something to keep Lazarus from dying?" At most, the weeping of Jesus might reflect the same kind of anger at wailing that was shown toward the lament for Jairus's daughter (Mk 5:38ff.).[54]

An opposing view is taken by Schnackenburg, who is willing to see anger in v. 33, but not in the weeping of Jesus at v. 35: "The weeping here has no connection with the surge of anger."[55] Schnackenburg refers to this passage as possibly related to the use of the noun *dakrúon* in Hebrews 5:7: "In the course of his earthly life he offered up prayers and petitions, with loud cries and *tears*, to God who was able to deliver him from death" (cf. Esau's tears at Heb 12:17); and in neither case does anger seem to be the primary motivation of Christ's weeping.

Had Schnackenburg not already let the *turbavit se ipsum* of v. 33 be so strongly interpreted by the anger of *fremuit in spiritu*, he could have underscored his interpretation of Jesus' weeping as an expression of sadness by reference to the close tie admitted between sadness and that *turbatio* which is ascribed to Jesus in the following two chapters. "Now my soul *is in turmoil*" (Jn 12:27). "Jesus exclaimed *in great distress:* in very truth I tell you: one of you is going to betray me" (13:21). There is at least an indirect parallel here to the synoptic portrayal of Jesus on the Mount of Olives, which from Maximus Confessor to Thomas More's *De tristitia Christi* was the *locus classicus* for the eminently human dimensions of Christ's will. As Raymond Brown puts it: "John 12:27, 'My soul is troubled *(tarassein),*' is parallel to Mark 14:34, 'My soul is sorrowful *(perilypos).*' Both reflect Ps. 42:5 'Why are you so sorrowful

---

53. Bultmann, 406f.
54. For Bultmann's rejection of older exegesis on the weeping of Christ, cf. also 406, n. 4.
55. Schnackenburg, *Gospel,* vol. 2, 336.

(perilypos), my soul, and why do you trouble *(syntarassein)* me?'"⁵⁶ The *Vulgata* makes the association alluded to by Brown all the more apparent to its readers: "Quare tristis es anima mea et quare conturbaras me." Yet even here in the context of chapters 12 and 13 of John, Schnackenburg is more interested in contrasting *turbatio* to any fear of death⁵⁷ than he is keen to associate *turbatio* with that sadness of Jesus which he sees expressed in the tears of chapter 11.

Despite their disagreement on whether to include the images of Christ's *turbatio* in that depiction of Christ's sadness that both admit is intended by his weeping, Thomas and Schnackenburg agree on a more basic point. It is because Schnackenburg can see the theological *significance* that John attaches to Christ's sadness that he is willing to oppose Bultmann's complete denial that the gospel is claiming there to be sadness in Jesus.

If we compare other New Testament passages in which tears on the part of Jesus (Heb 5:7) or people following him (Acts 20:19; Rev 7:17; 24:24) are mentioned—the verb is used only in this passage—the reason seems to be the sadness and darkness of the present world, the situation of trial and persecution. On the sad journey to the tomb, Jesus too is moved by the darkness of the inevitability of death. The evangelist does not gloss over the horror of death, but believes that it is conquered in faith (cf. vv. 25c, 39). The scale of Jesus' act can only be recognised if the bitterness of physical death is not minimised. The short remark that Jesus began to weep is the dark precursor of his confident prayer to the Father (v. 41), just as in 12:27–28 the momentary "confusion" of his soul gives way to the calm and confident prayer to the Father to glorify his name. It is in this sense that the Johannine Jesus is one with men and not impervious to their distress. The Johannine community is also aware of the darkness of the earthly journey, which ends in physical death, and from out of this knowledge its members lift their eyes in faith to the never-ending future of the life given by Jesus (cf. 8:51; 12:25).⁵⁸

Thomas is more willing than most of our contemporaries to admit in principle that the Gospel is portraying something of the psychological reactions of Jesus to the events that he experiences.⁵⁹ Oddly enough, our contemporaries

---

56. Raymond E. Brown, *The Gospel according to John I–XII* (Garden City, N.Y.: Doubleday, 1966), 470.

57. Schnackenburg, *Johannesevangelium*, 2, 484f.; and *Gospel*, vol. 2, 386ff. The English translation here brings "terror," where Schnackenburg eliminates from Christ not just "terror," but even "Todesangst." By way of contrast to the synoptic Garden scene, "In John we have only (!) 'My soul is troubled (erschüttert).'"

58. Schnackenburg, *Gospel*, vol. 2, 337; cf. 387.

59. Cf. *Ioan.* 11, lect. 5, n. 1531: "consequenter cum dicit, *Iesus ergo, ut vidit eam plorantem . . . infremuit spiritu et turbavit se,* ponuntur ea quae pertinent ad affectum Christi." "Primo ergo ponitur affectus Christi ostensus Mariae."

are quicker to moralize the text; and yet Thomas agrees with them that what is portrayed always has a theological point. Where contemporary writers ascribe these intentions to the Gospel author, who might have chosen to portray Christ otherwise, Thomas presents them as the intention of Christ himself, who could have chosen not to be so affected by the sadder side of life and death.[60] Like Bultmann and Schnackenburg, Thomas, too, sees in the expression *infremuit spiritu* an indication of Jesus' indignation and anger:[61] but Thomas is closer here to Schnackenburg than to Bultmann in holding for the compatibility of sadness with indignation and anger; indeed, Thomas describes sadness as the necessary condition of anger.[62] And yet Thomas goes beyond both of these more recent exegetes by adding to Christ's anger and sadness a moment of fear as well.[63] While seeing in the upset of Christ as portrayed in John a mix of sadness, anger, and fear, Thomas sees sadness as the dominant emotion among the three.[64]

Why Jesus Is Shown to Be Sad: The Significance of the *Tristitia Christi*

Unlike the more recent commentaries, for which the passages quoted above from R. Bultmann are paradigmatic, Thomas does not read Christ's anger as directed against those who are mourning;[65] quite to the contrary, Thomas sees the mourning of the Jews with Martha and Mary as commend-

---

60. Unlike Schnackenburg, Bultmann shares one of the exaggerated dimensions of Thomas's reading of how Christ "commanded" himself to have emotions; cf. *Ioan.* 11, lect. 5, n. 1535: "quia ipse suo imperio turbavit semetipsum," etc.

61. Cf. *Ioan.* 11, lect. 5, n. 1534: "Sed quid significat fremitus Christi? Videtur quod significet iram; *Prov. XIX*, 12: Sicut fremitus leonis, ita et ira regis. Item. Videtur quod significet indignationem; secundum illud *Psalmi CXI* 10: *Dentibus suis fremet et tabescet.* Responsio dicendum quod hic fremitus in Christo iram quamdam et indignationem cordis significat."

62. Cf. ibid., "Omnis autem ira et indignatio ex aliquo dolore et tristitia causatur."

63. Cf. *Ioan.* 12, lect. 5, n. 1651: "secundum hoc ergo est sensus: *Nunc anima mea turbata est;* idest, affecta est passionibus timoris et tristitiae, quantum ad sensitivam, quibus tamen ratio non turbabatur, nec suum ordinem deserebat, *Mc.* XIV 33: *Coepit Iesus pavere et taedere.*"

64. Cf. *Ioan.* 13, lect. 4, n. 1796: "Inter omnes autem affectiones seu passiones appetitus sensitivi, tristitia magis vim commotionis habet. Delectatio enim, cum dicat quietem in bono praesenti, magis rationem quietis habet quam commotionis. Timor etiam, cum sit de malo futuro, minus movet quam tristitia, quae est de malo praesenti. Et inde est quod turbatio animi praecipue dicitur tristitia. Turbatus est ergo Iesus, idest tristatus." In *ST* III, q. 15, where Thomas again defends the presence of sadness, fear, and anger in Christ (adding "admiratio," surprise or puzzlement, to them), he again describes *tristitia* as foundational for fear (a. 7, resp. et ad 2: fear as *tristitia* transposed from a present to a future but not entirely inevitable *nocivum*) and for anger (a. 9: "Ira est effectus tristitiae. . . . Et sic ira est passio composita ex tristitia et appetitu vindictae").

65. *Ioan.* 11, lect. 5, n. 1534: "Duo autem hic suberant: unum de quo Christus turbabatur, quod erat mors hominis, inflicta propter peccatum; aliud autem de quo indignabatur, erat saevi-

able[66] and the mourning of Jesus throughout these chapters as parenetic. Over the course of his comments, Thomas will argue for at least five senses in which the significance of Christ's sadness must be understood.

First: with reference to the ontology of death and the rationality of Jesus' sadness. Unlike many of his contemporaries, such as Bonaventure in his own commentary on John, Thomas sees this upsetting sadness not merely as compassion for human infirmity, blindness, and wickedness,[67] but as sadness about human death itself: something that Bonaventure expressly denies.[68] Like Bonaventure, Thomas sees the *turbatio Christi* as remaining within the

---

tia mortis et diaboli. Unde, sicut quando aliquis vult repellere hostem, dolet de malis illatis ab ipso, et indignatur ad animadvertendum in eum, ita et christus doluit et indignatus est."

66. cf. *Ioan.* 11, lect. 5, n. 1527: "in quo quidem Iudaei commendandi sunt, quia, ut dicitur *Eccl.* VII, 38, *Non desis plorantibus in consolatione.*"

67. Bonaventura, *Commentarius in Evangelium S.Ioannis*, c. XI, n. 57, Opera omnia, vol. 6 (Quaracchi: Ad Claras Aquas, 1893), 404b. Although Bonaventure is willing to read the *turbatio* of Christ here as a form of sadness, his unwillingness to read this sadness as mourning about death leaves him with little motivation to develop the idea of *tristitia* beyond the conventions of the monastic tradition; cf. Rainer Jehl, *Melancholie und Acedia. Ein Beitrag zur Anthropologie und Ethik Bonaventuras* (Paderborn: Schoeningh, 1984). Thomas, too, knows of the destructive power of sadness or melancholy and the traditional interpretation of *tristitia* as a vice or at least as a passion to be overcome (cf. *ST* I-II, q. 37, a. 3; q. 39, a. 1, and the unspoken presupposition behind the preceding question 38 as well), and he will see in Christ's sadness a model of not being overwhelmed by the possible excesses of mourning; but he also can point to positive modifications of *tristitia* that, under certain conditions and within certain bounds, let it become part of a virtue of genuinely Christian mourning.

68. Bonaventura: "Intelligendum tamen, quod Christus non flevit propter mortem Lazari, sed propter nostram miseriam, quae in morte Lazari significabatur." Thomas differs from Bonaventure not only by stressing the possibility of a virtuous qualification of sadness, but by defining the possibility of virtuous mourning, where the object of Christ's sadness is first and foremost the *nocivum* of suffering and death; cf. also *ST* III, q. 15, a. 6: "Potuit autem anima Christi interius apprehendere aliquid ut nocivum: et quantum ad se, sicut passio et mors eius fuit; et quantum ad alios, sicut peccata discipulorum vel etiam Iudaeorum occidentium ipsum." The immediate meaning of mourning death thus remains the foundation of the extended senses of mourning injustice. Jesus' willingness to accept death as somehow a part of God's salvific plan was indirect, presupposing the more basic rejection of death in itself; cf. *ST* III, q. 15, a. 6, ad 4: "Et hoc modo mors Christi et eius passio fuit, secundum se considerata, involuntaria et tristitiam causans." In his *ST* III, q. 18, a. 3, Thomas deepens the Patristic critique of Monothelitism to show that, within the human will of Jesus, the *voluntas ut natura*, including the preference for life over death, is no less rational than the so-called *voluntas rationis*, the will of something good only on the basis of some additional reason. Cf. Tomas Alvira, *Naturaleza y Libertad. Estudio de los conceptos tomistas de voluntas ut natura y voluntas ut ratio* (Pamplona: University of Navarra Press, 1985). The indirectness of Jesus' acceptance corresponds for Thomas to the indirect contribution of Christ's death to our salvation; the accent remains on the resurrection: *ST* III, q. 50, a. 6, ad 1: "Mors Christi est operata salutem nostram ex virtute divinitatis unitae et non ex sola ratione mortis"; *ST* III, q. 53, a. 4: "Si autem consideremus corpus et animam Christi mortui secundum virtutem naturae creatae, sic non potuerunt sibi invicem reuniri, sed oportuit Christum resuscitari a Deo." Neither Christ's sufferings nor his

limits of reason, not as a *perturbatio* that would have eclipsed it; but, unlike Bonaventure, Thomas includes the evil of death in the objects about which Jesus is sad, precisely because Jesus rationally knows what death is.[69] It is here that Thomas could best presuppose the philosophical work he had already done on the anthropological significance of death. Unlike some of our own contemporary theologies of death, such as Karl Rahner's,[70] it is not the hiddenness of death that calls for mourning, but the insight into this *nocivum*.

Second: a sense of the piety and justice of Jesus' mourning. Given the rational insight into the *nocivum* of death, it was then a matter of piety towards those whom he loved that Jesus would mourn their deaths or the deaths of their loved ones. Thomas interprets the sadness of Jesus as paying this justice of piety both to Lazarus[71] and to his mourning sister, Mary. By mourning with Mary, Jesus is far from displaying anger at her sadness; rather, by sharing it, he affirms it.[72]

Third: with reference to the Christological significance of Jesus' sadness. By allowing himself to be truly moved by sadness about death, and by showing us how churned up he is in the face of death, the Christ reveals his true humanity:[73] an anti-docetic theme especially well-known to Thomas from his Patristic research.[74] Thomas goes on to reject any contradiction between high

---

death would have been salvific of themselves: "non satisfactio . . . nisi ex caritate" (cf. *ST* III, q. 14, aa. 1–4).

69. *Ioan.* 13, lect. 4, n. 1797ff.: "Et haec turbatio fuit in Christo: unde signanter dicit Evangelista, quod *turbatus est spiritu*, idest turbatio quae fuit in appetitu sensitivo, in Christo fuit ex iudicio rationis. Unde supra XI, 33, dicit quod *turbavit semetipsum*. In Christo enim omnia ex deliberatione rationis etiam in inferiori appetitu sensitivo proveniebant: unde nec subiti motus sensualitatis in Christo fuerunt. Voluit autem hic Iesus turbari propter duo. Primo quidem propter fidei nostrae instructionem. Nam imminebat ei passio, et mors, quam naturaliter refugit natura humana, et, cum eam sibi sentit imminere, tristatur tamquam de malo et nocivo sibi praesente."

70. On the "Verhuelltheit des Todes," death's "hiddenness, its darkness" cf. Karl Rahner, *Zur Theologie des Todes* (Freiburg: Herder, 1958), 36ff.; trans. Charles H. Henkey as *On the Theology of Death* (New York: Herder and Herder, 1961), 46ff.

71. *Ioan.* 11, lect. 5, n. 1537: "Consequenter Dominus affectum suum lacrymis demonstrat; unde subditur *Et lacrymatus est Iesus:* Quae quidem lacrymae non erant ex necessitate, sed ex pietate et causa. Fons enim pietatis erat."

72. Ibid., n. 1533: "Circa quam quidem turbationem primo quidem attende pietatem, secundo discretionem, tertio potestatem. Pietatem quidem ex causa, quae est iusta. Tunc enim iuste turbatur quis, si ex aliorum tristitia et malo turbetur: et quantum ad hoc dicit *Ut vidit eam plorantem;* Rom. XII, 15: *Gaudere cum gaudentibus et flere cum flentibus.*"

73. *Ioan.* 12, lect. 5. n. 1652: "Sciendum est quod Dominus turbari voluit propter duo: primo quidem propter fidei documenta, ut scilicet veritatem humanae naturae approbaret: et ideo iam ad passionem appropinquans omnia humanitus agit."

74. Thomas opposes the *turbatio Christi* to the later error of Apollinaris, *Ioan.* 12, lect. 5, n. 1654); and 13, lect. 4, n. 1798.

and low Christologies, arguing that it is rather the coincidence of both that underscores the significance of each. The raising of Lazarus by the power of Christ's divinity is given its full significance only by the "weakness" of Christ's humanity revealed in his sadness at death.

We should note here that Christ is truly divine and truly human. And so in his actions we find almost everywhere that the divine is mingled with the human, and the human with the divine. And if at times something human is mentioned about Christ, something divine is immediately added. Indeed, we read of no weakness of Christ greater than his passion; yet as he hangs on the cross divine events are manifested: the sun is obscured, rocks are rent, and the bodies of saints that had been asleep arise. Even at his birth, as he lay in the manger, a star shines in the heavens, the angels sing his praises, and the magi and kings offer gifts. We have a similar situation here: for Christ experiences a certain weakness in his human affections, becoming disturbed over the death of Lazarus. We read, *he was deeply moved in spirit and troubled himself*.[75]

Fourth: with reference to the soteriological significance of Jesus' sadness. By choosing to share our sadness at death, Jesus reveals not only his own human nature, but also his love for humankind. Jesus reveals not only the subjective side of his love, but also the object of his salvific will. In revealing his enmity to the powers of death, he also reveals his will for the restoration of fully human life. Precisely because this emotion of Jesus and its portrayal by the evangelist could have been avoided, its mention underlines all the more the salvific intentionality of the Christ.

I answer that Christ's being deeply moved here indicates a certain anger and resentment of the heart. For all anger and resentment are caused by some kind of pain and sadness. Now there are two things involved here: the one about which Christ was troubled was death, which was afflicted upon the human race on account of sin; the other, which he resented, was the cruelty of death and of the devil. Thus, just as, when one wants to repel an enemy, he is saddened by the evils inflicted by him, and indignant at the very thought of him, so too Christ was saddened and indignant. There was also power (signified by Christ's being deeply moved) here, because Christ

---

75. *Ioan.* 11, lect. 5, n. 1532: "Ubi notandum est Christum verum Deum esse et verum hominem. Et ideo ubique fere in factis suis mixta leguntur humana divinis et divina humanis: et si quandoque ponitur aliquid humanum de Christo statim additur aliquid divinum. Nihil enim infirmius de Christo legimus quam eius passionem; et tamen eo in cruce pendente divina facta patent, quod sol obscuratur, petrae scinduntur, corpora sanctorum qui dormierant resurgunt. In nativitate etiam et eo iacente in praesepio, sidus de caelo fulget, angelus laudes cecinit, magi et reges munera offerunt. Simile autem habemus in hoc loco: nam Christus secundum humanitatis affectum aliquid infirmum patitur turbationem quamdam de morte Lazari concipiens; unde dicit *infremuit spiritu et turbavit semetipsum,*" trans. Weisheipl and Larcher, *Commentary on the Gospel of Saint John*, Part 2, 181.

troubled himself by his own command. Sometimes such emotions arise for an inappropriate reason, as when a person rejoices over something evil, or is saddened over what is good.... But this was not the case with Christ; thus he says, *When Jesus saw her weeping, ... he troubled himself.* And sometimes such emotions arise for a good reason, but are not moderated by reason. So he says, *he was deeply moved in spirit ...* (as if to say): He took on this sadness by a judgement of reason.[76]

Fifth: with attention to the parenetic significance of Jesus' sadness. Even before he began his commentary on *John*, Thomas had argued that not every deed of Jesus narrated by the Gospels was meant to offer us an example for our literal imitation.[77] It is thus all the more striking that Thomas devotes so much space and energy to stressing the parenetic purpose of the passages on Jesus' *turbatio*. Underscoring again the freedom with which this turmoil of Jesus is manifested here,[78] Thomas insists that, far from displaying anger at the mourning of death, Jesus shared this mourning in order to offer us an example for our imitation, avoiding the dual danger of our mourning too much[79] or too little. The arguments for exemplarity extend here the logic de-

---

76. *Ioan.* 11, lect. 5, n. 1534ff. "Responsio. Dicendum quod hic fremitus in Christo iram quamdam et indignationem cordis significat. Omnis autem ira et indignatio ex aliquo dolore et tristitia causatur. Duo autem hic suberant: unum de quo Christus turbabatur, quod erat mors homini inflicta propter peccatum; aliud autem de quo indignabatur erat saevitia mortis et diaboli. Unde, sicut quando aliquis vult repellere hostem, dolet de malis illatis ab ipso, et indignatur ad animadvertendum in eum, ita et Christus doluit et indignatus est. (Fremitus significat etiam) potestatem autem, quia ipse suo imperio turbavit semetipsum. Nam huiusmodi quidem passiones aliquando insurgunt ex causa indebita; sicut cum aliquis de malis gaudet et de bonis tristatur; *Prov.* II, 14: *Qui laetantur cum male fecerint et exultant in rebus pessimis;* et hoc non fuit in Christo. Unde dicit *Ut vidit eam plorantem ... turbavit seipsum.* Aliquando insurgunt ex aliqua causa bona, non tamen ratione moderantur: et propter hoc dicit *infremuit spiritu ...* , quasi dicat: Iudicio rationis hanc sibi tristitiam assumpsit": Weisheipl and Larcher 2, 181ff.

77. Cf. Richard Schenk, "*Omnis Christi actio nostra est instructio:* The Deeds and Sayings of Jesus as Revelation in the view of Thomas Aquinas," in *La doctrine de la révélation divine de saint Thomas d'Aquin*, ed. Leo Elders, *Studi Tomistici* 37 (Vatican City: Libreria Editrice Vaticana, 1990), 104–31.

78. Cf. *Ioan.* 12, lect. 5, n. 1651: "Huiusmodi autem passiones aliter sunt in nobis et aliter fuerunt in Christo. In nobis enim sunt ex necessitate, inquantum quasi ab extrinseco commovemur et afficimur; in Christo non sunt ex necessitate, sed ex imperio rationis, cum in eo nulla passio fuerit nisi quam ipse concitavit. Nam intantum inferiores vires erant subditae rationi in Christo quod nihil agere et pati poterant, nisi quod eis ratio ordinabat. Et ideo dicitur supra, XI, 33, quod *Iesus infremuit spiritu et turbavit* semetipsum; *Ps. LIX,* 4: *Commovisti terram* (idest, humanam naturam) *et turbasti eam.* Sic ergo turbata est anima Christi quod nec contra rationem, sed secundum rationis ordinem turbatio in eo fuit."

79. *Ioan.* 11, lect. 5, n. 1534: "secundum iudicium rationis turbatur; unde dicit *fremuit spiritu,* quasi iudicium rationis servans. In turbatione enim spiritus dicitur mens, vel ratio, secundum illud *Eph.* IV, 23: *Renovamini spiritu mentis vestrae.* Quandoque autem contingit quod huiusmodi passiones sensitivae partis nec fiunt spiritu, nec servant moderamen rationis, quin potius ipsam perturbant: quod quidem in ipso non fuit, quia *infremuit spiritu.*"

veloped in the other four senses of why Christ is revealed as experiencing sadness in the face of death.

Note that Christ willed to be troubled for two reasons. First, to show us a doctrine of the faith. . . . Secondly, he wanted to be an example for us. For if he had remained unmoved and had felt no emotions in his soul, he would not have been a satisfactory example of how we should face death. And so he willed to be troubled in order that when we are troubled at the prospect of death, we will not refuse to endure it, we will not run away: *For we have not a high priest who is unable to sympathize with our weakness, but one who in every respect has been tempted as we are, yet without sinning* (Heb 4:15). The relationship of this to what came before is clear. He encouraged his disciples to suffer when he said: *He who hates his life in this world will keep it for eternal life.* But some might say to him: *Lord, you can calmly discuss and philosophize about death because you are above human sorrows, and death does not trouble you.* It was to counter this that he willed to be troubled.[80]

Developing a brief suggestion by Augustine already recorded in the *Catena aurea*,[81] Thomas focuses his sense of the exemplarity meant here by contrasting the parenetic meaning of Christ's sadness with the Stoic exclusion of sadness from the ideal of wisdom.

A thing is said to be troubled whenever it is greatly agitated. Hence, when the sea is very agitated, it is said to be troubled. And so whenever a thing oversteps the bounds of its repose and tranquillity, it is said to be troubled. Now in the human soul there is a sentient area and a rational one. The sensitive area of the soul is troubled when it becomes strongly affected by certain movements. For example, when it is contracted

---

80. *Ioan.* 12, lect. 5, n. 1652: "Sciendum est quod Dominus turbari voluit propter duo: primo quidem propter fidei documenta . . . ; secundo propter exemplum: nam si omnia constanter egisset et nullam passionem sensisset in anima, non fuisset sufficiens exemplum ad mortem sustinendam hominibus. Et ideo turbari voluit, ut, cum turbamur, non recusemus mortem sustinere, nec deficiamus; *Hebr.* IV, 15: *Non habemus pontificem qui non possit compati infirmitatibus nostris, tentatum per omnia, pro similitudine absque peccato.* Unde ex hoc apparet continuatio cum praecedentibus. Quia enim dixerat: *Qui odit animam suam in hoc mundo, in vitam aeternam custodit eam,* in quo ad passionem discipulos exhortatus fuerat, ne dicant aliqui: *O Domine, securus potes disputare et philosophari de morte, qui extra dolores humanos existens, propter mortem non turbaris:* et ideo ut hoc excluderet, turbari voluit." Thomas is able to synthesize here elements of the Greek theology he discovered in the course of collating his own gloss on the Gospel, paraphrasing for the *Catena aurea* John Chrysostom's *Hom. 66 Ioan.*: "Chrysostomus *Ioannem:* Quia Dominus ad passionem discipulos exhortatus fuerat, ne dicant, quod ipse extra dolores existens humanos facile de morte philosophatur, et nos admonet, propter hoc quod ipse est sine periculo, ostendit quod et ipse in agonia sit, et tamen propter utilitatem mortem non renuit; unde dicit *Nunc anima mea turbata est.*"

81. Citing and yet going beyond the *Tract. 60 Ioan.* for John 13:21: "Augustinus. Pereant igitur argumenta Stoicorum, qui negant in sapientem cadere perturbationem animorum; qui profecto, sicut vanitatem aestimant veritatem, sic stuporem deputant sanitatem; turbetur plane animus Christiani non miseria, sed misericordia."

by fear, raised up by hope, dilated with joy, or otherwise affected by one or other of the emotions. Sometimes this perturbation remains within the bounds of reason, and sometimes it exceeds the bounds of reason, namely, when reason itself is troubled. And although this latter condition quite often occurs in us, it is not found in Christ, since he is the Wisdom of the Father. Indeed, it is not found in any wise person; thus the Stoic tenet that one who is wise is not troubled, i.e. in his reason. Accordingly, the meaning of *Now my soul is troubled,* is this: My soul is affected by the emotions of fear and sadness in its sentient part; but these emotions do not trouble my reason: it does not abandon its own order. *He began to be greatly distressed and troubled* (Mk 14:33).[82]

The Patristic and post-Patristic sources edited by Thomas for his Gloss offer several authorities for the Christological and soteriological senses of Christ's mourning as well as for wider metaphorical interpretations; but the parenetic sense is underdeveloped in the Patristic sources.[83] By contrast,

---

82. *Ioan.* 12, lect. 5, n. 1651: "proprie dicitur turbari aliquid quando commovetur: unde et mare commotum, dicimus esse turbatum. Quandocumque ergo aliquid excedit modum suae quietis et tranquillitatis, tunc illud dicitur turbari. In anima autem humana est pars sensitiva et pars rationalis. In sensitiva quidem parte animae accidit turbatio, quando aliquibus motibus commovetur: puta cum timore contrahitur, spe elevatur, gaudio dilatatur, seu aliqua alia passione afficitur. Sed haec quidem turbatio quandoque quidem sub ratione sistit; quandoque vero limitem rationis excedit, cum scilicet ipsa ratio perturbatur. Quod quidem pluries in nobis contingit, sed in Christo hoc locum non habet, cum sit ipsa sapientia Patris; nec etiam in aliquo sapiente: Unde sententia Stoicorum est quod sapiens non turbatur, scilicet quantum ad rationem. Secundum hoc ergo est sensus: *Nunc anima mea turbata est;* idest, affecta est passionibus timoris et tristitiae, quantum ad sensitivam, quibus tamen ratio non turbabatur nec suum ordinem deserebat; *Mc.* XIV, 33: *Coepit Iesus pavere et taedere.*" Cf. 13, lect. 4, n. 1797: "Sed attendendum, quod quidam philosophi fuerunt, scilicet Stoici, dicentes, quod huiusmodi turbatio et huiusmodi passiones in sapientem non cadunt; quamvis enim sapiens secundum eos timeat, gaudeat, et desideret, nullo modo tamen tristatur. Sed horum falsitas manifeste apparet ex hoc quod Iesus, qui est summa sapientia, turbatur. Sciendum tamen, quod duplex est turbatio. Quaedam procedit ex carne, quando scilicet quis turbatur praeter iudicium rationis ex apprehensione sensuali, quae quidem turbatio quandoque quidem consistit intra limites rationis, in nullo eam obnubilans. Quae non perfecta passio, sed propassio dicitur a Hieronymo; et haec in sapientem cadit. Quandoque autem rationis limitem excedit, et eam turbat, et est non solum passio, sed etiam turbatio; et haec in sapientem non cadit. Alia est turbatio quae procedit ex ratione, quando scilicet ex rationis iudicio et deliberatione turbatur quis in appetitu sensitivo. Et haec turbatio fuit in Christo: unde signanter dicit evangelista, quod *turbatus est spiritu,* idest turbatio quae fuit in appetitu sensitivo, in Christo fuit ex iudicio rationis."

83. Cf. the *Catena aurea* at the critical passage, John 11:33–38: Thomas cites Augustine with the short phrase, "Quare autem flevit Christus, nisi quia homines flere docuit?" After stressing the Christological sense of Christ's turmoil, Theophylact of Ohrid is quoted as then pointing to the parenetic sense as well: "tum etiam nos monendo, ac metam moestitiae et iucunditati imponendo. Nam ex toto nec compati nec moerere ferinum, ac horum exuberantia muliebre." Referring to Christ's turmoil about the exclusion of Judas (John 13:21), Thomas cites but does not develop another parenetic interpretation suggested by Augustine in his Johannine treatises: "etiam Dominus significare sua turbatione dignatus est, quod quando ex falsis fratribus aliquos separari, etiam ante messem, urgens causa compellit, fieri sine ecclesiae turbatione non possit. Turbatus est autem non carne, sed spiritu: spiritus enim in huiusmodi scandalis non perversitate,

Thomas is so intent on portraying the exemplary nature of Christ's sadness that he is willing to reverse the immediate sound of the texts, *Let not your hearts be troubled.* Thomas asks if Jesus is guilty here of hypocrisy, being troubled at death himself, but not granting to his followers the same concession:

Let not your hearts be troubled (John 14:1). . . . But above, John 13:21, it says that *Jesus was troubled in spirit.* How can he tell his disciples not to be troubled, when he himself was troubled? I answer that he did not teach the opposite of what he did. It was stated above that he was troubled *in spirit,* not that his spirit was troubled. He is not forbidding them to be troubled in spirit, but he is forbidding that their hearts, that is, their spirits, be troubled. For there is a troubled state which arises from reason; that is to be praised and not forbidden: *For godly grief produces repentance that leads to salvation* (2 Cor 7:10). Yet there is a different grief or troubled state of the reason itself; this is not laudable because it draws reason from its proper course. . . .[84]

. . . (A further reason for manifesting his sadness was) so that, by controlling his own sadness, he might teach us to moderate our sadness. The Stoics had taught that a wise man is never sad. But it is very inhuman not to be sad at the death of another. However, there are some who become excessively sad over the evils which afflict their friends. Now our Lord willed to be sad in order to teach us that there are times when we should be sad, which is contrary to the opinion of the Stoics; and he preserved a certain moderation in his sadness, which is contrary to the excessively sad type. . . . The third reason (for manifesting his sadness) is to tell us that we should be sad and weep for those who physically die: *I am utterly spent and crushed* (Ps 38:8).[85]

---

sed caritate turbatur; ne forte in separatione aliquorum zizaniorum, simul aliquod eradicetur et triticum." The citation continues in a sense more congenial to Thomas's reflections: "sive ergo ipsum Iudam pereuntem miserando, sive sua morte appropinquante, turbatus est: non animi infirmitate, sed potestate turbatur. Non enim aliquo cogente turbatur, sed turbavit semetipsum, ut supra dictum est. Quod autem turbatur, infirmos in suo corpore, hoc est in sua ecclesia, consolatur, ut si qui suorum morte imminente turbantur, non se reprobos putent."

84. *Ioan.* 14, lect. 1, n. 1850: "*Non turbetur cor vestrum* . . . Sed supra XIII, 21, dicitur: *Turbatus est Iesus spiritu,* etc. Quomodo ergo docet non turbari qui primo turbatus est? Responsio. Dicendum quod non docuit contrarium eius quod fecit. De eo autem dicitur quod *turbatus est spiritu,* non quod spiritus eius sit turbatus. Hic autem non prohibet quin turbentur spiritu, sed prohibet quod eorum cor, idest spiritus, non turbetur. Est enim quaedam turbatio ex spiritu, ex ratione procedens, quae laudabilis est, nec prohibetur. *II Cor.* VII, 10: *Quae enim secundum Deum tristitia est, poenitentiam in salutem stabilem operatur.* Alia est tristitia seu turbatio ipsius rationis; quae non est laudabilis, quia abducit a propria rectitudine"; Larcher, Part 2, p. 328.

85. *Ioan.* 11, lect. 5, n. 1535: "Secundo, ut dum tristatur et cohibet seipsum, doceat modum servandum esse in tristitiis. Stoici enim dixerunt quod nullus sapiens tristatur. Sed valde inhumanum esse quod aliquis de morte alicuius non tristetur. Aliqui autem sunt qui in tristitiis de malo amicorum nimis excedunt. Sed Dominus tristari voluit, ut significet tibi quod aliquando debeas contristari, quod est contra Stoicos; et modum in tristitia tenuit, quod est contra secundos. . . . Tertia ratio est, ut insinuet quod nos pro mortuis corporaliter tristari et plorare debemus: secundum illud *Ps. XXXVII,* 9: *Afflictus sum, et humiliatus sum nimis*"; Larcher, Part 2, p. 182.

Against the immediate sound of the words taken outside their context, *Let not your hearts be troubled,* Thomas reads the meaning of the Gospel as Christ's teaching us by word and example to allow ourselves to be troubled enough to mourn both death and sin, that other destruction of genuinely human possibilities:

> Christ wept in order to show us that it is not blameworthy to weep out of compassion: *My son, let your tears fall for the dead* (Sir 38:16). He wept with a purpose, which was to teach us that we should weep because of sin: *I am weary with my moaning; every night I flood my bed with tears* (Ps 6).[86]

Although there are types of mourning inconsistent with the ideal of Christian life, there could be no completely Christian existence without a genuine sense of mourning.

IMAGINING THE GOAL OF THE INVESTIGATION—ANEW

Despite the well-known seriousness of death that follows from Thomas's anthropology and despite the lesser known but demonstrable intentionality evident in his theology of mourning, especially in the Johannine commentary, there has not yet been a reception of Thomas's suggestions that even comes close to the programmatic nature of his own remarks.[87] The future reception of the suggestions evident in Thomas's *Commentary on the Gospel of St. John* will be possible only if, beyond the immediate context of mourning the loss of personal loved ones, new contexts are opened up that Thomas anticipated only in part. Two such contexts may be suggested here in closing.

First: the context of interreligious dialogue. Among the many goals of interreligious dialogue is the self-critical attainment of a more genuine sense of one's own religion. The weaknesses perceived in other religions can help interlocutors thematize the all too familiar weaknesses thus easily overlooked by them in their own religion. This goal of self-correction is of special promise

---

86. *Ioan.* 11, lect. 5, n. 1537: "Ideo flebat, ut ostenderet non esse reprehensibile si aliquis ploret ex pietate; *Eccl.* XXXVIII, 16: *Fili, super mortuum produc lacrymas.* Flevit ex causa, ut doceret hominem propter peccatum fletibus indigere, secundum illud Ps. VI, 7: *Laboravi in gemitu meo, lavabo per singulas noctes* lectum meum."

87. Among the most instructive presentations cf. Hermann Volk, "Das christliche Verständnis des Todes," in *Gesammelte Schriften III* (Mainz: Gruenewald, 1978), 185–235; J. B. Lotz, "*Magis anima continet corpus . . . quam e converso* (*ST* I q. 76, a. 3). Zum Verhaeltnis von Seele und Leib nach Thomas von Aquin," *Zeitschrift fuer katholische Theologie* 110 (1988): 300–309; and Leo Scheffczyk: *"Unsterblichkeit" bei Thomas von Aquin auf dem Hintergrund der neueren Diskussion* (Munich: Bayerische Akademie der Wissenschaften, 1989).

to Christianity in its dialogue with non-Abrahamic religions. In his own self-understanding, Thomas articulated his theology of mourning in opposition to both Platonic spiritualism and Stoic indifference: against both, Thomas argues that death is a *nocivum* that calls for compassionate mourning. In our own day, the discourse with Buddhism can lead Christianity back to the unfinished task of wrestling with its own Stoic inheritance, while the discourse with Hinduism can lead a Christian theology back to the unfinished task of dealing with its own Platonic influences.[88] The significance that Thomas sees in John for the purification of Christianity from its Platonic and its Stoic temptations can be further developed by interreligious dialogue of this kind.

The idea of compassion is central to both Buddhism and Christianity, but in different understandings. Thomas's idea of compassion shows how *tristitia* can be developed into a virtue of "misericordia" capable of correcting and purifying Christianity of its Stoic temptation to view suffering distantly from the perspective of the entire cosmos. From this self-distancing perspective of the entire cosmos, the Stoics attempted to view their own sufferings as if they were the sufferings of others, rather than, quite to the contrary, to view the sufferings of others as if they were one's own sufferings: *Quia autem tristitia seu dolor est de proprio malo, intantum aliquis de miseria aliena tristatur aut dolet inquantum miseriam alienam apprehendit ut suam.*[89] For this purpose, the anti-Stoic idea of compassion needs to work out the idea of a qualified self (to view sufferings "as one's own," *ut suam*). The discourse with Buddhism can clarify how this idea of compassion needs still to be developed by Christianity in order to provide in a future synthesis a genuine and adequate alternative helpful to human and non-human beings alike. A similar impetus to Christian self-critique can come from Christian conversations with Hinduistic traditions. While the term "Platonic" is widely viewed in a pejorative light by Christian theologians today, the temptation has not vanished to spiritualize (at times by "existentializing") hopes for perfection generally, even for post-mortal salvation. Popular theories of a "resurrection-in-death" have tended to reduce the *nocivum* of death to a hypothetical possibility that is avoided in fact, as is claimed, by a spiritualized perfection into which earthly existence

---

88. For a more detailed account of this possibility of interreligious dialogue, cf. Richard Schenk, "The Progress and End of History, Life after Death, and the Resurrection of the Human Person in the World Religions: An Attempt at a Synthesis from a Christian Perspective," in Peter Koslowski, ed., *The Progress, Apocalypse, and Completion of History and Life after Death of the Human Person in the World Religions* (Dordrecht: Kluwer Academic Publishers, 2002), 104–20.

89. *ST* II-II, q. 30, a. 2.

organically grows, without rupture.[90] The dialogue with Hinduistic traditions can help Christian theology continue to recover its ideal of a uniquely embodied personality and history.

Second: the context of the quest for justice. In his Johannine commentary, Thomas distinguished and linked two objects of Christ's turmoil: death and a broader sense of injustice and sin, which, like death, render impossible human possibilities.[91] In his later, post-Thomistic work, Johann Baptist Metz has done much to show to Catholic theology what the programmatic sense of seeking a future from the memory of suffering could look like.[92] The resources within Thomas for developing this potential of the *memoria passionis* for the quest of peace and justice have been largely overlooked; less so, the significance for interreligious dialogue. As Metz writes:

> The mysticism of apocalyptically inspired traditions is at its heart a mysticism of open eyes with its unconditional obligation to see the sufferings of others. From the founding legends of Buddhism, it is clear that Buddha, too, was changed by encountering the sufferings of strangers; but, in the end, he flees into the royal palace of his inner self, finding in a mysticism of shut eyes an interior landscape immune to suffering and immune to the provocation of a limited time. Contrasted with this, the mysticism of Jesus is a kind of "weak" mysticism. Jesus cannot transport himself outside and beyond the landscape of suffering. His mysticism leads to an apocalyptic outcry.[93]

In his commentary on John, Thomas, too, has offered us a vision of Christ—and a Christianity—of "open eyes." The commentary teaches us in a

---

90. Cf. in the work of the later Karl Rahner, especially after his shift to the theory of resurrection-in-death, the Platonic interpretation of death as self-perfection ("Selbstvollendung"), as maturation ("Reife"/"Zeitigung"), and as the fruition ("Frucht") and harvest ("Ernte") of time, so, e.g., in K. Rahner, *Grundkurs des Glaubens. Einführung in den Begriff des Christentums* (Freiburg: Herder, 1976), 267ff., 419ff. For a critique of the interpretations of death as self-perfective cf. Wolfhart Pannenberg, "Tod und Auferstehung in christlicher Sicht," *Kerygma und Dogma* 20 (1974): 167–80. On the internal development of Rahner's theology of death cf. Luyten, *Todesverstaendnis und Menschenverstaendnis;* and Schenk, *Die Gnade vollendeter Endlichkeit,* 458–77.

91. *Ioan.* 11, lect. 5, n. 1534: "Duo autem hic suberant: unum de quo Christus turbabatur, quod erat mors homini, inflicta propter peccatum; aliud autem de quo indignabatur, erat saevitia mortis et diaboli. Unde, sicut quando aliquis vult repellere hostem, dolet de malis illatis ab ipso, et indignatur ad animadvertendum in eum, ita et christus doluit et indignatus est."

92. Cf. J. B. Metz, *Glaube in Geschichte und Gesellschaft* (Mainz: M. Gruenewald, 1980), 136–48; idem, "Gott und Zeit—Zur Zukunft des apokalyptischen Erbes," in Richard Schenk and Wolfgang Vögele, eds., *Apokalypse. Vortragsreihe zum Ende des Jahrtausends* (Loccum: Evangelische Akademie, 2000), 289–302.

93. Johann Baptist Metz, "Gott. Wider den Mythos von der Ewigkeit der Zeit," in Tiemo Rainer Peters and Claus Urban, eds., *Ende der Zeit? Die Provokation der Rede von Gott* (Mainz: Grünewald, 1999), 32–50, here 44ff.

unique way how to hear the fourth Gospel and to live that central *exemplum, mandatum,* and *praeceptum* it proclaims (Jn 13:15,34; 15:12,17). The same love that teaches us to mourn the losses of humankind teaches us to hope for the salvation of human goods. A hope for goods whose loss would not be mourned would be hollow. A Church that could not mourn is one that could not hope; but also: a Church that could not hope is one that could not mourn for long. The future vitality of Christianity will depend on the revival of these twin virtues.

PART 5

The Person and Work of Jesus Christ

FOURTEEN

The Extent of Jesus' Human Knowledge according to the Fourth Gospel

BENEDICT M. ASHLEY, O.P.

THE PROBLEM

The First and Second Parts of the *Summa theologiae* of St. Thomas Aquinas prepare for his exploration of the mystery of the Person and work of Jesus Christ our Savior. His treatment of the Church, the sacraments, and the goal of history are all considered as the completion of his own work during his earthly and risen life. In his exploration in the Third Part of his *Summa theologiae* of the Person and work of Jesus, St. Thomas Aquinas drew heavily on his previous study of the fourth Gospel.[1] In the *Prologue* of his commentary on this Gospel (n. 1) he cites the words of St. Augustine that "While the other Gospel writers inform us in their Gospels about the active life of Jesus, John in his Gospel informs us also as to his contemplative life." Note that "also," since St. Thomas tells us that the task of a member of the Dominican Order, as he was, must be to imitate the Lord by "giving to others what one has first contemplated."

This was in accord with Aquinas's philosophy in which the nature of anything is revealed through what it does. Hence it is through the

---

1. The *Commentary on the Gospel of St. John*, of which the prologue and first five chapters are by Aquinas and the rest a *reportatio* by Reginald of Piperno, was probably written 1270–1272 during St. Thomas's second period of teaching at Paris. The Third Part of the *Summa theologiae* was written at Naples, about 1272 until left uncompleted in 1273. See James A. Weisheipl, O.P., *Friar Thomas D'Aquino: His Life, Thought and Works* (Garden City: Doubleday, 1974), 246–47, 361–62, 372, and Jean-Pierre Torrell, O.P., *Saint Thomas Aquinas*, vol. 1, *The Person and His Work*, 198–201, 261–66, 333, 339f. At least the first 20, or perhaps 35, questions of the Third Part, however, were already completed when he went to Naples, and it is with this part we are chiefly concerned here. Yet it remains probable that the Commentary is the earlier work.

work of Christ that we best recognize who he is. As a Person he is the Son of God, the Second Person of the Trinity, entirely equal with the Father and that Person through whom the Holy Spirit proceeds from the Father as the source of both Son and Spirit. Yet in obedience to the Father and in the power of the Holy Spirit he has chosen to become human like us in all but sin, in order not only to redeem us from our sins but also to raise us up with him to eternal life in the community of the Trinity.

This truth raises for us the difficult theological problem much discussed today as to the nature of Jesus' human contemplation of the Father in the Holy Spirit during his earthly life. Did he in his humanity enjoy the beatific vision of his Father even in this life, or only in his divine nature?

Gerald O'Collins, S.J., and Daniel Kendall, S.J., have reviewed this question in their article, "The Faith of Jesus."[2] They are concerned to refute the thesis defended by St. Thomas that Jesus, since even in his earthly life he had the beatific vision of the Trinity, unlike Christians, did not have the virtue of faith. Collins and Kendall carefully discuss the three documents of the Holy See that are sometimes quoted as adopting Aquinas's view, held also by other medieval theologians. They conclude, however, that, as the International Theological Commission has also seemed to recognize, these documents do not constitute a definitive magisterial pronouncement on the subject, which thus remains open for theological debate.

In reviewing the various theological opinions on the question, the authors list six principal difficulties for the assumption that Jesus had the beatific vision in this life:

1. How could he have truly suffered if he was already beatified?
2. How could he have had free will?
3. How could he have been tempted and gained merit through trials?
4. How could he have experienced the human process of learning?
5. The Gospels (e.g., Mk 5:30–32; 13:32) seem to indicate that his human knowledge was limited.
6. The hypostatic union in Christ of a divine and human nature does not necessarily imply that Jesus possessed the beatific vision in his human nature.

On this question the Holy See declared in *Lamentabili* (1907) that

A critic cannot assert that Christ's knowledge was unlimited unless by advancing the hypothesis, which is historically inconceivable and morally repugnant, that Christ as

---

2. *Theological Studies* 53 (1992): 403–23.

man had God's knowledge and yet was unwilling to communicate so much knowledge to his disciples and posterity (DS 3434).

The Holy Office in 1919 declared that it could not be "taught safely" that

It is not certain that the soul of Christ during his life among men had the knowledge that the blessed, that is, those who have achieved their goal *(comprehensores)*, have (DS 3645).

Pius XII in *Mystici Corporis* (1943) affirms that Christ in his human intellect possessed the beatific vision and knew all future members of the Church from conception. On this last statement and the previous ones, however, O'Collins and Kendall comment:[3]

Yet it needs to be pointed out that the encyclical was concerned with the mystery of the Church and not as such with doctrines about Christ. In short, contemporary Catholics should continue to give these documents a respectful hearing. But we fail to see any clear obligation to endorse the view that Christ during his earthly existence enjoyed the beatific vision. Neither his unique personal dignity as Son of God nor his unique function for revelation and redemption necessarily and clearly requires such extraordinary knowledge.

They then add that

The International Theological Commission in its Christological documents, "Select Questions of Christology" (1979), "Theology, Christology and Anthropology" (1981), and "The Consciousness of Christ Concerning Himself and His mission" (1985), does not assert beatific vision but only that "the consciousness that Jesus had of his mission implied an awareness of his 'preexistence.'" (Cf. *Catechism of the Catholic Church* 471–74)

These difficulties were certainly known to Aquinas, although as regards the fifth, concerning the exegesis of the Gospels, he was not acquainted with modern exegetical methods. Yet he firmly maintains in the *Summa theologiae* III, q. 9, a. 2 that Jesus, even as he journeyed to God in this life in his human nature, possessed the beatific vision in its fullness.[4] In q. 7, a. 3 he concludes

---

3. Ibid., 410.
4. See also "A man is called a pilgrim *(viator)* from tending to beatitude and a beholder *(comprehensor)* from having already obtained beatitude. . . . Now man's perfect beatitude consists in that of both soul and body—in the soul as regards what is proper to it inasmuch as the mind sees and enjoys God—in the body inasmuch as the body will be resurrected. . . . Now before his passion Christ's mind saw God perfectly and thus he had beatitude as far as regards what is proper to the soul, but beatitude was lacking as regards all else, since his soul could suffer and his body was both liable to suffering and to death. Hence he was at once beholder inasmuch as he had the beatitude proper to the soul and at the same a pilgrim inasmuch as was still tending to beatitude as regards what lacking for his beatitude." (*ST* III, q. 15, a. 10)

that therefore Jesus did not have the virtue of faith since he possessed what is superior to faith, namely vision.

It is easy to see why such a thesis is unacceptable to many theologians today, when the trend is to work out a "Christology from below" that emphasizes the truth of Jesus' humanity. This is believed to be necessary both to avoid Gnostic and Monophysite heresy and to make Jesus more credible and lovable to our secular humanist culture. These are good intentions, but of course, as in all matters of Christology, they involve the risk of minimizing the *mystery* of the Incarnation. My purpose in this essay is not to answer all these difficulties nor to evaluate O'Collins and Kendall's quite nuanced proposal for a solution, but to consider how Aquinas's *Commentary on John* enabled Aquinas to present his final views in the *Summa theologiae*.

In his commentary on the *Prologue* Aquinas explains that when in John 1:4b it is said of the Divine Word "And that Life was the light of men," this can be understood in two ways:

> First it is called the light of man as an object visible only to men, because only intelligent creatures can see it, since only they are capable of the divine vision.... Second it can be called the light in which all men participate. For we are only able to see the Word and that light through that participation that is in our nature in the superior part of our soul, namely the light of the intellect. (*Ioan.* 1, lect. 3, n. 101)

And later he adds that this is true not only as regards our creation but also regards our restoration from sin: "And the light was the light of all men, not simply of the Jews, because the Son of God in becoming flesh came into the world that he might illuminate all men with grace and truth" (*Ioan.* 1, lect. 3, n. 101). As to the words "Full of grace and truth" (Jn 1:14b) said of the Word made flesh, Aquinas comments that

> Anyone is given grace as he united to God. Therefore that one is full of grace who is most perfectly united to God. But others are joined to God through the sharing of a natural likeness (Gen 1:16, "Let us make man in our image and likeness"), others through faith (Eph 3:17, "May Christ dwell in your hearts through faith"), and others through charity since he who "remains in charity remains in God," as is said 1 Jn 4:16. But these ways are not perfect since neither through natural participation is anyone perfectly united to God, nor is God seen through faith as he is, nor loved through charity as he is loveable; since He is infinitely good and therefore infinitely lovable, and this infinite lovableness no creaturely love can match, and therefore [in these ways] no perfect union is possible. In Christ, however, in whom human nature is united to divinity in the unity of person is to be found a complete and perfect union to God, since that union was such that all acts both of the divine and human nature were acts of that one person. He was, therefore, full of grace in that he did not receive from God some special gift of grace, but was God himself (Phil 2:9, "The Father gave

the Son that name that is above every name" and Rom 1:4, "He who was predestined the Son of God in power"). He was also full of truth, since the human nature in Christ attained to the divine truth itself so that a man was the divine truth itself. For in other men are many particular shared truths by which the First Truth shines in their minds in many representations, but Christ is the Truth itself. Hence it is said in Col 2:3 that "in him are hidden all the treasures of wisdom." (*Ioan.* 1, lect. 8, n. 188)

Thus for Aquinas Christ in his human nature possesses Truth in the fullest way possible. On another verse, "For God does not give the Spirit according to measure" (Jn 2:34), he similarly comments,

This is said of Christ both as God and as man. . . . God the Father gives the Spirit without measure since he gives Christ both the strength and power of breathing forth the Holy Spirit whom, since the Holy Spirit is infinite, the Father gives without limit; and indeed gives the Holy Spirit to the Son just as he, the Father himself possesses the Spirit so that the Spirit proceeds "also from the Son." And the father gives the Holy Spirit to the Son through the Son's eternal generation. Similarly also Christ, as he is man has the spirit without measure, for to other humans the Holy Spirit is given according to measure since his grace is given to them within limits. But Christ as man does not receive grace according to measure and therefore he does not receive the Holy Spirit according to measure. (*Ioan.* 3, lect. 6, n. 543)

Jesus has this grace in three ways: (1) as the grace of the union of his human nature to his divinity, (2) as his habitual grace as an individual man, and (3) as his grace as the Head of the Church. His grace of union is infinite, but his habitual grace as an individual man and his grace of the Head of the Church have certain limits. Nevertheless, it can still be said that Christ received these graces "without measure" in three senses: (1) as regards the total capacity of his human nature; (2) as regards the infinity of the gift received; (3) and as he is the cause through whom others receive grace. As to the last of these three senses, St. Thomas comments:

It is evident from all that has been said, that the grace of Christ that is called the grace of headship according to which Christ is the head of the Church is infinite as to its influence. For from the fact that he himself possesses the gifts of the Spirit "without measure," he has the power of pouring them out without measure. In other words, the grace of Christ is sufficient not only for some men but for all men, according to 1 Jn 2:2, "He is the propitiation for our sins and not for our sins only but for those of whole world" and even of many worlds, if such exist. (*Ioan.* 3, lect. 6, n. 544)

Thus Aquinas derived two fundamental principles from this Gospel that he used to answer the two important questions with which we are here concerned. These principles are: (1) that Jesus by reason of the union of his human nature to his divine person had the fullness of grace and truth in the unlimited degree possible to a created nature, and (2) that this was necessary for his mission of redemption as head of the Church of those predestined to be redeemed.

In *Summa theologiae* III, q. 9, a. 2, which asks, "Whether Christ had any science other than that of a blessed one or *comprehensor?*," the *sed contra* cites the words of John 8:55, "For I know Him and I keep his word." Aquinas in his commentary says that this applies both to Christ's speculative intellectual knowledge and to his affective consent to the Father's will. He then says in his reply to the question,

That which is in potency is reduced to act through that which is in act; for others are heated only through that which is hot. Human beings, however, are in potency to that beatific knowledge that is the vision of God as they are ordered to it as to their end: for it is only rational creatures that are capable *(capax)* of that beatific vision inasmuch as they are images of God. Humans are brought back to this ultimate end through the humanity of Christ, according to Hebrews 2:10, "For it was fitting that He [God the Father], for whom and by whom all things exist, in bringing many sons to glory, should make the pioneer of their salvation [Christ] perfect through suffering." And it was also fitting that the beatific knowledge that consists in the vision of God should belong to Christ in the most excellent manner, since a cause should always be more powerful than its effect. (*Ioan.* 8, lect. 8, n. 1286)

To the objection (ad 3) that such a knowledge is beyond human nature, Aquinas replies,

The beatific vision or knowledge is in a certain way beyond the nature of the rational soul insofar as that soul cannot attain to it by its own power; but in another way. . . . it is in accord with that nature insofar as according to its nature it is made in the image of God and hence capable of that vision. Yet [God's] uncreated knowledge is in every way above the nature of the human soul.

Aquinas then in *Summa theologiae* III, q. 7 asks about the individual habitual grace of Christ in his human person and declares that he had all the virtues and gifts, including hope and love, but not faith (a. 3).

It is written (Heb. 11:1): "Faith is the evidence of things unseen." But there was nothing that was not visible to Christ, according to what Peter said to Him (John 21:17): "Thou knowest all things." Therefore there was no faith in Christ. . . . As was said above (II-II, q. 1, a. 4), the object of faith is a something divine that is unseen. Now a virtuous habit, as every other habit, takes its species from its object. Hence, if we deny that the something divine was unseen, we exclude the very essence of faith. Nevertheless, Christ, as will be made clear (III, q. 34, a. 4) from the first moment of His conception saw God's Essence fully. Hence he could not have had faith.

In replying to the obvious objections to this answer he concedes that faith is a nobler virtue than the moral virtues, yet unlike them it implies a deficiency that Christ could not have had. Nor did Christ lack the merit of faith since he obeyed God in all matters, as do the blessed in heaven, who also no longer need the virtue of faith, since it is replaced by the beatific vision.

What then are we to think of O'Collins and Kendall's objections to this view so confidently argued by the Angelic Doctor? It is noteworthy that they do not explicitly raise the difficulty that has so troubled those who want to emphasize a "low" Christology so as to emphasize Jesus' humanity, namely, "Doesn't this make the earthly Jesus less human?" The answer to that of course is that if we attain the beatific vision in heaven we will be no less human than we are; we will be perfectly human. "Grace perfects nature" and restores us to the perfect humanity that God intended for us in the creation. It is true that Aquinas does not claim that Adam and Eve had the beatific vision, since they too had to be prepared for it by a meritorious life of faith. Nor does Aquinas ever suggest that Our Lady, the new Eve, had that vision in this life. Nevertheless, it cannot be argued that its possession would diminish rather than complete Jesus' perfect humanity.

O'Collins and Kendall avoid stating any such direct argument, but implicitly raise it in the first three and seemingly strongest of their objections. If Jesus was already possessed of the beatific vision, how could he have merited our salvation by freely obeying his Father, an obedience that involved many trials and suffering, "even death on the Cross"? The answer to this is found in Aquinas's teaching that it is not the simple fact of trials and suffering that gain anyone merit before God, but the obedience with which the trials and suffering are accepted.[5] Jesus' obedience was perfect and therefore every action he performed had infinite merit. The reason that God required that he undergo such great trials and suffering was not that any one of his simple acts of love was insufficient to save the whole world, but it was rather to manifest to us the perfection of his obedience, since this would not have been sufficiently evident to us in his more ordinarily human acts. Furthermore Aquinas points out in III, q. 34, a. 4, ad 1 that Christ did not need to merit the glory of his human soul but only the glorification of his human body. Thus, since we are the "Body of Christ," we need his merit on our behalf.[6]

---

5. In *ST* III, q. 46, a. 3 Aquinas argues that although Christ's death on the cross was for many reasons appropriate to his mission (cf. a. 2), it was not absolutely necessary for our salvation, since we could have been saved in other ways.

6. In *ST* III, q. 19, a. 3 Aquinas shows Christ merited for himself and also for his outward glory, while in a. 4 he shows that as Head of the Church he merited for all; in III, q. 48 he

Moreover, from a psychological perspective, Aquinas argues in III, q. 34 that although in this life human intellectual activity is dependent on the senses, this is not absolutely necessary, since the separated soul will have knowledge in somewhat the same manner as the angels or pure spirits. Hence at the very moment of conception Christ could have human knowledge and thus could have human freedom.[7]

Hence also Jesus, even as he enjoyed the beatific vision in this life, retained his free will by which he carried out his mission in perfect obedience to his Father. Our freedom is given to us in our human nature to enable us to be happy; we are not free with respect to happiness itself. Yet in this life we can sin because the nature of our happiness remains somewhat obscure. Hence we can choose goods that are more evidently desirable than true happiness although in conscience we know that they are only deceptive. In the beatific vision, however, we will experience a happiness that is so perfect that we will no longer be free to sin. Yet we will not lose our freedom, since we can still choose for enjoyment among created goods whatever is not inconsistent with our love of God and neighbor. In this life also we do not lose our freedom by basing every decision on the love of God and neighbor, but remain free as to the virtuous ways in which this love can be expressed. Thus Jesus by reason of the beatific vision could not sin, but this did not make him less free, but more free in his willing obedience to the plan of God. Indeed perfect obedience to a superior is not robotic, but should be an application of our gifts of intelligence and ingenuity to realize the superior's command in the best way possible in the circumstances. A good workman follows the blueprint in building a house, but not just mechanically. He shows his own craftsmanship.

A further consideration concerning Christ's consciousness is that human consciousness has many levels of awareness. I am only dimly conscious of the room in which I am writing but fully conscious of the page before me. The great writers on the mystical life tell us that in the unitive state the presence of God is evident to the mystic even when she or he is engaged in very ordinary practical matters, and perhaps even in sleep.[8] In this state of union God

---

shows he merited (a. 1) as Head of Church, (a. 2) as to atonement, (a. 3) as a worthy sacrifice, (a. 4) as our redeemer, and (a. 5) as a divine Person acting through his human nature as his instrument.

7. In *ST* III, q. 18, a. 4 Aquinas argues for Christ's free will, and shows in a. 5 that this will, though free, was always conformed in obedience to God's will in such a way that there was no contrariety between it and Christ's virtuous human passions, even his natural human fear of death (a. 6). See also III, q. 20, a. 1, in which Aquinas holds that Christ was perfectly subject to his Father in his human nature, although equal to him in his divinity.

8. On the accounts given by mystics of the unitive state see Juan Gonzalez-Arintero, O.P.,

is still known only in the darkness of faith. Yet faith has become like the sky at dawn and the beatific vision of God, like the sight of the sun, is just below the horizon.

From such facts of mystical experience, it is evident that there is no contradiction in supposing that Jesus had ordinary human knowledge by which he engaged in the daily routine of life, even as in the depths of his consciousness he was fully aware of himself as a divine Person, the Son of God who is "known only to the Father, and whom alone the Father knows as His Son" in the unity of Holy Spirit.[9] Thus Karl Rahner, who dealt profoundly with this question in view of his own transcendental philosophy of the human subject, argued that the hypostatic union required that Jesus be immediately aware that he was the Son of God.[10] The reason Rahner gave for this was that it belongs to human nature and human intelligence to have an indirect self-consciousness of the knowing subject in every direct act of knowledge. Since the human Jesus was a divine Person, he therefore must have had—precisely in order to be human—an immediate awareness of his own Person. For Rahner, however, this was not a direct, objective awareness, as would be the beatific vision, but a background awareness, or "horizon" of consciousness that we possess as subjects.

In this way Rahner sought to reconcile the background awareness that he claims Jesus had of his own divine Person with Jesus' human life of learning, willing, and acting in an entirely human manner. Rahner based this solution on his Transcendental Thomistic philosophy that seized on Aquinas's teaching that we have an indirect self-consciousness in all our direct consciousness of the material world and our own body. This direct awareness of the world and our bodily selves is the proper object of human intelligence that acquires all it knows only through the senses. Most Thomists, however, do not accept this interpretation of Aquinas, since it colors his thought with the philosophy of Kant, who claimed for us an *a priori* element in human knowledge independent of the senses.

For Aquinas our indirect self-consciousness is in no wise *a priori*, since it arises in us only through and in our direct consciousness of the material world. Only reflexively do we know ourselves directly and clearly. For

---

The Mystical Evolution in the Development and Vitality of the Church, vol. 2 (St. Louis: Herder, 1951), 170–303.

9. In *ST* III, q. 46, a. 7, Aquinas argues that Christ had joy in the highest part of his soul even on the cross.

10. Karl Rahner, "Dogmatic Reflections on the Knowledge and Self-Consciousness of Christ," in *Theological Investigations*, vol. 5 (Baltimore: Helicon Press, 1966), 193–218.

Aquinas, therefore, Christ's self-awareness of his divinity would have been possible only through the objective beatific vision of God. Yet there is no contradiction in claiming that at the same time he had ordinary human thought processes. Nevertheless, Aquinas's claim that Jesus knew himself as God in the beatific vision attributes to him a more perfect way of knowing his divine Person than the merely indirect, background mode that Rahner suggests. A child has an indirect self-consciousness but very little direct self-understanding. Human maturity, on the other hand, consists in achieving a direct objective understanding of one's self. In Aquinas's theory Jesus had that mature knowledge from the moment of his conception and hypostatic union with the divine Son; yet this did not prevent him from also acquiring knowledge in the ordinary human way in the course of a maturing lifetime.[11]

---

11. Aquinas's claim that Jesus had not only the beatific vision but also mature human knowledge at the moment of his conception does indeed seem extravagant. One must take into account his Aristotelian embryology that today concerns the abortion question; see my articles "A Critique of the Theory of Delayed Hominization," in D. G. McCarthy and A. S. Moraczewski, *An Ethical Evaluation of Fetal Experimentation* (St. Louis, Mo.: Pope John Center, 1976), Appendix I, 113–33, and "Delayed Hominization: Catholic Theological Perspective," in *The Interaction of Catholic Bioethics and Secular Society*, Proceedings of the Eleventh Bishops' Workshop, Dallas, Texas, ed. Russell E. Smith (Braintree, Mass.: Pope John Center, 1992), 163–80, and with Albert S. Moraczewski, O.P., "Is the Biological Subject of Human Rights Present from Conception?" in *The Fetal Tissue Issue: Medical and Ethical Aspects*, ed. Peter J. Cataldo and Albert S. Moraczewski, O.P. (Braintree, Mass.: Pope John Center, 1994) and "Cloning, Aquinas, and the Embryonic Person," *National Catholic Bioethics Quarterly* 1 (2001): 189–202. St. Thomas thought that God creates the human spiritual soul with its intelligence only when its bodily instrument is sufficiently formed but that this occurred only some weeks after conception ("delayed hominzation"). This instrument is the central organ or prime mover of the body that is the organ of sensation: for Aristotle and Aquinas the heart, for us the brain. Hence for Aquinas the child from the first moment it exists could have the sense of touch that is the minimal requirement of intellection. Since, however, Jesus' conception was miraculous, St. Thomas supposed that this happened for him at the moment of Mary's consent to Gabriel's message. With modern embryology we must conclude that human conception and creation of the soul naturally occurs at fertilization of the ovum when the human genome is complete since from then on the human person develops itself. Yet for several weeks the brain does not yet exist. However, what is primordial to the brain is the information in the nucleus of the zygote that will build the brain. Hence, contrary to Aquinas, it seems impossible to attribute to the zygotic body any actual capability of sensation. This, however, does not negate Aquinas's *principal* argument, namely, that Jesus' human intelligence could have had "infused" knowledge, like the separated soul or an angel, since that is not derived form the senses, while the beatific vision is the direct presence of God in the *lumen gloriae* (*ST* III Suppl., q. 92, a. 1). Hence Jesus, in the womb of Mary, even before his body had developed a brain, could have been miraculously conscious of his Father, his own divine Person as Son, and his mission from his Father, and could have freely committed himself to that mission for our sake. Since John the Baptist at a later stage in the womb was already a prophet (Lk 1:41), why would we deny this was more perfectly true of Jesus? To assert this in no way minimizes the humanity either of John or of his Lord.

O'Collins and Kendall raise two other related difficulties for Aquinas's teaching. The Gospels seem to indicate that Jesus in his earthly life experienced the human process of learning, and certain passages such as Mark 5:30–32 and 13:32 seem to indicate that his human knowledge was limited. Thus we read in Mark: "And Jesus, perceiving in himself that power had gone forth from him, immediately turned about in the crowd, and said, 'Who touched my garments?' . . . And he looked around to see who had done it" (5:30, 32) and also that Jesus said of the Last Judgment, "But of that day or that hour no one knows, not even the angels in heaven, nor the Son, but only the Father" (13:32). There are similar passages in all four Gospels.

Aquinas, of course, was well aware that these passages had been troubling to the Church Fathers. He did not claim that the human intelligence of Christ was comprehensively omniscient as he was in his divinity, since the human soul, while by grace it is open to the vision of God as he truly is, finds his infinite truth inexhaustible.[12] Yet Jesus in the beatific vision that he possessed in this life knew all about creatures that there is to know.[13] In addition to this, according to Aquinas, Jesus acquired knowledge in the human manner by the intellectual analysis of the information received through his bodily senses.[14] We humans learn in two ways, one by finding out the truth for ourselves, the other by being taught. Aquinas says that the former way is the superior one and therefore, "It was more fitting for Christ to have his acquired knowledge by his own efforts than from teaching."[15] This does not seem absolutely to exclude that Jesus learned from others, but simply to say that he was first and foremost a teacher, not a pupil.

The fourth Gospel is more insistent than the Synoptic Gospels on Jesus' "clairvoyance." Thus, on John 6:15, "Then Jesus, because he knew they were going to come and seize him by force to make him king, withdrew again up the mountainside alone," Aquinas comments,

> In Christ was a threefold knowledge. First, he had sense knowledge and in this respect was like the Prophets in that certain sensible images could be formed in Christ's imagination by which future or hidden things could be represented which was appropriate to his state in this life. Second was an intellectual knowledge and in this he was unlike the Prophets but was above the angels because he was in more excellent possession [of the beatific vision] than any creature. Third was the divine cognition and in respect to this he was the inspirer of the Prophets and the angels, since all cognition is a participation in the Divine Word. (*Ioan.* 6, lect. 2, n. 868)

---

12. *ST* III, q. 10, a.3.
13. *ST* III, q. 9, a. 1.
14. *ST* III, q. 9, a. 4.
15. *ST* III, q. 9, a. 4, ad 1.

For Aquinas the first of the foregoing texts in Mark and others like them refer to Jesus' behavior that was appropriate to his human nature in ordinary situations, in this case, to ask those about him to point out the women who had touched him when he was not looking, just as any prophet might do even if he at the same time was clairvoyant. As Jesus did not work miracles except for a special reason, so he would not have used his clairvoyance openly except for some special reason. As for the second statement that even the Son does not know the time of the judgment, the Fathers of the Church recognized that this is a rhetorical way of emphasizing that Jesus' mission from the Father did not permit him to make this particular revelation and cannot be taken literally.

The final objection of our authors is their assertion that the hypostatic union in Christ of a divine and human nature does not necessarily imply that Jesus possessed the beatific vision in his human nature. On this fundamental problem a distinction, based on Aquinas's statements already quoted, is necessary. If we consider only the ontology of this unfathomable mystery we find no absolute reason to say that it would have been impossible for the divine Word to have assumed human nature without bestowing the beatific vision on its intellectual power. Yet if we take into consideration, as Aquinas does, the purpose of the Incarnation, then Aquinas's argument for his thesis has great force. The Word became incarnate in order to make it possible again for all humanity to attain the beatific vision. Since the cause must contain what it effects—a fountain must be filled with water—and it is the Word in his human nature that is the source of the gift of the beatific vision that we hope to enjoy, Christ must himself enjoy it in a supreme way.

It could still be objected that while this argument holds for the risen Christ ascended to the Father in eternity it need not have been so during his earthly life, since our salvation comes after his resurrection. I believe that is really what O'Collins and Kendall have in mind. But this would not satisfy Aquinas. For him Christ's salvific mission and meriting of our salvation begins as soon as he assumes human nature. It is not the risen Christ that merits our salvation but the earthly Christ as present among us. Every moment of his life is the fulfillment of his saving mission and this is possible only because he already has attained in his human nature the goal that he has been sent to bring us to at last.

At the very end of the fourth Gospel (21:25) we read that "There are many other things that Jesus did. If every one of them were written down, I suppose the whole world would not have room for the books that would be written." St. Thomas comments on this:

To write down one by one the signs and works of Jesus Christ is to summarize the power of each and all these words and doings; but the words and works of Christ are also those of God. And if anyone might wish to explain each of them, he would be utterly unable; for the whole world could not do this, because all the words we humans have cannot say as much as the One word of God. Thus from the beginning of the Church all writing was about Christ but it was never enough; furthermore if the world should endure for hundred thousand years not enough books can be written about Christ to perfectly sum up what he has done and said. As it is said at the end of Ecclesiasticus 12, "There is no end to writing books," and Psalm 40:5 says, "I have uttered these things and spoken them, but they are too numerous to recount!" (*Ioan.* 21, lect. 6, n. 2660)

Thus with Aquinas we must humbly kneel in contemplation and adoration before the mystery of the Word made flesh.

FIFTEEN

Anti-Docetism in Aquinas's *Super Ioannem*
St. Thomas as Defender of the Full Humanity of Christ

PAUL GONDREAU

 Biblical scholars have long noted the anti-docetic overtones of John's Gospel. These overtones targeted the latent tendencies in the primitive Christian community to deny, in varying degrees, the reality of Christ's humanity. (From the Greek δοκέω, "to seem," docetism, which was the first great challenge to Christological faith, alleges that Christ only *appeared* to have come in the flesh.)[1] What is less known, and what remains one of the most unappreciated elements of his thought, is St. Thomas's own rather pronounced anti-docetism.[2]

---

1. For the anti-docetism of the Johannine writings (cf., e.g., 2 Jn 7: "many deceivers . . . will not acknowledge the coming of Jesus Christ in the flesh"), cf. R. E. Brown, *The Community of the Beloved Disciple* (New York: Paulist Press, 1979), 109–16, and 155–58; idem, *The Gospel According to John, I–XII*, Anchor Bible, vol. 29 (Garden City: Doubleday, 1966), lxxvi–lxxvii; U. Schnelle, *Antidocetic Christology in the Gospel of John* (Minneapolis: Fortress Press, 1992); and G. J. Riley, *I Was Thought to Be What I Am Not: Docetic Jesus and the Johannine Tradition* (Claremont: Institute for Antiquity and Christianity, 1994). Providing evidence of docetic currents in ancient Christianity, Riley (pp. 5–6) cites the third-century *Apocalypse of Peter* from the Nag Hammadi library, which asserts (*Apoc. Peter* 81.7–24): "The Savior said to [Peter], 'He whom you saw on the tree glad and laughing, this is the living Jesus. But this one into whose hands they drive the nails is his fleshly part, which is the substitute being put to shame, the one who came into being in his likeness.'" As Riley observes, such a passage "illustrate[s] one of the common strategies of relieving Jesus of the humiliation of the crucifixion: providing a substitute who is merely human and undergoes what the spiritual Jesus, given the theological presuppositions of the . . . writer, cannot be allowed to undergo."

2. Some have the opposite, and quite erroneous, impression of Aquinas. An example is J. A. T. Robinson (*The Human Face of God* [Philadelphia: Westminster, 1973], 40, n. 14), who, when it comes to Thomas's Christology, equates Aquinas with a "glorified Hilary [of Poitiers]." As for those few Thomist scholars who have underscored

Aquinas's anti-docetism is borne out of his reading of the New Testament, and in particular of the Gospel of John. In his prologue to the *Commentary on the Gospel of St. John,* Aquinas observes that John composed his Gospel to refute certain Christological heresies. Though most of these heresies, Thomas admits, concern Christ's divinity, some are directed against his humanity. As a result, Aquinas shows a penchant for emphasizing the fourth Gospel's condemnation, usually implicit, of any heresy that cheapens in any docetic manner the full human consubstantiality of Christ, such as Apollinarianism, Arianism, Monophysitism, Monothelitism, Manichaeism, and the like.[3]

This penchant adheres strictly to Aquinas's biblical exegesis. Consistent with his medieval day, Thomas's reading of Scripture aims above all at drawing out the ultimate theological truth imparted through the Bible. Reading the Gospel of John—the "anti-docetic" Gospel of John—with St. Thomas provides, then, the occasion for retrieving Aquinas's appreciation of the theological truth regarding Christ's full humanity as disclosed through the Sacred Page. The *Commentary on John* stands as a telling testament to Aquinas's efforts to show, to quote J.-P. Torrell, "wherever possible that Christ is a man fully subject to the laws of humanity."[4]

Examining the Christology of Aquinas's commentary on John's Gospel offers insight as well into the theological method of Aquinas. Ever the consummate theologian, St. Thomas at all times begins his theological reflection with the revealed word of the Sacred Page, the wellspring of all theology: "the entire theology of St. Thomas," Etienne Gilson explains, "is a commentary on the Bible; he advances no conclusion without basing it somehow on the

---

Aquinas's anti-docetism, J.-P. Torrell merits singular acclaim; cf. his *Le Christ en ses mystères. La vie et l'oeuvre de Jésus selon saint Thomas d'Aquin,* 2 vols. (Paris: Desclée, 1999). Cf. as well G. Lafont, *Structures et méthode dans la "Somme théologique" de saint Thomas d'Aquin* (Paris: Les Éditions du Cerf, 1996), 349. Also, for a fuller theological and historical treatment of Aquinas's esteem for the fullness of Christ's humanity with respect to his human affectivity, cf. my own *The Passions of Christ's Soul in the Theology of St. Thomas Aquinas,* Beiträge zur Geschichte der Philosophie und Theologie des Mittelalters 61 (Münster: Aschendorff, 2002).

3. Though I shall refer to docetism as a defined system of belief, R. E. Brown (*The Gospel According to John, I–XII,* lxxvi) reminds us that, in reality, "[d]ocetism was not so much a heresy by itself as it was an attitude found in a number of heresies," such as in gnosticism and Manichaeism. This explains why Thomas never mentions docetism by name in the *Commentary on John;* instead, by singling out the heresies of the ancient Church, he indicates the lingering presence of docetism all throughout Church history, particularly in the crucial period when the defining formulation of Christological doctrine was being forged.

4. Torrell, *Le Christ en ses mystères,* vol. 1, 118. For more on how Scripture was read and taught in the medieval schools and how one was professionally qualified as a Master of theology to expound on the Bible in an authoritative fashion, cf. J. A. Weisheipl, Introduction to *Commentary on the Gospel of St. John,* trans. Weisheipl and Larcher, Part 1, 6–7.

word of sacred Scripture, which is the Word of God."⁵ Put another way, since the study of theology is distinguished as such by its formal examination of divine revelation, the incontrovertible source of which is Scripture, Aquinas asserts nothing concerning Christ that is not at least implied by Scripture: "we should not say anything about God," Thomas writes in a query on the Holy Spirit that applies equally to Christ, "that is not found in sacred Scripture, either explicitly or implicitly."⁶

This statement is easily verified by even the casual glance at Thomas's commentary on John's Gospel. Here Aquinas performs a true *exegesis* (rather than an eisegesis), inasmuch as he lets the revealed word of God, especially the words and actions of Christ, dictate and determine his thinking, particularly on Christ's human nature.

At the same time, however, Aquinas's understanding of Christ's humanity is forged from an anthropological framework that is thoroughly Aristotelian in inspiration. With the *Commentary on John*'s presentation of the humanity of Christ, we witness an exemplary expression of St. Thomas's intertwining of revealed and natural truth, an intertwining of John's witness of the human Christ with an Aristotelian metaphysics of human nature.

Subsequently, in light of the Pontifical Biblical Commission's recent call for a renewal of theology through a union of biblical studies with the speculative theological disciplines, we can see how Aquinas's own method of joining biblical exegesis with speculative theology stands out as the model for such a renewal.⁷ We need look no further than the *Commentary on John*—a work that M.-D. Philippe ranks as St. Thomas's preeminent theological tract—for Thomas's own finest expression of such a union.⁸

---

5. E. Gilson, *Les tribulations de Sophie* (Paris: J. Vrin, 1967), 47, cited in J.-P. Torrell, *Saint Thomas d'Aquin, maître spirituel* (Fribourg, Switz.: Éditions Universitaires, 1996), 505. Cf. *ST* I, q. 1, aa. 1–2, and a. 8, ad 2.

6. *ST* I, q. 36, a. 2, ad 1: "de Deo dicere non debemus quod in sacra Scriptura non invenitur, vel per verba, vel per sensum." Cf. as well *Contra errores Graecorum*, I, 1.

7. The 1993 Pontifical Biblical Commission, "The Interpretation of the Bible in the Church," *Origins* 23 (1994): 518–20. In *Toward Understanding Saint Thomas*, 240–60, M.-D. Chenu explains how the thirteenth century was at a crucial theological crossroads on account of the tension, present in the universities, between speculative theology and Biblical exegesis. Though Thomas would make a valiant effort at keeping the two united (after all, the master in theology at Paris only lectured on Scripture), they would eventually become permanently divorced.

8. Philippe, "Préface" to *Saint Thomas d'Aquin*, 14.

DOCETISM, A TWO-HEADED MONSTER

"It must be said," Thomas writes in his gloss on John 1:14 ("And the Word became flesh"), "that the Word is man in the way that anyone is man, namely, as having human nature" (*Ioan.* 1, lect. 7, n. 172).[9] These remarks place us at the heart of the docetic debate, a debate that has ravaged Christianity since its very inception in various, sometimes diluted or masked, forms: whether the Word truly assumed a real human nature. Or whether, as is more often the case for the semi-docetist of today, the doctrine of the Incarnation means nothing more than an abstract dogma whose far-reaching existential ramifications on the human experience of Jesus need secure minimal, if any, consideration from the common believer.

Lest we dismiss the docetic position without giving it its rightful due, however, we should realize that docetism does choose a more amenable road to trod. For, proclaiming, really, that God *is man,* that is, that the all-powerful uncreated Lord of the universe has entered into substantial union with his creation, has always and continues to scandalize the religious and philosophical world alike. Even Thomas admits in the *Commentary on John* (on Jn 10:33) that the mystery of the Incarnation "surpasses all understanding" *(opus incarnationis excedens omnem mentem)* on account of the inestimable gulf separating man from God and the incredulity of the claim that a man—though he is no common man—bridges this gulf *(tanta est distantia Dei et hominis, quod incredibile eis erat quod idem qui est homo, esset Deus).*

Yet the truth of Christian revelation announces just this: "Nothing more marvelous could be accomplished," Aquinas proclaims in the *Commentary on John,* "than that God should become man" (*Ioan.* 2, lect. 3, n. 398).[10] By denying the authenticity of the Incarnate Word's assumed manhood, docetism seeks to deliver a deathblow to this truth. No one perceives this better than St. Thomas. Aquinas, in fact, understands that the threat docetism poses comes from two fronts, the first soteriological and the other metaphysical.

The soteriological peril follows from the fact that, by denying the reality of Christ's humanity, docetism denies the very salvation of the human race wrought by Christ. As Thomas explains: "Christ gives life to the world through the mysteries he accomplished in his flesh" (*Ioan.* 6, lect. 4, n. 914).[11]

---

9. I use St. Thomas Aquinas's *Commentary on the Gospel of Saint John,* Part 1, trans. Weisheipl and Larcher, 86–87, making modifications where necessary.

10. Cf. *SCG* IV, ch. 27 for almost the identical wording: "Nothing more wonderful can be considered than the divine achievement of true God, the Son of God, becoming true man."

11. Cf. as well *Ioan.* 5, lect. 5, n. 791: "through the mysteries Christ accomplished in his flesh

God saves us not as a deceptive heavenly being masquerading in illusory visible form, but as a real life-and-blood man who suffered and died at the hands of his true human brethren. *This* is why God became man—to save us from our sins—and this is what docetism disavows. Thomas suggests this when he writes in the Commentary, in words that echo the opening prologue of the *Summa theologiae:* "the *humanity of Christ* is the way that leads us to God" (*Ioan.* 7, lect. 4, n. 1074; emphasis mine).[12] Without the humanity of Christ, without the true incarnate flesh of the second Person of the Trinity, there is no way to God, there is no reconciliation with God. Docetism causes the bottom to fall out on any meaningful proclamation of a redeemer Christ.

The metaphysical pitfall presented by docetism is no less grave: the view that physical reality amounts to nothing less than miserable wastage. This results from the fundamental contempt most docetists harbor for material reality. The idea that the immaterial God assumes that which is inherently opposed to the supreme goodness of his being (matter) could therefore not be more abhorrent to the docetic conception of things. Commenting on John 1:14, Aquinas explains this when he writes:

> the truth of the Incarnation [disproves] the Manichees, who said that the Word did not assume true flesh, but only imaginary flesh, since it would not have been fitting for the Word of *the good God* to assume flesh, *which they regarded as created by the devil.* (*Ioan.* 1, lect. 7, n. 169; emphasis added; cf. *Ioan.* 2, lect. 1, n. 358)

Such a view of material creation, always popular in the history of human thought, squarely opposes the mind-set of Aquinas. St. Thomas holds tenaciously to the absolute and fundamental goodness of *all* created being, material as well as immaterial. This has led G. K. Chesterton to dub Aquinas, rightly, as St. Thomas of the Creator.[13] In a passing but highly illuminative remark made in reference to the miracle at Cana, Thomas offers a glimpse

---

we are restored not only to an incorruptible life in our bodies, but also to a spiritual life in our souls"; and *ST* III, q. 9, a. 2. Already Ignatius of Antioch († *c.* 107) understood this quite well, as he criticizes severely (in *Ad Trall.,* chs. 9–10, and *Ad Smyrn.,* ch. 2) those who allege that Jesus only "seemed" to have suffered and died; cf. R. E. Brown, *Community of the Beloved Disciple,* 113 n. 221.

12. Cf. *ST* I, q. 2, prol. Thomas elaborates on this *Ioan.* 6, lect. 5, nn. 936, 939: "As man, Christ is the way: 'I am the way' (Jn 14:6); and as the Christ, he leads us to the Father as a way leads to its end. . . . For we obtain the fruit of the resurrection through those things which Christ did in his flesh." Cf. as well *Ioan.* 14, lect. 2, nn. 1868, 1872: "He is the way by reason of his human nature. . . . And so Christ, who is our way, became the way even for himself, this is, for his flesh, to go to the truth and the life."

13. See Chesterton, *Saint Thomas Aquinas* (Garden City: Image Books, 1956), 119. Among those who have insightfully highlighted this aspect of Aquinas's thought, J. Pieper (*Guide to Thomas Aquinas* [San Francisco: Ignatius Press, 1991], 120–33) merits first mention.

into this side of his thought: Christ created wine out of water rather than out of nothing, Aquinas explains, "in order to show that material or visible substances are good and created by God" (*Ioan.* 2, lect. 1, n. 358).[14] *Because* they are created, that is, because they issue from the creative hand of God, material substances *must* be considered good (cf. 1 Tim 4:4). No substance that has its source in God can be evil as such. That the second Person of the holy Trinity has substantially united himself to genuine living, breathing, feeling human flesh only confirms, definitively, this very fact.

There is, then, a hidden irony in docetism: God would *not* have clothed himself in human flesh if material reality were somehow evil or inherently subversive of the spiritual. However, since he did, the response is not to distrust the authenticity of the Incarnation, as the docetists do, but to affirm, as Aquinas does, the goodness of material creation. The dogma of the Incarnation stands as a pointed rebuttal to those who either refuse to take material reality seriously or cannot bring themselves to recognize the nobility of that which God finds worthy enough to take on himself.

In sum, it is the conviction both to uphold the reality of Christian salvation and to repudiate the ever-present human tendency to demean the physical that accounts for St. Thomas's lifelong defense of the full humanity of Christ.

VERITAS HUMANAE NATURAE CHRISTI

To make his case against docetism, Aquinas appeals time and again to what he terms in the *Commentary on John* (and elsewhere) the "truth of the human nature" *(veritas humanae naturae)* assumed by Christ (*Ioan.* 4, lect. 1, n. 563).[15] To properly grasp the thrust of Aquinas's anti-docetic argument, we must therefore examine how he sees in the Jesus of the Fourth Gospel a man who exhibits a "true human nature." Most broadly speaking, and taking an Aristotelian metaphysics of human nature as our guide, this would be a man who possesses a body and a soul substantially (or hylemorphically) united. To the Jesus of body and soul, then, we turn our attention.

---

14. Cf. *Ioan.* 6, lect. 1, n. 860: "sensible things do not come from the devil, as the Manichean error maintains. For if this were so, our Lord would not have used sensible things to praise God."

15. Cf. as well *Ioan.* 11, lect. 5, n. 1535: "Voluit etiam Christus . . . ad probandum conditionem et veritatem humanae naturae"; *Ioan.* 12, lect. 5, n. 1652: "Dominus turbari voluit propter . . . veritatem humanae naturae approbaret"; *Ioan.* 13, lect. 4, n. 1798: "Ut ergo ostenderet se veram naturam humanam habere"; *Ioan.* 19, lect. 5, n. 2458: "Christus ostenderet id quod erat, scilicet verus homo"; and *Ioan.* 1, lect. 7, n. 169: "ad ostendendum veritatem incarnationis."

Corpus Verum Christi

John 1:14 ("And the Word was made flesh [*sarx* in Greek, *caro* in Latin] and dwelt among us") leaves little room for doubt as to whether Jesus possesses a true body.[16] Yet, it is Christ's *body* or *flesh* that the docetists, given their disdain for the physical, see as the most objectionable element of the Incarnation. Thomas thus wastes little time in exploiting this passage from John's Prologue to serve an anti-docetically charged exegesis. He insists that, if genuinely human, Jesus *must* own an organic, that is, materially composed, body: "the body of Christ derives from the earth as regards its material composition" (*Ioan.* 3, lect. 5, n. 533).[17] In the *Summa* Aquinas's wording becomes even stronger, to the point of stressing the "carnal and earthly" nature of Christ's body *(corpus carneum et terrenum)*, and Christ's body's composition of "flesh and bones and blood" *(caro et ossa et sanguis).*[18]

The reality of Jesus' suffering, death, and resurrection offers the greatest evidence for the Word's assumption of a real human body. Without a true body, Jesus can undergo no actual death (death implies a separation of the soul from the body), and with no death, there can be no resurrection, and, hence, no salvation.[19] As a result, Aquinas sees anti-docetic rejoinders all throughout the crucifixion scene, as when Jesus exclaims from the cross "I thirst" (Jn 19:28): "By these words," Thomas explains, "Jesus proves that his death is real and not illusory" *(ostendit mortem suam esse veram, non phantasticam).* The same goes for the discharge of blood and water from the pierced side of Jesus in John 19:34: "this happens to show that Christ was a true man" *(quidem factum est ut Christus ostenderet id quod erat, scilicet verus homo).* And

---

16. Commenting on John 1:14, R. E. Brown (*Community of the Beloved Disciple*, 114) explains: "There is no doubt from 1:14 that the Johannine Jesus has a real humanity." Brown treats this verse in greater depth in *Gospel according to John, I–XII*, 30–35. The weighty impact of John 1:14 can be seen in the *Tertia pars* of the *Summa*, where the term "flesh" *(caro)* occurs in reference to Christ 228 times (a prime example is q. 16, a. 2, *sed contra:* "Christ is man according to the flesh" *[Christus secundum carnem est homo]*). Cf. G. Lafont, *Structures et méthode dans la "Somme théologique,"* 349–58.

17. Cf. as well *Ioan.* 16, lect. 7, n. 2162: "Christ came into the world [cf. Jn 16:28], inasmuch as the body of the human nature he assumed originates with the world."

18. *ST* III, q. 5, aa. 1–2. In III *Sent.*, d. 12, q. 3, a. 1, sol. 1, Thomas affirms that part and parcel of Christ's bodily nature is his male sex: "it was necessary that Christ assume everything following upon human nature, namely, all the properties and parts of human nature, among which is sex; and therefore it was proper for him to assume a sex." For more on this issue, cf. my *The Passions of Christ's Soul*, 145–50.

19. For death involving a separation of the soul from the body, cf. *ST* III, q. 50, aa. 4 and 6, and q. 56, aa. 1–2. Note that in *ST* III, q. 50, a. 1, Aquinas holds that it was fitting for Christ to die "in order to show the truth of his assumed [human] nature."

the link between the body of the mortal Jesus before the cross and the body of the resurrected Christ after the cross—so vital because the mystery of human salvation hinges on it—is established when the resurrected Christ shows his side and hands to the apostle Thomas in John 20:27; as Aquinas explains: "[By this gesture Christ wished] to show that his resurrected body is *of the same nature* as that which was previously corruptible" (*Ioan.* 20, lect. 6, n. 2559; emphasis added).[20] Any meaningful proclamation of Christian redemption hinges strictly on the realism of the tortuous crucifixion and death of Christ's body.

This ascribes immeasurable soteriological significance to Christ's bodily nature. In fact, since the whole purpose of the Incarnation is to save the human race from its sins (cf. the prologue to the *Tertia pars* of the *Summa*), Christ's body *must* share in the soteriological aim of the Incarnation if it is to avoid being assumed in vain:

> It is clear that the flesh of Christ, as united to the Word and to the Spirit, does profit very much and in every way; otherwise, *the Word would have been made flesh in vain, and the Father would have made him known in the flesh in vain.* (*Ioan.* 6, lect. 8, n. 993; emphasis added)

In addition to his mortality, the other physical weaknesses Jesus exhibits (hunger, thirst, fatigue) betray the reality of his humanness as well. This Aquinas affirms in his gloss on John 4:6, where Jesus sits down at Jacob's well because "he was tired from his journey":

> [In his fatigue] Jesus manifests his weakness . . . in order to show the truth of his assumed [human] nature. . . . In this way Christ, wishing to show the truth of his human nature, allowed it to act and suffer in ways that properly belong to men. . . . Thus he became hungry and tired. (*Ioan.* 4, lect. 1, n. 563)

We should note that Thomas's statement, "Christ allowed his human nature to act and suffer in ways that properly belong to men," gives witness to the vibrant patristic voice that often reverberates in Aquinas's writings. This locution echoes the celebrated Christological axiom penned by Leo the Great (†461): "Each form accomplishes in concert with the other what is appropri-

---

20. Thomas makes this argument more explicit in *ST* III, q. 54, a. 1 (cf. a. 3): "Christ's body after his resurrection was a true body, and of the same nature as it was before. For had it been an imaginary body, his resurrection would not have been true, but only apparent." In the *sed contra* of this article, Thomas quotes Luke 24:37 rather than John 20:27, as the former supplies more anti-docetic material: "when Christ appeared to his disciples, 'they were troubled and frightened, and supposed that they saw a spirit,' as if his body were not true but illusory. But to remove their fears he then added: 'Touch me and see, for a spirit has not flesh and bones as you see that I have.' Consequently, he had not an illusory but a true body."

ate to it, the Word performing what belongs to the Word, and the flesh carrying out what belongs to the flesh."[21] This axiom, which was formulated to counter the Monophysitic denial of the full integrity of Christ's humanity, was appropriated and employed to great end by John Damascene (†749), whose own Christology exerted a profound influence on Aquinas.[22]

Thomas's reliance upon Leo's axiom also explains why John's focus on Christ's divinity gives Aquinas little cause for concern, since Christ's divinity in no way threatens the integrity of his humanity: "the flesh carries out what belongs to the flesh." Those statements that Jesus utters in John's Gospel, then, that intimate his divinity, such as John 8:58 ("Before Abraham was, I am"), do not of themselves derogate from Christ's humanity. If anything, they serve to remind us that, though *verus homo,* Jesus is not *purus homo,* to quote Jacques Maritain.[23] They remind us that Christ is the one divine Person of the Word united to two natures, human and divine, to use the terminology of the Council of Chalcedon.

For Aquinas, this means Christ's humanity is safeguarded and understood *only* when seen in direct relation to the *whole* of the mystery of the Incarnation, the *totus Christus.* This means Christ must at all points be looked upon as the divine Person of the Word subsisting in an assumed human nature. This includes the Jesus of the New Testament, the Jesus of John's Gospel. And it matters little that such a regard for Christ is the fruit of a conciliar decree formulated long after the Evangelists had penned their Gospels. For the God who acts as the primary author of Scripture is the same God who guides the decisions of the ecumenical councils (in this case Chalcedon). If St. Thomas weaves the Chalcedonian doctrine of the hypostatic union all throughout his reading of John, it is because what John asserts with respect to

---

21. Leo the Great, *Tomus ad Flavianum* (DS 294): "Agit enim utraque forma cum alterius communione quod proprium est. Verbo scilicet operante quod Verbi est et carne exsequente quod carnis est." The ultimate foundation for this axiom can be found in Tertullian, *Adversus Praxean* 27, 11 (CCSL 2, 199).

22. One can find the equivalent of Leo's axiom all throughout John Damascene's *De fide orthodoxa,* Bk. III, chs. 19–20 (ed. Buyt., 256–60). Though Thomas does cite Leo's axiom itself (cf. *ST* III, q. 19, a. 1), he prefers Damascene's use of it: cf., e.g., *ST* III, q. 14, a. 2; q. 46, a. 6; III *Sent.,* d. 15, q. 2, a. 2, sol. 2, ad 2. For the influence of Leo's *Tome* on Aquinas's Christology, cf. C. G. Geenen, "The Council of Chalcedon in the Theology of St. Thomas," in *From an Abundant Spring: The Walter Farrell Memorial Volume of "The Thomist,"* ed. Staff of *The Thomist* (New York: P. J. Kenedy, 1952), 172–217, at 185. For Damascene as the leading Patristic source in Aquinas's theology of the human weaknesses assumed by Christ, cf. my *Passions of Christ's Soul,* 58–60, and 111–13.

23. J. Maritain, *On the Grace and Humanity of Jesus* (New York: Herder and Herder, 1969), 70.

the mystery of Christ *must* correlate with the teachings of Chalcedon, as with all the Christological councils.

The fact that God unites himself substantially to a bodily nature means that Christ's body, far from the unseemly disgrace the docetists consider it to be, acts as the visible sign and tabernacle of his divinity. This Jesus intimates when he refers to his own body as a temple in John 2:19 ("Destroy this temple, and in three days I will raise it up"):

Christ calls his body a temple because a temple is something that God dwells in ... and he dwells in Christ according to a union in person, a union that includes not only the soul, but the body as well. *And so the very body of Christ is God's temple.* (*Ioan.* 2, lect. 3, n. 399; emphasis added)

To further underscore the authenticity of Christ's body, St. Thomas appeals to Jesus' real human parentage (his mother), since human lineage extends by way of blood lines, or, more precisely, by bodily descent: "Christ was born deriving his flesh materially from the flesh of his mother," Aquinas writes in the Commentary (*Ioan.* 3, lect. 1, n. 448).[24] This explains Thomas's affinity for St. Paul's assertion that "God sent his Son, made *(factum)* from a woman" (Gal 4:4), a passage cited no fewer than nine times in the *Commentary on John*.

Whenever Jesus appears in the Gospel with his mother, then, we are reminded of his lineage according to the flesh, and, hence, of his genuine humanness. This Aquinas observes in his gloss on the wedding at Cana. Here Aquinas points to the presence of Jesus' mother as proof of the Word's true humanity. Evidence of having a mother stands as a pointed retort to all those who claim—take note of Thomas's anti-docetic wording—"that Christ had only an imaginary body, not a real one," or "that Christ assumed a celestial body that was in no way related to the Virgin" (*Ioan.* 2, lect. 1, n. 349).[25]

That affirming Christ's bodily descent from the Virgin involves paramount mystical and ecclesiological significance Aquinas does not fail to mention. As St. Thomas knows, there must be a real historical body of Jesus *before* there can be the mystical Body of Christ, the Church:

---

24. Cf. *Ioan.* 4, lect. 1, n. 560: "Christ descended from them [the Patriarchs] according to the flesh."

25. Cf. *Ioan.* 3, lect. 2, n. 467; and *ST* III, q. 5, aa. 1–2. When commenting on Jesus' statement in John 6:62 that the Son of man will ascend "to where he was before," Aquinas censures the view that Christ assumed a "heavenly body" again (*Ioan.* 6, lect. 8, n. 990): "It is according to his human nature that it becomes him to ascend 'to where he was before,' namely, to heaven, where he had not been in his human nature. This stands in opposition to the teaching of [the 2nd-century Gnostic] Valentinus, who claimed that Christ had assumed a heavenly body."

[I]n the mystical sense, marriage signifies the union of Christ and the Church. . . . And this marriage was begun in the womb of the Virgin, when God the Father united a human nature to his Son in a unity of person. Thus, the chamber of this union was the womb of the Virgin. (*Ioan.* 2, lect. 1, n. 338)

Anima Vera Christi

To be human requires the possession of a soul, the animating principle of man, though not just any soul, but a full rational or intellectual soul. Rooted in an Aristotelian-inspired anthropology, Aquinas's view of the human soul includes not only intellectual powers (a mind and will), but also the subsumption of lower operational capacities that correspond to the sensitive (or animal) soul (sense knowledge and desire) as well as to the vegetative soul (growth, nourishment through the assimilation of nutrients, and generation).[26]

To establish this in Christ, Aquinas turns to the witness of the fourth Gospel, as, indeed, of all the Gospels (Thomas's exegesis always operates in light of the whole of Scripture).[27] That Jesus possesses a soul (at least) is implied by John's statement that the Word was made flesh. As Thomas explains, the Evangelist speaks nonsensically if by "flesh" he does not mean a body united to a soul. This follows from the fact that human flesh is truly such only if it is animated or ensouled, a fact supported by Jesus' own words in reference to himself in the Synoptics:

[Some] have said that the Word assumed flesh without a soul. . . . This was the error of Arius. . . . The falsity of this opinion follows from the clear evidence of sacred

---

26. Cf. *ST* I, q. 78, a. 1; cf. as well Aristotle, *De anima*, Bk. II, chs. 3–4 (414a28–415b28); and, for those authors who appropriate this aspect of the Stagirite's thought and who have an influence on Thomas, Nemesius of Emesa, *De natura hominis*, ch. 14 (ed. Verbeke-Moncho, pp. 91–2); Damascene, *De fide orth.*, Bk. II, ch. 12 (ed. Buyt., 118–9); and Albert the Great, *De homine*, q. 67, a. 2.

27. Though the modern exegete might wince at the ease by which Thomas not only reverts to the Synoptics in order to explain a passage in John, but also moves between the Johannine world and the rest of Scripture, including the Old Testament, his method excels at observing what the 1984 Pontifical Biblical Commission (*Scripture and Christology: A Statement of the Biblical Commission with a Commentary,* trans. J. A. Fitzmyer [New York: Paulist Press, 1986], 31) calls the "principle of totality." This principle, the Commission states, "the Fathers and the medieval theologians well recalled, even though they were reading and interpreting the biblical texts according to the methods suited to the culture of their own times." In *Dei verbum*, §12, Vatican Council II sanctions recourse to this principle in the interpretation of Scripture when it asserts that "a right understanding of the sacred texts demands attention . . . to the content and coherence of Scripture as a whole." For more of the same, cf. the 1993 Pontifical Biblical Commission, "Interpretation of the Bible in the Church," 513–16.

Scripture, which frequently mentions Christ's soul (cf. Mt 26:38: "My soul is sorrowful . . ."), and because certain passions of the soul are said of Christ which can in no way exist in the Word of God or in flesh alone: "Jesus began to be sorrowful and troubled" (Mt 26:37). . . . Furthermore, flesh clearly does not obtain the specific nature of flesh except through its soul. (*Ioan.* 1, lect. 7, n. 168)[28]

Continuing the same line of argument, and still in his gloss on John 1:14, Thomas insists that the flesh assumed by the Word, if authentically human, must be animated not by any soul but by a full rational soul. Here the opponent in mind is Apollinaris, who affirmed a sensitive soul in Christ but not a rational one. For Aquinas, this position is tantamount to a denial of the dogma of the Incarnation, and he appeals to the force of reason and the authority of Scripture (specifically Mt 8:10, which attests to the experience of wonder in Jesus) to demonstrate this:

This [view of Apollinaris] is plainly false, since it conflicts with the authority of sacred Scripture, which attributes certain things to Christ that cannot belong to his divinity, nor to his sensitive soul, nor to his flesh, such as Christ's experience of wonder as recounted in Mt 8:10. For, wonder is a passion that arises from a rational or intellectual soul, since it pertains to the desire to know the hidden cause of an observed effect. Therefore, just as sorrow forces one to affirm, contra Arius, a sensitive soul in Christ, so does the experience of wonder compel one to posit, contra Apollinaris, an intellectual soul in Christ. The same conclusion can be reached by reason. For just as there is no flesh without a soul, so neither is there true human flesh without a human soul, which is intellectual. So if the Word assumed flesh that was animated by a merely sensitive soul to the exclusion of a rational soul, he did not assume human flesh; consequently, one could not say God became man. (*Ioan.* 1, lect. 7, n. 168)[29]

---

28. For Aquinas's remarks on Christ's possession of a soul in the *Summa theologiae*, cf. III, q. 5, a. 4, and q. 19, a. 2. J. P. Galvin ("Jesus Christ," in *Systematic Theology: Roman Catholic Perspectives*, ed. F. Schüssler Fiorenza and J. P. Galvin [Dublin: Gill and Macmillan, 1992], 249–324, at 265) agrees with this reading of John 1:14, as he notes that the term "flesh" (*sarx*) in John 1:14 affirms "[not so much] body as distinguished from soul, but rather full human reality."

29. Thomas offers the same argument in *SCG* IV, c. 33; and *ST* III, q. 5, a. 4; cf. John Damascene, *De fide orth.*, Bk. III, chs. 3 and 6 (ed. Buyt., 176–88). Since wonder (*admiratio*) is a kind of "desire to know," one can speak meaningfully of *admiratio* in Christ only if one affirms a real growth in knowledge in him. For this reason, Thomas's own confessed change of opinion on the issue of Christ's acquired knowledge (he reverses his earlier denial of such knowledge in Christ in *ST* III, q. 9, a. 4) will spur him on to give unparalleled attention to Christ's *admiratio* in *ST* III, q. 15, a. 8 (a singular achievement for his day). For a closer look at the development in Thomas's thought on Christ's knowledge, cf. J.-P. Torrell, O.P., "S. Thomas d'Aquin et la science du Christ: une relecture des Questions 9–12 de la *Tertia Pars* de la 'Somme de théologie,'" in *Recherches thomasiennes*. Études revues et augmentées (Paris: J. Vrin, 2000), 198–213, at 207–10. For a comparison with Thomas's contemporaries, cf. Alexander of Hales, III *Sent.*, d. 13, n. 10 (ed. Quar., p. 131); Albert the Great, III *Sent.*, d. 13, a. 10; and d. 14; and Bonaventure, III *Sent.*, d. 14, a. 1, qq. 1–2; and a. 3, q. 2 (ed. Quar., 318–23).

Thomas carries the same argument further, this time to cover the powers of Christ's soul. More specifically, Aquinas argues, contra Monothelitism (the heresy denying a human will in Christ), that the soul of Jesus, as with any human soul, was endowed with an intellectual appetite or will (i.e., with an inclination to, and subsequent ability to, choose the good as known by reason): "there are two wills in our Lord Jesus Christ: one is a divine will, which is the same as the Father's, and the other is a human will, which belongs to himself, *just as it belongs to him to be a man*" (*Ioan.* 5, lect. 5, n. 796; emphasis added).[30]

Central to Thomas's concerns in speaking of a human will in Christ are the soteriological stakes. It is, after all, by his human will that Jesus freely accepts his cross—"not as I will, but as you will" (Mt 26:39)—and, hence, freely chooses to redeem the human race. Thomas goes to great lengths to explain this at all major points in his career, including his gloss on this passage from Matthew 26:39 in the *Lectura super Matthaeum*.[31] Unless Christ's soul is endowed with a human will, it is fanciful to speak of the salvation of the human race.

As the above-cited passages have suggested, the subsumption of lower animal or sentient powers in Jesus' soul is implied by the movements of passion he undergoes. For Aquinas, the passions enter into the essential makeup of the human being, since they are the appetitive movements of the sensitive (or animal) part of the soul. The passions denote any degree of affective inclination toward that which the senses perceive as good and desirable, or avoidance of that which the senses perceive as harmful and undesirable. To be human is to feel pulled affectively by the world around us, to have likes and dislikes, hopes and fears, sorrows and joys, to be subject in multiple ways to affective wounds. All of this corresponds to the human experience of Jesus in the fourth Gospel (cf., e.g., John 11:33, where Jesus is "deeply moved in spirit and troubled" upon learning of Lazarus's death). For this reason, Aquinas can insist that Christ's display of passion serves as an apt reminder of his genuine humanity: "the Lord [exhibited passions] . . . for the deposit of faith, namely,

---

30. Cf. as well *Ioan.* 6, lect. 4, n. 923: "in Christ there were two wills. One pertains to his human nature, and this will is proper to him, both by nature and by the will of the Father"; and *ST* III, q. 18, a. 1: "It is clear that the Son of God assumed an integral human nature. Now the will pertains to an integral human nature, since it is one of its natural powers. . . . Hence, we must say that the Son of God assumed a human will, together with human nature." A seventh-century heresy, Monothelitism was officially condemned at the Third Council of Constantinople (680–81) with the help of the theology of Maximus the Confessor.

31. Cf. *In Matt.* 26, lect. 5; III *Sent.*, d. 15, q. 2, a. 3, sol. 2; *De ver.*, q. 26, a. 9 ad 7; *ST* III, q. 18, aa. 1–6 (especially a. 1, ad 1, and a. 5); q. 47, a. 2, ad 2; and a. 3, ad 1 and ad 2.

to prove the truth of his human nature, *since the passions certainly pertain to every human being*" (*Ioan.* 12, lect. 5, n. 1652; emphasis added).[32]

Jesus' display of passion not only attests to his possession of a genuine soul, it also provides an example for us to imitate in that very domain of human life that is noted for its two extremes. The first extreme, inspired by the Stoic view that the passions count as nothing more than "sicknesses of the soul," esteems the passions as worthy of pure contempt and suppression. The second extreme, which characterizes our own age especially, sees nothing wrong with movements of passion dictating our actions irrespective of the demands of reason. With this in mind, Thomas writes in his gloss on John 11:33:

Christ suffers certain weaknesses in his human affections, such as being troubled in spirit when he learned of Lazarus's death. . . . Now Christ wished to be troubled and sorrowful for three reasons. First, *to prove the condition and truth of his human nature*. Second, so that by controlling his own sorrow, he might show us the proper way in which we should undergo sorrow. For the Stoics say that sorrow cannot befall the wise or virtuous individual. *But it is exceedingly inhuman* (valde inhumanum) *to witness the death of someone and not feel some sorrow.* Certainly, some undergo excessive sorrow over a friend's misfortune. But the Lord willed to feel sorrow not only to show us that, contrary to the Stoics, we should be sorrowful at certain times, but also to show us how to control our sorrow. . . . The third reason is to suggest that we too should mourn and weep for those who physically die. . . . Consequently, the Lord shows the affections of his heart both by his words, "Where have you laid him?" [Jn 11:34] . . . and by his tears: "And Jesus wept" [Jn 11:35]. (*Ioan.* 11, lect. 5, nn. 1532, 1535–37; emphasis added)[33]

Human sin, of course, has left in its wake a particularly crippling affective condition, whereby the passions, lying at the heart of the inner conflict of flesh against spirit, frequently overstep the bounds of moral propriety. For this reason, Thomas, drawing upon the doctrine of Christ's sinlessness, is quick to point out, as he does whenever broaching the subject, that "the pas-

---

32. Thomas repeats this in *Ioan.* 13, lect. 4, n. 1798. For an extensive analysis of this aspect of Aquinas's Christology, cf. my *Passions of Christ's Soul.*

33. Cf. as well *Ioan.* 12, lect. 5, n. 1652, and *Ioan.* 13, lect. 4, nn. 1797–98. Aquinas's criticism of the Stoic contempt for the passions surfaces throughout Thomas's entire *opera*: cf., e.g., *ST* I-II, q. 24, a. 3; q. 59, a. 2; III, q. 15, a. 4 ad 2; *In Roman.* 9, lect. 1; *Sent. Libri Ethic.*, Bk. II, lect. 3; *De malo*, q. 12, a. 1; *De ver.*, q. 26, a. 8 ad 2; and IV *Sent.*, d. 49, q. 3, a. 4; cf. as well E. K. Rand, *Cicero in the Courtroom of St. Thomas Aquinas* (Milwaukee: Marquette University Press, 1946), 51–52. The same stratagem of using Christ's affective example to refute the Stoic position, a stratagem that clearly echoes Augustine (cf. *De civ. Dei*, Bk. XIV, ch. 9 [CCSL 48, 426–27], and *Tract. in Ioh. LX*, n. 3 [CCSL 36, 479]), occurs in *ST* I-II, q. 59, a. 3, *sed contra*; *ST* III, q. 46, a. 6 ad 2; *De malo*, q. 12, a. 1, arg. 12, and *sed contra* 4; and *Expos. super Iob ad litt.*, on 3:1.

sions are in us in one way and in Christ in another" (*Ioan.* 12, lect. 5, n. 1651).[34] Jesus' enjoyment of perfect moral integrity means his passions "always observed the order and rule of reason," or that his passions never "disquieted his reason nor abandoned the order of reason" (*Ioan.* 11, lect. 5, n. 1534; cf. *Ioan.* 12, lect. 5, n. 1651). Such remarks make sense only in light of the tenet of Christ's immunity to all sin. Aquinas notes that it is the very disproportion between the moral quality of Jesus' passions and our own that allows Christ, a real man subject to real movements of passion, to act as "the supreme model of perfection" *(summum exemplar perfectionis)*, to quote his gloss on John 12:6.

As we can see, St. Thomas's remarks on Christ's human affectivity steer a middle course in a terrain littered with the hazards left, on the one side, by the docetic misgivings of Christ's real humanity (Arius denied a soul in Christ because of the passions he exhibited), and, on the other, the Stoic disdain for the passions (along with its residual effects on Christian spirituality). This attests not only to Aquinas's sound metaphysics of human nature, whereby he refuses to equate passion with moral transgression as such, but also and especially to his faithful reading of the fourth Gospel, as with all the Gospels.

Before leaving the subject of Christ's human soul, we should recall that, for Aquinas, body and soul unite as matter and form not in a merely loose Cartesian fashion (an excessive spiritualist anthropology), but in a wholly substantial or hylemorphic way. An integrated whole, the human being is a unified composite of body and soul: "a man is not a man without his body, just as he is not a man without his soul," G. K. Chesterton writes while commenting on this aspect of St. Thomas's anthropology.[35]

The same holds for Christ. To be sure, because he was sinless, Jesus partook in the same harmony between body and soul that prelapsarian man enjoyed before the introduction of sin into the world, that is, before the disruptive impact of sin on human nature. As a result, Aquinas speaks often of a dynamic hylemorphic exchange between Jesus' body and his soul, such that the experiences of one (like the bodily pain he endured in his tortuous crucifixion) always affected (or "redounded into") the other. As Thomas pens early

---

34. This wording is standard for Aquinas throughout his entire career: cf. *ST* III, q. 15, a. 4; *Comp. theol.*, ch. 232; *De ver.*, q. 26, a. 8; and III *Sent.*, d. 15, q. 2, a. 2, sol. 1. On the issue of Christ's sinlessness, Thomas notes that Jesus' interrogatory statement in John 8:46, "Which of you convicts me of sin?" should evoke "wonder" at the "excellence of Christ's singular purity." For Christ's immunity to the effects of original sin, cf. *ST* III, q. 13, a. 3 ad 2; q. 14, a. 3; q. 31, a. 7 ad 2; *Comp. theol.*, ch. 224; *De ver.*, q. 26, a. 8, arg. 6; etc.

35. Chesterton, *Saint Thomas Aquinas*, p. 37.

in his career: "Christ possessed perfect hylemorphic union, so that what he underwent on account of the greatness of his soul corresponded in equal measure to his body united to it."[36]

With Aquinas entirely committed to an image of Christ the man who *is* his body and his soul, we can appreciate how this Master theologian's hylemorphic anthropology only adds greater force to his already stalwart anti-docetism.

CREDIBILITY IN THE INCARNATION

St. Thomas's anti-docetism surfaces in another recurring theme in the *Commentary on John:* the need for credibility in the Incarnation, that is, the need for Christ to appear as a true and genuine human being. This need follows from the fact that faith in a God incarnate is little served if the human family cannot fully *believe* that Christ's humanity accurately reflects the truth of human nature.[37] On this score, John's Gospel clearly suggests that Jesus was regarded as a common human being by those who saw and heard him, at least if the constant rejection Jesus encountered when intimating his divinity is to make proper sense. Christ's possession of a credible humanity explains, so Thomas states, why the Samaritan woman at Jacob's well believes she sees in Jesus what any bystander sees—a common man—as implied by her utterance "come and see the man" (Jn 4:29): "at first," Aquinas writes, "the woman says things about Christ that were believable and openly manifest, namely, that he was a man *(dixit ea de Christo quae credibilia erant et in propatulo, scilicet quod esset homo),* 'made in the likeness of men' (Phil 2:7)." By asserting that Christ's manhood was "openly manifest" *(propatulo)* to all, Aquinas supplies us with one of his most anti-docetically charged statements. He offers as well his conviction that the fourth Gospel puts Christ's integral humanity on full display for all to behold.

Aquinas sees the need to give credibility to the Incarnation at work whenever Jesus attempts, for whatever reason, to shield his divinity. This begins already in his infancy and adolescence. Jesus refrains from performing miracles

---

36. III *Sent.,* d. 15, q. 2, a. 3, qc. 3, *sed contra* 2: "Christus fuit optime complexionatus, quod patet ex hoc quod habuit nobilissimam animam, cui respondet equalitas complexionis in corpore." Cf. *ST* III, q. 19, a. 2. For the redounding effects of Christ's body into his soul, or vice versa, cf., e.g., *ST* III, q. 14, a. 1 ad 2; q. 15, a. 6; *Comp. theol.,* ch. 231; *De ver.,* q. 26, a. 10; III *Sent.,* d. 15, q. 2, a. 1, sol. 3 ad 3, and a. 2, sol. 1; etc.

37. For this theme of credibility in the Incarnation in the *Summa,* cf. III, q. 14, a. 1, and ad 4; and q. 15, a. 7 ad 2. Here Aquinas is indebted to Peter Lombard (III *Sent.,* d. 15, c. 1 [ed. Coll. Bonav., 94]) and Bonaventure (III *Sent.,* d. 15, a. 1, q. 1 [ed. Quar., 331]), who also accentuate the need for Christ's humanity to be seen as fully believable.

in his boyhood, since the exercise of divine power at a young age might have induced onlookers to doubt the authenticity of his humanity. An appreciation of the docetic dangers posed by a miracle-performing wonder boy leads St. Thomas to censure the *Protevangelium* (or what Thomas calls *The Infancy of the Savior*), an apocryphal infancy narrative from the mid second century which alleges that the puerile Jesus performed multiple miracles. As Thomas writes in his commentary on the miracle at Cana, the first that Jesus performs:

> This [miracle] shows the error of the book, *The Infancy of the Savior*. The reason he performed no miracles during this interim period [between his infancy and his public ministry] was that if he had not been like other infants, the mystery of the circumcision and Incarnation might have been regarded as pure illusion. He thus postponed showing his knowledge and power for another time, corresponding to the age when other men reach the fullness of their knowledge and power. (*Ioan.* 1, lect. 14, n. 264)[38]

Aquinas advances the same argument in his exegesis of John 7:1, in which Jesus avoids going to Judea in order to evade the Jews that wish to kill him. Explaining why Jesus declined to use his divine power to subdue his enemies, Thomas points his argument of credibility squarely at those who march to the beat of the docetic drum:

> Christ did not want to do this [i.e., use his divine power to stop his persecutors] all the time, for while this would have shown his divinity, it might have cast doubt on his humanity. Therefore, as a man he showed his humanity by sometimes fleeing his persecutors, *in order to silence all those who would say that he was not a true man*. (*Ioan.* 7, lect. 1, n. 1012; emphasis added)[39]

Christ's possession of a fully believable human nature fits hand-in-glove with the need for a true human model or exemplar to imitate. Inspired by Scripture (1 Pet 2:21: "Christ suffered for you, leaving you an example, that you should follow in his steps") and rooted in a rich Patristic tradition, this notion of Christ's exemplarity resounds all throughout Aquinas's works. Evidence for this is found in his penchant for the expression "Christ's action is

---

38. Cf. as well *Ioan.* 2, lect. 1, n. 346: "The reason [Mary did not encourage Christ to perform miracles before the wedding at Cana] is that before this time he lived like any other person." Later in *ST* III, q. 43, a. 3, Thomas will maintain the same view, namely, that the miracle at Cana helps undergird credibility in Christ's humanity. Torrell (*Le Christ en ses mystères*, vol. 1, 272) notes that Thomas's anti-docetic polemic with the *Protevangelium* runs throughout the entire *Commentary on John*.

39. Later in John 7:10 (n. 1027) when Jesus does finally go to Judea, but this time "in secret" (*in occulto*), Aquinas invokes the same argument of credibility: "[Jesus did this] so that he would not disclose his divinity, and so perhaps makes his Incarnation less certain.... Thus, Christ hid himself as a sign of his humanity, and as an example of virtue for us."

our instruction."⁴⁰ In the *Commentary on John,* the theme of credibility leading to exemplarity emerges especially when Thomas addresses Christ's affectivity. In each passage in which John recounts some movement of passion in Jesus, Aquinas does not fail to underscore the exemplary significance of such movements: "the Lord wished to be troubled," Thomas writes in his gloss on John 12:27 ("Now is my soul troubled"), "for two reasons: first, for the deposit of faith, namely, to prove the truth of his human nature . . . and, second, to provide an example for us."⁴¹ Because we have seen God in authentic human form, we can know precisely how we should mold our lives.

From this it is clear how coupling the need for credibility in the Incarnation with the exemplary value of Christ's actions appends greater soteriological punch to Thomas's anti-docetic argument. Jesus can be a true model for us, that is, he can be useful for our salvation, only if his human actions are real and not illusory. That Aquinas recognizes this indicates the personal impact Christ's humanity had on his own salvation. This Master theologian appreciates what it means to say God has taken on the same physical apparatus as we possess, including its appetitive drives, if only to allow us to see God with our eyes and hear him speak in a language we speak, making it all the easier to model our lives after God's own visibly cast ideal of human excellence and holiness. For Aquinas, the spiritual life is wholly "Christic," that is, Christ centered, or Christo-conforming.⁴²

To further underscore the need for credibility in the Incarnation, Thomas turns to the notion of *conveniens,* or "fittingness." For Aquinas, this notion of *conveniens* plays a key role in the coherence and beauty of the divine wisdom that unfolds in the joining of an integral human nature to the divine Person

---

40. *ST* III, q. 40, a. 1, ad 3: "Christi actio fuit nostra instructio." For more on this expression, which occurs 17 times in Aquinas's works, cf. Schenk, "*Omnis Christi actio nostra est instructio,* 103–31. For other texts affirming Christ's exemplarity (other than in the *Commentary on John,* which shall be noted immediately below), cf. *ST* III, q. 40, a. 2 ad 1; q. 50, a. 1; q. 51, a. 1; *In Matt.,* ch. 4, lect. 2; *In ad Cor.,* ch. 11, lect. 1; *Contra err. Graec.* VII, 23–25; *In ad Cor.,* ch. 11, lect. 1; *Comp. theol.,* chs. 227–28; and *CG* IV, ch. 55. Torrell (*Saint Thomas d'Aquin, maître spirituel,* 156–57) notes that "Christ's exemplarity is always in the forefront of Master Thomas's mind." Cf. I. Biffi, *I Misteri di Cristo in Tommaso d'Aquino,* vol. 1 (Milan: Jaca Books, 1994), 391–93; Torrell, "'Imiter Dieu comme des enfants bien-aimés'. La conformité à Dieu et au Christ dans l'oeuvre de saint Thomas," in *Recherches thomasiennes,* 325–35.

41. *Ioan.* 12, lect. 5, n. 1652: "Dominus turbari voluit propter duo. Primo quidem propter fidei documenta, ut scilicet veritatem humanae naturae approbaret. . . . Secundo propter exemplum." For the other passages maintaining the same, cf. *Ioan.* 11, lect. 5, n. 1535; *Ioan.* 13, lect. 1, n. 1727, *Ioan.* 13, lect. 3, n. 1781, and *Ioan.* 13, lect. 4, n. 1798; *Ioan.* 15, lects. 2–3, nn. 2003 and 2010; etc.

42. This point is stressed by T. F. O'Meara, "Jean-Pierre Torrell's Research on Thomas Aquinas," *Theological Studies* 62 (2001): 787–801, at 798.

of the Word, and as such stands outside the docetic conception of things. God remains absolutely free in choosing the means by which to redeem the human race. The means chosen—becoming a true man—must therefore represent the most "fitting" or "suitable" way of achieving the end of human salvation. In view of God's economic plan of salvation, it was more fitting for the Word to substantially unite himself to a human nature. Aquinas has little difficulty in affirming the full manhood of God because he recognizes the eminent coherence of this assumed manhood. In Thomas's vocabulary, then, *conveniens* signifies not only fittingness but also coherence, or even ordered beauty. Aquinas gives such priority to the notion of the *conveniens* of the Incarnation that he makes it the opening object of inquiry in the definitive Christological study he offers in the *Tertia pars* of the *Summa*.[43]

If God fittingly assumes a human nature, all the more fittingly does he assume a fully credible human nature. Put another way, once one appreciates the coherence *(conveniens)* of the dogma of the Incarnation, it becomes easier to give assent to the veracity (or credibility) of Christ's humanity. For this reason, one finds several passages in the *Commentary on John* in which the notion of the *conveniens* of Christ's full manhood appears.[44] We might note that Aquinas's admiration for the sublime beauty *(conveniens)* of the divine logic disclosed in the Incarnation offers another glimpse into how profoundly the humanity of Christ must have marked the heart of Aquinas's spiritual life.

---

43. G. Narcisse ("Les enjeux épistémologiques de l'argument de convenance selon saint Thomas d'Aquin," in *Ordo sapientiae et amoris*. Image et message de saint Thomas d'Aquin à travers les récentes études historiques, herméneutiques et doctrinales, ed. C.-J. Pinto de Oliveira [Fribourg, Switz.: Éditions Universitaires, 1993], 143–67, at 146–47) affirms that a "torrent of suitabilities" runs throughout Aquinas's Christology. The *Tertia pars* of the *Summa* alone offers 108 uses of *conveniens* in relation to Christ's ontology and psychology. Thomas is not alone on this: Peter Lombard, Alexander of Hales, Albert the Great, and Bonaventure all affirm the fittingness of the Incarnation. For more on the notion of *conveniens* in Aquinas's Christology, cf. Torrell, *Le Christ en ses mystères*, vol. 1, 34–38; O. H. Pesch, *Thomas von Aquin. Grenze und Grösse mittelalterlicher Theologie. Eine Einführung*, 2nd ed. (Mainz: Matthias-Grünewald-Verlag, 1989), 318–22; and M.-D. Chenu, *La théologie comme science au XIIIe siècle* (Paris: J. Vrin, 1969), 92–99.

44. Cf., e.g., *Ioan*. 1, lect. 7, n. 169. One could also point to Thomas's gloss on John 5:26–27 (*Ioan*. 5, lect. 5, n. 789), in which the Father gives the Son "authority to execute judgment" on account of his being the Son of Man, i.e., on account of his being human. Here Aquinas finds it fitting that Christ as a man should exercise this judgment for three reasons: first, because it will give human bodily form to the judgment, thereby making it visibly seen by all; second, because it is only right that the very man who "was falsely found guilty should condemn the truly guilty"; and, third, because it intimates the mercy by which Christ will judge, as it "gives confidence for a man to have another man as judge."

ANTI-DOCETISM AND THE EUCHARIST

This look into Aquinas's defense of Christ's full humanity in the *Commentary on John* closes with a few remarks on the anti-docetism inherent in Thomas's commentary on the Bread of Life discourse in John 6 (a discourse that Raymond Brown acknowledges may have been anti-docetic in inspiration).[45] Aware that denying the reality of Christ's humanity leads to a denial of the reality of the Eucharist, Aquinas takes the occasion of this discourse to draw on the intrinsic relation, almost too obvious to point out, between Christ's flesh in his human nature and his flesh in the Eucharist. Simply put, if Christ's humanity is not real, then neither is it truly the body of Christ present in the Eucharist. If Christ's body is not real and life-giving, then neither can the Eucharist be real and life-giving. This Thomas suggests in his exegesis of Jesus' statement in John 6:35, "I am the bread of life":

> Because the flesh of Christ is united to the Word of God, his flesh is life-giving. Thus, his body, sacramentally received, is also life-giving, for Christ gives life to the world through the mysteries that he accomplished in his flesh. . . . And so Christ's flesh is called bread. (*Ioan.* 6, lect. 4, n. 914)

Aquinas elaborates on this in his gloss on John 6:51, in which Jesus declares, "the bread which I shall give for the life of the world is my flesh":

> he shows that even his flesh is life-giving, for it is the instrument *(organum)* of his divinity. And since an instrument acts by the power of the agent, then just as the divinity of Christ is life-giving, so too (as Damascene says) does his flesh give life by the power of the Word to which it is united. . . . What he is saying here pertains, then, to the sharing in his body, i.e., to the sacrament of the Eucharist. (*Ioan.* 6, lect. 6, n. 959)

It bears insisting: the realism of the Eucharist, the true nourishment of our souls, *requires* the realism of the humanity of Christ.

The ecclesiological ramifications of this should not be neglected. Like the Eucharist, the realism of the Church also requires the authenticity of Christ's humanity. If Christ's humanity, his body, is not real, then neither can the Church be considered his true *mystical* Body. The Church is the extension of the Incarnation, the extension of the glorified humanity of Christ.

Brief mention must be made of Thomas's assertion, cited immediately above, that Christ's flesh acts as the "instrument"—the *organum*—of his divinity. Though he inherits the notion of Christ's humanity acting as the *or-*

---

[45]. "The Docetists seem to have neglected the Eucharist and to have denied that it was the flesh of Jesus (Ignatius, *Smyrnaeans*, vii, 1). Therefore, the eucharistic realism of John 6:51–58 may also have been anti-docetic in tendency." Brown, *Gospel according to John, I–XII*, lxxvi.

ganum of his divinity from John Damascene (cf. *De fide orthodoxa*, Bk. III, chs. 15 and 19), Aquinas could bring himself to reproduce these words of Damascene only later in his career (the *De veritate* marks the decisive turning point). As a young theologian, Thomas quite rightly understood that only God can, to quote the *Commentary on John*, "give life," that is, cause grace. However, to say Christ's humanity acts as the instrument of his divinity is tantamount to saying his humanity also gives life (or causes grace). For, whenever an instrumental agent is at work, the effect produced (in this case grace) comes about *only through* the proper mediated action of the instrumental cause (even though the instrumental cause, on its own, is never proportioned to the effect as such). The young Aquinas, then, wanted to make sure that we not attribute to a mere human nature (though it is the human nature assumed by Christ) what properly belongs to the divine Person of the Word, namely, the giving of grace or of eternal life.

Aristotelian metaphysical principles allowed Thomas to overcome the dilemma. Since grace ranks as a quality (or accidental form) rather than as a substance (or subject) as such, grace does not require God's *immediate* causal action. God's immediate causal action is required *only* when a substantial change is effected. However, since grace effects an accidental rather than a substantial change on the part of the soul, the metaphysical (and, hence, theological) obstacle preventing one from saying God can cause grace through a mediated (human) instrument is removed.

Aided by this understanding, Aquinas affirms—and he stands alone among his scholastic contemporaries in doing so, though Damascene was known and used by all—that Christ's humanity, moved by the divine Person of the Word (like a brush moved by a painter), truly produces or causes grace.[46] This is unique to Christ, since it is only inasmuch as it subsists in a

---

46. For Aquinas's definitive position on this matter, cf. *ST* III, q. 19, a. 1, and ad 2 (the definition of instrumental causality comes in I, q. 45, a. 5); for the first change in opinion, cf. *De ver.*, q. 27, a. 4; for the earlier view, cf. III *Sent.*, d. 13, q. 2, a. 1, ad 3. Other scholars who have treated this issue, including the development of Thomas's thought and the reasons thereof, include: J.-P. Torrell, O.P., "La causalité salvifique de la résurrection du Christ selon saint Thomas," in *Recherches thomasiennes*, 214–41 (originally published in *Revue thomiste* 96 [1996]: 179–208); É.-H. Wéber, *Le Christ selon saint Thomas d'Aquin* (Paris: Desclée, 1988), 179–87; and T. Tschipke, *Die Menschheit Christi als Heilsorgan der Gottheit unter besonderer Berücksichtigung der Lehre des hl. Thomas von Aquin* (Freiburg im Breisgau: Herder, 1940), 116–45. For the position of Thomas's contemporaries on the matter, cf. Albert the Great, *De resurrectione*, tr. 2, q. 1, sol. (ed. Colon., vol. 26, p. 259); and Bonaventure, IV *Sent.*, d. 43, a. 1, q. 6, *corpus* and ad 4 (ed. Quar., 895) (Torrell ["La causalité salvifique," 220 n. 3] observes that Bonaventure "sees [in Christ's humanity] no proper causality" with respect to the accomplishments proper to his divinity).

divine Person that Christ's humanity can enjoy the noble privilege of acting as the instrumental cause of grace. Both the principal cause (the divine Person of the Word, the one proportioned to the effect as such) and the instrumental cause (Christ's humanity) together produce the effect of grace, just as a Caravaggio and his hand must work jointly to produce the chiaroscuro style of painting. The Son of God acts as savior of the human race *through* his assumed human nature, not apart, around, or in abstraction from it.

What we find formulated in the *Commentary on John,* then, stands as a testament to Aquinas's commitment to probe ever deeper the human dimension of the Incarnation: "Christ's flesh is life-giving, for it is the *organum* of his divinity. And since an instrument acts by the power of the agent, then just as the divinity of Christ is life-giving, so too does his flesh give life by the power of the Word to which it is united."

These remarks on the instrumental realism of the flesh of the Incarnate Word show Aquinas at his anti-docetic best.

CONCLUSION

In sum, we can say that for St. Thomas, one fails to grasp the plain sense of John if one misses this Gospel's anti-docetic witness of Christ as a full human being, consubstantial to us in all things: "nothing implanted in our nature by God was lacking in the human nature assumed by the Word of God," is how Aquinas puts it in the *Summa*.[47] Aquinas's keen awareness of the soteriological and metaphysical sacrifices offered up at the altar of the docetic Christ keeps him close to the dogma of the Incarnation at all points in his career, as his reading of John shows. It is no exaggeration to say that Christian tradition knows of no greater defender of Christ's full humanity than St. Thomas Aquinas.

The Christ of Aquinas is no *pure* human being, however. He is a divine Person, the second Person of the holy Trinity, in whom his humanity subsists. One must therefore never lose sight of the fact that, as the fourth Gospel attests, Christ is the true eternal Son of the Father, just as he is a man of true flesh and blood: "our faith is in both the divinity and the humanity of Christ," Thomas writes in the *Summa,* "such that belief in one is not sufficient without belief in the other."[48]

He goes further in the *Commentary on John.* Taking as his springboard the

---

47. *ST* III, q. 9, a. 4: "nihil eorum quae Deus in nostra natura plantavit defuit humanae naturae assumptae a Verbo Dei."

48. *ST* III, q. 53, a. 2: "Est autem fides nostra et de divinitate et de humanitate Christi: non enim sufficit alterum sine altero credere."

confession of faith of the apostle Thomas in John 20:28, "My Lord and my God," Aquinas expressly identifies the "good theologian" *(bonus theologus)* with the one who believes in *both* Christ's humanity, captured by the words "my Lord" (this is what the apostles called him before his death and glorified resurrection) *and* his divinity, signified by "my God" (*Ioan.* 20, lect. 6, n. 2562). In his reading of John's Gospel, Aquinas strives assiduously to give credence and intelligibility to the revealed tenets of both the full humanity and the true divinity of Christ. In so doing, St. Thomas qualifies as that "good theologian" he himself describes.

SIXTEEN

Aquinas and Christ's Resurrection
The Influence of the *Lectura super Ioannem* 20–21 on the *Summa theologiae*

PIM VALKENBERG

When I published a revised version of my dissertation on *Place and Function of Holy Scripture in the Theology of St. Thomas Aquinas,* I realized that the choice of this subject was to a large extent determined by the ecumenical atmosphere of my theological education at the Catholic Theological University of Utrecht, now the home of the Thomas Institute at Utrecht.[1] First, therefore, let me make some preliminary remarks on the theological significance of reading John with Aquinas, issuing from my present theological position at the Catholic University of Nijmegen, in which I am involved in interreligious dialogue and the Christian theology of religions.

JOHN AND THE OTHERS

When I investigated the bibliographical resources on the theology of St. Thomas Aquinas some years ago, I could not find many studies about Aquinas as commentator of Scripture. But the majority of these few studies were concerned with his *Commentary on John,* and the same holds true for translations of Aquinas's commentaries or parts thereof. In this respect, *Reading John with St. Thomas Aquinas* pursues an estimable tradition. Let me explain why I find this tradition both appealing and ambiguous.

In the first place, both the Gospel according to John and the *repor-*

---

1. Wilhelmus G. B. M. Valkenberg, *Words of the Living God: Place and Function of Holy Scripture in the Theology of St. Thomas Aquinas* (Leuven: Peeters, 2000).

tatio[2] of Aquinas's commentary on this Gospel have an outstanding value as theological works. In his well-known prologue, Aquinas elaborates on Isaiah 6:1, "I saw the Lord seated on a throne, high and exalted," saying that John gives us such a contemplative vision of God incarnate, mainly because he pays special attention to the divinity of Christ, while the other authors of the Gospels mainly deal with the mysteries of his humanity (*Ioan.* prol., n. 10). Aquinas recognizes John as a real theologian, someone who speaks about Christ as God incarnate. Therefore, the real subject of this type of God-talk is not Christ but God the Savior.[3] In his *Commentary on John,* Aquinas is keen on discovering this deep structure of theological meaning in the words of the Apostle, and therefore he constantly refers to terms such as *mysterium* and *signum.*

Of course, the theological depth of the fourth Gospel has been the main reason for its success in the history of the Church. But this medal has its reverse as well. If the theological depth of St. John's Gospel is no longer seen as a complement to the other Gospels, as Aquinas sees it, the divinity of Christ will be separated from his humanity, and the theological tradition might become one-sided. It could be argued, for instance, that the *Catechism of the Catholic Church* stresses in certain parts of its Christology the descending approach of St. John to such an extent that the plurality of apostolic testimonies in the New Testament is in danger.[4] Likewise, someone who is acquainted with Aquinas's *Commentary on John* is better equipped to see him as a biblical theologian than someone who knows only his *Summa contra gentiles* and his *Summa theologiae.* But if one really wants to know Aquinas as a biblical theologian, one should consider at least his commentaries on St. Paul[5] or on the Psalms, and preferably his *Glossa continua super Evangelia* as well. In this respect, one should once again treat John as a witness of Christ among the others.

It is interesting to know that Aquinas deals with this issue of "John and the

---

2. A *reportatio* means that the text has been written down by one of Aquinas's secretaries or pupils. For some time, Aquinas's *Commentary on the Gospel of St. John* has been thought of as an *expositio,* which would mean that Aquinas would have rewritten this text by his own hand; but this is deemed improbable by J.-P. Torrell in his *Initiation à saint Thomas d'Aquin* (Paris: Cerf, 1993), at 289.

3. See the prologue to the third part of his *Summa theologiae:* "de ipso omnium Salvatore ac beneficiis eius humano generi praestitis nostra consideratio subsequatur."

4. See J. Dupuis, S.J., "The Incarnation of the Son of God," in *Commentary on the Catechism of the Catholic Church,* ed. M. J. Walsh (London: Chapman, 1994), 112–26.

5. Which is, in part, an *expositio,* unlike his *reportatio* on John. This means that one has a better chance to encounter the real theologian in his commentary on Romans than in his commentary on John.

others" several times in his *Commentary on John* 20–21. In John 20:2 the author mentions the presence of Simon Peter and of "the other disciple whom Jesus loved," that is, John himself according to an old tradition. At this point, Aquinas pays close attention to the plot of the story:[6] while John outruns Peter coming to the sepulcher, he waits to let Peter go in first. On the level of the *littera,* this is a kind of behavior that behooves younger people with their elder companions. But on the spiritual level, the two disciples signify the Jews (Jn) and the Gentiles (Peter) (*Ioan.* 20, lect. 1, nn. 2480–87). The same indication, "the disciple whom Jesus loved" returns in John 21:7 and 21:20. Again, Aquinas takes the opportunity to draw a comparison between John and Peter. For instance, he says that while John has a deeper intellect, Peter has a more passionate affect (*Ioan.* 21, lect. 2, n. 2594, citing Chrysostom). Or, with reference to the question "Simon son of John, do you love me?" (Jn 21:15), he says that Christ loved John because of three reasons: his intellect, his virginity, and his young age. But he loved John more with a human love, and Peter more with a divine love. This is because Peter signifies active life, while John signifies contemplative life (*Ioan.* 21, lect. 5, nn. 2639–43).

Finally, I would like to mention a third aspect with reference to "John and the others," namely the rather bad reputation of the Gospel according to John in interreligious dialogue. Of course, the issue of interreligious dialogue is a modern issue, and therefore one should not expect to receive any direct answer from either John or Thomas Aquinas in this field.[7] But the awareness that one cannot go on theologizing as if Christianity were the only religion determines our contemporary theological horizon to a large extent. Therefore, it is necessary to acknowledge that the fourth Gospel has its dark sides and should be read in the context of the New Testament in its entirety. It is a well-known fact that the famous words "I am the way; I am the truth and I am life" (Jn 14:6) have functioned as one of the major underpinnings of exclusivist claims by Christians, although this text can and must be explained in a different fashion.[8] Apart from that, the Gospel according to John is itself a part of that horrifying anti-Jewish tradition that seems to be the dark side of

---

6. He says: "nota quod non sine causa Evangelista etiam particularia diligenter narrat" (*Ioan.* 20, lect. 1, n. 2480; cp. n. 2485).

7. Cf. P. Valkenberg, "How to Talk to Strangers: Aquinas and Interreligious Dialogue in the Middle Ages," *Jaarboek 1997* (Utrecht: Thomas Instituut), 9–47.

8. This text is not meant as a judgment on outsiders who do not know Christ, but as a direction for his disciples who do know him but not the specific way to the Father; cf. P. Valkenberg, "Christ and the Other Ways," in *Die widerspenstige Religion* (*Festschrift* for Hermann Häring), ed. T. van den Hoogen, H. Küng, and J.-P. Wils (Kampen: Kok, 1997), 377–96, at 385f.

the Christian tradition in most of its historical forms. In particular, John 8 has been a point of departure for classical forms of anti-Judaism, hatred of the Jews, and even demonization of them.[9] One has to say, however, that Aquinas is rather reticent on this issue in his *Commentary on John* 8. When Christ says to his Jewish opponents, "Your father is the devil" (Jn 8:44), Aquinas warns against a dualistic interpretation in the vein of the Manichees. Rather, following Origen he stresses an ethical interpretation: the Jews are called sons of the devil because they do not do the works of the Father (*Ioan.* 8, lect. 6, n. 1240).[10]

So, while enjoying the spiritual richness and the theological depth of both John and Thomas, we should not forget that they are part of a rich and sometimes ambiguous Christian tradition, and that their voices should be remembered as key-notes in the chorus of saints—but not without second voices.

AQUINAS AS MASTER OF SACRED SCRIPTURE

Coming now to the main topic of this essay, I want to show how Aquinas's daily task as *Magister in sacra Pagina* influenced his systematic theology, as can be seen in the basic structure of his *Summa theologiae*. It is my contention that Father M.-D. Chenu was right when he characterized Aquinas's theology on the mysteries of the life of Christ in *Summa theologiae* III, qq. 27–59 as a specimen of biblical theology.[11] But I think that it is possible to show that his systematic theology in its entirety has a biblical character. This can be demonstrated by a quantitative analysis of the place of Scripture—the number of quotations from Scripture in Aquinas's systematic-theological works—but also and more importantly, by a qualitative analysis of the functions of Scripture, which shows that it is the main source of Aquinas's theology. In this qualitative analysis, I distinguish between a number of theologically secondary functions of Scripture, in which it may be used in a theological text like any other source, and an underlying theologically primary function in which Scripture determines the theological text as its source and framework, because it determines the possibility of theological knowledge concerning God's revelation.[12]

---

9. "Johannes 8 is het klassieke aanknopingspunt van de Jodenhaat," P. Tomson, "*Als dit uit de Hemel is . . .*": *Jezus en de schrijvers van het Nieuwe Testament in hun verhouding tot het Jodendom* (Hilversum: B. Folkertsma Stichting voor Talmudica, 1997), 364.

10. "non ut mali Iudaei dicuntur filii diaboli, sed imitatione."

11. See M.-D. Chenu, *Introduction à l'étude de Saint Thomas d'Aquin* (Montréal/Paris: Vrin, 1950), 222; also M. Corbin, *Le chemin de la théologie chez Thomas d'Aquin* (Paris: Beauchesne, 1974), 800.

12. For this distinction, see Valkenberg, *Words of the Living God*, 51.

In the remainder of this contribution, I want to limit myself to the relation between Aquinas's *Commentary on the Gospel of St. John,* chapters 20 and 21, and his systematic theology about the resurrection of Christ in *Summa theologiae* III, qq. 53–56. After having unfolded my theory about the relation between Aquinas's exegetical works and his systematic-theological works in general and his *Summa theologiae* in particular, I want to give you some concrete examples of the manner in which his *Commentary on John* influenced his theological *quaestiones.*

First of all, it is important to distinguish between two types of theological reflection on Scripture, leading to two literary genres in Aquinas's days. On the one hand, there is the older literary form of the *expositio,* which means that the theologian follows the order of the subject matters as they are presented in the biblical text. Usually, this *expositio litterae* is preceded by a *divisio litterae* in which the text is analyzed as to its logical order, and it is concluded by one or more confirmative quotations from Scripture. In Aquinas's commentaries on Scripture, however, one can easily find traces of another literary genre: the *quaestio,* in which attention is drawn to a certain problem of a theological or exegetical nature. In a certain sense, the emancipation of theological *quaestiones* from their direct relation to Scripture is one of the significant characteristics of the emerging *scholae* in the twelfth and thirteenth centuries: it distinguished the manner in which Scripture was read at the universities from the manner in which it was read in the abbeys and convents. Therefore, one would expect that the style of the *quaestio* would be more characteristic of Aquinas's mature systematic-theological works, such as his *Summa theologiae,* than the works of his youth, such as his *Scriptum super Sententiis.* But the reverse is the case: when comparing these theological works, one can demonstrate that the influence of the literary genre of *expositio* is greater in his *Summa theologiae* than in his *Scriptum super Sententiis.* Let me try to explain this.

In a historical perspective, one could agree with Beryl Smalley in saying that Aquinas moved from the traditional spiritual reading of Scripture in the *expositio* to the more rigidly scientific reading of Scripture in the *quaestio* or even the *disputatio;* from the "monastic" stress on spiritual senses towards the "Aristotelian" stress on the literal sense of Scripture.[13] Another eminent scholar, Michel Corbin, gives a largely convincing explanation of the apparent contradiction that Aquinas, growing more acquainted with Aristotle and sci-

---

13. See B. Smalley, *The Study of the Bible in the Middle Ages,* 3rd ed. (Oxford: Basil Blackwell, 1983), 301. On the senses of Scripture, see also the contribution by John Boyle in this volume.

entific theological procedures, introduces a more traditional manner of explaining Scripture in his *Summa theologiae* when he says that Aquinas rediscovered, thanks to Aristotle, the dependency of theological knowledge on God's revelation through Scripture. To the extent that Aquinas understood Aristotle better, he relied less on the Philosopher and more on Scripture in his theological works.[14]

My research, however, while endorsing Corbin's analysis, suggests that there is an explanation for this shift that is even more decisive: Aquinas's growing acquaintance with Scripture through his daily lecturing on Scripture as *Magister in sacra Pagina,* and his daily praying and singing of Scripture as a Friar Preacher. A comparative analysis of literary genres learns that Aquinas's *expositiones* on Scripture prove to be the main factor determining the differences between his theology on the resurrection of Christ in the *Scriptum super Sententiis* at the beginning of his teaching career, and the text in the *Summa theologiae* at the end of his teaching. This can be demonstrated by six characteristics of an *expositio* that are more prominent in his *Summa* than in his other systematic-theological works:

- extensive explanations of a text from Scripture, which was quoted in an argument, in the reply to this argument;
- the use of Patristic commentaries on Scripture, sometimes derived from Aquinas's *glossa continua* on the Gospels;
- the interpretation of the *littera* of Scripture by explaining the meaning of some specific word in the original text of Scripture;
- the singular place of quotations from Scripture in the arguments *sed contra;*
- the greater number of quotations from the Psalms, the letter to the Romans, and the Gospel according to St. John: Aquinas lectured on these books simultaneously with writing the third part of his *Summa theologiae;*
- the greater number of confirmative quotations from Scripture.

It is in this sense that Chenu wrote that Aquinas's *Summa theologiae* may be characterized as "biblical theology" because it is an offspring of his theological exegesis.[15] The characteristic of "biblical theology" is but loosely connected with the presence of many explicit quotations from Scripture; it is mainly based on the theologically primary function of Scripture as source and framework of Aquinas's theology. The results of my research show that Scripture

---

14. See Corbin, *Le chemin de la théologie chez Thomas d'Aquin,* 720 and 841.
15. See Chenu, *Introduction à l'étude de Saint Thomas d'Aquin,* 221f.

has such a primary function everywhere in Aquinas's theology; it is more or less clearly expressed in relation to subject matter and literary genre, but it can be discovered anywhere in a theological reading of Aquinas's theological texts. In this respect, the scriptural character of his theology is expressed most clearly in the *Summa,* but it is present in his earlier works as well. The *Summa theologiae* may be described as a concentration on the heart of the matter in Aquinas's theology, not only because it is a work for beginners in theology who should know the basic *auctoritates,* but also because Aquinas lectured on Scripture and used Scripture progressively as normative source and framework in his theology.

THE INFLUENCE OF HIS *COMMENTARY ON JOHN* 20–21 ON HIS *SUMMA THEOLOGIAE*

Aquinas's *Commentary on John* can be dated as posterior to his commentary on St. Matthew, probably between 1270 and 1272.[16] Since the third part of his *Summa theologiae* is usually dated in the year 1272–1273, it is rather likely that we can find some traces from his *expositio* on chapters 20 and 21 of St. John's Gospel in his systematic-theological *quaestiones* in the third part of his *Summa theologiae.* While Aquinas remains rather traditional in his approach to the resurrection of Christ in his *Scriptum super III Sententiarum,* d. 21, q. 2, his approach in *Summa theologiae* III, qq. 53–56 remains without precedent.[17] Although Aquinas was the first to introduce a *quaestio* on the resurrection of Christ in a commentary on the third book of the Sentences by Peter Lombard, this question is influenced as to its contents by the *Summa fratris Alexandri* and, indirectly, by the *Summa aurea* written by William of Auxerre. But in the case of the *Summa theologiae,* I could not find such systematic-theological sources. This is another indication that his main sources for his *quaestiones* on the resurrection of Christ in *ST* III, qq. 53–56 were his own *expositiones* on the last chapters of the Gospels, including his Patristic documentation in the *Glossa continua.*

However, before I will give some instances of this influence of the theological exegesis in Aquinas's commentary on John 20–21 on his systematic theology in his *Summa theologiae,* I would like to give an example from the same context that shows that there is also an influence of Aquinas's systematic approach on his theological exegesis. My example refers to the fact that Aquinas

---

16. See James A. Weisheipl, *Friar Thomas d'Aquino: His Life, Thought and Works* (Garden City, N.Y.: Doubleday, 1974), 246; J.-P. Torrell, O.P., *Initiation à saint Thomas d'Aquin: sa personne et son oeuvre* (Fribourg: Editions Universitaires, 1993), 288.

17. For more details, see Valkenberg, *Words of the Living God,* 190–206.

notices that the Gospels seem to speak differently about the way in which the apostles perceive Christ after his resurrection. While St. Paul, for instance, stresses the fact that resurrection leads to a reality that is no longer corporeal but spiritual, some of the Gospels, notably St. Luke and St. John, stress the fact that Christ had a real body after his resurrection. This is the case, for instance, in the encounter between Christ and Thomas the Apostle, on the occasion of which Christ says: "Reach your finger here; see my hands. Reach your hand here and put it into my side. Be unbelieving no longer, but believe" (Jn 20:27). But in the same story, it is told that Christ came and stood in their midst, while the doors were closed (Jn 20:26). In his commentary on the Sentences, Aquinas endorsed a contemporary explanation that he found in his sources, namely that Christ could enter while the doors were shut because he possessed the endowments of glorified bodies, among which is *subtilitas,* the power to be together with another body at one and the same place.[18] In his *Summa theologiae,* however, he prefers a more theological solution: the body of Christ could suddenly appear and disappear because of the power of the divinity united with it.[19] In this case, it is quite clear that Aquinas inserted a theological *quaestio* while commenting on John 20:19 that made him change from the more "anthropological" explanation that he accepted in his *Scriptum* to the more theological explanation he gives in his *Summa.* This theological *quaestio* goes as follows:

One should know that some people have said that to enter through closed doors is characteristic of a glorified body, because it has a condition in which it is able to be together with another body at the same place. They say that this can happen without a miracle. This opinion, however, is to be rejected because such a condition would be contrary to the nature of a human body that is always spatial, according to Aristotle. And therefore, one has to say that Christ could do this miraculously, because of his divinity. And if such a thing sometimes happens with the bodies of saints, one has to call this a miracle. Aquinas ends this excursus by saying that Augustine and Gregory teach the same thing; Augustine connects this miracle of closed doors with the miracle of the virgin birth of Christ in which the maidenhead of the Virgin Mary was not violated either.[20]

Once again, Aquinas uses the non-theological insights of Aristotle in order to arrive at a more theological solution. In his *Summa theologiae,* Aquinas repeats the same *auctoritates* by Augustine and Gregory, but he seems to leave

---

18. See III *Sent.,* d. 21, q. 2, a. 4., sol.1, resp ad. 2–3. Aquinas found the attribution to Praepositinus in the *Summa aurea* by William of Auxerre and in the *Summa fratris Alexandri.*

19. See *ST* III, q. 54, a. 1, ad 1.

20. This is my paraphrase of Aquinas's *Ioan.* 20, lect. 4, n. 2527.

somewhat more room for the other solution as well, since he announces that he will discuss the theory according to which a glorified body can be at one place together with another body when he would discuss resurrection in general—which he never did, as we know.[21] With reference to Christ, however, Aquinas says that he came through closed doors, although he had a real body, not because of the nature of this body, but because of the power of the divinity united with it.

The next example of an influence from Aquinas's *Commentary on John* on his *Summa theologiae* is concerned with the beautiful story of the encounter between Christ and Mary Magdalene (Jn 20:11–18) that formed the major source for one of the most interesting ways to interpret the resurrection of Christ in the history of Christian art.[22] Just like the *Noli me tangere* ("Do not touch me") paintings of Fra Angelico in Florence, it shows the resurrection of Christ as an encounter in which the human dimension is stressed, while suggesting that this human dimension is, in the end, not sufficient.[23] For instance, commenting on Mary Magdalene's question to the gardener, "If it is you, sir, who removed him, tell me where you have laid him, and I will take him away" (Jn 20:15), Aquinas asks: "Why does she say 'him', supposing the gardener to know to whom she refers, while not having mentioned his name?" (*Ioan.* 20, lect. 3, n. 2511). He answers that the power of love is such that one cannot imagine others to be ignorant of the beloved. That is why the men of Emmaus said to Christ, who seemed not to know what had happened: "Are you the only person staying in Jerusalem not to know what has happened there in the last few days?" (Luke 24:18). With reference to the same words, Aquinas adds: "What a courage in this woman, who was not afraid of the sight of a corpse; and who dared to take up a load that she couldn't possibly bear!" And with reference to the famous words, "Do not cling to me, for I have not yet ascended to the Father" (Jn 20:17), Aquinas adds: "he wanted to lead her to a higher kind of faith." Again, Aquinas shows his theological approach: a keen attention to the human dimensions of the Gospel narratives is connected with its deeper theological meaning: the encounter with the living Christ is a mystery of God's love and grace (*Ioan.* 20,

---

21. My edition of *ST* III, q. 54, a. 1 refers to q. 83 a. 2 in the *Supplementum*, but this text is not authentic.

22. On the importance of the notion of an encounter with Christ, see also the contribution by Dr. Janet Smith in this volume.

23. For a theological reflection on this interpersonal character of the appearances of the risen Christ, see P. Schoonenberg, *Wege nach Emmaus: unser Glaube an die Auferstehung Jesu* (Graz, 1974); H. Kessler, *Sucht den Lebenden nicht bei den Toten: die Auferstehung Jesu Christi in biblischer, fundamentaltheologischer und systematischer Sicht* (Düsseldorf, 1985).

lect. 3, nn. 2517–18). In his *Summa theologiae,* Aquinas pays some special attention to the fact that Christ has manifested himself to a woman, while women were not able to testify according to Jewish law.[24] Aquinas replies in the words of St. Cyril that they will be equal to men in the state of glory, a quotation that can also be found in his *Catena* on Luke 24:8. This text may be seen as a small but ambiguous contribution toward a more equal treatment of men and women in the Church: while women will be equals in the state of glory, they still are subordinate in the meantime.[25] The theological insight that the state of glory began in Christ, however, should have some consequences for the members of his Mystical Body.[26]

The attentiveness to the human dimension of the Gospel narratives about the appearances of Christ after his resurrection leads to another characteristic that may be found explicitly in Aquinas's theology on the resurrection of Christ in his *Summa theologiae:* the notion of a companionship of Christ with his disciples.[27] In his *Commentary on John,* Aquinas mentions this issue on the occasion of the words, "A week later his disciples were again in the room, and Thomas was with them. Although the doors were locked, Jesus came and stood among them, saying, 'Peace be with you!'" (Jn 20:26; *Ioan.* 20, lect. 6, n. 2552). He asks: "Why did Christ come after eight days since his last appearance (see John 20:19) on the day of his resurrection?" He gives a literal and a mystical reason; the latter has to do with the meaning of the number eight, signifying the time of the glorified. But the literal reason has to do with the fact that Christ did not want to be with them continuously, but did appear to them several times. The reason is that he did not rise to the same way of life as before. So, a companionship with the disciples suggests a kind of familiarity that is evaded by Christ, just as he avoided being touched by Mary Magdalene. But, on the other hand, he had to meet with them a few times in order to comfort their faith. In the *Summa theologiae,* Aquinas makes this clear as follows: "Christ had to keep them company in order to comfort them. But he could not be with them continuously, because in that case they would have thought that he lived a normal life just like before. So, he had to appear sometimes in order to manifest the truth of the resurrection; but he had to disappear in order to manifest the glory of the resurrection."[28] This di-

---

24. See *ST* III, q. 55, a.1, ad 3.
25. See Kari Elisabeth Borresen, *Subordination and Equivalence. The Nature and Role of Woman in Augustine and Thomas Aquinas* (Washington, D.C.: The Catholic University of America Press, 1981).
26. See *ST* III, q. 53, a. 2.　　　　27. See *ST* III, q. 55, a. 4.
28. *ST* III, q. 55, a. 3, ad 2.

alectical relationship between the truth and the glory of Christ's resurrection determines Aquinas's reading of John 20–21 at many places, just as it determines the question about the quality of the body of the risen Christ in his *Summa theologiae*.[29] In his true and glorious body, Christ manifests himself as God incarnate. That is why Aquinas rejected the eschatological reference to the subtlety of glorified bodies: Christ is truly God and truly a human being at the same time.

A bit further on, in comments on the next verse, "Then he said to Thomas, 'Reach your finger here; see my hands. Reach your hand here and put it into my side. Be unbelieving no longer, but believe'" (Jn 20:27), two short questions come up in Aquinas's commentary. In the first place, there is a doubt concerning the scars in Christ's body: since glorified bodies should be without defects, why did Christ have any scars? In his commentary, Aquinas quotes a beautiful text from Augustine that he quotes again in his *Summa theologiae*.[30] It goes as follows:

> Of course, Christ could have removed the stains of his scars from his glorified body. But he knew why he preserved the scars in his body. In the first place, this was to show them to Thomas who did not believe unless he would touch and see; in the second place, this is to show them to his enemies and to the sinners on the day of judgement. Then, He will say to them: See the man whom you have crucified, see the wounds that you have inflicted; recognize the side that you have pierced. It has been opened by you and for you; but you did not want to go in.[31]

When discussing the scars in the body of Christ after his resurrection in the *Summa*, Aquinas gives a number of Patristic quotations that show the improvement in his Patristic documentation in comparison with his *Scriptum super Sententiis*, where he quoted freely by mediation of the glosses; in the *Summa*, he quotes extensively and literally from firsthand sources.[32]

The second question is related to the wounds in the bodies of martyrs: will

---

29. Aquinas's systematic approach makes him think that every appearance by Christ has a certain meaning, and he keeps on enumerating the number of appearances while commenting on John 20 and 21. So, for instance, John 21:,1 "Some time later, Jesus showed himself," refers to glory, because he appeared only sometimes; John 21:5, where Christ asks something to eat, refers to truth because of the *familiare convivium* between Christ and the Apostles (n. 2597). Finally, John 21:14, "This makes the third time that Jesus appeared," gives occasion for enumerating the number of appearances (n. 2613; cf. n. 2525) by quoting Augustine, just as in *ST* III, q. 55, a. 3, ad 3.

30. *Ioan.* 20, lect. 6, n. 2557; *ST* III, q. 54, a. 4. The text is from *De Symbolo ad Catechum.* II 8.

31. For an interpretation of this text and its biblical allusions, see Valkenberg, *Words of the Living God*, 99–100 n. 160.

32. See ibid., nn. 158 and 159.

their bodies bear these wounds in the state of beatitude? "Yes," Augustine answers, "but they will appear as signs not of defects but of dignity." Although this second question is not directly connected with the body of Christ, Aquinas quotes it in the same context as the previous quotation from Augustine.[33] This order of quotations, which can be complemented by many others, seems to indicate that Aquinas had his commentary on John 20 in his mind when he wrote his theology on the resurrection of Christ in his *Summa*. It also indicates that quotations from the Fathers often function as a bridge between Aquinas's commentaries on Scripture and his systematic-theological works.

Finally, I would like to point out that Aquinas's *Commentary on John* on John 20–21 not only influenced his systematic theology, but also influenced him in the third task of a theological Master, next to reading and discussing Scripture, namely preaching Scripture.[34] At some places in Aquinas's commentaries on Scripture, one may find short *collationes,* schemes for sermons consisting of *distinctiones* and *auctoritates.* Here, Aquinas probably used his commentary on Scripture for one of his sermons. To end this essay, I want to show you such a *collatio* that might have been used for a sermon on the feast of St. Peter or for a sermon *ad praelatos:* to those who bear responsibility in the Church. With reference to John 21:15—"After breakfast, Jesus said to Simon Peter, 'Simon son of John, do you love me more than all else?' 'Yes, Lord,' he answered, 'you know that I love you.' 'Then feed my lambs', he said"—Aquinas (*Ioan.* 21, lect. 3, n. 2616) distinguishes three things necessary for a superior in the Church: obedience, knowledge, and grace. But above all, love is necessary. Aquinas not only takes the opportunity to distinguish between several kinds of love that a superior in the Church should have, but also tells us how we should elect such a superior. This is just a little example that shows that Aquinas's commentary on John 20–21 is connected not only with his systematic theology on the resurrection of Christ, but also with his other duties as Master of the sacred Page, including his preaching office. In a certain sense, preaching is another way of reading Scripture, as reading the Scriptures should influence one's life, as Stephen Fowl has made clear in his beautiful book *Engaging Scripture*.[35] I find the theological reading of Scripture by Thomas Aquinas convincing not only because he points to the theo-

---

33. *ST* III, q. 54., a. 4. The quotation is from XXII *De Civitate Dei*.

34. *Legere, disputare, praedicare (Scripturam):* these were the tasks of a *Magister in sacra Pagina;* see Torrell, *Initiation à saint Thomas d'Aquin,* 79.

35. Fowl, *Engaging Scripture* (Oxford: Blackwell, 1998).

logical depth of St. John's Gospel, but also because he is aware that a theological reading of Scripture cannot be limited to one's study. If I want to read Scripture theologically as a Christian, I have to make this reading of Scripture inform my life as a Christian. The encounter between Christ and his disciples should become my encounter with Christ, mediated by John and Thomas Aquinas.

PART 6

Church and Sacraments

SEVENTEEN

"That the Faithful Become the Temple of God"

The Church Militant in Aquinas's *Commentary on John*

FREDERICK CHRISTIAN BAUERSCHMIDT

 Where *did* Thomas Aquinas put his ecclesiology? Theologians today generally accept the claim that Thomas has no "ecclesiology" as we would understand that term, by which I mean that he never takes up the Church as a distinct locus for comprehensive theological discussion.[1] Did the famously absent-minded saint simply misplace it? One searches the *Summa theologiae* in vain for a treatise *de ecclesiae*.[2] The situation seems even less promising in his *Commentary on the Gospel of St. John*, where the commentary genre itself does not tend to the systematic treatment of anything. Yet this does not mean that Thomas's commentary has nothing to do with the Church. In his introduction to the *Lectura*, Thomas writes, "The end of this Gospel is also clear, and it is that the faithful become the temple of God and be filled with the majesty of God; and so John says below (20:31), 'These things are

---

1. See, *inter alia*, George Sabra, *Thomas Aquinas's Vision of the Church: Fundamentals of an Ecumenical Ecclesiology* (Mainz: Matthias-Grünewald-Verlag, 1987), 19.

2. This of course begs the question of whether any of the so-called treatises of the *Summa* are intended to be comprehensive treatments. For example, if the discussion of the Trinity in the first part is supposed to be comprehensive, it is decidedly lopsided, focusing entirely on the intra-Trinitarian processions and relations and giving scant attention to the missions (or, to use modern terminology, focusing on the "immanent Trinity" to the detriment of the "economic Trinity"). For a balanced discussion of the Trinity, one must also take into account, *inter alia*, the discussions of the incarnation in the third part and of the gifts of the Spirit in the second part. See Herwi Rikhof, "Aquinas's Authority in the Contemporary Theology of the Trinity" in *Aquinas as Authority*, ed. Paul van Geest, Harm Goris, and Carlo Leget (Leuven: Peeters, 2002), 213–34.

written so that you may believe that Jesus is the Christ, the Son of God'" (*Ioan.* prol., n. 10).³ In what follows, I wish to argue that Thomas's reading of John's Gospel is one that is throughout concerned with the "edification" or "upbuilding" of the Church as a community of disciples who follow the risen Lord—what Thomas and the tradition typically call "the Church militant."⁴ Indeed, Thomas sees John's aim in writing his Gospel to be the formation and hallowing of that community. Further, Thomas's own purpose in writing his *Commentary on John* is the continuing formation of a community of disciples.

While Aquinas did not think the Church theologically uninteresting, he also does not appear to have approached it as a topic to be treated systematically. Rather, he saw theological reflection on the Church to be what we might call an "occasional" enterprise, something to be discussed as need arose, but not itself a major topic of discussion.⁵ Remarks about the Church are scattered throughout the *Summa theologiae,* cropping up in some obvious places (e.g., the discussion of the sacraments in the third part) and in some not so obvious ones (e.g., the discussion of duties and states of life that concludes the second part). One must therefore do a bit of excavating and piecing together in order to come up with anything like what we would call an ecclesiology.

This is no less true in Aquinas's *Commentary on John.* Indeed, his remarks on the Church are here, if anything, *more* occasional, prompted as they are by the specific requirements of textual exposition. If one combs through the text looking for references to the Church, the result seems like nothing more than an unpromising pile of scraps: a remark from the story of the Wedding at Cana of Galilee, bits from the Last Supper discourse, and so on. Perhaps it is possible to cobble these together into some sort of ecclesiology, particularly if one were to supplement them with bits from the *Summa theologiae.* But is that the best this text has to offer?

While the scattered remarks Aquinas makes about the Church in the *Commentary on John* are not without interest, one must look at his overall in-

---

3. English translations are from St. Thomas Aquinas, *Commentary on the Gospel of St. John,* trans. Weisheipl and Larcher.

4. In this essay I am concerned primarily with the Church militant and not the Church suffering (the souls in Purgatory) or the Church triumphant (the saints and angels).

5. On the "occasional" nature of Aquinas's ecclesiology, see Nicholas M. Healy, *Church, World and the Christian Life: Practical-Prophetic Ecclesiology* (Cambridge: Cambridge University Press, 2000), 56–58. In this entire essay I am much in debt to Healy's "practical-prophetic" approach to ecclesiology for helping me to understand what Thomas is up to in his *Commentary on John.*

"That the Faithful Become the Temple of God" 295

terpretation of the narrative if one wishes to fully grasp what he has to say about the nature of the Church. And the first thing that one must see is that for Thomas the whole purpose of John's Gospel is not simply the conversion of individuals, but the edification and sanctification of the Church as the new temple of Jesus' body.[6] In his comments on John 2:19–21—"Destroy this temple, and in three days I will raise it up"—Aquinas refers to Origen's ecclesiological interpretation of the "Temple" in this passage, and goes on to note that, interpreted in this way, the "three days" refer to three phases of divine pedagogy: the law of nature, the written law, and the law of grace (*Ioan.* 2, lect. 3, n. 404).[7] It is through this process of pedagogy that God forms his household, "built upon the foundation of the apostles and prophets, with Christ Jesus himself as the cornerstone" (Eph 2:19–20). One might say that, through this threefold pedagogy (i.e., the natural law, the old law, and the new law), God creates and hallows a space within the fallen world in which an acceptable sacrifice—doing good, seeking justice, rescuing the oppressed, defending the orphan, pleading for the widow—can be offered to God.[8]

Thus when Aquinas says that John's purpose in writing his Gospel "is that the faithful become the temple of God," he is indicating that the ecclesiological importance of John's Gospel (and of his commentary on it) is found not so much in what it says about the Church, but in the way in which the Gospel (and his commentary) function as a means of ecclesial edification for the Church militant. In fact, the Gospel is not really *about* the Church at all; Thomas says that the "matter" of the Gospel is the humanity and divinity of

---

6. George Sabra's survey of ecclesiological images and metaphors in Aquinas (*Thomas Aquinas's Vision of the Church*, 34–71) mentions "temple" only in passing (40) and focuses on *congregatio fidelium* and *corpus mysticum* as the dominant descriptions of the Church (69). While his comments are accurate of Aquinas's work as a whole, they do not take into account the importance that a particular terminology (i.e., temple) might have in a particular context (a commentary on John).

7. See Origen's *Commentary on John* 10.20 ("Now, both of these two things, the temple and the body of Jesus, appear to me, in one interpretation at least, to be types of the Church, and to signify that it is built of living stones, a spiritual house for a holy priesthood, built on the foundation of the Apostles and prophets, Christ Jesus being the head corner-stone; and it is, therefore, called a temple"), which Aquinas excerpts in the *Catena Aurea*. See *Catena Aurea: Commentary on the Four Gospels Collected out of the Works of the Fathers by Thomas Aquinas*, vol. 4: *St. John*, trans. John Henry Newman (London: Saint Austin Press, 1997 [1841]), 98. As far as I have been able to determine, the interpretation of the three days as three phases of ecclesial pedagogy come not from Origen, but from Aquinas himself, perhaps reflecting a particular Dominican interest in teaching.

8. See Isaiah 1:16–17. Thomas says in *ST* II-II, q. 188, a. 2: "those services which we render to our neighbor, in so far as we refer them to God, are described as sacrifices." In the *Commentary on John*, he quotes Isaiah 1:16 in his discussion of the cleansing of the temple (*Ioan.* 2, lect. 2, n. 389).

Christ (*Ioan.* prol., n. 10).⁹ But the *goal* of the Gospel is the formation of the Church as a community of disciples, a goal that is achieved through the proclamation of the humanity and divinity of Jesus.

One might object that, however important Aquinas thinks the Church is, such an interpretation of his commentary is trying a bit too hard; that a much more obvious approach is to begin where Aquinas begins, with John as the contemplative *par excellence.* Comparing John to the other evangelists, Thomas notes that whereas they instruct us on the active life (or, as he also puts it, about the humanity of Jesus), John in addition instructs us on the contemplative life (or, as he also puts it, about the divinity of Christ) (*Ioan.* prol., nn. 1, 9). Whereas the other evangelists are symbolized by such earth-bound figures as an ox, a lion, and a human being, John's symbol is a lofty eagle, which flies, "above the cloud of human weakness and looks upon the light of unchanging truth with the most lofty and firm eyes of the heart" (*Ioan.* prol., n. 11). Thus John's Gospel is, in Thomas's eyes, preeminently a *contemplative* text: a text that is the fruit of and food for contemplation.

I have no counter-objection to any of this, provided we guard against the resonances that the word "contemplation" has in modern ears. Particularly as used in the religious context, contemplation (and its cousin "mysticism") is often portrayed as a universal, trans-confessional phenomenon practiced by individuals who are connected only accidentally to any particular religious tradition or body. Therefore it ought to be stressed that this is emphatically *not* what Aquinas means by contemplation. The contemplative life is not equivalent to some sort of non-ecclesial "mysticism." To be a contemplative is to have a particular role within the Christian community. If we understand what is entailed in this state of life, we can begin to see how this "contemplative" Gospel is also an "ecclesial" Gospel.

On the one hand, contemplation is inextricably intertwined with the sacramental and ascetical activities of the Church. Indeed, Aquinas associates the perfection of John's contemplation with "moral science" (*Ioan.* prol., n. 9); one cannot know God without a comprehensive reshaping of the affections through sacraments and ascesis.[10] In this regard, one might say that John's contemplation is "perfect" because it does not separate knowledge and love. On the other hand, the most perfect religious state is not that of the contemplative who knows and loves God, but rather that of the teacher who

---

9. As the late Hans Frei put it, Jesus Christ, not the Church, is the "ascriptive subject" of the narrative.
10. See *ST* II-II, q. 180, a. 2.

seeks actively to share that knowledge with others. As Thomas says in the *Summa theologiae*, "even as it is better to enlighten than merely to shine, so it is better to give to others the fruits of one's contemplation than merely to contemplate."[11] In the *Commentary on John*, Thomas harmonizes the story of Mary of Bethany anointing Jesus in John 12:3 with Mark 14:3 and Matthew 26:7, to depict Mary (who traditionally represents the contemplative life) anointing both the head and the feet of Jesus. Commenting on this dual anointing, Thomas says, "one who honors Christ himself anoints the head of Christ; and one who serves his faithful anoints our Lord's feet" (*Ioan.* 12, lect. 1, n. 1599).[12] For Thomas, John's purpose in writing his Gospel is identical with the purpose of any good Dominican's preaching: to share the fruits of contemplation. Thus, in Thomas's view, John cannot be described simply as a "contemplative," but as a particular kind of contemplative: a teacher of sacred doctrine—that is, one who initiates others into God's own self-knowing by initiating them into the evangelical language of the Christian community. As Thomas puts it, John's office was "to give testimony" (*Ioan.* 21, lect. 6, n. 2654).

Therefore there is no problem with accepting Aquinas's portrayal of John as a contemplative and still maintaining that the overall purpose of both the Gospel and Thomas's *Commentary on John* is the formation of the community of Christian disciples. Certainly part of what it means to be a disciple of Jesus is to seek always to fix him in one's vision, so that one may ever more faithfully follow him. Certainly what makes the shared life of Christians possible is not superficial friendliness but rather the shared experience of prayer. In this sense, the vocation of the contemplative is absolutely central to the life of the Church; it is the contemplative vision that sees the temple not made with hands (2 Cor 5:1; Heb 9:11) after which the Church militant is patterned.

It is not without purpose that Aquinas begins his *Commentary on John* with an exegesis of the opening verse of Isaiah's vision in the temple: "I saw the Lord seated on a high and lofty throne, and the whole house was full of his majesty, and the things that were under him filled the temple."[13] He reads

---

11. *ST* II-II, q. 188, a. 6.

12. This interpretation is not found in either Augustine or Chrysostom, the two chief sources Aquinas draws on in his commentary, nor can it be found in any of the other patristic sources collected in the *Catena aurea*. What we seem to have here is a novel interpretation by Thomas that reflects his concern to commend the Dominican mode of life.

13. Aquinas returns to this text in passing in the penultimate paragraph of the *Commentary on John* (*Ioan.* 21, lect. 6, n. 2659).

this as coming from the mouth of John the evangelist and attesting to the height, fullness, and perfection of John's contemplation.[14] What is perhaps of greater interest is this identification of John and Isaiah. Isaiah—whose vision of God's glory in the temple is the occasion for his call to bring the message of God's judgment and consolation to the people of Israel—is the typological prefiguring of John—whose encounter with God's glory in the Word made flesh is the foundation of his proclamation to the Church of the judgment passed by that incarnate glory. Isaiah speaks of the "days to come" when "the mountain of the Lord's house shall be established as the highest of the mountains, and shall be raised above the hills; [and] all the nations shall stream to it" (Is 2:2). John speaks of the "hour" when Jesus was lifted up in his glorification on the cross, as it were "raised above the hills" so as to draw all people to himself (cf. Jn 12:32). Isaiah looks to the future and John looks to the past, but both bear witness to the same thing: the day of Zion's lifting up and the gathering of the nations at the temple of true sacrifice.

What does it mean to speak of John and Isaiah "bearing witness" (see Jn 21:24)? While Aquinas does speak of John's apostolic office as one of "witness" (e.g. *Ioan.* 21, lect. 6, n. 2654), more typically he speaks simply of "teaching." John, like Christ, is first and foremost a teacher. However, as in the case of what Thomas means by "contemplation," modern readers must be careful not to misunderstand what he means by "teaching": to modern ears it has quite misleading, overly cognitive, connotations. In particular, we cannot identify Thomas's use of "teaching" with the modern notion of a detached imparting of information, in which the teacher is, or should be, separable from what is taught. When a nineteenth-century liberal such as Harnack presents Jesus as a teacher of the "higher righteousness," this is precisely in order to separate the *person* of Jesus from the *content* of his teaching. This is clearly not what Thomas means when he speaks of Jesus in the *Summa* as "the most excellent of teachers."[15] For, as he says in the *Commentary on John,* "the doctrine [i.e., teaching] of the Father is the Son himself" (*Ioan.* 7, lect. 2, n. 1037).[16]

Teaching is always a self-involving activity. Particularly in the case of one who teaches a "way" of life, the greatness of a teacher is judged by how fully

---

14. Speaking specifically of the phrase "the things that were under him filled the temple," Aquinas says that these "things" are the sacraments of his humanity, which fill the faithful, "who are the temple of God" (*Ioan.,* prol., n. 8).

15. *ST* III, q. 43, a. 4.

16. On *doctrina* as an activity rather than a "thing," see the comments of Jean-Pierre Torrell, *Le Christ en ses mystères: la vie et l'œuvre de Jésus selon saint Thomas d'Aquin,* vol. 1 (Paris: Desclée, 1999), 242.

he or she embodies the teaching.[17] Indeed, Jesus is the best of all teachers precisely because he quite simply *is* the content of his teaching. Commenting on John 14:6, where Jesus says, "I am the way," Thomas writes, "Christ is the way to arrive at the knowledge of the truth, while still being the truth itself" (*Ioan.* 14, lect. 2, n. 1868). Similarly, the effectiveness of teaching is judged not so much by the quantity of information absorbed as it is by the degree to which the truth embodied in the teacher comes to be embodied in the pupil. If Christian teaching is instruction in a certain way, it cannot be said to be learned until one actually follows this way.[18] So to speak of Jesus or John or Aquinas himself as a teacher is not to imply a disengaged communication of information. "Teaching" must always be placed within the martyriological context of bearing witness with one's life in order to form others to bear witness with their lives. Christian teaching is about the formation of disciples; it is about the "edification" or "building" of God's temple.[19]

If we wish to see what Aquinas has to say about the formation of disciples in the *Commentary on John,* we ought to look first at some of what he says about that "most excellent of teachers," Jesus. In his commentary, Thomas repeatedly stresses that Jesus' teaching is a comprehensive project of formation in which both his words and his actions are of crucial importance (e.g., nn. 1555, 1652, 1781, 1870). In the case of Jesus, teaching by example is particularly

---

17. At one point Thomas speaks of "two things which are necessary for preachers if they are to lead others to Christ. The first is clear, orderly speech. . . . The second is virtue, manifested in good actions" (Ioan. 12, lect. 4, n. 1634). We ought to note, however, that the necessity of the teacher embodying the truth applies primarily when one is teaching a "way of life." It obviously is not true, for example, when teaching basic math concepts, precisely because we don't normally think of there being a "mathematical way of life."

18. Here I am putting forward a version of what Bruce Marshall describes as a "weak pragmatic thesis." One's claim to have learned the Christian "way" can be *dis*proved by a failure of practice, though successful practice is not itself sufficient proof that one has learned it. My claim is slightly different from the one Marshall himself examines, which has to do with the justification of Christian truth claims themselves. For a contrast between "strong" and "weak" versions of the pragmatic thesis, see *Trinity and Truth* (Cambridge: Cambridge University Press, 2000), 182–91. In terms of Thomas's own way of putting things, Christian teaching (i.e., *sacra doctrina*) has as its ultimate aim the communication of "formed faith." This is not to say that faith without love is nothing, but it is not what Christian teaching aims at.

19. The Dominican ideal, articulated by Fra Humbert of Romans, general of the order during Thomas's lifetime, was *docere verbo et exemplo:* to teach by word and example. This meant that Dominicans saw their total deportment as part of their preaching, and consequently that their formation as Dominicans was as much, if not more, focused on bodily practices as it was on the conveying of information. For an example of this, see the discussion of how the iconography in the novices' cells at the convent of San Marco in Florence was key in this "bodily" formation in William Hood, *Fra Angelico at San Marco* (New Haven: Yale University Press, 1993), 200–207.

fitting, since the union of humanity and divinity in Jesus means that the truth about God that Jesus wishes to teach is embodied in his human deeds and suffering. Referring to Jesus' saying, "I am the way, and the truth, and the life," Thomas notes, "[Christ] is the way by reason of his human nature, and the destination [i.e., truth and life] because of his divinity. . . . Christ is the way to arrive at the knowledge of the truth, while still being the truth itself" (*Ioan.* 14, lect. 3, n. 1868).

One might describe the teaching that is Jesus' life as a "theandric" performance, in which his divine person is both communicated and received in a pattern of human action and passion.[20] Commenting on Jesus' invitation to the two disciples of John the Baptist to "come and see" where he lives (Jn 1:39), Thomas notes that he issues this invitation "because the dwelling of God, whether of glory or grace, cannot be known except by experience: for it cannot be explained in words" (*Ioan.* 1, lect. 15, n. 292). Regarding Jesus' words in John 14:4, "where I am going you know, and the way you know," Thomas comments, "they knew the Father through Christ, and they knew Christ by living with him" (*Ioan.* 14, lect. 2, n. 1864). Not only does Jesus teach the truth of God by example, but also his disciples learn by imitating that example. Therefore, knowing the truth of God is not something in addition to the life of discipleship—as it were, a kind of reward for faithfulness. Rather, in the faithful following of Jesus through imitation of his example, the truth of God is embodied in the life of the disciple. Thomas quotes Augustine: "Walk like this human being and you will come to God" (*Ioan.* 14, lect. 2, n. 1870).[21]

But how does one "walk like this human being"? Certainly Aquinas is not suggesting that we can simply slap on our "What Would Jesus Do?" wristbands and step out into the life of discipleship. The imitation of Christ is central to Thomas's understanding of the Christian life and discipleship, but he also knows that we must discern *which* of Jesus' actions are exemplary in a given circumstance and *how* they are to be imitated. Key to this discernment is the practice of Christian teaching within a structured community of teachers and learners, all of whom seek to be disciples, taught by Jesus and the Spirit.

---

20. On Jesus' "theandric activity" see *ST* III, q. 19, a. 1, ad 1; on his "action and passion" (*acta et passa*) see the end of the prologue to the *Tertia pars* and the comments of Jean-Pierre Torrell, O.P., *Le Christ en ses mystères*, 15.

21. One ought also to note the role of the Spirit in this. Thomas writes, "since the Holy Spirit is from the Truth [i.e., Christ], it is appropriate that the Spirit teach the truth, and make those he teaches like the one who sent him" (Ioan. 16, lect. 3, n. 2102 [Weisheipl and Larcher, Part 2, 443]).

The communal life of discipleship is non-negotiable as the context for Christian teaching and learning. Aquinas says that we ought to imitate the disciples who gathered in the upper room on the evening of Easter and on Pentecost, "for Christ came to them when they were united together, and the Holy Spirit descended on them when they were united together, because Christ and the Holy Spirit are present only to those who are united in charity" (*Ioan.* 20, lect. 4, n. 2529). If the teaching activity of the Church is to manifest the ongoing teaching of Christ and the Spirit, and not simply be our best guess about what Jesus would do, then it must occur within a community of disciples to whom Christ and the Spirit are present. Thomas writes that "all who are in the Church are taught, not by the apostles nor by the prophets, but by God himself" (*Ioan.* 6, lect. 5, n. 944). We see here a certain circularity in which the fitting context for the teaching of Christ and the Spirit is the community that is itself established by that teaching. Just as Christ is both the "way" and the "destination" for Christians, the Church militant is both the means and the goal of the edification of disciples.

Further, the Church is understood by Aquinas as a community united in love.[22] The language of "the Church militant" may conjure for some today the image of crusaders cleaving the heads of infidels with cries of *Christus est Dominus*, but this is not what Thomas means.[23] He writes, "anyone who wants to be in the army of Christ should be stamped with the emblem of charity," since "the special sign of a disciple of Christ is charity and mutual love" (*Ioan.* 13, lect. 7, n. 1839). Thomas's injunction that preachers should "go forward in charity within the unity of the Church" (*Ioan.* 21, lect. 1, n. 2582) is less about guarding one's theological orthodoxy than it is about having one's teaching emerge from the context of unity in love that is a sign of the presence of Christ and the Spirit. Even more than this, the unity in love of the community of disciples is an icon of the love shared by Father, Son, and Holy Spirit. Thomas says, "our unity resembles that of the divine nature, by which the Father and the Son are one. . . . That is why we are invited to imitate divine love: 'Be imitators of God, as beloved children, and walk in love, as Christ loved us' [Eph 5:1]" (*Ioan.* 17, lect. 5, n. 2240; cf. 17, 3, n. 2214).

22. George Sabra writes, "If one were to study all of Thomas' ecclesiological statements in all of his writings with the intention of discovering which mark of the Church occupied him most, the result would be quite clear: unity" (*Thomas Aquinas's Vision of the Church*, 70).

23. The reference to the crusader is obviously a reference to the now famous (or notorious) example given by George Lindbeck in his book *The Nature of Doctrine* (Philadelphia: Westminster Press, 1984). For a subtle discussion of the issues regarding truth, meaning, and the justification of truth claims raised by the example, see Bruce Marshall, *Trinity and Truth*, 191–204.

The unity in love of the community of disciples is itself a preaching of God's nature as a community of love.

If the communal life of disciples as a unity in charity is to be a preaching of God's nature as love, then it must be an empirical reality, discernible through and fostered by concrete practices. Part of the point of a temple is to order and make holy the space around it through its visible presence. Though Aquinas will speak of Christ's mystical body as comprising "the predestined, the called, and the sanctified" (*Ioan.* 6, lect. 7, n. 972), this should not be confused with the view that the true Church of Christ is an invisible fellowship of believers. The Church is ultimately that friendship between human beings made possible through friendship with God, and, as Thomas notes, "it is of the very nature of friendship that it is not imperceptible; otherwise, it would not be friendship, but merely good will" (*Ioan.* 13, lect. 7, n. 1837). So if the friendship of disciples with each other in God is to be genuine, it must have some practices that are visible markers.

The key practices are sacramental ones, just as the chief activity of the Temple on Mount Zion was the worship of Israel's God through the offering of sacrifice. It is through the sacraments, as Thomas puts it (quoting 1 John 4:16), that the Church militant "abides in God" and that the grace of Christ given through the Spirit "proliferates" (*Ioan.* 20, lect. 4, n. 2539; cf. 6, 8, n. 993). In particular, the Eucharist, which Thomas calls "the Church's meal" (*Ioan.* 21, lect. 2, n. 2599) and "the food of harmony" (*Ioan.* 6, lect. 7, n. 966), is "a food capable of making man divine and inebriating him with divinity" not only because it contains and signifies Christ, but also because it signifies the unity in love of the mystical body (*Ioan.* 6, lect. 7, n. 972). Sacramental actions are irreplaceable precisely because they make clear that the mutual love that is the special sign of Christ's disciples is never a human achievement, something that the Church can make itself be, but is always fundamentally something received.[24] The sacraments, adapted as they are to our normal means of learning through the sensual apprehension of material objects (see *Ioan.* 3, lect. 1, n. 443), also have a pedagogical function; they not only display but also engender the unity in love of Jesus' disciples. They are a means by which Christ and the Spirit make the community of disciples a visible reality.

But as irreplaceable as sacramental actions are, they are not sufficient of themselves for the edification of the community of disciples. This can be seen

---

24. Speaking of the "Church's meal," Aquinas says, "The ministers of the Church should also bring something to this meal; but whatever it is, it has come from God" (*Ioan.* 21, lect. 2, n. 2599).

in Thomas's own distinction between "sacramental eating" and "spiritual eating" in the Eucharist.[25] While Thomas in no way denies that anyone who receives the sacrament of the Eucharist truly receives the body and blood of Christ by way of "sacramental eating," he just as clearly maintains that this is something different from the "spiritual eating" of Christ. He writes, "that person eats the flesh of Christ and drinks his blood in a spiritual way who shares in the unity of the Church; and this is accomplished by the love of charity" (*Ioan.* 6, lect. 7, n. 969). Aquinas goes so far as to say "this sacrament has no effect on one who is insincere" (*Ioan.* 6, lect. 7, n. 976).

Does this appeal to "sincerity" amount to a retreat from visible markers of discipleship into an indiscernible interiority? I think not. While we may have a cultural aversion to passing judgment on anyone's sincerity, such judgment clearly is possible, though of course not infallible. The way in which we normally judge someone's sincerity is not by means of some special ability to see inner attitudes, but rather is by observing the entire ensemble of his or her visible actions. In particular, we can observe the coherence or incoherence of a person's behavior in the diverse spheres of life. The prophets of Israel pointed out that if one shows devotion to God in a ritual context but abuses God's "little ones" in the context of economic transactions, then one shows oneself to be insincere. Similarly, Aquinas notes that, at the Last Supper, "Judas, along with the other disciples, ate bread with Christ, even consecrated bread" (*Ioan.* 13, lect. 3, n. 1790), yet Judas's subsequent action of betrayal reveals the insincerity with which he eats that bread. Therefore we can make the judgment that he eats Christ's body sacramentally, but not spiritually.[26]

The insincerity with which Judas eats Christ's sacramental body is contrasted with Christ's total surrender of his life, displayed in the humility with which he washes his disciples' feet, even the feet of Judas (*Ioan.* 13, lect. 1, n. 1741). This action of washing feet is for Aquinas a kind of summing up of the total practice of Jesus that we are called to imitate. Thomas, following Augustine, commends the literal practice of footwashing itself, "for when a person

---

25. See, for example, *Ioan.* 6, lect. 7, n. 972. It is striking how blessedly free Aquinas is from any compulsion to constantly assert his Catholic orthodoxy on the question of the *ex opere operato* nature of sacramental actions. Perhaps this is because he lived in a time after the controversy over Berengar's teachings on the Eucharist and prior to the sixteenth-century debates, in which (apart from the Albigensians) this was not being seriously questioned, thus allowing Thomas to explore the "spiritual" dimension of the sacraments without worrying about compromising sacramental realism.

26. Of course this is, like all the Church's judgments, a penultimate one (what Julian of Norwich called "the lower doom"), subject itself to the eschatological judgment of God (what Julian called "the higher doom").

stoops down to the feet of his neighbor, humility is awakened in his heart, or if it is already there it is made stronger" (*Ioan.* 13, lect. 3, n. 1779).[27] At the same time, the power of this example, since it is "the example of the Son of God, which cannot be in error and is adequate for all situations" (*Ioan.* 13, lect. 3, n. 1781), extends beyond the specific action of washing feet to all of those practices that flow from the humility displayed and engendered by that action: "one who gives bread to the hungry washes his feet, as does one who practices hospitality, or gives food to one in need" (n. 1779). We might say that the Church militant is called to a comprehensive imitation of Jesus' example in the upper room, obeying not only his command to receive him through sacramental eating, but also his command to "wash each other's feet." Or, to put it in terms that are more familiar to us but would probably puzzle Thomas himself (since for him worship is an act of justice), the visible markers of the community of disciples are not only ritual ones but also ethical ones.

The visibility of the Church militant entails its concrete ordering as a community. This community is ordered *synchronically* according to various offices in the Church by which authority is exercised. While I think Thomas Gilby was correct in saying that Aquinas was less "clericalist" than many in his day (particularly the canonists), it is also clear that he saw the Church as a structured community in which some are given the office of teacher and can therefore teach with authority.[28] Indeed, the diversity of ecclesiastical offices "is for the beauty and completion of the Church" (*Ioan.* 6, lect. 5, n. 938; cf. 1, 4, n. 119) because they are the occasion for the decorous ordering of the community. In discussing the characteristics requisite for the pastoral office in the context of Peter's encounter with the risen Christ by the sea of Tiberius, Thomas quotes Aristotle's *Politics* to the effect that "it is the natural order of things that the one who cares for and governs others should be better" (*Ioan.* 21, lect. 3, n. 2619). This applies in the Church militant no less than in Aristotle's *polis*.

But we must also bear in mind that the Church is not the *polis*. What it means for Peter to be "better" is not for him to be Aristotle's magnanimous

---

27. Cf. Augustine, *Tractatus in Evangelium Iohannis* 58.4. There is something about that particular behavior, placed within the context of the story of Jesus, that has an almost sacramental power, even in cultures where it is not a normal custom. I suspect that, like many thirteenth-century mendicants, Thomas thought the greater danger lay not in following Jesus' example too literally, but in not following it literally enough.

28. Thomas Gilby, *St. Thomas Aquinas: Theological Texts* (London: Oxford University Press, 1955), 337, n. 1.

man, but for him to love Jesus as Jesus wishes to be loved. What this means gets unfolded in a variety of ways, much of it associated with Peter's denial of Jesus and subsequent forgiveness. Because he himself has denied Christ and been forgiven, Peter can be compassionate towards sinners (*Ioan.* 18, lect. 3, n. 2309). He has learned the depths of humility in not presuming even to know his own heart. Peter says to the risen Christ, "Lord, you know everything; you know I love you," and Thomas comments, "He is saying in effect: I do love you; at least I think I do. But you know all things, and perhaps you know something else that will happen" (*Ioan.* 21, lect. 4, n. 2627). It is this humbled Peter to whom Jesus gives the task of leadership in the Church militant, precisely because in his humility he embodies what Christ taught by his example.

This community of disciples is ordered *diachronically* by the succession of apostolic office and by the normative status that the apostolic witness, as contained in Scripture, has in the process of communal discernment and teaching (*Ioan.* 21, lect. 6, n. 2656).[29] Aquinas scarcely mentions apostolic succession in the *Lectura,* though he seems to presume it in discussing Jesus' command to Peter, "Feed my lambs" (*Ioan.* 21, lect. 3, nn. 2623–25). He shows more interest in the normativity of apostolic witness. For Thomas, the incarnation of the Word forms, as it were, the hinge upon which history turns, the point of reference that makes it possible to understand both what comes before and what follows. Thomas writes, "Christ's actions are in a way midway between the events of the Old Testament and of the New Testament. . . . Christ's actions are the rule and exemplar of the things that are done in the New Testament, and they were prefigured by the fathers of the Old Testament" (*Ioan.* 12, lect. 3, n. 1626). The event of the Word made flesh is to the Church as the Holy of Holies was to the Temple: it is that around which the structure is organized; it contains the "law" by which the people of God are sanctified.[30] Whether one is a prophet like John the Baptist who comes before, or an apostle like John the Evangelist who follows, the closer in time one is to this crucial event the more authoritative one's witness.[31] What this means for the synchronic structure of the community of disciples is that those who lead the community in discernment by virtue of pastoral office must always seek to teach in accord with the apostolic witness and in the manner of the apostles and prophets.

---

29. *ST* I, q. 1, a. 8, ad 2.
30. Note that Thomas says, "the Son himself is the commandment of the Father" (*Ioan.* 12, lect. 8, n. 1725).
31. See *ST* II-II, q. 174, a. 6.

Part of what teaching in the manner of the apostles means is attending to the narrative structure of the apostolic witness.[32] Just as Jesus speaks and acts not simply as a way of imparting information about God, but rather as a "theandric performance" of his divine personhood, so too John's gospel is an "evangelical performance" in which God's self-donation in the incarnation is re-presented to us—performed anew—in the gospel narratives. It is striking that Aquinas says that in his prologue John "insinuates" *(insinuat)* Christ's divinity, while in the remainder of the Gospel "he shows *(manifestat)* it by the things Christ did in the flesh" (*Ioan.* 1, lect. 1, n. 23).[33] Despite the prologue's clear declaration that "the Word was God," this remains an indirect stating, an insinuation of what can better be shown in the story of Jesus' action and passion. The narrative genre of the gospel is uniquely suited to the proclamation of this theandric performance because it is in what is said and done by and to Jesus of Nazareth that the self-diffusive goodness of God is communicated to us (see *ST* III, q. 1, a. 1). At the end of his *Commentary on John* Aquinas says, "to write about each and every word and deed of Christ is to reveal the power of every word and deed" (*Ioan.* 21, lect. 6, n. 2660). The gospel narrative is a conduit of the divine power of the words and deeds of Jesus.[34]

Of course one might well object to the attempt to claim that Aquinas has any interest in narrative at all, seeing this as simply an attempt to graft a once trendy theological category onto an unwilling recipient. Is not Thomas's approach to theology much more conceptual than narrative? It certainly seems that Aquinas goes to great lengths in the *divisio* that opens each lecture to dismember any narrative continuity in John's Gospel so that the following *expositio* may treat the text as a series of conceptual points.[35] In fact, Thomas so dismembers the narrative that it is very difficult, when reading Thomas's *Commentary on John,* to keep track of the story.

In response to this objection, let me make clear that the claim that Thomas is cognizant of and concerned with the narrative character of the

32. Bear in mind that even non-narrative apostolic writings, such as the letters of Paul, all presume the story of Jesus (even if they were written before the actual Gospel narratives). See Stephen Fowl, *The Story of Christ in the Ethics of Paul: An Analysis of the Function of the Hymnic Material in the Pauline Corpus* (Sheffield, England: JSOT Press, 1990), 198–202, especially 200 n. 1.

33. Weisheipl and Larcher's translation reads "states" for *insinuat,* but Thomas's typical use of this term indicates an indirect form of assertion.

34. In his *Commentary on Paul's Letter to the Romans,* Thomas says that "the Gospel itself contains the power of God." (*In Rom.,* n. 98). Cf. ibid., n. 100, where he seems to ascribe healing power to the very material on which the Scriptures are written.

35. See Valkenberg, *Words of the Living God,* 167.

apostolic witness is simply to say, first, that for him the claims made about Jesus' person are inseparable from the scriptural stories of "the things Christ did in the flesh" (*Ioan.* 1, lect. 1, n. 23) and, second, that the claims made by and for Jesus are unintelligible apart from the larger narrative structure of God's providence over creation.[36] It is not to claim that Thomas thinks that one can do theology simply by "telling stories" or that one does not need conceptual clarification. He is well aware that John's Gospel itself is not simply a chronicle of events; rather, it is a narrative that is structured in a particular way so as to convey a particular theological meaning. It is not simply an account of what Jesus said and did; it is an *interpreted* account that has a conceptual structure.[37] Thomas repeatedly shows us how John leads his readers through events so that they can avoid the conceptual (and moral) blind alleys and missteps that afflict Nicodemus, the Samaritan woman, Peter, and others in the story. As readers, we are not in the same position as the characters in the narrative because we have the benefit of John's interpretation of the events he recounts.

Likewise, in his *Commentary on John,* Thomas leads *his* students through John's narrative, helping them to avoid the missteps and blind alleys that have afflicted earlier readers of John's Gospel, such as Arius or Nestorius. At the same time, just as John's interpretation must adhere to the events he recounts, so too Thomas's commentary must adhere to John's interpretation of those events. The *divisio* that opens each lecture is not a peeling off of the narrative husk so as to reveal the conceptual kernel; rather, it is more like sketching a road map of the country ahead, so that we will not take a wrong turn or fail to attend to those parts of the landscape that previous pilgrims have considered most significant. Looking at the map is in no way a substitute for following on the journey itself. In other words, Thomas's commentary presumes readers already familiar with the narrative.

This process of commentary indicates that, while the apostolic witness of Scripture is normative, it continues to be interpreted by being reflectively lived out in the Church militant, which is a community of both saints and sinners. Referring to the story of Jesus calling Phillip, Aquinas says, "a disci-

36. See Thomas Hibbs, *Dialectic and Narrative in Aquinas: An Interpretation of the Summa Contra Gentiles* (Notre Dame, Ind.: University of Notre Dame Press, 1995), especially 30–34.

37. Not only does Thomas see John as offering a more "contemplative" narrative than the other three evangelists, he also shows an awareness that John might have ordered events in a particular way in order to make a particular point. See, for example, *Ioan.* 21, lect. 1, n. 2571, where Aquinas discusses John's reasons for telling the story of Jesus' appearance to the disciples beside the Sea of Tiberias after he seemed to have brought his Gospel to a conclusion.

ple's vocation is to follow" (*Ioan.* 1, lect. 16, n. 311). What John and Thomas are both trying to do is to teach us to be disciples of Jesus by faithfully "following" his story. The normative interpretive account of Jesus' example as contained in the Scriptures must be interpreted by the exemplary performance of the saints (*Ioan.* 18, lect. 4, n. 2321). In the diverse ways that disciples have followed this story, new light has constantly been shed on *how* to follow it in shifting contexts. For example, Thomas is able to confidently extend the application of Jesus' example of washing feet to included the spiritual and corporal works of mercy—forgiving our enemies, praying for them, practicing hospitality, giving food to one in need (*Ioan.* 13, lect. 3, n. 1779)—because this is how Jesus' example has been interpreted by the saints. It is attention to the lives of the saints, which we might think of as reading the "narrative" of the Holy Spirit, that makes the imitation of Christ something more than just the mechanical repetition of Jesus' actions.

The activity of continually identifying exemplary lives of holiness is crucial for the Church militant's ability to know what it means to "walk like this human being" in diverse contexts. Again, we have a kind of circularity: the holiness of the saint can be recognized only in the light of past examples, but at the same time each new saint sheds light on what the imitation of Christ looks like in his or her particular time and place. Thérèse of Lisieux's holiness is recognizable because of such predecessors as Theresa of Avila, but she also reveals what it means to be crucified with Christ in the age of modern atheism, when the world seems to obscure rather than reveal the presence of God. Maximilian Kolbe conforms in some ways to the pattern of the Christian martyr, while at the same time showing us what it means in the midst of the *shoah* to bear witness to Christ's work of breaking down the dividing wall between Jew and Gentile.

But of course the Church is not simply the Church of the saints; it is also the Church of sinners. Aquinas is startlingly blunt in his acknowledgment of the shortcomings of the Church. We find in him no attempt to distance an idealized Church from the flawed empirical Church.[38] In his allegorical interpretation of the storm that besets the disciples' ship (6:17–18), Thomas, citing Augustine, says that the storms that beset the ship are "the trials and persecutions which would afflict the Church due to a lack of love" (*Ioan.* 6, lect. 2, n. 879).[39] Whereas Augustine interprets this story in an apocalyptic context, seeing it as a prefiguring of the winnowing tribulations at the end of time,

---

38. The attempt to do this is a characteristic of what Nicholas Healy calls "blueprint ecclesiologies." See *Church, World, and the Christian Life,* 37–38.

39. Cf. Augustine, *Tractatus in Evangelium Iohannis* 25.5–6.

"That the Faithful Become the Temple of God" 309

Aquinas seems to see in it an allegory of the *current*—dare one say *persistent*—lack of love that besets the Church. When Thomas says that true friendship must be "not imperceptible" (*Ioan.* 13, lect. 7, n. 1837), his employment of the double negative shows an unblinking realism about life within the community of disciples (a realism perhaps born of his own experience in religious community), where human viciousness and vanity are sometimes held in check but never vanquished, where "affectionate" nicknames like "the dumb ox" are given. As Thomas says, the unity in love of the Church is not the perfected unity of the Church triumphant, but a "unity which is taking shape" (*Ioan.* 17, lect. 5, n. 2242).

But the failure to which the Church is subject reaches beyond mere lukewarmness in love; it reaches all the way to the betrayal of Christ. Regarding Jesus' saying, "truly, truly, I say to you, one of you will betray me," Aquinas notes, "He is careful to say, 'one of you,' i.e., one of those chosen for this holy society, so that we might understand that there would never be a society so holy that it would be without sinners and those who are evil" (*Ioan.* 13, lect. 4, n. 1799). While Thomas goes on to say that Jesus is reproving Judas and not the group as a whole, since "we should not think a group bad because one member is bad," he then adds, "although if several are bad the group could be considered bad." Thomas makes no attempt to distinguish between the "objective" holiness of the Church and the "subjective" sinfulness of her members. While one bad member does not make the Church as a whole evil, neither does the Church as a whole appear immune from implication in the evil of her members. The Church militant is, for Thomas, Christ's bride, wedded to him in the womb of the Virgin Mary (nn. 338, 518), but it is also an instance of "human society" (*Ioan.* 13, lect. 3, n. 1791), subject to the same risks as other human societies.[40] Thomas believes, of course, in the holiness of the Church: that the Church lives by grace and the promise of Jesus that the gates of hell shall not prevail against her. But this is something different from the view, heard these days in certain ecclesiastical circles, that, while *Christians* may sin, the *Church* cannot, because she is objectively holy in her structures and sacraments.[41] As we saw in looking at Thomas's views on sacramen-

---

40. This is the theme explored at great length by Hans Urs von Balthasar in his 1948 essay "Casta Meretrix" (i.e. "the chaste whore") in *Explorations in Theology II: The Spouse of the Word* (San Francisco: Ignatius Press, 1991), 193–288.

41. In his commentary on Matthew's Gospel, Thomas interprets the "gates of hell" verse (Matthew 16:18) in what seems at first glance a rather triumphalist manner, using it as an occasion to claim that while the Church of Constantinople had at times fallen into heresy, the Church founded on Peter—not just Rome but the whole Western Church—had not. But two things should be pointed out. First, Thomas's focus in this verse is doctrinal orthodoxy, not

tal and spiritual communion, the sacraments of the New Covenant are, absent love, as capable as the sacrifices of Israel of spiritual emptiness, of becoming an abomination in the eyes of God.[42] The same could be said of the other structures of the Church.

Though Thomas does not work out the details, his comments indicate that one can maintain belief in the holiness of the Church without positing a "Church itself" that is somehow other than the saints and sinners who make up the Church militant. And much is at stake in our ability to see the Church militant exemplified in her sinners as well as in her saints. If the Church, *as Church,* celebrates in the life and witness of Maximilian Kolbe the fruit of the tradition of the saints, ought it not also, *as Church,* repent of the life and witness of Christians who perpetrated the Holocaust as the fruit of the tradition of Christian anti-Jewish polemics? Ought not the Church be able to see in such sinners not simply the failure of individual Christians, but the failure of the community of disciples as a whole? If we cannot see this then we have blinded ourselves to the paradoxical light cast by our shadows and have deprived the community of disciples of the edification of repentance.

The final thing that must be said is that, for Thomas, while the end of the Gospel is the unbuilding of the faithful as the temple of God, the Church militant is not an end in itself. God's ultimate purpose is not the sanctification of the Church, but the blessing of creation as a whole. The community of disciples teaches and learns not simply for its own edification, but "so that the world might believe." If the world is to believe in the Gospel, then it must have some convincing reason to believe it to be true. Providing such a

---

sinfulness. Thomas's notion of unformed faith makes clear that one can believe and still sin. Second, when he comes to Matthew 16:23 ("get behind me Satan") he emphasizes Peter's constant need of grace in order to know the truth of Christ. In other words, while Thomas believes that the Church founded on Peter shall not have the gates of hell prevail against it, this belief is not couched in terms of a distinction between "the Church itself" and her members. See S. Thomae Aquinatis, *Super Evangelium S. Matthae, lectura,* P. Raphaelis Cai, O.P., ed. (Rome: Marietti, 1951), n. 1385 and n. 1504. Of course, just because Aquinas did not hold this view does not mean it is wrong. After all, Thomas did not believe that Mary was conceived without sin either. The distinction between the holy Church and her sinful members may be a case of genuine doctrinal development. I don't think it is, largely based on the reasons sketched in the next paragraph, but it cannot be ruled out *a priori* as a possibility. At the same time, perhaps Aquinas is an indication that one can have a robust doctrine of the holiness of the Church without making such a distinction.

42. In this regard, Catholic Christians would do well to ponder what Paul means when he tells the Corinthian Christians, "When you come together, it is not really to eat the Lord's supper" (1 Cor 11:20). We ought not let our fear of being accused of Donatism keep us from taking Paul with all seriousness.

reason is the task of the Church.⁴³ Aquinas writes, "Nothing shows the truth of the gospel better than the charity of those who believe" (*Ioan.* 17, lect. 5, n. 2241). The unity in love of the community of disciples is not simply to provide them with a foretaste of heaven. It is to be a light to the nations that displays the truth of God and awakens in others the desire for communion with God and each other. So we return to Isaiah's vision of the lifting up of Jerusalem and the pilgrimage of the nations. It is the fidelity of the people of God to the life of discipleship, a fidelity visibly displayed in their love for one another, that is the instrument by which the gospel is made credible in the eyes of the world.

But while the Church has the task of showing the truth of the gospel, it is of itself in no way adequate to this task. Aquinas is clear that the community of disciples is a thoroughly penultimate reality, possessed of a true but cloudy vision of the mystery it is called to embody. Thomas says, "we do see the kingdom of God and the mysteries of eternal salvation, but imperfectly" (*Ioan.* 3, lect. 1, n. 433). On the day when "the saying that is written will be fulfilled: 'Death has been swallowed up in victory'" (1 Cor 15:54), we will see face to face, and there will be no more need for the enigmatic seeing through signs that characterizes the Church militant.⁴⁴ And even prior to that day, the words of its stories are always exceeded by the Word of God; the boundaries of its identity are constantly being transgressed by God's will to save; its rituals and structures are but a pale image of the heavenly worship of the saints and angels who stand before the lamb.

This should not be taken as a slight to the significance of the Church, which is, after all, the temple filled with the majesty of God. But it is an indication of what it means for it to be filled with the majesty of God. It means that it is like Isaiah, blessed and afflicted with a vision that shakes the doorposts of the Temple, and called by God to proclaim his word. It is like Peter, who stands in all his inadequacy before the risen Lord and receives his command: feed my sheep. It is like St. Thomas, reduced to the silence of learned ignorance in the face of the mystery of God. Finally, it is like John, blessed above all the other apostles with a keen understanding, but in the end proclaiming only love. Thomas writes of John, "as an old man he was carried to the Church by his followers to teach the faithful. He taught only one thing: 'Little children, love one another.' This is the perfection of the Christian life" (*Ioan.* 21, lect. 5, n. 2653). This, we might say, *is* the majesty of God.

---

43. Of course, it is ultimately the task of the Spirit. The Church, however, is an instrumental cause.

44. *ST* III, q. 61, a. 4.

EIGHTEEN

"And They Shall All Be Taught by God"
Wisdom and the Eucharist in John 6

Michael Dauphinais

John 6 offers a unique view of Jesus Christ. It begins with a miracle of the loaves and fishes, continues with a miracle of Jesus walking on water, and then culminates with the bread of life discourse. Almost all biblical scholars and theologians recognize some connection between the miraculous multiplication of physical bread and the subsequent discourse on the bread of life. But what is the character of that living bread come down from heaven? Is the bread of life simply equivalent to Jesus' wisdom from on high, or is it the Eucharistic flesh of Jesus? Although some contemporary biblical scholars have seen these as mutually exclusive options, St. Thomas leads us to contemplate the inner connections of the mysteries of Incarnate Wisdom and the Eucharist.

RAYMOND BROWN'S BIFURCATION OF THE BREAD OF LIFE DISCOURSE: TO DISTINGUISH IN ORDER TO DIVIDE

The late Catholic biblical scholar Raymond Brown, in his magisterial two-volume commentary on John in the Anchor Bible Series, emphasizes the distinction between the sapiential (wisdom) and Eucharistic meanings of the overall bread of life discourse. Brown discerns in the present bread of life discourse two discourses that were later compiled together. Thus John 6:35–50 forms the original discourse. 6:51–58 is a later discourse on the bread of life. The first is primarily sapiential in character, although it may have some Eucharistic undertones. The latter is primarily Eucharistic.

The original discourse according to Brown—6:35–50—begins with Jesus saying, "I am the bread of life; he who comes to me shall not

"And They Shall All Be Taught by God" 313

hunger, and he who believes in me shall never thirst." The original discourse ends with Jesus saying, "This is the bread which comes down from heaven, that a man may eat of it and not die" (6:50). In this first discourse, to eat the bread of life is to believe in Jesus. As Jesus says in 6:47–48, "Truly, truly, I say to you, he who believes has eternal life. I am the bread of life." Jesus is the wisdom from on high who has come down from heaven so that by believing in him we may have eternal life. Brown argues that the meaning of this original discourse is primarily sapiential.

Brown sees in John 6:51–58 a different discourse. Here Jesus begins by saying, "I am the living bread which came down from heaven; if any one eats of this bread, he will live for ever; and the bread which I shall give for the life of the world is my flesh." Brown admits that this second discourse is clearly Eucharistic in tone. The bread here signifies the Eucharistic flesh of Jesus. "Truly, truly, I say to you, unless you eat the flesh of the Son of man and drink his blood, you have no life in you" (6:53). This second discourse, according to Brown, ends with the verse, "He who eats me will live because of me. This is the bread which came down from heaven; he who eats this bread will live for ever" (6:58).

In both discourses, consuming the bread come down from heaven results in eternal life. In the first discourse, the bread of life is simply Jesus himself and his teaching. In the second discourse, the bread of life is clearly the Eucharistic flesh of Jesus. Brown argues that since the sapiential and Eucharistic means are divergent, that what we now see as one discourse was originally two. Brown goes so far to hypothesize that the second, overtly Eucharistic discourse stemmed from a tradition within the Johannine community about the Last Supper of Jesus with his disciples. Such a hypothesis about where the second discourse originally came from cannot be proved correct or false. But Brown clearly states that there is no way to interpret accurately the present discourse in John 6 as a united whole. What he has distinguished, Brown has no ability to unite.

OPTIONS AVAILABLE FROM ST. THOMAS

Since St. Thomas focuses his attention on the canonized form of the biblical text, he accepts the unity of the present form of the bread of life discourse. What kind of unity does he discern? Is it a false unity that denies some of the distinctive elements highlighted by Brown? For instance, does St. Thomas force an exclusively Eucharistic meaning on the whole text and thereby deny the importance of belief in Jesus as the divine revelation of God? Or does he harmonize the entire discourse to the acceptance of Jesus' teaching? As I will argue, St. Thomas does neither. Instead, he discerns fundamental interrelationship between the sapiential and the Eucharistic elements of John 6. I will identify three central themes for displaying this interrelationship. First, in his exegesis of the miracle of the loaves and fishes, St. Thomas shows how Jesus' teaching comes as spiritual food. Second, St. Thomas discerns in Jesus' initial teaching about the bread of life the necessity of the Incarnation in order for us to receive wisdom from on high. Third, St. Thomas teaches that the Eucharistic flesh must be received as divine wisdom to lead to eternal life.

The Multiplication of the Loaves as Symbolic of Jesus' Teaching

In John 6, Jesus initiates the multiplication of the loaves. He asks, "How are we to buy bread, so that these people may eat?" St. Thomas accepts that this question primarily concerns the fact that people were physically hungry for physical bread. Nevertheless, St. Thomas also sees the symbolism of the surface narrative in John. The question of how to refresh people physically leads, for St. Thomas, to the deeper question of how to refresh people spiritually. St. Thomas thus cannot get through the beginning of the multiplication of the loaves without speaking of the true wisdom that refreshes (*Ioan.* 6, lect. 1, n. 849). He quotes Sirach 15:3, "Wisdom will feed him with the bread of life and understanding."[1] St. Thomas thus interprets the miraculous multiplication of loaves in light of Jesus' mission to refresh us completely.

After commenting on the literal meaning of the loaves and fishes, St. Thomas shifts attention to its mystical meaning. Although his use of numbers may appear strange to our contemporary way of reading Scripture, it is clear St. Thomas uses number correlations to teach deeper theological points. The mystical meaning of the miraculous feeding, according to St. Thomas, is that no human wisdom will suffice to make man happy. Only Christ, the true wisdom of God, can bring us to a complete knowledge of the truth. When Phillip remarks, "200 denarii would not suffice [to feed the crowds]" (Jn 6:7), St. Thomas says that the number 100 symbolizes perfection. The number 200 symbolizes the double perfection necessary for wisdom—through both experience and contemplation. St. Thomas uses the number symbolism to state clearly our need for Christ: even the perfection of human wisdom would not suffice. When Andrew suggests a boy who has five barley loaves and two fishes, St. Thomas compares this to the Old Testament. The five loaves represent the five books of Moses; the two fishes, which give a

---

1. The RSV reads, "She will feed him with the bread of understanding" (Sir 15:3). It would appear that the context of John 6 colored St. Thomas's practice of quoting from memory—thus the insertion of the bread of life.

pleasant flavor to the bread, represent the teaching of the Psalms and the prophets. But Andrew remarks, "What are these among so many?" (Jn 6:9), mystically revealing that the teaching of the Old Law cannot bring man to a complete knowledge of the truth (*Ioan.* 6, lect. 1, n. 854). Again, St. Thomas uses the mystical meaning of the text as a means to instruct us that Christ alone can bring the perfection of wisdom. Even the fact that Christ uses the five loaves and the two fish for his miraculous feeding becomes an occasion for St. Thomas to teach that the Old Testament was good and that the New Testament is prefigured and contained in the Old.

St. Thomas interprets the symbolism of the miraculous feeding in a thoroughly sapiential way. Christ is the revelation of God, the true wisdom, who alone can completely satisfy the human creature.

The Necessity of the Incarnation for Us to Receive Wisdom— or Why Wisdom Must be Eucharistic

St. Thomas follows the narrative unity of John 6 as an interpretive key. After the miraculous feeding, the crowds seek to make Jesus king, but he flees from them. Eventually the crowds catch up with him, but Jesus gently admonishes them for following him simply because he filled their bellies with food. He says, "Do not labor for the food which perishes, but for the food which endures to eternal life, which the Son of Man will give you" (Jn 6:27). St. Thomas shows how Jesus lifts his listeners from desiring physical bread to working for spiritual bread; just as he did with the Samaritan woman at the well when he led her to consider the living water that quenches thirst forever (cf. Jn 4:13). St. Thomas does not exclusively identify this spiritual food with the Eucharist. Instead, he shows that this spiritual food has at least three meanings: first, "the food is God himself, insofar as he is the Truth which is to be contemplated and the Goodness to be loved"; second, "this food is the obedience to the divine commands: [as when Jesus says] 'my food is to do the will of him who sent me'"; third, it is Christ himself "insofar as the flesh of Christ is joined to the Word of God, which is the food by which the angels live" (*Ioan.* 6, lect. 3, n. 895). The spiritual food that leads to eternal life is God himself, our obedience to God, and the Incarnate Word.

According to St. Thomas, when Jesus says, "the food which endures to eternal life, which the Son of Man will give you" (6:27), Jesus' reference to himself as "the Son of Man" focuses our attention on the Incarnation. Why is the spiritual food that we need given to us through the Incarnation, which is obviously a physical reality? St. Thomas answers, "The Son of Man gives this good in a spiritual way, because human nature, weakened by sin, found spiritual food distasteful, and was not able to take it in its spirituality. Thus it was necessary for the Son of Man to assume flesh and nourish us with it: 'You have prepared a table before me' (Ps. 23:5)" (*Ioan.* 6, lect. 3, n. 897). Notice that St. Thomas speaks of both the Incarnation and the Eucharist here: "it was necessary for the Son of Man *to assume flesh and to nourish us with it.*" Sin has blocked us from receiving the true wisdom, who is God, in His spiritual nature. God becomes a man so that we can see his physical nature and so be led to contemplate his divine nature. Nevertheless, this sapiential meaning naturally leads to the Eucharistic meaning since St. Thomas says not only did the Son of Man assume flesh, but he also nourishes us with his flesh.

The mystery of the Incarnation leads into the mystery of the Eucharist. The Word becomes flesh so that we can perceive the Word in order to receive the Word. Then the Word feeds us with his assumed flesh so that we can receive the Word not only according to our intellectual nature, but also according to our physical nature. St. Thomas can hardly speak of the flesh of Christ without referring to both the Incarnation and the Eucharist. He writes, "the Word of God is especially called the bread of life" (*Ioan.* 6, lect. 4, n. 914). He then interprets the manna first as "bread of divine wisdom." The manna also signifies the flesh of Christ. St. Thomas observes that "manna" means "what is this?" He continues: "nothing is more a source of wonder than the Son of God made man. . . . It is also a cause for wonder how Christ can be present in the sacrament" (*Ioan.* 6. lect. 4, n. 914). When St. Thomas discusses the bread of life, we see that he holds together what he distinguishes. The bread of life is the Word of God. The bread of life is the Incarnate Word. The bread of life is the Eucharistic Word.

Why the Eucharist Must be Sapiential

St. Thomas distinguishes between the sapiential and the Eucharistic meanings of Jesus' words in John 6:51, "I am the living bread which came down from heaven; if any one eats of this bread, he will live for ever; and the bread which I shall give for the life of the world is my flesh." St. Thomas argues that the phrase "I am the living bread" pertains to the power of the Word, whereas the second part, "the bread which I shall give for the life of the world is my flesh" pertains to the sacrament of the Eucharist (*Ioan.* 6, lect. 6, n. 959). By maintaining this distinction, St. Thomas instructs us that the Eucharist cannot be understood apart from its connection to the Word of God. He states that Christ's body, sacramentally received, is life-giving because the flesh of Christ is united to the Word of God.

St. Thomas distinguishes the Word from the Eucharistic flesh in order to unite them in a proper understanding of the Eucharist. He draws upon a traditional distinction between receiving the Eucharist sacramentally and receiving it spiritually when he interprets John 6:55, "He who eats my flesh and drinks my blood abides in me, and I in him." To eat sacramentally is to receive the sacrament. To eat spiritually is to attain to the reality of the sacrament: Christ himself, primarily as his body, blood, soul, and divinity (both signified and contained) and secondarily as his mystical body (signified, but not contained). St. Thomas writes, "one eats his flesh and drinks his blood in a spiritual way if he is united to him through faith and love, so that one is transformed into him and becomes his member. . . . And so this is a food capable of making man divine and inebriating him with divinity" (*Ioan.* 6, lect. 7, n. 972). To eat sacramentally and spiritually is to receive more than merely Christ's flesh, but to receive Christ's divinity as well and so be transformed into Christ.

St. Thomas interprets Jesus' words in John 6:63, "It is the spirit that gives life, the flesh is of no avail," by means of a similar distinction between a material meaning and a spiritual meaning. To receive Christ's flesh in a material way would not give life since flesh in and of itself has no power to give eternal life—not even Christ's flesh. To receive Christ's flesh in a spiritual way, however, does give life because Christ's flesh is understood to be united to the Word and to the Spirit (*Ioan.* 6, lect. 8, nn. 992–93). The Eucharist cannot be separated from the revelation of God in Jesus Christ, which includes both his verbal teachings and his passion and death. St. Thomas clearly states this connection: "since this is the sacrament of our Lord's passion, it contains in itself the Christ who suffered. Thus, whatever is an effect of our Lord's passion is also an effect of this sacrament. For this sacrament is nothing other than the application of our Lord's passion to us" (*Ioan.* 6, lect. 6, n. 963). According to St. Thomas's interpretation of John 6, the Eucharist must be received in both a sacramental and a spiritual way—in other words, the Eucharist must be received in its fully sapiential reality.

CONCLUSION

While St. Thomas distinguishes the sapiential and Eucharistic elements of John 6, he also shows how each presupposes the other. Wisdom from on high requires that it can be received by fallen human beings; the reception of the Eucharistic flesh saves only insofar as it unites human beings to the eternal Word. Unlike some contemporary biblical scholars, we see that what St. Thomas distinguishes, he is also able to unite. The scholastic motto, "to distinguish in order to unite," is a motto that needs to be retrieved for contemporary theology of the Bible.

NINETEEN

The Role of the Apostles in the Communication of Revelation according to the *Lectura super Ioannem* of St. Thomas Aquinas

SERGE-THOMAS BONINO, O.P.

TRANSLATED BY TERESA BEDE AND MATTHEW LEVERING

 God does not need human beings. The First Cause has no need of secondary causes to accomplish his ends. In the government of the universe, however, God has recourse to secondary causes in order to communicate in a hierarchical way the perfections that he imparts to creatures and in order to bring them to himself. In particular, God employs intermediaries in order to communicate to spiritual creatures the perfection that is supernatural knowledge.

Now, as Dionysius says (Coel. Hier. iv), the divinely established law of such things is that they be revealed immediately by God to higher persons, through whom they are imparted to others, as is evident in the ordering of the heavenly spirits.[1]

The universal law of mediation rests on two fundamental principles dear to Aquinas. He makes reference to these principles when explaining, in regard to John 1:6, why the Light, which can manifest itself on its own, nevertheless wished to use witnesses (*Ioan.* 1, lect. 4, n. 119). The first is the metaphysical principle of the generosity of act. The more a subject is in act—that is to say the more being, perfection,

---

1. *ST* III, q. 55, a. 1: "Ut Dionysius dicit, in libro Caelest. Hier. [§3, PG 3, 181], haec est lex divinitus instituta, ut a Deo immediate superioribus revelentur, quibus mediantibus deferantur ad inferiores"; II-II, q. 172, a. 2. Cf. W. J. Hankey, "'Dionysius dixit, Lex divinitatis est ultima per media reducere': Aquinas, Hierocracy and the 'augustinisme politique,'" *Medioevo* 18 (1992): 119–50.

Role of the Apostles in the Communication of Revelation

and goodness it has—the more it tends to communicate itself. And the more it communicates itself, the more it assimilates to itself the object on which it exerts its influence, insofar as it makes it participate in its own dignity as cause. Therefore the sign that a subject has attained its perfection is its aptitude to produce another like itself and, more particularly, another acting subject. For example, a teacher is perfect when he is capable not only of instructing a disciple, but above all of making a teacher out of his student. This principle is applied analogically to natural agents and to free agents. It imposes upon the latter no strict necessity in the Neoplatonic manner. God freely employs the mediation of secondary causes, thereby manifesting his supreme liberality[2] and communicating to creatures a greater likeness of his perfection:[3]

> God wanted to have certain witnesses, not because he needed their testimony, but to ennoble those whom he appointed witnesses. Thus we see in the order of the universe that God produces certain effects by means of intermediary causes, not because he himself is unable to produce them without these intermediaries, but he deigns to confer on them the dignity of causality because he wishes to ennoble these intermediate causes. Similarly, even though God could have enlightened all men by himself and [led] them to a knowledge of himself, yet to preserve due order in things and to ennoble certain men, he willed that divine knowledge reach men through certain other men. "'You are my witnesses,' says the Lord" (Is 43:10). (*Ioan.* 1, lect. 4, n. 119)

The second principle that grounds the law of mediation is the requirement of a proportion between the cause and the effect. In the order of the communication of knowledge, this principle requires that the teacher place himself at the level of understanding of his students, in order to raise them bit by bit nearer to his level. In this way, he can, by pedagogical condescension, have recourse to the intermediaries nearest to the receiver of his teaching. The intermediaries receive knowledge from him and transmit it to the beneficiary in the most suitable way.

> [C]ertain men of weak understanding are unable to grasp the truth and knowledge of God by themselves. And so the Lord chose to come down to them and to enlighten certain men before others about divine matters, so that these others might obtain from them in a human way the knowledge of divine things they could not reach by themselves. (*Ioan.* 1, lect. 4, n. 119)[4]

---

2. Cf. *ST* I, q. 103, a. 6, and parallel places.

3. Cf. *In IV Sent.*, d. 24, q. 1, a. 1, qla 1: "Et ideo, ut in suis operibus repraesentaretur non solum secundum quod in se est, sed etiam secundum quod aliis influit, hanc legem naturalem imposuit omnibus, ut ultima per media perficerentur et media per prima, ut Dionysius dicit."

4. Cf. a similar notation of the same verse from St. Albert, which refers to Denys, *In Evangelium secundum Ioannem Expositio*, ed. Borgnet, *Opera omnia*, 24 (Paris, 1899), 41.

The law of mediation, as a general structure of Thomas's thought, profoundly illumines his theological reflection on the role of the apostles in the communication of *sacra doctrina,* of supernatural and salvific knowledge.[5]

The Teacher *par excellence,* the chief mediator in the order of supernatural knowledge, is the incarnate Word, Jesus Christ.[6] "No one has ever seen God; the only Son, who is in the bosom of the Father, he has made him known" (Jn 1:18). His teaching surpasses all other teaching.[7] In fact, by virtue of the hypostatic union, Jesus is Truth itself (Jn 14:6):

> He was also full of truth, because the human nature in Christ attained to the divine truth itself, that is, that this man should be the divine Truth itself. In other men we find many participated truths, insofar as the First Truth gleams back into their minds through many likenesses; but Christ is Truth itself. Thus it is said: "In whom all the treasures of wisdom are hidden" (Col 2:3). (*Ioan.* 1, lect. 8, n. 188; 1, 3, n. 103; 1, 10, n. 207)

The human soul of Jesus participates in a unique manner in the subsistent Truth that he is in person, and so he becomes the witness of this truth.[8] As much as a human intelligence could be, the intelligence of Christ is filled with the knowledge of God:

> [F]rom the very instant of his conception the most holy soul of Christ was full with all knowledge of the truth, "full of grace and truth" (1:14), that is, with the knowledge of every truth: "In whom are hid all the treasures of wisdom and knowledge" (Col 2:3). (*Ioan.* 17, lect. 2, n. 2201)[9]

Consequently, in virtue of the principle of the causality of the maximum, which holds that the subsisting perfection must be the cause of the existence

---

5. On the role of the apostles in the transmission of Revelation, cf. A. Lemonnyer, "Les Apôtres comme Docteurs de la foi d'aprés saint Thomas," in *Mélanges thomistes,* Bibliothéque thomiste, 3 (Paris, 1923), 153–73; Y. Congar, "L'apostolicité de l'Eglise selon s. Thomas d'Aquin," RSPT 44 (1960): 209–24; C. Halligan, "The Teaching of St. Thomas in Regard to Apostles," *American Ecclesiastical Review* 144 (1961): 32–47; E. Ménard, *La Tradition, Révélation, Ecriture, Eglise selon saint Thomas d'Aquin* (Paris: Desclée de Brouwer, 1964), 88–99.

6. Cf. A. Cirillo, *Cristo Rivelatore del Padre nel Vangelo di S. Giovanni secondo il Commento di San Tommaso d'Aquino,* Diss. Angelicum, Rome, 1998. The term *mediator* is applied to Jesus Christ in the order of knowledge, *Ioan.,* n. 2201.

7. Cf. *Ioan.* 1, lect. 11, n. 221: "Haec doctrina ideo omnibus aliis doctrinis supereminet dignitate, auctoritate et utilitate, quia ab unigenito Filio, qui est prima sapientia, immediate est tradita."

8. Cf. *Ioan.* 3, lect. 5, n. 533: "Christus enim inquantum Deus est ipsa veritas; sed inquantum homo, est testis veritatis"; infra 18, 37: "In hoc natus sum, et ad hoc veni, ut testimonium perhibeam veritati."

9. The title *rabbi* often attributed to Jesus in *John* is interpreted by St. Thomas in the sense of this plenitude of knowledge, cf. *Ioan.* 1, lect. 16, n. 327. On the human knowledge of Christ, cf. *ST* III, qq. 9–12.

Role of the Apostles in the Communication of Revelation

of the participated perfection in all the subjects who participate in it,[10] Christ is constituted as the source of all supernatural knowledge of God: "And all who know God, owe this to Christ" (*Ioan.* 13, lect. 6, n. 1830). "From his fullness have we all received" (Jn 1:16).

The root and fountain of our knowledge of God is the Word of God, that is, Christ: "The foundation of wisdom is the word of God" [Sir 1:5]. Human wisdom consists in knowing God. But this knowledge flows to us from the Word, because to the extent that we share in the Word of God, to that extent do we know God. . . . From this knowledge of the Word, which is the root and fountain, flows, like rivulets and streams, all the knowledge of the faithful. (*Ioan.* 17, lect. 6, n. 2267–68)

Now Jesus Christ has freely chosen to communicate his own proper fontal knowledge of the mystery of God through human mediations. Among these, the apostles hold the first place. "[I]t is through the disciples that the knowledge of the truth has come to us" (*Ioan.* 6, lect. 1, n. 856). The apostles have benefited from a direct and eminent participation in Jesus Christ's knowledge.

"I have given them the words which thou gavest me" (Jn 17:8). Saint Thomas makes explicit this double subordinate communication, which follows a structure frequently found in the Gospel of John, in which the relation Father/Son is extended and reflected in the relation Son/disciples. In a first moment, the Father communicates his *doctrina* to the Son, either in the eternal instant of generation or at the conception of his human nature. This is the first gift.

The other giving of knowledge is from Christ to his disciples, so he says, "I have given them," by teaching them, both from without and from within: "For all that I have heard from my Father I have made known to you" (Jn 15:15). By saying this he shows that he is the mediator between God and man (1 Tim 2:5), because what he received from the Father he passed on to the disciples: "I stood between the Lord and you at that time, to declare to you the word of the Lord" (Deut 5:5). (*Ioan.* 17, lect. 2, n. 2201)

---

10. There is an abundance of literature about this principle. Cf. for example, G. Isaye, "La Théorie de la mesure et l'existence d'un maximum selon saint Thomas," *Archives de philosophie* 16 (1940): 1–136; L.-B. Geiger, *La Participation dans la philosophie de s. Thomas d'Aquin,* Bibliothéque thomiste, 23 (Paris: Vrin, 1953), 472; V. de Couesnongle, "La Causalité du maximum," *RSPT* 38 (1954): 433–44. It is approached in different forms: *De ver.*, q. 3, a. 7, s. c. 2: "Omne quod est in aliquo genere oportet reduci in primum illius generis"; q. 5, a. 9, s.c. 3: "Illud quod est primum in aliquo genere est causa eorum quae sunt post in illo genere"; *SCG*, III, 17 (n. 1991): "Quod est maximum in unoquoque genere, est causa omnium illorum quae sunt illius generis"; *De subst. sep.*, 9 (n. 49): "Si quis ordinem rerum consideret, simper inveniet id quod est maxime semper causam esse eorum quae sunt post ipsum."

As the first beneficiaries of the teaching of Christ, and the ones who must communicate it to all men, the apostles are by rights the solid and permanent foundations of the *congregatio fidelium,* of the Church gathered together by the apostolic faith[11]—"the Church, which was built on [Peter's] confession of faith" (*Ioan.* 1, lect. 15, n. 306)—and of which the *doctrina apostolorum* is one of the great riches (cf. *Ioan.* 2, lect. 2, n. 383).

> The Church is firmly established. A house is said to be firmly established when it has good foundations. Now the Church's chief foundation is Christ. . . . The Apostles and their doctrine are the Church's secondary foundation, from which She derives Her stability. This is described where it is said that the city had "twelve foundations, wherein were inscribed the names of the twelve apostles" (Rev 21:14). Hence the Church is called *apostolic.*[12]

Saint Thomas never believed it necessary to compose a treatise *De apostolis,* but he nevertheless possesses implicitly a firm theology of the apostolate. My purpose in this study is to make explicit portions of this theology, but in light of three limits. First of all, a textual limit: I will hold myself to the teaching of *Commentary on the Gospel of St. John.* With regard to the theology of the apostolate, this work of his maturity (1270–72) presents several points of interest:

First, its object, the Gospel of John, like the other Gospels, directly describes the apostles, even if curiously the noun *apostle* does not appear in this Gospel. It already contains several "Acts" of the apostles.

Second, the Gospel of John, especially in the discourse after the Last Supper, is filled with an elaborate theology of the apostolate as a participation in the work of Christ.

Third, in an epoch in which Johannine authenticity was not in question, St. Thomas sees in the Gospel of John the unparalleled witness of an apostle in the act of teaching. His reflection on the mission of the evangelist John and the nature of his writings is a key element of his theology of the apostolate.

A methodological limit follows. The *Commentary on John* is inscribed in a long tradition of interpretation and it would be necessary, in order to best discern the originality of Thomas's theology, to compare it to his sources. I did not wish to undertake this in a systematic manner, particularly because of the absence of any critical edition and of any developed *apparatus fontium.*

---

11. Cf. Ephesians 1:20 and St. Thomas's commentary on this passage, *In Eph.,* n. 127–128.
12. *In Symbolum,* a. 9 (Marietti, n. 985); cf. the remarks of Y. Congar, "L'apostolicité de l'Eglise selon s. Thomas d'Aquin."

Finally, a thematic limit. The *Commentary on John* contains some precious indications on the ideal of the *vita apostolica,* the apostolic mission of the shepherds of the Church. I have chosen, however, to concentrate on the essential theme: the role of the apostles in the transmission of revelation. In fact, the theme of revelation is at the heart of a Gospel that, as St. Thomas explains, recounts few miracles but whose "main object was to present the teaching of Christ" (*Ioan.* 6, lect. 1, n. 844).

In order to present the wide variety of teachings in the *Commentary on John* on this question, I will proceed in two stages. First, I will consider what the commentary teaches on the knowledge that the apostles had: its object, nature, causes, modalities, and so forth. I will then examine what it says about the communication of this knowledge, which defines the apostolic mission.

Before diving into this subject, let us make precise what we understand by "apostles." "Apostle" means sent forth.[13] More precisely, the apostle is sent in order to witness, to announce. Such is his function *(officium).* In this broad sense, Christ himself is called an apostle.[14] Likewise the Samaritan woman[15] and Mary Magdalene, who had the privilege of receiving "the office of an apostle; indeed, she was an apostle to the apostles insofar as it was her task to announce our Lord's resurrection to the disciples" (*Ioan.* 20, lect. 3, n. 2519).

In a strict sense, however, the apostles constitute a particular category of disciples. The "disciples" are all the believers who follow Christ's teaching. Thus, with regard to Joseph of Arimathea, St. Thomas distinguishes between the three notions of believer, disciple, and apostle: "[He] was a disciple of Jesus, not one of the twelve, but one of the many other believers, for at first all those who believed were called disciples" (*Ioan.* 19, lect. 6, n. 2464). Among these disciples, certain ones were chosen by Jesus Christ to be apostles. They constitute an *ordo* in the Church,[16] that is to say, a socially recognizable group[17] that is defined by its proper hierarchical *officium*—the preaching of the truth—for which they were delegated.[18] It is this *officium* that communicates its name to the group.[19] To this office, which implies a particular style of

---

13. Cf. *Ioan.* 20, lect. 4, n. 2537: "Habebant officium proprium apostolorum: Apostolus enim idem est quam missus."

14. Cf. Hebrews 3:1 and *Ioan.* 13, lect. 3, n. 1782.

15. Cf. *Ioan.* 4, lect. 3, n. 624: "Apostolorum annuntiando assumens."

16. Cf. *Ioan.* 15, lect. 3, n. 2026: Dicit ergo "Posui vos," idest, dedi vobis ordinem in Ecclesia mea, 1 Co 12, 28.

17. On social structures in the Church, cf. *ST* II-II, q. 183: De officiis et statibus hominum in generali.

18. Cf. *Ioan.* 17, lect. 4, n. 2231: "officium, ad quod deputantur."

19. Cf. *Ioan.* 13, lect. 3, n. 1782: "Officium eorum est quod sint Apostoli."

life, a more radical manner of following Christ by abandoning everything,[20] is also attached a *dignitas*.[21] The group made up of apostles is called a college,[22] which, St. Thomas tells us, is a structured ensemble of which Peter is the chief.[23] As we will see, the college of the apostles is also called the Twelve, with a particular signification.

CONTEMPLARI

Directly Revealed Knowledge

In the priestly prayer of chapter 17, the apostles occupy a well-determined place. In fact, in his *divisio textus,* St. Thomas did not fail to point out the threefold structure of this prayer.[24] Jesus prays for himself first (vv. 1–6). Then he prays for the "group of disciples"[25] or "group of apostles"[26] (vv. 7–19). Finally, he prays "for all the faithful,"[27] "in general for all the faithful,"[28] "for the entire community of the faithful"[29] (vv. 20–23). This threefold structure emphasizes the mediating role of the apostles between Christ and his faithful people. The faithful are those "who believe in me *through their word*" (Jn 17:20). Thus:

> [B]elief comes in two ways. Sometimes by instruction from another; and this is the usual way.... Sometimes it comes by a divine revelation; and this is the special way.[30]

The faithful believe, therefore, on the word of the apostles. St. Thomas dwells for some time on the objections raised against this universal mediation of the

---

20. Cf. *Ioan.* 6, lect. 8, n. 984: "Multi erant in populo Iudaeorum qui adherebant Christo, credentes ei, et sequebantur eum non tamen relictis omnibus, sicut duodecim, qui omnes dicebantur discipuli." In prol., n. 14, St. Thomas points out that the apostles have reached their true state of apostleship at the moment when they leave everything to follow Jesus. In 16, 8, n. 2171, he sees a sign of the weakening of the apostles during the passion in the fact that they take back their own belongings. In short, the apostolic office is intrinsically linked to poverty. Thus when the Samaritan woman assumes the office of the apostles, St. Thomas likes to note that when she leaves her water jug, she leaves everything (cf. 4, 3, n. 625).

21. Cf. *Ioan.* 20, lect. 5, n. 2546: "Thomas erat electus ad eam dignitatem quam Deus sacraverat duodenario numero"; 20, 4, n. 2537.

22. Cf. *Ioan.* 13, lect. 4, n. 1799: "sanctum collegium"; 13, 5, n. 1821; 17, 2, n. 2193.

23. Cf. *Ioan.* 21, lect. 3, n. 2623: "eximius apostolorum, vertex collegii."

24. Cf. *Ioan.* 17, lect. 1, n. 2177.   25. Ibid.

26. *Ioan.* 17, lect. 2, n. 2193.   27. *Ioan.* 17, lect. 1, n. 2177.

28. *Ioan.* 17, lect. 5, n. 2232.   29. *Ioan.* 17, lect. 5, n. 2233.

30. *Ioan.* 12, lect. 7, n. 1693. The context and the end of n. 1696 attest that this special way concerns, among others, the apostles. Cf. *ST* II-II, q. 6, a. 1: "Quibusdam quidem revelantur immediate a Deo, sicut sunt revelata apostolis et prophetis. Quibusdam autem proponuntur a Deo mittente fidei praedicatores."

apostles.[31] It is applied neither to the righteous of the Old Covenant nor, it seems, to those who, like St. Paul and the good thief, believed directly in the words of Christ himself, without passing through the apostles' preaching.[32] St. Thomas, however, distinguishes between the preaching of the apostles and its objective content: not only those who were taught by the apostles themselves (or their successors) have believed "through the word of the apostles," but also all those who believed through the "word of faith," which is the objective content of the apostles' preaching and which is called the word of the apostles "because they were especially *(principaliter)* commissioned to preach it" (*Ioan.* 17, lect. 5, n. 2235). If in a general manner, adhesion to the objective faith of the apostles comes by welcoming the preaching of the apostles, it can in certain cases be dissociated from their preaching, which opens some interesting perspectives concerning the salvation of those who cannot be in direct contact with apostolic preaching as such. The law of mediation, therefore, does not have an unrelenting Neoplatonic rigor.

Whatever the case might be, the faith of the apostles, by its nature, calls attention to this "special way" of believing, which consists in seeing[33]—immediate knowledge *par excellence*—and drawing the truth directly from the Source.[34] This immediacy establishes the value and certitude of their teaching.

From this point of view, the apostles are in a situation analogous to that of the prophets of the Old Testament and John the Baptist, who benefited from direct revelation. This being said, by comparing the sowers (the patriarchs and the prophets) and the harvesters (the apostles), which is the topic of the fourth chapter of the Gospel, St. Thomas underlines two major differences between the apostles and their predecessors the prophets, which are in fact two differences between the Old Covenant and the New Covenant. First, the mission of the apostles realizes efficaciously what the prophets tried, but were not able to accomplish: to bring men to Christ.[35] Second, the apostles received a revelation at the time more profound and clearer than the

---

31. The question has already been extensively examined by St. Augustine, *In Iohannis Evangelium tractatus CXXIV,* tr. CIX, CCL, 36 (Turnhout: Brepols, 1954), 618–21.

32. Cf. *Ioan.* 17, lect. 5, nn. 2234–35.

33. Cf. *Ioan.* 1, lect. 8, n. 179: "Innotuit autem Apostolis Verbum incarnatum dupliciter. Primo quidem per visum acceperunt de eo notitiam"; n. 180; n. 191: "Posita evidentia Verbi, quia ipsis Apostolis innotuit per visum"; n. 200: "quomodo Apostolis innotuit visu, quasi a Christo accipientibus."

34. Cf. *Ioan.* 1, lect. 11, n. 221.

35. Cf. *Ioan.* 4, lect. 4, n. 651: "Apostoli messuerunt, quia ipsi [Prophetae] quod intendebant, scilicet homines adducere ad Christum, efficere non potuerunt, quod tamen apostoli fecerunt."

prophets.[36] Elsewhere, St. Thomas typically contrasts the witness of the apostles, which rests on what they saw in the past, to the witness of the prophets, which rests on what they have foreseen for the future.[37]

The knowledge from which the apostles benefited is a supernatural knowledge that corresponds to the very object of the Christian faith. It is supernatural in its object, which transcends all the knowledge of philosophers, whose imperfection St. Thomas emphasizes above all with regard to the knowledge of God.[38] It is also supernatural in its cause. St. Thomas, in line with the Pauline passage from 1 Corinthians 1, strongly insists on the apostles' natural ignorance, their unrefined character *(rudes)*,[39] their natural slowness of understanding, of which the Gospel offers numerous examples,[40] in order to show better by contrast the supernatural origin of their teaching. This is the reason why Nathaniel was not chosen to be an apostle: he was too intelligent!

Christ did not want the conversion of the world to the faith to be attributed to human wisdom, but solely to the power of God. And so he did not choose Nathanael as an apostle, since he was very learned in the law; he rather chose simple and uneducated men.[41]

However, the supernatural knowledge, with which they have been gifted, establishes the grandeur of the apostles. It places them above "the entire world," which arouses in them a profound astonishment that bears witness to their humility: "How is it that you will manifest yourself to us, and not to the world" (John 14:22).[42]

---

36. Cf. *Ioan.* 4, lect. 4, n. 651: "Prophetae seminantes sunt, quia multa de divines tradiderunt; messores vero sunt apostolie, qui ea quar non manifestaverunt Prophetae hominibus, praedicando et docendo revelaverunt, Ep 3, 5: 'Quod aliis generationibus non est agnitium . . . sicut nunc revelatum est sanctis Apostolis suis.'" *Ioan.* 1, lect. 8, n. 183, St. Thomas refers to the analogous difference between shadow and figures, and the full light.

37. Cf. *Ioan.* 1, lect. 8, n. 183; 1, 15, n. 282.

38. Cf., for example, *Ioan.* 1, lect. 5, n. 125.

39. Cf. *Ioan.* 11, lect. 3, n. 1499.

40. Cf. *Ioan.* 4, lect. 3, n. 633; n. 636; n. 1497: "Tarditatem autem intellectus discipulorum ponitt Evangelista cum dicit"; n. 1499, here talking about Philip, cf. n. 852: "Sciendum . . . quod Philippus inter alios magis tardus et rudis erat."

41. *Ioan.* 1, lect. 16, n. 334. Cf. also nn. 310, 629, and the exception that confirms the rule in n. 426 (Nicodemus). This theme, entirely classical in the Christian apologetics of the Church Fathers, is very present in St. Thomas, cf., for example, *De rationibus fidei*, c. 7: *Ut manifestum fieret opus divinae virtutis, omnia abiecta et infirma in mundo elegit: pauperem matrem, vitam inopem, discipulos et nuntios idiotas;* CG, I, 6.

42. Cf. *Ioan.* 14, lect. 6, n. 1939.

The Progressive Acquisition of This Knowledge

The apostles did not immediately benefit from the perfect knowledge of the Christian mysteries that made them permanent foundations of the Church. As we shall see, they fully enjoyed it (that is, in a way to be able to communicate it) only on the day of Pentecost. They were, however, progressively disposed to this knowledge, and the manner in which St. Thomas renders account of their progress is exemplary for a pedagogy of the faith.

The Role of the Heart in the Acquisition of Apostolic Knowledge

The knowledge that the apostles acquired about the mystery of God engages not only the mind, but also the heart. Certainly, St. Thomas, who speaks formally, teaches that moral goodness is not of itself required in order to prophesy, as Caiaphus proves,[43] and even that knowledge of the faith can subsist without charity. This situation, however, is possible only for inferior forms of supernatural knowledge. The more that one is raised in the order of supernatural knowledge, the more the agreement between love and knowledge of God becomes a necessity, to the point that the perfection of knowledge cannot be achieved without love.

> For contemplation is perfect when the one contemplating is led and raised to the height of the thing contemplated.... So in order that it might be perfect it is necessary that it rise and attain the end of the thing contemplated, adhering and assenting by affection and understanding to the truth contemplated. (*Ioan.* prol., n. 8)

Without entering into the study of the diverse modalities according to which love can determine knowledge, let us note the insistence with which St. Thomas, in many places, underlines the profound link between the friendship of the apostles with Jesus and the revelation which gives them the secrets of God. The key text here is John 15:15: "No longer do I call you servants, for the servant does not know what his master is doing, but I have called you friends, for all that I have heard from my Father I have made known to you." St. Thomas comments:

> For the true sign of friendship is that a friend reveals the secrets of his heart to his friend. Since friends have one mind and heart, it does not seem that what one friend reveals to another is placed outside his own heart: "Argue your case with your neighbor" (Prov 25:9). Now God reveals his secrets to us by letting us share in his wisdom: "in every generation she [Wisdom] passes into holy souls and makes them friends of God and prophets" (Wis 7:27). (*Ioan.* 15, lect. 3, n. 2016)

---

43. Cf. *Ioan.* 11, lect. 7, n. 1579; *ST* II-II, q. 172, a. 4.

It is the friendship that they have with God that explains why Christ specially manifests himself to the apostles (cf. John 14:22–23). In fact, charity alone renders man apt to benefit from divine revelation:[44]

> The reason is obvious why God will manifest himself to his own, and not to the world. It is because his own really have love, and it is love which distinguishes the saints from the world: "He hides the light from the proud. He shows his friend that he owns it" (Job 36:32). (*Ioan.* 14, lect. 6, n. 1949)[45]

This link between revelation and friendship is eminently verified in the case of the apostle John:

> [A]mong the other disciples of the Lord, John was more loved by Christ. . . . And because secrets are revealed to friends . . . , Jesus confided his secrets in a special way to that disciple who was specially loved. Thus it says in Job (36:32): "From the savage" that is, the proud, "he hides his light," that is, Christ hides the truth of his divinity, "and shows his friend," that is, John, "that it belongs to him." (*Ioan.* prol., n. 11)

Thomas elsewhere establishes a very beautiful parallel between the repose of John, during the Last Supper, on Jesus' bosom, where he draws out the secrets of God, and the repose of the only Son in the bosom of the Father (Jn 1:18; cf. *Ioan.* 13, lect. 4, n. 1804). And he comments further on:

> As for the mystical interpretation, we can see from this that the more a person wants to grasp the secrets of divine wisdom, the more he should try to get closer to Christ, according to: "Come to him and be enlightened" [Ps 34:5]. For the secrets of divine wisdom are especially revealed to those who are joined to God by love: "He shows his friend that it is his possession" [Job 36:33]. (*Ioan.* 13, lect. 4, n. 1807)

Agents of the Apostles' Acquisition of Knowledge

The apostles' progress in the knowledge of God is the work of grace in them and therefore, in the last analysis, of the Holy Trinity. In his *Commentary on John*, St. Thomas attributes this perfecting, according to diverse modalities, to the Incarnate Word and to the Holy Spirit.

At times, he seems to distribute the roles: Christ transmits doctrine exteriorly, and the Spirit assures its interior assimilation.[46] In fact, the acquisition of knowledge always assumes two elements: exterior communication of an

---

44. Cf. *Ioan.*, n. 1940: "Duo ponit, quae reddunt hominem idonem ad Dei manifestationem. Primum est caritas."

45. The quasi totality of the citations from Job 36:32 in Thomas's *corpus* is concentrated in our commentary. One can deduce that Aquinas was spiritually fascinated by this verse at the time when he was writing *Commentary on John*.

46. Cf. *Ioan.* 14, lect. 6, n. 1958: "Filius ergo tradit nobis doctrinam, cum sit Verbum; sed Spiritus sanctus doctrinae eius nos capaces facit."

objective teaching and the interior action of subjectively assimilating this teaching. In the supernatural order, where human intelligence is not directly proportioned to the truths taught, the necessity of a subjective revelation is added to that of an objective revelation that consists in the teaching of Christ.[47]

But in fact, the action of the Incarnate Word and the action of the Spirit are not two juxtaposed and simply concurrent actions. There is only a single action, only an integral teaching: that of Christ, who gives the words he received from the Father (Jn 17:8) "by teaching them, both from without and from within" (*Ioan.* 17, lect. 2, n. 2201). In fact, the word of Christ is particular in that it also acts in the interior and procures the understanding and love of its own content.[48] In this, the authority of Christ as teacher absolutely transcends that of any purely human teacher.[49] This privilege comes to him from the hypostatic union: as man, Christ acts on the exterior through the teaching that he dispenses and, as God, he gives the inspiration,[50] the Spirit who, interiorly, effects the assimilation of his words. The illuminating action of the Spirit is thus subsumed within the integral teaching of the incarnate Son.[51]

The Incarnate Word

Christ, in his humanity, is a teacher, and St. Thomas freely projects on him the ideal traits of a medieval professor. Thus, in order to teach his disciples after having washed their feet, Christ begins by putting his vestments back on because "a teacher, who should be serious and of great authority, ought also to be suitably dressed"! (*Ioan.* 13, lect. 3, n. 1770). Similarly, his preferential love for the apostle John is, among other things, like that of every professor for the best in the class: "Teachers especially love their intelligent students" (*Ioan.* 21, lect. 5, n. 2639).

Jesus Christ teaches the disciples by his exemplary behavior—*Omnis*

---

47. Cf. *Ioan.* 13, lect. 5, n. 1816: "Verba Christi adeo profunda sunt et humanum intellectum excedentia, quod non plus inde capere possumus nisi inquantum ipse revelat."

48. Cf. *Ioan.* 1, lect. 16, n. 313: "Non enim vox Christi solum exterioribus dicebatur, sed fidelium interiora ad eius inflammabat amorem."

49. Cf. *Ioan.* 3, lect. 1, n. 428: "Alii enim magistri docent tantum exterius, sed Christus etiam interius, quia, ut dicitur supra 1, 9 'erat lux vera, quae illuminat omnem hominem"; et ideo ipse solus dat sapientiam; Lc XXI, 15: 'Ego dabo vobis os et sapientiam.' Et hoc nullus purus homo dicere potest"; n. 1775.

50. Cf. *Ioan.* 5, lect. 4, n. 780.

51. Saint Thomas indicates that, in the Gospel of John, the effects attributed to the Spirit are often attached to the Son (and vice versa). Cf. *Ioan.* 14, lect. 7, n. 1961: "Quia vero Spiritus sanctus a Filio procedit, ideo que Spiritus sanctus appropriate facit, attribuitur Filio."

Christi actio est nostra instructio[52]—and displays a consummate pedagogical art, of which St. Thomas loves to make mention. Thus Jesus takes the apostles away from the crowds so that they may be more attentive to his teaching.[53] He adapts to their weakness,[54] to the progressive character of their knowledge, only revealing what they can bear at a given moment.

Above all, Christ maintains with his apostles an atmosphere of *familiaritas*,[55] born of mutual knowledge and love, which create favorable conditions for the reception and personal assimilation of the truth taught. Christ's exceptional familiarity with St. John is not foreign to the doctrinal depth of his Gospel.[56] This familiarity as a condition of salvific revelation brings to its fulfillment the logic of the Incarnation:

For he not only willed to be like men in nature, but also in living with them on close terms without sin, in order to draw to himself men won over by the charm of his way of life. (*Ioan.* 1, lect. 7, n. 178)

The Holy Spirit[57]

The interior work of the Holy Spirit in the apostles is twofold: he enlightens their intelligence and purifies their heart.

First, he instructs them,[58] teaches them,[59] enlightens their intelligence,[60] and leads them to the truth about faith and morals.[61] He does this not by bringing to them new objective knowledge, but by assuring their personal subjective assimilation of the teachings of Christ. "From the coming of the Holy Spirit they will receive great things, namely, an understanding of all the

---

52. For instance, *Ioan.* 4, lect. 1, n. 570, Jesus Christ, by accepting solitude, gives his disciples an example of humility. On the theological axiom *Omnis Christi actio est nostra instructio*, cf. *Ioan.* 11, lect. 6, n. 1555, where it is connected with John 13:15: "I gave you an example so that you would act as I have acted toward you," and R. Schenk, *"Omnis Christi actio est nostra instructio,"* 104–31.

53. Cf. *Ioan.* 14, lect. 8, n. 1977.

54. Saint Thomas sees an example (more contestable) of this pedagogy in the fact that Jesus speaks for a longer time to the Samaritan woman than to the apostles, therefore adapting himself to the intellectual weakness of woman, cf. *Ioan.* 4, lect. 4, n. 639.

55. The use of the term *familiaritas* by St. Thomas merits a more in-depth study. One finds 28 significant occurrences of it in the *Commentary on John.*

56. Cf. *Ioan.* 13, lect. 7, nn. 1803, 1807.

57. Concerning the pneumatology of the *Commentary on John*, cf. G. Ferraro, *Lo Spirito e l'ora di Cristo.*

58. Cf. *Ioan.* 16, lect. 3, n. 2099.

59. Cf. *Ioan.* 16, lect. 7, n. 2152: "Per Spiritum sanctum edocti."

60. Cf. *Ioan.* 16, lect. 3, n. 2103: "non corporaliter, sed intrinsecus in mente illuminando."

61. Cf. *Ioan.* 17, lect. 4, n. 2229: "Sanctifica eos, immitendo eis Spiritum sanctum, et hoc in veritate, idest in cognitione veritatis fidei et tuorum mandatorum."

words of Christ" (*Ioan.* 14, lect. 6, n. 1952). St. Thomas loves to cite Job 32:8 in this context: *Inspiratio Omnipotentis dat intelligentiam*.[62] Thomas explains, contrary to the idea dear to heretics of an esoteric teaching of Christ reserved to an elite, that "the Lord presented all matters of faith to his disciples, but not in the way he later revealed them" (*Ioan.* 16, lect. 3, n. 2101): if they progress, however, it is not by attaining to other truths, but by receiving a more profound manner of understanding the truth already received. The connection between the teaching of Christ and the action of the Spirit is well defined when St. Thomas comments on the verse, "He will teach you all things" (John 14:26):

> Just as the effect of the mission of the Son was to lead us to the Father, so the effect of the mission of the Holy Spirit is to lead the faithful to the Son. Now the Son, since he is begotten Wisdom, is Truth itself.... And so the effect of this kind of mission [of the Spirit] is to make us sharers in the divine wisdom and knowers of the truth. The Son, since he is the Word, gives teaching to us; but the Holy Spirit enables us to grasp it. He says, "He will teach you all things," because no matter what a person may teach by his exterior actions, he will have no effect unless the Holy Spirit gives an understanding from within. For unless the Spirit is present to the heart of the listener, the words of the teacher will be useless: "The breath of the Almighty makes him understand" (Job 32:8). This is true even to the extent that the Son himself, speaking by means of his human nature, is not successful unless he works from within by the Holy Spirit. (*Ioan.* 14, lect. 6, n. 1958)[63]

The action of the Spirit consists at the same time in purifying the apostles of their overly carnal love in order to lead them toward the moral perfection of spiritual friendship, indispensable to the understanding of the mystery:

> The Spirit makes us to know all things by inspiring us from within, by directing us and lifting us up to spiritual things. Just as one whose sense of taste is tainted does not have a true knowledge of flavors, so one who is tainted by love of the world cannot taste divine things. (*Ioan.* 14, lect. 6, n. 1959)

> It is a characteristic of the Holy Spirit to reveal the truth because it is love which impels one to reveal his secrets: "I have called you friends, for all that I have heard from my Father I have made known to you" (Jn 15:15); "He showed it," the truth, "to his friend" (Job 36:33). (*Ioan.* 14, lect. 4, n. 1916)

The apostles' simultaneous progress in the love and knowledge of Jesus Christ is therefore in a strict dependence on the action in them of the Spirit.

---

62. Three of the ten appearances of this verse in the work of St. Thomas are found in *Ioan.*, nn. 1628, 1958, 2062.

63. Cf. also n. 2102: "Cum enim sit a veritate, eius est docere veritatem et facere similes suo principio."

It is an essential theme of the Gospel of John that the gift of the Spirit is an effect of the glorification of Jesus Christ, that is to say of his Pasch: "as yet the Spirit had not been given, because Jesus was not yet glorified" (Jn 7:39).[64] St. Thomas returned many times to the question of the moment in which the apostles received the Spirit. In order to avoid all simplistic, binary responses—Spirit or no Spirit!—it is fitting to distinguish different effects and therefore different "missions" of the Spirit. On one hand, the invisible mission of interior sanctification of souls certainly anticipates the glorification of Christ,[65] even if it depends logically on it and is indeed more perfect afterward. On the other hand, against St. John Chrysostom[66] and with St. Augustine,[67] St. Thomas thinks that there were certain authentic manifestations of the Spirit—prophecy, miracles—before the resurrection and that the exorcisms done by the apostles during Jesus' ministry were indeed works of the Spirit. This being said, the difference between the time that preceded Easter and the time that followed it consists in the difference between the limited character and the fuller—superabundant—character of the gift of the Spirit to the apostles.[68] After the resurrection, the Spirit is no longer given, as it were, in passing, but he establishes between himself and the apostles in whom he dwells a true *familiaritas*.[69]

The understanding of Christ's words[70] and of the meaning of the Scrip-

---

64. This verse from John is often cited: *Ioan.*, iiii. 554, 1093, 1637, 1859, 1902, 2088.

65. Cf. *Ioan.* 4, lect. 1, n. 554, where St. Thomas defends the idea that the baptism administered by Christ and his disciples before the passion certainly gave the Holy Spirit, having a sanctifying value: "Non erat datus visibilibus signis, sicut post resurrectionem Christi datus est discipulis; sed tamen datus est, et dabatur, per internam sanctificationem, credentibus." In *ST* I, q. 43, a. 1, ad 1, St. Thomas forthrightly affirms this invisible action of the Holy Spirit in the saints of the Old Testament.

66. Cf. Jean Chrysostome, *Homélies sur l'Evangile de saint Jean,* LI, Oeuvres complètes, 14, (Paris: Vivès, 1869), 60–61.

67. Cf. Augustin, *In Iohannis Evangelium,* tract. XXXII, 302–4.

68. Cf. *Ioan.* 7, lect. 5, n. 1093: "Et ideo dicendum est, secundum Augustinum, quod ante resurrectionem Apostoli habuerunt Spiritum sanctum etiam quantum ad dona prophetica et miraculorum. Et hic quod dicitur 'nondum erat Spiritus datus', intelligendum de abundanti datione, et visibilibus signis; sicut datus fuit eis post resurrectionem et ascencionem in linguis igneis"; similar doctrine in n. 1902 concerning signs accomplished by the apostles: "Antequam Jesus esset glorificatus, Spiritus non fuit datus discipulis in ea plenitudine in qua datus est postmodum; supra VII, 39"; *ST* I-II, q. 106, a. 3; III, q. 72, a. 1, ad 1.

69. Cf. *Ioan.* 14, lect. 4, n. 1920.

70. Before the plenary gift of the Spirit, the apostles "nondum perfectum sensum habuerunt de verbis Christi" (*Ioan.* 16, lect. 5, n. 2122). The spiritual knowledge of the words of Christ is linked to the gift of the Spirit that makes the apostles "spiritual," cf. *Ioan.* 16, lect. 7, n. 2152: "Discipuli autem a principio quasi animales erant, et quae dicebantur eis, obscura erant et sicut proverbia; sed postmodum a Christo spirituales effecti et per Spiritum sanctum edocti, spiritualia aperte capiebant."

Role of the Apostles in the Communication of Revelation 333

tures,[71] which is an essential effect of the gift of the Spirit, contains, it seems, three major stages for Aquinas. The final stage will be the full revelation of the mystery in the immediacy of the vision, which Aquinas makes the ultimate end of the promises of Christ that bear on the knowledge of God.[72] The first two stages are distinguished as imperfect and perfect in a certain order, that of the knowledge of faith. Saint Thomas recognizes that the apostles have, before Easter, a certain knowledge of the mysteries of Christ, but this knowledge attains its perfection only with the glorification of Jesus and the full coming of the Holy Spirit. Concerning John 17:8, where Jesus says, "they . . . know in truth that I came from thee; and they have believed that thou didst send me," Thomas comments:

All these things had already begun, but they still remained to be completed. Thus, in reference to what has already begun, he speaks in the past tense, but in reference to their completion he speaks in the future, because they would be accomplished by the coming of the Holy Spirit. (*Ioan.* 17, lect. 2, n. 2203)

This full knowledge, therefore, is the effect of the glorification of Christ and of the consequent gift of the Spirit. St. Thomas explains this by commenting on John 12:16 ("His disciples did not understand this at first; but when Jesus was glorified, then they remembered"):

The reason why they knew only after he had been glorified was because it was then that they received the power of the Holy Spirit, which made them wiser than all the wise: "The breath of the Almighty makes a man understand" (Job 32:8). (*Ioan.* 12, lect. 3, n. 1628)

St. Thomas situates very precisely this fullness of the gift of the Spirit and the knowledge that results from it at Pentecost, distinguished (but not separated) from the resurrection and the ascension. Thus he points out that one of the possible meanings of the adverb "then," in the expression "*then* you will know the Father" (John 14:7), refers to the achievement of the Paschal mystery:

[A]fter my resurrection and ascension and after I have sent the Holy Spirit, "you shall know him," with the perfect knowledge of faith, for when the Spirit, the Paraclete, comes, "he will teach you all things, and bring to your remembrance all that I have said to you" (14:26). (*Ioan.* 14, lect. 2, n. 1880)

Similarly, Aquinas interprets *mystice* the different moments of the washing of the feet as an anticipation of the different stages of the Pasch. The washing of

---

71. Cf. *Ioan.* 16, lect. 3, n. 2102: "omnem veritatem figurarum legis, quam adepti sunt discipuli per Spiritum sanctum. Unde Daniel 1, 17 dicitur quod dedit Dominus pueris illis sapientiam et intelligentiam." Cf. n. 2101 with reference to Luke 24:45.

72. Cf. *Ioan.*, nn. 1880, 2101, 2203.

the feet properly corresponds to the Passion; the fact that Christ puts his garments back on corresponds to the resurrection; his return to his place at the table corresponds to his ascension and to his sitting at the right hand of the Father. It is only after all this that Jesus teaches his disciples, which, for St. Thomas, corresponds to the full teaching procured through the gift of the Spirit at Pentecost.

> When Christ sends the Holy Spirit to his disciples he will be giving them complete teaching.... But three things are to take place before the Spirit is sent.... And so, before sending into them the Holy Spirit, who would perfectly teach them, Christ would wash them with the blood he shed; take up his garments by rising; and resume his place by ascending in glory. (*Ioan.* 13, lect. 3, n. 1771)

The proof that Pentecost "adds" something to Easter is that during the time of the appearances after the resurrection, the apostles did not yet have perfect knowledge, because they posed questions. Saint John Chrysostom[73] identified the day, of which Jesus had said, "In that day you will ask nothing of me" (John 16:23), as the day of the resurrection of Christ, but St. Thomas considers that this day includes Pentecost:

> [O]ur Lord "calls that day" not only the day of his resurrection, but also that day the disciples were to be taught by the Holy Spirit: "When the Spirit of truth comes, he will teach you all truth" [16:13]. And so by speaking in a vague manner of that time, our Lord also includes the coming of the Holy Spirit. It is like saying: "In that day," once the Holy Spirit has been given, "you will ask nothing of me," because you will know all things by the Holy Spirit: "His anointing teaches you about everything" (1 Jn 2:27). (*Ioan.* 16, lect. 6, n. 2137)

We know, however, that Pentecost in the Gospel of John takes place on the evening of Easter when Jesus breathes on his disciples (Jn 20:22–23). But, commenting on this passage,[74] St. Thomas intends to preserve the primacy of Pentecost by reserving for it properly some essential aspect of the gift of the Spirit. Certainly, with St. John Chrysostom,[75] he rejects the thesis of some theologians who reduce this episode to a simple preparation for receiving the Spirit on the day of Pentecost. However, he does strive to limit the gift of this evening of Easter to a particular effect of the gift of the Spirit. It confers only the power of forgiving sins, according to the interpretation of Chrysostom; or according to Augustine and Gregory, it only signifies one of the two aspects

---

73. Cf. Jean Chrysostome, *Homélies sur l'Evangile de saint Jean*, LXXIX, 322–23.
74. Cf. *Ioan.* 20, lect. 4, n. 2540. St. Thomas seems to attribute no pneumatological value to John 19:30: "he gave up his spirit" (n. 2452).
75. Cf. Jean Chrysostome, *Homelies sur l'Evangile de saint Jean*, LXXXVI, 403.

of the mystery of charity, that of love of neighbor. It is, therefore, only on the day of Pentecost that the apostles attained through the Spirit the fullness and perfection of the knowledge of faith.

Among the many reasons of fittingness that explain why Christ did not communicate the Spirit to his disciples while he was still among them on earth—since he could have communicated the Spirit to them—the first is taken, according to St. Thomas, from the "indisposition" of the apostles: their faith was imperfect and they were not yet capable of loving Christ as God, with a spiritual love of charity.[76] Is this not a vicious circle? It is necessary to have received the Holy Spirit in order to be able to receive him! But in fact this paradox returns to Thomas's typical conception of the dynamic relationships between God's love for man and man's love for God, which follows from his central thesis on the absolute primacy of grace. The manifestations of man's love for God (observing the commandments, loving the Father . . .) are always the effect and sign of God's anterior love for man.[77] The love of God for man is primary, unconditioned, and it arouses in man the love for God that disposes him to receive the even greater gift that God wants to give him. It is in this line that St. Thomas explains how the merits of the apostles are the cause of their growth in the reception of the Holy Spirit:

No one can love God unless he has the Holy Spirit: because we do not act before we receive God's grace, rather, the grace comes first: "He loved us first" [1 Jn 4:10]. We should say therefore, that the apostles first received the Holy Spirit so that they could love God and obey his commands. But it was necessary that they make good use, by their love and obedience, of this first gift of the Holy Spirit in order to receive the Spirit more fully. (*Ioan.* 14, lect. 4, n. 1909)[78]

---

76. *Ioan.* 16, lect. 2, n. 2088: "Noluit eum [Spiritum] dare discipulis existens cum eis, quadruplici ratione. Primo propter eorum indispositionem: nam Spiritui sancto, cum sit amor spiritualis, contrarietur amor carnalis. Discipuli autem quodam carnali amore afficiebantur ad Christi humanitatem, necdum elevate erant spirituali amore ad eius divinitatem, et ideo nondum capaces erant Spiritus sancti." Cf. n. 2093: "Quamdiu enim discipuli carnaliter ad Christum afficiebantur, Sanctus spiritus non erat in eis, ut dictum est, eo modo quo postea fuit."

77. Cf. *Ioan.* 15, lect. 2, n. 2002, as regards the correct interpretation of the conditional proposition, "If you keep my commandments, you will remain in my love" (Jn 15:10); n. 2159, in regard to the verse: "The Father loves you because you love me" (Jn 16:27), Aquinas shows that the disciples' love for Jesus is the sign and effect of the logically anterior love of God for them; nn. 2019–24 commenting on John 15:16: "It is not you who chose me, but I who chose you": here, the key text is 1 John 4:10: "ipse prior dilexit nos," which appears no less than 12 times in the *Commentary on John*.

78. It is necessary to specify that this good usage is also a gift of grace.

The Moral Perfecting of the Apostles

The apostles' access to perfect knowledge in the order of faith is inseparable from their moral perfecting in the order of charity. Following the lead of the Gospels, however, St. Thomas likes to emphasize that the acquisition of this moral perfection was very progressive. Certainly, from the moment he called them, the apostles loved Jesus sincerely. "The good disciples"—the apostles by contrast with Judas—"had very great love for Christ,"[79] and St. Thomas does not miss an opportunity to highlight the fervor of the love of Peter,[80] John,[81] or Thomas.[82] This love shows itself through immense respect for Jesus.[83]

This love, which is already a fruit of divine election, unites the apostles to Christ. In so doing, it separates them from the world[84] (which pledges them thenceforth an implacable hatred) and confers on them a certain perfection. Saint Thomas also affirms that even before the Passion, "after Christ, the apostles were more perfect than others" (*Ioan.* 13, lect. 1, n. 1749). This perfection, however, remains very relative. Thus Jesus, in John 13:33, calls the apostles "little children":

> He says, "little children," to show their imperfection, for they were not yet perfectly children, because they did not yet perfectly love. They were not yet perfect in charity.... Still, they had grown somewhat in perfection, because from slaves they became little children, as he calls them here, and brethren. (*Ioan.* 13, lect. 7, n. 1832)

The imperfection of their love comes from the fact that it is still too carnal and is grounded on an insufficient knowledge of the true identity of Christ. The sadness they show at the idea of being physically separated from Jesus is proof.[85] The very earthly nature of their questions also demonstrates their at-

---

79. *Ioan.* 13, lect. 4, n. 1801: "Boni discipuli habebant ad Christum maximam caritatem."

80. Cf. *Ioan.* 6, lect. 8, n. 1002: "Verbum Petri multum amicitiae est ostensivum: iam enim Christus eis erat honorabilior quam patres et matres"; n. 1761: ferventissimus amor eius ad Christum; n, 1817: "Petrus ita fervidus erat in amore Christi quod si pro certo scivisset Iudam fuisse Christum traditurum, statim occidisset eum"; nn. 2478, 2593, 2594: "Ioannes altior intellectu, Petrus ferventior affectu" (from Chrysostome, *Homélies sur l'Évangile de saint Jean*, LXXXVII, 411).

81. Cf. *Ioan.* 13, lect. 4, n. 1804: "Propter vehementer fervorem affectus sui ad Christum"; Prov. 8: 17: "Ego diligentes me diligo."

82. Cf. *Ioan.* 11, lect. 3, n. 1504.

83. Cf. *Ioan.* 4, lect. 3, n. 623; 16, 5, n. 2122: "In quo commendenda est eorum reverentia ad Christum, quae tanta erat ut non praesumerent eum interrogare"; 21, 2, n. 2593.

84. Cf. *Ioan.* 15, lect. 5, n. 2043: "Apostoli electi erant et elevati supra mundum, inquantum erant effecti participes divinitatis, et coniuncti Deo."

85. Cf. *Ioan.* 16, lect. 2, n. 2085: "Gaudebant enim de praesentia Christi quodam modo carnali affecti ad humanam eius speciem, sicut homo delectatur de praesentia amici."

Role of the Apostles in the Communication of Revelation

tachment to fleshly realities,[86] which impedes their access to superior revelations.

On account of these aspects, before Easter, the apostles remained weak. They did not have the desire to die for Christ, which is the sign of perfect charity.[87] They were not even capable of imagining the sufferings that they would undergo for Christ because "their spirits were weak" (*Ioan.* 16, lect. 3, n. 2101). In this condition, they could only be scandalized by the Passion:

> And it is fitting that our Lord restrains them from falling after promising the Holy Spirit, because the Holy Spirit is love—"God's love has been poured into our hearts through the Holy Spirit which has been given to us" (Rom 5:5)—and the Holy Spirit prevents stumbling: "Great peace have those who love your law; nothing can make them stumble" (Ps 119:165). Now it is characteristic of friends that they disregard any loss for the sake of one another, as stated in Proverbs [12:26]. So, for one who is a friend of God, to suffer punishment and loss is no reason to fall away. Yet because the disciples had not yet received the Holy Spirit before the death of Christ, they did fall away during his passion. . . . But after the Holy Spirit came there was no falling away. (*Ioan.* 16, lect. 1, n. 2069)

The apostles' behavior when faced with the Passion of Christ possesses, therefore, a revelatory role. Despite the fact that "their faith was very strong" (*Ioan.* 13, lect. 4, n. 1801), the apostles sinned. They hid themselves, having lost their confidence.[88] Even on the evening of Easter, they were still "hesitant in their faith" (*Ioan.* 20, lect. 4, n. 2532). Peter, who at first had shown his pride by considering himself greater than the other apostles,[89] proved, by the fear that he displayed and that led him to deny Jesus, that perfect love had not yet taken possession of him as would be the case after the resurrection.[90] Only the complete gift of Pentecost would confirm the apostles in perfect charity and allow them to have access to perfect knowledge.

Toward Perfect Knowledge

Perfect knowledge consists in the knowledge of the divinity of Jesus Christ and his consubstantiality with the Father, which constitutes, for St. Thomas, the summit of New Testament revelation.

---

86. Cf. *Ioan.* 16, lect. 6, n. 2144, where St. Thomas concludes: "nec dum Spiritum adoptionis acceperant, quo ad spiritualia et caelestia anhelerent."

87. Cf. *Ioan.* 13, lect. 7, n. 1834: "Non potestis me sequi, quia non estis perfecti in caritate, ut velitis mori pro me: ego enim per mortem iturus sum. Item ego iturus sum ad gloriam Patris, ad quam nullus venire potest nisi sit caritate perfectus."

88. Cf. *Ioan.* 19, lect. 6, n. 2464.
89. Cf. *Ioan.* 21, lect. 3, n. 2621.
90. Cf. *Ioan.* 21, lect. 3, n. 2617.

From the start, the apostles have faith,[91] even a faith of great spiritual quality since it rests more on Jesus' teaching than on his miracles.[92] Nonetheless, their knowledge of Jesus' identity remains superficial. They stop at the humanity of Jesus, perceived as a man of God, a holy man.[93] When, then, did they have access to the knowledge of the divinity of Jesus? The response is complex. In paragraph 1886 of the *Commentary on John,* in order to reconcile some apparently contradictory affirmations concerning the faith of the apostles—"You know where I am going" (John 14:4), "If you had known me, you would have known the Father also" (John 14:7)—St. Thomas first sets forth the solution presented by St. Augustine, who refers to the individual differences between the apostles.[94] Certain apostles knew Christ as the Word of God.[95] This was the case with Peter who, in virtue of an internal revelation, confessed him as the Christ, the Son of the living God at Caesarea Philippi.[96] But others, such as Philip,[97] did not truly know him. However, Saint Thomas at once proposes another solution: all the apostles knew Christ as man, but none of them yet knew him *perfectly* as regards his divine nature.[98]

While only imperfectly knowing the true personality of Jesus, the apostles were still ignorant of the different aspects of the mystery of the Trinity. They

---

91. The call at the lakeshore, to which the first disciples responded, is a call to faith, cf. *Ioan.* 1, lect. 15, n. 308.

92. Cf. *Ioan.* 2, lect. 3, n. 418.

93. This is still, for example, the "faith" of Mary Magdalene on the morning of Easter. Cf. *Ioan.* 20, lect. 3, n. 2517: "Mulier autem haec aliquam fidem habebat de Christo sicut de sancto viro, unde et magister eum vocabat: necdum ad hoc pervenerat ut cognosceret eum aequalem Patri et unum cum Deo."

94. Cf. Augustine, *In Iohannis Evangelium,* tract. LXX, 503.

95. *Ioan.* 2, lect. 1, n. 365, St. Thomas indicates that the manifestation of Jesus at the wedding of Cana could have been decisive for certain apostles' faith in the divinity of Jesus since John said that "his disciples believed in him" (Jn 2:11): "Vel dicendum quod ante crediderunt ei sicut bono viro, iusta et recta praedicanti; sed modo crediderunt in eum tanquam in Deum." Nathaniel confessed only a divine filiation of Jesus by adoption (cf. *Ioan.* 1, lect. 16, n. 328).

96. Cf. *Ioan.* 6, lect. 5, n. 935; 20, 6, n. 2562. This is also Martha's confession of faith in John 11:27, of which Aquinas explains, *Ioan.* 11, 4, n. 1520, that it is a confession of perfect faith, implying in particular the recognition of Jesus' divine nature and his equality with the Father.

97. Philip seemed to be the most limited of all the apostles. Cf. *Ioan.* 6, lect. 1, n. 851: "Philippus inter alios magis tardus et rudis erat, et ideo frequenter interrogabat."

98. *Ioan.* 14, lect. 3, n. 1886: "Christus dupliciter cognosci poterat; scilicet secundum humanam naturam, et sic omnes sciebant. . . . Et secundum divinam, et sic eum nondum perfecte cognoverant." Cf. n. 1866: "Licet Christum perfecte secundum hominem scirent, eius tamen divinitatem imperfecte cognoscebant." It is in this sense of an *imperfect* knowledge of the divinity that one must understand certain texts that suggest that the apostles (some apostles?) had faith in the divinity of Christ, cf. nn. 2096, 2168, where the apostles affirm that they now know that Christ came from God, *consubstantialis Patri et verus Deus.*

Role of the Apostles in the Communication of Revelation

have only an imperfect knowledge of the Father.[99] They did not know him as Father,[100] nor did they know how the Father is in the Son and the Son in the Father. According to St. Thomas, this is the source of the misunderstandings during the discourse after the Last Supper.[101] Still less did they know the equality of the Father and the Son.[102] As regards the Spirit, the apostles have before Easter only a rudimentary knowledge.[103]

Everything changed at Easter. The very apostle Thomas who, on the evening of Holy Thursday, vowed his ignorance—"We do not know where you are going, how can we know the way?" (Jn 14:5)—took the decisive step when the risen Lord manifested himself to him eight days after Easter:

> Thomas quickly became a good theologian by professing a true faith. He professed the humanity of Christ when he said, My "Lord," for he had called Christ this before the passion: "You call me Teacher and Lord" (Jn 13:13). And he professed the divinity of Christ when he said, "and my God." Before this, the only one who had called Christ God was Peter: "You are the Christ, the Son of the living God" (Mt 16:16). (*Ioan.* 20, lect. 6, n. 2562)

This perfect knowledge of Jesus Christ as a divine person is surely the work of the Spirit:

> "[The Spirit] will glorify me," that is, give a clear knowledge of me. He will do this, first of all, by enlightening the disciples: for they were still carnal and attached to Christ in a carnal way, that is, in the weakness of his flesh, not realizing the grandeur of his divinity. Later, they were able to grasp this through the Holy Spirit: "God has revealed to us through the Spirit" (1 Cor 2:10). (*Ioan.* 16, lect. 4, n. 2106)

This brings about personal knowledge of the Father precisely as he is Father of the only-begotten Son, within the Trinity. The Father "was made so known through his Son when the apostles believed that Christ was the Son of God" (*Ioan.* 17, lect. 2, n. 2195).[104] Consequently, this also brings about knowledge of the Son as equal and coessential with the Father.[105]

---

99. Cf. *Ioan.* 14, lect. 2, n. 1880; 16, lect. 7, n. 2148.

100. Cf. *Ioan.* 17, lect. 2, n. 2195.

101. Cf. *Ioan.* 14, lect. 5, n. 1926: "Quae quidem causabantur ex ignorantia unius rei: ex hoc scilicet quod ignorabant quomodo Pater in Filio, et Filius in Patre."

102. Cf. *Ioan.* 14, lect. 8, n. 1972: "Nondum noverant quid sit resurrectio, nec eum aequalem Patris existimabant"; 16, 3, n. 2101: "plena cognitio divinorum quam non habebant tunc, puta aequalitatem Filii ad Patrem et huiusmodi."

103. *Ioan.* 14, lect. 5, n. 1921: "Apostoli non multum ad notitiam Spiritus Sancti conscenderant."

104. Cf. n. 30; n. 2222: "Vel 'dedi,' idest dabo, per inspirationem Paracliti, 'sermonem tuum,' idest de te," where one sees that the Son made the Father known through the Spirit.

105. Cf. *Ioan.* 16, lect. 7, n. 2154: "quia manifeste eum cognoscentes, scietis me esse ei aequalem et coessentialem."

In the *Commentary on John*, this faith in the divinity of Jesus, which leads to the knowledge of the Trinity, appears at many places connected to the resurrection. The resurrection manifests the divinity of Christ:

> Jesus gives [to those who ask of him a sign justifying his attitude toward the money changers in the Temple] the sign of his future resurrection because this shows most strikingly the power of his divinity. For it is not within the power of mere man to raise himself from the dead. Christ alone, who was free among the dead, did this by the power of his divinity. (*Ioan.* 2, lect. 3, n. 397)[106]

The apostles therefore could hardly imagine the resurrection before it happened since they knew only very imperfectly the divinity of Jesus.[107] Nevertheless, the plain fact of the resurrection does not suffice to explain faith in Jesus' divinity;[108] during the time after Easter, Jesus wanted to "strengthen in the hearts of the apostles their faith in his resurrection and in his divinity" (*Ioan.* 20, lect. 3, n. 2518), the gift of the Spirit imprinting a definitive seal on his teaching.

In this theological perspective, where the Trinity is seen as the objective center and the historic summit of revelation,—the *fides sanctae Trinitatis* is the very object of apostolic preaching[109]—one understands the primacy that the Gospel of John possesses and the exceptional importance that St. Thomas accords to its Prologue: "For while the other Evangelists treat principally of the mysteries of the humanity of Christ, John, especially and above all, makes known the divinity of Christ" (*Ioan.* prol., n. 10).[110]

John treats of that which is at the same time the most profound and the most hidden in Christian revelation.[111] At the heart of his Gospel he places

---

106. Cf. n. 414; n. 1830: "Hanc gloriam incepit habere [Christus] in resurrectione et in passione in quibus homines cognoscere coeperunt suam virtutem et suam divinitatem"; n. 1927: "Tunc videntes eum resurrexisse, et esse cum eis, certissimam fidem de eo habuerunt, praecipue qui acceperunt Spiritum Sanctum, qui omnia docebat"; n. 1972; n. 2151: "Cum iam per fidem resurrectionis eum firmiter Deum verum esse credentes elevati essent ad altiora."

107. Cf. *Ioan.* 16, lect. 5, nn. 2123, 2133.

108. Saint Thomas interprets in a very restrictive sense the "He saw and he believed" from John 20:8. According to Aquinas, John, at the very most, believed in the resurrection (n. 2489, following Chrysostom) and more probably only he believed in the truth of Mary Magdalene's words (n. 2488, following Augustine, *In Iohannis Evangelium*, tract. CXX, 664).

109. Cf. *Ioan.* 6, lect. 1, n. 865; 6, 8, n. 1007.

110. Cf. ibid.: "Patet etiam materia huius Evangelii, quae est cognitio divinitatis Verbi; n. 23: Evangelista Ioannes . . . intendit principaliter ostendere divinitatem Verbi incarnat; et ideo dividitur istud evangelium in partes duas. Primo enim insinuat Christi divinitatem."

111. Cf. *Ioan.* 3, lect. 1, n. 430: "Ioannes vero ea quae ad divinitatem Christi pertinent principaliter tractat, quae cum occulta sint, et a cognitione hominum remota, maiori assertione indigebant."

Role of the Apostles in the Communication of Revelation

the ultimate expression of the apostolic faith, the divinity of Christ, the *fides Trinitatis*. In this way he appears truly as the Theologian, one who considers all the highest things, *sub ratione Dei*.

CONTEMPLATA ALIIS TRADERE

As soon as they have been fully enlightened by Christ, the apostles become in their turn light for other men, but by virtue of *lux illuminata*.[112] Every fullness seeks to communicate itself—it is better to enlighten than simply to shine.[113] They assume therefore the "very great" function of witnesses, a sign that their knowledge of God, participated from that of Christ, has from now on attained its perfection.[114]

In this way the apostles participate in the salvific mission of Christ, especially in his work of preaching. They extend it, and they accomplish it. "As you sent me into the world, so I send them into the world" (John 17:18; cf. 20, 21). Consequently, according to the great Dionysian principles that structure his vision of divine government, St. Thomas attributes to the apostles an important role in the return of men to their Principle, since "it belongs to the divine order that lower things be led back to God through those that are higher" (*Ioan.* 12, lect. 4, n. 1634). They are the attendants of the Church, who bring the faithful to Christ.[115] As soon as Andrew knew Christ, he announced him to Peter. Indeed, the sign of perfect conversion to Christ is to work to bring others to him.[116] St. Thomas carefully notes that the movement of conversion must not stop in the participated perfection that is found in the apostle as secondary cause, but rather it is achieved only in union with subsistent perfection itself.[117] The practical consequence: the apostle must efface himself; he must in no way interpose himself or turn toward himself the movement that carries the believer toward God.[118]

---

112. Cf. *Ioan.* 12, lect. 8, n. 1713: "Licet Apostoli dicantur lux, Mt 5, 14: 'Vos estis lux mundi,' non tamen ea ratione qua Christus: ipsi enim sunt lux illuminata; quamvis aliquo modo, scilicet ministerio, illuminantes essent."

113. Cf. *ST* II-II, q. 188, a. 6.

114. Cf. *Ioan.* 1, lect. 4, n. 116: "Illi qui participant non solum dona Dei in seipsis per gratiam Dei bene operando, sed etiam diffundunt ad alios dicendo, movendo et exhortando, specialius sunt testes Dei"; n. 117: "Hoc autem officium Ioannis, scilicet testificandi, est valde magnum, quia nullus potest de aliquo testificari, nisi eo modo quo illud participat.... Unde testimonium perhibere divinae veritatis, indicium est cognitionis Veritatis"; n. 123.

115. Cf. *Ioan.* 2, lect. 1, n. 343.

116. Cf. *Ioan.* 1, lect. 16, n. 316: "Sicut Andreas perfecte conversus studuit adducere fratrem suum ad Christum, ita et Philippus fratrem suum Nathanaëlem ... quod fuit signum perfectae conversionis."

117. Cf. *Ioan.* 1, lect. 4, n. 122, concerning John the Baptist.

118. Cf. *Ioan.* 4, lect. 3, n. 626: "Nihilominus tamen in hoc veri praedicatoris imitatur

The apostles accomplished this missionary work through their dignity as free and conscious secondary causes: the mere instrument communes with the principal agent in the single action, but the secondary cause communes more profoundly in the very plan—the *ratio operis*—of the principal agent, of which the secondary cause must have a certain knowledge, in order voluntarily to engage himself in the action.[119] The preaching of the apostles is therefore, on their part, a work of highest charity looking to the good of the faithful.[120]

This preaching first consists in giving testimony to what they had seen and heard "since the beginning" (Jn 15:27). They attest *de visu et auditu* to the deeds and signs of Jesus Christ, his preaching and his miracles.[121] They expose them not in the manner of brute facts but with solicitude for instructing, for bringing out the meaning, for emphasizing that which contributes to the edification of the Church.[122] This direct testimony of the apostles, of St. John for example, is for believers a source of certitude in faith.[123] In writing, it also extends to the future.[124] There follows the exceptional authority of the canonical writings, which, as an expression of apostolic testimony, are absolutely sure, are inerrant,[125] and constitute the rule of the faith.[126]

As is the acquisition of perfect knowledge, so also its diffusion by the activity of the apostolic testimony is placed under the influence of grace[127] and

---

exemplum, non ad se, sed ad Christum vocando; II Cor. IV, v. 5. 'Non enim praedicamus nosmetipsos, sed Christum'"; and also n. 662, where St. Thomas explains that faith parts from the testimony in order to rejoin the attested truth.

119. Cf. *Ioan.* 15, lect. 3, n. 2015: "Instrumentum autem communicat cum artifice in opere, sed non in operis ratione. Sic ergo tales servi participant solum in opere; sed quando servus operatur ex propria voluntate, necesse est quod rationem operis sciat, et quod revelentur ei occulta, per quae scire possit quae agit. . . . Apostoli autem . . . a se movebantur ad bona opera facienda, scilicet ex propria voluntate per amorem inclinata; et ideo Dominus secreta sua revelat eis."

120. Cf. *Ioan.* 17, lect. 3, n. 2226: the apostles remain in the world "propter utilitatem fidelium, qui per eos credituri erant."

121. Cf. *Ioan.* 15, lect. 5, n. 2067.

122. Cf. *Ioan.* 2, lect. 3, n. 419: "Non fuit intentio Evangelistarum omnia signa Iesu conscribere, sed tot quot necessaria erant ad Ecclesiam fidelium instruendam"; 21, 6, n. 2655.

123. Cf. *Ioan.* 19, lect. 5, n. 2459: "Ponitur certitudo narrationis, et primo ex apostolico testimonio"; n. 2461: "ex testimonio apostolico certificatur."

124. Cf. *Ioan.* 21, lect. 6, n. 2655.

125. Cf. *Ioan.* 21, lect. 6, n. 2656: "Notandum autem quod cum multi scriberent de catholica veritate, haec est differentia, quia illi, qui scripserunt canonicam Scripturam, sicut Evangelistae et Apostoli, et alii huiusmodi, ita constanter eam asserunt quod nihil dubitandum relinqunt"; 13, 1, n. 1730: "Haereticum est dicere, quod aliquid falsum, non solum in Evangeliis, sed etiam in quacumque canonica scriptura inveniatur."

126. Cf. *Ioan.* 21, lect. 6, n. 2656: "Sola canonica scriptura est regula fidei."

127. Cf. *Ioan.* 1, lect. 4, n. 114, concerning John the Baptist: "Ad officium namque testimonii

Role of the Apostles in the Communication of Revelation 343

of the Holy Spirit who assures the *idoneitas* of the apostles to the apostolic office.[128] In particular, the Spirit guarantees the objective fidelity of the testimony despite the passing of time;[129] he confers on the apostles the courage necessary to announce it and disposes the hearts of the hearers to accept it.[130]

By their activity of witness and teaching, the apostles continue Christ's mission of teaching. They prolong it and imitate it.[131] They do so not as delegates of an absent one but in virtue of their union of love with Jesus who acts even now, that is, in virtue of their mystical configuration to Christ.[132] Fully taking up the Pauline theme of the mystical body, St. Thomas shows how the mission of the members is not other than the mission of the Son. Christ "speaks in and through the apostles" (*Ioan.* 16, lect. 3, n. 2093);[133] the reception given to the apostles' preaching is the image of the one given to the teaching of Christ;[134] the hatred of the world for the apostles is in fact a rejection of Christ.[135]

However, if the apostolic mission has the same purposes as that of Christ—to convert the world to the faith[136]—it presents an essential novelty in relation to the historical mission of Jesus: it is extended to the pagans, while Jesus preached only to the Jews. The work of the conversion of pagans presumes that the paschal mystery has been fully accomplished.[137] It happens, therefore, through the apostles. The episode of the Greeks who, seeking to see Jesus, encounter the apostles (Jn 12:21) permits St. Thomas to insist on this apostolic mediation in the conversion of pagans:

---

requiritur idoneitas: nam nisi testis sit idoneus, qualitercumque mittatur ab alio, non est sufficiens testimonium eius. Homo autem efficitur idoneus ex gratia Dei."

128. Cf. *Ioan.* 20, lect. 4, n. 2538: "Datur eis idoneitas officii per dationem Spiritus sancti."

129. Cf. *Ioan.* 14, lect. 7, n. 1960: "Quomodo enim Evangelista Ioannes post quadraginta annos potuisset omnium verborum Christi, quae in Evangelio scripsit, habere memoriam, nisi ei Spiritus sanctus suggessisset."

130. Cf. *Ioan.* 15, lect. 5, n. 2066: "Testimonium perhibet instruendo discipulos et fiduciam eis praebendo ad testificandum . . . doctrinam suam communicando credentibus in Christum . . . emolliendo audientium corda."

131. Thus their preaching, like Christ's, is itinerant, cf. *Ioan.* 1, lect. 15, n. 281.

132. Cf. *Ioan.* 10, lect. 2, n. 1398: "Esse autem pastorem, aliis communicavit, et membris suis dedit: nam et Petrus pastor, et ceteri Apostoli pastores fuerunt. . . . Nullus enim est pastor bonus nisi per caritatem efficiatur unum cum Christo, et fiat membrum veri pastoris."

133. Saint Thomas here implicitly rejects the error according to which the mission of the Spirit takes the place of the mission of the Son in the age of the apostles.

134. Cf. *Ioan.* 13, lect. 3, n. 1793; 15, 4, n. 2042.

135. Cf. *Ioan.* 15, lect. 4, n. 2035–38.

136. Cf. *Ioan.* 15, lect. 3, n. 2027: "'Ut eatis,' per mundum discurrendo, ut totum convertatis ad fidem; Mc ult., 15: 'Euntes in mudum, praedicate Evangelium omni creaturae.'"

137. Cf. *Ioan.* 12, lect. 4, n. 1637.

[W]e should note that Christ personally preached only to the Jews . . . ; but he preached to the Gentiles through the apostles. . . . This was now being indicated beforehand inasmuch as the Gentiles who wanted to see Christ did not come to him first, but to one of his disciples, to Philip. (*Ioan.* 12, lect. 4, n. 1637)

Following the metaphor of the body, along with St. Augustine, St. Thomas thus sees the apostles as "the feet" by which Christ went to the pagans.[138] It is through them that he goes to the pagans to convert them[139] and to bring them back to God as a shepherd gathers his sheep.[140] The universal dimension of the apostolic mission (as well as its object) is signified by the name of the Twelve, according to a symbolism of numbers dear to the medievals: "They were called the twelve because the faith in the Holy Trinity had to be preached by them to the four corners of the world" (*Ioan.* 6, lect. 1, n. 856).[141] How can one distinguish in the mission between the ministerial action proper to the apostles and the divine action? Saint Thomas has recourse here to the distinction between the interior and the exterior. God (Christ) acts directly on the interior of hearts and indirectly, through the mediation of the apostles, on the exterior.[142] It therefore belongs to the apostles to continue the exterior preaching of Jesus: they "exteriorly" transmit the objective truth of the faith and exhort men to adhere to it. This teaching, however, can only attain its end through Christ's interior action in the hearts of the hearers:

[A]s long as God's help and the interior Preacher are not there, the words of the preacher have no effect. (*Ioan.* 21, lect. 1, n. 2582)

The net by which the fish are taken is the teaching of the faith, by which God draws us by inspiring us from within: "No one can come to me unless the Father who sent me draws him" (6:44). The apostles also draw us by their exhortations. (*Ioan.* 21, lect. 2, n. 2596)

In order to lead well this work of teaching, the apostles are endowed by the Spirit with, in addition to perfect knowledge, the virtues and charisms neces-

---

138. Cf. *Ioan.* 7, lect. 4, n. 1081: "Iturus [erat] ad gentes, non praesentia corporis, sed pedibus suis, scilicet Apostolis. Misit ad nos membra sua et fecit nos membra sua." Cf. Augustine, *In Iohannis Evangelium*, tract XXXI, p. 299.

139. Cf. *Ioan.* 10, lect. 6, n. 1469.

140. Cf. *Ioan.* 10, lect. 4, n. 1418.

141. Cf. 6, 8, n. 1007: "Hic enim numerus congrue consecratur eis qui fidem sanctae Trinitatis per quattuor mundi cardines praedicaturi erant."

142. Cf. *Ioan.* 21, lect. 2, n. 2608: "Invitat autem ad convivium Christus interius inspirando per seipsum . . . et exterius docendo et exhortando per alios." It is similar in sacramental action where the minister performs the "exterior" acts while Christ works the interior sanctification, cf. 6, 1, n. 861.

Role of the Apostles in the Communication of Revelation 345

sary to proclaim the Gospel. First of all, there is the apostolic boldness born of that perfect love which, as it is said, chases away fear:

> Before this the disciples were so timid that they did not dare to profess Christ publicly, but when they were filled with the Holy Spirit fear was cast out, and they proclaimed Christ to the people, being somehow impelled by that same Spirit. (*Ioan.* 16, lect. 4, n. 2106)

Henceforth they experience joy even in the trials that they endure for Christ.[143]

Second, there are signs and miracles, which aim at confirming the apostles' teaching. The apostles work them *in virtute Christi,* Christ fulfilling his promise in them: "He who believes in me will do the works I do and even greater ones" (Jn 14:12).[144] In them, the Spirit glorifies Jesus "by accomplishing marvelous works in and through the apostles"[145] because, in Aquinas's logic of participation, the dignity of secondary causes reflects the First Cause: "For the strongest sign of great power is when a person does extraordinary things not only by himself but also through others."[146] In order to avoid any ambiguity, however, this power shows itself in weakness; St. Thomas, following St. Paul, loves to highlight the very humble modes, humanly speaking, of the apostolic preaching.[147]

The ministry of the apostles is not limited to this teaching of the faith. By the administration of the sacraments, where the grace of the Holy Spirit is communicated, they also assure, in some manner, the fruitful reception of the Word. Saint Thomas sees in the two "Pentecosts" (the evening of Easter in John and Pentecost in Luke) the sign of this double aspect of the one apostolic mission:

> [T]he grace of Christ, which is given by the Holy Spirit, was to be distributed to us by being proliferated through the sacraments . . . and through teaching. . . . The Spirit descended on the apostles the first time through a breath to indicate the proliferation of grace through the sacraments, whose ministers they were. . . . The second time the Spirit descended on them in tongues of fire to indicate the proliferation of grace through teaching, and so we read in Acts (2:4) that right after they were filled with the Holy Spirit they began to speak. (*Ioan.* 20, lect. 4, n. 2539)

---

143. Cf. *Ioan.* 10, lect. 3, n. 1390; 14, 6, n. 1955, in reference to Acts 5:41.

144. Cf. the commentary on this verse, *Ioan.* 14, lect. 3, nn. 1898–9. Cf. 16, 4, n. 2106: "Dominus per Apostolos plura et maiora facit quam per semetipsum."

145. *Ioan.* 16, lect. 4, n. 2106: "Opera mirifica in Apostolis et per Apostolos faciendo."

146. *Ioan.* 14, lect. 3, n. 1898: "Potissimum enim signum magnae virtutis est ut homo non solum per se sed etiam per alios eximia operatur."

147. Cf., for example, *Ioan.* 4, lect. 3, n. 629.

At the end of this inquiry into the theological status of the apostles in the *Commentary on John,* it is evident that Aquinas's exegesis is an integral exegesis. First, St. Thomas explores the intelligibility of the Word of God by freely clarifying Scripture by means of Scripture and by returning in a systematic manner to the tradition of Patristic interpretation (in this case, Augustine and Chrysostom). Second, faith, in its search for understanding, calls largely upon metaphysical reasoning. Aquinas's reading of Scripture assumes metaphysical presuppositions that profoundly structure it. Thus, the great themes of his metaphysics of causality and participation, as integrated within a theology of divine government, are thoroughly present in his reflection on the role of the apostles. Third, this exegesis leads into the spiritual life. In the *Commentary on John,* the apostles appear as the archetype of Christian perfection, so that imitation of the apostles is the exemplary path to holiness for every Christian and especially for the Friar Preachers who constitute the audience of St. Thomas and assume by profession the *vita apostolica.* In short, the exegesis of St. Thomas is an act of preaching: an exegesis that is itself apostolic.

About the Contributors

Benedict M. Ashley, O.P. is professor of moral theology emeritus at Aquinas Institute of Theology in St. Louis. He has recently served as a research Fellow at the John Paul II Cultural Center in Washington, D.C. He is the author of numerous distinguished books and articles on moral theology. Among his recent books are *Justice in the Church* (Catholic University of America Press), *Choosing a Worldview and Value System* (Alba House), and *Living the Truth in Love* (Alba House).

Frederick Christian Bauerschmidt is associate professor of theology at Loyola College in Maryland and serves as co-editor of the journal *Modern Theology*. In addition to numerous articles, he has authored *Julian of Norwich and the Mystical Body Politic of Christ* (University of Notre Dame Press) and *Why the Mystics Matter* (Sorin Books), and he is currently preparing an anthology of and commentary on selected texts by Aquinas, primarily from the *Tertia pars* of the *Summa theologiae*.

Serge-Thomas Bonino, O.P. serves as dean of the Catholic University of Toulouse, where he teaches philosophy. Fr. Bonino is also the director of studies for the Dominicans in Toulouse and a founding member of the Institut Saint-Thomas d'Aquin, a center for advanced studies in Thomistic theology. He is the author of numerous studies on St. Thomas and the history of Thomism. He serves as the editor of the *Revue thomiste*.

John F. Boyle is professor of theology at the University of St. Thomas in St. Paul, Minnesota. Dr. Boyle is presently editing St. Thomas Aquinas's *Roman Commentary* on Book I of Peter Lombard's *Sentences*. He has published numerous scholarly articles in Thomistic studies.

Stephen F. Brown is professor of systematic theology at Boston College. In addition to numerous articles on topics in medieval philosophy and theology, he has published critical editions of the works of

Ockham, and has edited the English translation of St. Bonaventure's *Journey of the Mind to God*. He is the director of the Medieval Institute for Philosophy and Theology at Boston College.

David B. Burrell, C.S.C. is the Theodore Hesburgh Professor in Philosophy and Theology at the University of Notre Dame. Fr. Burrell has written numerous books and articles in comparative philosophical theology, including *Aquinas: God and Action* (University of Notre Dame Press), *Knowing the Unknowable God* (University of Notre Dame Press), *Freedom and Creation in Three Traditions* (University of Notre Dame Press), and *Friendship and Ways to Truth* (University of Notre Dame Press). He has co-translated *Al-Ghazali on the Ninety-Nine Beautiful Names of God* (Islamic Texts Society) and has translated Al-Ghazali's *Book of Faith in Divine Unity and Trust in God's Providence* (Fons Vitae).

Michael Dauphinais is associate dean of faculty and assistant professor of theology at Ave Maria University. His dissertation, "Christ the Teacher in St. Thomas Aquinas: The Pedagogy of the Incarnation," is under review for publication. With Matthew Levering, he has authored *Knowing the Love of Christ: An Introduction to the Theology of St. Thomas Aquinas* (University of Notre Dame Press) and *Holy People, Holy Land: A Theological Introduction to the Bible* (Brazos Press). He is the co-editor of the English edition of *Nova et Vetera*.

Gilles Emery, O.P. is professor of dogmatic theology at the University of Fribourg. In addition to numerous scholarly articles, he has authored *La Trinité créatrice* (Vrin), *Thomas d'Aquin, Traités: Les raisons de la foi, les articles de la foi* (Cerf), and *Trinity in Aquinas* (Sapientia Press). He co-edited, with Pierre Gisel, *Le Christianisme est-il un monotheisme?* (Labor et Fides). He is a member of the editorial board of the *Revue thomiste*.

Paul L. Gondreau is assistant professor of theology at Providence College, where he teaches in both the undergraduate and graduate programs. He is the author of *The Passions of Christ's Soul in the Theology of St. Thomas Aquinas* (Aschendorff). He is a member of the editorial board of the English edition of *Nova et Vetera*.

Matthew L. Lamb is professor of theology at Boston College and Ave Maria University. He has published more than 125 articles and essays in a variety of journals and has authored *History, Method, and Theology* and *Solidarity with Victims* (Crossroad). He is the translator of St. Thomas Aquinas's *Commentary on St. Paul's Letter to the Ephesians* (Magi Books).

About the Contributors 349

Carlo Leget is associate professor of medical ethics at the University Medical Centre Nijmegen. He is an active member of the Thomas Instituut at Utrecht, and a frequent contributor to the Instituut's *Jaarboek*. In addition to numerous articles, his publications include *Living with God: Thomas Aquinas on the Relation between Life on Earth and "Life" after Death* (Peeters), a bilingual (Latin-Dutch) edition of Aquinas's Sermons on the Ten Commandments (Meinema), and a bilingual edition of Aquinas's Sermons on the Lord's Prayer and Hail Mary (Meinema). He is co-editor of *Aquinas as Authority* (Peeters).

Matthew Levering is associate professor of theology at Ave Maria University. He has authored *Christ's Fulfillment of Torah and Temple: Salvation according to St. Thomas Aquinas* (University of Notre Dame Press) and *Scripture and Metaphysics: Aquinas and the Renewal of Trinitarian Theology* (Blackwell), and co-authored with Michael Dauphinais *Knowing the Love of Christ: An Introduction to the Theology of St. Thomas Aquinas* (University of Notre Dame Press) and *Holy People, Holy Land: A Theological Introduction to the Bible* (Brazos Press). He serves on the editorial board of Catholic University of America Press's Thomas Aquinas in Translation series, and is co-editor of the English edition of *Nova et Vetera*.

Steven A. Long is assistant professor of philosophy at the University of St. Thomas in St. Paul, Minnesota. He has published numerous important articles in scholarly journals—including among many others *The Thomist, International Philosophical Quarterly,* and *Revue thomiste*—and has lectured widely in the United States and Europe on questions of metaphysics and ethics. Presently he is preparing a collection of essays for publication. He serves as an associate editor of the English edition of *Nova et Vetera*.

Bruce D. Marshall is professor of historical theology at the Perkins School of Theology at Southern Methodist University. He has played an important role in the ecumenical dialogue between the Evangelical Lutheran Church in America and the Standing Conference of Canonical Orthodox Bishops in the Americas. In addition to numerous scholarly and popular articles, he is the author, most recently, of *Trinity and Truth* (Cambridge University Press).

Richard A. Schenk, O.P. completed his studies in Munich with a dissertation on the anthropology of St. Thomas, before teaching theology in Germany, in Switzerland, and at the Dominican School of Philosophy and Theology in Berkeley, California. Between 1991 and 2000 he served as director of the Hannover Institute of Philosophical Research. He is currently director of the

Intercultural Forum for Studies in Faith and Culture at the John Paul II Cultural Center in Washington, D.C. The critical editor of Robert Kilwardby's *Quaestiones in librum IV Sententiarum*, he is the author of numerous articles in contemporary systematic theology, comparative theology, and medieval theology. For the Catholic University of America Press, he is preparing a new edition of Aquinas's *Commentary on Hebrews*.

Michael Sherwin, O.P. is associate professor of moral theology at the University of Fribourg, Switzerland. He has also taught at the Dominican School of Philosophy and Theology in Berkeley, California. Fr. Sherwin's translation of *Morality: A Catholic View* from the French edition by Servais Pinckaers, O.P. has been recently published by St. Augustine's Press. Fr. Sherwin is the author of a forthcoming monograph, *"By Knowledge and by Love": Charity and Knowledge in the Moral Theology of St. Thomas Aquinas* (Catholic University of America Press).

Janet E. Smith holds the Michael J. McGivney Chair in Life Issues Ethics at Sacred Heart Major Seminary, in Detroit, Michigan. In addition to many scholarly and popular articles, she has published *Humanae Vitae: A Generation Later* (Catholic University of America Press) and *Why Humanae Vitae Was Right: A Reader* (Ignatius Press).

Pim Valkenberg is associate professor of dogmatic theology and theology of religions at the Department of Theology and Religious Studies, Catholic University of Nijmegen. In addition, he is visiting professor for theology in the M. Phil. program at St. Augustine College of South Africa, Johannesburg, South Africa. He is a member of the Thomas Instituut at Utrecht and is a frequent contributor to its *Jaarboek*. In addition to his numerous articles in medieval theology, Christology, and comparative theology, he has authored *Words of the Living God: Place and Function of Holy Scripture in the Theology of St. Thomas Aquinas* (Peeters).

Michael Waldstein is the president of the International Theological Institute in Gaming, Austria. A frequent writer on topics pertaining to the genesis of Christianity, he has co-authored with Frederik Wisse, *The Apocryphon of John: Synopsis of Nag Hammadi Codices II,1 III,1 and IV,1 with BG 8502,2* (Brill). He is the author of numerous scholarly articles regarding the Gospel of John, Gnosticism, Rudolf Bultmann, St. Thomas Aquinas, and Hans Urs von Balthasar. He is working on a book, *Common Good and Gift of Self: The Communion of Persons in Thomas Aquinas and John Paul II*.

Selected Bibliography
St. Thomas Aquinas and the Bible
COMPILED BY CHRISTOPHER T. BAGLOW

Works by St. Thomas Aquinas on Scripture—Latin Editions and Corresponding English Translations. (All of the Latin editions listed below are contained in database form with both reading and search capacities on Roberto Busa, S.J., ed., *Thomae Aquinatis opera omnia cum hypertextibus in CD-ROM,* 2nd ed. Milan: Licosa-Editel, 1996.)

1. *Expositio super Isaiam ad litteram.* Vol. 28, Leonine Ed. Rome: 1974.
"Commentary on the Book of the Prophet Isaiah." Trans. Matthew Rzeczkowski. In *Thomas Aquinas, The Gifts of the Spirit: Selected Spiritual Writings,* ed. Benedict Ashley, 87–91. Hyde Park, N.Y.: New City Press, 1995: 87–91. (On Is 11.2.)

2. *Super Ieremiam et Threnos.* In vol. 14, Parma Ed., 577–667; 668–685. Parma: 1863. (No published translation.)

3. *"De commendatione et partitione sacrae scripturae"* [Principium "Rigans montes de superioribus" and "Hic est liber mandatorum Dei"]. In vol. 1, *Opuscula theologica,* ed. R. Verardi, 435–43. Turin: Marietti, 1954.
"The Inaugural Sermons." In *Thomas Aquinas, Selected Writings,* ed. and trans. Ralph McInerny, 5–17. Harmondsworth: Penguin, 1998. (Includes both inaugural lectures.)
"Inaugural Lecture (1256)." In *Albert and Thomas: Selected Writings,* ed. and trans. Simon Tugwell, 355–60. Classics of Western Spirituality. New York: Paulist Press, 1988. (Includes the first inaugural lecture.)

4. *Expositio super Iob ad litteram.* Vol. 26, Leonine Ed. Rome: 1965.
The Literal Exposition on Job: A Scriptural Commentary Concerning Providence. Trans. with an introduction by Martin D. Yaffe and Anthony Damico. Atlanta, Ga.: Scholars Press, 1989.

5. *Glossa continua super Evangelia (Catena Aurea).* 2 vols., ed. by A. Guarienti. Turin: Marietti, 1953.
Catena Aurea: Commentary on the Four Gospels Collected out of the Works of the Fathers by S. Thomas Aquinas, trans. John Henry Newman. 4 vols. Oxford: Parker, 1841–45; reprinted in 7 vols., Albany, N.Y.: Preserving Christian Publications, 1993–96; reprinted in 4 vols., London: St. Austin Press, 1997.
Catena Aurea. Trans. M. F. Toal. Mercier Press, 1955; reprinted in 4 vols. as *The Sunday*

Sermons of the Great Fathers, Chicago: Regnery, 1957–63; Swedesboro, N.J.: Preservation Press, 1996.

6. *Lectura super Matthaeum.* Turin: Marietti, 1951. [Includes spurious text in nos. 444–582 and 603–10; cf. MS Basel, *Bibl. Univ.* B.V. 12 for complete text of the commentary.]
"From the Lectures on St. Matthew." In *Albert and Thomas: Selected Writings,* ed. and trans. Simon Tugwell, 445–75. Classics of Western Spirituality. New York: Paulist Press, 1988. (On Mt 6.5–15.)

7. *Lectura Super Evangelium S. Ioannis lectura.* Ed. Raffaele Cai. Turin: Marietti, 1952.
Commentary on the Gospel of St. John, Part 1. Trans. James A. Weisheipl and Fabian R. Larcher. Albany, N.Y.: Magi Books, 1980. (Contains lectures on John 1–7.)
Commentary on the Gospel of St. John, Part 2. Trans. Fabian R. Larcher. Petersham, Mass.: St. Bede's Publications, 1999. (Contains lectures on John 8–21.)

8. *Super Epistolas S. Pauli lectura.* Vols. 1–2, ed. by Raphael Cai. Turin: Marietti, 1952. [Includes spurious text in vol. 1, nos. 336–582 of *In I Cor.*]
Commentary on St. Paul's Epistle to the Galatians. Trans. Fabian R. Larcher. Albany, N.Y.: Magi Books, 1966.
Commentary on St. Paul's Epistle to the Ephesians. Trans with an introduction by Matthew L. Lamb. Albany, N.Y.: Magi Books, 1966.
Commentary on St. Paul's First Letter to the Thessalonians and the Letter to the Philippians. Trans. Fabian R. Larcher and Michael Duffy. Albany, N.Y.: Magi Books, 1969.
Commentary on St. Paul's First Letter to the Corinthians. Trans. Fabian R. Larcher and ed. Daniel A. Keating. Posted at www.aquinas.avemaria.edu
Commentary on St. Paul's Second Letter to the Corinthians. Trans. Fabian R. Larcher and ed. Daniel A. Keating. Posted at www.aquinas.avemaria.edu.
Commentary on the Letter to the Hebrews. Trans. Fabian R. Larcher and ed. Daniel A. Keating. Posted at www.aquinas.avemaria.edu.
Commentary on the Letter to the Colossians. Trans. Fabian R. Larcher and ed. Daniel A. Keating. Posted at www.aquinas.avemaria.edu.
"Exposition of Paul's Epistle to Philemon." In *Thomas Aquinas, Selected Writings,* ed. and trans. Ralph McInerny, 812–21. New York: Penguin, 1998.
"Selections from Thomas Aquinas' *Commentary on Romans.*" Trans. Eugene F. Rogers, Jr. In *The Theological Interpretation of Scripture: Classic and Contemporary Readings,* ed. Stephen Fowl, 325–35. Blackwell Readings in Modern Theology. Oxford: Blackwell, 1997. (Parts of the commentary on Romans 9–11.)
"Commentary on Paul's First Epistle to the Corinthians." Trans. Matthew Rzeczkowski. In *Thomas Aquinas, The Gifts of the Spirit: Selected Spiritual Writings,* ed. Benedict Ashley, 21–78. Hyde Park, N.Y.: New City Press, 1995. (On 1 Cor 12–13.)
"From the First Lectures on St. Paul" and "From the *Commentary on Romans.*" In *Albert and Thomas: Selected Writings,* ed. and trans. Simon Tugwell, 433–38. Classics of Western Spirituality. New York: Paulist Press, 1988. (On 1 Cor 14.13–15, 1 Tim 2.1, and Rom 8.26–27.)

9. *Postilla super Psalmos.* In vol. 14, Parma Ed., 148–553. Parma: 1863.
St. Thomas's Commentary on the Psalms. Trans. Hugh McDonald, Stephen Loughlin, et al. Posted at www.niagara.edu/aquinas and faculty.niagara.edu/loughlin/Translation.html, with mirror site at www4.desales.edu/~philtheo/loughlin/ATP/index.html. (In progress; Latin and English.)
"Commentary on the Psalms of David." Trans. Matthew Rzeczkowski. In *Thomas Aquinas, The Gifts of the Spirit: Selected Spiritual Writings,* ed. Benedict Ashley, 95–133. Hyde Park, N.Y.: New City Press, 1995. (Prologue, and commentary on Ps 45.)

Selected Bibliography

Secondary Works

Aillet, Marc. *Lire le Bible avec S. Thomas*. Fribourg: Editions Universitaires, 1993.

Arges, Michael. "New Evidence Concerning the Date of Thomas Aquinas' *Lectura* on Matthew." *Medieval Studies* 49 (1987): 517–23.

Arias Reyero, Maximino. *Thomas von Aquin als Exeget*. Einsiedeln: Johannes Verlag, 1971.

Ausín, S. "La providencia divina en el libro de Job. Estudio sobre la 'Expositio in Job' de Santo Tomás de Aquino." *Scripta Theologica* 8 (1976): 477–550.

Baglow, Christopher T. "*Modus et Forma*": *A New Approach to the Exegesis of Saint Thomas Aquinas with an Application to the* Lectura super Epistolam ad Ephesios. Analecta Biblica 149. Rome: Pontifical Biblical Institute Press, 2002.

———. "Sacred Scripture and Sacred Doctrine in St. Thomas Aquinas." In *Aquinas on Doctrine: A Critical Introduction*, ed. Thomas G. Weinandy, Daniel A. Keating, and John P. Yocum, 1–25. Edinburgh: T&T Clark, 2004.

Basevi, C. "La justificatión en los comentarios de Pelagio, Lutero y santo Tomás a la epistola a los Romanos." *Scripta Theologica* 19 (1987): 113–76.

Bataillon, L.-J. "De la *lectio* à la *praedicatio*. Commentaires bibliques et sermons au XIIIe siècle." *Revue des sciences philosophiques et théologiques* 70 (1986): 559–75.

———. "La diffusione manoscritta e stampata dei commenti biblici di san Tommaso d'Aquino." *Angelicum* 71 (1994): 579–90.

———. "Les sermons de saint Thomas et la *Catena Aurea*." In *St. Thomas Aquinas 1274–1974: Commemorative Studies*. Vol. 1, ed. A. Maurer, 67–75. Toronto: 1974.

———. "Saint Thomas et les Pères: de la *Catena* à la *Tertia Pars*." In *Ordo sapientiae et amoris*, ed. C.-J. Pinto de Oliveira, 15–36. Fribourg: Editions Universitaires, 1993.

Bellemare, R. "La Somme de Théologie et la lecture de la Bible." In *Colloque commémoratif saint Thomas d'Aquin 1274–1974*. Vol. 5, 257–70. Ottawa: 1974.

Benoit, P. *Inspiration and the Bible*. Trans. Jerome Murphy-O'Connor and M. Keverne. London, Melbourne, and New York: Sheed and Ward, 1965.

Berceville, G. "Exégèse biblique, théologie et philosophie chez Thomas d'Aquin et Luther commentateurs de Rm 7:14–25." *Recherches de science religieuse* 91 (2003): 373–95.

———. "L'étonnante alliance: Evangile et miracles selon saint Thomas d'Aquin." *Revue Thomiste* 103 (2003): 5–74.

———. "L'*Expositio continua* sur les quatre Evangiles de saint Thomas d'Aquin *(Catena Aurea)*: le commentaire de Marc." Mémoire de D.E.A., 1988, deposited at Le Saulchoir.

Berchtold, Christoph. *Manifestatio Veritatis. Zum Offenbarungsbegriff bei Thomas von Aquin*. Münster: LIT-Verlag, 2000.

Berger, David. "Die Quellen der Summa theologiae: Die Heilige Schrift." In David Berger, *Thomas von Aquins Summa theologiae*, 67–75. Darmstadt: Wissenschaftliche Buchgesellschaft, 2004.

———. "*Sacra doctrina*—Die zentrale Bedeutung der q.1 der Ia der *Summa theologiae* des Aquinaten." *Gregorianum* 84 (2004): forthcoming.

Bermudez, Catalina. "Hijos de Dios por la Gracia en los comentarios de Santo Tomás a las cartas paulinas." In *Storia del tomismo*, 78–89. Studia Tomistici 45. Vatican City: Libreria Editrice Vaticana, 1992.

———. "Predestinazione, grazia et libertà nei Comenti di San Tommaso alle Lettere di San Paolo." *Annales Thelogici* 4 (1990): 399–421.

Biffi, Inos. "I misteri della vita Cristo nei commentari biblici di San Tommaso d'Aquino." *Divus Tomas* 79 (1976): 217–54.

Billy, Dennis J. "Grace and Natural Law in the *Super epistola ad Romanos lectura*: A Study in Thomas' Commentary on Romans 2:14–16." *Studia Moralia* 26 (1988): 15–37.

Black, C. Clifton. "St. Thomas' Commentary on the Johannine Prologue: Some Reflections on Its Character and Implications." *Catholic Biblical Quarterly* 48 (1986): 681–98.

Blanche, F.-A. "Le sens littéral des Écritures d'après saint Thomas d'Aquin." *Revue Thomiste* 14 (1906): 192–212.

Blanco, A. "Word and Truth in Divine Revelation. A Study of the Commentary of St. Thomas Aquinas on John 14,6." In *La doctrine de la révélation divine de saint Thomas d'Aquin*, ed. Leo Elders, 27–48. Vatican City: Libreria Editrice Vaticana, 1990.

Boadt, Lawrence. "St. Thomas Aquinas and the Biblical Wisdom Tradition." *Thomist* 49 (1985): 575–611.

Bouthillier, D. "Le Christ en son mystère dans les *Collationes* du *Super Isaiam* de saint Thomas d'Aquin." In *Ordo sapientiae et amoris*, ed. C.-J. Pinto de Oliveira, 37–64. Fribourg: Editions Universitaires, 1993.

Boyle, John F. "St. Thomas Aquinas and Sacred Scripture." *Pro Ecclesia* 4 (1996): 92–104.

———. "The Theological Character of the Scholastic 'Division of the Text' with Particular Reference to the Commentaries of Saint Thomas Aquinas." In *With Reverence for the Word: Medieval Christian Exegesis in Judaism, Christianity and Islam*, ed. Jane Dammen McAuliffe, Barry D. Walfish and Joseph W. Goering, 276–83. Oxford: Oxford University Press, 2002.

Callan, Charles J. "The Bible in the Summa Theologica of St. Thomas Aquinas." *Catholic Biblical Quarterly* 9 (1947): 33–47.

Caprioli, P. M. "Il sacerdozio di Christo nella *Somma Teologica* e nel commento *Super Epistolam ad Hebraeos*." In *Storia del tomismo*, 96–105. Studi Tomistici 45. Vatican City: Libreria Editrice Vaticana, 1992.

Castagnoli, Pietro. "Regesta Thomistica: Saggio di chronologia della vita e scritti di S. Tommaso d'Aquino." *Divus Thomas* 30 (1927): 704–24; 31 (1928): 249–68.

Cessario, Romanus. *The Godly Image: Christ and Salvation in Catholic Thought from Anselm to Aquinas*. Petersham, Mass.: St. Bede's Publications, 1990.

Chardonnens, D. "*Dei providentia circa hominem*. Providence divine et condition humaine selon l'*Expositio super Iob ad litteram* de Thomas d'Aquin. Diss., Fribourg, 1995.

———. "La loi ancienne selon S. Thomas." *Revue Thomiste* 61 (1961): 485–97.

———. "L'espérance de la résurrection selon Thomas d'Aquin, commentateur du Livre de Job. 'Dans ma chair, je verrai Dieu.'" In *Ordo sapientiae et amoris*, ed. C.-J. Pinto de Oliveira, 65–83. Fribourg: Editions Universitaires, 1993.

———. *L'homme sous le regard de la providence: Providence de Dieu et condition humaine selon l'Exposition littérale sur le livre de Job de Thomas d'Aquin*. Paris: J. Vrin, 1997.

Chenu, M.-D. "Lecture de la Bible et Philosophie." In *Mélanges offerts à Étienne Gilson*, 161–71. Toronto/Paris, 1959.

———. "Théologie symbolique et exégèse scolastique aux XIIe–XIIIe siècles." In *Mélanges J. de Ghellinck*. Vol. 2, 509–26. Gembloux, 1951.

———. *Toward Understanding St. Thomas*. Trans. A.-M. Landry and D. Hughes. Chicago: Henry Regnery, 1964.

Childs, Brevard S. *The Struggle to Understand Isaiah as Christian Scripture*. Grand Rapids, Mich.: Eerdmans, 2004.

———. *Biblical Theology of the Old and New Testaments: Theological Reflection on the Christian Bible*. Minneapolis, Minn.: Fortress Press, 1992.

Cipriani, S. "Riflessioni esegetiche su *super S. Ioannis Evangelium Lectura* di S. Tommaso." In *Atti del VIII Congresso Tomistico Internazionale*. Vol. 1, 172–88. Vatican City: Libreria Editrice Vaticana, 1981.

Cirillo, A. "Cristo Rivelatore del Padre nel Vangelo di S. Giovanni secondo il Commento di San Tommaso d'Aquino." Diss., Angelicum, 1988.

Coggi, R. "Le caratteristiche fondamentali dell'esegesi biblica di san Tommaso." *Sacra doctrina* 35 (1990): 533–44.

Colosio, Innocenzo. "La lode divina nel commento di S. Tommaso ai Salmi." *Rassegna di Ascetica e Mistica* 25 (1974): 179–94.

Colunga, A. "La vida eterna en san Juan según los comentarios de san Alberto Magno y santo Tómas." *Ciencia tomista* 65 (1943): 121–43.

———. "Los sentidos de los Salmos según S. Tomas." *Ciencia Tomista* 39 (1917): 353–62.

Congar, Y-M. "Le sens de l'économie salutaire dans la théologie de S. Thomas." In *Festgabe Joseph Lortz*. Vol. 1, 73–122. Baden-Baden: B. Grimm, 1957.

———. "Sur la trilogie: Prophète-roi-prêtre." *Revue des sciences philosophiques et théologiques* 67 (1983): 97–115.

———. "Tradition und Sacra Doctrina bei Thomas von Aquin." In *Kirche und Ueberlieferung: Festgabe J.R. Geiselmann*, ed. J. Betz and H. Fries, 170–210. Freiburg: 1960.

Conticello, C. G. "San Tommaso ed i padri: La *Catena aurea super Ioannem*." *Archives d'histoire doctrinale et littéraire du moyen âge* 65 (1990): 31–92.

Corbin, Michel. "Le Pain de la Vie. La lecture de Jn 6 par S. Thomas d'Aquin." *Recherches de Science Religieuse* 65 (1977): 107–38.

Cuéllar, Miguel Ponce. *La Naturaleza de la Iglesia según Santo Tomas. Estudio del Tema en el Comentario al "Corpus Paulinum."* Pamplona: Ediciones Universidad de Navarra, 1979.

Cueppens, Franziscus. "Quid S. Thomas de multiplici sensu litterali in s. Scriptura senserit?" *Divus Thomas* 33 (1930): 164–73.

Dahan, Gilbert. *L'exégèse chrétienne de la Bible en Occident médiéval, XIIe–XIVe siècle*. Paris: Cerf, 1999.

———. "Saint Thomas d'Aquin et la métaphore. Rhétorique et herméneutique." *Medioevo* 18 (1992): 85–117.

———. "Thomas d'Aquin commentateur de la première épître aux Corinthiens." In Thomas d'Aquin, *Commentaire de la première Epître aux Corinthiens*, trans. Jean-Eric Stroobant de Saint-Eloy, i–xxxvii. Paris: Cerf, 2002.

Daly, Mary S. "The Notion of Justification in the Commentary of St. Thomas Aquinas on the Epistle to the Romans." Diss., Marquette University, 1971.

Davies, Brian. "Is 'Sacra Doctrina' Theology?" *New Blackfriars* 71 (1990).

Decker, Bruno. "Schriftprinzip und Ergänzungstradition in der Theologie des hl. Thomas von Aquin." In *Schrift und Tradition*, 191–221. Essen, 1962.

———. "Sola Scripture bei Thomas von Aquino." In *Universitas: Dienst an Wahreit und Leben (Festschrift für Bischof Dr. Albert Stohr)*. Vol. 3, 117–29. Mainz: Matthias Grünewald, 1960.

Denifle, H. "Quel livre servait de base à l'enseignement des maîtres en théologie dans l'université de Paris?" *Revue Thomiste* 2 (1894): 149–61.

Di Marco, A. "San Tommaso e la pluralità dei sensi biblici nella problematica odierna." In *Atti del congresso internazionale Tommaso d'Aquino nel suo settimo centenario*. Vol. 4, 60–69. Naples, 1976.

Domanyi, Thomas. *Der Römerbriefkommentar des Thomas von Aquin: Ein Beitrag zur Untersuchung seiner Auslegungsmethode*. Bern: Peter Lang, 1979.

Dondaine, A. Preface to *Expositio super Job. Tom. XXVI, Opera Omnia*, by Thomas Aquinas: 420–30.

Donneaud, Henri. "Insaisissable sacra doctrina?" *Revue Thomiste* 98 (1998): 179–224.

Dubois, M. "Mystical and Realistic Elements in the Exegesis and Hermeneutics of St. Thomas Aquinas." In *Creative Biblical Exegesis: Christian and Jewish Hermeneutics through the Centuries*, ed. Benjamin Uffenheimer and H.G. Reventlow, 39–54. Sheffield, England: JSOT Press, 1988.

Elders, Leo J. "Aquinas on Holy Scripture as the Medium of Divine Revelation." In *La doctrine de la révélation divine de saint Thomas d'Aquin*, ed. Leo Elders, 132–52. Vatican City: Libreria Editrice Vaticana, 1990.

———. "Der Wahrheitsbegriff in den Bibelkommentaren des Thomas von Aquin." In *Im Ringen um die Wahrheit*, ed. Remigius Baumer et al., 35–52 Bierbronnen: Hochschulverlag der Gustav Siewerth Akademie, 1997.

———. "La relation entre l'Ancienne et la Nouvelle Alliance selon saint Thomas." *Revue Thomiste* 100 (2000): 580–602.

———. "Les citations de saint Augustin dans la *Somme théologique* de saint Thomas d'Aquin." *Doctor Communis* 40 (1987): 115–67.

———. "St. Thomas and the Bible." In *Aquinas's Sources: The Notre Dame Symposium,* ed. Timothy L. Smith. South Bend, Ind.: St. Augustine's Press, forthcoming.

Emery, Gilles. *La Trinité créatrice.* Paris: Vrin, 1995.

———. *Trinity in Aquinas.* Ypsilanti, Mich.: Sapientia Press, 2003.

Eschmann, I. T. "The Quotations of Aristotle's *Politics* in St. Thomas' *Lectura super Matthaeum.*" *Medieval Studies* 18 (1956): 232–40.

Fernandez, A. "Système exégétiques de saint Thomas." *España y America* 10 (1909).

Ferraro, G. "Aspetti di penumatologia nell'esegesi di S. Tommaso d'Aquino dell'espistola ai Romani." *Euntes docete* 36 (1983): 51–78.

———. "Il tema dello Spirito Santo nel Commento di San Tommaso d'Aquino all'Epistola agli Ebri." In *Atti del VII Congresso Tomistico Internazionale: Tommaso d'Aquino nel suo settimo centenario.* Vol. 4, 41–59. Naples, 1976.

———. "La pneumatologia di san Tommaso d'Aquino nel suo commento al quarto vangelo. Aspetti di dottrina e di esegesi del dottore angelico." *Angelicum* 66 (1989): 193–263.

———. "L'ora di Cristo e della Chiesa nel commento di san Tommaso d'Aquino al quarto vangelo. Aspetti di esegesi thomista." In *San Tommaso e l'odierna problematica teologica,* 125–55. Studi Tomistici 2. Vatican City: Libreria Editrice Vaticana, 1974.

———. *Lo Spirito e l'"ora" di Cristo: L'esegesi di San Tommaso d'Aquino sul quarto Vangelo.* Vatican City: Libreria Editrice Vaticana, 1996.

———. "Lo Spirito Santo nel commento di san Tommaso d'Aquino ai capitoli XIV–XVI del quarto vangelo." In *Atti del VII Congresso Tomistico Internazionale: Tommaso d'Aquino nel suo settimo centenario.* Vol. 4, 79–91. Naples, 1976.

———. "San Giovanni Crisostomo come fonte di san Tommaso. La sua esposizione dei testi pneumatologici nel commento del quarto vangelo." *Angelicum* 62 (1985): 194–244.

Froehlich, Karl. "Aquinas, Thomas." In *Historical Handbook of Major Biblical Interpreters,* ed. Donald K. McKim, 85–91. Downers Grove, Ill.: Intervarsity Press, 1998.

Gaboriau, Florent. *Au seuil de la Somme. Un quiproquo chez Thomas d'Aquin?* Paris: FAC, 1999.

Gardeil, A. "Les procédés exégétiques de S. Thomas." *Revue Thomiste* 11 (1903): 428–57.

Garrigues, Jean-Miguel. "Les prérogatives inaliénables du peuple juif selon saint Thomas commentant saint Paul. À propos de La Promesse par le Cardinal J.-M. Lustiger." *Revue Thomiste* 103 (2003): 145–58.

Geenen, G. "Le fonti patristiche come autorità nella teologia di san Tommaso." *Sacra doctrina* 20 (1975): 7–67.

———. "The Place of Tradition in the Theology of St. Thomas." *Thomist* 15 (1962): 110–35.

Gélinas, Y. D. "La critique de Thomas d'Aquin sur l'exégèse de Joachim de Fiore." In *Atti del VII Congresso Tomistico Internazionale: Tommaso d'Aquino nel suo settimo centenario.* Vol. 1, 368–76. Naples, 1975.

Glorieux, P. "Essai sur les commentaires scripturaires de saint Thomas et leur chronologie." *Recherches de théologie ancienne et médiévale* 17 (1950): 237–66.

Grijs, F. de. "Het schriftgebruik in *De Regno* van Thomas van Aquino." In *Jaarboek 1985,* ed. Werkgroep Thomas van Aquino, 34–72. Utrecht: Thomas Instituut, 1986.

———. "Thomas' Schriftgebruik bij de systematische overdenking van het willen van Christus." In *Jaarboek 1981,* ed. Werkgroep Thomas van Aquino, 38–84. Utrecht: Thomas Instituut, 1981.

Guindon, Roger. "La *Lectura super Matthaeum incompleta* de saint Thomas." *Revue de l'Université d'Ottawa* 25 (1955): 213–19.

———. "La Théologie de Saint Thomas d'Aquin dans le rayonnement due *Prologue* de saint Jean." *Revue de l'Université d'Ottawa* 29 (1959): 5–23; 121–42.

———. "L'*Expositio in Isaiam* est-elle une oeuvre de Thomas d'Aquin <<bachelier biblique>>?" *Recherches de théologie ancienne et médiévale* 21 (1954): 312–21.

Haggard, Frank Powell. "An Interpretation of Thomas Aquinas as a Biblical Theologian with Special Reference to his Systematizing of the Economy of Salvation." Diss., Drew University, 1972.

Healy, Nicholas M. *Thomas Aquinas: Theologian of the Christian Life*. Aldershot, England: Ashgate, 2003.

Hendrickx, M. *Sagesse de Dieu et sagesse des hommes. Le commentaire de 1 Co 1–4 et sa confrontation avec la grande glose de Pierre Lombard*. Louvain-la-Neuve, 1987.

Hood, John Y. B. *Aquinas and the Jews*. Philadelphia: University of Pennsylvania Press, 1995.

Horst, Ulrich. *Die Gaben des Heiligen Geistes nach Thomas von Aquin*. Berlin: Academie Verlag, 2001.

———. "Über die Frage einer heilsökonomischen Theologie bei Thomas von Aquin: Ergebnisse und Probleme der neuren Forschung." *Münchener Theologische Zeitschrift* 12 (1961): 97–111.

Imbach, Rudi. "La filosofia nel prologo di san Giovanni secondo sant'Agostino, san Tommaso e Meister Eckhart." In *Studi 1995*, ed. D. Lorenz and S. Serafini, 161–82. Rome: 1995.

Johnson, Mark F. "Another Look at the Plurality of the Literal Sense." *Medieval Philosophy and Theology* 2 (1992): 117–41.

———. "God's Knowledge in Our Frail Mind: The Thomistic Model of Theology." *Angelicum* 76 (1999): 25–45.

Jordan, Mark. "Préface." In St. Thomas Aquinas, *Commentaire sur les Psaumes*, trans. J.-E. Stroobant, 7–12. Paris: Cerf, 1996.

———. "Thomas Aquinas." In *Dictionary of Biblical Interpretation: K–Z*, ed. John H. Hayes, 573–75. Nashville: Abingdon Press, 1999.

Kaczynsky, Edward. "'Lex spiritus' in S. Paolo e la sua interpretazione in S. Tommaso." In *Credo in Spiritum Sanctum: Atti del congresso telogico internazionale di Pneumatologia*. Vol. 2, 1207–22. Vatican City: Libreria Editrice Vaticana, 1983.

Kealy, Sean P. *Matthew's Gospel and the History of Biblical Interpretation*. Lewiston: Edwin Mellen Press, 1997.

Keaty, Anthony. "The Demands of Sacred Doctrine on 'Beginners.'" *New Blackfriars* 84 (2003): 500–509.

———. "Thomas's Authority for Identifying Charity as Friendship: Aristotle or John 15?" *Thomist* 62 (1998): 581–601.

Kennedy, Robert G. "Thomas Aquinas and the Literal Sense of Sacred Scripture." Diss., University of Notre Dame, 1985.

Kerr, Fergus. "Recent Thomistica: I." *New Blackfriars* 83 (2002): 245–51.

Klünker, W.-U. *Thomas von Aquin. Der Prolog des Johannes-Evangeliums*. Stuttgart, 1986.

Koster, M.-D. "Das Schriftzeugnis in der Mariologie des Thomas von Aquin." In *Heilige Schrift und Maria*, ed. Deutschen Arbeitsgemeinschaft für Mariologie, 80–94. Essen, 1963.

Kühn, Ulrich. *Via caritatis: Theologie des Gesetzes bei Thomas von Aquin*. Göttingen: Vandenhoeck and Ruprecht, 1965.

Lamb, Matthew. Foreword to St. Thomas Aquinas, *Commentary on St. Paul's Epistle to the Ephesians*, 3–36. Albany, N.Y.: Magi Books, 1966.

La Soujeole, Benoit-Dominique de. "Les *tria munera Christi*: Contribution de saint Thomas à la recherche contemporaine." *Revue Thomiste* 99 (1999): 59–74.

Légendre, A. "La bible dans la Somme théologique." *Revue fac. Cath. de l'Ouest* 21 (1911): 9–33.

Levering, Matthew. *Christ's Fulfillment of Torah and Temple: Salvation according to Thomas Aquinas*. Notre Dame: University of Notre Dame Press, 2002.

———. *Scripture and Metaphysics: Aquinas and the Renewal of Trinitarian Theology.* Oxford: Blackwell, 2004.

———. "St. Thomas Aquinas and the Pontifical Biblical Commission." *Pro Ecclesia* 13 (2004): 25–38.

Lubac, Henri de. *Exégèse Médiévale: Les Quatre Sens de L'Écriture.* 4 vols. Paris: Aubier, 1959–63. (See especially vol. 4, 272–302.)

———. "Spiritual Understanding." In *The Theological Interpretation of Scripture: Classic and Contemporary Readings,* ed. Stephen E. Fowl, 2–25. Oxford: Blackwell, 1997.

Lyonnet, S. "L'actualité de Saint Thomas exégète. L'opposition paulinienne entre 'la lettre et l'Esprit' à la lumière de l'interprétation de saint Thomas." In *Atti del VII Congresso Tomistico Internazionale: Tommaso d'Aquino nel suo settimo centenario.* Vol. 4, 9–28. Naples, 1976.

MacGough, A. C. "Los signos del cuarto evangelio según santo Tomás de Aquino." Diss., Pamplona, 1979.

Mahoney, I. D. J. "The Spirit of God and the Sons of God: The Power of the Holy Spirit in Christian Behaviour according to the Scripture Commentaries of Saint Thomas Aquinas." Diss., Gregorianum, 1974.

Mailhiot, M.-D. "La pensée de saint Thomas sur le sens spirituel." *Revue Thomiste* 59 (1959): 613–63.

Maillard, Pierre-Yves. *La vision de Dieu chez Thomas d'Aquin: Une lecture de l'In Ioannem à la lumière de ses sources augustiniennes.* Paris: J. Vrin, 2001.

Mandonnet, P. "Chronologie des écrits scripturaires de saint Thomas d'Aquin." *Revue Thomiste* 33 (1928): 222–45.

Manzanedo, M. F. "La antropologia filosofica nel commentario tomista al libro de Job." *Angelicum* 62 (1985): 419–71.

———. "La antropologia teologica en el commentario tomista al libro de Job." *Angelicum* 64 (1987): 301–31.

Maquart, F.-X. "S. Thomas commentateur de la Saint Ecriture." *Cahiers du Cercle Thomiste* 1 (1926): 153–69.

Marco, A. "S. Tommaso e la pluralità dei sensi biblici nella problematica odierna." In *Atti del VII Congresso Tomistico Internazionale: Tommaso d'Aquino nel suo settimo centenario.* Vol. 4, 60–69. Naples, 1976.

Margerie, Bertrand de. "Mort sacrificielle du Christ et peine de mort chez Thomas d'Aquin, commentateur de Saint Paul." *Revue Thomiste* 83 (1983): 394–417.

Martin, Francis. "*Sacra Doctrina* and the Authority of Its *Sacra Scriptura* according to St. Thomas Aquinas." *Pro Ecclesia* 10 (2001): 84–102.

McCarthy, Brian. "El modo del conocimiento profético y escriturístico según Sto. Tomás de Aquino." *Scripta Theologica* 9 (1977): 425–84.

McGuckin, Terence. "St. Thomas Aquinas and Theological Exegesis of Sacred Scripture." *Louvain Studies* 16 (1991): 99–120.

Meinhold, P. "Zur Auffassung des hl. Thomas von Aquin von der Geschichte, insbesondere der Heilsgeschichte: Die Auseinandersetzung mit der Geschichtstheologie des Joachim von Fiore." In *Atti del VII Congresso Tomistico Internazionale: Tommaso d'Aquino nel suo settimo centenario.* Vol. 3, 153–64. Naples, 1977.

Ménard, Etienne. *La Tradition: Révélation, Écriture, Église selon saint Thomas d'Aquin.* Paris: Desclée de Brouwer, 1964.

Morard, Martin. "À propos du *Commentaire des Psaumes* de saint Thomas d'Aquin." *Revue Thomiste* 96 (1996): 653–70.

———. "Les expressions '*corpus mysticum*' et '*persona mystica*' dans l'oeuvre de saint Thomas d'Aquin." *Revue Thomiste* 95 (1995): 653–64.

———. "Sacerdoce du Christ et sacerdoce des chrétiens dans le *Commentaire des Psaumes* de saint Thomas d'Aquin." *Revue Thomiste* 99 (1999): 119–42.

Ocker, Christopher. "Medieval Exegesis and the Origin of Hermeneutics." *Scottish Journal of Theology* 52 (1999): 328–45.
O'Connor, Donal J. "The Concept of Mystery in Aquinas' Exegesis, Pt. I-II." *Irish Theological Quarterly* 36 (1969): 183–210, 261–82.
O'Hara, Mary L. "Truth in Spirit and in Letter: Gregory the Great, Thomas Aquinas and Maimonides on the Book of Job." In *From Cloister to Classroom: Monastic and Scholastic Approaches to Truth*, ed. E. Rozanne Elder. Vol. 3, 47–79. Kalamazoo, Mich.: Cistercian Publications, 1986.
Paissac, H. *Théologie du Verbe. Saint Augustin et saint Thomas*. Paris: Cerf, 1951.
Pandolfi, Carmelo. *San Tommaso filosofo nel* Commento ai Salmi: *Interpretazione dell'essere nel modo 'esistenziale' dell'invocacione*. Rome: Edizione Studio Domenicano, 1993.
Panella, E. "La *Lex nova* tra storia ed ermeneutica. Le occasioni dell' esegesi di S. Tommaso d'Aquino." *Memorie Dominicane* 6 (1975): 11–106.
Parenti, S. "Il pensiero letterale della Scrittura secondo S. Tommaso." *Sacra Doctrina* 20 (1975): 69–97.
Paretzky, A. "The Influence of Thomas the Exegete on Thomas the Theologian. The Tract on Law (I-II, qq. 90–108) as a Test Case." *Angelicum* 71 (1994): 549–77.
Pelster, Franz. "Echtheitsfragen bei den exegetischen Schriften des hl. Thomas von Aquin." *Biblica* 3 (1922): 328–38; 4 (1923): 300–311.
Perotto, Lorenzo. "La mistica del dolore nel Commento di S. Tommaso al Libro di Giobbe." *Divinitas* 46 (2003): 53–67.
Perrella, G. "Il pensiero di S. Agostino e S. Tommaso circa il numero del senso letterale nella Scrittura." *Biblica* 26 (1945): 277–302.
Persson, Per Erik. *Sacra Doctrina: Reason and Revelation in Aquinas*. Trans. Ross Mackenzie. Philadelphia: Fortress Press, 1970.
Pesch, Otto Herman. "Paul as Professor of Theology: The Image of the Apostle in St. Thomas' Theology." *Thomist* 38 (1974): 584–605.
Phillippe, M.-D. "Préface" to *Thomas d'Aquin, Commentaire sur l'Evangile de saint Jean*. Vol. 1, 7–49. Versailles: Buxy, 1981.
Pinckaers, Servais. *The Sources of Christian Ethics*. Trans. Mary Thomas Noble from the 3rd ed. Washington, D.C.: The Catholic University of America Press, 1995.
Poffet, J.-M. *Les chrétiens et la Bible. Les anciens et les modernes*. Paris: Cerf, 1998.
Pontifical Biblical Commission (1993). "The Interpretation of the Bible in the Church." *Origins* 23 (1994): 497–524.
Pope, Hugh. *St. Thomas as Interpreter of Holy Scripture*. Oxford: Basil Blackwell, 1924.
Potvin, T. R. *The Theology of the Primacy of Christ according to St. Thomas and Its Scriptural Foundations*. Fribourg: Editions Universitaires, 1973.
Preus, James. *From Shadow to Promise: Old Testament Interpretation from Augustine to the Young Luther*. Cambridge, Mass.: Harvard University Press, 1969.
Principe, Walter H. "'Tradition' in Thomas Aquinas' Scriptural Commentaries." In *The Quadrilog: Tradition and the Future of Ecumenism*, ed. Kenneth Hagen, 43–60. Collegeville, Minn.: Liturgical Press, 1994.
Renard, J. P. "La Lectura super Matthaeum V, 20–28 de Thomas d'Aquin (Edition d'après le ms. Bâle, Univ. Bibl. B.V. 12)." *Recherches de théologie ancienne et médiévale* 50 (1983): 145–90.
Revuelta, Jose M. "Los Comentarios Bíblicos de Santo Tómas." *Scripta Theologica* 3 (1971): 539–79.
Riché, Pierre, and Guy Lobrichon, eds. *Le Moyen Age et la Bible*. Paris: Beauchesne, 1984.
Riedlinger, H. "Zur Unterscheidung der Verstehensbereiche der geschichtlichen Schriftauslegung: Anmerkungen zu Thomas von Aquin, Summa Theologiae p.I, q.1, a.10." In *Veritati Catholicae. Festschrift für Leo Scheffczyk*, 697–711. Aschaffenburg, 1985.

Rogers, Eugene F., Jr. *Thomas Aquinas and Karl Barth: Sacred Doctrine and the Natural Knowledge of God.* Notre Dame: Notre Dame University Press, 1995.

———. "The Virtues of an Interpreter Presuppose and Perfect Hermeneutics: The Case of Thomas Aquinas." *Journal of Religion* 76 (1996): 64–81.

Rossi, Margherita Maria. "(L')Attenzione a Tommaso d'Aquino esegeta." *Angelicum* 76 (1999): 73–104.

———. "La 'divisio textus' nei commenti scritturistici di S. Tommaso d'Aquino: Un procedimento solo esegetico?" *Angelicum* 71 (1994): 537–48.

———. "Teoria e metodo esegetici in S. Tommaso d'Aquino. Analisi del Super Epistolas sancti Pauli Lectura ad Romanos, c.1,1.6." Diss., Angelicum, 1992.

Ryan, Thomas F. *Thomas Aquinas as Reader of the Psalms.* Notre Dame: University of Notre Dame Press, 2000.

Salguero, J. "Santo Tomás de Aquino y la hermeneútica bíblica." In *Atti del VII Congresso Tomistico Internazionale: Tommaso d'Aquino nel suo settimo centenario.* Vol. 4, 29–40. Naples, 1976.

Santi, F. "L'esegesi biblica di Tommaso d'Aquino nel contesto dell' esegesi biblica medievale." *Angelicum* 71 (1994): 509–35.

Saul, D. "Thomas von Aquino als Ausleger des A.T." *Zeitschrift für wissenschaftliche Theologie* (1895): 603–25.

Schenk, Richard. "*Omnis Christi actio nostra est instructio:* The Deeds and Sayings of Jesus as Revelation in the View of Thomas Aquinas." In *La doctrine de la révélation divine de saint Thomas d'Aquin,* ed. Leo Elders, Studi Tomistici 37, 104–31. Vatican City: Libreria Editrice Vaticana, 1990.

Seckler, M. *Das Heil in der Geschichte: Geschichtstheologisches Denken bei Thomas von Aquin.* Munich: Kösel Verlag, 1964.

Selden, J. "Aquinas, Luther, Melancthon and Biblical Apologetics." *Grace Theological Journal* 5 (1984): 181–95.

Sheets, John. "The Scriptural Dimension of St. Thomas." *American Ecclesiastical Review* 144 (1961): 154–73.

Shooner, H.-V. "La *Lectura in Matthaeum* de S. Thomas (Deux fragments inédits et la *Reportatio* de Pierre d'Andria)." *Angelicum* 33 (1956): 121–42.

Siedl, H. "Thomas von Aquin und die moderne Exegese." *Zeitschrift für katholische Theologie* 93 (1971): 29–44.

Smalley, Beryl. *The Gospels in the Schools, c. 1100–c. 1280.* London: Hambledon Press, 1985.

———. *The Study of the Bible in the Middle Ages.* 2nd ed. Notre Dame: University of Notre Dame Press, 1964; 3rd ed. Oxford: Basil Blackwell, 1983.

Smith, John Clark. "Christ as 'Pastor,' 'Ostium' and 'Agnus' in St. Thomas Aquinas." *Angelicum* 56 (1979): 93–118.

Somme, Luc-Thomas. *Fils adoptifs de Dieu par Jésus Christ: La filiation divine par adoption dans la théologie de saint Thomas d'Aquin.* Paris: Vrin, 1997.

Spicq, Ceslas. "*Saint Thomas d'Aquin Exégète.*" In *Dictionnaire de Théologie Catholique,* ed. A. Vacant, E. Mangenot and E. Amann. Vol. 15, col. 694–738. Paris: Libraire Letouzey et Ané, 1946.

Stump, Eleonore. "(Aquinas') Biblical Commentary and Philosophy." In *The Cambridge Companion to Aquinas,* ed. Norman Kretzmann and Eleonore Stump, 252–68. Cambridge: Cambridge University Press, 1993.

Sweeney, E. M. "Divine Revelation in the Commentary of Saint Thomas Aquinas on Saint John's Gospel." Diss., Pamplona, 1981.

Swierzawski, Waclaw. "Christ and the Church: *Una Mystica Persona* in the Pauline Commentaries of St. Thomas Aquinas." In *S. Tommaso Teologo,* ed. A. Piolanti, 239–50. Vatican City: Libreria Editrice Vaticana, 1995.

———. "Faith and Worship in the Pauline Commentaries of St. Thomas Aquinas." *Divus Thomas* 75 (1972): 389–412.

———. "God and the Mystery of his Wisdom in the Pauline Commentaries of St. Thomas Aquinas." *Divus Thomas* 74 (1971): 466–500.

———. "L'exégèse biblique et la théologie spéculative de s. Thomas d'Aquin." *Divinitas* 18 (1974): 138–53.

Synan, Edward. "The Four 'Senses' and Four Exegetes." In *With Reverence for the Word: Medieval Christian Exegesis in Judaism, Christianity and Islam,* ed. Jane Dammen McAuliffe, Barry D. Walfish and Joseph W. Goering, 225–36. Oxford: Oxford University Press, 2002.

Synave, P. "La Doctrine de saint Thomas d'Aquin sue le sens littéral des Ecritures." *Revue Biblique* 35 (1926): 40–65.

———. "Les Commentaires scripturaires de saint Thomas d'Aquin." *Vie Spirituelle* 8 (1923): 455–69.

———. *Prophecy and Revelation. A Commentary on the Summa Theologica II-II, Questions 171–178.* Trans. Avery Dulles and Thomas L. Sheridan. New York: Desclée, 1961.

Tabet, M. A. "El lenguaje de Dios en la Biblia segùn la doctrina de Santo Tomás." In *Atti del VIII Congresso Tomistico Internazionale.* Vol. 4, 126–35. Vatican City: Libreria Editrice Vaticana, 1977.

Tholuck, A. *De Thoma Aquino et Abaelardo S. Scripturae interpretibus.* Halle: E. Anton, 1842.

Ti-Ti Chen, J. "La unidad de la Iglesia según el Comentario de Santo Tomás a la Epístola a los Efesios." *Scripta Theologica* 8 (1976): 111–230.

Torrance, T. F. "Scientific Hermeneutics, according to St. Thomas Aquinas." *Journal of Theological Studies* 13 (1962): 259–89.

Torrell, J.-P. "La traité de la prophétie de S. Thomas d'Aquin." In *Recherches sur la théorie de la prophétie au mayen age, XIIe–XIVe siècles: etudes et texts,* 205–31. Fribourg: Editions Universitaires, 1992.

———. "Quand saint Thomas méditait sur le prophète Isaïe." *Revue Thomiste* 90 (1990): 5–47.

———. *Saint Thomas Aquinas.* Vol. 1: *The Person and His Work,* trans. Robert Royal. Washington, D.C.: The Catholic University of America Press, 1996.

———. *Saint Thomas Aquinas.* Vol. 2: *Spiritual Master,* trans. Robert Royal. Washington, D.C.: The Catholic University of America Press, 2003.

Torrell, J.-P., and D. Bouthillier. "Le traité de la prophétie de s. Thomas d'Aquin et la théologie de la révélation." *Studi Tomistici* 37 (1990): 171–95.

Valkenberg, Wilhelmus G. B. M. "Did Not Our Heart Burn? Place and Function of Holy Scripture in the Theology of St. Thomas Aquinas." Diss., Utrecht, 1990.

———. "The Functions of Holy Scripture in Aquinas' Theology on the Resurrection of Christ." In *Atti del IX Congresso Tomistico Internazionale VI: Storia del Tomismo, Fonti e Reflessi,* 13–22. Vatican City: Libreria Editrice Vaticana, 1992.

———. "Verslag van het onderzoeksproject naar het gebruik van de H. Schrift in de theologie van Thomas van Aquino." In *Jaarboek 1985,* ed. Werkgroep Thomas van Aquino, 142–44. Utrecht: Thomas Instituut, 1986.

———. *Words of the Living God: Place and Function of Holy Scripture in the Theology of St. Thomas Aquinas.* Leuven: Peeters, 2000.

Van Ackeren, Gerald F. *Sacra Doctrina: The Subject of the First Question of the Summa Theologica of St. Thomas Aquinas.* Rome: Catholic Book Agency, 1952.

Van Banning, Joop. "Saint Thomas Aquinas et l'Opus imperfectum in Matthaeum." In *S. Tommaso nella storia del pensiero,* 73–85. Vatican City: Liberia Editrice Vaticana, 1982.

Van der Ploeg, J. "The Place of Holy Scripture in the Theology of St. Thomas." *Thomist* 10 (1947): 398–422.

Vass, G. T. "'Secundum illud Apostoli . . .': A Study of the Use of Biblical Authorities in the Systematic Theology of Thomas Aquinas." Diss., Pont. Univ. Gregorianae, 1963.

Venard, Olivier-Thomas. "Croire en savant—Saint Thomas bibliste." In *Thomistes ou de l'actualité de saint Thomas d'Aquin,* ed. Serge-Thomas Bonino, 37–48. Paris: Parole et Silence, 2003.

———. *Thomas d'Aquin Poète Théologien.* Vol. 1: *Littérature et Théologie. Une saison en enfer.* Genève: Ad Solem, 2002.

Vera, José Loza. "Santo Tomás de Aquino intérprete de la Sagrada Escritura." *AnáMnesis* 13 (2003): 29–46.

Verger, Jacques. "L'exégèse de l'Université." In *Le Moyen Age et la Bible,* ed. Pierre Riché and Guy Lobrichon, 199–232. Paris: Beauchesne, 1984.

Vooght, P. de. "Le rapport écriture-tradition d'après Saint Thomas d'Aquin et les théologiens du XIIIe siècle." *Istina* 9 (1962): 499–510.

Vosté, J.-M. "Exegesis Novi Testamenti et sancti Thomae Summa Theologica." *Anglicum* 24 (1947): 3–19.

———. "S. Thomas epistularum S. Pauli interpres." *Angelicum* 19 (1942): 256–76.

Waldstein, Michael. "On Scripture in the *Summa Theologiae.*" *Aquinas Review* 1 (1994): 73–94.

Weisheipl, James A. Introduction to *Commentary on the Gospel of St. John* by Thomas Aquinas. Vol. 1, trans. by Fabian R. Larcher. Albany: Magi Books, 1980.

———. "The Johannine Commentary of Friar Thomas." *Church History* 45 (1976): 185–95.

———. "The Meaning of Sacra Doctrina in Summa Theologiae I, q.1." *Thomist* 38 (1974): 49–80.

Wiesman, H. "Der Kommentar des hl. Thomas von Aquin zu den Klageliedern des Jeremias." *Scholastik* 4 (1929): 82–86.

Worrall, Peter. "St. Thomas and Arianism." *Revue théologie ancienne et médiévale* 23 (1956): 211.

Zarb, Seraphim. "De ubertate sensus litteralis in sacra Scriptura secundum doctrinam sancti Thomas Aquinatis." *Analecta Gregoriana* 68 (1954): 251–73.

———. "Utrum S. Thomas unitatem an vero pluralitatem sensus litteralis in sacra Scriptura docuerit?" *Divus Thomas* 33 (1930): 337–59.

Zawilla, R. "The Biblical Sources of the *Historiae Corporis Christi* attributed to Thomas Aquinas." Diss., University of Toronto, 1985.

———. "Saint Thomas d'Aquin et la théologie biblique de l'Eucharistie du Xie au XIIIe siècle." Communication to the Journée thomiste de Saint-Jacques, Paris, 24 November 1987 (unpublished).

Zedda, S. "Christo e lo Spiritu Santo nell'adozione a figli secondo il commento di S. Tommaso alla lettera ai Romani." In *Tommaso d'Aquino nel suo settimo centenario.* Vol. 4, 105–12. Naples: Edizioni Domenicane Italiane, 1976.

Index

Note: Boldface type beside authors' names indicates starting pages of articles. Boldface numbers in the entry for "John (Bible)" indicate chapter numbers from the Gospel of St. John.

abduction, 117–18
actions, 28, 58, 68n12, 241–42; human, 155, 176, 192, 207, 210, 303; unity of, 36, 69–71. *See also* Christ, actions of; God, actions of; Holy Spirit, actions of; notional acts; Word, actions of
Adam and Eve, 247
advocate, 70
Albert the Great, Saint, 7, 39, 56
alta. See height
Ambrose, Saint, 19, 49
amor. See love
amplitudo. See fullness
Andrew (Apostle), 207, 341
angels, 20, 250n11, 251, 311, 315
anger, 223–24, 226, 228–30
Apollinarianism/Apollinaris, 20, 255, 265
apostles, xxiii–xxiv, 139, 208, 221, 295, 301, 305–7; Christ's resurrection and, 284, 286–87; ministry of, 318–46; reception of Holy Spirit by, 63, 65–66. *See also* disciples; faith, apostolic; witness, apostolic
apostolic life *(vita apostolica)*, 190, 323, 346
apprenticeship, xix, 174–75, 177, 190–92. *See also* discipleship
appropriations, doctrine of, xv, 33, 69–71, 123
Aquinas. *See* Thomas Aquinas, Saint
Arianism/Arius, xvii, 103, 134, 255, 268, 307; refutation of, 18–20, 29, 50–52, 54, 122, 264–65
Aristotle, xix, 6, 12, 18–19, 56, 281–82; on causality, 125–26; on eternity, 130, 134n13, 135; on friendship, 191; on governance, 304–5; on learning, 182, 187–88; on life, 154–56, 161–62; metaphysics of, 201, 256, 259, 274, 284; philosophy of, 117, 194–96, 201–5, 211; theology of, 10, 48–49; on words, 19, 26
ascension, of Christ, 333–34
Ashley, Benedict M., xx–xxi, **241**
Athanasius of Alexandria, Saint, 41, 53, 104
atheism, 308

Augustine, Saint, 14, 17, 90, 95; on the apostles, 338, 344; Aquinas influenced by, xiv; on the Church, 308; on the crucifixion, 185; on eternity, xvii, 134n13; on evil, 124; exegesis of, 19–20, 101, 127, 196, 210; on faith, 180; on Gospel of John, 156–57; on the Holy Spirit, 62, 334; on life, 154-56, 161-62; on mourning, 213; on obedience, 98; on Person of Christ, 241, 284, 300; on the resurrection, 287–88; theology of, 119–22, 129; Trinitarian theology of, 42, 44, 47, 49–50, 52–53, 69, 132–33; on washing of feet, 303. *See also individual writings of*
Aureoli, Peter, xiv, 10–15, 19
authorial intention, 3–8. *See also* literal sense

Balthasar, Hans Urs von, xvi, 79, 90
baptism, 163, 332n65; of Christ, 63, 66, 68n12, 126, 206, 208
Barth, Karl, 79n5
Basil of Caesarea, Saint, 39, 49, 121, 133
Batholomew of Capua, xxiv
Bauerschmidt, Frederick Christian, xxii–xxiii, **293**
Bede, Teresa, **318**
being. *See* existence *(esse)*
biblical exegesis, xiii–xxiii, 23–61, 80–82, 153-54, 168–72, 221, 280–83. *See also* Augustine, Saint, exegesis of; Fathers of the Church, exegesis of; Thomas Aquinas, Saint, exegesis of
blind man, healing of, 166, 210, 224
body: glorified, 139, 261, 284–88; human, 163–66, 243n4, 249, 284; mystical, xxi, 243; 343; soul and, 259–60, 264, 268
Body of Christ. *See* Church
Boethius, xvii, 30, 48, 129, 135
Bonaventure, Saint, 40, 227–28, 274n46
Bonino, Serge-Thomas, xxiii–xxiv, **318**
Book of Life, 19
Boyle, John F., xiv, **3**

364 Index

Boyle, Leonard, 118
Bread of Life discourse. *See* Eucharist
Broglie, Guy de, 116
Brown, Raymond, xxiii, 224–25, 273, 312–13
Brown, Stephen F., xiv, **9**
Buddhism, 235–36
Bultmann, R., xx, 223–26
Burrell, David B., xvii, **115**

Calvinists, 146–47
Catechism of the Catholic Church, 106–7, 278
Catena aurea (Aquinas), 14, 42, 50–53, 59, 222, 231, 286
Catholicism. *See* Roman Catholicism
causality, 47, 123–26, 160, 196, 246, 252, 274; divine, xviii, 40, 121, 136, 140–49, 157, 203; secondary, 318–20, 342, 345–46
Cerinthus, 18
charity, xix–xx, 244, 301, 327–28, 335–37, 342. *See also* love
chastity, 200
Chenu, M.-D., 280, 282
Chesterton, G. K., 258, 268
Christ, xv–xvii, 17–18, 80–81, 106, 120–21, 243–44, 246, 285; acceptance of, 194–211; actions of, 40–44, 58, 64–74, 77, 81–82, 123, 305–8, 344; betrayal of, 303, 305, 309; divine nature of, 28, 41–42, 158, 163, 184–85, 195–96, 229, 263, 278, 284, 337–41; dual nature of, xviii, 14–15, 66, 179, 242, 245, 287, 295–96, 300–301, 316–17; glorification of, 93, 332–33, 345; human nature of, 45n58, 68n12, 85, 95, 102–4, 137, 185, 188–89, 228–29, 241–76, 278, 320, 338–40; relationship of, to God, 26–32, 35–37, 42–43, 47–54, 56–58, 63, 85–91, 93–95, 99–106, 111–12, 133–37, 159, 203; as teacher, xix, xxii–xxiii, 89–90, 129, 173–93, 251, 299, 317, 319–22, 329–31, 334, 343. *See also under* baptism; Church; death; grace; life; mission; passion; power; resurrection; suffering; truth; way
Christianity, 10–12, 18, 60, 172, 175, 215–16, 235–37, 326; interreligious dialogue and, 279–80, 310
Christology, 34, 228–29, 232, 261–63; low, 244, 247; Roman Catholic, 278; of Thomas Aquinas, xxi, 36, 79n5, 255
Church, xxii–xxiii, 149, 170, 237, 241, 304, 322, 342; Christ as head of, 137–39, 245–47, 263–64, 273, 302; human leadership of, 288, 324; militant, 293–311; mission of, 128; women in, 286

closed doors, miracle of, 284–86
clothing, symbolism of, 187–88, 329, 334
co-eternity, 26, 28, 47, 51–52, 94, 121, 133–34. *See also* divine persons, equality of
coherence, 271–72, 303
Colossians (Bible), 32, 97
commandments, 99–100, 102–3, 108, 112, 315, 335
Commentary on Boethius's De Trinitate (Aquinas), 11–12
Commentary on the De Anima (Aquinas), 187–88
Commentary on the Gospel of St. John (Aquinas), 14–20, 307; compared to *Summa theologiae*, xxi–xxii, 23–61, 80, 116–19, 127, 244, 277–89; ecclesiology of, 293–311; intention of, 157, 294, 297; Prologue to, xviii, 129, 156–68, 194, 241, 255–56, 293; theology of, xiii–xvii, xxiii–xxv, 92–112
Commentary on the Sentences (Aquinas), 50
compassion, 234–35
conception, of Christ, 250, 284, 320–21
concertatio, 181n10
concupiscence, 203–4
Confessions (Augustine), xx, 4–5, 213–15
connaturality, 199–200
consciousness, human, 249–50. *See also* intellect; self-knowing
consolation, 44, 69–70, 74, 298
consubstantiality, xxi, 16, 18, 109, 119, 121–22, 132–34, 255, 275, 337. *See also* Christ, relationship of, to God; hypostatic union
contemplation, xxii, 187–88, 192, 195–96, 314, 327. *See also* John, Saint, contemplative nature of; life, contemplative
contemporary theology, 153, 168–72, 317
conveniens. *See* coherence
conversion, 166–67, 195, 205–10, 295, 326, 341, 343
Corbin, Michel, xxii, 281–82
correctories dispute, 218
Council of Chalcedon, 262–63
covenant, 80–81, 325
creation, xvii–xviii, 4, 15, 27, 35, 80, 110, 115–26; goodness of, 147–48, 247, 258–59
crucifixion. *See* death, of Christ
Cyril, Saint, 286

Dauphinais, Michael, xxiii, **312**
death, xix–xx, 213–25, 227–29, 234–36, 243n4, 267–68; of Christ, xvi, 78–85, 89–91, 128,

138–39, 161, 185–86, 247, 258, 260–61, 298, 317, 336–37
De civitate Dei (Augustine), 215–16
declarative theology, xiv, 10–20
De Magistro (Augustine), 183
Democritus, 134
De perfectione vitae spiritualis (Aquinas), 97
De potentia (Aquinas), xiv, 4–7, 31, 50
De Trinitate (Augustine), 16
dialogue, interreligious, 234–37, 277, 279
Dionysius the Pseudo-Areopagite, 20, 49, 216, 341
disciples, 81, 110, 179–81, 184–93, 206, 220, 231; Christ's relationship to, 321, 323, 334, 336, 345; community of, 294, 296–97, 302–5, 308–11. *See also* apostles
discipleship, xix, 173–82, 300–301, 303. *See also* learning
disciplina. *See* instruction
discovery, 182
divisio litterae, 281, 306–7
divisio textus, xiv, xxiii, 3–8, 324
Docetism, xxi–xxii, 228, 254–76
doctrine, sacred, 9, 56, 60, 108, 174, 188, 297, 320–22
Dominicans, xxiv, 190, 241, 297, 299n19
dove, 63, 68n12, 126
dulia, 97, 104
Durandus, xiv, 10, 13, 19

Easter, 301, 332–34, 337, 339–40, 345
Ebionites, 18
Ecclesiasticus (Bible), 199–200
economic Trinity, 40–41, 58–59, 293n1
education, xix, 96, 173, 184. *See also* learning
Emery, Gilles, xiv–xv, **23**, 108–9, 111
emotions, 222–32, 265–68, 271
epistemology, 126, 196–98, 201, 211
erat, 47
errors. *See* heresies
eternity, xvii, 127–39, 159. *See also* co-eternity; life, eternal
etiological sense, 196
Eucharist, xxi–xxiii, 93–94, 138–39, 164–65, 171, 273–75, 302–4, 312–17
Eunomius of Cyzicus, 18, 43, 51–52
evangelical teaching, 306. *See also* teaching
evil, 122, 124, 137, 199, 201–6, 209, 259, 309; divine permission of, xviii, 143–48
example *(exemplar),* 110–11, 175, 184, 186–89; of Christ, 230–31, 233, 237, 270–71, 299–300, 304–5, 308, 329–30

exegesis. *See* biblical exegesis
existence *(esse),* 125, 130–33, 135–39, 141, 145, 148–49, 154–55, 160–63
Exodus (Bible), 80, 133, 138
expositio litterae, 281–83, 306

faith, 20, 32, 55, 59–60, 115–17, 172, 206, 210–11; apostolic, 110, 322, 325, 338, 341–42; articles of, xiv, 10–12; in Christ, 158, 167, 269, 271, 340; death conquered by, 224–25, 231; gift of, 175–76, 178, 185; knowledge and, 333, 335–36; learning and, xix, 177–82; love and, 128, 165; not possessed by Christ, xx, 242–44, 246–47, 249; reason and, 13–14, 119, 126, 134, 346; salvation through, 42, 163; taught by Holy Spirit, 330–31; Trinitarian, 76, 86, 344; unity through, 317
faithful, 293–311, 324, 342
Father. *See* God
fatherhood, 96–97, 104
Fathers of the Church, xiii–xiv, xxiv, 39–42; exegesis of, 44–55, 100, 188, 221–22, 232, 252, 261, 270, 282–83, 287–88; theology of, 14–20, 59, 61, 78, 129, 134, 228
Filioque, 38, 39, 62. *See also* Christ
First Cause, 140–43, 203, 318–19, 345. *See also* causality
I Corinthians (Bible), 97, 208, 310n42, 326
First Truth, 10, 13, 245, 320. *See also* truth
flesh, 267, 339; Word made, 28, 254, 260–65, 298, 305–7, 315–16. *See also* Eucharist; Incarnation
food, spiritual, 164–65, 302, 314–15. *See also* Eucharist
forgiveness. *See* sin, forgiveness of
Fowl, Stephen, xiii, xix, 170, 288
free will, xvii–xviii, 140–50, 156, 210, 217; possessed by Christ, 242, 248, 266
friendship, 88, 107, 157–58, 302, 309; love of, 200, 203–4; revelation and, 190–92, 327–28
fullness, 157, 161–66

Galatians (Bible), 97
Gauthier, R.-A., 55
Geach, Peter T., xv, 73–75
generation, 29, 86–88, 96, 121, 125, 133, 321; eternal, 50, 64n5, 67n10, 102–4, 106–9, 203, 245. *See also* creation; Incarnation; regeneration
generosity of act, 318–19

Genesis (Bible), 5, 118
Gentiles, 164, 205, 209, 279, 308, 344. *See also Summa contra gentiles* (Aquinas)
gifts, 32, 104–5, 207, 321. *See also* Holy Spirit, gifts of; self-giving
Gilbertus of Poitiers, 48
Gilby, Thomas, 304
Gilson, Etienne, 255–56
glory, 80, 182, 298, 300. *See also* Christ, glorification of
Glossa continua super Evangelia (Aquinas), 47, 278, 282, 283
Gnosticism, 53, 244, 263n25
God, xvii, 10, 12, 17–19, 49, 115, 121, 160; actions of, xv–xvi, xviii, 41, 58, 70–74, 77–78, 109, 163, 274; as author of Scripture, 6, 128, 262; as creator, 43, 96, 117–20, 132, 135, 157–59, 164, 171; as First Cause, 140–43, 203, 318-19, 345; Holy Spirit sent by, 64, 66–67, 245; knowledge of, 75–77, 89, 205–8; kyriarchal, xvi, 82–85, 91; love of, 335; person of, 26–27, 39, 110; plan of, 84–85, 310; relationship of, to Christ, 26–32, 35–37, 42–43, 47–54, 56–58, 63, 85–91, 93–95, 99–106, 111–12, 133–37, 159, 203; as teacher, xix, 68n12, 175–77, 182; triune, xiv–xv, xvii, 71–80, 86, 126, 129, 135. *See also under* gifts; grace; knowledge
Godfrey of Fontaines, 9
gods, 131, 134, 137
Gondreau, Paul, xxi–xxii, **254**
goodness, 142, 144–49, 195–202, 210–11, 258–59, 266, 319; of God, 12, 123–24, 162, 306, 315; moral, 207–8, 327
Good Shepherd, 166, 344
grace, xxi, xxiii, 27–28, 110–11, 116, 125–27, 208–11, 274–75, 288, 295, 300, 328, 335; of Christ, 37, 63, 137–38, 244–47, 302, 345; of God, 157–58, 160, 171–72, 181, 189, 285; of the Holy Spirit, 180, 342, 345; life of, 161, 163, 166, 168
Grant, Sara, 125
Greeks, 41, 51, 55, 343
Gregory (Nazianzen), 95
Gregory the Great, Saint, 19–20, 49, 92, 284, 334–35
Gui, Bernard, xxiv
guilt, 144–45, 165

habituation, xix, 195
happiness, 177, 248, 314
hatred, 199, 203–4. *See also* Jews, hatred of
healing, 166, 183, 209–10, 221. *See also* miracles

height, 157–61
Henry of Ghent, 9
heresies, 12, 14, 17–19, 30, 122; refutation of, 44, 46, 49, 60, 134; Trinitarian, 51–57, 59. *See also specific heresies*
hermeneutics, 153, 156–58, 166–72, 206, 220–22
Hilary (Saint), 19–20, 103–4, 110, 112, 121, 158; Trinitarian theology of, 42–43, 49–50, 52–53, 133
Hinduism, 235–36
Hittinger, Russell, xviii, 149
holiness, xix–xx, 195, 308–9
Holocaust, 310
Holy Spirit, xv–xvi, xxii, 52, 80, 85–86, 88–89, 105, 208; actions of, 38–44, 62–77, 109, 163–64, 168, 180, 329–35, 339; gifts of, 53, 118, 127, 210, 293n1, 302, 332–35, 343–45; as love, 31–36, 63, 65–66, 70, 191–92, 301, 337; person of, 26–27, 29–32, 33, 35, 43; as teacher, xix, 66–68, 100–101, 129, 176, 188–90; unity of, 111–12, 317. *See also under* grace; mission; procession
Hugh of Saint-Victor, 45
human beings, 155–56, 168, 197–98, 203, 216–17, 219, 247. *See also* existence *(esse)*; nature, human
humility, 83–85, 147, 172, 184, 186, 303–5, 326, 330n52
Hunt, Anne, 78–79, 85
hylemorphic union, 259, 268–69
hypostatic union, 29–30, 62, 68n12, 112, 138, 242, 249–50, 252, 262, 320, 329

identity, xvii, 28, 71–77, 80–91
image, of God, 32, 86, 129, 244, 246
imitation, of Christ, 241, 300, 303–4, 308. *See also* example *(exemplar)*
immanent Trinity, xvi, 28, 40–42, 59, 79, 293n1
immorality, 204–5. *See also* moral life
immortality, 198, 219
Incarnation, xxi–xxiii, 11, 20, 52, 82, 137–39, 175–77, 190, 193, 314–16; doctrine of, 244, 252, 257–62, 269–75, 287. *See also* Word
Index thomisticus, 30n9
In principio, 49
instruction, 161–62, 165–67, 324, 342. *See also* learning
intellect, 131–34, 200–201, 205–6, 244, 316; actions of, 155–56, 197–98; of Christ, 251, 320; faith and, 128–29, 165; free will and, 124, 141–42; of God, 37, 159–60; human, 248–49, 329–30; learning and, 176; mode of, 31–34, 57. *See also* knowledge

International Theological Commission, 242–43
Irenaeus of Lyons, Saint, 39
Isaiah (Bible), 7, 80, 175, 177, 192, 211, 297–98, 311; 6:1, 156–57, 278
Israel, 80–82, 88, 91, 298, 303, 310
Jeremiah (Bible), 125
Jerome, Saint, 16
Jesus Christ. *See* Christ
Jews, 80–82, 164, 279, 344; hatred of, 280, 308, 310
Joachim of Fiore, 48
Job (Bible), 331
John (Bible): intention of, xiv, 7–8, 18–19, 56, 107–8, 157–58, 294–97, 307, 323; Prologue to, 26, 32, 47, 53–54, 154, 244, 260, 306, 340; **1**, xxi, 37, 46, 50, 64n5, 119–22, 125-26, 132, 134, 158, 162, 166, 175, 257–58, 265, 318; **2**, 263, 295; **3**, 42, 64, 87, 90, 105, 127, 159, 162-64, 204-5; **4**, 261, 325; **5**, 43, 50, 53, 87, 89, 104, 160, 164, 272n44; **6**, xxi–xxiii, 162–64, 171, 251, 273, 312–17; **7**, 165, 182, 270; **8**, 165, 246, 262, 280; **9**, 165–66; **10**, 53, 165; **11**, xx, 165, 220, 223, 225, 267; **12**, 268, 271, 333; **13**, 49, 53, 232, 336; **14**, 27, 43, 50, 53, 68, 74, 279, 299–300; **15**, 27, 53, 125, 140–50, 203, 327; **16**, 27, 47, 53, 68; **17**, 49, 53, 71n17, 88, 105-6, 111, 159–60, 324, 333; **20**, xxii, 63, 157, 261, 276, 279, 283-89; **21**, xxii, 279, 283-89. *See also Commentary on the Gospel of St. John* (Aquinas)
John, Saint, 305, 311, 322, 342; Christ's love for, 88, 328–29, 336; contemplative nature of, 55–56, 157–58, 161–62, 166, 296–98; holiness of, xix–xx, 195; theology of, 278–80
John Chrysostom, Saint, 16–19, 100, 121–22, 124, 158, 222, 332, 334; Trinitarian theology of, 42–43, 47, 49, 50, 52–53, 88
John of Damascus, 16, 19–20, 49, 95, 119–20, 262, 274
John of La Rochelle, 7
John Paul II, Pope, 105, 107, 150
John the Baptist, 250n11, 300, 305, 325
Joseph of Arimathea, 323
Judaism. *See* Jews
Judas, 303, 309, 336
judgment, 101, 104, 131–32, 136, 200–202, 209, 211, 298
justice, 83–84, 96, 145, 147, 228, 236, 304

Kant, Immanuel, 149, 249
Kendall, Daniel, xx, 242–44, 247, 251–52
Kilwardby, Robert, 218
knowledge, 174, 183, 197, 203, 209, 288, 325; acquisition of, 101, 328–29; divine, 108, 135–36, 147, 179, 246; of faith, 333, 335; about God, 89, 126, 129, 134, 142, 185, 191, 205–8; human, 168, 217, 241–53, 265n29; life and, 154–55, 157–63, 165–66, 171; love and, 58, 176–78, 193, 296, 327; perfect, 337–42, 344; supernatural, 318–21, 326–29; of the Trinity, 85–86, 118, 340; of truth, 180, 299, 314, 315; unity and, 35–37. *See also* like knows like; self-knowing
Kolbe, Maximilian, 308, 310

Lamb, Matthew L., xvii, **127**
Lamentabili (Pius X), 242–43
Larcher, Fabian, xxiv
Last Judgment, 251–52
Last Supper, xix, 53, 179, 185–89, 294, 322, 328, 339. *See also* Eucharist
law, xviii, 148–50, 200, 295, 305, 315
Lazarus, xx, 166, 181, 221, 224, 228–29, 266–67
learning, 96, 174, 182–84, 187, 192–93, 301–2, 310; by Christ, 242, 249, 251; faith and, 177–82. *See also* apprenticeship; discipleship; teaching
Leget, Carlo, xviii–xix, **153**
Leibnez's law, 71–75
Leo the Great, Saint, 261–62
Levering, Matthew, xvi, **78, 318**
life, 19, 153–72; Christ as, 89–90, 155, 166, 180, 190, 279, 300; contemplative, 14, 98, 127–28, 241, 279; eternal, xxi, xxiii, 100, 177, 184, 242, 274, 314–15, 317; mystical, 248–49; spiritual, 271, 346. *See also* apostolic life *(vita apostolica);* moral life
light, 19, 162, 165–66, 244, 318, 341
like knows like, xvii, 120, 197–200, 203–4
literal sense, xiv, 3–8, 15–18, 48, 169, 230, 286. *See also* Scripture, literal sense of
loaves and fishes, 164, 312, 314–15
Logos, xvii, 15, 17, 121. *See also* Word
Lombard, Peter, 48, 283
Long, Steven A., xviii, **140**
love, 27, 39, 80, 165, 199, 237, 246, 288, 328; for Christ, xvi, 98, 305, 317; divine, 58, 83–84, 87, 90–91, 100, 118, 167–69, 191–92; for God, 123, 248, 335; God as, 135, 159, 285; Holy Spirit as, 31–38, 44, 63, 65–68, 70, 86; knowledge and, 176, 178, 193, 296, 327; learning and, 189–90, 192; obedience and, 105–9, 184–86; perfection and, 96–97, 345; unity in, 36, 93–94, 112, 300–301, 309, 311; for the world, 203–5, 331

Lubac, Henri de, 79n5, 167
Luke (Bible), 97, 221, 284–85, 345
Luther, Martin, 223
Luyten, Norbert, xx
Macedonians/Macedonius, 51–52, 64
Manicheans, 19, 124, 158, 255, 258, 280
Marcellus of Ancyra, 53
Mare, William de la, 217–18
Maritain, Jacques, 146, 262
Mark (Bible), 7, 251–52
Marshall, Bruce D., xv, **62**
Martha (sister of Lazarus), 181, 226
martyrdom, 98, 308
Mary (mother of Christ), 180, 247, 263–64, 284, 309n41
Mary (sister of Lazarus), 226, 228, 297
Mary Magdalene, 178, 185, 285–86, 323
Matthew (Bible), 7, 95; Aquinas' commentaries on, 30, 32, 67, 183–84, 266, 309n41
Maximus the Confessor, Saint, 111, 266n30
mediation, law of, 318–21, 324–25, 344
mercy, 145, 147, 211, 308
Messiah, 80–82. *See also* Christ
metaphysics, xvi–xviii, 83, 133, 195, 258–59; of human nature, xxi, 268; of participation, xxiv, 40, 58. *See also* philosophy
Metz, Johann Baptist, 236
mind, human. *See* intellect
miracles, 207, 209, 223, 252, 269–70, 332, 338, 342, 345. *See also specific miracles*
mission, 92–112, 293n1, 344; of Christ, xxi–xxii, 39, 138–39, 191, 193, 314, 341; of divine persons, xv–xvi, 26, 28–29, 33, 37, 44, 57–58; of the Holy Spirit, 64–66, 127–28, 138–39, 331–32
modus significandi, xv, 76
Monophysitism, 244, 255, 262
Monothelitism, 255, 266
moral life, xviii–xx, 148–50, 167, 172, 204–6, 211, 330–31; education in, 174, 182
moral science, 195–96, 200–201
Moses, 5–6
mourning, xx, 212–37, 267
mystical sense, 3, 286, 328
Mystici Corporis (Pius XII), 243
mysticism, 236, 296

narrative theology, 80–81, 306–7
Nathanael, 207–8, 326
natural science, 195. *See also* science
nature, 28, 39, 43–44, 50–52, 57, 124–25, 158; divine, 30–31, 33, 87, 108–9, 111, 118, 132, 198; human, xxi, 108, 149, 247–49, 259, 316; reason and, 32, 143; unity of, 35–36, 69n15, 75, 112
Nedoncelle, 107
negation, 146–47
Nestorius, 307
New Testament, 81, 153n1, 221, 225, 255, 262, 278–79, 337. *See also* Old Testament; *individual books*
Nicene creed, 81, 121. *See also* Christology
Nicodemus, 155, 162–63, 167, 178, 180, 184, 208, 307
Nicomachean Ethics (Aristotle), 195–96, 201
non-duality, 122, 125
notional acts, 29, 33, 57, 105
nourishment, 161–62, 164, 166–67, 273, 316. *See also* Eucharist

obedience, xvi, 84–85, 90, 184–85, 207, 288, 315; of Christ, 242, 246–48; education and, 173–74, 189; mission and, 92–112
observantia, 96–97
O'Collins, Gerald, xx, 242–44, 247, 251–52
Oikonomia, xvi, 92–112
Old Latin African Bible, 15
Old Testament, 17, 43, 164, 179, 264n27, 305, 314–15, 325. *See also individual books*
order, divine, 40, 149–50
ordo disciplinae, 34, 42, 60
Origen, 121, 137, 158, 280, 295; Trinitarian theology of, 47, 49, 53, 64n5
origins, 27–28, 44, 64–65, 124

pagans, 343–44
Paraclete, 3, 43, 64, 128, 333. *See also* Holy Spirit
Parmenides, 130
participation, doctrine of, 37, 42, 51, 110–11, 184, 244, 346; and metaphysics, xxiv, 40, 58
Paschal mystery, xvi, 78–91, 138–39, 333, 343. *See also* death, of Christ; resurrection, of Christ
passion: of Christ, xxi, 95, 99, 190, 224, 229, 306, 317, 334; human, 196–98, 209, 265–67, 271, 300
Patristic traditions. *See* Fathers of the Church
Paul, Saint, 127, 179–80, 263, 284, 310n42, 325–26; Aquinas' commentaries on, 30, 32, 278, 343, 345
Paul of Samosata, 18, 51, 53
Pegis, Anton Charles, xx
Peirce, Charles Sanders, 117
Pentecost, 63, 94, 189–91, 301, 327, 333–35, 337, 345

perfection, 97–98, 166–68, 268, 318–21, 328, 333, 341; of contemplation, 298, 311, 314; of knowledge, 335–36; moral, 331

persons, divine, 106–10, 124, 133, 306; distinction of, 28, 87, 112; equality of, 35, 43, 50–52, 56–57, 93, 164, 242, 339; knowledge possessed by, 117–18; unity of, 83, 86, 301. *See also* mission, of divine persons; Trinity; *individual persons*

Peter (Apostle), 181, 307, 311, 336, 341; denial of Christ by, 304–5, 337; faith of, 246, 309n41, 338–39; as head of Church, 288, 324

Philip (Apostle), 207, 307–8, 338, 344

Philippe, M.-D., xxiv, 23, 256

Philippians (Bible), 92, 95

philosophy, 9–10, 18, 134, 203, 326; theology related to, xvii, 79n5, 115–17, 119, 129–31, 157–60, 211. *See also* Aristotle; Plato/Platonism

Photinus of Sirmium, 18, 51, 53

Pieper, Josef, 118–19

piety, 96–97, 104, 112, 228

Pius X, 242-43

Pius XII, 243

Plato/Platonism, 18, 130–31, 134, 160, 215–16, 235

pleasures, human, 202

Plotinus, 123–24, 130–31, 137, 214

pneumatological deficit, 62–65, 72

polytheism. *See* gods

Porphyry, 215

posture, symbolism of, 186–88

power, xix, 28, 43-44, 50; of Christ, 17, 64n5, 83–84, 101–3, 138, 166, 178, 184–85, 306; of God, 87, 103, 140–41, 160, 164, 326

Praepositinus of Cremona, 48

prayer, 128, 225, 297, 308, 324

preaching, 288, 302, 323, 340–42, 346. *See also* teaching

Pre-Socratic philosophers, 18, 134. *See also* philosophy

principium, 47

procession, 26–29, 31–34, 86–87, 94, 109–10, 118, 121–24, 293n1; of the Holy Spirit, 47–48, 55, 57–58, 66–68, 107, 242, 245

Proclus, 129, 131, 137, 216

prophets, 251–52, 295, 301, 303, 305, 315, 325–27, 332

Protestantism, 78

Proverbs (Bible), 122

Providence, xviii, 19, 85, 96, 135, 140–50, 183, 307

Psalms (Bible), 80, 106, 278, 282, 315

punishment, 144, 146–48

quaestiones, xxii, 46, 49–50, 54, 58, 281, 283–84

Rahner, Karl, 70, 71n17, 228, 249–50

reason *(ratio)*, 15, 17, 42, 115–21, 202n18, 209–10, 232, 265–68; faith and, 13–14, 119, 126, 134, 346; free will and, 142, 149; learning and, 183; nature and, 32, 143. *See also* intellect

redemption, 83–84, 109, 128–29, 137, 242–43, 266, 272. *See also* salvation

redoublement, 109, 111–12

reductio, 40

reduplication, 123–24

regeneration, 89n36, 162–67, 208

Reginald of Piperno, xxiv, 241n1

reincarnation, 215

relation, doctrine of, 27, 43, 57

relative opposition, 27, 33, 58–59

religion, 96–98, 104, 234, 277

reprobation, 144, 146–48

resurrection, 164, 166, 215–17, 220, 235; of Christ, xxi, 66, 128, 252, 260, 277–89, 332–34, 340; results of, 181, 188–90, 337.
    See also body, glorified; Paschal mystery

revelation, 116, 119–21, 129–30, 132, 149, 185, 211, 243; Christ as, xvi–xvii, xxiii, 80, 192, 313, 315, 317; communication of, 318–46; learning through, 182; theology of, xiii–xiv, 9–10, 280

Richard of Saint-Victor, 48, 106–7

Ricoeur, Paul, 169–70

Rogers, Eugene Jr., 168–69

Roman Catholicism, xix, 78, 134, 149–50, 236, 310n42

Romans (Bible), 32, 63, 92, 282

Rousseau, Mary F., xx, 219

Sabellianism/Sabellius, xvii, 18, 51–54, 134

sacra doctrina. *See* doctrine, sacred

sacraments, 138–39, 161, 241, 294, 296, 309–10, 345. *See also* baptism; Eucharist

sacrifice, 295, 298, 302, 310

sadness, of Christ, 199, 220–34, 265–67

saints, 308, 310–11, 328

salvation, 63, 78, 93, 97, 142, 198, 237, 311, 325; through Christ, 118, 180, 198, 229, 245–47, 252, 257–61, 271–72, 275; in Gospel of St. John, xiv, 153n1; through the Trinity, 35–36, 41–42, 58–59, 278; in the Word, 127, 138

Samaritan woman, 167, 208–9, 269, 307, 315, 323, 330n54
Schenk, Richard, xx, **212**
Schnackenburg, Rudolf, xx, 223–26
science, 50, 117, 179, 182, 195; of Christ, 36, 246; theology as, 9, 13. *See also* moral science
Scriptum super Sententiis (Aquinas), 56, 281–84, 287
Scripture, 10, 19, 126, 128, 138, 170, 305, 308; authority of, 12, 54, 211, 255–56, 262, 265, 342; etiological sense of, 196; exegesis of, xiii–xiv, xviii–xix, xxi, xxiv, 171, 264n27, 288–89, 346; goal of, 56–57, 59–61; literal sense of, 3–8, 45, 100, 108, 281–83, 332–33; spiritual sense of, 168–69; theology of, 34, 280; Trinitarian teachings in, 40–41
secularism, 150
Secunda secundae (Aquinas), 98
self-correction, 234–37
self-determination, xviii, 140, 143–44, 149, 155
self-giving, xvi, 80, 83, 86–91, 95, 97–98, 105, 306
self-knowing, 121, 132, 250, 297
senses, 197–98, 201–10, 217, 231, 248–51, 264, 266
sensus litteralis. *See* literal sense
sermo, 15, 17. *See also* Word
servant, example of, 186–87
Sherwin, Michael, xix, **173**
Simon (Apostle), 207
sin, 137, 145, 147, 206, 229, 234, 236, 308–10, 316; Christ free of, 242, 248, 267–68, 330; forgiveness of, 63–65, 139, 208–11, 244–45, 334
sincerity, 303
Smalley, Beryl, xiv, 3, 281
Smith, Janet E., xix, **194**
Sokolowski, Robert, 122
Son of God. *See* Christ
Son of Man, 315–16. *See also* Christ
sonship, xvi, 66, 96–97, 110–11, 163–64
soteriological dimension: of Christ's human nature, xxi, 257–58, 261, 266, 271; of Christ's sadness, 229, 232; of Trinitarian theology, xv, 35–39, 41–42, 58, 60, 79
soul, 170, 188, 209, 231–32; body and, 162–64, 259, 264, 268; of Christ, 20, 243, 247, 251, 265–68, 317, 320; immortality of, 115, 216–20; nature of, 16, 19, 246; separation of, 214, 248, 250n11, 260
speculative theology, xiii–xvii, xix–xxiii, 23–61, 81, 94, 108, 256

Spirit. *See* Holy Spirit
Stoicism/Stoics, xx, 15, 231–32, 235, 267
succession, apostolic, 139, 305
suffering, of Christ, 91, 165, 235–36, 242, 243n4, 246–47, 258, 260–61, 300, 337. *See also* passion, of Christ; sadness, of Christ
Summa contra gentiles (Aquinas), 135, 140, 150, 278; Trinitarian theology in, 23, 26–28, 30–31, 38n44, 55–56, 58, 60
Summa theologiae (Aquinas), xiv–xvii, xxiv, 7, 9, 103–4, 108, 200, 293–94; causality in, 145; compared to *Commentary on John*, xxi–xxii, 23–61, 80, 116–19, 127, 244, 277–89; creation in, 120, 126, 135; Eucharist in, 171; faith in, 11–13, 177; learning in, 178, 182–83; life in, 161; on mourning, 213; Paschal mystery in, 83–86, 91; Person of Christ in, 241–53, 258, 260, 272, 275, 298
synoptic Gospels, 18, 81–82, 99, 127, 156, 223, 264, 278, 296. *See also individual Gospels*
systematic theology, 153, 168–72, 280–84, 288

tarásso, xx, 220
teaching, 173–93, 296–301; by Apostles, 304–6, 310, 313–14, 325–26, 343–45. *See also* Christ, as teacher
temple of God, 293–311
Tertullian, 15–17
theandric teaching, xxii, 300, 306
theism/theists, 140, 148, 150
theology, xiii–xiv, 9–13, 78, 256; exegesis related to, 153–54; *Oikonomia* and, 92–112; philosophy related to, xvii, 79n5, 115–17, 119, 129–31, 157–60, 211. *See also* contemporary theology; narrative theology; speculative theology; systematic theology; Western theology
Theophylactus, 52
Third Council of Constantinople, 266n30
Thomas (Apostle), 179, 185, 261, 276, 284, 286–87, 311, 336, 339
Thomas Aquinas, Saint: anthropology of, 268–69, 284; on death, 216–20; ecclesiology of, 293; exegesis of, xiii–xiv, 3–8, 45, 48, 194, 255–56, 264, 277–89, 346; on life, 171–72; philosophy of, 115–19; sermons of, 34n26; on teaching, 182–84; theology of, 9, 23, 128, 168–72, 255–56, 274–77, 283–87, 306; Trinitarian theology of, xv–xvi, 70–71, 73–75, 79–80, 83–91, 108–9
Thomism/Thomists, 117, 146, 148, 218, 249

"through" (per), 122–23
time, xvii, 127–39
Tolomeo of Lucca, xxiv
Torah, 80, 82
Torrell, J.-P., xxiv–xxv, 255
totality, principle of, 264n27
Transfiguration of Christ, 63, 67
Trinity, xiv–xvi, 103–5, 132, 241–42, 275, 293n1; actions of, 68–76, 328; doctrine of, 11, 23–61, 93, 127–29, 338–39; faith in, 344; knowledge of, 117–18, 120; Paschal mystery and, 78–91. *See also* economic Trinity; immanent Trinity
tristitia. See sadness, of Christ
truth, xxi, 37n41, 59–60, 99, 129–30, 300, 311; acceptance of, 54–57, 115–16, 197, 204–6, 210–11; Christ as, 155, 180, 190, 279, 320, 331; human, 40, 89, 136, 149, 154, 160, 162, 217, 269; knowledge of, 176, 180, 299, 314–15, 319, 325; taught by the Holy Spirit, 66–68, 189–90, 330–31; of the Word, 106, 110, 244–45
turbatio, 220–225, 227–34, 265, 271

understanding, 13–14, 132–35, 166–68, 180, 330–33, 346. *See also* contemplation; knowledge
unity, 58, 93–95, 111–12, 317; of action, 69–71; of the Church, 301–3, 309, 311; divine, 91, 107–9

Valentinus, 53, 122, 263n25
Valkenberg, Pim, xxii, **277**
Vatican Council II, 264n27
Verbum, xvii, 15–17, 26, 36, 46–48, 70, 119–22. *See also* Word
Vigilius of Thapsus. *See* Athanasius, Saint
virtues, xix–xx, 84, 92, 96–97, 196, 202n18, 344–45; possessed by Christ, 246–47
vision, xxi; beatific, 242–44, 246–52; contemplative, 278; prophetic, 126; spiritual, 163, 208; supernatural, 182
Vulgata (Aquinas), 63, 64n5, 222, 225

Waldstein, Michael, xvi, **92**
washing of feet, 19, 186–88, 303–4, 308, 329, 333–34

water, symbolism of, 163, 208–9, 315
way, Christ as, 89, 155, 179–80, 190, 279, 299–301
wedding at Cana, 258–59, 263–64, 270, 294, 338n95
weeping, 223–25, 267. *See also* sadness, of Christ
Weisheipl, James A., xxiv
Western theology, xvi, 62, 72, 82–83, 95
will, xvi, 52, 106, 108, 124, 176; divine, 29, 36, 50, 83–84, 87, 99–105, 146, 203, 246, 311, 315; human, xx, 95, 98, 111, 144, 148, 264, 266; mode of, 31, 33–34
William of Auxerre, 13, 283
Williams, A. N., 79
wisdom, 175–76, 200, 231, 245; contemplative, 55–56, 60, 139, 188; divine, xxiii, 19, 85, 102, 123, 126, 128–29, 160, 177, 190–91, 271–72, 327–28; Eucharist and, 312–17; teaching of, xix, 183, 188–89
witness, 298–99; apostolic, 305–8, 319–20, 322–23, 326, 343
women, in the Church, 286
Word, 14, 17–20, 86–91, 106–7, 110, 205, 311, 338; actions of, 36–37, 39, 64n5, 109, 167, 176, 328–29; as creator, 118, 122–23, 125, 136–39, 195; divinity of, 7–8, 93, 120–21, 133, 153–54, 175, 251–52, 271–75; doctrine of, xv, xvii–xviii, 26–47, 53, 57–58, 170; generation of, 101–2, 132–35, 190, 257, 264; knowledge of, 321; made flesh, 28, 254, 260–65, 298, 305–7, 315–16; mission of, 127–28; nature of, 55–56, 70; reception of, 345; as teacher, 160, 188, 193, 320. *See also* Incarnation
words, human, 19–20, 26, 120, 132, 137, 139, 190, 311
wounds, of Christ, 261, 284, 287–88
Wright, N. T., xvi, 78, 80–91

Yeaog, David S., xiii
YHWH, 81–82, 91

Zechariah, 180, 221
Zeno, 130

www.ingramcontent.com/pod-product-compliance
Lightning Source LLC
Chambersburg PA
CBHW071852290426
44110CB00013B/1116